Excel 2002

ALL-IN-ONE DESK REFERENCE

FOR DUMMIES®

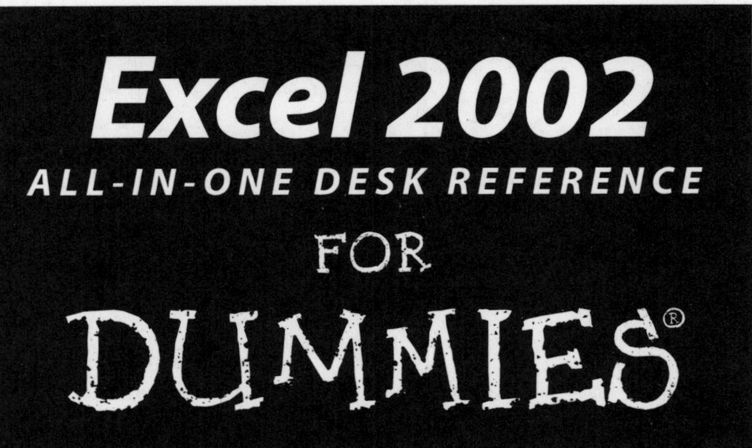

Excel 2002 All-in-One Desk Reference For Dummies

by Greg Harvey

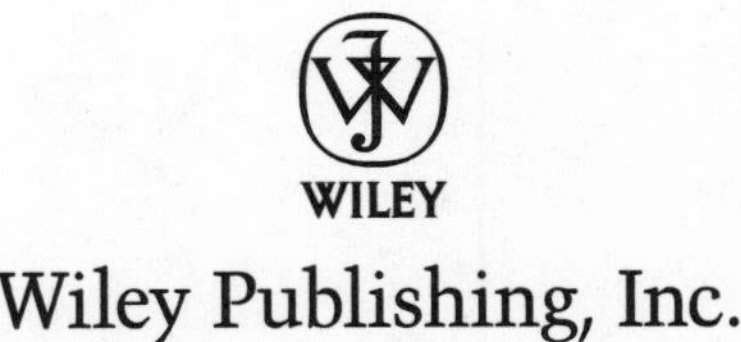

Wiley Publishing, Inc.

Excel 2002 All-in-One Desk Reference For Dummies®

Published by
Wiley Publishing, Inc.
909 Third Avenue
New York, NY 10022
`www.wiley.com`

Published by Wiley Publishing, Inc., Indianapolis, Indiana

Published simultaneously in Canada

For general information on our other products and services or to obtain technical support, please contact our Customer Care Department within the U.S. at 800-762-2974, outside the U.S. at 317-572-3993, or fax 317-572-4002.

Wiley also publishes its books in a variety of electronic formats. Some content that appears in print may not be available in electronic books.

Library of Congress Control Number: 2002110273

ISBN: 0764517945

Manufactured in the United States of America

10 9 8 7 6 5 4 3 2 1

IB/RS/RS/QS/IN

About the Author

Greg Harvey has authored tons of computer books, the most recent being *Excel 2002 For Dummies* and *Adobe Acrobat 5 PDF For Dummies.* He started out training business users on how to use IBM personal computers and their attendant computer software in the rough and tumble days of DOS, WordStar, and Lotus 1-2-3 in the mid-80s of the last century. After working for a number of independent training firms, he went on to teaching semester-long courses in spreadsheet and database management software at Golden Gate University in San Francisco.

His love of teaching has translated into an equal love of writing. *For Dummies* books are, of course, his all time favorites to write because they enable him to write to his favorite audience, the beginner. They also enable him to use humor (a key element to success in the training room) and, most delightful of all, to express an opinion or two about the subject matter at hand.

Dedication

To Ginger — thanks for taking such good care of me all these many years

Acknowledgments

I am always so grateful to the many people who work so hard to bring my book projects into being, and this one is no exception. If anything, I am even more thankful for the talents given the size and complexity of an All-In-One.

This time, special thanks are in order to Andy Cummings and Tiffany Franklin for giving me this opportunity to write and write and write about Excel in this great All-in-One format. Next, I want to express great thanks to my project editor, Christine Berman (a better one you couldn't ask for), and, to my partner in crime, Christopher Aiken (I really appreciate all your encouragement on this one). Thanks also go to Rebekah Mancilla for the great copy edit, Kerwin McKenzie for the great technical edit, Jennifer Bingham and Maridee Ennis for coordinating its production, and everybody at Wiley Publishing.

Publisher's Acknowledgments

We're proud of this book; please send us your comments through our online registration form located at `www.dummies.com/register/`.

Some of the people who helped bring this book to market include the following:

Acquisitions, Editorial, and Media Development

Project Editor: Christine Berman

Acquisitions Editor: Tiffany Franklin

Copy Editor: Rebekah Mancilla

Technical Editor: Kerwin McKenzie

Editorial Manager: Leah Cameron

Media Development Manager: Laura VanWinkle

Media Development Supervisor: Richard Graves

Editorial Assistant: Amanda Foxworth

Cartoons: Rich Tennant (`www.the5thwave.com`)

Production

Project Coordinators: Jennifer Bingham, Maridee Ennis

Layout and Graphics: Amanda Carter, Carrie Foster, LeAndra Johnson, Barry Offringa, Jacque Schneider, Jeremey Unger, Erin Zeltner

Proofreaders: John Tyler Connoley, Andy Hollandbeck, Arielle Carole Mennelle, Susan Moritz, Charles Spencer

Indexer: Sherry Massey

Publishing and Editorial for Technology Dummies

Richard Swadley, Vice President and Executive Group Publisher

Andy Cummings, Vice President and Publisher

Mary C. Corder, Editorial Director

Publishing for Consumer Dummies

Diane Graves Steele, Vice President and Publisher

Joyce Pepple, Acquisitions Director

Composition Services

Gerry Fahey, Vice President of Production Services

Debbie Stailey, Director of Composition Services

Contents at a Glance

Table of Contents

Book II: Worksheet Design 99

Introduction

The *Excel 2002 All-in-One Desk Reference For Dummies* brings together plain and simple information on using all aspects of Microsoft Excel designed to be of help no matter how much or how little experience you have with the program. As the preeminent spreadsheet and data analysis software for the personal computer, Excel offers its users seemingly unlimited capabilities too often masked in technical jargon and obscured by explanations only a software engineer could love. On top of that, many of the publications that purport to give you the lowdown on using Excel are quite clear on how to use particular features without giving you a clue as to why you would go to all the trouble.

The truth is that understanding how to use the abundance of features offered by Excel is only half the battle, at best. The other half of the battle is to understand how these features can benefit you in your work, in other words, "what's in it for you." I have endeavored to cover both the "how to" and "so what" aspects in all my discussions of Excel features, being as clear as possible and using as little tech-speak as possible.

Fortunately, Excel is well worth the effort to get to know as it's definitely one of the best data processing productivity tools that has ever come along. In short, Excel is a blast to use when you know what you're doing, and my great hope is that this "fun" aspect of using the program comes through on every page (or, at least, every other page).

About This Book

As the name states, The *Excel 2002 All-in-One Desk Reference For Dummies* is a reference (whether you keep it on your desk or use it to prop up your desk is your business). This means that although the chapters in each book are laid in a logical order, each stands on its own ready for you to dig into the information at any point.

As much as possible, I have endeavored to make the topics within each chapter stand on their own as well. When there's just no way around relying up some information that's discussed elsewhere, I include a cross-reference that gives you the chapter and verse (actually the book and chapter) for where you can find that related information if you're of a mind to.

Use the Contents at a Glance along with the full Table of Contents and Index to look up the topic of the hour and find out exactly where it is in this compilation of Excel information. You'll find that although most topics are introduced in a conversational manner, I don't waste much time cutting to the chase by laying down the main principles at work (usually in bulleted form) followed by the hard reality of how you do the deed (as numbered steps).

Foolish Assumptions

I'm only going to make one foolish assumption about you and that is that you have some need to use Microsoft Excel in your work or studies. If pushed, I further guess that you aren't particularly interested in knowing Excel at an expert level but are terribly motivated to find out how to do the stuff you need to get done. If that's the case, then this is definitely the book for you. Fortunately, even if you happen to be one of those newcomers who's highly motivated to become the company's resident spreadsheet guru, you've still come to the right place.

As far as your hardware and software goes, I'm assuming that you already have Excel 2002 (usually as part of Microsoft Office XP) installed on your computer, using a standard installation. I am not, however, assuming that you're running it under Windows XP (the latest and, I'm coming around to believe, the greatest version of Windows). Although the figures in this book all show Excel 2002 happily running on Windows XP, it makes no difference in the written instructions if you're still using a flavor of Window 9*x*, and in the very few instances where it does make a difference, I'm quite careful to point it out.

How This Book Is Organized

The *Excel 2002 All-in-One Desk Reference For Dummies* is actually nine smaller books rolled into one. That way, you can go after the stuff in the particular book that really interests you at the time, putting all the rest of the material aside until you need to have a look at it. Each book in the volume consists of two or more chapters, which consist of all the basic information you should need in dealing with that particular component or aspect of Excel.

In case you're the least bit curious, here's the lowdown on each of the nine books and what you can expect to find there.

Book I: Excel Basics

This book is for those of you who've never had the pleasure of firing up Excel and getting your bearings in the program window. Chapter 1 covers all the orientation material, including how to use the program's many menus, toolbars, and dialog boxes. Of special interest is the alternate way of issuing commands by voice.

Chapter 2 is your place to go to find out how to get online help in Excel. Believe or not, after you have the All-in-One basics down, some of the online help topics actually start making sense!

Chapter 3 is not to be missed, even by those of you who do not consider yourselves beginners by any stretch of the imagination. This chapter covers the many ways to customize Excel and make the program truly your own. It includes information on creating custom toolbars and menus as well as great information on how to use and procure add-in programs that can greatly extend Excel's considerable features.

Book II: Worksheet Design

Book II focuses on the crucial issue of designing spreadsheets in Excel. Chapter 1 takes up the call on how to do basic design and covers all the many ways of doing data entry (a subject that's been made all the more exciting with the addition of voice and handwriting input).

Chapter 2 covers how to make your spreadsheet look professional and read the way you want it through formatting. Excel offers you a wide choice of formatting techniques, from the very simple automatic formatting all the way to the very sophisticated conditional formatting.

Chapter 3 takes up the vital subject of how to edit an existing spreadsheet without disturbing its design or contents. Editing can be intimidating to the new spreadsheet user because most spreadsheets not only contain data entries that you don't want to mess up but formulas that can go haywire if you make the wrong move.

Chapter 4 looks at the topic of managing the worksheets that contain the spreadsheet applications that build in Excel. It opens the possibility of going beyond the two-dimensional worksheet with its innumerable columns and rows by organizing data three-dimensionally through the use of multiple worksheets (each Excel file already contains three blank worksheets to which you can add more). This chapter also shows you how to work with and organize multiple worksheets given the limited screen real estate afforded by your monitor and how to combine data from different files and sheets when needed.

Chapter 5 is all about printing your spreadsheets, a topic that ranks only second in importance to knowing how to get the data into a worksheet in the first place. As you expect, you find out not only how to get the raw data to spit out of your printer but also how to gussy it up and make it into a professional report of which anyone would be proud.

Book III: Formulas and Functions

This book is all about calculations and building the formulas that do them. Chapter 1 covers formula basics from doing the simplest addition to building array formulas and using Excel's built-in functions courtesy of the Insert Function feature. It also covers how to use different types of cell references when making formula copies and how to link formulas that span different worksheets.

Chapter 2 takes up the subject of preventing formula errors from occurring, and, barring that, how to track them down and eliminate them from the spreadsheet. This chapter also includes information on circular references in formulas and how you can sometimes use them to your advantage.

Chapters 3 through 6 concentrate on how to use different types of built-in functions. Chapter 3 covers the use of Date and Time functions, not only so you know what day and time it is, but actually put this knowledge to good use in formulas that calculate elapsed time. Chapter 4 takes up the Financial functions in Excel and shows you how you can use them to both reveal and determine the monetary health of your business. Chapter 5 is concerned with Math and Statistical functions (of which they are plenty). Chapter 6 introduces you to the powerful group of Lookup, Information, and Text functions. Here, you find out how to build formulas that automate data entry by returning values from a lookup table, get the lowdown on any cell in the worksheet, and combine your favorite pieces of text.

Book IV: Worksheet Collaboration

Book IV looks at the ways you can share your spreadsheet data with others. Chapter 1 introduces Excel's sophisticated features for sending out spreadsheets and having a team of people review and make comments on them. It also covers techniques for reviewing and reconciling the suggested changes.

Chapter 2 covers the important issue of security in your spreadsheets. Here, you find out how you can protect your data so that only those to whom you give permission can open or make changes to their contents.

Chapter 3 is concerned with sharing spreadsheet data with other programs that you use. It looks specifically at how you can share data with other Office programs such as Microsoft Word, PowerPoint, and Outlook. This chapter also discusses the role of smart tags in enabling you to automatically bring information into your spreadsheets from outside sources such as your Outlook address book and special Web sites on the Internet.

Book V: Charts and Graphics

Book V focuses on the graphical aspects of Excel. Chapter 1 covers charting your spreadsheet data in some depth. Here, you find out not only how to create great looking charts but also how to select the right type of chart for the data that you're representing graphically.

Chapter 2 introduces you to all the other kinds of graphics that you can have in your spreadsheets. These include graphic objects that you draw as well as graphic images that you import including Clip art included in Microsoft Office as well as digital pictures and images imported and created with other hardware and software connected to your computer.

Book VI: Data Management

Book VI is concerned with the ins and outs of using Excel to maintain large amounts of data in what are known as databases or, more commonly, data lists. Chapter 1 gives you basic information on how to set up a data list and add your data to it. This chapter also gives you information on how to reorganize the data list through sorting and how to total its numerical data with the Subtotal feature.

Chapter 2 is all about how to filter the data and extract just the information you want out of it (a process officially known as querying the data). Here, you find out how to perform all sorts of filtering operations from the simplest relying upon the AutoFilter feature to the more complex that use custom filters and specialized Database functions. Finally, you find out how to perform queries on external data sources such as those maintained with dedicated database management software for Windows such as Microsoft Access or dBASE as well as that run on other operating systems such as DB2 and Oracle.

Book VII: Data Analysis

Book VII looks at the subject of data analysis with Excel; essentially how to use the program's computational abilities to project and predict possible future outcomes. Chapter 1 looks at the various ways to perform what-if scenarios in Excel. These include analysis with one- and two-input variable Data tables, doing goal seeking, setting a series of different possible scenarios, and using the Solver add-in.

Chapter 2 is concerned with the topic of creating special data summaries called pivot table reports that enable you to analyze large amounts of data in an extremely compact and modifiable format. Here, you find out how to create and manipulate pivot tables as well as build pivot charts that depict the summary information graphically.

Book VIII: Excel and the Web

Book VIII brings you face to face with Excel's many Web features. Chapter 1 shows you how easy it is to save and publish your favorite spreadsheets or charts in the HTML, Web page format for use on the company's intranet or Internet Web site. Here, you also find out how to build truly interactive spreadsheet Web pages for users who have access to the later versions of the Internet Explorer and how to query Web pages to extract data for use in your standard Excel spreadsheets.

Chapter 2 takes up the subject of building and using hyperlinks in your standard Excel spreadsheets (the same kind of links that you know and love on Web pages on the World Wide Web). This chapter covers how to create hyperlinks for moving from worksheet to worksheet within the same Excel file as well as for opening other documents on your hard disk, or logging onto the Internet and browsing to a favorite Web page.

Book IX: Excel and Visual Basic for Applications

Book IX introduces the subject of customizing Excel through the use of its programming language called Visual Basic for Applications (VBA for short). Chapter 1 introduces to the use of the macro recorder to record tasks that you routinely perform in Excel for later automated playback. When you use the macro recorder to record the sequence of routine actions (using the program's familiar menus, toolbars, and dialog boxes), Excel automatically records the sequence in the VBA programming language.

Chapter 2 introduces you to editing VBA code in Excel's programming editor known as the Visual Basic Editor. Here, you find out how to use the Visual Basic Editor to edit macros that you're recorded that need slight modifications as well as how to write new macros from scratch. You also find out how to use the Visual Basic Editor to write custom functions that perform just the calculations you need in your Excel spreadsheets.

Icons Used in This Book

The following icons are strategically placed in the margins throughout all nine books in this volume. Their purpose is to get your attention and each has its own way of doing that.

This icon denotes some really cool information (in my humble opinion) that if you pay particular attention to will pay off by making your work just a lot more enjoyable or productive (or both).

This icon denotes a tidbit that you ought to pay extra attention to; otherwise, you may end up taking a detour that wastes valuable time.

This icon denotes a tidbit that you ought to pay extra attention to; otherwise, you'll be sorry. I reserve this icon for those times when you can lose data and otherwise screw up your spreadsheet.

This icon denotes a tidbit that makes free use of (oh no!) technical jargon. You may want to skip these sections (or, at least, read them when no one else is around).

Where to Go from Here

The question of where to go from here couldn't be simpler — why off to read the great Rich Tennant cartoons at the beginning of each of the nine books, of course. Which book you go to after that is a matter of personal interest and need. Just go for the gold and don't forget to have some fun while you're digging!

Book I

Excel Basics

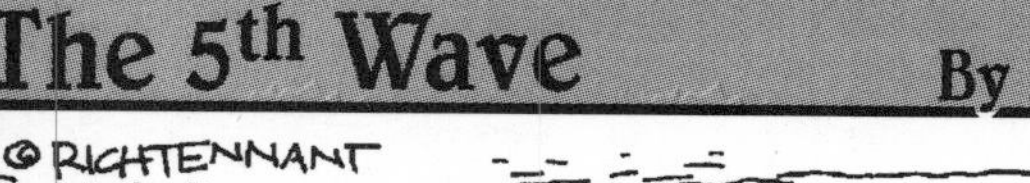

By Rich Tennant

Contents at a Glance

Chapter 1: Getting Acquainted with Excel

In This Chapter

- **Finding out what Excel can do for you**
- **Discovering the ways to start Excel**
- **Getting familiar with the Excel window**
- **Getting around the worksheet and workbook**
- **Issuing commands in Excel**

Before you go off trying to find out how to do things in Excel, you really need to know the things that the program is capable of doing. Therefore, I start this chapter with an ever-so-brief overview of the kinds of things that you can do with Excel 2002.

Also, without a sure grasp of the rock-bottom basics of Excel (such as loading the program, entering information in cells, choosing commands — that kind of stuff), moving on and trying to learn about some of the spiffier features in Excel can become not only frustrating but also just downright counterproductive. To ensure that this doesn't happen to you as you pick and choose among the many topics in the rest of this book, I have dedicated the first chapter of this first book to a review of Excel fundamentals.

By taking a second to glance over the material in this chapter, you can get yourself in a good position to really go through the exciting stuff found in the rest of the desk reference. By making sure that you're right on the money with your Excel basics, you'll have no trouble taking on new features of this spine-tingling program (and, hopefully, you can even have a lot of fun with them).

What's Up with Excel?

After Word, Microsoft's word processing powerhouse, Excel is the most popular program (also known as an *application program* or *application*) in the Microsoft Office suite. Excel holds this distinction, no doubt, because it entirely fulfills most people's number-crunching needs, which in modern business, comes right after their word processing needs.

Excel accomplishes this number crunching by combining sophisticated charting (also known as *graphing*) and data management capabilities with a sophisticated and powerful spreadsheet program. You're probably aware that, as a *spreadsheet program*, Excel merges the grid layout of an accountant's green sheet with the calculating power of his or her handheld calculator. This means that you can use the program's spreadsheet capabilities not only to lay out spreadsheet applications such as financial statements, expense reports, and the like in the common row/column grid arrangement, but you can also use the program's built-in calculating ability to compute all required subtotals, totals, and grand totals.

This combination of abilities makes Excel a natural for any type of application that uses some sort of tabular layout or relies on extensive calculations between the data required by the application. For example, you may use Excel to create many fill-in-the-blank paper forms that require no calculations at all. (Many people find that designing forms in Excel's grid layout is much easier than using Word's Table feature.) You may also use the program to create business-type forms, such as expense reports and sales and inventory sheets that involve extensive calculations.

The worksheet grid

The key to successfully using Excel as a spreadsheet program is in understanding its grid-like nature. Figure 1-1 shows you this grid in all its glory (without most of the program and sheet controls that normally appear when you start the program). By the way, in Excel, you always refer to this type of grid as a *worksheet*.

Note the following items about the grid shown in Figure 1-1:

- The columns of a worksheet are identified by letters (A, B, C, and so on) that appear across the Column header — when Excel runs out of letters (at column 26), it starts duplicating letters (so that column Z is followed by AA, AB, AC, and so on until it reaches column IV).
- The rows of a worksheet are identified by numbers (1, 2, 3, and the like until it reaches row 65,536) that appear down the Row header.
- The intersecting gridlines of each column and row form a rectangular box known as a *cell*.
- A totally blank worksheet is a pretty boring affair!

The most important thing to keep in mind about the worksheet is that each of its cells can hold its own data, depending upon the function and layout of the spreadsheet that you're building.

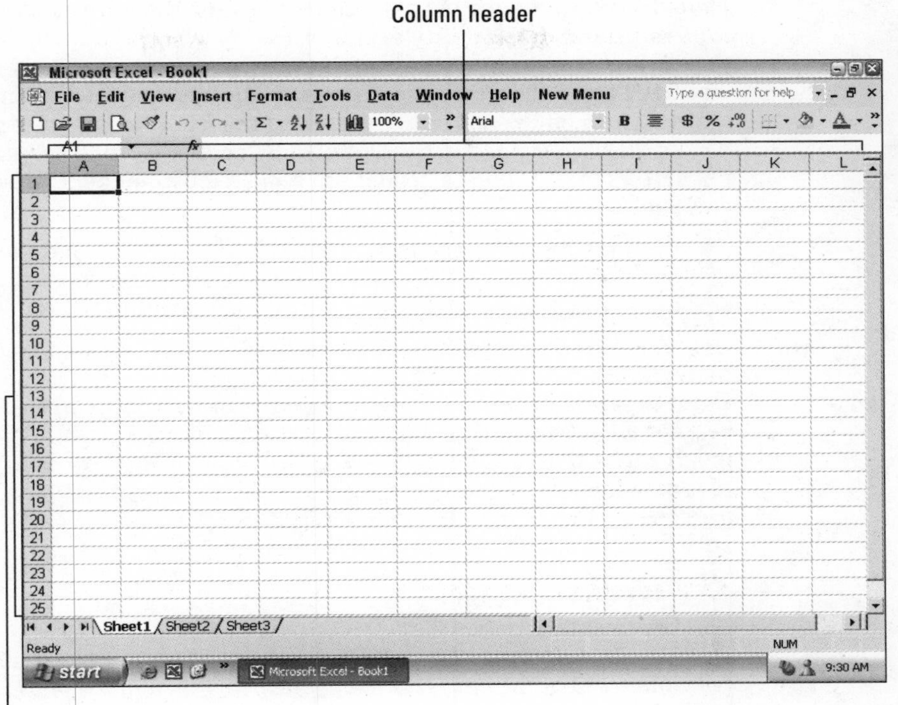

Figure 1-1: The basic Excel worksheet grid.

Getting a cell's address

Cells, by the way, are identified by their position in the grid; their so-called *cell address*. This address is normally noted by the cell's column letter followed by its row number so that the first cell (located at the intersection of the first column and row) in every Excel worksheet has the address A1, and the cell in the first row of the second column has the address B1, while the cell in the second row of the first column has the address A2, and so forth.

I say that a cell address is "normally" noted as a combination of its column letter and row number only because it is possible to switch to a different style of cell address notation, known affectionately as the *R1C1 reference style*. It has this wonderful appellation because in this system, R1C1 is the first cell of every worksheet instead of A1 (as in the normal, non-R1C1 reference style).

Note the following two big differences between the normal A1 style cell addresses and the R1C1 style addresses:

- ✦ R1C1 style addresses don't ever use the column letter — in fact, when you turn on this system (by clicking the R1C1 Reference Style check box on the General tab in the Options dialog box — Tools⇨Options), the letters in the column header are replaced by numbers, as shown in Figure 1-2.
- ✦ R1C1 style addresses always note the row position, and then the column position of each cell. Normal A1 style cell addresses do the opposite by first noting the position of the column position (by letter), and then the row.

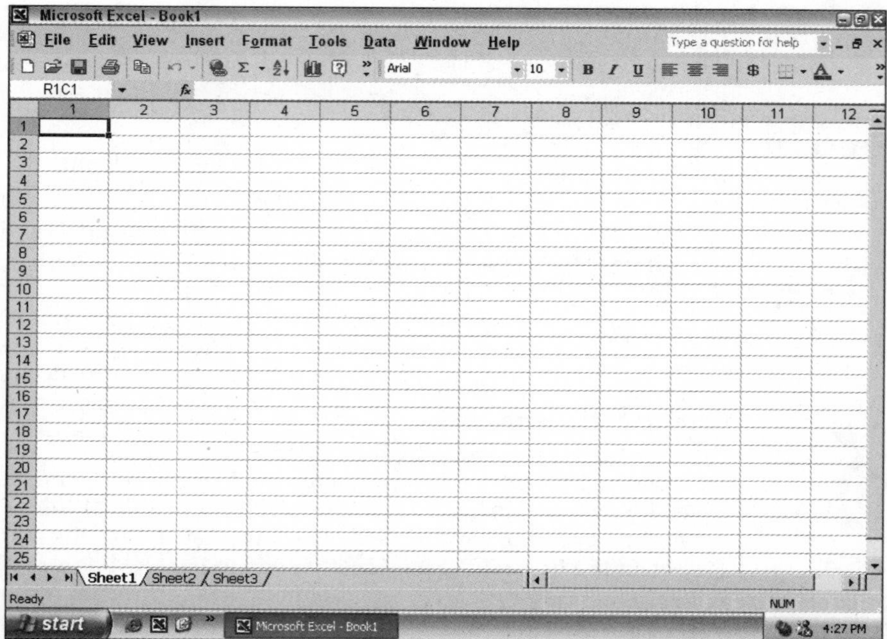

Figure 1-2: Basic Excel worksheet grid using the R1C1 style reference.

The big advantage of the regular A1 style cell addresses is they're shorter. Therefore, most people find them easier to deal with (especially in formulas) because their addresses don't have to include the R and C abbreviations (letters always designate columns and numbers always designate rows).

The big disadvantage of the A1 style cell address is that the cell addresses must duplicate letters in order to designate any column past 26 (and each worksheet contains a total of 256 columns). When referring to cell addresses hanging out in the wilds of a worksheet, the R1C1 cell address system suddenly doesn't seem so bad. For example, suppose that you're using the R1C1 style address system, and suppose I tell you that the data you want is in cell R1C52 of the worksheet; you have a good idea of its general location relative to the first cell. If, on the other hand, you're using the normal A1 style reference system, and I tell you that the data you want is in cell AZ1, you probably don't have a clue where that cell is located in relation to the first cell, A1, except that it's somewhere pretty far over in the same row.

Identifying the active cell

Regardless of which cell address system you have turned on, Excel indicates which cell you're working with at any given time (known as the *active cell* or *current cell*) in three ways:

- Listing its cell address at the beginning of the row immediately above the row with the worksheet's Column header (this area is known as the *Name box*)
- Highlighting the cell's column and row in the Column and Row header, respectively
- Displaying a heavy black border around the cell in the worksheet grid itself (known as the *cell pointer*)

Figure 1-3 illustrates these three ways of identifying the active cell. In this figure, you can bet your bottom dollar that cell C7 is the active cell in this worksheet because C7 appears in the Name box and the cell pointer is located at the intersection of column C and row 7, which, in turn, are both highlighted on the Column and Row borders of the worksheet.

Turning off R1C1 references in a worksheet

Most worksheets that you'll run across use the normal A1 style cell address system (because this is the program's default setting for cell addressing and most people don't even know the R1C1 system exists). Suppose that someone in the know switches to the R1C1 system and saves the Excel file with it turned on. When you open it, all cell references in the formulas of its worksheets use that system and the Column header contains numbers just like the Row header. You can always switch back to the normal cell reference style by choosing Tools➪Options and then clicking the R1C1 Reference Style check box on the General tab (to remove its checkmark). This check box is located at the top of the View tab in the Options dialog box. After you choose OK, all cell references in the formulas change back to the A1 style reference system and the Column header once again uses letters.

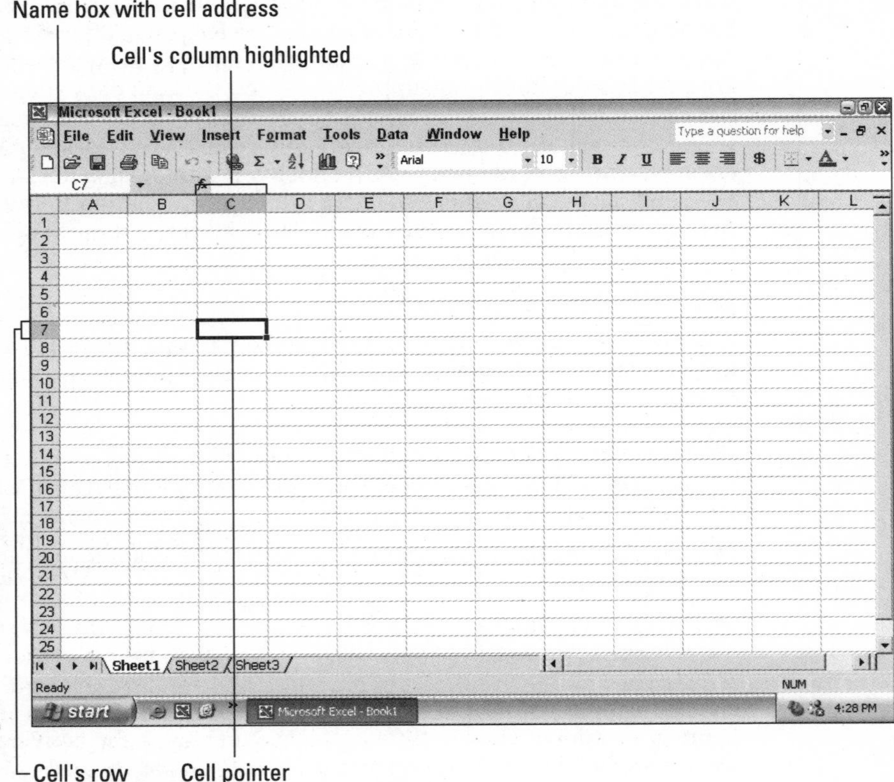

Figure 1-3: Identifying the active or current cell in the worksheet.

The three basic spreadsheet tasks

As I see it, you almost always end up doing the following three basic tasks when creating a new spreadsheet table or list:

- ✦ Entering the headings that define the layout of the spreadsheet table or list
- ✦ Entering the data in the table or list
- ✦ Formatting the data that you entered in the table or list

Note that most spreadsheet tables have both a row of column headings and a column of row headings that identify the different types of data that the tables contain. This stands in contrast to lists (also called *data lists* or *databases* in Excel) that use only a row of column headings at the top to identify their data.

The data that you enter in the cells of your table or list (see Book I, Chapter 2 for details) can consist of text, numbers, or even formulas that perform essential calculations (which, in turn, use values or even sometimes text entered in other cells of the table or list).

After you've entered all the data, the formatting of the table or list data is mostly done. In formatting the data, you actually change the formatting of the cells containing the data. In other words, instead of actually making the text that you've entered in a particular cell bold and italic (as you might do in a Word document), you assign these attributes to the cell that holds this text. This way, the bold and italic attributes remain associated with the cell even after you delete the text or replace it with a number or a formula that returns a calculated value. It is so important a task in building a spreadsheet in Excel that I devote an entire chapter to it (see Book II, Chapter 2).

Beyond the spreadsheet

Although working with spreadsheets is definitely Excel's strong suit (thus the worksheet as the underlying document), it is by no means the program's only claim to fame. As an adjunct to its basic spreadsheet abilities, Excel adds sophisticated charting and data analysis capabilities, along with a set of features that offer an uncomplicated approach to database management.

All of these extra features make some sort of use of the basic worksheet grid and, in the case of charting and data analysis, actually work with the data entered in spreadsheet applications (for details on charting, see Book V and for details on data analysis, Book VII). In the case of database management, Excel adds the ability to perform routine tasks, such as sorting and filtering, on data that you've actually entered in a worksheet in the form of a data list or have imported from other external sources, such as a dedicated database management program like Microsoft Access or the company's corporate database (see Book VI for details on performing these kinds of tasks).

Getting Excel Started

Excel is simply no fun at all if you can't get the blasted thing to run! So I want to begin this portion of the Excel "basics" material with an overview of the many ways you can get Excel up and running (then I discuss ways that you can catch it!).

Starting Excel 2002 is basically the same whether you are running the program under Windows XP or a version of Windows 98 (it just looks a little classier when you run it under XP — it being the latest and greatest version of the Microsoft Windows operating system). Regardless of your computer's OS (operating system), you have no lack of options when it comes to starting up Excel.

Starting from the Windows taskbar

The steps for starting Excel from the Windows taskbar, while simple, differ a bit depending upon which flavor of Windows you're using. For those of you using Windows XP, follow these steps:

1. **Click the Start button at the beginning of the taskbar.**

   The Start menu appears.

2. **Position the mouse pointer over the All Programs item at the bottom of the Start menu.**

   A cascading menu appears, showing the oodles and oodles of programs installed on your computer.

3. **Click the Microsoft Excel item on the Programs menu to fire up Excel.**

One nice thing about starting Excel from the Windows XP taskbar is that Windows automatically adds Excel to the Start menu, as shown in Figure 1-4, so that the next time you need to start the program, you can do it even more quickly by simply clicking the Start button and then clicking the Microsoft Excel item on the Start menu. Just keep in mind that Excel's appearance on the Windows XP Start menu is only a temporary advancement; as you continue to launch other programs besides Excel (such as Word, for example), Windows will eventually knock Excel off the Start menu and replace it with a more recently launched program.

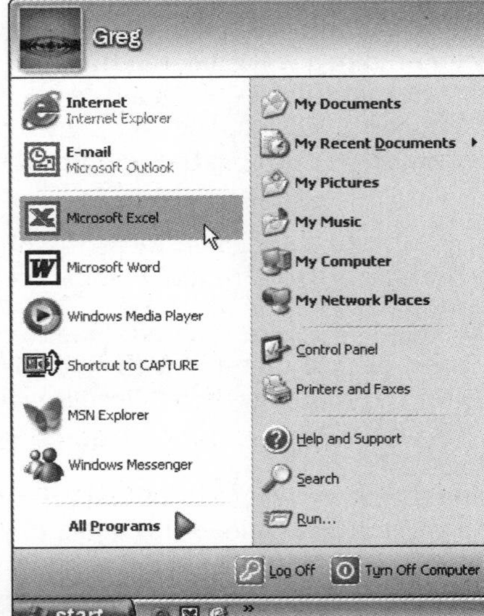

Figure 1-4: The Start menu in Windows XP after adding a Microsoft Excel item.

The steps for starting Excel from the Start menu of your Windows 98 or 95 taskbar are just a tiny bit different:

1. **Click the Start button at the beginning of the taskbar.**

   The Windows 98 or 95 Start menu appears.

2. **Position the mouse pointer over the Programs item near the top of the Start menu.**

   A cascading menu appears, showing the programs that you've installed on your computer.

3. **Click the Microsoft Excel item on the Programs menu to launch Excel.**

Starting Excel with a desktop or toolbar shortcut

If you use Excel extensively in your work, it probably won't take too long before the procedure for starting Excel using the Windows Start button wears a little thin. In such cases, you either need to add a desktop or Quick Launch toolbar shortcut for starting the Program or you need to start using the built-in Excel button on the Office Shortcut bar (described in the very next section).

To add a desktop shortcut for Excel, you need to find the program file that actually runs the Excel application (a nifty little executable file called excel.exe) and then use it to create a desktop shortcut. Here's how you do that:

1. **Click the Start button on the Windows XP or 9*x* (that *x* stands for 98 or 95) taskbar.**

   The Windows Start menu appears, containing a Search item.

2. **Click the Search item on the Start menu and then click All Files and Folders in the Search Results dialog box.**

   If you use Windows 9*x*, you vary this step a bit by positioning the mouse pointer over Search and then click For Files and Folders on the cascading menu that appears.

3. **Type** excel.exe **in the All or Part of File name text box (called the Search for Files or Folders Named text box in Windows 9*x*).**

4. **Click the Search button (called Search Now in Windows 9*x*).**

   Windows begins searching your computer's hard drive looking for the excel.exe file that starts the program.

5. **Click the Stop button (called Stop Search in Windows 9*x*) when the Excel file, listed as an Application type, appears in the Search Results dialog box.**

   Now, all you have to do is send a shortcut to this program file to your computer's desktop.

6. **Right-click the Excel file, then position the mouse pointer on Send To on the shortcut menu and click the Desktop (Create Shortcut) on the cascading menu.**

   Windows responds by creating a Shortcut to Excel on your desktop (that you see as soon as you close the Search Results dialog box).

7. **Click the Close button in the upper-right corner of the Search Results dialog box to get rid of it.**

As soon as you close the Search Results dialog box, you should see your Shortcut to Excel icon (just like the one shown in the left margin). To start Excel with this desktop shortcut, you simply double-click the icon or right-click it and then click the Open item on its shortcut menu.

The only drawbacks to desktop shortcuts are that you need to double-click them or right-click them and then click the Open item on their shortcut menus (which seems to me like a lot work to go through for a *shortcut!*), and they tend to move around and get lost as you add more and more desktop items (if your desktop is anywhere near as messy as mine, you may never find the blasted thing).

To avoid these kinds of hassles, you can copy the Excel desktop shortcut to your Quick Launch toolbar that appears to the immediate right of the Start button on your Windows taskbar. This way, you can always find your Excel shortcut, and you only have to single-click it (as you do with any other toolbar button in Windows) to get Windows to launch the program.

To add a copy of the Excel desktop shortcut to the Quick Launch toolbar at the beginning of your Windows taskbar, follow these steps:

1. **Drag the Shortcut to Excel icon from the desktop to the place on the Quick Launch toolbar where you want it to appear.**

   If you want the icon to appear at the very beginning of the bar right after the Start button, drag the icon until it's positioned on the Quick Launch bar and a thick black vertical bar, representing where the icon will be inserted, appears in front of the first button on the bar.

2. **Release the mouse button as soon as the vertical bar, indicating where the new button for the Excel shortcut will be added, appears at the place where you want it.**

As soon as you release the mouse button, Windows adds an Excel button (indicated by the Excel program icon shown in the left margin). After you've added this button to the Quick Launch bar, you can start Excel by clicking this button. If you ever need to remove it, simply drag the button off the Quick Launch bar. When you release the mouse button, the Excel button immediately disappears.

Starting Excel from the Office Shortcut bar

Office XP (which comes in both the Standard and the so-called Professional editions) contains an Office Shortcut bar that has built-in buttons for all the four major Office applications: Word, Excel, PowerPoint, and Outlook. The nice thing about using this toolbar to start Excel is that, after it's displayed, you only need to click its Excel button to fire up the program (there's none of this double-clicking that you have to do with desktop shortcuts). The bad thing about using this toolbar is that, like the Windows taskbar, unless you Auto Hide it, the thing remains displayed on-screen all the while you're using Excel, hogging up valuable screen space that can be otherwise used for displaying your valuable spreadsheet data.

To display the Office Shortcut bar, shown in Figure 1-5, you need to follow these steps:

1. **Click the Start button on the Windows XP or 9*x* (the *x* stands for 98 or 95) taskbar.**

   The Windows Start menu opens.

2. **Position the mouse pointer on the All Programs item (called Programs on Windows 9x).**

   The Programs cascading menu opens.

3. **Position the mouse pointer on the Microsoft Office Tools item.**

   The Microsoft Office Tools cascading menu opens.

4. **Click the Microsoft Office Shortcut Bar item on this menu.**

   Windows responds by displaying a Microsoft Office Shortcut Bar alert dialog box that asks if you want to configure the shortcut bar to start automatically each time you start Windows.

5. **Click the Yes button to have the Office Shortcut Bar automatically displayed each time you start Windows. Click the No button if you only want the bar displayed this one time.**

After you have the Microsoft Office Shortcut bar displayed, you can start Excel by just clicking the Microsoft Excel button (which uses the same icon as the Excel button on the Quick Launch bar).

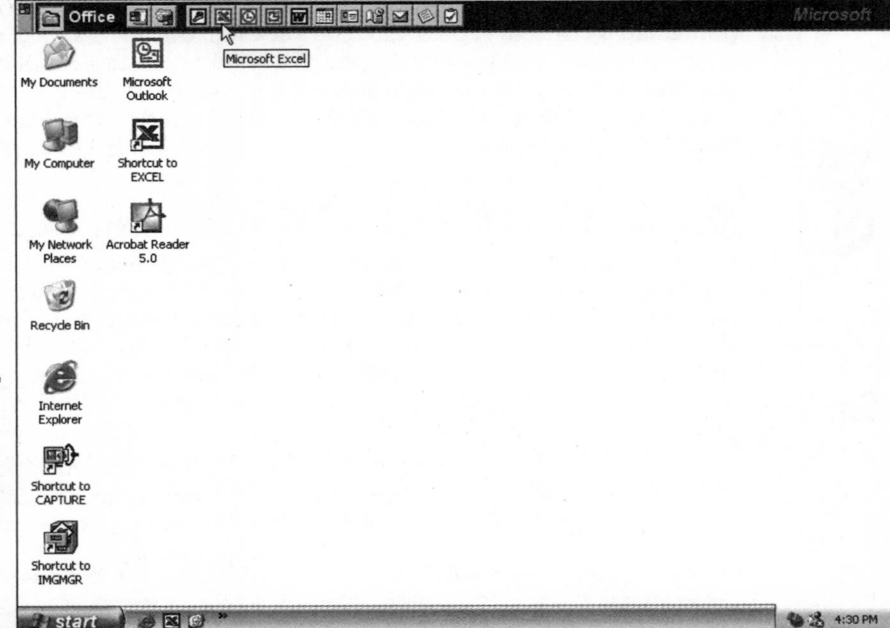

Figure 1-5: The Office Shortcut bar displayed at the top of the Windows XP desktop.

If you want the Microsoft Office Shortcut bar to automatically disappear as soon as you use it to start Excel, you need to turn on the Auto Hide feature. To do this, right-click somewhere on the bar (outside of any buttons) and then click the Auto Hide item on its shortcut menu. When Auto Hide is turned on, you can make the now normally invisible Office Shortcut bar temporarily reappear on the screen by positioning the mouse pointer on the edge of the screen where the bar originally appeared (top, left, or right side). After a second or two, the hiding toolbar suddenly reappears, enabling you to click its buttons. To make the toolbar disappear as fast as it appeared, simply move the mouse pointer off the toolbar.

Starting Excel by opening one of its document files

The last technique for starting Excel simply involves opening a document file created with the program. Windows, wisely following in the footsteps of the Apple Macintosh, associates each application program's executable file with all files that program generates. This means that as soon as you try to open an Excel document file (referred to as a *workbook* or *workbook file*), Windows checks to see if Excel is already running. If it is, Windows simply opens the selected workbook file in the application. If, however, Excel is not yet running, Windows automatically starts Excel before opening the selected workbook file in it.

To open a particular workbook file and, if necessary, launch the Excel program at the same time, simply locate and then double-click the workbook's file icon (similar to the one shown in the left margin) or right-click this icon and then click Open on its shortcut menu.

Don't forget that you can create desktop shortcuts to Excel workbook files that you routinely edit and print just as you do for the programs that routinely run. To create a shortcut icon for an Excel file, locate and open its folder, right-click the workbook file icon, and then highlight Send To on its shortcut menu before you click Desktop (Create Shortcut) on its cascading menu. Then, to open the file and launch Excel all in one stroke, you have only to double-click the Excel workbook desktop shortcut.

Getting to Know the Excel Window

When you start Excel, the program loads in a full-size program window entitled *Microsoft Excel*. As Figure 1-6 shows, the Excel program window is composed of several distinct areas, each of which contains its own elements. The Excel window is divided into the following areas:

- **Title bar.** Located in the first row at the top of the screen, it contains a Control menu button (that displays a pop-up menu of options for moving and resizing the screen), the title of the application (Microsoft Excel), a Minimize button, and a Restore Down button.
- **Menu bar.** Located in the next row, it contains the pull-down menus that enable you to select various Excel commands for use in doing your work in the program. This bar also contains the Ask a Question text box and the active document window's Minimize Window, Restore Window, and Close Window buttons.
- **Standard and Formatting toolbars.** Located side by side on the next row, each of these toolbars contains a series of buttons that, when clicked, perform commonly used Excel commands.
- **Formula bar.** This bar is comprised of three areas: the Name box, located at the far left, that displays the current cell reference; the Cancel and Enter boxes, located in the middle, for entering or editing data in the current cell, along with the Insert Function button (with the *fx* icon); and a third area, located to the right, that displays the contents that you're entering or have entered into the current cell.
- **Excel work area.** This area, located between the Formula and Status bars, contains all the document windows with the Excel workbooks that you have open — normally, Excel displays only the document window with the active worksheet in the active workbook in the middle of the work area.

- **Task Pane.** Located on the right side of the Excel work area, this pane contains one of four different panes: New Workbook (initially) — for opening new or existing workbook files for editing; Clipboard — for managing data that you store in the Windows clipboard; Search — for finding workbooks that you need to edit; and Insert Clip Art — for finding and using Windows clip art images in your worksheets
- **Status bar.** Located at the bottom of the Excel window, this is divided into two parts: the first part displays messages about the current state of the program or the Excel command that you are about to select; the second part contains five mode indicators that tell you when certain keys such as the Num Lock, Extend (F8), or Caps Lock keys or modes are engaged.

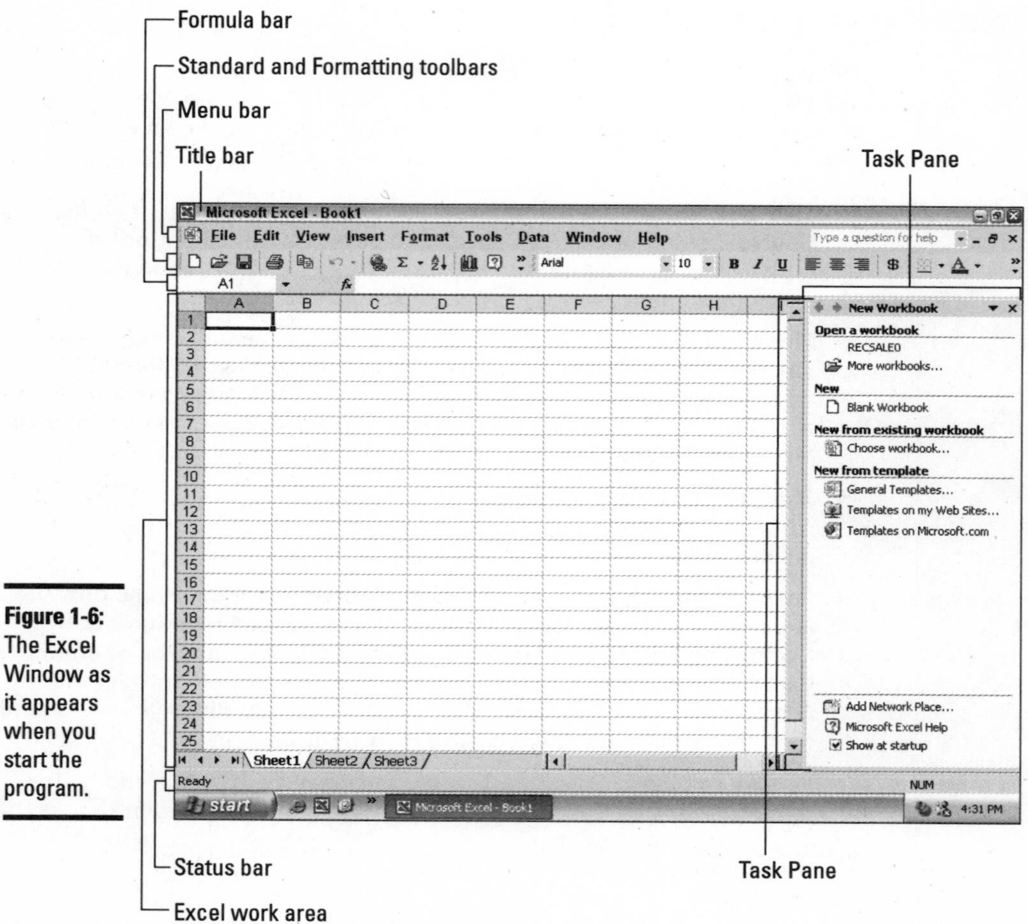

Figure 1-6: The Excel Window as it appears when you start the program.

Title bar

The title bar for the Excel window displays the name of the application (Microsoft Excel) between the program Control menu button (with the XL icon) on the left and two sizing buttons and the Close button on the far right. When you click the Control menu button, the program displays the Control menu. You can use the options on this menu to resize the Excel window, or to close the Excel window (and subsequently quit Excel).

When you first start Excel, the two sizing buttons located on the right side of the title bar consist of a Minimize and Restore Down button (shown respectively in the left margin). You click the Minimize button to reduce the Excel window to a button on the Windows taskbar (this is the equivalent of choosing the Minimize option on the Excel Control menu). You click the Restore Down button to reduce the Excel window down to a mid-size window in the middle of the Windows desktop (this is the equivalent of selecting the Restore option on the program Control menu).

When the Excel window is reduced to a button on the Windows taskbar, you can restore it to full size by clicking the button. When the Excel window is reduced to a mid-size window, the Restore Down button on the title bar changes to a Maximize button (shown in the left margin). You click the Maximize button to restore Excel window to full size (this is the equivalent of selecting the Maximize option on the program Control menu).

The Menu bar

The Menu bar contains nine pull-down menus (from File to Help) on the left side that you use to select the Excel commands necessary for creating your worksheets. On the right side of the Menu bar, you find the Ask a Question text box, which enables you to access the Excel online Help system by typing in a question (see Book I, Chapter 2 for more details). Located to the immediate right of the Ask a Question box, you find the Minimize Window, Restore Window, and Close Window buttons.

As with all the other Windows programs you use, you can choose the commands on the pull-down menus with the mouse or the keyboard. For more information on how to do this, see the "Making Menu Requests" section later in this chapter. As with the other applications in the Office XP suite, you can also choose menu commands by voice if your computer is equipped with a microphone. For detailed information on how to do this, see the "Issuing Voice Commands" section later in this chapter.

The Minimize Window, Restore Window, and Close Window buttons located on the right side of the Menu bar not only use the same icons as the

Minimize, Restore Down, and Close buttons located above on the Title bar, but they also work similarly:

- ✦ Click the Minimize Window button to reduce the active, full-size workbook window to a button at the bottom of the Excel work area.
- ✦ Click the Restore Window button to reduce the active full-size workbook window to a mid-size window with a title bar equipped with its own set of Minimize, Maximize, and Close buttons.
- ✦ Click the Close Window button to close the active workbook — Excel automatically prompts to save the file if you made changes to it since the last time you saved the workbook.

To restore a workbook that you've reduced to a mere button at the bottom of the Excel work area to its previous mid size, click its Restore Up button (using the same icon as the Restore Down button). To restore it to full size, click the Maximize button (you can also choose the Restore or Maximize items on the Control menu; these automatically pop up whenever you click the minimized workbook window button).

One of the easiest ways to restore a minimized workbook button is to use the Alt+Tab keystroke to cycle through all the windows (Excel and otherwise) that you currently have open; these are shown in an unnamed dialog box that appears in the middle of your screen. Continue pressing Alt+Tab until Windows selects the icon for the workbook that you want to restore (indicated by the filename that appears beneath the Excel file icon enclosed in a blue square in this unnamed dialog box).

Note that as soon as you click the Restore Window button, Excel removes the Minimize Window, Restore Window, and Close Window buttons from the Menu bar and the Ask a Question text box takes their place on the far right side of the bar. It does this because the newly restored, mid-size workbook window has its own set of Minimize, Maximize, and Close buttons on its own title bar. If you click the Maximize button on the active workbook window's title bar, the Minimize Window, Restore Window, and Close Window buttons magically reappear on the right side of the Menu bar, moving the Ask a Question text box back toward the middle.

The Standard and Formatting toolbars

The next bar in the Excel window contains two of the most basic toolbars in the program: the Standard toolbar on the left and the Formatting toolbar on the right. Because Excel 2002 automatically places both of these toolbars on the same row of the Excel window, you can't actually see all of the buttons on either toolbar.

To display buttons that aren't currently hidden on either of the two toolbars, you need to click the bar's Toolbar Options button (shown in the left margin) to display a pop-up menu that shows the rest of the buttons on that bar. Note that the two greater than symbols (>) that appear above the downward-pointing arrow form a continuation icon that indicates that not all of the buttons are displayed.

To see the name of any button on any toolbar in Excel, position the mouse on its icon until the name appears in a small box to the side. To display the Standard and Formatting toolbars on separate rows, one above the other, so that you always have access to all buttons on both bars, click the Toolbar Options button on either toolbar and then click the Show Buttons on Two Rows item on the pop-up menu. If you need more screen real estate, you can return to the two bars to their original row-sharing arrangement by clicking the Toolbar Options button on either toolbar (it's the last button on each bar whose icon now lacks a continuation icon and simply sports a lone downward-pointing arrow).

To use a Standard or Formatting toolbar button, simply click its icon (no need for you to double-click). If a button has a pop-up button (indicated by a smaller, square button with a downward-pointing arrow icon located to its immediate right), click this button to choose among a list of further options (for example, you can click the Font's pop-up button to select a new font size directly from its pop-up menu).

For information on how to move and size the Excel toolbars, see the "Taking the Toolbars to Task" section later in this chapter.

The Formula bar

The Formula bar is one of the most important rows in Excel. The first area, called the Name box, displays the address of the active or current cell (this address automatically changes as you move the cell pointer through a worksheet or select a group of cells for editing or formatting). Note that the Name box has its own pop-up button. You use this button in worksheets where you've given groups of cells (called *cell ranges*) common names, such as *sales tax*, *dividend*, and *grand total* (a technique covered in Book III, Chapter 1) to select the cell range by choosing its range name from the associated pop-up menu.

Located immediately to the right of the Name box, you find an area reserved for the Cancel, Enter, and Insert Function buttons. Note that Excel keeps the Cancel and Enter buttons hidden until you either start entering data in the active cell or start editing it, as shown in Figure 1-7. The Insert Function button (with the *fx* icon), however, is displayed on the Formula bar at all times.

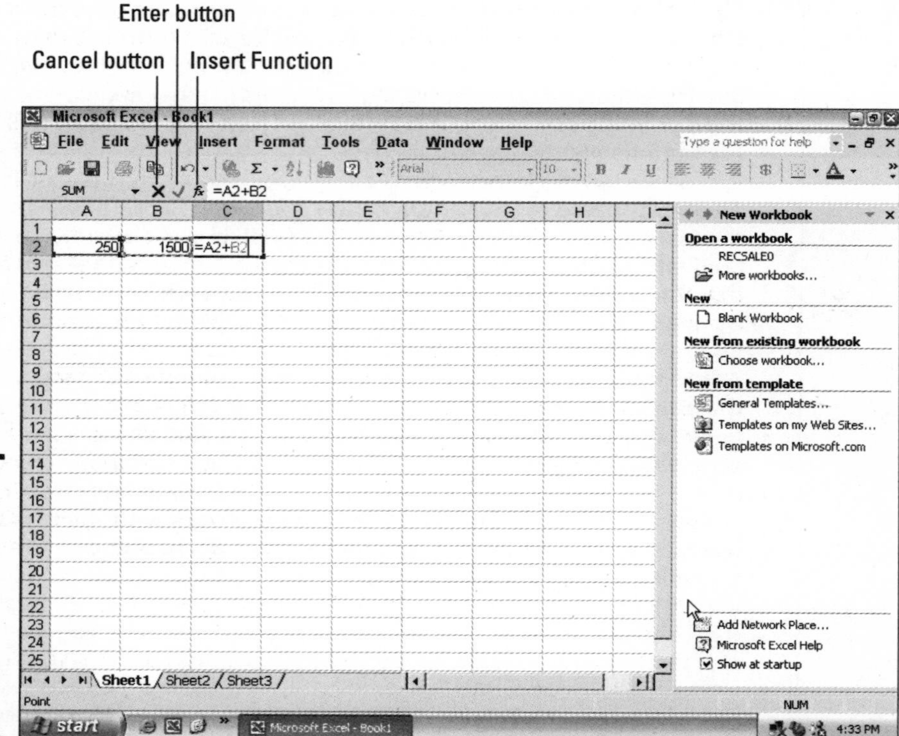

Figure 1-7: The Cancel and Enter buttons appear on the Formula bar during data entry or editing.

You click the Cancel button to abort the data entry or edits that you're making in the active cell. You click the Enter button to complete data entry or editing (note that this is by no means the only way to do this — see Book II, Chapters 1 for details). You click the Insert Function button to insert (or edit) one of Excel's many built-in functions in a formula that you're building (*functions* are ready-made formulas that perform specialized computations, some of which are quite complex — see Book III for complete information on their usage).

The Excel work area

The work area takes up most of the Excel window. As the name implies, this is the place that holds the workbook document windows where you build and edit your spreadsheets. Normally, only a single, full-sized worksheet appears in this space, although you can make Excel *do* windows, meaning that you can split the work area up into smaller window panes in which parts of other worksheets (in the same or different workbooks) can be displayed (see Book I, Chapter 4 for details on how to do this).

Even when a worksheet is displayed in a full-sized workbook window in the work area, you can see only a small fraction of the cells that it contains (each worksheet in every workbook that you open consists of 256 columns and 65,536 rows, giving you a grand total of 16,777,216 cells with which to work). To enable you to bring currently hidden columns and rows into view, the workbook window contains both a vertical and horizontal scroll bar (you use the horizontal bar to scroll back and forth through the columns and the vertical bar to scroll up and down the rows — see the "Getting Around the Worksheet" section later in this chapter for details).

Because each new workbook that you open automatically starts out with three blank worksheets (each with their own 16,777,216 cells arranged on a grid with 256 columns and 65,536 rows), you find sheet scroll button and sheet tabs to the immediate left of the horizontal scroll bar at the bottom of each workbook window. You use these controls to activate different worksheets in the workbook so that you can work with their cells (see the "Navigating the Workbook" section later in this chapter).

The Task Pane

The Task Pane is a new addition to the major productivity applications, such as Excel, Word, and PowerPoint in the Office XP suite. Whenever the Task Pane is displayed, it appears on the right side of the Excel work area obscuring part of the worksheet open below.

When you first start Excel, the program automatically opens the New Worksheet Task Pane to facilitate opening a new workbook or one that you have recently edited. As soon you select an existing workbook to edit or open a new workbook using the links it provides, Excel automatically closes the New Worksheet Task Pane for you. To then reopen the Task Pane, you just choose View⇨Task Pane from the Excel pull-down menus.

The New Worksheet is just one of four different task panes that you can use. In addition to New Worksheet, Excel offers a Clipboard, Search, and Insert Clip Art Task Pane. To switch to another task, click the Other Task Panes drop-down button, as shown in Figure 1-8, and then click the name of the pane that you want displayed. After you've used this pop-up menu to display a Task Pane other New Worksheet, you can then click the Forward and Back buttons at the top of the Task Pane window to jump back and forth between the one you selected and the original New Worksheet pane.

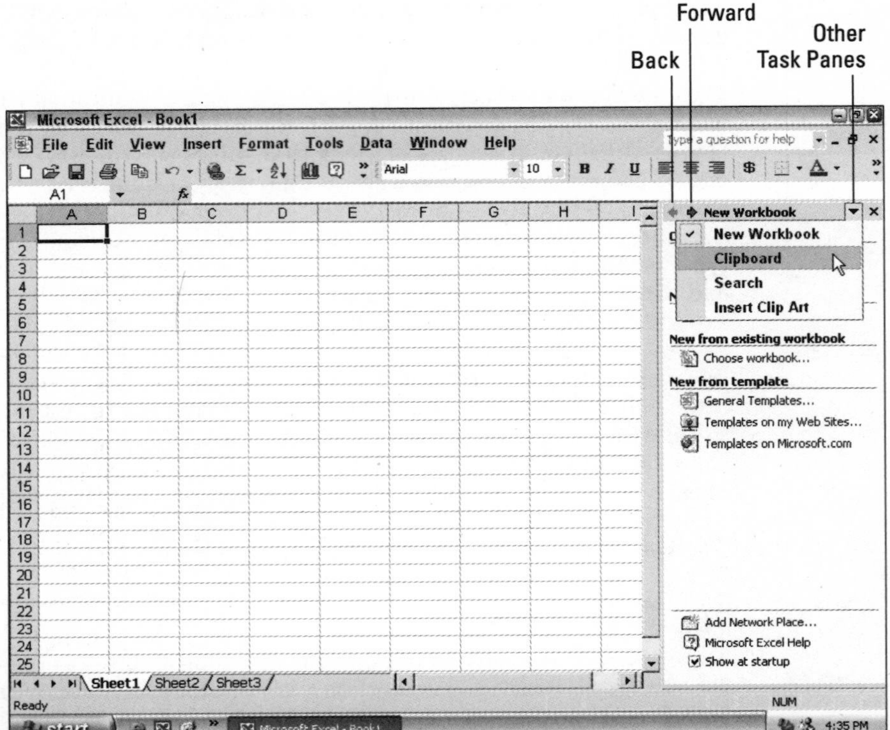

Figure 1-8: Selecting a new Task Pane to use.

The Status bar

Last but not least is the Status bar, the final element of the Excel window (the Windows taskbar located immediately beneath the Status bar does not, strictly speaking, belong to the Excel program, although it is continuously displayed as you use the application program). The Status bar keeps you informed of the current state of the program as you use it. The left side of the Status bar displays messages on the current state of the program. Usually, this area contains the Ready indicator, signifying that Excel is now fully prepared to accept new data in the current cell or some type of Excel command. The other important indicator that you often see in this area of the Status bar is the Edit indicator, signifying that the program is ready to accept the changes that you want to make to the contents of the current cell.

The right side of the status bar contains five *mode indicators*. These indicators tell you when certain lock keys, such as the Caps Lock, Num Lock, or Scroll Lock, are toggled on (these keys are called *toggle* keys because you turn them on by pressing the key once and they stay on until you turn them off by pressing the same key again). In addition to these keys, this area tells you when three other modes are active in Excel. Table 1-1 explains all the mode indicators that appear in this part of the status bar.

Table 1-1 The Various Modes of the Status Bar

Mode	*Key to Turn On/Off*	*Function*
EXT	F8	Extends the current cell range as you select other cells with the arrow keys
ADD	Shift+F8	Adds to the current cell range all cells you select with the arrow keys to the range
CAPS	Caps Lock	Types all letters in uppercase
NUM	Num Lock	Engages and disengages the numeric keypad on your keyboard
SCRL	Scroll Lock	Freezes the cell pointer in its current position as you scroll the worksheet
OVR	Insert	Types over existing text, replacing them with the characters you type
END	End	Combined with one of the four arrow keys (→, ←, ↓, or ↑), moves the cell pointer to the first cell with data that's adjacent to a blank cell in the direction of the arrow
FIX	(none)	Indicates that Excel is ready to automatically add a set number of decimal places to any value you enter in a cell (turned on and off by selecting Tools⇨Options and then selecting/deselecting the Fixed Decimal Places check box on the Edit tab of the Options dialog box)

Getting Around the Worksheet

Regardless of your computer screen size and screen resolution, very little of the total worksheet is displayed at any one time. Although you may create a few spreadsheets that utilize only the portion of the sheet that comes into view when you open it in Excel, chances are that most of your spreadsheets will be larger, either in terms of columns and rows of the worksheet, than can possibly be displayed at one time on your screen.

Because your average Excel spreadsheet is going to be too large to all fit on the screen at one time, you're going to be doing a combination of a lot of moving the cell pointer and scrolling new parts into view almost any time you sit down to work with this software. This being the case, I suggest that you take a second to review some of the more important shortcuts for moving the cell pointer and scrolling the worksheet.

Excel 2002 gives you several different basic ways of moving the cell pointer to different parts of the worksheet:

- ✦ Keyboard via the arrow keys and special cursor keys (Home, End, Page Up, and Page Down) alone and in combination with the Control key
- ✦ Mouse by moving new parts of the worksheet into view with workbook window's scroll bars and then clicking the cell
- ✦ Go To dialog box (which can be opened by pressing Ctrl+G or F5 or choosing Edit⇨Go To on the Menu bar)
- ✦ Voice command using Excel's Speech Recognition feature (see the "Issuing Voice Commands" section later in this chapter)

Keyboarding

Excel offers you plenty of ways to move the cell pointer with the keyboard; the most obvious way is to press the four arrow keys to move the cell pointer a cell at a time in the arrow's direction. Table 1-2 lays out all of your alternatives when it comes to moving the cell pointer from the keyboard.

Table 1-2 Keystrokes for Moving the Cell Pointer

Keystroke	*Movement*
→ or Tab	Next cell to the right
← or Shift+Tab	Next cell to the left
↑	Next cell up
↓	Next cell down
Home	Cell in column A of whatever row contains the cell pointer
Ctrl+Home	First cell (A1) of the worksheet
Ctrl+End or End, Home	Last cell in the active area of the worksheet
PgUp	Cell one screenful up in the current column
PgDn	Cell one screenful down in the current column
Ctrl+→ or End, →	First occupied cell to the right adjacent to a blank cell
Ctrl+← or End, ←	First occupied cell to the left adjacent to a blank cell
Ctrl+↑ or End, ↑	First occupied cell up adjacent to a blank cell
Ctrl+↓ or End, ↓	First occupied cell down adjacent to a blank cell

The keyboard shortcuts shown in Table 1-2 also automatically scroll the worksheet if scrolling is necessary to move to and select the cell. For example, suppose that the cell pointer is currently in the last column visible in the worksheet window and you press Tab or the → key; Excel scrolls the worksheet one column to the right when it selects the next cell over.

Likewise, if you press the Home key when the cell pointer is located in a column many columns to the right, Excel will scroll the entire screenful of data when it selects the cell in column A of the current row.

Among the many keystrokes for moving the cell pointer, the ones that combine the Ctrl or End key with an arrow key are among the most helpful for navigating large blocks of cells, such as tables, that span more than one screenful or for moving between tables in a complex worksheet.

TIP

When you use Ctrl and an arrow key to move around a table or between tables in a worksheet, you hold down Ctrl as you press one of the four arrow keys. When you use End and an arrow key, you press and release End before you press the arrow key. Pressing and releasing the End key causes Excel to display the END indicator on the status bar, indicating that the program is waiting for you to press one of the four arrow keys. Because you can keep the Ctrl key depressed as you press different arrow keys, the Ctrl+arrow key method provides a faster, less disjointed means of navigating blocks of cells than the End+arrow key method.

Mousing around

To use the mouse to move the cell pointer around a worksheet, first use the workbook window's scroll bars to move the part of the worksheet with the cell you want to view in the document window and *then* click that cell to make it active.

To scroll the worksheet grid one row at a time, click the scroll arrows on the vertical scroll bar (the up arrow to scroll up by a row and the down arrow to scroll down). To scroll the worksheet one column at a time, click the scroll arrows on the horizontal scroll bar (the left arrow to scroll left by a column and the right arrow to scroll right).

To scroll the worksheet one screen at a time, click the area on the scroll bar between the scroll box and the scroll arrows. To scroll the sheet up or down one screenful at a time, click the vertical scroll bar (above the scroll box to scroll up and below the scroll box to scroll down). To scroll the sheet left or right by one screenful, click the horizontal scroll bar (left of the scroll box to scroll left and right of the scroll box to scroll right).

For faster scrolling through a large worksheet, you can drag the scroll box. The size of the scroll box reflects the relative size of the *active area* of the worksheet, which is defined by the cell located at the intersection of the furthest column to the right and the row the furthest down in the worksheet that contains data entries (any cell in this column or row can contain the data entry — the cell at this intersection can, in fact, be empty).

Seeing is *not* the same as selecting!

When using the mouse to move the cell pointer, don't forget it's simply not enough to scroll the cell that you want to work with into view in the document window — you still have to remember to click the cell with the mouse pointer in order to activate the cell by moving the cell pointer to it. If you forget this essential step and start trying to enter data in the blank cell you're now staring at, Excel will suddenly scroll you back to the cell in the earlier part of the worksheet that does contain the cell pointer, which is where the characters you've been busily typing away appear.

Because the size of the worksheet's active area determines the relative size of the scroll box in both the vertical and horizontal scroll bar, it also indirectly determines how many columns and rows of the worksheet scroll as you drag the scroll box to a new position in the scroll bar. The bigger the active area, the faster you can scroll through it by dragging the scroll boxes in the vertical and horizontal scroll bars.

Go To

The Go To feature provides the most direct way to move to a distant cell or cell range in the worksheet. You can display the Go To dialog box, shown in Figure 1-9, by using any of the following techniques:

- ✦ Press Ctrl+G
- ✦ Press F5
- ✦ Choosing Edit➪Go To on the Excel Menu bar

To move the cell pointer to a particular cell in the worksheet, type its cell reference in the Reference text box, and then click OK or press Enter. Note that when you enter the cell reference, you can type the column letter(s) in upper- or lowercase.

Excel remembers the cell addresses of the cells that you visit and lists them in the Go To list box. The address of the very last cell that you selected is also automatically entered into the Reference text box. You can therefore quickly return to your previous place in a worksheet by pressing F5 and Enter. To return to another previously visited address in the list box of the Go To dialog box, simply double-click its address or click the address and then click OK.

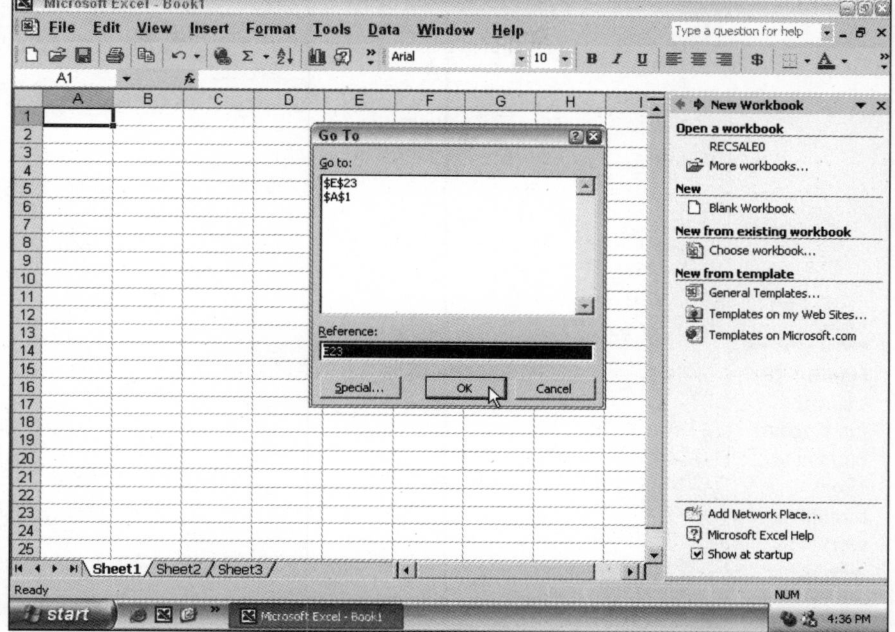

Figure 1-9: Using the Go To dialog box to move the cell pointer.

Navigating the Workbook

Each new workbook that you open in Excel contains three blank worksheets, which you can use as necessary in building your spreadsheet. Having more than one worksheet at your disposal enables you to separate different parts of a complex spreadsheet on individual worksheets in the workbook (as you do individual sections of a complex report on different pages of a word-processed document). If you find it necessary, you can also easily insert additional worksheets to the workbook to accommodate new sections of data (see Book II, Chapter 4 for details).

To make it easy to move to different sheets in a workbook, click the tabs, located at the bottom of the workbook document window, for each of the sheets to make any of the sheets active (meaning that its data is displayed in the work area as though the sheet were now sitting on top of the others in the workbook). You also find a series of tab scrolling buttons to the immediate left of the sheet tabs, shown in Figure 1-10, which enable you to scroll through the sheet tabs in workbooks. These workbooks contain so many worksheets that not all of their sheet tabs are visible at any one time at the bottom of the document window.

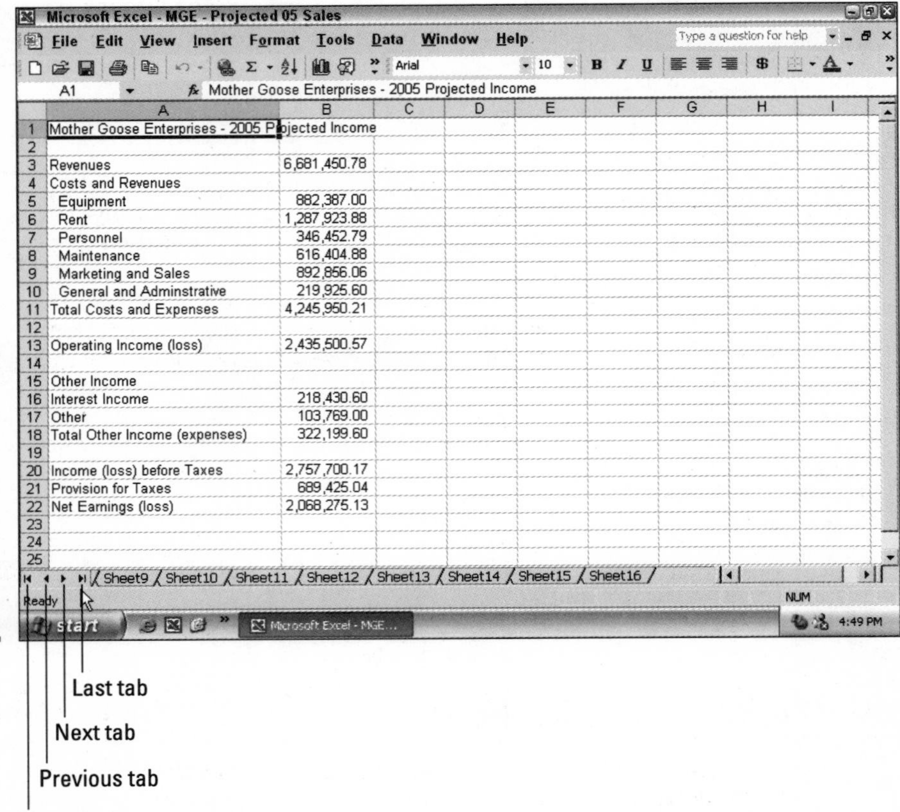

Figure 1-10: Using the tab scrolling buttons to scroll through a workbook with 16 worksheets.

The following are a couple of ways to move from one worksheet to another within the current workbook:

- ✦ Click the sheet tab of the sheet that you want at the bottom of the workbook's document window. If the sheet tab for the worksheet you want to move to isn't displayed, click the Next tab scroll button until the tab of the worksheet that you want to work with appears, and then click the sheet tab to activate the worksheet and display its data in the workbook document window. To redisplay a previous sheet tab, click the Previous tab instead.
- ✦ From the keyboard, hold down the Ctrl key as you press Page Down and Page Up to move from sheet to sheet. Pressing Ctrl+Page Down moves you to the same cell in the next sheet in the workbook. Pressing Ctrl+Page Up moves back up through the sheets in the workbook.

To scroll the last set of sheet tabs in a workbook into view, click the Last tab scroll button. To scroll the first set of sheet tabs into view, click the First tab button.

Making Menu Requests

Although the pull-down menus in Excel were specifically designed for using the mouse to select items, you can just as well use the keyboard if you prefer.

- ✦ To open a pull-down menu with the mouse, click the menu name. To display all the items on the menu, click the Continuation button at the bottom (indicated by two downward-pointing greater than symbols) or wait a few seconds. To select an item on the menu, click it. To open a cascading submenu attached to an item (indicated by a right-pointing triangle), highlight the item and then click the desired item on the submenu.
- ✦ To open a pull-down menu with the keyboard, press the Alt key plus the *hot key* (that is the letter that is underlined in the command) as in Alt+E to open the Edit menu or press F10 to activate the Menu bar, then press the right or left arrow key to select the desired menu and press the ↓ to open the menu. To display all the items on the menu, press ↓ until you highlight the Continuation button or wait a few seconds. To select a menu item, press ↓ to highlight it and then press Enter. To open a cascading menu attached to an item, press ↓ to highlight the item and then press → to open the submenu. To select an item from the cascading submenu, press ↓ to highlight it and then press Enter.

If you're one of the few remaining Lotus 1-2-3 users on the planet who is finally switching to Excel, you'll be happy to know that you can also press the / (slash) key instead of F10 to activate the pull-down menus.

After you've opened a pull-down menu, you can select any of its menu items by clicking the item with the mouse, typing its hot key, or pressing the ↓ key until the item is highlighted and then pressing the Enter key.

Some Excel commands have shortcut keys assigned to them. The shortcut keys assigned to a command are shown after the item's name on the appropriate pull-down menu. If you prefer, you can use the shortcut keys to select the command instead of using the pull-down menus. For example, to save an Excel document, you can press the shortcut keys Shift+F12 instead of choosing the Save option on the File menu.

Can we talk?

When using the Excel pull-down menus, you'll find that the selection of many menu items results in the display of a dialog box offering you oodles of further options from which to choose instead of actually executing a command. You can always tell that selecting a particular menu item will result in a dialog box of further options because the item name on the pull-down menu is followed by an *ellipsis* (...) or three periods in a row.

The controls found in the Excel dialog boxes comprise all the standard bells and whistles (actually buttons and boxes are more like it) that you find in any other Windows application (especially those in the Office XP suite). Complex dialog boxes, such as the Format Cells and the Options dialog box, offer so many options that they don't all fit in a single box. Therefore, these dialog boxes contain separate tabs that, after they are clicked, display a new slate of related options.

You can activate and/or select options in Excel's dialog boxes by clicking them, but don't forget that you can also do this by pressing the Tab key. If the options on a particular tab of a dialog box have hot keys (underlined letters), you can also select them by pressing the Alt key plus that key (note that you can't always just type the hot key letter because many dialog box options accept or respond to text entry).

When a menu item is off-limits

If a menu item appears in light gray on the menu (also referred to as being *dimmed*), this means that the item isn't currently available for selection because the conditions under which it operates are not yet in effect. For example, you find that the Paste item on the Edit menu remains dimmed as long as the Windows Clipboard is empty. As soon as you cut or copy some data to the Clipboard (with the Cut or Copy items on the Edit menu), the Paste menu item appears in normal bold type when you open the Edit menu letting you know that it is now ready to use.

When not all menu items are displayed

As Excel has become more and more sophisticated, the list of menu items on some of its pull-down menus has grown until they hang down almost to the bottom of the screen. In an attempt to tighten up the menus without dropping needed commands, Excel 2002 uses a system in which not all of the items on a given menu are immediately displayed the moment you first open the menu. You can always tell that you're looking at an abbreviated menu because a Continuation button (with two downward pointing greater than symbols, one on top of the other) appears immediately beneath the very last menu item.

To display all the items on an abbreviated menu, you can either wait a few seconds or click this Continuation button. Note that after you've expanded one menu to its full size, Excel automatically displays all items on any subsequent menus that you open (that is, until the next time you activate the Menu bar). If you prefer having all the menu items displayed whenever you open any pull-down menu (which is a very good idea when you're first becoming familiar with its commands), you can switch from abbreviated to a full-menu setting.

When deciding whether you want to work with these abbreviated menus, remember that Excel doesn't always display the same items on the abbreviated menu each time you open it. Because Excel watches which of the items you choose most often on any given menu, it always tries to make sure that these items are displayed on the abbreviated menu. This means that menu items you seldom use will most certainly be hidden until you expand the menu to its full form. Take it from me — this can make it very difficult to find an occasionally used item when you're not 100 percent sure which menu it's on. It's so much easier to track down a wayward menu item when you know that you're looking at the full menus.

To switch to full menus so that Excel shows you all the menu items each and every time you open any of its menus, follow these few steps:

1. **Right-click the Menu bar (or somewhere on the Standard/Formatting toolbar).**

   A long shortcut menu appears.

2. **Choose the Customize item at the very bottom of the shortcut menu by clicking it or typing** C.

   The Customize dialog box appears with the Options tab selected.

3. **Click the Always Show Full Menus check box on the Options tab.**

   This action automatically deselects and deactivates the Show Full Menus After a Short Delay check box (which now becomes dimmed).

4. **Click the Close button to close the Customize dialog box.**

Shortcut menus

In addition to the full-blown pull-down menus you find on the Excel Menu bar, the program offers a variety of specialized menus, called *shortcut menus*. Shortcut menus are attached to individual screen objects that you routinely encounter in the Excel window, such as the toolbars, worksheet cells, column and row headers, and sheet tabs.

To open an object's shortcut menu, simply right-click the object. An object's shortcut menu contains only menu items that are relevant to that object, so if you right-click one of the toolbars, the shortcut menu that appears contains only menu items for viewing and hiding and customizing the various Excel toolbars. Likewise, if you right-click one of the worksheet tabs, the shortcut menu that appears contains only menu items for doing stuff with sheet tabs, such as inserting and deleting tabs, renaming tabs, moving and copying tabs, and so on.

Figure 1-11 shows the shortcut menu that's attached to every cell in the worksheet displayed by right-clicking the cell. Note from this figure that items of shortcut menus often have hot keys (such as the *m* in the Insert Comment item) that you can press to select that item.

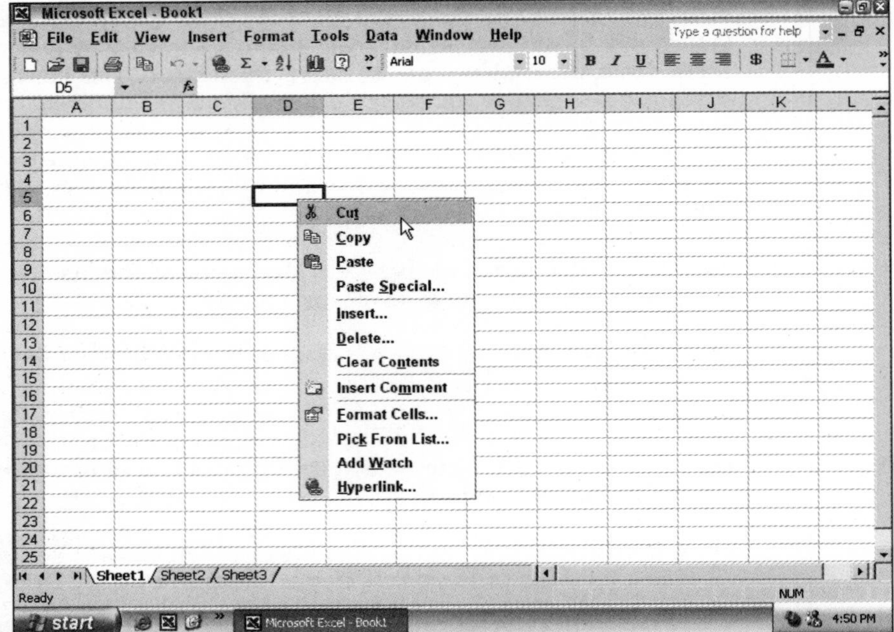

Figure 1-11: Right-clicking a cell to open its shortcut menu.

Shortcut menus are invaluable when working with hyperlinks and graphic objects that are embedded in a worksheet such as charts, comments, Clip Art, and other types of pictures. This is because shortcut menus give you fast, direct access to just the menu options you need in editing that particular kind of object. See Book VIII, Chapter 2 for details on using links and Book V, Chapters 1 and 2 for information on adding charts and graphics to the worksheet.

Issuing Voice Commands

Excel 2002 supports Speech Recognition, which enables you to issue voice commands that allow you to choose menu items, dialog box options, or even toolbar buttons by simply saying their names. According to Microsoft, to be able to use Speech Recognition in Excel, your computer must be at least a Pentium II running at a minimum speed of 300 MHz with a minimum of 128MB of RAM.

You also need a top quality microphone, preferably one that's attached to a headset (like the kind used by your office receptionist). The giveaway microphones that come with today's PCs are just not sensitive enough for today's speech recognition because they tend to pick up stray sounds, which frankly make it impossible to have your voice commands correctly processed.

For information on how to use the Dictation portion of the Speech Recognition feature to do data entry in your worksheet, see Book II, Chapter 1. While you're there, you can look up information on how to use the Text To Speech feature (a separate, but related new speech feature unique to Excel 2002) to validate the data entries that you make in a worksheet.

Installing and training Speech Recognition

If you or the person who installed Office XP on your computer performed a Standard installation, then Speech Recognition won't be installed until you first try to use the feature in Excel 2002 (or one of the other Office programs such as Word or PowerPoint). To install Speech Recognition, have your Office XP CD-ROM handy and then follow these steps:

1. **Choose Tools⇨Speech⇨Speech Recognition on the Excel menu bar.**

   An Alert dialog box displays, indicating that this feature isn't currently installed and asking if you want to install it now.

2. **Click the Yes button in the Alert dialog box.**

   Excel displays an Installing Components for Microsoft Excel dialog box, which is then replaced by a Microsoft Office XP dialog box, telling you to insert the Microsoft Office XP disk.

3. **Insert the CD with your Microsoft Office XP programs in the CD-ROM drive and then click OK.**

   Excel installs the Speech Recognition components while displaying its progress in an Installing Components for Excel dialog box.

Upon completion of this installation, a Welcome to Speech Recognition dialog box appears, indicating that you must adjust your microphone and train Office for speech recognition. To do this adjustment and training, you need to have your microphone and speakers properly hooked up. You also need about 15 minutes of uninterrupted time and a fairly quiet environment where you won't be disturbed. If you already have Speech Recognition installed, you can do this training by clicking the Tools button on the Language bar (Tools⇨Speech⇨Speech Recognition) and then clicking the Training option on its pop-up menu.

Click the Next button and then follow the onscreen instructions displayed in the Microphone and Voice Training Wizards. After you complete this initial microphone adjustment and speech recognition training, a new window appears with a brief multimedia presentation explaining how to make the best use of the Office XP Speech Recognition features. After that finishes playing, you're ready to begin using speech recognition for both entering data and issuing Excel voice commands.

If you're serious about using speech recognition to do data entry or to choose Excel commands, you should complete more than just the initial voice training because the more training you do, the higher the recognition accuracy rate. You can do more training sessions by clicking the More Training button that appears in the final Voice Training dialog box at the end of your initial training session. You can also do this at any later time by choosing Tools⇨Speech⇨Speech Recognition to display the Language bar, and then clicking the Tools button on this bar and Training on its pop-up menu. In the Training dialog box, you can select the passage that you want to read. By eventually reading all of the training sessions, you can really increase your accuracy rate, especially when dictating the data that you want entered in your spreadsheet.

Saying commands

After you've completed basic voice training, you can start using the Speech Recognition feature to issue your menu, toolbar, and dialog box selections verbally. To issue voice commands, you only need to put Speech Recognition into Voice Command mode:

1. **Choose Tools⇨Speech⇨Speech Recognition to display the Language bar.**

   If the Language bar is already displayed at the top of the Excel window, you can just click its Microphone button instead. If the Language bar is minimized on the Windows taskbar, click the Restore button (in Windows 9*x*, click the EN icon and then click Restore the Language Bar on its pop-up menu).

2. **Click the Voice Command button on the Language bar, shown in Figure 1-12.**

   Note that you can also say "voice command" to select this button.

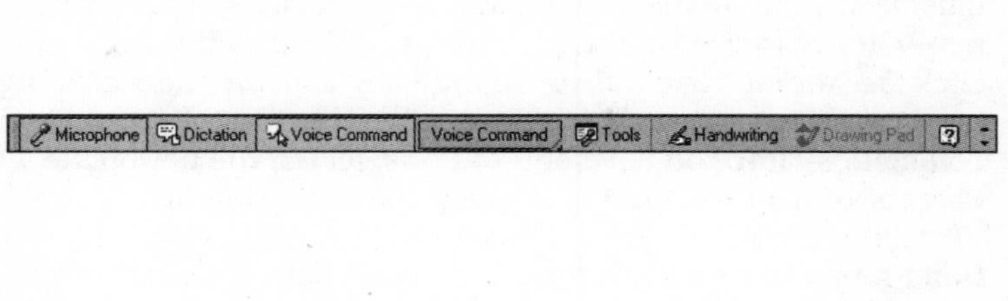

Figure 1-12: Click the Voice Command button on the Language bar before speaking commands.

After Speech Recognition is selected, you're ready to command your little heart out.

Choosing menu items, dialog box options, and toolbar buttons

To choose pull-down menus or to select buttons on an open toolbar (such as the Standard or Formatting toolbar), say the menu and item name or the toolbar's button name. For example, to choose File➪Save on the pull-down menus to save changes to the current workbook, you say "file," and then when Excel opens the File menu, you say "save" to choose the Save menu item. Alternately, you can just say the word *"save"* to have Excel perform exactly the same action — this time by selecting the Save button on the Standard toolbar.

If you say a menu command that opens a dialog box, you can select its tabs or options by saying their names. For example, if you say "format" and then say "cells," the Format Cells dialog box opens, and you can select the Font tab in this dialog box by saying "font" and then you can select the Strikethrough check box option by saying "strikethrough." To then close the Format Cells dialog box and apply the strikethrough attribute to the entry in the currently selected cell(s), say "Okay." To close a dialog box without putting into effect any of the options that you changed, say "cancel" instead (you can also say "escape" to close a dialog box without making changes).

Keep in mind that you can use Voice Command to select the dialog box option that you want to change. Say the word *"tab"* to have Excel advance through each of the options displayed on the current tab of a dialog box, selecting each option as it goes. When the dialog box option that you want to change is selected (indicated by highlighting in the case of text boxes and combo boxes, and dotted outlining in the case of radio buttons and check boxes), you can then say the new value or suspend Voice Command and enter the new value manually.

If you need to enter a new value in one of the text boxes in a dialog box (or select a value in a pop-up list when you don't already know its name), you must first turn off Voice Command temporarily and then enter or select the new value with the keyboard or mouse. To turn off Voice Command, simply click the Microphone button on the Language bar, thus causing the bar to hide the Dictation and Voice Recognition buttons. To resume giving voice commands after you have entered or selected the new value, click the Microphone button on the Language bar a second time.

Don't forget to turn off Voice Command before you start clicking objects in the Excel window with the mouse or typing something from the keyboard, because if you do — mark my words — you stand a good chance of having Voice Command decide that your mouse clicks or typing sounds like some Excel menu command or toolbar button. Having Excel choose a harmless command that you're not expecting can be bad enough, but having the program choose one that alters your worksheet can be devastating (usually when I forget to first turn Voice Command off, it responds by having Excel open up a new, blank worksheet, which totally throws me off because the worksheet with all my data is suddenly no longer onscreen!).

Note that the effects of many of the Excel commands that you choose (whether you do this by voice, keyboard, or mouse) are reversible by immediately using the program's Undo command (some commands such as saving changes in a document, are not reversible, however). If Speech Recognition ever messes up and chooses the wrong menu command, toolbar button, or dialog box option, immediately say the word *"undo."* Because Excel supports multiple levels of undo, you may have to repeat the word several times to get your worksheet back to the desired state.

Telling the cell pointer where to go

You can use Voice Command to move the cell pointer to new cells in the worksheet by saying the following words and phrases:

- "Right" or "right arrow" to move the cell pointer one column to the right
- "Left" or "left arrow" to move the cell pointer one column to the left
- "Up" or "up arrow" to move the cell pointer one row up
- "Down" or "down arrow" to move the cell pointer one row down
- "Home" to move the cell pointer to the beginning of the line
- "End," and then pause before you say the name of an arrow key ("up," "down," "left," or "right") to move the cell pointer to the edge of the next data region or worksheet boundary in that direction

You have a much better chance of having Excel's Speech Recognition feature understand your meaning if you say a phrase such as "left arrow" and "up arrow" rather than just saying solitary words such as "left" and "up."

Taking the Toolbars to Task

The Standard and Formatting toolbars that share the second row of the Excel window are by no means the only toolbars with which you'll be working. The program comes with a whole carload of ready-made toolbars that you can display or hide at any time while using the program. The easiest way to display a hidden toolbar is to right-click somewhere on the Menu bar or on one of the already displayed toolbars (such as the Standard/Formatting toolbar), and then click the toolbar's name on the shortcut menu that appears. You can also display a toolbar by choosing View⇨Toolbars and then choosing the toolbar's name on the cascading menu that appears.

In Excel, as with the Office programs, the toolbars that you display in the Excel window can be docked or free-floating. A *docked toolbar* is positioned either above the formula bar or on the left, right, or below the active document window (the Standard and Formatting toolbars are both docked side by side on the row below the Menu bar). A *floating toolbar* is displayed in its own window complete with title bar and Control menu button. Unlike a docked toolbar that remains stationary at the perimeter of the worksheet window, you can move and resize a floating toolbar as you want within the active document window.

To undock a docked toolbar, simply position the mouse pointer on the gray vertical bar in front of the very first button, then when the pointer changes into a four-headed arrow, drag the toolbar toward the center of the work area. As soon as the title bar appears, you can release the mouse button.

To dock a floating toolbar, simply position the mouse pointer somewhere on its title bar, then when the pointer changes to a four-headed arrow, drag the toolbar to one of the four edges of the screen. As soon as the toolbar's title bar disappears, you can release the mouse button. When docking a floater in an area that already contains other docked toolbars (such as the top area which already contains the Standard and Formatting toolbar on the same row), you can then reposition it on a new row by dragging it by the light gray vertical bar in front of the first button.

After you've undocked a toolbar, you can then move the newly floating toolbar around the Excel work area by dragging the title bar. You can also modify the shape of the toolbar window. To do this, either position the pointer on the right edge or the bottom edge of the toolbar window. When the pointer changes to a double-headed arrow, you then drag the mouse to change the shape of the toolbar.

If you've positioned the pointer on the right edge of the toolbar window, drag to the left to make the window narrower and longer or to the right to make the window wider and shorter. If you've positioned the pointer on the bottom edge of the window, you can accomplish the same thing by dragging the mouse down or up. Excel increases or decreases the number of rows of tools in the toolbar window to accommodate the change in shape.

To return a floating toolbar window to its previously docked position, simply double-click the toolbar. If you have modified the shape of a toolbar before you return the toolbar to its docked position, the toolbar will automatically resume this shape the next time you undock the toolbar. If you want to remove a toolbar window from the work area without docking it, click the Control menu button on the toolbar window. If you close a toolbar window without docking it, the toolbar will resume its previous position and shape in the work area the next time you display the toolbar.

In addition to moving and reshaping a toolbar, you can also customize the tools that it contains and even create your own toolbars. For complete information on how to customize Excel toolbars, refer to Book I, Chapter 3.

Chapter 2: Getting Help

In This Chapter

- **Becoming familiar with Excel's Help system**
- **Getting help from the Answer Wizard**
- **Looking up help topics in the Help system**
- **Putting the Office Assistant in his place**
- **Getting online help**
- **Getting online updates, downloads, and repairing Excel**

There's nothing quite like the feeling of getting just the help you need on using a new Excel feature right at the time your need arises. That's where the program's extensive online Help system comes in — at least in theory. The big problem is that between the strange animated paper clip (the default persona of the Office Assistant), tiled Help windows with about a gazillion help topics arranged the way a software engineer would like to see them, and a Help index jam-packed with obscure terms ranging from *ABS function* to *z-test*, you may really feel like you need help just in order to use Help.

In this chapter, I try to set you straight on the dos and don'ts of the Excel Help system so that instead of an intensely frustrating experience, you can get the help information you need right from the horse's mouth, so to speak, thus saving you from having to look up a topic in the many, many indexes in this book.

"Ask a Silly Question . . ."

The first place to go for help in Excel is the Ask a Question box that appears on the right side of the Excel Menu bar. This combo box is your ever-present key to accessing the Answer Wizard, a component of the Excel Help system that tries to respond intelligently to your queries by suggesting related help topics to which you may want to refer.

Although it's called the Ask a Question box, you really don't have to ask a formal question; entering a phrase with key terms will usually do just as well. For example, suppose that you want to find out how to print the columns in a spreadsheet table or data list at the top of each page. Instead of having to go through the trouble of typing out the formal question, "How do I get my spreadsheet headings to print on every page of my report?," you can simply enter the keyword phrase "print headings" in the Ask a Question box.

To use the Ask a Question box to consult the Answer Wizard, follow three easy little steps:

1. **Click the Ask a Question box to select whatever text it currently contains.**

   When you first use the Ask a Question box, it contains the phrase, "Type a question for help." When you click anywhere in this box, Excel selects all of the text in the box so that whatever you begin typing in the box replaces this original text.

2. **Type the keywords or a keyword phrase describing the topic that you want help with in the Ask a Question box.**

   Whatever you type in the Ask a Question box replaces the original text it contains.

3. **Press Enter to display a pop-up list of possible help topics (refer to Figure 2-1).**

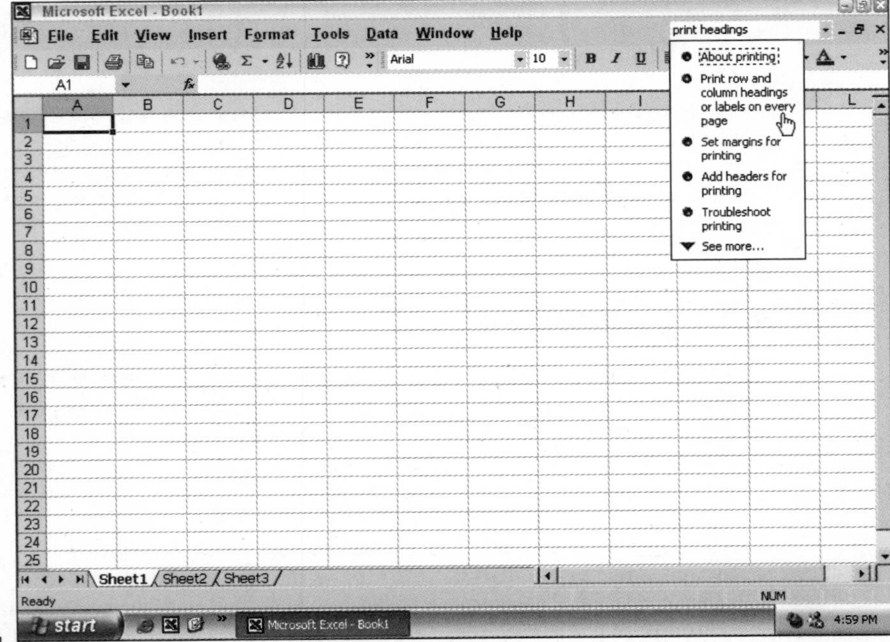

Figure 2-1: Selecting one of the help topics suggested by the Answer Wizard.

Simply click the topic to open the Help window and display information on one of the help topics listed in the Ask a Question box's pop-up menu. If none of the topics suggested by the Answer Wizard seem to fit the bill, click the See More button at the bottom of the list. If these further topics don't offer a good match, click the Ask a Question box and try using other keywords or more descriptive phrases — heck, you can even try asking it a real question — to try to get the Answer Wizard to cough up a pertinent topic or two this time.

Displaying a suggested help topic

When you click one of the topics in the list displayed below the Ask a Question box, Excel opens a separate Microsoft Excel Help window with information on the topic that you selected to the right of the Excel window (similar to the one shown in Figure 2-2). As you can see in this figure, this Help window contains a row of buttons (called out in the figure) beneath the title bar that you can use to manipulate the Help window and to print the help topic.

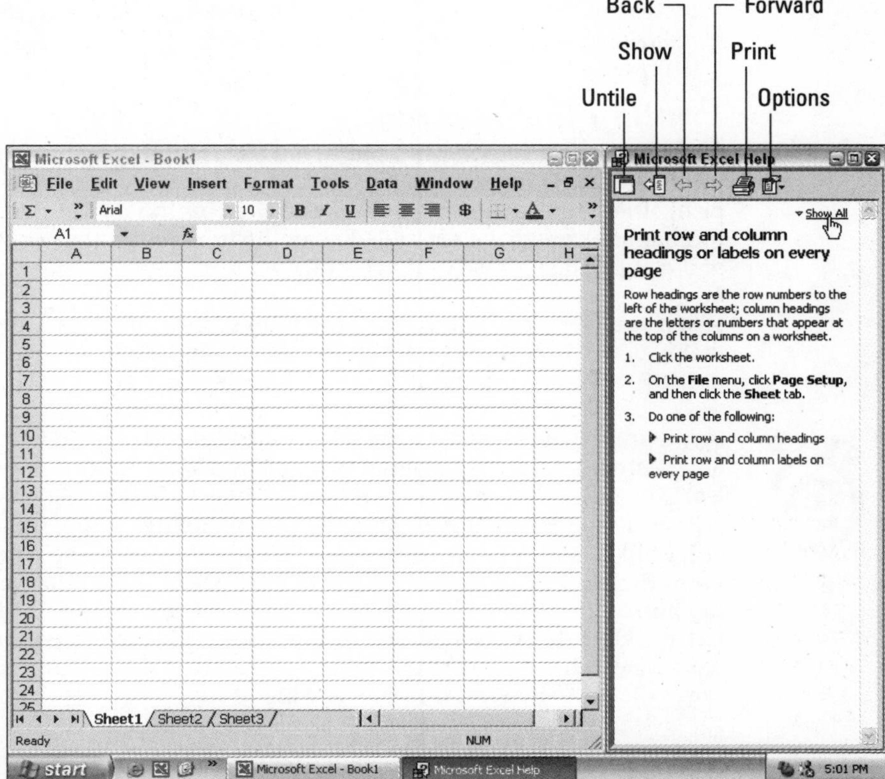

Figure 2-2: Displaying one of the suggested help topics in a tiled Help window.

This particular Help window about printing row and column headings on every page (shown previously in Figure 2-1) contains two topics located at the bottom of the general introductory text about this subject: Print row and column headings, and Print row and column labels on every page.

To display the information on both these topics, click the Show All link in the upper-right corner of the window (immediately below the row of toolbar buttons) to expand them. To display information on just one or the other topic, click its particular link — Print row and column headings, or Print row and column labels on every page.

To collapse a particular topic that you've expanded in order to hide its help information, simply click its link (you can distinguish an expanded topic from a collapsed topic because collapsed topics have blue triangles pointing to the right and expanded topics have triangles pointing downward).

After you're finished consulting the help information, you can close the Help window by clicking its Close button in the upper-right corner of the Microsoft Excel Help window. As soon as you do this, Windows automatically resizes the Excel window so that it once again takes up the entire screen.

Printing the help topic

In many situations, you will want to have a printed copy of the help topic information so that you can have it handy as you try out a new feature. To print a help topic, you simply click the Help button on the Help window's toolbar after you have expanded all of the help topics that you want printed and collapsed all those that you don't want.

When you click the Print button, the Help system displays a standard Print dialog box, where you can select the printer and print settings that you want used. To send the job to the printer, click OK.

If you prefer, you can also copy all or part of the displayed help information and paste it into other documents (such as a Word report or even an Excel worksheet) instead of printing it out. To copy help text, click the mouse pointer in the text and then drag the I-beam pointer through the text that you want to select (it appears highlighted). After you've selected the text, press Ctrl+C to copy it to the Windows clipboard. Switch to the window containing the document or worksheet into which the copied text is to be pasted, click the mouse pointer at the place in the document or cell in the worksheet where the first part of the copied text should appear, and then press Ctrl+V to insert it into the new file.

Resizing and moving the Help window

When you first open a Help window, it is automatically tiled on the right side of the Excel window (as shown previously in Figure 2-2). This arrangement enables you to see both the Help window and the worksheet that you have open in the Excel window. Because the windows are tiled, if you manually change the size of the Help window (for example, to make it somewhat wider by dragging its border to the left), the Excel window is automatically resized to accommodate the change (it is made narrower in the widening example).

If you don't want the Excel window resized each time you adjust the size of the Help window, click the Untile button on the Help window's toolbar. When you do this, the Help window immediately overlaps the Excel window so that if you make the Help window wider, it just obscures more of the Excel window underneath. If you want to view the online help information in a full screen, click the Help window's Maximize button.

After untiling the Help window, you can then manually reposition the window (by dragging its title bar) and resize it (by dragging one of its edges) in order to see various parts of the worksheet and/or the Excel menu bar, toolbars, and dialog boxes.

To once again have Windows tile the Excel program and Help windows side by side, you just need to click the Auto Tile button (this button automatically replaces the Untile button as soon as you click it).

Note that if you close the Excel Help window when auto tiling is turned off, Windows doesn't automatically resize the Excel program window for you (you have to do this yourself by clicking the window's Maximize button). For this reason, you may want to get in the habit of clicking the Auto Tile button before you click the Microsoft Excel Help window's Close button so that you're immediately ready to get back to work

Calling F1

F1 is the Help key in Excel. The first time you press this key (or choose Help⇨Microsoft Excel Help, its Menu bar equivalent), the Microsoft Excel Help window appears, displaying the list of general help topics, as shown in Figure 2-3. Note that the third topic from the top in this help window is called Getting Help — you click this link to get help on getting help, which may be just what the doctor ordered if you want an overview of the various help resources at your fingertips when you use the program.

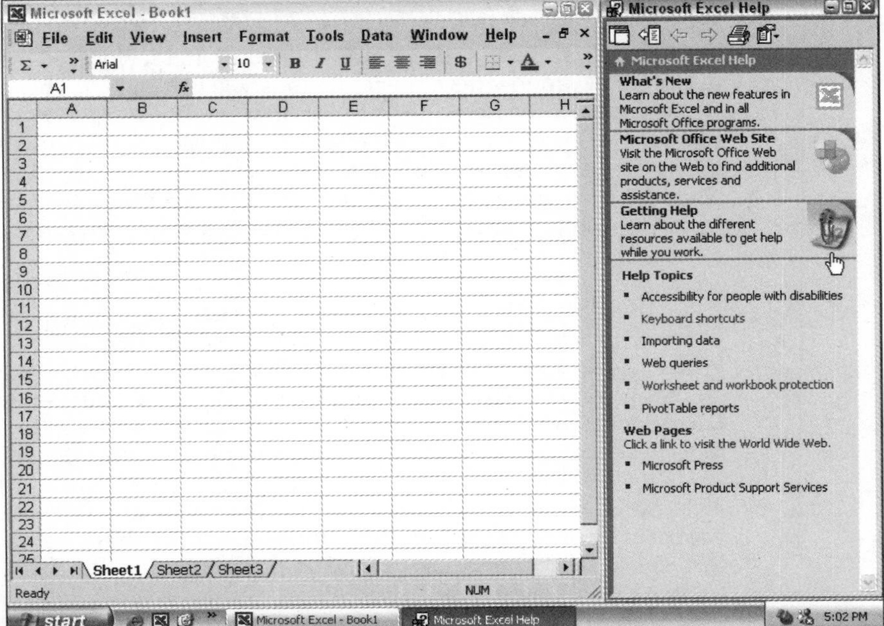

Figure 2-3: Displaying the general Excel Help window by pressing F1.

In addition to looking over the topics under the Getting Help heading, you may also want to check out the program's various keyboard shortcuts by clicking the Keyboard Shortcuts link under the Help Topics heading. When you click this link, a condensed list of all available major keyboard shortcuts, arranged in categories, appears in the Help window. To print the list of keyboard shortcuts so that you can refer to them as you work with Excel, click the Show All link located above and to the right of heading, Keyboard Shortcuts, and then click the Print button on the Help window's toolbar.

Note that when you click a topic link, such as the Getting Help topic in the general Help window, to pursue its information, the Back button on the Help window's toolbar becomes active (this button is initially dimmed because there is nowhere farther back to return to). You can click the Back button to return to the help screen from which you came (in this example, the General Help screen). After you use the Back button to return to a previous help screen, you automatically activate the Forward button on the toolbar, which you can click to go back to the help screen from which you just returned (whew!).

Looking up help topics the old fashioned way

The Microsoft Excel Help window that initially opens when you press F1 or choose Help⇨Microsoft Excel Help on the Menu bar is a condensed version of the window. To expand the window to a full version that includes the Contents, Answer Wizard, and Index tabs, click the Show button on the Help window's toolbar (or click the Options button and then click the Show Tabs item on its pop-up menu).

Figure 2-4 shows a full three-tab version of the Microsoft Excel Help window that appears after you click the Show button (which then automatically turns into a Hide button that you click to make the section with the tabs disappear). Note from Figure 2-4 that whenever you expand the Help window to include the Contents, Answer Wizard, and Index tabs, the Help system automatically turns off the auto tiling feature so that this expanded Help window obscures a good part of the Excel program window below.

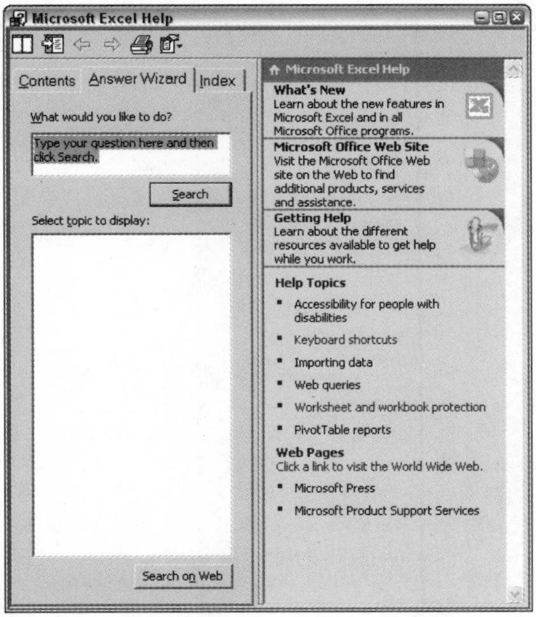

Figure 2-4: Expanded Microsoft Help window showing the Contents, Answer Wizard, and Index tabs.

Ask the Answer Wizard

When you first expand the Microsoft Excel Help window, the Answer Wizard tab in the middle of the three tabs is automatically selected, which enables you to type in a new question or enter new keywords or phrases to search for in the Help system (just like you do when using the Ask a Question box on the Excel menu bar).

There's a big difference between searching for a help topic on the Answer Wizard tab versus in the Ask a Question box. When you use the Answer

Wizard tab, you can continue to see all the help topics returned as a result of your search in the Answer Wizard tab as you read help information on the topic you've selected in the pane to the right.

Figure 2-5 illustrates how this works. In this figure, I entered "format data" in the What Would You Like to Do? text box and then clicked the Search button. As you can see, the Excel Help returned quite a long list of format-related topics. The first topic returned by the search, About Formatting Worksheets and Data, is automatically selected in the Select Topic to Display list box and its help information is displayed in the Help pane to the right. To display another help topic in this pane, simply click it in the Select Topic to Display list. To conduct a new search on this or a new topic, simply type the search keywords or phrase and then click the Search button.

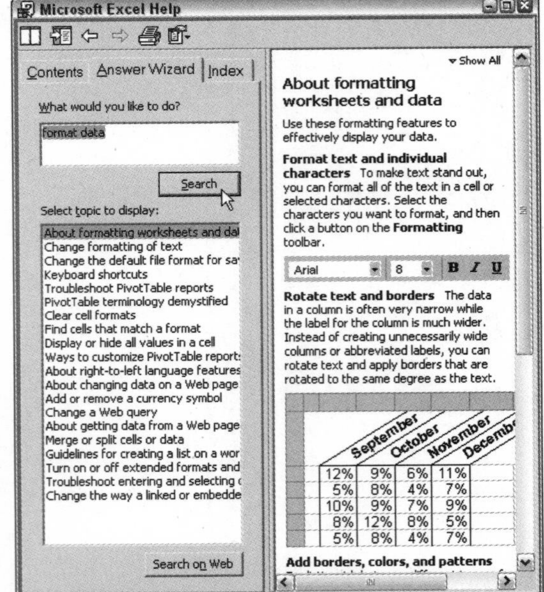

Figure 2-5: Searching for new help topics on the Answer Wizard tab.

Browsing topics with the Contents tab

The Contents tab contains a list of all Excel help topics arranged hierarchically in topical categories. When you first open this tab, all of the topics are collapsed under a single, all-encompassing category — Microsoft Excel Help. To expand the outline to display all the main categories within Microsoft Excel Help, click the Expand button (the one with the + sign) in front of the Microsoft Excel Help book icon on the Contents tab.

After you've displayed the main help categories on this tab, you can start burrowing deeper into a particular category by clicking its Expand button. Many main categories have subcategories and some subcategories have their own subcategories, but regardless of the number of nested levels, eventually you'll come to a list of help pages (indicated by the question mark on a page icon).

When you come to the level of individual help pages, you can display their help information in the main Help pane on the right by clicking the help page icon in the Contents pane. Figure 2-6 illustrates how this works.

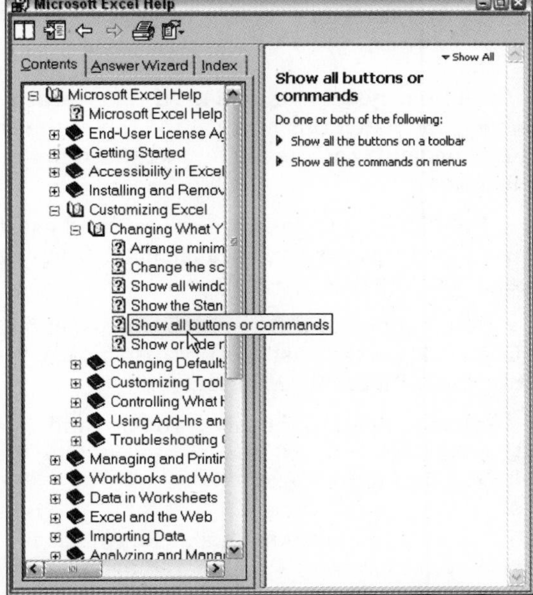

Figure 2-6: Browsing the help topics arranged hierarchically on the Contents tab.

In this figure, I first clicked the Expand button in front of the Customizing Excel category to display six subcategories: Changing What You See on the Screen, Changing Defaults and Settings, Customizing Toolbars and Menus, Controlling What Happens When You Start Excel, Using Add-Ins and Optional Components, and Troubleshooting Customizing Excel.

I then clicked the Expand button in front of the first Customizing subcategory, Changing What You See on the Screen, to display a list of six individual help pages. Finally, I clicked the fifth help page, Show All Buttons or Commands, to display its help information in the main Help pane to the right of Contents tab.

Looking up stuff from the Index tab

The Index tab in the expanded Microsoft Excel Help window contains a complete alphabetical list of keywords (starting with the cents symbol and ending with the ZTEST worksheet function). To browse through the keywords in this list, you can type your keywords in the Type Keywords text box, located at the top of the Index tab, or you can use the vertical scroll bar to scroll up the keywords in the Or Choose Keywords list box.

As you type keywords into the Type Keywords text box, Excel Help responds to each letter that you type by moving to the next term in the index that matches that character. For example, for Figure 2-7, I typed the letters *f-o-r-m* in the Type Keywords list box before clicking the keyword, *formula,* in the Or Choose Keywords list box. Here's a rundown on the sequence of events as they unfolded:

- ✦ When I typed *f*, the Help system jumped to the keywords *FACT Worksheet Function* and listed this entry at the top of the Or Choose Keywords list box because *FACT* is the first keyword in the Index that begins with the letter *f.*
- ✦ When I typed *o*, Help jumped to the keyword *fold* and listed it at the top of the Or Choose Keywords list box because it's the first keyword in the Index that begins with the two letters *fo*.
- ✦ When I typed *r*, Help jumped to the keyword *forecast* and listed it at the top of the Or Choose Keywords list box because it's the first keyword in the Index that begins with the three letters *for.*
- ✦ When I typed *m*, Help jumped to the keyword *form* and listed it at the top of the Or Choose Keywords list box because it's the first Index entry that begins with the four letters *form*.

After *form* was listed at the top of the Or Choose Keywords list box, I was able to just click the keyword *formula* (it appeared just five entries below *form*) in the Or Choose Keywords list box to add this term to the Type Keywords text box (no need to the type the characters *ula* onto *form*). With *formula* now entered into the Type Keywords text box, all I had to do was to click the Search button to have all the help topics in the Excel Help system searched for occurrences of that keyword.

As Figure 2-7 shows, the Excel Help system found 452 occurrences of the keyword *formula* in the various help topics (no surprises there). To explore the help topics that discuss formulas, you just scroll through the list shown in the Choose a Topic list box. To display help information on a particular topic shown in that list, you just click the topic in the Choose a Topic list box and the information appears in the main Help pane located to the right.

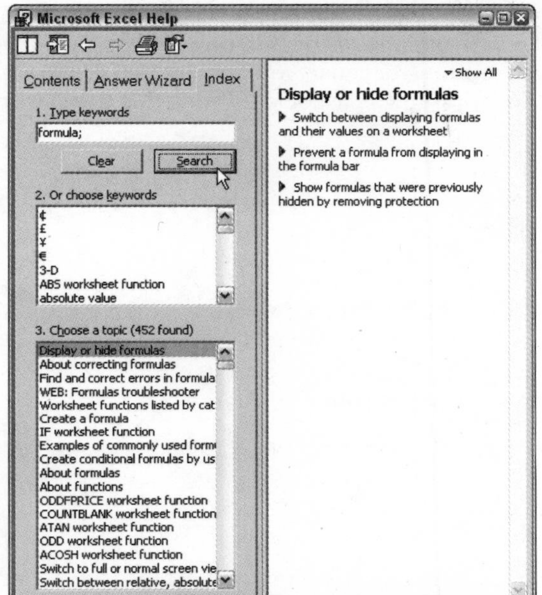

Figure 2-7: Looking up help topics on the Index tab.

What's up with this?

Shift+F1 is referred to as the "What's This?" shortcut key. When you press this key combination (or choose its menu equivalent, Help⇨What's This?) instead of opening an Excel Help window, the program simply adds a question mark to the normal arrowhead mouse pointer.

This new mouse pointer indicates that Excel is ready to display on-screen information about the next Menu item, toolbar button, or Task Pane item that you click. Figure 2-8 shows you how this works. For this figure, I pressed Shift+F1 and then clicked the Data menu on the Excel Menu bar followed Validation item on the Data menu with the "What's This" mouse pointer. As you can see, Excel responded by displaying a text box containing a brief description of the purpose and function of Excel's Data Validation feature.

You can make good use of the "What's This?" shortcut key to investigate the purpose of unfamiliar items on the Excel pull-down menus as well as those on the Excel taskbars. Note, however, that this Help feature is of very limited use with Excel toolbars; clicking a toolbar button with the "What's This?" mouse pointer doesn't really give you any better descriptions (often, not any different ones) than you get with the regular ScreenTip feature. (With the ScreenTip feature, the button's name appears next to the mouse pointer whenever you position it over a button for a second or two.) And don't even bother clicking the "What's This?" mouse pointer on any of the other screen real estate outside of the pull-down menu items, toolbar buttons, and Task Pane options because you only end up receiving the rather inane message, "No help topic is associated with this item" when you click anywhere else.

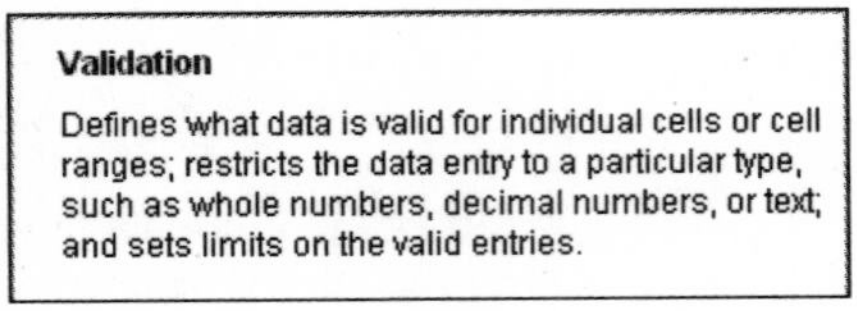

Validation

Defines what data is valid for individual cells or cell ranges; restricts the data entry to a particular type, such as whole numbers, decimal numbers, or text; and sets limits on the valid entries.

Figure 2-8: Displaying a short description of a menu item's function with the What's This? feature.

Getting Clippit to Find It

Nothing pains me more than having to discuss Clippit, your so-called "faithful" Office Assistant, but because he's officially still part of the Excel Help system, I have no choice but to bring him (it) up. In case you haven't figured it out, I'm not what you'd call a big fan of this attempt by Microsoft to create a personal computer assistant who watches your every move in Excel so as to be ready to come to your aid the moment you need help of any kind.

It's not just that I don't find Clippit particularly cute (I guess he's as cute as you'd expect an animated paper clip to be — it's just that I don't expect my paper clips to get bent out of shape unless I *do* the bending). It's also that aside from his bugging eyes and pretending that he's listening to your question and looking up an appropriate answer, he doesn't perform any different function from the Answer Wizard in the Ask a Question box or on the Answer Wizard tab (which never gives you any "attitude").

In fact, in my humble opinion, Clippit is nothing more than a failed holdover from earlier versions of the Office program that could have been retired from this latest version of Office without almost anyone missing him. All right, now that I've expressed it, that opinion does sound a bit harsh, and I don't mean to give you the impression that I don't have a soft spot for any of those cute, animated sprites out there in the world doing their darnedest to try and help us poor, deluded humans (after all, I'm one of the loudest voices saying, "I do believe in fairies," near the end of *Peter Pan* in that valiant group effort to save poor Tinkerbell's life).

So, what if you happen to like the little fellow and actually decide that you want to use him as a source for your Excel help? That's simple — just choose Help➪Show the Office Assistant on the Menu bar and voila, Clippit appears on the screen, ready to be of service.

After he's displayed on-screen, you can keep him out of the way as you work by dragging him anywhere in the Excel window. When you're ready to put him into service, all you do is click his cute, cuddly paper clip icon. Doing this causes a balloon to appear over Clippit's head in which you're cordially invited to type your question before clicking the Search button, as shown in Figure 2-9. As you type in your keywords or phrase (no more need here for real questions than when using the Ask a Question box), Clippit mimes the motions of writing your words down and studying them on a sheet of paper.

As soon as you click Clippit's Search button, he produces a new balloon, this time containing a list of suggested help topics for you to consult. To display information on a particular topic in the Microsoft Excel Help window, you click the topic of interest in the list. The help information then appears in a tiled Help window to the right of the Excel program window. The only difference is that good old Clippit appears at the beginning of the Help window's toolbar with his balloon still containing the list of suggested topics appearing to his left.

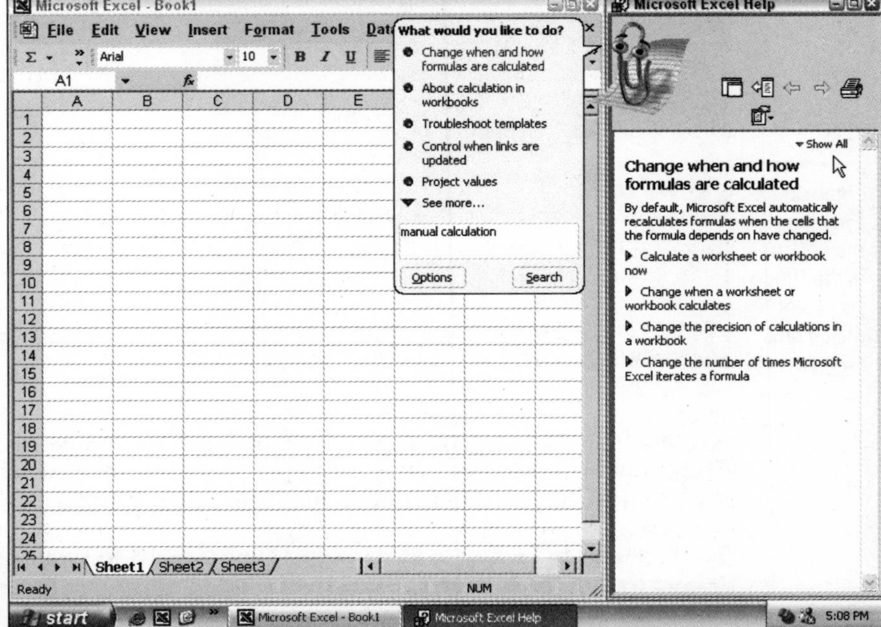

Figure 2-9: Asking Clippit, your friendly Office Assistant, for help on manual calculation.

When you finish exploring the help topics that Clippit has suggested to you, click the Close button in the Microsoft Excel Help window to close not only the Help window but also to close Clippit's help topic balloon, leaving only your favorite animated paper clip behind. Note that you can then leave Clippit hanging out in the Excel window or you can put him away either by choosing Help➪Hide the Office Assistant on the Menu bar or by right-clicking his icon and then clicking the Hide item on his shortcut menu.

Just when you thought Clippit's on-screen antics couldn't get any more annoying, you discover the Animate item on his shortcut menu. Heaven help you if you ever decide to actually choose this menu item and animate Clippit. Doing this turns this mild-mannered paper clip into a veritable crazy bail of wire, making it, at times, virtually impossible to ignore him and get any serious work done!

Limiting his options

If you do use Clippit to get help and tips on using Excel, you may want to change when and how he operates. To do this, open the Office Assistant dialog box with the Options tab selected, as shown in Figure 2-10. You can open this dialog box by clicking Clippit's icon and then clicking the Options button in the "What would you like to do?" balloon or you can right-click his icon and then click Options on his shortcut menu.

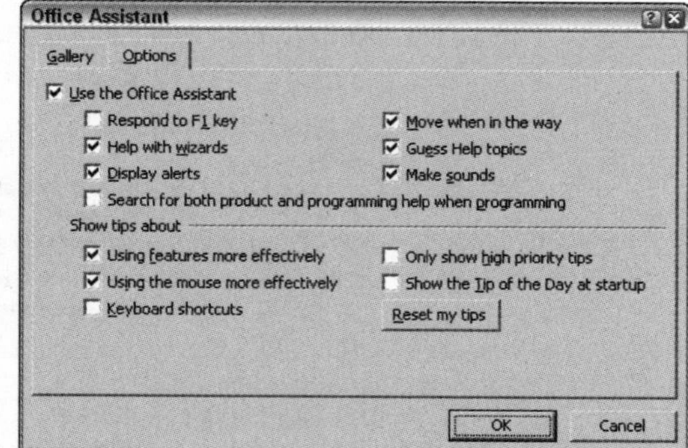

Figure 2-10: Changing the options in the Office Assistant dialog box.

As Figure 2-10 shows, most of the check box options on this tab are selected. The group of options located in the upper portion of the dialog box (under the Use the Office Assistant check box) determines how Clippit behaves:

- **Respond to F1 Key** to have Clippit appear ready for your question instead of the Microsoft Excel Help window when you press F1.

- **Move When in the Way** to have Clippit automatically move his body up to the toolbar at the top of the Microsoft Excel Help window and to move his balloon with the list of suggested help topics to the left so that you can see the help information displayed.
- **Help with Wizards** to have Clippit appear whenever you select an Excel command that invokes a *wizard* (Microsoft's name for a series of dialog boxes that walk you through the steps involved in a complicated procedure).
- **Guess Help Topics** to have Clippit attempt to guess what topics may be of interest when you type in a fairly vague question or general keywords in his "What would you like to do?" text box.
- **Display Alerts** to have Clippit display all your alert messages in one of his balloons (rather than using standard Excel dialog boxes).
- **Make Sounds** to have Clippit make all sorts of annoying sounds when he appears and disappears, when you save a workbook, and when he displays your messages (if the Display Alerts check box discussed previously is selected).
- **Search for Both Product and Programming Help When Programming** to have Clippit appear giving you his two cents when you try to get help using the VBA (Visual Basic for Applications) editor (see Book IX, Chapter 2 for details).

The group of options under the Show Tips About heading determines when and how Clippit gives you tips on using a program (see "A tip a day doesn't keep the assistant away" later in this chapter for details):

- **Using Features More Effectively** to have Clippit give you pointers on how to better use Excel commands to accomplish your objectives.
- **Only Show High Priority Tips** to have Clippit forego giving you advice on anything that the program doesn't consider as vital to the way you work in Excel (supposedly Clippit analyzes how you work to determine which tips are high priority and which aren't).
- **Using the Mouse More Effectively** to have Clippit give you pointers on improving your mouse techniques.
- **Show the Tip of the Day at Startup** to have Clippit appear whenever you first start Excel displaying a seemingly random (though often surprisingly useful) tip of the day.
- **Keyboard Shortcuts** to have Clippit remind you of keyboard shortcuts for certain Excel commands that you use.
- **Reset My Tips** to stop Clippit from endlessly recycling the same old stale tips when you start up Excel, if you are using the Show the Tip of the Day at Startup option discussed previously.

If you never ever want to see that twisted metallic body with those bugged-out eyes again, you can turn off the Office Assistant entirely by simply clicking the Use the Office Assistant check box to remove its checkmark. When this check box is unselected, all the check boxes on the Options tab of the Office Assistant dialog box are dimmed and Clippit won't bother you in any way. The only way to bring him back after this action is to choose Help⇨Show the Office Assistant on the Excel menu bar.

Getting a new assistant

Clippit, that twisted old clip, is not the only persona you can select for your Office Assistant. In fact, Microsoft has come up with a whole caste of kooky characters (once again proving it's no Disney Studios) from which you can choose. Believe it or not, in addition to Clippit, you have a choice among the following:

- Dot, a really cheesy red ball with a smiley face (don't get me started).
- F1, a really short-bodied robot with legs that look like they end in claws and, of all things, Clippit's eyes (he's certainly no R2D2).
- Office Logo, which simply consists of the four-color interlocking puzzle pieces used to designate Microsoft Office (oh so boring!).
- Merlin the magician (the only 3-D character in the bunch — he's shown in Figure 2-11).
- Mother Nature in the form of a globe on which images such as sunflowers and doves appear to grow (is nothing sacred?).
- Links, a kitty cat with big paws (my personal favorite because of the great purring sounds she makes).
- Rocky, a dog who looks absolutely nothing like the famous raccoon of the same name and who, at one point in the very early stages in the development of the Office Assistant, was set to replace Clippit as the default character (too bad they didn't stay with their first impulse).

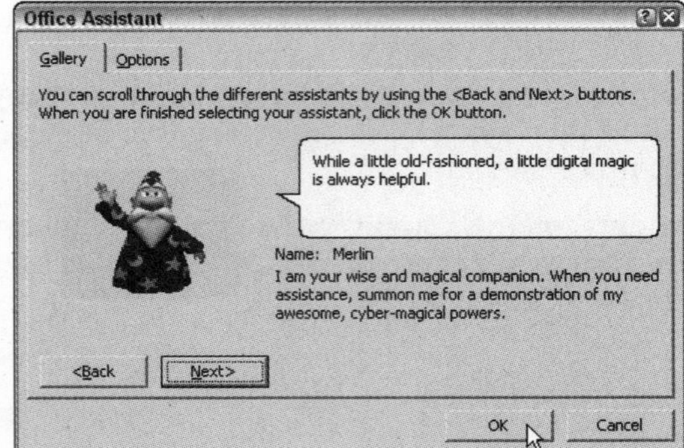

Figure 2-11: Looking for a new assistant on the Gallery tab of the Office Assistant dialog box.

So, what if you decide you've had enough of Clippit, but aren't quite ready to give up on the whole animated, personalized guide thing — how do you go about giving Clippit the boot and getting one of those other beauties to be your Office Assistant? Simple — just follow these steps:

1. **Click Clippit to display his "What would you like to do?" balloon.**

   If he's currently hidden, choose Help➪Show the Office Assistant before doing Step 1.

2. **Click the Options button.**

   The Office Assistant opens with the Options tab selected.

3. **Click the Gallery tab in the Office Assistant dialog box.**

   Doing this enables you to use the Next and Back buttons to scroll through and take a look at the different characters available.

4. **Click the Next button to go through the cast of available characters until you find the one that you want to use (use the Back button to go back through the list).**

5. **With the character that you want to use displayed on the Gallery tab, click OK.**

   Clippit is the only character installed when you do a standard installation of Office XP, so unless you've previously installed the character that you just selected, a Clippit alert balloon appears, asking whether you want to install the new character.

6. **Click Yes in the Clippit alert balloon to install the newly selected character. Otherwise, click OK in the Office Assistant dialog box to close it.**

Note that each character has its own quirks in terms of sounds and actions (especially if you click the Animate item on its shortcut menu) that you have to get used to. Of course, if you find your new Office Assistant just as annoying as Clippit but in different ways, you can turn him or her off by deselecting the Use the Office Assistant check box on the Options tab of the Office Assistant dialog box.

"A tip a day doesn't keep the assistant away"

As I discussed previously in the section, "Limiting his options," you can have Clippit (or whoever you currently use as your Office Assistant) not only give you help when you ask for it but also give you tips on using Excel. By default, the program selects the Using Features More Effectively and the Using the Mouse More Effectively check boxes in the Show Tips About section on the Options tab of the Office Assistant dialog box so that the Assistant only gives you suggestions on more efficient command procedures and mouse techniques based on the types of things you're actually doing in Excel.

If you want tips on keyboard shortcuts to be displayed, you need to select the Keyboard Shortcuts check box on the Options tab. If you also want the Assistant to display a general tip on using features more effectively each time you start Excel (which is what I call a random tip because it can't be based on anything you've done in the program since you just started it up), you need to select the Show the Tip of the Day at Startup check box on this tab.

When the Show the Tip of the Day at Startup check box is selected, Clippit (or whoever you're using) appears as soon as you start Excel, displaying his tip of the day in his familiar balloon dialog box. For the other tips, the Assistant is subtler; if he comes up with a tip for you based on what you're doing, a light bulb icon appears over his head. To see what tip the Assistant has cooked up for you, simply click the light bulb. To clear a tip that's displayed in the Assistant's balloon, click the OK button that appears at the bottom of the balloon.

If you click the Assistant instead of the OK button, Excel replaces the tip balloon with the familiar "What would you like to do?" dialog box. If you want to get the tip balloon back after getting your help suggestions, just press the Escape key to replace the "What would you like to do?" dialog box with the tip balloon.

Making Excel as Easy as 1-2-3

If you're one of the few remaining Lotus 1-2-3 users who are just now coming over to Excel, you can use the Help for Lotus 1-2-3 Users to ease your transition from Lotus to Excel. The Help for Lotus 1-2-3 Users can give you the Excel equivalents for any Lotus 1-2-3 command in one of two ways: as a demonstration that actually chooses the equivalent command on the Excel pull-down menus, and as an instruction in which the corresponding Excel procedure is displayed in a text box near the bottom of the Excel window.

To open the Help for Lotus 1-2-3 Users dialog box, shown in Figure 2-12, choose Help⇨Lotus 1-2-3 Help on the Excel menu bar. When you first open this dialog box, the Demo radio button is selected, meaning that Help will show you the Excel procedure for the 1-2-3 commands that you choose (note that you can slow down or speed up the rate at which this demonstration is played by clicking either the Slower or Faster button). To have Help display a list of the Excel steps that you must follow to do the corresponding 1-2-3 command, be sure that you click the Instructions radio button.

After choosing between the Demo and the Instructions option, you are ready to select the 1-2-3 menu command for which you want the Excel equivalent. To do this, you need to select the / (slash) command menu sequence in the Menu list box on the left side of the Help for Lotus 1-2-3 Users dialog box. First, select the 1-2-3 main menu with the arrow keys, or click it and then press Enter to display the list of available submenu options. Next, select the submenu option either from the keyboard or with the mouse, again by pressing the Enter key. Continue on in this manner until you've selected the entire 1-2-3 menu sequence and then click OK to have Excel either demonstrate the comparable procedure in Excel or display the steps in a comment box (depending upon whether the Demo or Instructions radio button is selected).

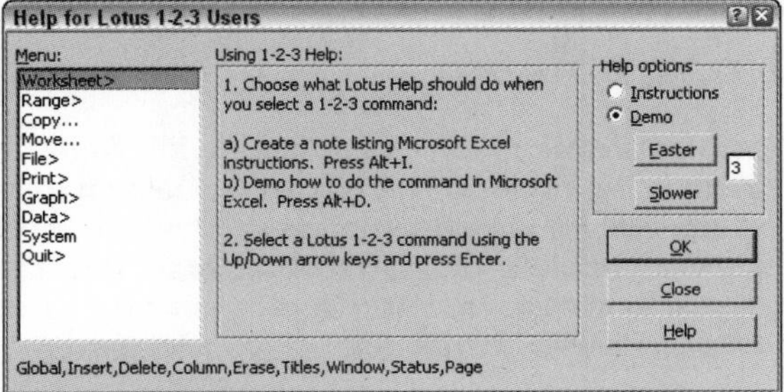

Figure 2-12: Setting up a command demo in the Help for Lotus 1-2-3 Users dialog box.

For example, suppose that you want Excel to demonstrate its procedure for formatting a group of cells with the Currency number format (a format that automatically adds a dollar sign, commas between thousands, and two decimal places to the values). To do this, open the Help for Lotus 1-2-3 Users dialog box and then follow these steps:

1. **Click the Demo radio button in the Help Options area.**
2. **Press the ↓ to highlight Range> or just click this option in the Menu list box and then press Enter.**

   The Menu list box now lists the submenu options Format> through Transpose with the Format> menu option already highlighted because it's the first submenu.
3. **With Format> selected in the Menu list, press Enter.**
4. **Press the ↓ to highlight Currency or just click this option in the Menu list box.**
5. **Click the OK button or press Enter to close the Help for Lotus 1-2-3 Users dialog box and start demonstrating the Excel procedure.**

When demonstrating some procedures, such as the procedure for formatting a group of cells with the Currency number format, Excel may pause at times and display a Help for Lotus 1-2-3 Users dialog box that prompts you for input. For example, in the Currency format example showcased in the previous steps, as soon as you click Close or press Enter the last time, one of these dialog boxes appears, asking you to verify the number of decimals (2 is the default number) and the cell range to which to apply this format (with the active cell's address given by default).

To use these defaults in the demonstration, just click the OK button. To modify the number of decimal places, click the Decimal Places text box and replace 2 with the desired number. To modify the cells to which the Currency format is applied, click the Range to Format text box in the Help for Lotus 1-2-3 Users dialog box and then click and drag through the cells to be formatted in the worksheet below the dialog box before you click its OK button.

Help Is Just a Web Site Away

Microsoft now maintains a Microsoft Office Worldwide Web site where you can go to get help on using Excel 2002, updates (usually in the form of bug fixes) to the program, and for goodies such as ready-made worksheet templates (see Book II, Chapter 1 for details) that facilitate the creation of specialized spreadsheets, as well as free Add-In programs (covered in Book I, Chapter 3) that extend Excel's feature set.

You can visit this Web site from within Excel itself (all you need is a dial-up or broadband connection to the Internet and a Web browser installed on your computer). To go online and explore the support offered by this Web site, follow these steps:

1. **Choose Help⇨Office on the Web from the Excel menu bar.**

   Excel responds by connecting you to the Internet, opening your Web browser, and going to the Home page of the Microsoft Office Worldwide Web site.

2. **Click the link on the map shown on the Microsoft Office Worldwide Home page for the area closest to your geographical location (Canada, United States, United Kingdom, or Hong Kong SAR).**

   When you click this link, Microsoft puts a cookie on your computer that automatically directs you to the site for that location (the United States, in most of your cases) whenever you choose Help⇨Office on the Web in the future. As soon as you click one of these geographical links, your Web browser takes you to the Microsoft Office Assistance Center site for that location.

Figure 2-13 shows you the Home page for the Microsoft Office Assistance Center site as it appeared at the time of this writing. As you can see in this figure, in the center of this page you find an Assistance by Product area (where you click the Excel link to get Excel help) plus links to Product Updates and to the Download center in the pane on the left. Note that this left pane also contains links to a Design Gallery Live, Template Gallery, and Office eServices.

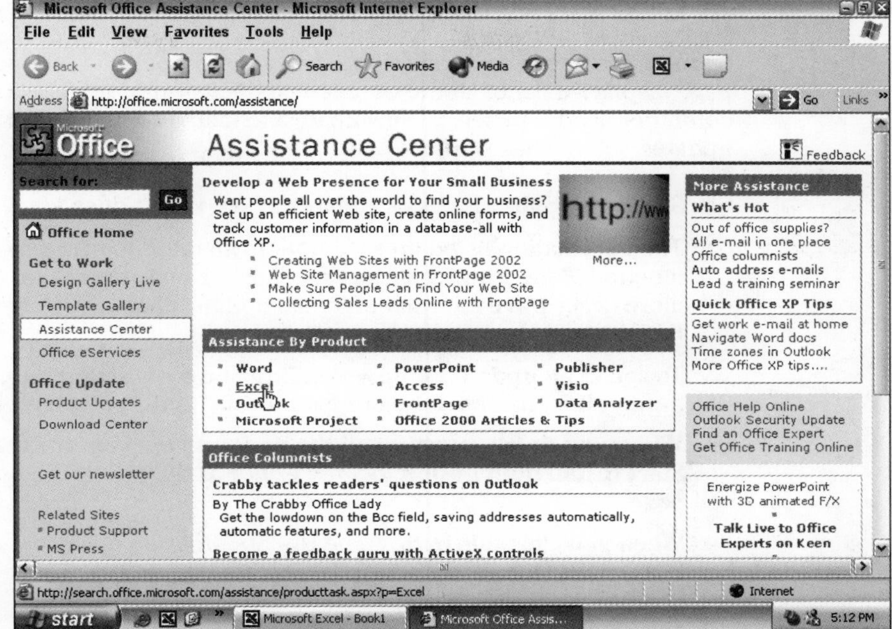

Figure 2-13: Visiting the Microsoft Office Assistance Center site's Home page.

If you click the Excel link in the Assistance by Product section of the Home page, your Web browser takes you to an Excel-specific page, which contains an alphabetical list of help topics (beginning with Analyzing Data and ending with Upgrade/Setup as of this writing) that are also hyperlinks; you can click these to visit pages with other links to specific articles on these topics.

Getting Excel updates

The Office Update section in the left pane of the Microsoft Office Assistance Center site's Home page, shown in Figure 2-13, contains two links: Product Updates and Download Center. To see whether Microsoft has posted any updates that may benefit your copy of Excel 2002, it's a good idea to follow this Product Updates link from time to time.

When you click the Products Update link, the Web browser opens a Product Updates page containing a link to an Automatic Detection program that can check your computer to see that it has the latest updates for Excel (and, indeed, all the Office XP programs). To use this detection program, just click the Go button near the top of the page.

When the Automatic Detection program finishes checking your computer for the latest updates (and you may have to deal with one or more security warning dialog boxes during this detection process), the Product Updates page displays a list of all the Office XP and Excel 2002 updates that your computer needs. To select, download, and install some or all of these updates, follow these steps:

1. **Scroll through this list of updates to see which ones you want.**

   The information listed on each update includes a brief description on its function along with its file size and approximate download time. To get more descriptive information on an update, click its Detailed Information About This Update link.

2. **To select an update for downloading and installation on your computer, click the check box in front of the update's name.**

3. **When you finish selecting all the updates you want to install, click the Start Installation button located either at the top or the bottom of the page.**

   When you click this button, the Update program opens the initial dialog box for the Office Product Updates Installation Wizard, where you must confirm your update selection.

4. **Look over the list of updates to be downloaded and installed and then, if everything checks out, click the Install Now button in the lower left corner.**

   Depending on the kind of Office updates that you selected, you may need to have your Office XP CD-ROM ready to pop in the drive. Make sure that you have your Office XP CD-ROM on hand before you take the next step.

5. **Click the Continue button in the next dialog box of the Office Product Updates Installation Wizard (it asks whether you have access to Office product CDs or a network installation connection).**

6. **Click the Accept button to accept the Microsoft Software end-user license agreement (you may even want to read it before moving on) that appears in the next dialog box of the Office Product Updates Installation Wizard.**

   After accepting the end-user license agreement (and you must if you want to get the updates), a Microsoft Office Product Updates dialog box appears that keeps you informed of the progress of both the downloading and installation of the updates.

   When the downloading of the updates finishes, the Microsoft Office XP Installer takes over, automatically installing them on your computer's hard drive. Note that you'll probably have to exit Excel before the

Installer can complete the update installation (to do this, just click on the Excel window and then choose File⇨Exit or press Alt+F4). After the Installer finishes installing the updates, a dialog box for the Microsoft Office Product Updates Wizard appears, informing you of a successful installation.

7. **Click the Close This Window button in the Microsoft Office Product Updates Wizard dialog box.**

   The Wizard dialog box closes and you are returned to the Product Updates page on the Microsoft Office Web site.

8. **If you're finished with this Microsoft Office Web site, click the Close button in the upper-right corner of your Web browser to return to Windows, where you can launch your updated copy of Excel. Otherwise, click the Return to Product Updates Catalog button to see about downloading and installing other Office or Excel product updates or to follow one of the other links, such as Assistance Center or Download Center, to see about what information or goodies you can get your hands on.**

Excel goodies for the downloading

Follow the Download Center link that appears on the left pane of the Microsoft Office Assistance Center site's Home page under the Office Update section heading (see Figure 2-13) to check out all the Excel goodies that you can download for free. When you click the Download Center link, your Web browser brings you to a Microsoft Office Download Center page, where you designate the type of downloads in which you're interested, along with the program and version for which they're intended.

After selecting the Product (Excel), the version (2002/XP), and the check boxes for all the types of downloads in which you're interested (Updates, Add-ins and Extras, and/or Converters and Viewers), click the Update List button to have them listed on this page.

The information on each item added to this list is arranged in three columns: Title, Date, and Type. To sort the items in the list by title, click the Title column heading. To sort them by the date on which they were offered for downloading, click the Date column heading. To sort the list by type of download (add-in, converter, update, or viewer), click the Type column heading.

Each item in the list gives its name, file size, and approximate download time, along with a brief description of its function. To get more information about a particular item, click the hyperlink attached to its name. To download an item, click the Download Now button that appears directly beneath its name.

A File Download dialog box appears, asking whether you want to open the downloaded file or just save it on your computer. Most of the time, you will want to save it on your desktop and then install it later, so click Save and select Desktop in the Save In text box of the Save As dialog box that next appears. After the file is successfully downloaded on your Windows desktop, you can then install it by simply double-clicking its file icon.

Don't try installing the Excel add-ins, updates, and other such items that you downloaded on your desktop from the Microsoft Office Download Center page until after you've exited all open programs, including Excel and your Web browser. Doing this makes it a lot more likely that the add-in, update, converter, or viewer installation will be successful while at the same time ensuring that no harm comes to your precious applications.

"Excel, heal thyself . . ."

As computer application programs such as Excel and operating systems such as Windows XP that run them become ever more sophisticated and complex, you run a greater and greater risk that at some point in their usage, something or other will suddenly start running amok and they will — how can I put this delicately — come unglued and go absolutely berserk on you (or at least, don't work like you know they should). In the past, when this kind of thing happened in Excel, you had no choice but to completely re-install the program.

Fortunately, Excel 2002 now offers an alternative to complete re-installation in the form of the new Detect and Repair command located on the Help menu. When you choose Help⇨Detect and Repair, Excel displays the Detect and Repair dialog box, shown in Figure 2-14, where you have a choice between retaining or discarding your shortcuts and custom settings during the repair.

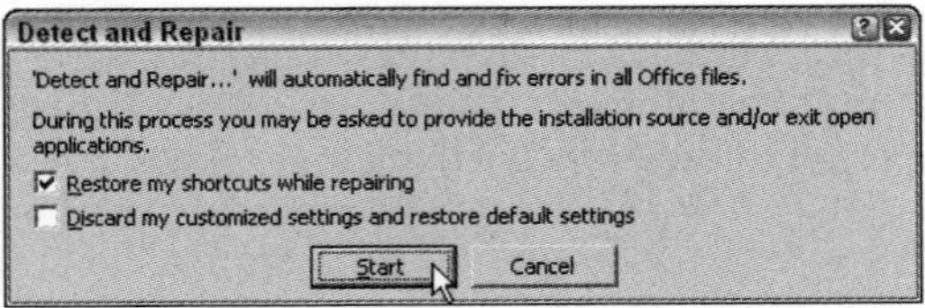

Figure 2-14: Using the Detect and Repair dialog box to try to fix a broken Excel.

To prevent Excel from restoring the shortcuts that you've set up, click the Restore My Shortcuts While Repairing check box to remove its checkmark. To have Excel dump all of your custom settings (described further in Book 1, Chapter 3), click the Discard My Customized Settings and Restore Default Settings check box to add a checkmark to it.

To have the Detect and Repair utility then begin its work, click the Start button in the dialog box. Note that you'll probably have to exit Excel if this utility finds serious enough problems to warrant reinstalling Excel (to do this, just click on the Excel window and then choose File⇨Exit or press Alt+F4). After Detect and Repair has finished its repair work, when you next restart Excel, you should find that it now runs as good as new.

Chapter 3: Customizing Excel

In This Chapter

- **Customizing the built-in toolbars**
- **Creating your own toolbars**
- **Making changes to the Excel menus**
- **Changing various and sundry program settings**
- **Extending Excel's capabilities with add-in programs**

Chances are good that Excel as it comes right out of the box is *not* always the best fit for the way you use the program. For that reason, Excel gives an amazing variety of ways to customize and configure the program's settings so that they better suit your needs and the way you like to work.

This chapter covers the most important methods for customizing Excel settings and features. It looks at three basic areas where you can tailor the program to your individual needs. The first place ripe for customization is in the arena of the many Excel toolbars and pull-down menus. Not only can you control which buttons and items appear on which built-in toolbar and menu, but you can also create custom toolbars and menus of your own design. The second place where you may want to make extensive modifications is to the default settings (also referred to as options) that control any number of program assumptions and basic behaviors. The third place where you can customize Excel is in the world of add-ins, those small, specialized utilities (sometimes called *applets*) that extend the built-in Excel features by attaching themselves to the main Excel program. Excel add-ins provide a wide variety of functions and are available from a wide variety of sources, including the original Excel 2002 program, the Microsoft Office Web site, and various and sundry third party vendors.

Tailoring the Toolbars

Excel 2002 makes it easy for you to make modifications to any of the built-in toolbars or pull-down menus (in Excel's mind, the Menu bar with all the pull-down menus is just another toolbar like the Standard toolbar or Formatting toolbar). In addition to modifying the buttons on a given toolbar or the items that appear on a particular pull-down menu on the Menu bar, you can also create new toolbars and add new pull-down menus to the Menu bar.

You can float or dock the new toolbars that you create just as you do any of the built-in toolbars. You can locate the new pull-down menus that you put together anywhere on the Menu bar.

When modifying or creating a new toolbar or pull-down menu, you use buttons or menu items to which three different types of elements are assigned:

- Built-in Excel commands
- Macros that you create (see Book IX, Chapter 1 for information on creating macros in Excel)
- Hyperlinks to other worksheets, workbooks, other application's documents, or Web pages (see Book VIII, Chapter 2 for details)

Note that when you select buttons for a toolbar that use the built-in commands, they use predefined icons. To assign a macro or hyperlink, you use a Custom Button (which, of all things, has a happy face icon). You can choose new icons for any of these buttons from those readily available to the program or you can even try your hand at the Button Editor, where you can design your own button icon.

Getting familiar with the Customize dialog box

Whether you're customizing or creating a new toolbar or pull-down menu, the first step that you take is always the same: You start by opening the Customize dialog box. To do this, you have a choice between these two methods:

- Choose View⇨Toolbars⇨Customize on the Menu bar.
- Right-click a toolbar or the Menu bar and then click the Customize item at the very bottom of the shortcut menu.

The Customize dialog box contains three tabs:

- **Toolbars:** Using this tab, you can display and hide any toolbar, create a new toolbar, rename or delete any toolbar that you create (not available for the built-in toolbars), reset the buttons on a modified built-in toolbar (not available for the toolbars you create), or attach a modified built-in or custom toolbar to another Excel workbook file (see Figure 3-1).

- **Commands:** Using this tab, you can add new buttons to the toolbars you're modifying or creating, or you can add new menu items to the built-in pull-down menus or custom menus to the Excel Menu bar (see Figure 3-2).
- **Options:** Using this tab, you can control whether or not the Standard and Formatting toolbars share a single row, the full pull-down menus are always displayed, large or small icons are used on the toolbars, the names of different fonts appear as examples of that font in all Font pull-down menus, ScreenTips that identify each button appear on the toolbars, and what type of animation, if any, is used in displaying the pull-down menus (see Figure 3-3).

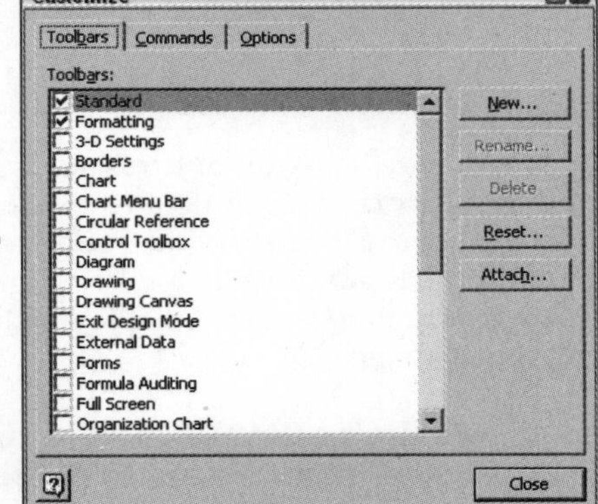

Figure 3-1: The Toolbars tab on the Customize dialog box.

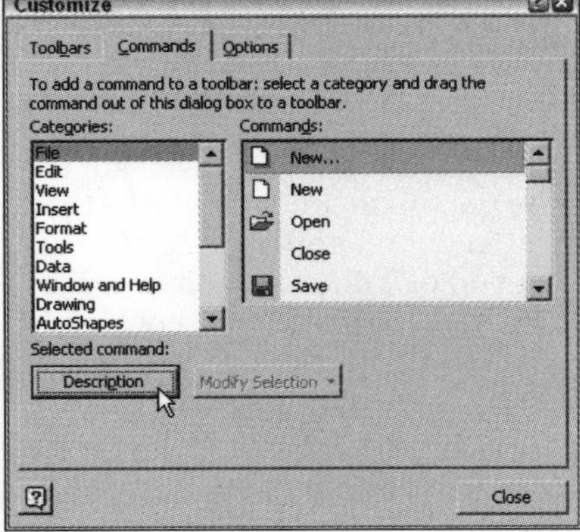

Figure 3-2: The Commands tab on the Customize dialog box.

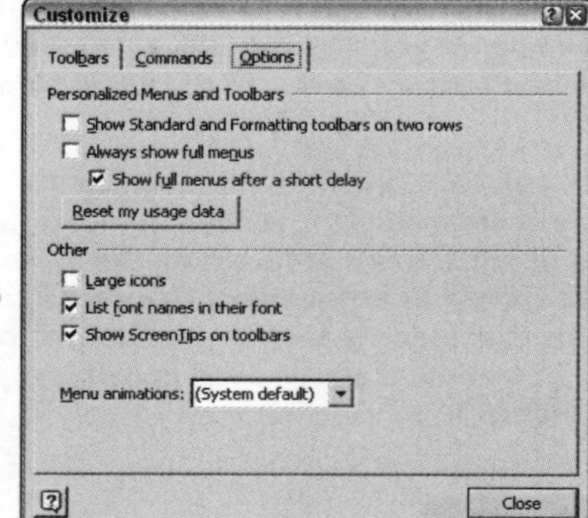

Figure 3-3: The Options tab on the Customize dialog box.

Modifying the toolbars

When modifying a toolbar, you can rearrange the buttons, add new buttons to it, or delete buttons from it. But before you can do any of these modifications, the toolbar you want to modify must be displayed somewhere in the Excel window and you must open the Customize dialog box. Note that you can combine opening the Customize dialog box and displaying the toolbar you want to modify by taking these steps:

1. **Choose View⇨Toolbars⇨Customize on the Menu bar or right-click the Menu bar and then click Customize at the bottom of the shortcut menu.**
2. **Click the Toolbars tab in the Customize dialog box if it's not already selected.**
3. **Click the check box in front of the name of the toolbar you want to display and modify.**

If the toolbar you mean to modify is already displayed somewhere in the Excel window, you can use the pop-up menu attached to that toolbar's Add or Remove Buttons item (located on the pop-up menu attached to the Toolbar Options button at the end of a docked toolbar and to the immediate left of the Close button on a floating toolbar) to add or remove buttons or to open the Customize dialog box. To add or remove buttons, position the mouse pointer over the Toolbar's name in the Add or Remove Buttons' pop-up menu and then click the desired check boxes on the cascading menu that appears (clicking a check box with a checkmark removes the button from the bar; clicking an empty check box adds the button). To open the

Customize dialog box so that you can perform other modifications to this or any other displayed toolbar, click the Customize item at the bottom of the Add or Remove Buttons' pop-up menu.

Rearranging buttons

You move buttons on the toolbar you're modifying by dragging them to new positions on the bar. As you drag a button, a shaded button icon appears on the mouse pointer at the tip of arrowhead, representing the button that you've selected. As you move this pointer, Excel indicates the places where you can insert the button by displaying a heavy I-beam pointer on the toolbar. When this I-beam appears at the place on the toolbar to which you want the button moved, release the mouse button to have the button appear at this new position.

Adding and deleting buttons

Adding and deleting buttons is similar to rearranging buttons on a toolbar except that, in this case, you're dragging buttons either on or off the toolbar rather than just dragging them to new positions on the bar.

To add a button, you first need to click the Commands tab of the Customize dialog box (see Figure 3-2) and locate the button or box for the command you want to add. The commands on this tab are arranged in categories according to their function. When you click a category in the Categories list box on the left, Excel then shows you all the commands you can choose from in the Commands list box on the right.

If you're not sure what a particular command does just by looking at its name and icon, you can display a short description of its function by clicking the command in the Commands list and then clicking the Description button. Excel responds by displaying a small text box with a brief description of what the button does. To close the text box, click anywhere outside of the box.

When you've located the button, box, or menu that you want to add in the Commands list box, you drag it from this box to the place on the toolbar where you want it inserted. As you drag the object from the Customize dialog box, Excel indicates when you can successfully drop the object into place by adding a box at the bottom of the mouse pointer. When this box contains an x and you drop the object, it is deleted. When this box contains a + sign and you drop the object, it is added to the toolbar (of course, you also see the I-beam at the tip of the mouse pointer indicating where the object will appear).

Although you're most apt to want to add new buttons to the toolbar you're modifying, keep in mind that you can also add pull-down menus. For example, say that you do a lot of e-mailing of Excel workbooks to coworkers and you don't want to always have to use the Send To sub-menu on the File pull-down menu, you could add a Send To pull-down menu to Standard toolbar so that you have access to the Mail Recipient command directly from this toolbar. All you have to do to make this change is to click Built-in Menus in the Categories list box on the Commands tab, then drag the Sent To menu item from the Customize dialog box to the place you want it to appear on the Standard toolbar.

To delete a button from a toolbar, you simply drag the button off the bar. As soon as the x appears in the box at the bottom of the mouse pointer, you can release the mouse button. The unwanted button then disappears from the toolbar, which adjusts the remaining buttons to fill in the gap.

If you ever mess up a toolbar by adding or getting rid of the wrong buttons or moving the buttons around into a jumble that you're not happy with, remember that you can reset the toolbar back to its original configuration by clicking the name of the toolbar on the Toolbars tab of the Customize dialog box to highlight the toolbar's name (don't click its check box) and then clicking the Reset button. An alert dialog box appears, asking you if you're sure that you want to reset the changes you made to the toolbar; click OK.

Modifying the pull-down menus

Because Excel considers the Menu bar to be just another toolbar (albeit one with text items rather than buttons with icons), you can modify any of its pull-down menus the same as you do the toolbars. When the Customize dialog box is displayed (View⇨Toolbars⇨Customize), you can move menu items to different positions on the menu (up or down) or even move items to another menu (something I don't recommend because this can be confusing for all but the most expert Excel users).

You can also delete menu items from a particular pull-down menu and even entire menus from the Excel Menu toolbar, if you find that you just have no use for a particular item or particular menu when you use Excel.

Of course, just because you *can* do something doesn't mean that you *should* do it. Instead of moving menu items all around the Menu bar or getting rid of menu items or entire menus that you think you'll never use, the most ambitious modifications you'll probably ever end up making to any of the Excel pull-down menu is simply modifying a menu or two by adding custom menu items to them.

Custom menu items are items to which you add macros that play back a sequence of Excel commands or hyperlinks that jump you to other documents or Web pages or even open new e-mail messages. To add a custom menu item to a pull-down menu, you follow these steps:

1. **Open the Customize dialog box (View⇨Toolbars⇨Customize) and then click the Commands tab.**
2. **Scroll down and then click Macros in the Categories list box.**

   The Macros category covers custom buttons and menu items to which you can attach either macros or hyperlinks that you create.
3. **Click Custom Menu Item in the Commands list box.**

   Because this item is intended for a pull-down menu, it doesn't use an icon.
4. **Drag the Custom Menu Item icon from the Customize dialog box to the place on the pull-down menu where you want it to appear and then release the mouse button.**

   As you drag through the desired pull-down menu on the Excel Menu bar, the menu opens and a heavy, now horizontal, I-beam appears indicating where the Custom Menu Item will be inserted when you release the mouse button. When you do release, a new item called Custom Menu Item appears on the menu above, below, or between the built-in menu items.
5. **Right-click the Custom Menu Item on the pull-down menu and then click Name on the shortcut menu that appears and type a short, descriptive name for the item. If you want a letter in the new name to be the hot key, type an ampersand (&) before that letter.**

   Remember that the hot key is the letter in the menu that the user can combine with the Alt key to choose the menu item from the keyboard without having to open the pull-down menus. This letter appears underlined on the pull-down menu. When assigning a hot key, choose a letter that is not already used on that menu.
6. **If you want the custom menu item separated from the other items on the menu with a light gray line, right-click the custom item and then click Begin a Group on the shortcut menu.**

   When you select Begin a Group, Excel adds a light gray separator bar above the menu item, indicating that the custom item begins a new group. This is helpful when you're adding a bunch of related custom menu items that need to appear as a distinct group.
7. **To assign a macro to the custom menu item, right-click the item, click Macros on the shortcut menu, and then select the macro to use (see Book IX, Chapter 1 for details). To add hyperlink to custom item instead, click Edit Hyperlink⇨Open on the shortcut menu and then select or create the hyperlink (see Book VIII, Chapter 2 for details).**

When you create a custom menu item that runs a macro, the macro must already exist before you perform Step 7. When creating one that accesses a hyperlink, you can create the hyperlink at the time you perform this step.

8. **Click the Close button in the Customize dialog box and then test out your new custom menu item by choosing it from the Menu bar.**

After adding a custom menu item to one of the pull-down menus, remember that you can still move it into a new position on that menu or even to a different pull-down menu. Simply drag it to the new position. If you decide that you no longer want the custom menu item to appear on the pull-down menus, delete the item by dragging it off the menus and then releasing the mouse button when the x appears at the bottom of the pointer.

Creating a new toolbar

Instead of monkeying around with the buttons available on the built-in toolbars, you're often better off just creating custom toolbars to use. That way, you can display the custom bar just when you're doing work in Excel that requires its particular set of buttons. Otherwise, you can have the custom toolbar hidden, keeping the Excel work area as uncluttered as possible.

To illustrate how easy it is to create a custom toolbar, I show you an example toolbar that contains a veritable potpourri of useful tools called Choice Tools (see Figure 3-4). To create a custom toolbar, you follow these steps:

1. **Choose View⇨Toolbars⇨Customize on the Excel Menu bar.**

   Doing this opens the Customize dialog box, the first step in doing any work with editing or creating toolbars or menus.

2. **Click the Toolbars tab in the Customize dialog box.**

   The Toolbars tab contains a New button that you use to start a new, custom toolbar.

3. **Click the New button on the Toolbars tab.**

   Doing this opens the New Toolbar dialog box where you name your custom toolbar. For this example, I named the new toolbar Choice Tools.

4. **Type a short, descriptive name for your toolbar in the Toolbar Name text box and then click OK.**

   Excel responds by closing the Toolbar Name text box. The program adds the name of your new custom toolbar to the bottom of the Toolbars list box in the Customize dialog box while at the same time displaying a blank, floating toolbar somewhere to the right of the Customize dialog box in the Excel work area. The title bar of this baby toolbar contains only two buttons, Close and Add or Remove Buttons, plus the first two letters of the name you gave (more of the name appears as the toolbar lengthens to accommodate the buttons that you add to it).

5. **Click the Commands tab in the Customize dialog box.**

   You are now ready to add buttons (or even pull-down menus) to your custom toolbar. To do this, you select the various command buttons you want to add and then drag them into a desired placement on the blank, baby toolbar.

6. **Click the category of the first button (or set of buttons) that you want to add to the toolbar in the Categories list box on the left.**

   For this example, I clicked Edit in the Categories list box because the first set of buttons I want on the custom Choice Tools bar are found in this group.

7. **Locate the button you want to add from the selected category in the Command list and then drag it to the blank toolbar, dropping it when the + sign appears at the bottom of the mouse pointer.**

   Note that if you want to add a button that runs a macro or jumps to a hyperlink, you select Macros in the Categories list box and then drag the Custom Button in the Commands list to the toolbar to add a generic button with a happy face icon. (You can then assign a macro or link to this button and change its icon.) To add a built-in menu to the toolbar, click Built-in Menus in the Categories list and then drag the desired menu to the toolbar. To add a custom menu to the custom toolbar, click New Menu in the Categories list and then drag New Menu from the Commands list to the new toolbar. (You can then rename the custom menu and add menu items to it, as described in the next section of this chapter, "Making a new menu.")

   In the Choice Tools example, I dragged the Go To... button to the first position on the new toolbar. To build the rest of the toolbar, you continue on in this manner, selecting the category and then dragging the tool to its desired position. As you add more tools, the toolbar gets longer and longer, displaying more of the toolbar's name in the title bar.

8. **Repeat Steps 6 and 7 until you've added all the buttons you want on the new toolbar.**

   Remember that you can move tools around after adding them to the new bar by just dragging them to new positions. You can also remove buttons that you decide you really don't need by dragging them off the bar.

Note that you can also group buttons by adding a light gray vertical separator (like the ones you see in the Standard and Formatting toolbars). To do this, you simply drag the button in front of where you want a separator to appear slightly to the right on the toolbar until a light gray vertical bar appears. To get rid of a separator that you decide you really don't need, you drag the button behind the separator to the left until the vertical gray bar disappears.

9. **When you finish making all the necessary additions and modifications to your new toolbar, click the Close button to close the Customize dialog box.**

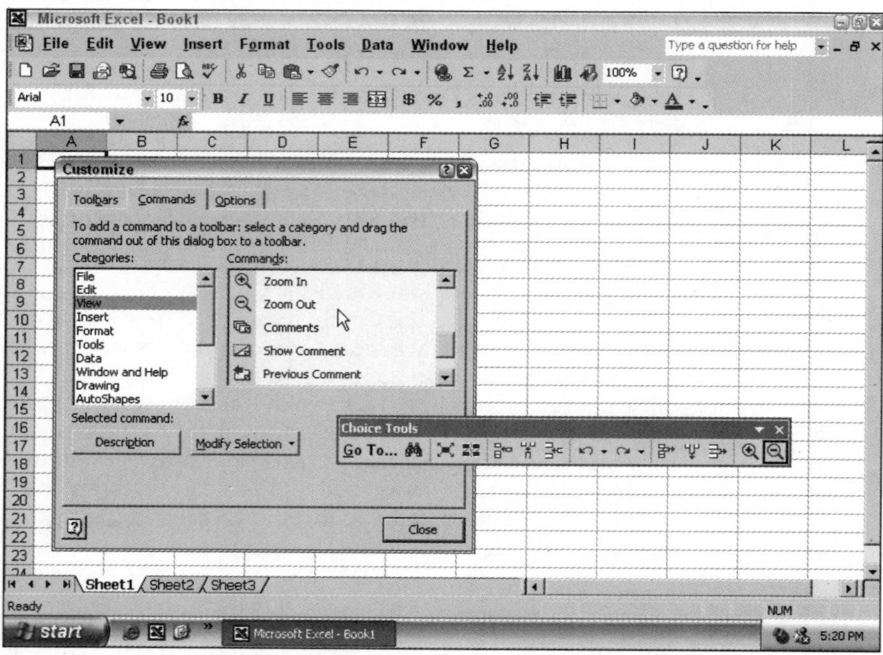

Figure 3-4: Creating a Choice Tools custom toolbar loaded with useful buttons.

In the Choice Tools example toolbar shown in Figure 3-4, I ended up adding a total of 14 buttons and separating them into the following six groups:

- The first group contains the Go To... and Find button from the Edit category.
- The second group contains the Select Current Region and Select Visible Cells buttons from the Edit category.

- ✦ The third group contains the Insert Cells, Insert Columns, and Insert Rows buttons from the Insert category.
- ✦ The fourth group contains Undo and Redo buttons from the Edit category.
- ✦ The fifth group contains Delete, Delete Columns, and Delete Rows buttons from the Edit category.
- ✦ The sixth group contains the Zoom In and Zoom Out buttons from the View category.

I use this custom toolbar when doing heavy editing to the structure of worksheets (see Book II, Chapters 3 and 4). The Undo and Redo buttons are there in case I use the various Insert and Delete buttons in error and end up accidentally inserting or deleting cells, columns, or rows. The Zoom In and Zoom Out buttons enable me to quickly zoom in and out on various regions in the worksheet after locating them with the Go To... and Find buttons.

Making a new menu

To create a new menu for the Menu bar, you follow these steps:

1. **Choose View⇨Toolbars⇨Customize on the Excel Menu bar.**

   Doing this opens the Customize dialog box, the first step in building a new menu.

2. **Click the Commands tab in the Customize dialog box.**

   To create a new menu, you must first select New Menu in the Categories list box.

3. **Scroll down and then click New Menu category in the Categories list box on the left side of the Commands tab.**

   Next, you must drag the New Menu item displayed in the Commands list box to the place on the Excel Menu bar where you want the custom menu to appear.

4. **Drag the New Menu item in the Commands list box to the right to the place on the Excel Menu bar where you want the custom menu to appear.**

   Now, you're ready to rename the menu.

5. **Right-click New Menu on the Excel Menu bar, click Name on its shortcut menu, type the name you want to appear on the Menu bar, and press Enter. If you want a letter in the menu name to be the hot key, type an ampersand (&) before that letter.**

After you've named the custom menu, you're ready to start adding your built-in submenus, macros, and/or hyperlinks.

6. **To add a submenu, click Built-in Menus in the Categories list box and then drag the desired menu from the Commands list box to the custom menu on the Menu bar. To add a macro or hyperlink, click Macros in the Categories list box and then drag Custom Menu Item to the custom menu on the Menu bar.**

   If you add a Custom Menu Item for a macro or hyperlink, you need to rename the menu item and then assign the macro or link to it.

7. **Right-click the Custom Menu Item on the pull-down menu, click Name on shortcut menu that appears, and type a short, descriptive name for the item. If you want a letter in the new name to be the hot key, type an ampersand (&) before that letter.**

8. **To assign a macro to the custom menu item, right-click the item, click Macros on the shortcut menu, and select the macro to use (see Book IX, Chapter 1 for details). To add hyperlink to custom item instead, click Edit Hyperlink⇨Open on the shortcut menu and then select or create the hyperlink (check out Book VIII, Chapter 2 for details).**

   You continue in this manner, adding submenus and Custom Menu Items as needed. Remember that you can move menu items simply by dragging them up or down on the custom menu. You can also separate groups of menu items with a light gray horizontal separator. To insert a separator above a menu item, right-click the item and then click Begin a Group on its shortcut menu.

9. **Repeat Steps 5 through 8 as needed until you've added all the necessary items to the custom menu.**

   Now you're ready to close the Customize dialog box and start using your new menu.

10. **Click the Close button in the Customize dialog box to close it so you can test out the items on your custom menu.**

Figure 3-5 shows a custom Web menu that I added to the Excel Menu bar. Notice that "b" is the hot key for opening this menu from the keyboard in combination with the Alt key (so that the menu's name is really We&b). The Web custom menu contains three items: the built-in Send To submenu, along with two Custom Menu Items (renamed to Mind Over Media and Excel Examples, respectively) to which hyperlinks are assigned. I use the Mind Over Media menu item to open the Internet Explorer and go directly to the home page of my Web site. I use the Excel Examples menu item to open a Worksheets folder on the network server that contains example spreadsheets that appear in the figures throughout this reference.

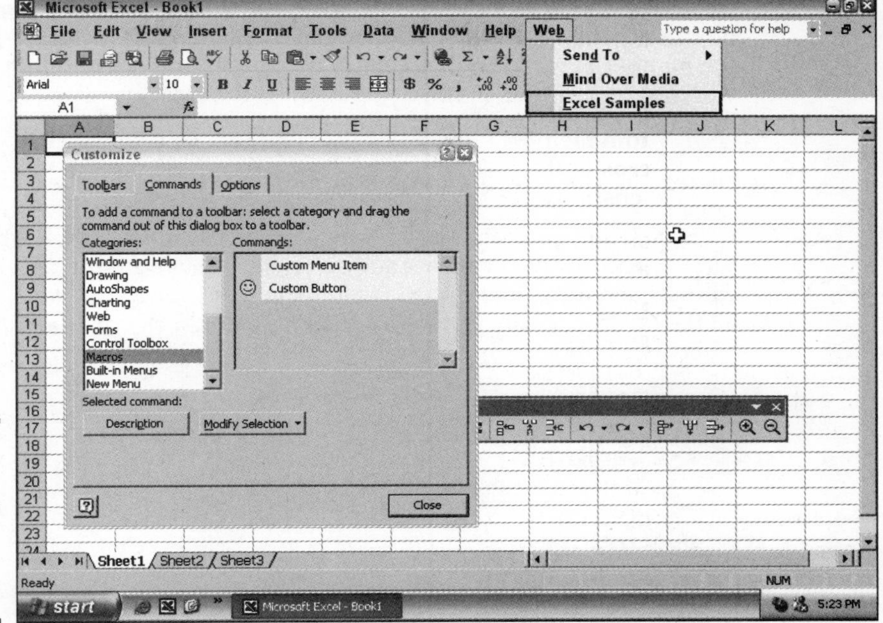

Figure 3-5: Creating a custom Web menu for the Excel Menu bar.

Exercising Your Options

Each time that you open a new workbook, Excel makes a whole bunch of assumptions about how you want the spreadsheet and chart information you enter into it to appear on-screen and in print. These assumptions may or may not fit the way you work and the kinds of spreadsheets and charts you need to create.

In the following four sections, you get a quick rundown on how to change the default or *preference* settings in the Options dialog box. This is the biggest dialog box in Excel, with a billion tabs (thirteen actually). From the Options dialog box, you can see what things appear on-screen and how they appear, as well as when and how Excel calculates worksheets.

Nothing discussed in the following four sections is critical to your being able to operate Excel. Just know that if you find yourself futzing with the same setting over and over again in most of the workbooks you create, then it's high time to get into the Options dialog box and modify that setting so that you won't waste anymore time tinkering with the same setting in future workbooks.

View options

Excel gives you a lot of control over what appears on-screen and how it looks. The options for controlling the appearance of the Excel program and workbook windows mostly show up on the View tab of the Options dialog box. In addition, you can customize the cell-reference style, the menus used, the number of worksheets to a new workbook, and the font that each new workbook uses — all in the General tab of the Options dialog box (discussed in the next section, "General options").

Figure 3-6 shows the options on the View tab of the Options dialog box. To open this dialog box, choose Tools➪Options on the pull-down menus and then click the View tab. The View tab contains a mess of check boxes that turn on and off the display of various elements in both the Excel program window and a particular workbook document window. As you would expect, all the options that have check marks in their check boxes are displayed, whereas all the options with empty check boxes are hidden.

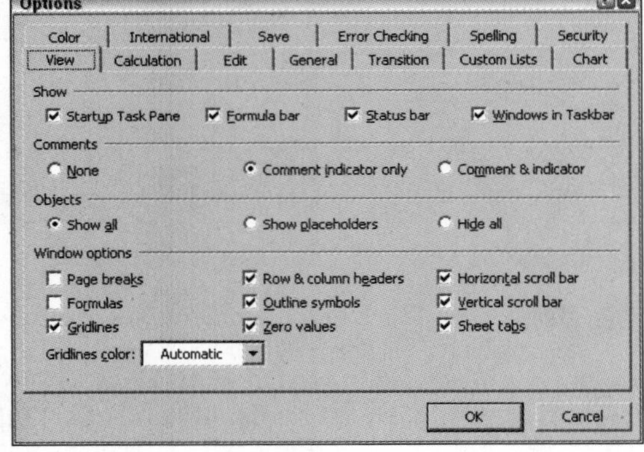

Figure 3-6: The View tab of the Options dialog box controls what appears on screen.

The Show section of the Options dialog box contains four check boxes, controlling the display of the following elements:

- **Startup Task Pane:** Shows the Task Pane each time you start Excel.
- **Formula Bar:** Shows the formula bar right below the Formatting toolbar at the top of the program window.
- **Status Bar:** Shows the status bar at the bottom of the program window.
- **Windows in Taskbar:** Displays multiple buttons on the Windows Taskbar for all the workbooks you have open.

In the Comments area, you find these three radio buttons:

- **None:** Hides both the comment indicators (the little red triangle in the upper-right corner) and the display of their text boxes.

- **Comment Indicator Only:** Shows just the comment indicators in the cells without displaying the text boxes with their comments (see Book IV, Chapter 1 for information on creating comments).
- **Comments & Indicator:** Displays both the comment indicators and the text boxes with the comments in the workbook.

In the Objects area, you find these three radio buttons (see Book V, Chapter 2 for more on graphics objects in Excel):

- **Show All:** Displays all graphic objects (such as charts, clip art, and other types of graphics) in the workbook.
- **Show Placeholders:** Represents graphic objects with grayed out rectangles (doing this speeds up the workbook display on slower computers).
- **Hide All:** Removes the display of all graphic objects in the workbook.

The check-box options in the Window options area of the View tab determine whether or not a number of elements in the current worksheet are displayed. Keep in mind that turning off a particular element in the current worksheet does not turn it off in any other worksheet in that workbook. All of the following option settings are saved as part of your worksheet when you save the workbook except for the Automatic Page Breaks option (which always reverts to the default of being hidden):

- **Page Breaks:** Shows the page breaks that Excel puts in the worksheet when you print it or look at it in Print Preview mode.
- **Formulas:** Shows the formulas in the cells of your worksheet by automatically widening all the columns and left aligning all the information in the cells.
- **Gridlines:** Shows the column and row separators that define the cells in your worksheet.
- **Gridlines Color:** Changes the color of the gridlines (when they're displayed, of course) by clicking a new color on the color palette that appears when you click its drop-down list button. (I find that navy blue is rather fetching.)
- **Row & Column Headers:** Shows the row of column letters at the top of the worksheet and the column of row numbers at the left.
- **Outline Symbols:** Shows all the various symbols that appear when you outline a worksheet table (something you only do with really large tables so that you can collapse the table to its essentials by hiding all but particular levels) or when you use the Subtotals feature to calculate subtotals, totals, and grand totals for certain fields in a database.

- **Zero Values:** Displays entries of zero in the worksheet. Deselect this check box if you want to suppress the display of all zeros in a worksheet (as you might in a worksheet template if you don't want to see all those zeros in a new worksheet generated from the template).
- **Horizontal Scroll Bar:** Displays the horizontal scroll bar to the right of the worksheet tabs at the bottom of the workbook document window. When you hide the horizontal scroll bar and leave the sheet tabs displayed (see Sheet Tabs, following), Excel fills the area normally reserved for the horizontal scroll bar with more sheet tabs. Note that this option affects the display of every worksheet in your workbook.
- **Vertical Scroll Bar:** Displays the vertical scroll bar on the right side of each worksheet in the workbook document window.
- **Sheet Tabs:** Displays the tabs that enable you to activate the various worksheets in your workbook. Note that if you remove the display of the sheet tabs, you can still use Ctrl+PgDn and Ctrl+PgUp to move between worksheets. However, without the tabs, you won't know which worksheet you're looking at unless you can recognize the sheet from its data alone.

General options

The General tab in the Options dialog box (shown in Figure 3-7) contains a number of program-setting options that you might want to change (if not right away, then after working with Excel a little more). Of special interest to some might be the Sheets in New Workbook option that sets the number of blank worksheets in each new workbook (you might routinely need more than 3 and want to choose a more realistic number: hey, like 5, or maybe, if you're feeling wild, 10); the Standard Font option that sets the font used in every cell of a new workbook; and the Default File Location that determines which directory Excel automatically chooses when you try to open or save a workbook document.

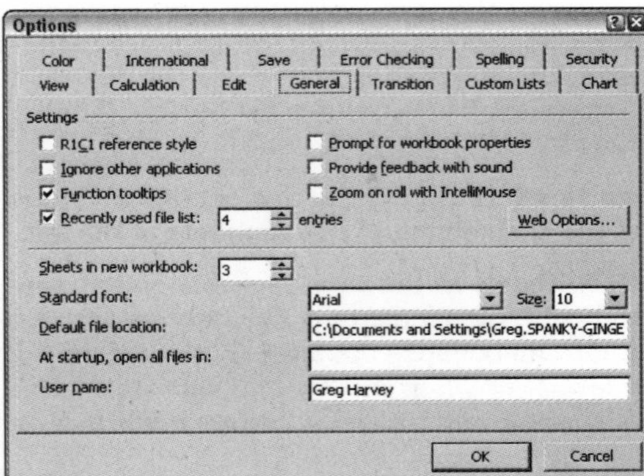

Figure 3-7: The General tab of the Options dialog box controls a variety of default settings.

- **R1C1 Reference Style:** This box switches you in and out of the A1, B1, and so on cell reference system that Excel normally uses into the creepy R1C1 alternate style, in which each column is numbered just like the rows, and the row (that's the R part) reference number precedes the column (that's the C part) reference number. In this system, the cell you know and love as B2 would be cell R2C2. (Hey, wasn't that the name of that vacuum-cleaner-like droid in *Star Wars*?! No, wait, that was R2-D2.)
- **Ignore Other Applications:** When this check box contains a check mark, Excel ignores requests made from other programs using DDE (which stands for Dynamic Data Exchange, as if you care). This is of interest only if you are using data created with other programs in your Excel workbooks (in which case, you definitely want to leave this check box alone).
- **Function ToolTips:** When this check box contains a checkmark, Excel displays brief descriptions of the buttons and boxes on the various built-in toolbars. To display a ToolTip when this option is selected, you must rest the mouse pointer on the button or box for a second or two.
- **Prompt for Workbook Properties:** Normally, Excel does not display a Properties dialog box where you can enter summary information about the subject of the workbook as well as key words that you later use when searching for the file. That can all change if you put a check mark in this check box, because Excel will then automatically remind you to enter summary information for each new workbook that you save.
- **Provide Feedback with Sound:** When you select this check box, Excel plays available sounds associated with routine events, such as opening and saving workbooks, and displaying alert dialog boxes. Note that if you deselect this check box, it not only turns off sound feedback in Excel 2002 but in all other Office XP application programs (like Word 2002, PowerPoint 2002, and so on) as well.
- **Zoom on Roll with IntelliMouse:** If you're using a Microsoft IntelliMouse with a wheel in between the two mouse buttons and you select this check box, you can zoom in and out on the current worksheet just by rolling its wheel. When you roll the wheel down one click, Excel zooms out on the worksheet by reducing the magnification by 15 percent (until the magnification reaches 10 percent). When you roll the wheel up one click, Excel zooms in on the worksheet by increasing the magnification by 15 percent (until the magnification reaches 100 percent).
- **Web Options:** Click this button to display the Web Options dialog box, where you can modify the options that control how your Excel data appear when viewed with a Web browser, such as Internet Explorer. (See Book VIII, Chapter 1 for more on how to publish Excel data on the Internet.)

- **Recently Used File List:** When you select this check box, Excel lists the last four documents you opened (in order from most recently used to least recently used) at the bottom of the File menu. You can then open any of these four files simply by selecting its name (or number) after you open the File menu.
- **Sheets in New Workbook:** Normally, Excel puts three blank worksheets in each new workbook you open. If you're never in a million years gonna use more than one or two worksheets, you can select this option and reduce the number. On the other hand, you could also use this option to increase the number of worksheets in a new workbook if you find that you're routinely using more than three sheets, and you're getting tired of having to manually add worksheets. (See Book II, Chapter 4 for information on manually inserting and removing worksheets from a workbook.)
- **Standard Font** and **Size:** Use these options to change the font and/or font size that Excel automatically assigns to all the cells in a new workbook. If you have a favorite font you like to see in most of the worksheets you create (and Arial ain't it), this is the way to select your font of choice, rather than having to call upon the Font tool on the Formatting toolbar all the time (see Book II, Chapter 2).
- **Default File Location:** If you don't specify a directory for this option when you first start Excel, the program looks for each workbook that you try to open or puts each new workbook that you save in a folder named My Documents on your hard drive. Use this option to select another folder as the repository of your precious documents by entering the path name of the folder (such as `C:\Greg\Excel Stuff`). Note that this folder must exist prior to using this option — it can't be one that you intend to create but just haven't gotten around to yet. Remember that you can create a new folder at the time you first save a new workbook by clicking the Create New Folder button on the Save As dialog box toolbar.
- **At Startup, Open All Files In:** Normally, Excel opens any document that you put in the special Startup folder called XLStart whenever you start Excel. If you don't feel that one Startup folder is enough, you can use this option to specify another one. Again, this folder must already exist before you can designate it as your alternate startup location by entering its path in its text box.
- **User Name:** In my copy of Excel, this is usually Greg Harvey (unless I'm using my nom de plume, I.M. Shakes Peer), but it will differ in your copy unless you happen to go by the same name or alias that I do. If you want to change your user name to Greg Harvey or I.M. Shakes Peer, this is where you do it.

Edit options

The Edit tab of the Options dialog box (shown in Figure 3-8) contains options that determine how editing works. As you notice when you first select the Edit tab, most of these check-box options are already turned on for you.

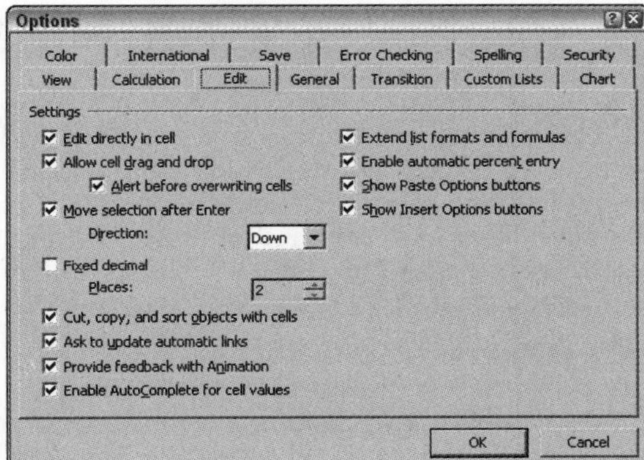

Figure 3-8: The Edit tab of the Options dialog box controls how Excel behaves when editing cells.

- **Edit Directly in Cell:** If you deselect this option, you can't do any more editing within the cell. Instead, you have to edit the cell's contents on the formula bar after either double-clicking the cell or selecting it and then pressing F2.
- **Allow Cell Drag and Drop:** If you deselect this option, you can no longer use the drag-and-drop method to copy or move cells around a worksheet, from worksheet to worksheet within a workbook, or from workbook to workbook.
- **Alert Before Overwriting Cells:** If you deselect this option (which I really don't recommend), Excel no longer warns you when a drag-and-drop operation is about to obliterate stuff that you've already entered in the worksheet.
- **Extend List Formats and Formulas:** When this check box has a checkmark, Excel automatically formats new items added to the end of a list and copies formulas that are repeated in rows above when you use the same formatting or copy the same formula in at least three of the last five preceding rows.
- **Enable Automatic Percent Entry:** When this check box has a checkmark, Excel automatically multiplies all numbers less than 1 by 100 when you apply the Percent number format to their cells. If you want numbers greater than 1 also multiplied by 100 when you format their cells with the Percent format, remove the checkmark from this check box.

- **Show Paste Options Buttons:** When this check box has a checkmark, Excel automatically displays a Paste Options button when you paste cells, which enables you to select special options such as Keep Source Formatting and Match Destination Formatting.
- **Show Insert Options Buttons:** When this check box has a checkmark, Excel automatically displays an Insert Options drop button when inserting cells, rows, or columns in a worksheet that enables you to select special options such as Format Same As Left or Above and Clear Formatting.
- **Move Selection after Enter** and **Direction:** If you deselect this option, Excel no longer moves the cell pointer when you press the Enter key to complete a cell entry. If you still want Enter to complete an entry and move the cell pointer but don't want it to move to the next cell down, leave the Move Selection after Enter check box selected and choose a new direction (Right, Up, or Left) in the Direction drop-down list box.
- **Fixed Decimal** and **Places:** Select this option only when you want to set all values in the worksheet to the decimal precision indicated in the associated edit box (see Book II, Chapter 1 for more information). When selecting this check box, you can modify the number of decimal places from the default of 2 by entering the new value in the edit box or using the spinner buttons.
- **Cut, Copy, and Sort Objects with Cells:** Deselect this editing option only when you don't want graphic objects (like text boxes, arrows, and imported images) to move around when you cut, copy, or sort the cells underneath them.
- **Ask to Update Automatic Links:** Deselect this option when you don't want Excel to bother you before going ahead and updating links between formulas in different workbooks.
- **Provide Feedback with Animation:** Select this option when you want Excel to animate the process of making room for insertions or the process of pulling up and over cells to close gaps in the worksheet when making deletions.
- **Enable AutoComplete for Cell Values:** Deselect this option if you find that the AutoComplete feature gets in your way when entering columns of data in a worksheet. (See Book II, Chapter 2 for information on what the heck AutoComplete is, let alone what it does.)

Save options

The settings on the Save tab of the Options dialog box (shown in Figure 3-9) control the program's AutoRecover settings. The AutoRecover feature enables Excel to save copies of your entire Excel workbook at the interval displayed in the Minutes text box (10 by default) in the folder on the disk specified in the AutoRecover Save Location text box.

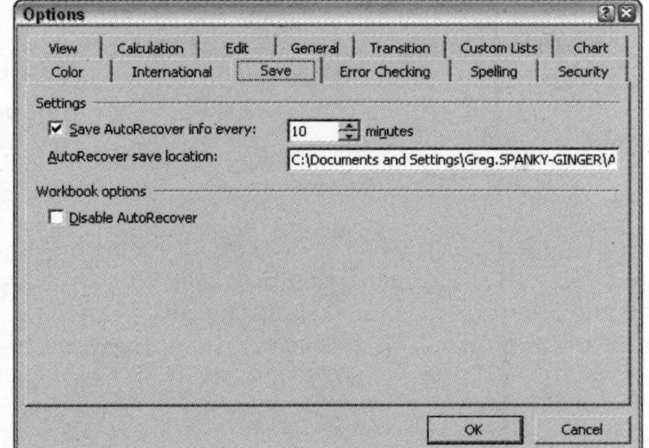

Figure 3-9: The Save tab of the Options dialog box controls the Auto-Recover settings.

If your computer should crash or you suddenly lose power, the next time you start Excel, the program then automatically displays an AutoRecover pane from which you can open a copy of the workbook file that you were working on when this crash or power loss occurred. If this recovered workbook (saved at the time of the last AutoRecover), contains information unsaved in the original copy the last time you used the Save command before the crash or power loss, you can then use the recovered copy rather than manually reconstructing and reentering the otherwise lost information.

You may also use the recovered copy of a workbook, should the original copy of the workbook file become corrupted in such a way so that Excel is no longer able to open it. (This happens very rarely, but it *does* happen.)

Don't disable the AutoRecover feature by selecting the Disable AutoRecover check box on the Save tab, even if you have a battery backup system for your computer that gives you plenty of time to manually save your Excel workbook during any power outage, because this in no way protects you from data loss if your workbook file becomes corrupted or you hit the computer's power switch by mistake.

Add-in Mania

Add-ins are small, specialized programs that extend Excel's built-in features in some way. Most of the add-in programs created for Excel offer you some kind of specialized function or group of functions that extend Excel's computational abilities. Before you can use any add-in program, the add-in must be installed in the proper folder on your hard drive, and then you must select the add-in in the Excel Add-Ins dialog box.

Excel add-in programs are saved in a special file format identified with the .XLA (for Excel Add-in) filename extension. These XLA files are normally saved inside the Library folder (sometimes in their own subfolders) that is located in the Office10 folder. This folder, in turn, is located in your Microsoft Office folder inside the Program Files folder on your hard drive (often designated as the C:\ drive).

After an add-in program has been installed in the Library folder, its name then appears in the list box of the Add-Ins dialog box that you open by choosing Tools➪Add-Ins on the Excel Menu bar. To activate any of the add-in programs (by putting them into the computer's memory), you click the check box in front of their name in the Add-ins Available list box (see Figure 3-10) and then click OK.

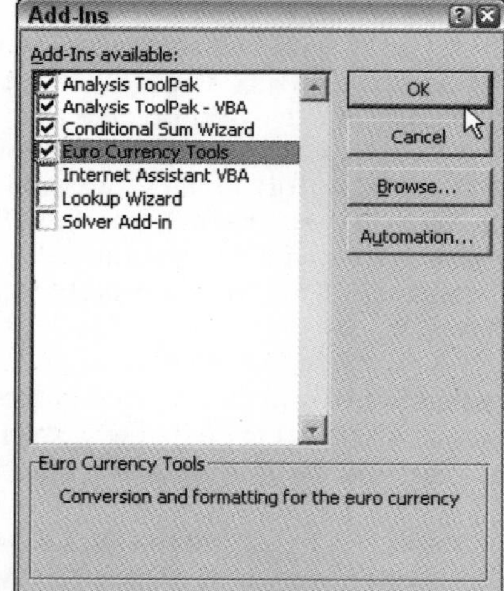

Figure 3-10: Activating the Add-in programs that come with Excel 2002.

If you ever copy an XLA add-in program to a folder other than the Library folder in the Office10 folder on your hard drive, its name won't appear in the Add-ins Available list box when you open the Add-Ins dialog box. You can, however, activate the add-in by clicking the Browse button in this dialog box and then selecting the add-in file in its folder in Browse dialog box before you click OK.

Installing the add-ins included with Excel

Whether you know it or not, you already have a group of add-in programs waiting for you to install and activate. The following add-in programs are included with Excel 2002:

- **Analysis ToolPak:** Adds extra financial, statistical, and engineering functions to Excel's pool of built-in functions.
- **Analysis ToolPak VBA:** Enables VBA programmers to publish their own financial, statistical, and engineering functions for Excel.
- **Conditional Sum Wizard:** Helps you set up formulas that sum data only when the data meets the criteria you specify (see Book II, Chapter 1).
- **Euro Currency Tools:** Enables you to format worksheet values as Euro currency and adds a EUROCONVERT function for converting other currencies into Euros.
- **Internet Assistant VBA:** Enables VBA programmers to publish Excel data to the Web.
- **Lookup Wizard:** Helps you set up formulas that return data from an Excel list by using known data in that list (see Book III, Chapter 6).
- **Solver Add-In:** Calculates solutions to what-if scenarios based on cells that both adjust and constrain the range of values (see Book VII, Chapter 1).

The first time you activate any of these add-ins included with Excel, the program immediately displays an alert dialog box, telling you that the add-in is not currently installed and asking you if you want to install it. (All the included add-ins are marked for installation on first use so that they show up in the list box in the Add-Ins dialog box but do not actually take up disk space until you're ready to use them.) Click the Yes button in this alert dialog box to have the selected add-in (or add-ins) in this list installed. Keep in mind that Excel needs to access to your Office XP CD-ROM or its files on your network in order to install any of these included add-in programs.

When you install and activate these add-in programs, Excel displays new menu items for most of them on the Tools pull-down menu that you choose when you want to use them. So, for example, you choose Tools⇨Conditional Sum when you want to use the Conditional Sum Wizard add-in and Tools⇨Data Analysis when you want to use one of the additional statistical functions added as part of the Analysis TookPak add-in.

You can save computer memory (RAM) that may be needed for doing calculations in the workbook that you're editing by deactivating any and all add-in programs that you're not currently using (simply open the Add-Ins dialog box and click the check box in front of the add-in program's name in the Add-ins Available list box and click OK). Note that deactivating an add-in does not uninstall it (that is, remove it from the Library folder on your hard drive); it only removes the add-in from the computer's RAM memory. If you do deactivate add-ins to save memory, you must remember to open the Add-Ins dialog box and activate them again when you do need access to their functions.

Downloading free add-ins

In addition to the add-ins automatically included with Excel 2002, Microsoft offers a number of Excel add-ins that you can download and use for free. To browse these freebies and perhaps download and install some of them, you follow these steps:

1. **Choose Help⇨Office on the Web on the Excel Menu bar.**

   Doing this launches your Web browser, connects you to the Internet (assuming that you do have access to it), and then takes you to the home page of the Microsoft Office Assistance Center.

2. **Click the Download Center link in the panel on the left.**

   Doing this opens the Download Center page, where you select the product and the version for which you want add-ins.

3. **Click the Product drop-down button and then click Excel on its pop-up menu.**

   Next, you need to make sure that 2002/XP is listed in the Version combo box to the immediate right of the Product combo box. If not, click the Version drop-down button and click 2002/XP on its pop-up menu.

4. **Click the check box in front of the Add-ins and Extras under the heading, Choose Which Type(s) of Downloads You Want Displayed in the Boxes Below.**

   Now, you need to update the list.

5. **Click the Update List button to display a list of all the available Excel 2002 add-ins.**

   Scroll through the list of add-ins, reading its description, file size, and approximate download times.

6. **To download a particular add-in, click its Download Now! button, click the Save button in the File Download dialog box, and select the Desktop as the location in the Save As dialog box before you click the Save button.**

   After the add-in file is successfully downloaded on your computer's desktop, you can continue downloading other add-ins.

7. **To download other Excel add-ins in the list, repeat Step 6.**

   As soon as you finish downloading the Excel add-ins, you're ready to install them.

8. **When you finish downloading Excel add-ins, click the Close button in your Web browser to close it.**

   To install an add-in, you simply double-click its icon on the Windows desktop.

9. **Double-click the icon for the add-in you want to install, click Yes when asked if you want to install it, and then click Yes again when asked if you accept the License agreement (after you've read every word of it, of course).**

   Follow whatever prompts appear to complete the installation process. Often, you see a dialog box asking you where to install the add-in. Accept the default location (the Library folder in the Office10 folder).

10. **Click the OK button in the alert dialog box indicating that your add-in has been successfully installed.**

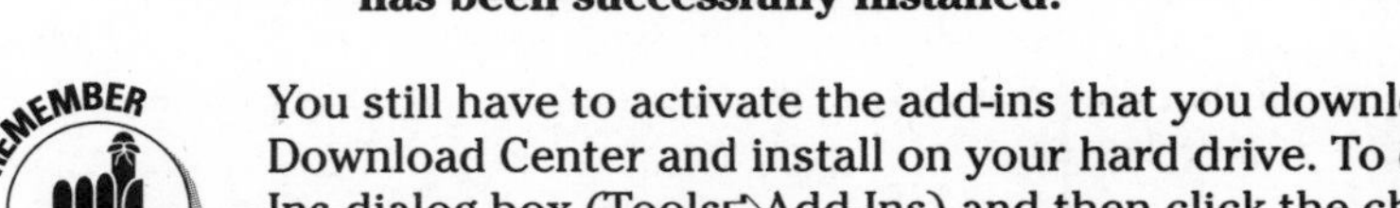

REMEMBER

You still have to activate the add-ins that you download from the Microsoft Download Center and install on your hard drive. To do this, open the Add-Ins dialog box (Tools⇨Add-Ins) and then click the check box in front of the add-in you want to activate before you click OK.

TIP

If, after installing and activating one of the Microsoft add-ins you downloaded, you are unable to locate the add-in program when you use Excel, first check the Tools menu for any new items. Then check the list of toolbars (View⇨Toolbars) to see if any new toolbars have been added. If you still can't find the command, click the Ask a Question box, type the name of the add-in, and press Enter. Often, Microsoft Excel Web Help has information on a particular add-in, including the menu where it should appear.

For example, if you type **Report Manager add-in** in the Ask a Question box and then press Enter (to get help on locating and using the Report Manager add-in that you've downloaded, installed, and activated), the topic WEB: Create and Print Reports with the Report Manager appears on the pop-up menu. When you click this topic, help information from the Microsoft Office Assistance Center appears in the Microsoft Help window, telling you that the Report Manager command should show up on the View menu and giving you lots of information on how to use this valuable utility.

Purchasing third-party add-ins

The add-ins included with Excel and the freebie add-ins on the Microsoft Web site available for downloading are not the only Excel add-ins that you can lay your hands on. Many third-party vendors sell Excel add-ins that you can often purchase online and then immediately download onto your hard drive.

To find third-party vendors and get information on their add-ins, open your Web browser and do a search for

```
Excel add-ins
```

Even before you do a Web search, you may want to visit Macro Systems Web site at

```
www.add-ins.com
```

This online outfit offers a wide variety of useful Excel add-ins, such as the Duplicate Finder add-in that quickly finds and selects all duplicate data entries in a worksheet based on entries in one or more cells (which you can then get rid of in one swoop by choosing the Edit⇨Delete command), and the Name Splitter that automatically splits full names that have been entered into single cells into individual cells with first names, middle names or initial, and last names (so that the list can then be better sorted and filtered by parts of the names).

Note that you can expect to pay Macro Systems between $25.00 and $50.00 for add-in programs like these (really reasonably priced if you consider how many man-hours it would take to manually hunt down and eliminate duplicates or to split up names into separate cells in huge worksheets).

Book II

Worksheet Design

"The top line represents our revenue, the middle line is our inventory, and the bottom line shows the rate of my hair loss over the same period."

Contents at a Glance

Chapter 1: Building Worksheets

In This Chapter

- **Tips for designing worksheets**
- **Understanding the different types of cell entries**
- **Different ways of entering data in the worksheet**
- **Restricting the type of entries that you can make in cells**
- **Saving worksheets**

Before you can begin building a new spreadsheet in Excel, you must have the design in mind. As it turns out, the design aspect of the creative process is often the easiest part because you can borrow the design from other workbooks that you've already created or from special workbook files, called *templates*, which provide you with the new spreadsheet's form, along with some of the standard, or *boilerplate,* data entries.

After you've settled upon the design of your new spreadsheet, you're ready to begin entering its data. In doing the data entry in a new worksheet, you have several choices regarding the method to use. For this reason, this chapter not only covers all the methods for entering data — from the most basic to the most sophisticated — but it also includes hints on when each is the most appropriate. Note, however, that this chapter doesn't include information on building formulas, which comprises a major part of the data entry task in creating a new spreadsheet. Because this task is so specialized and so extensive, you find the information on formula building covered in Book III, Chapter 1.

Designer Spreadsheets

Each and every time you start Excel without also opening an existing workbook file, the program presents you with a new workbook (with the generic filename, Book1), consisting of three totally blank worksheets. At this point, you can either launch into building your new spreadsheet by using the workbook's three blank worksheets, or you can open a spreadsheet template or existing workbook file and then adapt the template's or workbook file's design by entering the data for the new spreadsheet.

Take it from a template

Spreadsheet templates are the way to go if you can find one that fits the design of the spreadsheet that you're building. You can choose from a couple of good sources for ready-made spreadsheet templates. First, you can try using the spreadsheet templates created by an Excel spreadsheet design firm called Spreadsheet Solutions, which are included with the Excel program. Second, you can also download free spreadsheet templates from the Microsoft Office Web site.

Instead of using ready-made templates, you can create your own templates from your favorite Excel workbooks. After you save a copy of a workbook as a template file, Excel automatically generates a copy of the workbook whenever you open the template file. This way, you can safely customize the contents of the new workbook without any danger of inadvertently modifying the original template.

Using the Spreadsheet Solutions templates

Excel includes the following five templates, courtesy of Spreadsheet Solutions:

- Balance Sheet
- Expense Statement
- Loan Amortization
- Sales Invoice
- Timecard

As with the add-in programs included with Excel 2002, these template files are marked for "installation on first use," meaning that you have to try to open a new workbook generated from the template before it's installed on your computer. As with all components that are installed on first use, be sure that you have your original Office XP CD-ROM on hand when you do this or make sure that Excel has access to the Office XP files on a network drive.

Installing the Spreadsheet Solutions templates

Follow these steps to install and then immediately use any of the five Spreadsheet Solutions templates:

1. **Start Excel and then click the General Templates link in the New Workbook Task pane that appears in the pane to the right of the document window with the worksheets for Book1.**

If the New Workbook Task pane is not displayed, choose View⇨Task Pane on the Excel menu bar to open it. When you click the General Templates link, Excel responds by opening the Templates dialog box that contains two tabs: General and Spreadsheet Solutions.

2. **Click the Spreadsheets Solutions tab in the Templates dialog box.**

   The Spreadsheets Solutions tab shows the template file icons (notice how they differ from regular workbook files by placing the XL icon on top of a tablet with multiple sheets rather than a single sheet). To install the template and then generate a new workbook file from it, you need to select the icon.

3. **Double-click the icon of the template that you want to install and use or click it and then click the OK button, as shown in Figure 1-1.**

   Excel responds by installing all of the Spreadsheet Solutions templates (after you supply the CD-ROM or indicate where the Office XP files are located on your network) and then opening a copy of the template that you selected in the Excel document window.

4. **Fill in the missing information in the appropriate cells in the new workbook and then save your changes with the File⇨Save command.**

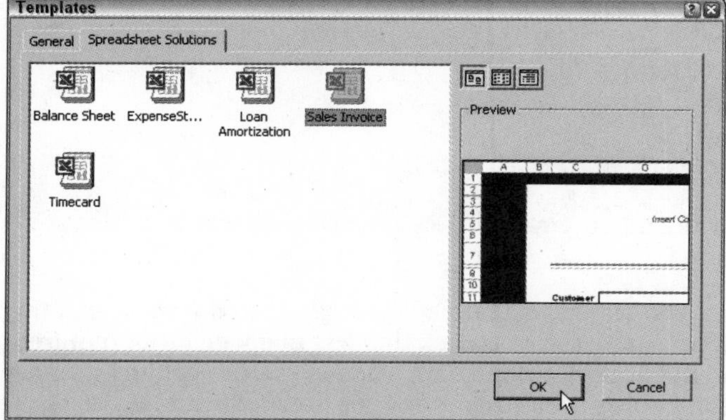

Figure 1-1: Selecting a Spreadsheet Solutions template from which to generate a new workbook.

Figure 1-2 shows a copy of a blank sales invoice generated from the Sales Invoice template located on the Spreadsheet Solutions tab of the Templates dialog box. As you can see on the Excel window title bar in this figure, when Excel generated this first copy of the Sales Invoice workbook from the original template file, the program also gave it the temporary filename, Sales Invoice1. If you were to then create a second copy of the sales invoice by once again opening the Sales Invoice template, the program would name that copy Sales Invoice2. This way, you don't have to worry about one copy overwriting another and you never risk mistakenly saving changes to the original Sales Invoice template file itself (which actually uses a completely different filename extension — `xlt` for Excel template as opposed to `xls` for Excel worksheet).

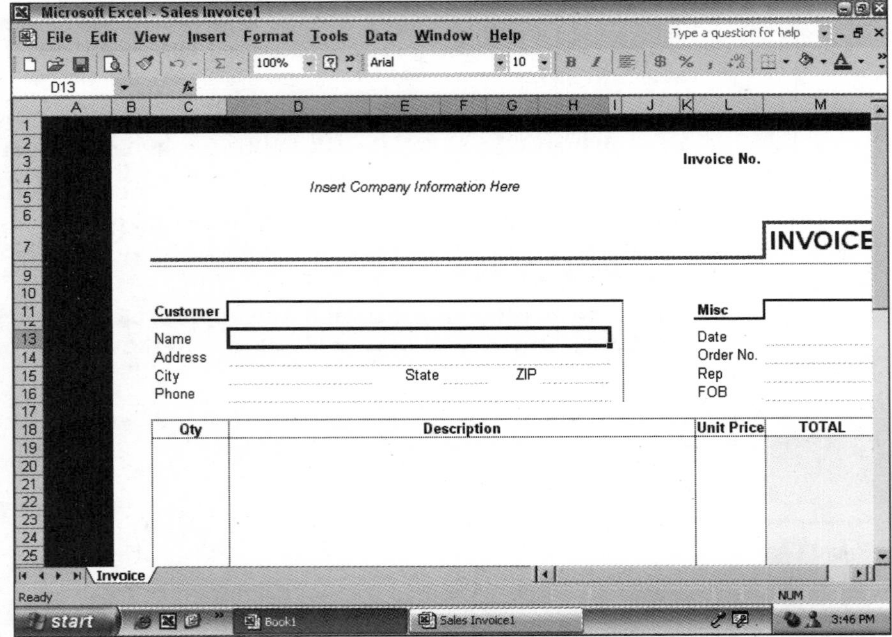

Figure 1-2: A new sales invoice worksheet generated from the generic Sales Invoice template.

To fill in the blanks in a spreadsheet generated from one of the Spreadsheet Solutions templates, you click the first blank cell that requires a data entry, type in the necessary data, and then press Tab or the Enter key to advance to the next blank cell (either over or down, depending on the template's design). If pressing Tab or Enter to advance takes you past a blank cell in the worksheet that needs data, simply click the cell, type in the data, and then press Enter to complete the entry and advance to the next blank.

Note that when filling in a spreadsheet generated from a Spreadsheet Solutions template, you only have access to the cells that require personalized data entry. This means that you don't have access to the cells in the worksheet that contain the generic headings or to the cells that contain the formulas that calculate new subtotals, taxes, and grand totals based on the particular values that you enter into the cells used in doing these calculations.

After you finish filling in the personalized data, save the workbook just as you would a workbook that you had created from scratch (see the "Saving the Data" section at the end of this chapter for details on saving workbook files).

You can customize the Spreadsheet Solutions template to make them easier to fill out and then save those modifications in a new template that you save on your hard drive. For example, you can make your own custom sales invoice template from one generated by the Spreadsheet Solutions Sales Invoice template by filling in your company name and address in the top section and your billing terms and a thank-you message in the bottom sections.

Saving changes to your customized templates

To save your changes as a new template file, follow these steps:

1. **Click the Save button on the Standard toolbar (the one with the disk icon), choose File⇨Save on the Excel menu bar, or press Ctrl+S.**

   Doing any one of these methods opens the Save As dialog box, where the temporary filename (such as Sales Invoice1) appears in the File Name text box.

2. **Edit the filename for your new template in the File Name text box.**

   Next, you need to change the file type from a regular Microsoft Excel Workbook to a Template in the Save as Type combo box.

3. **Click the Save as Type drop-down button and then click Template in the pop-up menu.**

   Note that Excel automatically selects the Templates folder (indicated by the appearance of Templates in the Save In combo box) as the place to save your template. All spreadsheet template files that you save in this folder automatically appear on the General tab of the Template dialog box.

4. **Click the Save button to close the Save As dialog box and save your customized template in the Templates folder.**

   After the Save As dialog box closes, you still need to close the customized template file in the Excel work area.

5. **Choose File⇨Close on the Excel Menu bar or press Ctrl+W to close the customized template file.**

After saving the customized template file in the Template folder, you can generate new workbooks from it by simply clicking the General Templates link in the New Workbook Task pane. The file icon for the customized template appears on the General tab of the Templates dialog box. To generate a new workbook from the customized spreadsheet template, double-click this template file icon or, if you prefer, click the icon and then click OK.

Figure 1-3 shows the General tab of the Templates dialog box after I customized the Spreadsheet Solutions Sales Invoice template and then generated a new template from it. I saved a copy of the Sales Invoice template in the same folder under the name MOM Sales Invoice (MOM stands for *Mind Over Media,* the name of my company) after adding the company name and address at the top, and the company's billing terms and a nice thank-you message at the bottom. With all this boilerplate information already in place in each invoice generated from this template, I bypass a lot of tedious (and very unnecessary) data entry whenever I need to get a bill out.

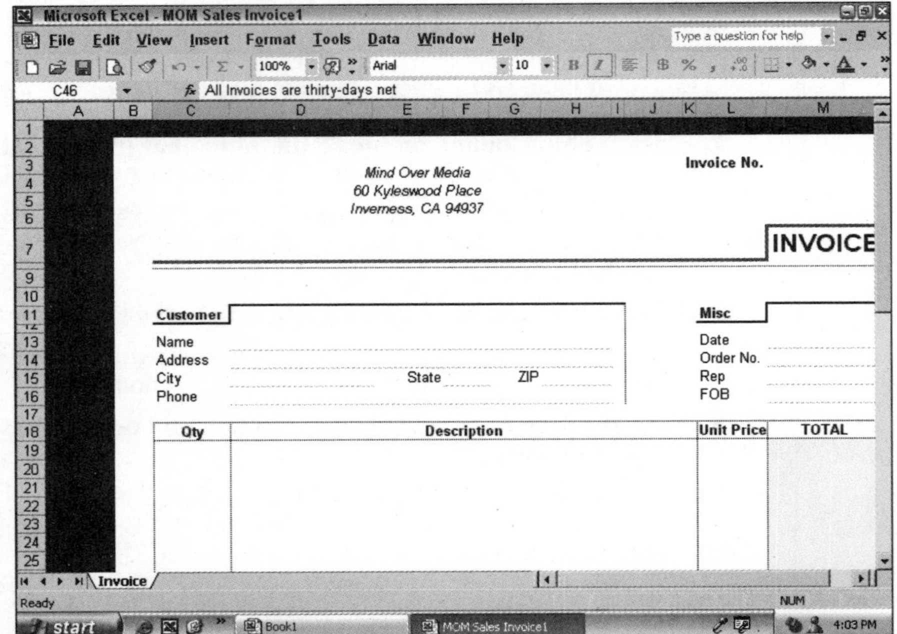

Figure 1-3: A new workbook generated from the customized Sales Invoice template.

Downloading Microsoft spreadsheet templates

You can easily check out and download any of the spreadsheet templates offered by Microsoft. As long as you have Internet access, you can do it right from within Excel by clicking the Templates on Microsoft.com link, located near the bottom of the New Workbook Task pane. When you click this link, Excel opens your Web browser, which connects you to the Internet and then opens the Microsoft Template Gallery Home page, shown in Figure 1-4.

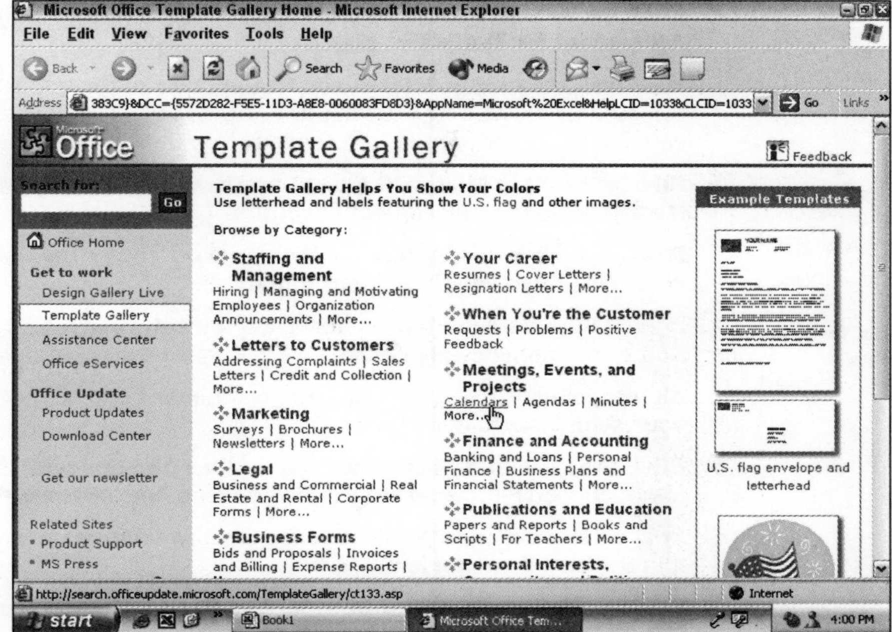

Figure 1-4: Visiting the Microsoft Template Gallery in search of cool spreadsheet templates.

As Figure 1-4 shows, the Template Gallery is arranged by categories, some of which — Resumes, Cover Letters, and so forth — don't pertain to Excel at all (indeed, all the templates in these categories are Word templates). Others, such as Invoices and Billing, Financial Statements, and Investments pertain as much — if not more — to Excel than to the other Office programs, including Word, PowerPoint, and Access (only the templates in the Investments category are 100 percent for Excel). Still others in categories such as Managing and Motivating Employees, Calendars, and Payroll (which you can access by clicking the More button under Staffing and Management) are a mixed bag with just as many non-Excel templates as Excel templates.

When you find a spreadsheet template that you think you may want to use, follow these steps:

1. **Click the template's Go to Preview link, located to the right of its description.**

   The first time you access the Template Gallery you have to accept a general End User License Agreement for using their templates (oh, Microsoft and their licensing agreements!).

2. **Click the Accept button, located at the bottom of the End User License Agreement for Templates page.**

   Your Web browser now takes you to a preview of the template that you selected, showing how the template appears in Excel. If you're still interested in using the template, you need to open it in Excel.

3. **Click the Edit in Microsoft Excel button on the Preview page to open the template in your copy of Excel.**

   When you click this button, the Web browser copies the template to your hard drive and then opens it in Excel.

4. **Personalize the template as necessary by entering your own information in the appropriate cells.**

   All that remains to do is to save the customized spreadsheet template in your Templates folder.

5. **Click the Save button on Standard toolbar (the one with the disk icon), choose File⇨Save on the Excel menu bar, or press Ctrl+S.**

   Now enter a descriptive filename for the new template before you save it in the Templates folder.

6. **Edit the filename for your new personalized Microsoft template in the File Name text box.**

   Next, you need to remember to change the file type from a regular Microsoft Excel Workbook to a Template in the Save as Type combo box.

7. **Click the Save as Type drop-down button and then click Template in the pop-up menu.**

   Verify that you're saving the new spreadsheet template in the Templates folder, and then you're ready to save it.

8. **Make sure that Templates is the folder shown in the Save In combo box and then click the Save button.**

   Now all that remains to do is to close the template file.

9. **Choose File⇨Close on the Excel Menu bar or press Ctrl+W to close the customized template file.**

After saving a personalized version of the template that you've downloaded (as described in the preceding steps), you can use the template to generate new workbooks by opening it from the General tab of the Templates dialog box (open this dialog box by clicking the General Templates link in the New Workbook Task pane).

Creating your own spreadsheet templates

You certainly don't have to rely on spreadsheet templates created by other people. Indeed, many times you simply can't do this because even though other people may generate the type of spreadsheet that you need, their design doesn't incorporate and represent the data in the manner that you prefer or that your company or clients require.

When you can't find a ready-made template that fits the bill or that you can easily customize to suit your needs, create your own templates from sample workbooks that you've created or that your company has on hand. The easiest way to create your own template is to first create an actual workbook prototype, complete with all the text, data, formulas, graphics, and macros that it requires to function.

When readying the prototype workbook, make sure that you remove all headings, miscellaneous text, and numbers that are specific to the prototype and not generic enough to appear in the spreadsheet template. You may also want to protect all generic data, including the formulas that calculate the values that you or your users input into the worksheets generated from the template and headings that never require editing (see Book IV, Chapter 3 for information on how to protect certain parts of a worksheet from changes).

After making sure that both the layout and content of the boilerplate data are hunky-dory, save the workbook in the template file format (`xlt`) in the Templates folder so that you can then generate new workbooks from it by opening it on the General tab of the Templates dialog box (for details on how to do this, refer to the steps in the previous section, "Saving changes to custom templates").

As you may have noticed when looking through the Spreadsheet Solutions templates included in Excel (see Figure 1-2, for example) or browsing through the templates available from the online Microsoft Template Gallery, many spreadsheet templates abandon the familiar worksheet grid of cells, preferring a look very close to that of a paper form instead. When converting a sample workbook into a template, you can also remove the grid, use cell borders to underscore or outline key groups of cells, and color different cell groups to make them stand out (for information on how to do this kind of stuff, refer to Book II, Chapter 2).

Keep in mind that you can also customize the toolbars or create custom toolbars that offer easy access to the commands needed in preparing the type of spreadsheet generated from the template (see Book I, Chapter 3 for details on customizing and creating custom toolbars). Also keep in mind that you can add online comments to parts of the template that instruct coworkers who are unfamiliar with the template and may be less skilled in using Excel on how to properly fill in and save the data (see Book IV, Chapter 1 for details on adding comments to worksheets).

If you create a custom toolbar to be used in workbooks generated from a template file, be sure to associate the toolbar with the template file by using the Attach button, located on the Toolbars tab of the Customize dialog box, to attach the toolbar to copy the toolbar into the workbook (you can do this before saving the prototype workbook as a template file). This way, you can always be sure that everyone who builds a workbook from the template has access to your custom tools.

Designing a workbook from scratch

Not all worksheets come from templates. Many times, you need to create rather unique spreadsheets that aren't intended to function as standard models from which certain types of workbook are generated. In fact, most of the spreadsheets that you create in Excel may be of this kind, especially if your business doesn't rely on the use of highly standardized financial statements and forms.

Planning your workbook

When creating a new workbook from scratch, you need to start by considering the layout and design of the data. When doing this mental planning, you may want to ask yourself some of the following questions:

- Does the layout of the spreadsheet require the use of data tables (with both column and row headings) or lists (with column headings only)?
- Does the spreadsheet require the use of multiple data tables and/or lists?
- Do these data tables and lists need to be laid out on a single worksheet or can they be placed in the same relative position on multiple worksheets of the workbook (like pages of a book)?
- Do the data tables in the spreadsheet use the same type of formulas?
- Do some of the columns in the data lists in the spreadsheet get their input from formula calculation or do they get their input from other lists (called *lookup tables*) in the workbook?
- Will any of the data in the spreadsheet be graphed, and will these charts appear in the same worksheet (referred to as *embedded charts*) or will they appear on separate worksheets in the workbook (called *chart sheets*)?
- Does any of the data in the spreadsheet come from worksheets in separate workbook files?

- How often will the data in the spreadsheet be updated or added to?
- How much data will the spreadsheet ultimately hold?
- Will the data in the spreadsheet be shared primarily in printed or online form?

All these questions are an attempt to get you to consider the basic purpose and function of the new spreadsheet before you start building it, so you can come up with a design that is both economical and fully functional.

Economy

Economy is an important consideration because when you open a workbook, all of its data is loaded into your computer's dynamic memory (also known as *RAM memory*). This may not pose any problems if your computer is one of the latest generation of PCs with more memory than you can conceive of using at one time, but it can pose quite a problem if you share the workbook file with someone whose computer is not so well equipped. Also, depending on just how much data you cram into the workbook, you may even come to see Excel creep and crawl the more and more you work with it.

To help guard against this problem, make sure that you don't pad the data tables and lists in your workbook with extra empty "spacer" cells. Keep the tables as close together as possible on the same worksheet (with no more than a single blank column or row as a separator, which you can adjust to make as wide or high as you like), or — if the design allows — keep them in the same region of consecutive worksheets.

Functionality

Along with economy, you must pay attention to the functionality of the spreadsheet. This means that you need to allow for future growth when selecting the placement of its data tables, lists, and charts. This is especially important in the case of data lists because they have a tendency to grow longer and longer as you continue to add data, requiring more and more rows of the same few columns in the worksheet. This means that you should usually consider all the rows of the columns used in a data list as "off limits." In fact, always position charts and other supporting tables to the right of the list rather than somewhere below the last used row. This way, you can continue to add data to your list without ever having to stop and first move some unrelated element out of the way.

This spatial concern is not the same when placing a data table that will total the values both down the rows and across the columns table — for example, a sales table that sums your monthly sales by item with formulas that calculate monthly totals in the last row of the table and formulas that calculate item totals in the last column. In this table, you don't worry about having to move other elements, such as embedded charts or other supporting or unrelated data tables, because you use Excel's capability of expanding the rows and columns of the table from within so that as the table expands or contracts, surrounding elements move in relation to and with the table expansion and contraction. You do this kind of editing to the table because inserting new table rows and columns ahead of the formulas ensures that they can be included in the totaling calculations. In this way, the row and column of formulas in the data table acts as a boundary that floats with the expansion or contraction of its data but which keeps all other elements at bay.

Finalizing your workbook

After you've more or less planned out where everything goes in your new spreadsheet, you're ready to start establishing the new tables and lists. Here are a few general pointers on how to set up a new data table that includes simple totaling calculations:

- Enter the title of the data table in the first cell, which forms the left and top edge of the table.
- Enter the row of column headings in the row below this cell, starting in the same column as the cell with the title of the table.
- Enter the row headings down the first column of the table, starting in the first row that will contain data (doing this leaves a blank cell where the column of row headings intersect the row of column headings).
- Construct the first formula that sums columns of (still empty) cell entries in the last row of the table, and then copy that formula across all the rest of the table columns.
- Construct the first formula that sums the rows of (still empty) cell entries in the last column of the table, and then copy that formula down the rest of the table rows.
- Format the cells to hold the table values, and then enter them in their cells or enter the values to be calculated and then format their cells (this is really your choice).

When setting up a new data list in a new worksheet, enter the list name in the first cell of the table, and then enter the row of column headings in the row below. Then, enter the first row of data beneath the appropriate column headings (see Book VI, Chapter 1 for details on designing a data list and inputting data into it).

Generating a new workbook from another workbook

The New Workbook Task pane contains a nifty link called Choose Workbook that you can use to open a copy of an existing workbook that you want to modify and then save as a new workbook. Use Choose Workbook when you have access to an existing workbook that contains a spreadsheet, which is very similar to the spreadsheet that you now need to build and it would be faster to modify the data in the original workbook than to spend time copying extensive sections of the original data into a blank workbook.

When you click the Choose Workbook link, Excel opens the New from Existing Workbook dialog box, where you select the original Excel workbook that you want to modify. After selecting its file icon and then clicking the Create New button, Excel opens a copy of the original file (indicated by adding a number to the original filename) that you can then safely modify to your heart's content without any danger of corrupting the original.

Please don't open the original workbook and start making modifications to its spreadsheet with the intention of then using the File➪Save As command to save your changes in a copy of the original file. It's just far too easy to select the File➪Save command by mistake and thereby save your changes in the original workbook. Always play it safe and use the Choose Workbook link in the New Workbook Task pane instead.

Opening new blank workbooks

Although Excel automatically opens a new workbook (called Book1 when you first start the program) that you can use in building a new spreadsheet from scratch, you will encounter occasions in using Excel when you need to open your own blank workbook. For example, if you launch Excel by opening an existing workbook that needs editing and then move on to building a new spreadsheet, you'll need to open a blank workbook (which you can do before or after closing the workbook with which you started Excel).

The easiest way to open a blank workbook is to click the New button on the Standard toolbar (this is the very first button with the blank-sheet-of-paper icon) or press Ctrl+N. Excel responds by opening a new workbook, which is given a generic Book name with the next unused number (Book1, if you opened Excel with a blank Book1).

You can also open a blank workbook by choosing File➪New on the Excel Menu bar. Unlike when clicking the New button or pressing Ctrl+N, Excel responds to this action by opening the New Workbook Task pane so that you can then click the Blank Workbook link to open a new workbook (or you can click one of the other links to open an existing workbook or a copy based on an existing workbook or template). Note that if this Task pane is already displayed, choosing File➪New has absolutely no effect in the Excel window.

As soon as you open a blank workbook, Excel makes its document window active. To then return to another workbook that you have open (which you would do if you wanted to copy and paste some of its data into one of the blank worksheets), click its button on the Windows taskbar or press Alt+Tab until its file icon is selected in the dialog box that appears in the middle of the screen.

If you ever open a blank workbook by mistake, you can just close it right away by pressing Ctrl+W or choosing File⇨Close on the Excel menu bar to make its document window disappear and to automatically return you to the workbook window that was originally open at the time you mistakenly opened the blank workbook.

It Takes All Kinds (Of Cell Entries)

Before covering the many methods for getting data into the cells of your new spreadsheet, you need to understand which type of data that you're entering. To Excel, everything that you enter in any of the cells of any of its worksheets is either one of two types of data: *text* (also known as a *label*) or a *number* (also known as a *value* or *numeric entry*).

The reason that you should care about what type of data you're entering into the cells of your worksheet is that Excel treats your entry differently, depending on what type of data it thinks you've entered:

- **Text** entries are automatically left-aligned in their cells, and if they consist of more characters than fit within the column's current width, the extra characters spill over and are displayed in blank cells in columns on the right (if these cells are not blank, Excel cuts off the display of any characters that don't fit within the cell borders until you widen its column).
- **Numbers** are automatically right-aligned in their cells, and if they consist of more characters (including numbers and any formatting characters that you add) than fit within the column's current width, Excel displays a string of number signs across the cell (######), telling you to widen the column (in some cases, such as decimal numbers, Excel will truncate the decimal places shown in the cell instead of displaying the number-sign overflow indicators).

So, now all you have to know is how Excel differentiates text data entries from numeric data entries.

What's in a label?

Here's the deal with text entries:

- All data entries beginning with a letter of the alphabet or a punctuation mark are considered text.

- All data entries that mix letters (A–Z) and numbers are considered text, even when the entry begins with a number.
- All numeric data entries that contain punctuation other than commas (,), periods (.), and forward slashes (/) are considered text, even when they begin with a number.

This means that in addition to regular text, such as *First Quarter Earnings* and *John Smith*, nonstandard data entries, including *C123*, *666-45-0034*, and *123C* are also considered text entries.

However, a problem exists with numbers that are separated by hyphens (also known as *dashes*): if the numbers that are separated by dashes correspond to a valid date, then Excel converts it into a date (which is most definitely a kind of numeric data entry — see the "Dates and times" section in this chapter for details). For example, if you enter *1-2-3* in a cell, Excel thinks that you want to enter the date January 2, 2003 in the cell, and the program automatically converts the entry into a date number (displayed as 1/2/2003 in the cell).

If you want to enter a number as text in a cell, you must preface its first digit with the apostrophe (') mark. For example, if you're entering a part number that consists of all numbers, such as 12-30-05, and you don't want Excel to convert it into the date December 30, 2005, you need to preface the entry with an apostrophe by entering into the cell:

```
'12-30-05
```

Likewise, if you wanted to enter 3/4 in a cell, meaning three out of four rather than the date March 4th, you enter

```
'3/4
```

(Note that if you want to designate the fraction, three-fourths, you need to input =3/4, in which case, Excel displays the value 0.75 in the cell display.)

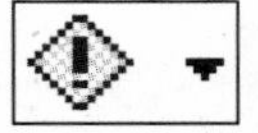

When you complete an entry that starts with an apostrophe, the apostrophe is not displayed in the cell (it does appear, however, on the Formula bar) and a tiny green triangle appears in the upper-left corner of the cell and an alert symbol appears to the immediate left (as long as the cell pointer is in this cell). When you position the mouse pointer on this alert indicator, a drop-down button appears to its right (shown in the left margin). When you click this drop-down button, a pop-up menu, shown in Figure 1-5, appears, which indicates that the number is currently stored as text and also enables you to convert it back into a number (by removing the apostrophe).

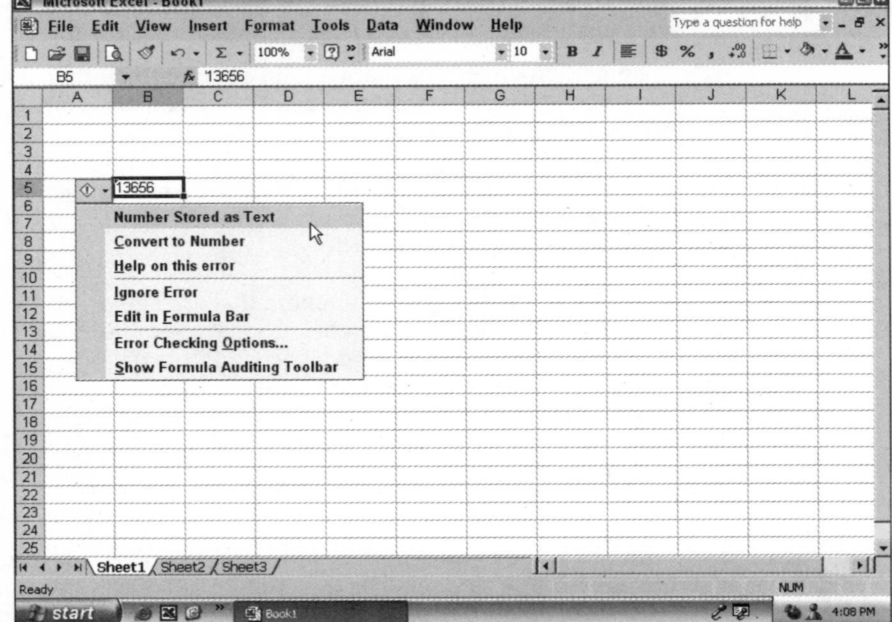

Figure 1-5: Opening the pop-menu attached to Number Stored as Text alert.

If you start a cell entry with the equal sign (=) or the at symbol (@) followed by other characters that aren't part of a formula, Excel displays an error dialog box as soon as you try to complete the data entry; Excel uses the equal sign to indicate the use of a formula and what you have entered is not a valid formula. The program knows that Lotus 1-2-3 used the @ symbol to indicate the use of a built-in function and what you have entered is not a valid built-in function. This means that you must preface any data entry beginning with the equal sign and at symbol that isn't a valid formula with an apostrophe in order to get it into the cell.

What's the value?

In a typical spreadsheet, numbers (or numeric data entries) can be as prevalent as the text entries — if not more so. This is because traditionally, spreadsheets were developed to keep financial records, which included plenty of extended item totals, subtotals, averages, percentages, and grand totals. Of course, you can create spreadsheets that are full of numbers that have nothing to do with debits, credits, income statements, invoices, quarterly sales, and dollars and cents.

Number entries that you make in your spreadsheet can be divided into three categories:

✦ **Numbers that you input** directly into a cell (you can do this with the keyboard, your voice — if you use the Speech Recognition feature, or even by handwriting if your keyboard is equipped with a writing tablet).

✦ **Date and time numbers** that are also input directly into a cell but are automatically displayed with the default Date and Time number formats and are stored behind the scenes as special date serial and hour decimal numbers.

✦ **Numbers calculated by formulas** that you build yourself by using simple arithmetical operators and/or Excel's sophisticated built-in functions.

Input numbers

Numbers that you input directly into the cells of the worksheet — whether they are positive, negative, percentages, or decimal values representing dollars and cents, widgets in stock, workers in the Human Resources department, or potential clients — don't change unless you specifically change them, either by editing their values or replacing them with other values. This is quite unlike formulas with values that change whenever the worksheet is recalculated and Excel finds that the values upon which they depend have been modified.

When inputting numbers, you can mix the digits 0–9 with the following keyboard characters:

```
+ - () $ . , %
```

You use these characters in the numbers you input as follows:

✦ Preface the digits of the number with a plus sign (+) when you want to explicitly designate the number as positive, as in +(53) to convert negative 53 into positive 53 — Excel considers all numbers to be positive unless you designate them as negative.

✦ Preface the digits of the number with – or enclose them in a closed pair of parentheses to indicate that the number is a negative number, as in –53 or (53).

✦ Preface the digits of the number with a dollar sign ($), as in $500, to format the number with the Currency style format as you enter it (you can also apply this format after it's entered).

✦ Input a period (.) in the digits of the number to indicate the position of the decimal point in the number, as in 500.25. (Note that you don't have to bother entering trailing zeros after the decimal point because the General number format automatically drops them, even if you type them in.)

✦ Input commas (,) between the digits of a number to indicate the position of thousands, hundred thousands, millions, billions, and the like, and to assign the Comma style number format to the number, as in 642,153 (you can also have Excel add the commas by assigning the Comma format to the number after you input the number.

- Append the percent sign (%) to the digits of a number to convert the number into a percentage and assign the Percent number style to it, as in 12%.

The most important thing to remember about the numbers that you input is that they inherit the type of number formatting currently assigned to the cells in which they're entered. When you first open a blank workbook, the number format appropriately called General (which some have called the equivalent of no number formatting because it doesn't add any special format characters, such as a constant number of decimal places or thousands separators) to each cell of the worksheet. You can override the General format by adding your own formatting characters as you input the number in a cell or later by selecting the cell and then assigning a different number format to it (see Book II, Chapter 2 for details).

Dates and times

Excel stores dates and times that you input into a spreadsheet as special values. Dates are stored as serial numbers and times are stored as decimal fractions. Excel supports two date systems: the 1900 date system used by Excel for Windows (also used by Lotus 1-2-3) which uses January 1, 1900 as serial number 1, and the 1904 system used by Excel for the Macintosh, which uses January 2, 1904 as serial number 1.

If you use Excel on the IBM-compatible PCs and Macintosh computers in your office, you can switch from the default 1900 date system to the 1904 date system for those worksheets that you create in the Windows version and then transfer to the Macintosh version. To switch to the 1904 date system, click the Calculation tab of the Options dialog box (Tools⇨Options) and then click the 1904 Date System check box.

By storing dates as serial numbers representing the number of days that have elapsed from a particular date (January 1, 1900 or January 2, 1904), Excel can perform arithmetic between dates. For example, you can find out how many days there are between February 15, 1949 and February 15, 2005 by entering 2/15/05 in one cell, 2/15/49 in the cell below, and then creating a formula in the cell below that one that subtracts the cell with 2/15/49 from the one containing 2/15/05. Because Excel stores the date 2/15/05 as the serial number 38398 and the date 2/15/49 as the serial number 17944, it can calculate the difference and return the result of 20454 (days, which is equal to 56 years).

When you use a date directly in a formula that performs date arithmetic, you must enclose the date in quotation marks. For example, if you want to enter a formula in a cell that calculates the number of days between February 15, 1949 and February 15, 2005, in the cell you have to enter the following formula:

```
="2/15/05"-"2/15/49"
```

Times of the day are stored as decimal numbers that represent the fraction of the 24-hour period starting with 0.0 for 12:00 midnight through 0.999 for 11:59:59 p.m. By storing times as decimal fractions, Excel enables you to perform time calculations such as those that return the elapsed time (in minutes) between any two times of the day.

Inputting dates and times using recognized formats

Although Excel stores dates as serial numbers and times as decimal fractions, luckily, you don't have to use these numbers to enter dates or times of the day into cells of the worksheet. You simply enter dates by using any of the recognized Date number formats that are used by Excel and times by using any of the recognized Time number formats. Excel then assigns and stores the appropriate serial number or decimal fraction at the same time the program assigns the date or time format that you used to this value. Table 1-1 shows you typical date and time entries that you can use as examples when entering dates and times in the cells of a worksheet.

Table 1-1 Common Ways to Enter Dates and Times

What you enter	*Date or time Recognized by Excel*
1/6/2004	January 6, 2004
1/6/04	January 6, 2004
1-6-04	January 6, 2004
6-Jan-04	January 6, 2004
6-Jan	January 6
Jan-04	January, 2004
1/6/04 5:25	January 6, 2004 5:25 a.m.
5:25	5:25 a.m.
5:25 P	5:25 p.m.
5:25 p.m.	5:25 p.m.
17:25	5:25 p.m.
17:25:33	5:25:33 p.m.

Understanding how Excel treats two-digit years

The only thing that's a tad bit tricky about inputting dates in a spreadsheet is understanding when you have to input all four digits of the year and when you can get away with entering only two. As Table 1-1 shows, if you input the date 1/6/04 in a cell, Excel recognizes the date as 1/6/2004 and not as 1/6/1904. In fact, if you enter the date January 6, 1904 in a spreadsheet, you must enter all four digits of the year (1904).

Here's how Excel decides whether a year for which you enter only the last two digits belongs to the 20th or 21st century:

- 00 through 29 belong to the 21st century, so Excels interprets 7/30/29 as July 30, 2029.
- 30 through 99 belong to the 20th century, so Excel interprets 7/30/30 as July 30, 1930.

This means that you don't have to enter the four digits of the year for dates in the years 2000 through 2029 or for dates in the years 1930 through 1999.

Of course, if you can't remember these cutoffs and are just generally confused about when to enter two digits versus four digits, just go ahead and enter all four digits of the year. Excel never misunderstands which century the date belongs to when you spell out all four digits of the year.

Numeric formulas

Many numeric entries in a typical spreadsheet are not input directly but are returned as the result of a calculation by formula. The numeric formulas that you build can do anything from simple arithmetic calculations to complex ANOVA statistical analysis (see Book III for complete coverage of all types of numeric formulas). Most spreadsheet formulas use numbers input into other cells of the worksheet in their calculations. Because these formulas refer to the address of the cell containing the input number rather than number itself, Excel is able to automatically recalculate the formula and return a new result anytime you change the values in the original cell.

The most important thing to remember about numeric formulas is that their calculated values are displayed in their cells in the worksheet while the contents of the formulas (that indicate how the calculation is done) is displayed on the Formula bar whenever its cell contains the cell pointer. All numbers returned by formulas inherit the nondescript General number format. The only way to get these calculated numbers to appear the way you want them in the worksheet is to select them and apply a new, more appropriate number format to them (see Book II, Chapter 2 for details).

Data Entry 101

I want to pass on to you a few basic rules of data entry:

- ✦ You must select the cell where you want to make the data entry before you can make the entry in that cell.
- ✦ Any entry that you make in a cell that already contains data replaces the original entry.
- ✦ Every data entry that you make in any cell (whether you do this from the keyboard, with voice, or by handwriting) must be completed with some sort of action (such as clicking the Enter button on the Formula, pressing the Enter key, or clicking a new cell) before the entry is officially entered in that cell.

I know that the first rule sounds so obvious that it should go without saying, but you'd be surprised how many times you look at the cell where you intend to add new data and then just start entering that data without realizing that you haven't yet moved the cell pointer to that cell. As a result, the data entry that you're making is not destined to go into the cell that you intended. In fact, you're in the process of making the entry in whatever cell currently contains the cell pointer, and if that cell is already occupied, you're in the process of replacing its entry with the one you meant to go somewhere else!

This is where the third rule is so important because even if you're in the process of messing up your spreadsheet by entering data in the wrong cell (and, if that cell is occupied, you're destroying a perfectly good entry), you haven't done it until you take the action that completes the entry (such as clicking the Enter button on the Formula bar or pressing the Enter key). This means that you can recover simply by clicking the Cancel button on the Formula bar or by pressing the Escape key on your keyboard. As soon as you do that, the errant data entry disappears from the Formula bar (and the original data entry — if it exists — returns), and you're then free to move the cell pointer to the desired cell and redo the entry there.

Data entry keyboard style

The only trick to entering data from the keyboard is to figure out the most efficient way to complete the entry in the current cell (and Excel gives you many choices in this regard). You can, of course, complete any data entry by clicking the Enter button on the Formula bar (presumably this is what Microsoft intended; otherwise, why have the button?), but clicking this button is not at all efficient when the mouse pointer isn't close to it.

You should know of another potential drawback to clicking the Enter button on the Formula bar to complete an entry: When you do this, Excel doesn't move the cell pointer but keeps it right in the cell with the new data entry. This means that you still have to move the cell pointer before you can safely make your next data entry. You're better off than pressing the Enter key because doing this not only completes the entry in the cell, but also moves the cell pointer down the cell in the next row.

Of course, pressing the Enter key is efficient only if you're doing the data entry for a table or list down each row across the succeeding columns. If you want to enter the data across each column of the table or list down succeeding rows, pressing Enter doesn't work to your advantage. Instead, you'd be better off pressing the → key or the Tab key to complete each entry (at least until you get to the cell in the last column of the table) because pressing these keys completes the entry and moves the cell pointer to the next cell on the right.

Take a look at Table 1-2 to get an idea of the keys that you commonly use to complete data entries. Keep in mind, however, that any key combination that moves the cell pointer (see Table 1-2 in Book I, Chapter 1 for a review of these keystrokes) also completes the data entry that you're making, as does clicking another cell in the worksheet.

Table 1-2 Keys Used in Completing Data Entry

Keys	*Cell pointer movement*
Enter	Down one row
↓	Down one row
Tab	Right one column
→	Right one column
Shift+Tab	Left one column
←	Left one column
↑	Up one row

If you have more than one cell selected (see Book II, Chapter 2 for more on this) and then press Ctrl+Enter to complete the data entry that you're making in the active cell of this selected range, Excel simultaneously enters that data entry into all of the cells in the selection. You can use this technique to enter a single label or value in many places in a worksheet at one time.

If you have more than one worksheet selected (see Book II, Chapter 4) at the time that you make an entry in the current cell, Excel makes that entry in the corresponding cells of all the selected worksheets. For example, if you enter the heading *Cost Analysis* in cell C3 of Sheet1 when Sheet1 through Sheet3 are selected, Excel enters *Cost Analysis* in cell C3 of Sheet2 and Sheet3 as well.

You AutoComplete this for me

Excel automatically makes use of a feature called AutoComplete, which attempts to automate completely textual data entries (that is, entries that don't mix text and numbers). AutoComplete works this way: If you start a new text entry that begins with the same letter or letters as an entry that you've made recently in the same region of the worksheet, Excel completes the new text entry with the characters from the previous text entry that began with those letters.

For example, if you enter the spreadsheet title *Sales Invoice* in cell A1 of a new worksheet and then start entering the table title *Summary* in cell A3, as soon as you type *S* in cell A3, Excel completes the new text entry so that it also states *Sales Invoice* by adding the letters *ales Invoice.*

When the AutoComplete feature completes the new text entry, the letters that it adds to the initial letter or letters that you type are automatically selected (indicated by highlighting). This way, if you don't want to repeat the original text entry in the new cell, you can replace the characters that Excel adds just by typing the next letter in the new (and different) entry. In the previous example, in which Sales Invoice was repeated in the cell where you want to input *Summary*, the *ales Invoice* text appended to the *S* that you type disappears the moment you type *u* in *Summary*.

To make use of automatic text completion rather than override it as in the previous example, simply press a key (such as Enter or an arrow key), click the Enter button on the Formula bar, or click another cell to complete the completed input in that cell. For example, when building a sales table in which you're inputting sales for three different account representatives — George, Jean, and Alice — after entering each of their names manually in the appropriate rows of the Account Representative column, you only need to type in their first initial (*G* to get George, *J* to get Jean, and *A* to get Alice) in subsequent cells and then press the ↓ or Enter key to move down to the next row of that column. Of course, in a case like this, AutoComplete is more like automatic typing, and it makes filling in the Account Representative names for this table extremely quick and easy.

If the AutoComplete feature starts to bug you when building a particular spreadsheet, you can temporarily turn it off; simply click the Enable AutoComplete for Cell Values check box, and remove the checkmark on the Edit tab of the Options dialog box (Tools➪Options).

You AutoCorrect this right now!

Along with AutoComplete, Excel has an AutoCorrect feature that automatically fixes certain typos that you make in the text entries as soon as you complete them. For example, if you forget to capitalize a day of the week, AutoCorrect does this for you (turning *friday* into *Friday* in a cell as soon as you complete the entry). Likewise, if you mistakenly enter a word with two initial capital letters, AutoCorrect automatically lowercases the second capital letter (so that *QUarter* typed into a cell becomes *Quarter* upon completion of the cell entry).

In addition to these types of obvious capitalization errors, AutoCorrect also automatically takes care of common typos, such as changing *hsi* to *his* (an obvious transposition of two letters) or *inthe* to *in the* (an obvious case of a missing space between letters). In addition to the errors already recognized by AutoCorrect, you can add your own particular mistakes to the list of automatic replacements.

To do this, open the AutoCorrect dialog box and then add your own replacements in the Replace and With text boxes located on the AutoCorrect tab, shown in Figure 1-6, as follows:

1. **Choose Tools⇨AutoCorrect Options from the Excel Menu bar.**

   The AutoCorrect dialog box opens for your language, such as English (U.S.).

2. **If the AutoCorrect options aren't already displayed in the dialog box, click the AutoCorrect tab to display them.**

3. **Click the Replace text box and then enter the typo exactly as you usually make it.**

4. **Click the With text box and enter the replacement that AutoCorrect should make (with no typos in it, please!).**

   Check the typo that you've entered in the Replace text box and the replacement that you've entered in the With text box. If everything checks out, go on to Step 5.

5. **Click the Add button to add your new AutoCorrect replacement to the list of automated replacements.**

6. **Click the OK button to close the AutoCorrect dialog box.**

You can use the AutoCorrect feature to automatically replace favorite abbreviations with full text, as well as to clean up all your personal typing mistakes. For example, if you have a client with the name Great Lakes Securities, and you enter this client's name in countless spreadsheets that you create, you can make an AutoCorrect entry so that Excel automatically replaces the abbreviation *gls* with *Great Lakes Securities*. Of course, after you use AutoCorrect to enter Great Lakes Securities in your first cell by typing *gls*, the AutoComplete feature kicks in, so the next time you type the *g* of *gls* to enter the client's name in another cell, it fills in the rest of the name, leaving you with nothing to do but complete the entry.

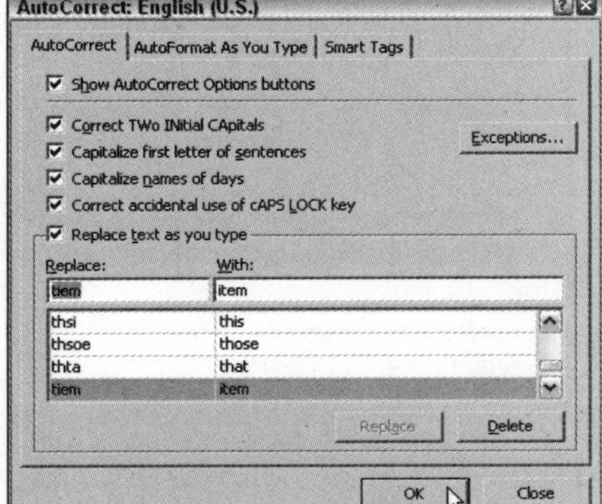

Figure 1-6: You can add your own automated replacements to the AutoCorrect tab.

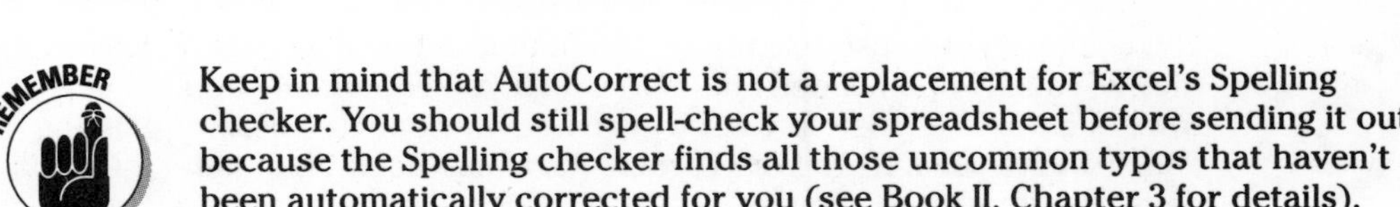

Keep in mind that AutoCorrect is not a replacement for Excel's Spelling checker. You should still spell-check your spreadsheet before sending it out because the Spelling checker finds all those uncommon typos that haven't been automatically corrected for you (see Book II, Chapter 3 for details).

Constraining data entry to a cell range

One of the most efficient ways to enter data into a new table in your spreadsheet is to pre-select the empty cells where the data entries need to be made and then enter the data into the selected range. Of course, this trick only works if you know ahead of time how many columns and rows the new table requires.

The reason that pre-selecting the cells works so well is that doing this constrains the cell pointer to that range, provided that you press *only* the keystrokes shown in Table 1-3. This means that if you're using the Enter key to move down the column as you enter data, Excel automatically positions the cell pointer at the beginning of the next column as soon as you complete the last entry in that column. Likewise, when using the Tab key to move the cell pointer across a row as you enter data, Excel automatically positions the cell pointer at the beginning of the next row in the table as soon as you complete the last entry in that row.

Table 1-3	Keystrokes for Moving Within a Selection
Keystrokes	*Movement*
Enter	Moves the cell pointer down one cell in the selection (moves one cell to the right when the selection consists of a single row)
Shift+Enter	Moves the cell pointer up one cell in the selection (moves one cell to the left when the selection consists of a single row)
Tab	Moves the cell pointer one cell to the right in the selection (moves one cell down when the selection consists of a single column)
Shift+Tab	Moves the cell pointer one cell to the left in the selection (moves one cell up when the selection consists of a single column)
Ctrl+period (.)	Moves the cell pointer to from corner to corner of the cell selection

This means that you don't have to concentrate on repositioning the cell pointer at all when entering the table data. This way, you can keep your attention on the printed copy from which you're taking the data.

You can't very well use this pre-selection method on data lists because they're usually open-ended affairs to which you continually append new rows of data. The most efficient way to add new data to a new or existing data list is to use Excel's Data Form feature (see Book VI, Chapter 1 for details on its use).

Getting Excel to put in the decimal point

Of course, if your keyboard has a ten-key entry pad, you'll want to use it rather than the numbers on the top row of the keyboard to make your numeric entries in the spreadsheet (make sure that the Num Lock key is engaged or you'll end up moving the cell pointer rather than entering numbers). If you have a lot of decimal numbers (suppose that you're building a financial spreadsheet with loads of dollars and cents entries), you may also want to use Excel's Fixed Decimal Places feature so that Excel places a decimal point in all the numbers that you enter in the worksheet.

To turn on this feature, click the Fixed Decimal Places check box on the Edit tab of the Options dialog box (Tools➪Options) to put a checkmark in it. When you do this, the text box that determines the number of decimal places that the program is to add to each number entry is activated. You can then specify the number of places by changing its value (2 is, of course, the default).

After turning on Fixed Decimal Places, Excel adds a decimal point to the number of places that you specified to every numeric data entry that you make at the time you complete its entry. For example, if you type the digits 56789 in a cell, Excel changes this to 567.89 at the time you complete the entry.

Note that when this feature is turned on and you want to enter a number without a decimal point, you need to type a period at the end of the value. For example, if you want to enter the number 56789 in a cell and *not* have Excel change it to 567.89, you need to type

```
56789.
```


Ending the number in a period prevents Excel from adding its own decimal point to the value when Fixed Decimal Places is turned on. Of course, you need to turn this feature off after you finish making the group of entries that almost all require the same number of decimal places. To do this, click the Fixed Decimal Places check box on the Edit tab of the Options dialog box (Tools➪Options) to remove its checkmark.

You AutoFill it in

Few Excel features are more helpful than the AutoFill feature, which enables you to fill out a series of entries in a data table or list — all by entering only the first item in the series in the spreadsheet. You can sometimes use the AutoFill feature to quickly input row and column headings for a new data table or to number the records in a data list. For example, when you need a row of column headings that list the 12 months for a sales table, you can enter *January* or *Jan.* in the first column and then have AutoFill input the other 11 months for you in the cells in columns to the right. Likewise, when you need to create a column of row headings at the start of a table with successive part numbers that start at L505-120 and proceed to L505-128, you enter L505-120 in the first row and then use AutoFill to copy the part numbers down to L505-128 in the cells below.

The key to using AutoFill is the Fill handle, which is the small black square that appears in the lower-right corner of whatever cell contains the cell pointer. When you position the mouse pointer on the Fill handle, it changes from the normal thick, white-cross pointer to a thin, black cross pointer (shown in the left margin). This change in shape is your signal that when you drag the Fill handle in a single direction, either down or to the right, Excel will either copy the current cell entry to all the cells that you select or use it as the first entry in a consecutive series, whose successive entries are then automatically entered in the selected cells.

Note that you can immediately tell whether Excel will simply copy the cell entry or use it as the first in a series to fill out by the ToolTips that appear to the right of the mouse pointer. As you drag through subsequent cells, the ToolTip indicates which entry will be made if you release the mouse button at that point. If the ToolTip shows the same entry as you drag, you know Excel didn't recognize the entry as part of a consecutive series and is copying the entry verbatim. If, instead, the ToolTips continue to change as you drag through cells showing you successive entries for the series, you know that Excel has recognized the original entry as part of consecutive series.

Figures 1-7 and 1-8 illustrate how AutoFill works. In Figure 1-7, I entered January as the first column heading in cell B2 (using the Enter button on the Formula bar so as to keep the cell pointer in B2, ready for AutoFill). Next, I positioned the mouse pointer on the AutoFill handle in the lower-right corner of B2 before dragging the Fill handle to the right until I reached cell G2 (and the ToolTip stated June).

Figure 1-8 shows the series that was entered in the cell range B2:G2 when I released the mouse button with cell G2 selected. For this figure, I also clicked the drop-down button attached to the AutoFill Options button that automatically appears whenever you use the Fill handle to copy entries or fill in a series to show you the items on this pop-up menu. This menu contains a Copy Cells radio button that enables you to override Excel's decision to fill in the series and have it copy the original entry (January, in this case) to all the selected cells.

Note that you can also override Excel's natural decision to fill in a series or copy an entry before you drag the Fill handle. To do so, simply hold down the Ctrl key (which adds a tiny plus sign to the upper-right corner of the Fill handle). Continue to depress the Ctrl key as you drag the Fill handle and notice that the ToolTip now shows that Excel is no longer filling in the series or copying the entry as expected.

When you need to consecutively number the cells in a range, use the Ctrl key to override Excel's natural tendency to copy the number to all the cells you select. For example, if you want to number rows of a list, enter the starting number (1 or 100, it doesn't matter) in the first row, then press Ctrl to have Excel fill in the rest of the numbers for successive rows in the list (2, 3, 4, and the like, or 102, 103, 104, and so on). If you forget to hold down the Ctrl key and end up with a whole range of cells with the same starting number, click the Auto Fill Options' drop-down button and then click the Fill Series radio button to rectify the mistake and convert the copied numbers to a consecutively numbered series.

Figure 1-7: Dragging the Fill handle to fill in a series with the first six months of the year.

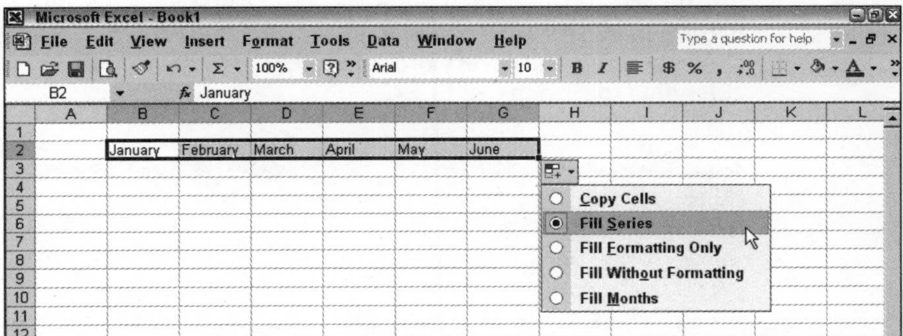

Figure 1-8: The series of monthly column headings with the Auto Fill Options pop-up menu.

When using AutoFill to fill in a data series, you don't have to start with the first entry in that particular series. For example, if you want to enter a row of column headings with the last six months of the year (June through December), you enter *June* first and then drag down or to the right until the mouse pointer selects the cell where you enter *December* (indicated by the December ToolTip). Note also that you can reverse-enter a data series by dragging the Fill handle up or the left. In the June-to-December-column-headings example, if you drag up or the left, Excel will enter June to January in reverse order.

Keep in mind that you can also use AutoFill to copy an original formula across rows and down columns of data tables and lists. When you drag the Fill handle in a cell that contains a formula, Excel automatically adjusts its cell references to suit the new row or column position of each copy (see Book III, Chapter 1 for details on copying formulas with AutoFill).

Filling series with increments other than one

Normally, when you drag the Fill handle to fill in a series of data entries, Excel increases or decreases each entry in the series by a single unit (a day, month, hour, or whatever). You can, however, get AutoFill to fill out a series of data entries that uses some other increment, such as every other day, every third month, or every hour-and-a-half.

Figure 1-9 illustrates a number of series all created with AutoFill that use increments other than one unit. The first example in row 3 shows a series of different times all 45 minutes apart, starting with 8:00 a.m. in cell A3 and extending to 2:45 p.m. in cell J3. The second example in row 6 shows a series of days of the week that use every other day of the week starting with Monday in cell A6 and extending to Saturday in cell G6. The third example in row 9 shows a series of numbers, each of which increases by 15, that starts with 35 in cell A9 and increases to 170 in cell J9. The last example in row 13 shows a series with every other month, starting with Jan. in cell A13 and extending to Nov. in cell F13.

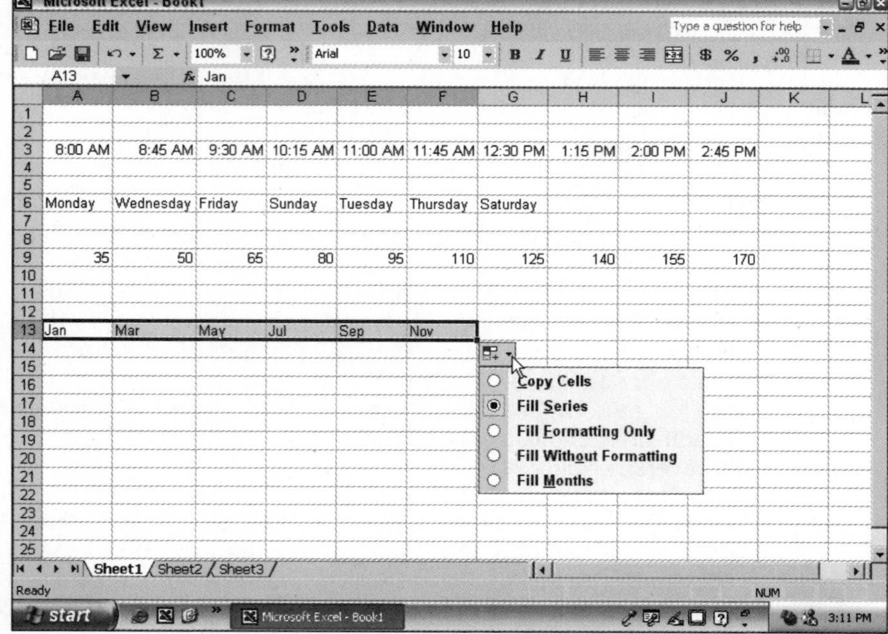

Figure 1-9: Various series created with AutoFill by using different increments.

To create a series that uses an increment other than one unit, follow these four general steps:

1. **Enter the first two entries in the series in consecutive cells above one another in a column or side by side in a row.**

   Enter the entries one above the other when you intend to drag the Fill handle down the column to extend the series. Enter them side-by-side when you intend to drag the Fill handle to the right across the row.

2. **With the cell pointer in the cell with the first entry in the series, drag through the second entry.**

   Both entries must be selected (indicated by being enclosed within the expanded cell pointer) before you use the Fill handle to extend the series. Excel analyzes the difference between the two entries and uses its increment in filling out the data series.

3. **Drag the Fill handle down the column or across the row to extend the series by using the increment other than one.**

   Check the ToolTips to make sure that Excel is using the correct increment in filling out your data series.

4. **Release the mouse button when you reach the desired end of the series (indicated by the entry shown in the ToolTip appearing next to the black-cross mouse pointer).**

Creating custom AutoFill lists

Just as you can use AutoFill to fill out a series with increments different from one unit, you can also get it to fill out custom lists of your own design. For example, suppose that you often have to enter a standard series of city locations as the column or row headings in new spreadsheets that you build. Instead of copying the list of cities from one workbook to another, you can create a custom list containing all the cities in the order in which they normally appear in your spreadsheets. After you create a custom list in Excel, you can then enter all or part of the entries in the series simply by entering the first item in a cell and then using the Fill handle to extend out the series either down a column or across a row.

To create a custom series, you can either enter the list of entries in the custom series in successive cells of a worksheet before you open the Custom Lists tab of the Options dialog box, or you can type the sequence entries for the custom series in the List Entries list box located on this tab, as shown in Figure 1-10.

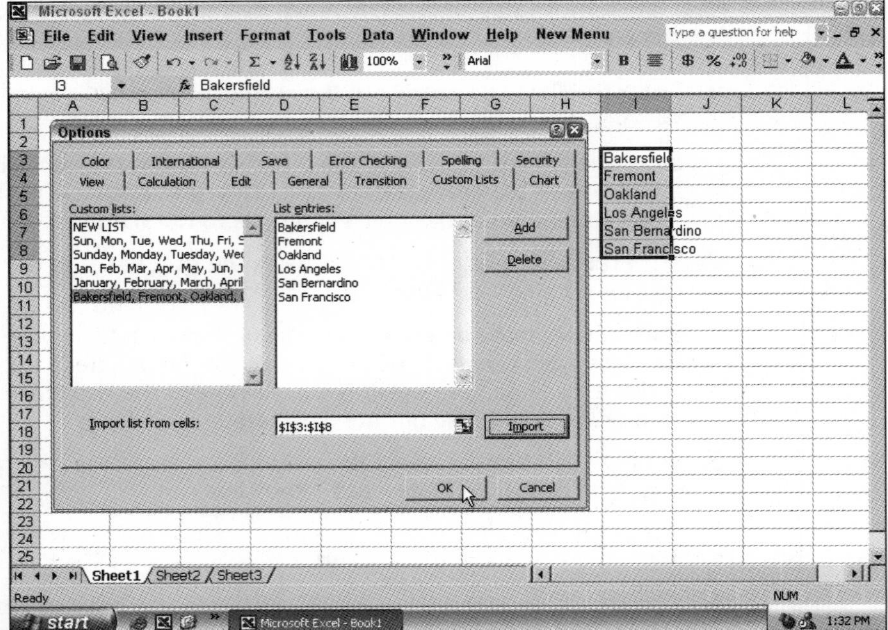

Figure 1-10: Creating a custom list of cities for AutoFill.

If you already have the data series for your custom list entered in a range of cells somewhere in a worksheet, follow these steps to create the custom list:

1. **Click the cell with the first entry in the custom series and then drag the mouse pointer through the range until all the cells with entries are selected.**

   The expanded cell pointer should now include all the cells with entries for the custom list.

2. **Choose Tools⇨Options from the Excel Menu bar.**

   The Options dialog box opens, where you need to display the Custom Lists tab.

3. **Click on the Custom Lists tab in the Options dialog box to activate it.**

   Now you should check the accuracy of the cell range listed in the Import List from Cells text box (the range in this box lists the first cell and last cell in the current selected range separated by a colon — you can ignore the dollar signs following each part of the cell address). To check that the cell range listed in the Import List from Cells text box includes all the entries for the custom list, click the Collapse Dialog Box button, located to the right of the

Import List from Cells text box (shown in the left margin). When you click this button, Excel collapses the Options dialog box down to the Import List from Cells text box and puts a marquee (the so-called marching ants) around the cell range.

If this marquee includes all the entries for your custom list, you can expand the Options dialog box by clicking the Expand Dialog box button (which replaces the Collapse Dialog Box button and is shown in the left margin) and proceed to Step 4. If this marquee doesn't include all the entries, click the cell with the first entry and then drag through until all the other cells are enclosed in the marquee. Then, click the Expand Dialog box button and go to Step 4.

4. **Click the Import button to add the entries in the selected cell range to the List Entries box on the right and to the Custom Lists box on the left side of the Custom Lists tab.**

   As soon as you click the Import button, Excel adds the data entries in the selected cell range to both the List Entries and the Custom Lists boxes.

5. **Click the OK button to close the Options dialog box.**

If you don't have the entries for your custom list entered anywhere in the worksheet, you have to follow the second and third steps listed previously and then take these three additional steps instead:

1. **Click the List Entries box and then type each of the entries for the custom list in the order in which they are to be entered in successive cells of a worksheet.**

   Press the Enter key after typing each entry for the custom list so that it appears on its own line in the List Entries box or separate each entry with a comma.

2. **Click the Add button to add the entries that you've typed into the List Entries box on the right to the Custom Lists box, located on the left side of the Custom Lists tab.**

   Note that when Excel adds the custom list that you just typed to the Custom Lists box, it automatically adds commas between each entry in the list — even if you pressed the Enter key after making each entry. It also automatically separates each entry on a separate line in the List Entries box — even if you separated them with commas instead of carriage returns.

3. **Click the OK button to close the Options dialog box.**

After you've created a custom list by using one of these two methods, you can fill in the entire data series by entering the first entry of the list in a cell and then dragging the Fill handle to fill in the rest of the entries. If you ever decide that you no longer need a custom list that you've created, you can delete it by clicking the list in the Custom Lists box on the Custom Lists tab of the Options dialog box and then clicking the Delete button. Excel then displays an alert box indicating that the list will be permanently deleted when you click OK. Note that you can't delete any of the built-in lists that appear in this list box when you first open the Options dialog box and then click the Custom Lists tab.

Keep in mind that you can also fill in any part of the series by simply entering any one of the entries in the custom list and then dragging the Fill handle in the appropriate direction (down and to the right to enter succeeding entries in the list or up and to the left to enter preceding entries).

Limiting data entry with Data Validation

The Data Validation feature in Excel can be a real timesaver when doing repetitive data entry and can also go a long way in preventing incorrect entries in your spreadsheets. When you use Data Validation in a cell, you indicate what type of data entry is allowed in the cell. As part of restricting a data entry to a number (which can be a whole number, decimal, date, or time), you also specify the permissible values for that type of number (a whole number between 10 and 100 or a date between January 1, 2004 and December 31, 2004, for example).

When you restrict the data entry to text, you can specify the range of the minimum and maximum text length (in characters), or — even better — a list of permissible text entries that you can select from a pop-up menu (opened by clicking a pop-up button that appears to the right of the cell whenever it contains the cell pointer).

When using Data Validation to restrict the type of data entry and its range of acceptable values in a cell, you can also specify an input message that is automatically displayed next to the cell when you select it and/or an error alert message that is displayed if you try to put the wrong type of entry or a number outside of the permissible range.

To use the Data Validation feature, put the cell pointer in the cell where you want to restrict the type of data entry that you can make there, and then choose Data⇨Validation on the Excel Menu bar. The Data Validation dialog box opens with the Settings tab selected (similar to the one shown in Figure 1-11).

You then click the pop-up button attached to the Allow combo box and select among the following items:

- **Whole Number** to restrict the entry to a whole number that falls within a certain range or adhere to particular parameters that you specify.

- **Decimal** to restrict the entry to a decimal number that falls within a certain range or adhere to particular parameters that you specify.
- **List** to restrict the entry to one of several text entries that you specify, which you can select from a pop-up menu that's displayed by clicking a pop-up button that appears to the right of the cell whenever it contains the cell pointer.
- **Date** to restrict the entry to a date that falls within a certain range or on or before a particular date.
- **Time** to restrict the entry to a time that falls within a certain range or on or before a particular time of the day.
- **Text Length** to restrict a text entry so that its length in characters doesn't fall below or go above a certain number or falls within a range that you specify.
- **Custom** to restrict the entry to the parameters specified by a particular formula entered in another cell of the worksheet.

To specify an input message after selecting all the items on the Settings tab, click the Input Message tab of the Data Validation dialog box where you enter a short title for the Input Message (such as *How to Proceed*) in the Title text box and then enter the text of your message in the Input Message list box below.

To specify an alert message, click the Error Alert tab of the Data Validation dialog box, where you can choose the kind of warning in the Style drop-down list: Stop (the default, which uses a red button with a cross in it), Warning (which uses a yellow triangle with an exclamation point in it), and Information (which uses a balloon with a blue *I* in it). After selecting the type of alert, you then enter the title for its dialog box in its Title text box and the text of the alert message in the Error Message list box.

By far the most popular use of the Data Validation feature is to create a drop-down menu from which you or someone who uses your spreadsheet can select the appropriate data entry. Figures 1-11 and 1-12 illustrate this type of usage.

As Figure 1-11 shows, on the Settings tab of the Data Validation dialog box, I choose List in the Allow combo box and then in the Source text box, I designated the cell range J2:J7, which just happens to contain the list of allowable entries (you can type them in the Source text box separated by commas if the list doesn't already exist someplace on the worksheet). Notice in this figure that as soon as you select List in the Allow combo box, an in-cell, drop-down check box appears. Keep this check box selected because it tells Excel to create a drop-down list (or pop-up menu, as it's also called) containing only the entries specified in the Source text box.

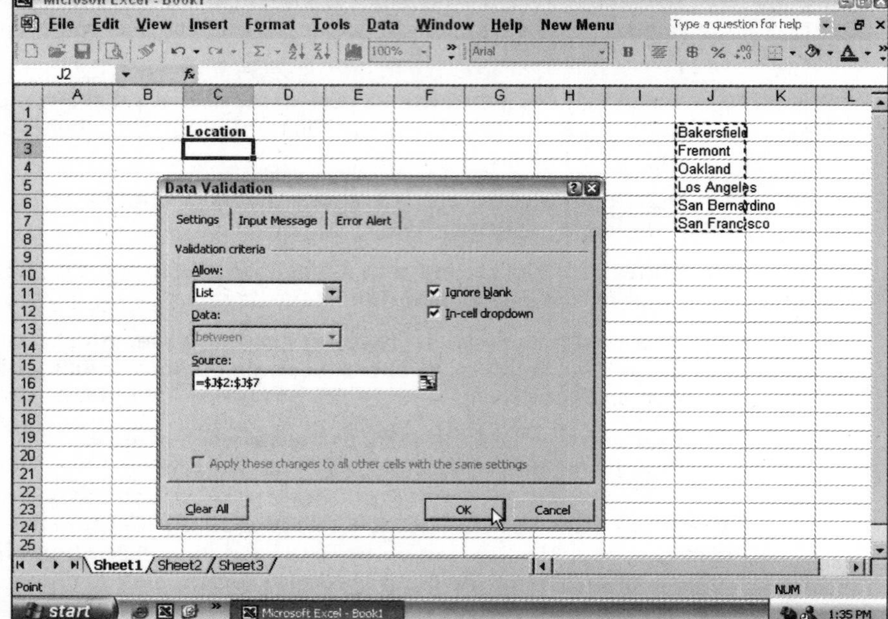

Figure 1-11: Creating a custom drop-down list in the Data Validation dialog box.

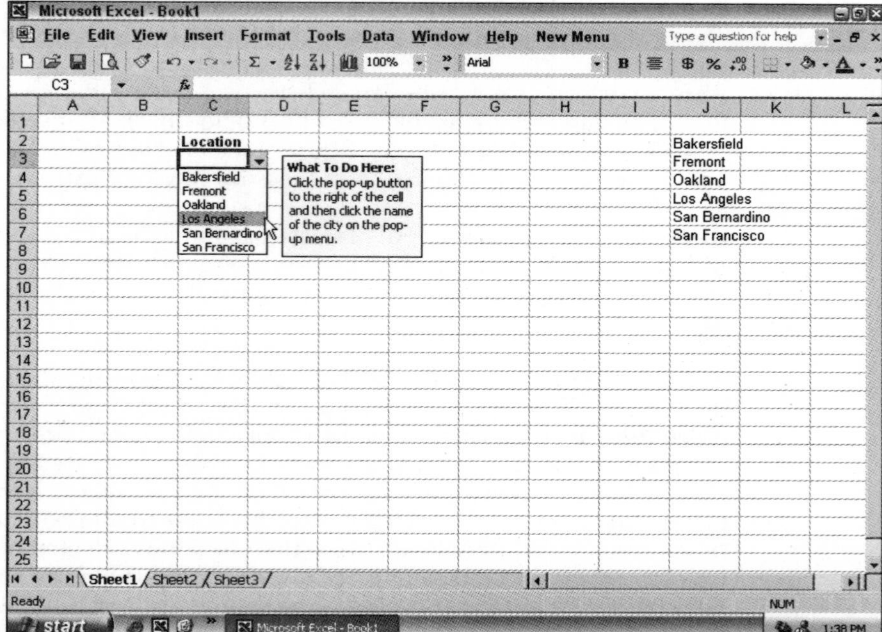

Figure 1-12: Selecting a city from the custom drop-down list.

Figure 1-12 shows you what happens in the spreadsheet after you close the Data Validation dialog box. Here, you see the pop-up menu (with a list of cities taken from the cell range J2:J7) as it appears when you click the cell's new pop-up button. In this figure, you can also see the input message box that I created for this cell by using the options on the Input Message tab of the Data Validation dialog box. Note that you can reposition this message box (officially known as a *comment box*) so that it's close to the cell, but doesn't get in the way of selecting an entry, simply by dragging it with the mouse pointer.

Figure 1-13 demonstrates what happens if you try to input an entry that isn't on the drop-down list. For this figure, I deliberately disregarded the input instructions and typed *Las Vegas* as the location. As soon as I pressed the Enter key, the custom alert dialog box (which I named *Unacceptable Entry*) appears. I created this alert dialog box by using the options located on the Error Alert tab of the Data Validation dialog box.

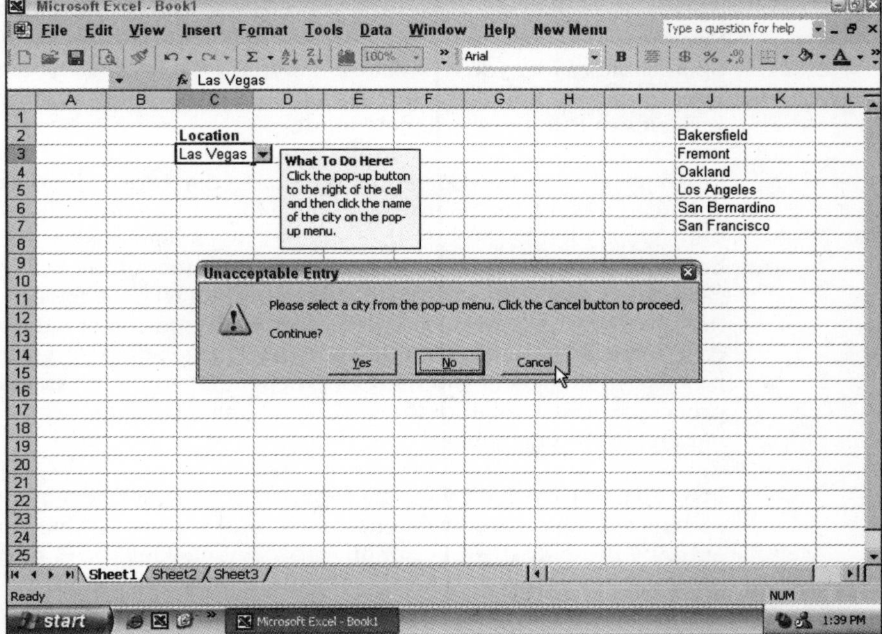

Figure 1-13: Getting an error message after trying to input a city that's not on the list.

In data lists or tables that require a text or number entry within a particular range, use the Data Validation feature to set up the type of entry and permitted range in the first cell and then use the Fill handle to copy that cell's Data Validation settings to subsequent cells in the same column or row.

To find cells to which Data Validation has been applied, open the Go To dialog box (Ctrl+G or F5), and then click the Special button and click the Data Validation radio button in the Go To Special dialog box. Click the Same radio button under Data Validation to have Excel go to the next cell that uses the same Data Validation settings as the active cell. Leave the All radio button under Data Validation selected to go to the next cell that uses any kind of Data Validation setting.

To get rid of Data Validation settings assigned to a particular cell, put the cell pointer in that cell, click Clear All button in the Data Validation dialog box (Data⇨Validation) and then click OK.

Speaking of data entry

Excel's Speech Recognition feature enables you to do completely hands-free data entry by dictating the text or numbers that you want entered in the current cell. The keys to successful dictation are training and more voice training and having a quiet environment in which to dictate (for information on installing and training Speech Recognition, see the "Issuing Voice Commands" section in Book I, Chapter 1). If you're in one of those wonderful open cubicles and you're still awaiting that private office, you may find that Speech Recognition picks ambient noises from the surrounding office area and tries to turn them into data input.

When using Speech Recognition to dictate your spreadsheet data entries, you need to keep the microphone close to your mouth and in the same position as you dictate (be sure that you're using a high quality microphone on a headset). Speak normally and in a low but not monotone voice (use the same voice and intonation that you used when training Speech Recognition), pausing only when you come to the end of a thought or the data entry for that cell. Keep in mind that it takes time for your computer to process your speech, and therefore, depending upon the speed of your processor, it may take some time before your words appear on the Formula bar and in the current cell.

Be prepared to turn off your microphone as soon as Speech Recognition has recognized the cell entry (accurately or not) so that you can complete the entry by pressing the Enter or an arrow key, clicking the Enter box, or clicking another cell. If your mike doesn't have a physical off/on switch, you do this by clicking the Microphone button at the beginning of the Language bar, shown in Figure 1-14. Note that you can also complete a data entry by clicking the Voice Command button on the Language bar and then saying something like "down arrow" or "enter."

Figure 1-14: Click the Dictation button on the Language bar to say the data entry for a cell.

When dictating cell entries, you can include punctuation and special symbols in your entries by calling the symbol by the word that Speech Recognition understands. Table 1-4 gives you a list of these symbols and what you should say when dictating them as part of the cell entry.

Table 1-4 Dictating Punctuation and Special Symbols

To Enter	*You Dictate*
,	"Comma"
.	"Period" or "dot"
...	"Ellipsis"
:	"Colon"
;	"Semicolon"
?	"Question mark"
/	"Slash"
'	"Single quote"
'	"End quote"
"	"Quote" or "open quote"
"	"Close quote" or "end quote"
~	"Tilde"
!	"Exclamation point"
@	"At sign" or "at"
#	"Pound sign"
$	"Dollar sign"
%	"Percent sign"

(continued)

<table>
<tr><th colspan="2">Table 1-4 (continued)</th></tr>
<tr><th>To Enter</th><th>You Dictate</th></tr>
<tr><td>^</td><td>"Caret"</td></tr>
<tr><td>&</td><td>"Ampersand"</td></tr>
<tr><td>*</td><td>"Asterisk"</td></tr>
<tr><td>(</td><td>"Paren"</td></tr>
<tr><td>)</td><td>"Close paren"</td></tr>
<tr><td>-</td><td>"Hyphen" or "dash"</td></tr>
<tr><td>_</td><td>"Underscore"</td></tr>
<tr><td>=</td><td>"Equals"</td></tr>
<tr><td>+</td><td>"Plus sign" or "plus"</td></tr>
<tr><td>[</td><td>"Open bracket"</td></tr>
<tr><td>]</td><td>"Right bracket"</td></tr>
<tr><td>\</td><td>"Backslash"</td></tr>
<tr><td>|</td><td>"Vertical bar"</td></tr>
<tr><td>></td><td>"Greater than"</td></tr>
<tr><td><</td><td>"Less than"</td></tr>
<tr><td>Enter</td><td>"New line"</td></tr>
</table>

When dictating numeric entries in your cells, you need to keep the following idiosyncrasies in mind:

- ✦ Speech Recognition spells out all numbers below 20 so that when you say "seven," the program inputs *seven* and not *7* in the cell.
- ✦ Speech Recognition enters all numbers 21 and higher as digits so that when you say "thirty-five," the program inputs *35* in the cell.
- ✦ To have Speech Recognition enter the fraction 1/2 in the cell, you say "one-half."
- ✦ To have Speech Recognition enter other fractions, you say the number of the numerator, "slash," followed by the number of the denominator as in "one slash four" to insert 1/4 into the cell.
- ✦ When you say ordinal numbers ("first," "second," and so on), Speech Recognition inputs 1st, 2nd, and the like in the cell.

Doing handwritten data entry

Instead of making your cell entries by typing them with the keyboard or dictating them with the Speech Recognition feature, you can use the

Handwriting Recognition feature to write them into the cell. When using Handwriting Recognition to input cell entries, you can either use the mouse to write the text and numbers or use a special graphics tablet equipped with a stylus attached to your computer. Please note that although I say you *can* use the mouse with Handwriting Recognition to write out your entries, I am not at all saying that you would *want* to use it. In fact, I want to emphasize that if you are serious about using Handwriting Recognition to do data entry in your spreadsheet, the first thing you should do is invest in a graphics tablet and get it connected to your computer.

The second thing that you should do is install the Handwriting Recognition feature (this is one of the Office XP features that isn't set to install on your first use). To do this, open Add/Remove Programs in the Windows Control panel, and then click Microsoft Office XP in the Add/Remove Programs dialog box followed by the Add/Remove button (called Change on Windows XP). Follow the prompts in the Microsoft Office XP Setup Wizard and then expand the Alternative User Input item under Office Shared Features in the Features to Install list box to display the Handwriting item. Click Run From My Computer on this item's pop-up menu and then click the Update button to do the installation. Be sure that you have the Office XP CD-ROM at hand or you can tell the Office Installer where the program files are located on your network before you click this button.

After the Handwriting Recognition feature is installed, the next time you open the Language bar in Excel (Tools⇨Speech⇨Speech Recognition) you notice that it contains two new buttons: Handwriting and Drawing Pad (see Figure 1-15). When you click the Handwriting button on the Language bar, a pop-up menu with the following menu items appears:

- **Writing Pad:** Choose this item to do your handwriting within a Writing Pad dialog box, which contains a horizontal line that you can use as a guide.
- **Write Anywhere:** Choose this item to do your handwriting freehand anywhere on the Excel screen.
- **Drawing Pad:** Choose this item to display a Draw dialog box where you can hand-draw text or images that are inserted into the document as graphics (this menu item doesn't work in Excel).
- **On-Screen Standard Keyboard:** Choose this item to display a miniature on-screen virtual keyboard that enables you to enter characters by clicking its keys.
- **On-screen Symbol Keyboard:** Choose this item to display a miniature on-screen virtual symbol keyboard that enables you to enter common accented characters by clicking its keys.

Before you start trying to handwrite any cell entries, be sure that the microphone is turned off on the Language bar so that you don't end up using Speech Recognition at the same time you're trying to use Handwriting Recognition (not the most perfect combination). You know that the mike is turned off if the Dictation and Voice Commands buttons are not visible on the bar. If you do see these buttons, click the Microphone button to hide these buttons before you click the Handwriting button and click either the Writing Pad or the Write Anywhere item on its pop-up menu.

When you choose the Writing Pad menu item, a Writing Pad window opens. On the right side of this window, you find a group of buttons that you can use when doing your handwriting. When you choose the Write Anywhere menu item, a Write Anywhere dialog box containing only these buttons appears. The last button on both the Writing Pad window and the Write Anywhere dialog box is an Expand button (with two greater than symbols — >>), which you can click to display even more buttons.

Figure 1-15 shows the Writing Pad window as it appears after you click its Expand button (which then automatically turns into a Reduce button) to display all of its buttons. When you choose the Write Anywhere item on the Handwriting button's pop-up menu, you can begin writing your cell entry anywhere on the screen as large as you like (it won't affect any of the data displayed in the worksheet underneath). When you choose the Writing Pad item, you must keep your writing within the window (although you don't have to go as far as keeping the baselines of your letters and numbers on the blue guideline).

To write with a stylus on a graphics tablet, simply begin tracing the letters on the tablet as you would write with a pen on a piece of paper. To write with the mouse, you must hold down the mouse button as you trace the letters on your desktop (no easy feat, to say the least).

As soon as you pause your writing or the Handwriting Recognition feature recognizes a chunk of what you have written, the converted text appears in the current cell at the insertion point. If you are writing in the Writing Pad dialog box, you must pause at the end of the line and have your writing converted in order to clear the box and continue. You can also force the Handwriting Recognition feature to convert your writing by clicking the Recognize Now button (the one with *T* in back of the page and the curved arrow showing it going onto the page) in the Writing Pad window or the Write Anywhere dialog box.

If the Handwriting feature correctly recognizes the text for your cell entry (and it's pretty good about this unless you're one of those illegible writers that drove your teachers crazy), you can complete it as you normally would by pressing Enter or an arrow key, or by clicking the Enter button on the Formula bar. You can also complete the entry by clicking the Enter button in the Writing Pad window or the Write Anywhere dialog box.

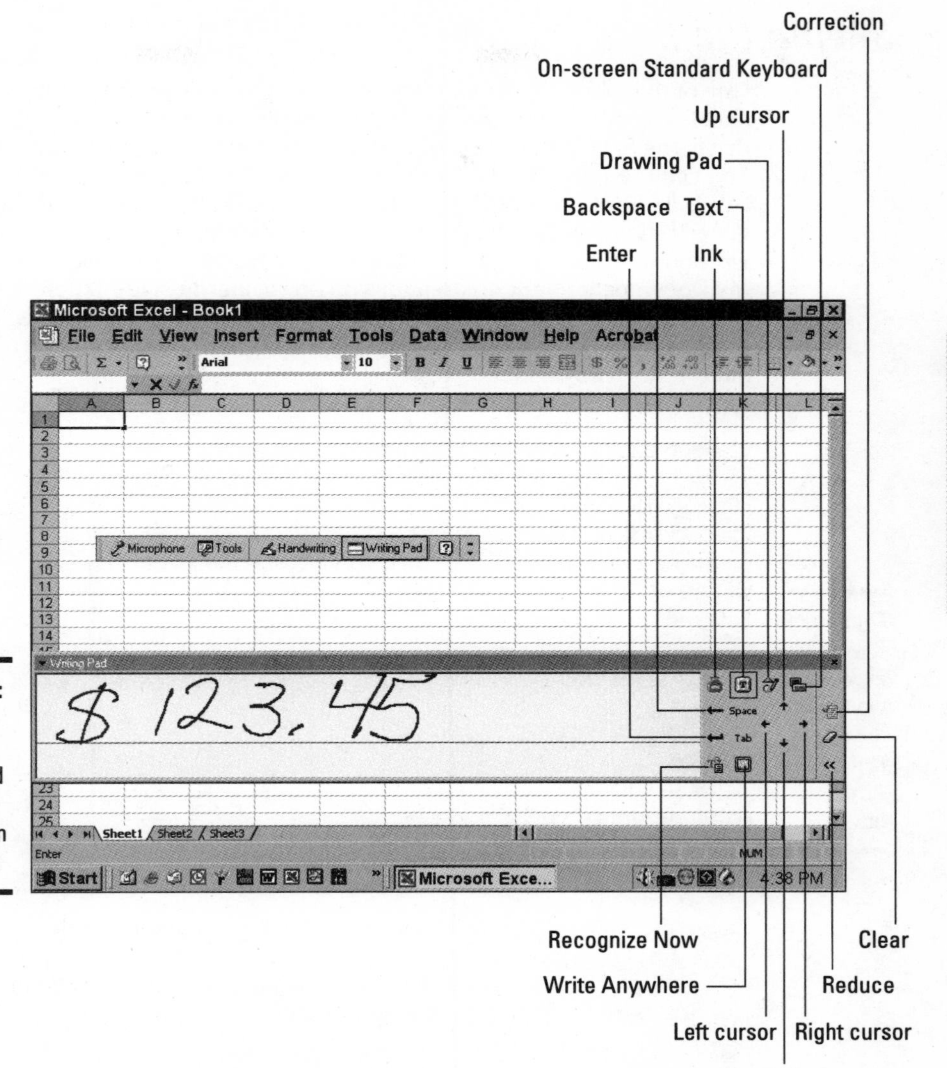

Figure 1-15: Using the expanded Writing Pad to create a handwritten cell entry.

If Handwriting Recognition incorrectly converts some of your writing, correct the incorrect text by clicking the Backspace button to erase the incorrect characters and then try rewriting the garbled text. If Handwriting Recognition still can't correctly interpret your handwritten characters, erase them as before and then use the on-screen or physical keyboard to enter them. Remember to display the on-screen keyboard, you click the Handwriting button the Language bar and then click the On-Screen Standard Keyboard menu item.

Saving the Data

One of the most important tasks you ever perform when building your spreadsheet is *saving your work*! The first time you save a new workbook on the hard drive, the Save As dialog box, similar to the one shown in Figure 1-16, appears. You can then rename the workbook file to something a tad bit more descriptive than Book1 or Book2 by clicking the File Name text box and replacing the generic filename. You can also select a new folder in which you want the new workbook saved (by default, Excel saves any new workbook file in the My Documents folder created for you on the hard drive). When selecting a new folder, you can use the big folder buttons in the panel located on the left of the Save As dialog box or you can select and open the folder from the Save In drop-down menu.

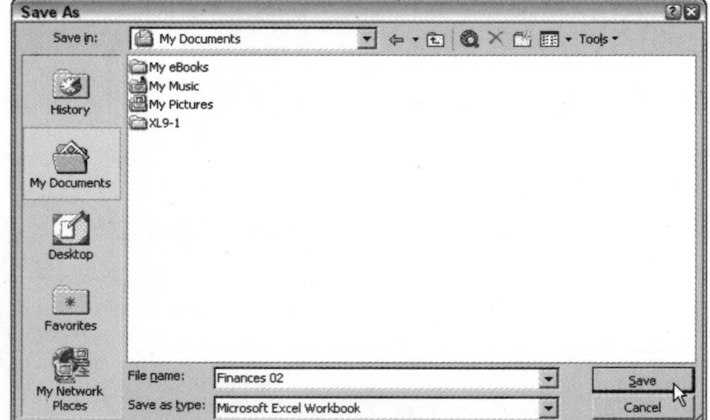

Figure 1-16: Saving a new workbook the first time in the Save As dialog box.

Excel offers two different ways to invoke the Save command:

- ✦ Choose File⇨Save from the Excel menu bar, click the Save button on the Standard toolbar (the one with the disk icon), or press Ctrl+S.
- ✦ Choose File⇨Save As from the Excel menu bar or press F12.

The former methods are used to save changes to your workbook. The latter methods are used when you want to save the workbook with a new filename, in a new folder, and/or as a new type of file. The first time you use the File⇨Save command (or its equivalent shortcuts), Excel opens the Save As dialog box as though you had chosen File⇨Save As (or pressed F12).

After you've saved your new workbook file at least one time, the Save As dialog box no longer appears when you choose File⇨Save or its shortcuts — the program simply saves all unsaved changes in the workbook in the originally selected folder under the originally designated name. From that point on, you need to choose File➪Save As on the Menu bar (or press F12) when you want to open the Save As dialog box to save a copy of the workbook file with a new filename, in a new folder, or as a new file type.

Get in the habit of using the Save command very soon after starting work on a new workbook file. This way, Excel's AutoRecover feature can get started saving copies of your file at the preset interval that you can use if the workbook file ever become corrupted or if you experience a power or machine failure that prevents you from using the Save command.

You can save a copy of your workbook file as a different file type by clicking the new file format from the pop-up menu that's attached to the Save as Type combo box in the Save As dialog box. The file types available on this pop-up menu include options for saving the workbook as a Web page, text file, or in workbook formats used by earlier versions of Excel, Lotus 1-2-3, and Quattro Pro.

Chapter 2: Formatting Worksheets

In This Chapter

- **Selecting cell ranges for formatting**
- **Using AutoFormat to quickly format tables**
- **Assigning number formats**
- **Changing data alignment, fonts, and other attributes**
- **Changing the colors, borders, and patterns in cell ranges**
- **Using conditional formatting**
- **Using the Format Painter and styles to format data**

Formatting — the subject of this chapter — is the process by which you determine the final appearance of the worksheet and the data that it contains. Excel's formatting features give you a great deal of control over the way the data appears in your worksheet. To all types of cell entries, you can assign a new font, font size, font style (such as bold, italics, underlining, or strikeout), or color. You can also change the alignment of entries in the cells in a variety of ways, including the horizontal alignment, the vertical alignment, or the orientation; you can also wrap text entries in the cell or center them across the selection. To numerical values, dates, and times, you can assign one of the many built-in number formats or apply a custom format that you design. To the cells that hold your entries, you can apply different kinds of borders, patterns, and colors. And to the worksheet grid itself, you can assign the most suitable column widths and row heights so that the data in the formatted worksheet are displayed at their best.

Making Cell Selections

Although you have to select the cells of the worksheet that you want to work with before you can accomplish many tasks used in building and editing a typical spreadsheet, perhaps no task requires cell selection like that of formatting. With the exception of the special AutoFormat feature (which automatically selects the table to which its multiple formats are applied), selecting the cells whose appearance you want to enhance or modify is always your first step in their formatting.

In Excel, you can select a single cell, a block of cells (known as a *cell range*), or various discontinuous cell ranges (also known as a *nonadjacent selection*).

Figure 2-1 shows a nonadjacent selection that consists of four different cell ranges (the smallest range is the single cell A1).

Selecting cells with the mouse

Excel offers several methods for selecting cells with the mouse. With each method, you start by selecting one of the cells that occupies the corner of the range that you want to select. The first corner cell that you click becomes the *active cell* (indicated by its cell reference in the formula bar) and the cell range that you then select becomes anchored on this cell.

After you select the active cell in the range, drag the pointer to extend the selection until you have highlighted all of the cells that you want to include. Here are some tips:

- To extend a range in a block that spans several columns, drag left or right from the active cell.
- To extend a range in a block that spans several rows, drag up or down from the active cell.
- To extend a range in a block that spans several columns and rows, drag diagonally from the active cell in the most logical directions (up and to the right, down and to the right, up and to left, or down and to the left).

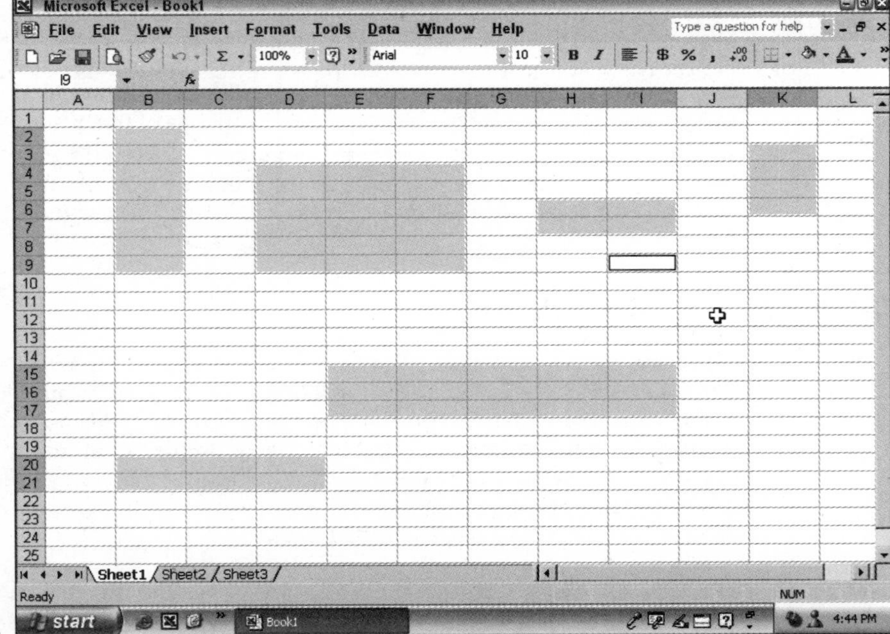

Figure 2-1: Worksheet with a nonadjacent cell selection made up of several different sized ranges.

A range by any other name

Cell ranges are always noted in formulas by the first and last cell that you select, separated by a colon (:); therefore, if you select cell A1 as the first cell and cell H10 as the last cell, the cell range is noted as A1:H10. This same block of cells can just as well be noted as H10:A1 if you selected cell H10 before cell A1. Likewise, the same range can be equally noted as H1:A10 or A10:H1, depending upon which corner cell you select first and which opposite corner you select last. Keep in mind that despite the various range notations that you can use (A1:H10, H10:A1, H1:A10, and A10:H1), you are working with the same block of cells, the main difference being that each has a different active cell whose address appears in the Name box on the Formula bar (A1, H10, H1, and A10, respectively).

If you ever extend the range too far in one direction, you can always reduce it by dragging in the other direction. If you've already released the mouse button and you find that the range is incorrect, click the active cell again (clicking any cell in the worksheet deselects a selected range and activates the cell that you click) and select its cells again.

You can always tell which cell is the active cell forming the anchor point of a cell range because it is the only cell within the range that you've selected that isn't highlighted and is the only cell reference listed on the formula bar. As you extend the range by dragging the thick white-cross mouse pointer, Excel indicates the current size of the range in columns and rows on the Formula bar (as in 5R x 2C when you've highlighted a range of five rows long and two columns wide). However, as soon as you release the mouse button, Excel replaces this row and column notation with the address of the active cell.

You can also use the following shortcuts when selecting cells with the mouse:

- ✦ To select a single-cell range, click the thick white-cross mouse pointer somewhere inside the cell.
- ✦ To select all cells in an entire column, position the mouse pointer on the column letter in the column header and then click the mouse button. To select several adjacent columns, drag through their column letters in the column header.
- ✦ To select all cells in an entire row, position the mouse pointer on the row number in the row header and then click the mouse button. To select several adjacent rows, drag through the row numbers in the row header.
- ✦ To select all the cells in the worksheet, click the box in the upper-left of the worksheet at the intersection of row and column headers.

- To select a cell range composed of partial columns and rows without dragging, click the cell where you want to anchor the range, hold down the Shift key, and then click the last cell in the range and release the Shift key (Excel selects all the cells in between the first and the last cell that you click). If the range that you want to mark is a block that spans several columns and rows, the last cell is the one diagonally opposite the active cell. When using this Shift+click technique to mark a range that extends beyond the screen, use the scroll bars to display the last cell in the range (just make sure that you don't release the Shift key until after you've clicked this last cell).
- To select a nonadjacent selection comprised of several discontinuous cell ranges, drag through the first cell range, and then hold down the Ctrl key as you drag through the other ranges. After you have marked all of the cell ranges to be included in the nonadjacent selection, you can release the Ctrl key.

Selecting cells with the keyboard

Excel also makes it easy for you to select cell ranges with the keyboard by using a technique known as *extending a selection*. To use this technique, you move the cell pointer to the active cell of the range, and then press F8 to turn on Extend mode (indicated by EXT on the Status bar) and use the direction keys to move the pointer to the last cell in the range. Excel selects all the cells that the cell pointer moves through until you turn off Extend mode (by pressing F8 again).

You can use the mouse as well as the keyboard to extend a selection when Excel is in Extend mode. All you do is click the active cell, press F8, and then click the last cell to mark the range.

You can also select a cell range with the keyboard without turning on Extend mode. Here, you use a variation of the Shift+click method by moving the cell pointer to the active cell in the range, holding down the Shift key, and then using the direction keys to extend the range. After you've highlighted all the cells that you want to include, release the Shift key.

To mark a nonadjacent selection of cells with the keyboard, you need to combine the use of Extend mode with that of Add mode. To turn on Add mode (indicated by ADD on the status bar), you press Shift+F8. To mark a nonadjacent selection by using Extend and Add mode, follow these steps:

1. **Move the cell pointer to the first cell of the first range you want to select.**
2. **Press F8 to turn on Extend mode.**

3. **Use the arrow keys to extend the cell range until you've highlighted all its cells.**
4. **Press Shift+F8 to turn off Extend mode and turn on Add mode instead.**
5. **Move the cell pointer to the first cell of the next cell range you want to add to the selection.**
6. **Press F8 to turn off Add mode and turn Extend mode back on.**
7. **Use the arrow keys to extend the range until all cells are highlighted.**
8. **Repeat Steps 4 through 7 until you've selected all of the ranges that you want included in the nonadjacent selection.**
9. **Press F8 to turn off Extend mode.**

You AutoSelect that range!

Excel's AutoSelect feature provides a particularly efficient way to select all or part of the cells in a large table of data. AutoSelect automatically extends a selection in a single direction from the active cell to the first nonblank cell that Excel encounters in that direction.

You can use the AutoSelect feature with the mouse or keyboard. The general steps for using AutoSelect to select a table of data with the mouse are as follows:

1. **Click the first cell to which to anchor the range that you are about to select.**

   In a typical data table, this cell may be the blank cell at the intersection of the row of column headings and the column of row headings.

2. **Position the mouse pointer on the edge of the cell in the direction that you want the range extended.**

   To extend the range up to the first blank cell to the right, position the pointer on the right edge of the cell. To extend the range left to the first blank cell, position the pointer on the left edge of the cell. To extend the range down to the first blank cell, position the pointer on the bottom edge of the cell. And to extend the range up to the first blank cell, position the pointer on the top edge of the cell.

3. **When the pointer changes shape from a cross to an arrowhead, hold down the Shift key and then double-click the mouse.**

   As soon as you double-click the mouse, Excel extends the selection to the first occupied cell that is adjacent to a blank cell in the direction of the edge that you double-clicked.

To get an idea of how AutoSelect works, consider how you use it to select the data table (in the cell range A2:J7) shown in Figures 2-2 and 2-3. With the cell pointer in cell A3 at the intersection of the row with the Date column headings and the column with the Part row headings, you can use the AutoSelect feature to select all the cells in the table in two operations:

- ✦ In the first operation, hold down the Shift key and then double-click the bottom edge of cell A2 to highlight the cells down to A7, selecting the range A2:A7 (see Figure 2-2).
- ✦ In the second operation, hold down the Shift key and then double-click the right edge of cell range A2:A7 to extend the selection to the last column in the table (selecting the entire table with the cell range A2:J7, as shown in Figure 2-3).

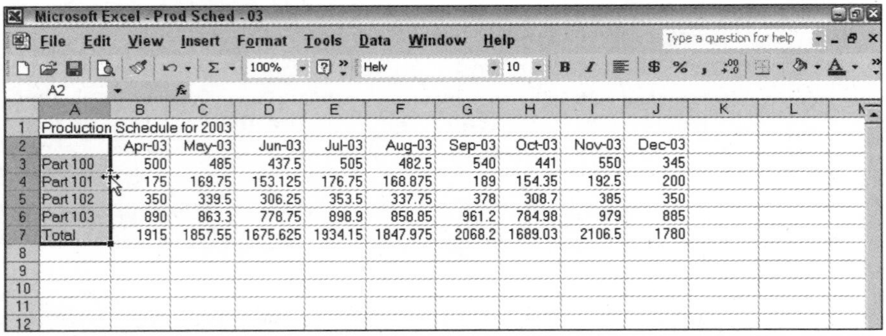

Figure 2-2: Selecting the cells in the first column of the table with AutoSelect.

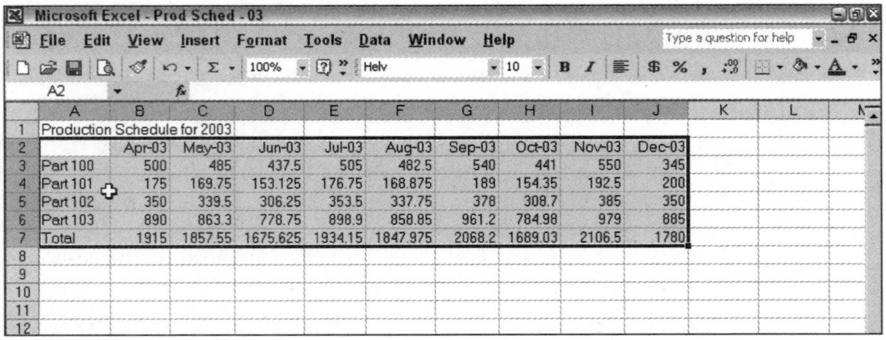

Figure 2-3: Selecting all the remaining columns of the table with AutoSelect.

If you select the cells in the first row of the table (range A2:J2) in the first operation, you can then extend this range down the remaining rows of the table by double-clicking the bottom edge of one of the selected cells (it doesn't matter which one).

To use the AutoSelect feature with the keyboard, press the End key and one of the four arrow keys as you hold down the Shift key. When you hold down Shift and press End and an arrow key, Excel extends the selection in the direction of the arrow key to the first cell containing a value that is bordered by a blank cell.

In terms of selecting the table of data shown in Figures 2-2 and 2-3, this means that you would have to complete four separate operations to select all of its cells:

1. **With A2 as the active cell, hold down Shift and press End+↓ to select the range A2:A3.**

   Excel stops at A3 because this is the first cell containing a value bordered by a blank cell.

2. **Hold down Shift and press End+↓, again extending the range down to cell A7.**

   Excel stops at A7 because this is the last occupied cell in that column. At this point, the cell range A2:A7 is selected.

3. **Hold down Shift and then this time, press End+→.**

   Excel extends the range only to column B (because B2 is the first cell to the right of the active cell that contains a value and is bordered by the blank cell, A2). At this point, the cell range A2:B7 is selected.

4. **Hold down Shift and then press End+→ again.**

   This time, Excel extends the range all the way to column J (because cell J3 contains an entry and is bordered by a blank cell). Now all of the cells in the table (the cell range A2:J7) are selected.

Selecting cells with Go To

Although you usually use the Go To feature to move the cell pointer to a new cell in the worksheet, you can also use this feature to select a range of cells. When you choose Go To on the Edit menu (or press Ctrl+G or F5), Excel displays a Go To dialog box similar to the one shown in Figure 2-4. To move the cell pointer to a particular cell, enter the cell address in the Reference text box and click OK (Excel automatically lists the addresses of the last four cells or cell ranges that you specified in the Go To list box).

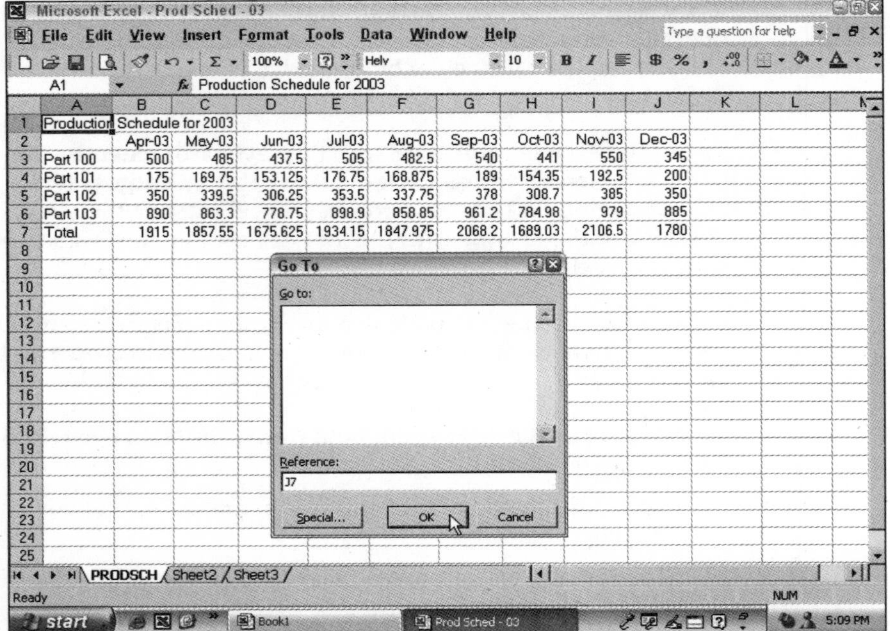

Figure 2-4: Selecting the cell range with the Go To feature.

Instead of just moving to a new section of the worksheet with the Go To feature, you can select a range of cells by taking these steps:

1. **Select the first cell of the range.**

   This becomes the active cell to which the cell range is anchored.

2. **Choose Edit ⇨Go To on the Menu bar or press Ctrl+G or F5.**

   The Go To dialog box opens.

3. **Type the cell address of the last cell in the range in the Reference text box.**

   If this address is already listed in the Go To list box, you can enter this address in the text box by clicking it in the list box.

4. **Hold down the Shift key as you click OK or press Enter to close the Go To dialog box.**

   By holding down Shift as you click OK or press Enter, you select the range between the active cell and the cell whose address you specified in the Reference text box.

Instead of selecting the anchor cell and then specifying the last cell of a range in the Reference text box of the Go To dialog box, you can also select a range simply by typing in the address of the cell range in the Reference text box. Remember that when you type a range address, you enter the cell reference of the first (active) cell and the last cell in the range separated by a colon. For example, to select the cell range that extends from cell B2 to G10 in the worksheet, you would type the range address b2:g10 in the Reference text box before clicking OK or pressing Enter.

Name that range!

One of the easiest ways to select a range of data is to assign a name to it and then choose that name on the pop-up menu attached to the Name box on the Formula bar or in the Go To list box in the Go To dialog box. Of course, you reserve this technique for cell ranges that you work with on a somewhat regular basis; for example, ranges with data that you print regularly, consult often, or have to refer to in formula calculations. It's probably not worth your while to name a range of data that doesn't carry any special importance in the spreadsheet.

To name a cell range, follow three simple steps:

1. **Select all the cells in the range that you intend to name.**

   You can use any of the cell selection techniques that you prefer. When selecting the cells for the named range, be sure to include all the cells that you want selected each time you select its range name.

2. **Click the Name box on the Formula bar.**

   Excel automatically highlights the address of the active cell in the selected range.

3. **Type the range name in the Name box and then press Enter.**

   As soon as you start typing, Excel replaces the address of the active cell with the range name that you're assigning. As soon as you press the Enter key, the name appears in the Name box instead of the cell address of the active cell in the range.

When naming a cell range, however, you *must* observe the following naming conventions:

- ✦ Begin the range name with a letter of the alphabet rather than a number or punctuation mark.
- ✦ Don't use spaces in the range name — instead, use an underscore between words in a range name (as in Qtr_1).

- Make sure that the range name doesn't duplicate any cell reference in the worksheet by using either the standard A1 or R1C1 notation system.
- Make sure that the range name is unique in the worksheet.

After you've assigned a name to a cell range, you can select all of its cells simply by clicking the name on the pop-up menu attached to the Name box on the Formula bar. The beauty of this method is that you can use it from anywhere in the same sheet or a different worksheet in the workbook because as soon as you click its name on the Name box pop-up menu, Excel takes you directly to the range, while at the same time automatically selecting all its cell.

Range names are also very useful when building formulas in your spreadsheet. For more on creating and using range names, see Book III, Chapter 1.

Adjusting Columns and Rows

Along with knowing how to select cells for formatting, you really also have to know how to adjust the width of your columns and the heights of your rows. Why? Because often in the course of assigning different formatting to certain cell ranges (such as new font and font size in boldface type), you may find that data entries that previously fit within the original widths of their column no longer do and that the rows that they occupy seem to have changed height all on their own.

In a blank worksheet, all of the columns and rows are the same standard width and height. All columns start out 8.43 characters wide (or 64 pixels) and all rows at 12.75 characters high (or 17 pixels). As you build your spreadsheet, you end up with all sorts of data entries that can't fit within these default settings. This is especially true as you start adding formatting to their cells to enhance and clarify their contents.

Most of the time, you don't need to be concerned with the heights of the rows in your worksheet because Excel automatically adjusts them up or down to accommodate the largest font size used in a cell in the row and the number of text lines (in some cells, you may wrap their text on several lines). Instead, you'll spend a lot more time adjusting the column widths to suit the entries for the formatting that you assign to them.

Remember what happens when you put a text entry in a cell whose current width isn't long enough to accommodate all its characters. If the cells in columns to the right are empty, Excel lets the display of the extra characters spill over into the empty cells. If these cells are already occupied, however, Excel cuts off the display of the extra characters until you widen the column sufficiently. Likewise, remember that if you add formatting to a number so that its value and formatting can't both be displayed in the cell, those nasty overflow indicators appear in the cell as a string of pound signs (#####) until you widen the column adequately.

You AutoFit the column to its contents

The easiest way to adjust the width of a column to suit its longest entry is to use the AutoFit feature. AutoFit determines the best fit for the column or columns selected at that time, given their longest entries.

- To use AutoFit on a single column, position the mouse pointer on the right edge of that column in the Column header and then, when the pointer changes to a double-headed arrow, double-click the mouse.
- To use AutoFit on multiple columns at one time, select the columns by dragging through them in the Column header or by Ctrl+clicking the column letters, and then double-click the right edge of one of the selected columns when the pointer changes to a double-headed arrow.

These AutoFit techniques work well for adjusting all columns except for those that contain really long headings (such as the spreadsheet title that often spills over several blank columns in row 1), in which case, AutoFit makes the columns far too wide for the bulk of the cell entries.

For those situations, use the AutoFit Selection command, which adjusts the column width to suit only the entries in the cells of the column that you have selected. This way, you can select all the cells except for any really long ones in the column that purposely spill over to empty cells on the right and then have Excel adjust the width to suit all but them. After you've selected the cells in the column that you want the new width to fit, choose Format⇨Column⇨AutoFit Selection on the Menu bar.

Adjusting columns the old fashioned way

AutoFit is nothing if not quick and easy. The only problem with AutoFit is that it's totally based on the width of the longest entry currently in that column. If you need more precision in adjusting your column widths, you have to do this manually either by dragging its border with the mouse or by entering new values in the Column Width dialog box.

To manually adjust a column width with the mouse, drag the right edge of that column onto the Column header to the left (to narrow) or to the right (to widen) as required. As you drag the column border, a ToolTip appears above the mouse pointer indicating the current width in both characters and pixels. When you have the column adjusted to the desired width, release the mouse button to set it.

To adjust a column width in the Column Width dialog box, position the cell pointer in any one of the cells in the column that you want to adjust and then choose Format⇨Column⇨Width on the Menu bar to open the Column Width dialog box, shown in Figure 2-5, where you enter the new width (in the number of characters between 0 and 255) in the Column Width text box before clicking OK.

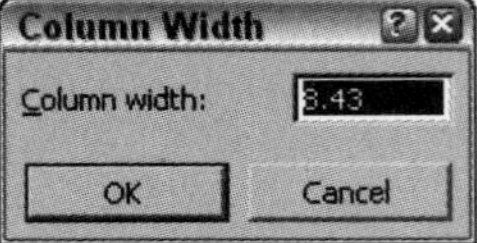

Figure 2-5: Adjusting the column width in the Column Width dialog box.

You can apply a new column width that you set in the Column Width dialog box to more than a single column by selecting the columns (either by dragging through their letters on the Column header or holding down Ctrl as you click them) before you open the Column Width dialog box.

Setting a new standard width

You can use the Standard Width command to set all the columns in a worksheet to a new uniform width (other than the default 8.43 characters). To do so, simply choose Format⇨Column⇨Standard Width on the Menu bar to open the Standard Width dialog box, replace the default 8.43 in the Standard Column Width text box with your new width (in characters), and then click OK or press Enter.

Note that when you set a new standard width for the columns of your worksheet, this new width doesn't affect any columns whose width you've previously adjusted either with AutoFit or in the Column Width dialog box.

Hiding out a column or two

You can use the Hide command to temporarily remove columns of data from the worksheet display. When you hide a column, you're essentially setting the column width to 0 (and thus, making it so narrow that for all intents and purposes, the sucker's gone). Hiding columns enables you to remove the display of sensitive or supporting data that needs to be in the spreadsheet but may not be appropriate in printouts that you distribute (keeping in mind that only columns and rows that are displayed in the worksheet get printed).

To hide a column, put the cell pointer in a cell in that column and then choose Format⇨Column⇨Hide on the Menu bar. To hide more than one column at a time, select the columns either by dragging through their letters on the Column header or by holding down Ctrl as you click them before you choose Format⇨Column⇨Hide.

Excel lets you know that certain columns are missing from the worksheet by removing their column letters from the Column header so that if, for example, you hide columns D and E in the worksheet, column C is followed by column F on the Column header.

To restore hidden columns to view, simply choose Format⇨Column⇨Unhide on the Menu bar, and Excel immediately redisplays all previous hidden columns in the worksheet. Because Excel also automatically selects all the redisplayed columns, you need to deselect the selected columns before you select any more formatting or editing commands that will affect all of their cells. You can do this by clicking on a single cell anywhere in the worksheet or by dragging through a particular cell range that you want to work with.

Keep in mind that when you hide a column, the data in the cells in all of its rows (1 through 65536) are hidden (not just the ones you can see on your computer screen). This means that if you have some data in rows of a column that need printing and some in other rows of that same column that need concealing, you can't use the Hide command to remove their display until you've moved the cells with the data to be printed into a different column (see Book II, Chapter 3 for details).

Rambling rows

The controls for adjusting the height of the rows in your worksheet parallel those that you use to adjust its columns. The big difference is that Excel always applies AutoFit to the height of each row so that even if you find an AutoFit menu item on the Format⇨Row cascading menu, you won't find much use for it (personally, I've never had any reason to use it).

Instead, you'll probably end up manually adjusting the heights of rows with the mouse or by entering new height values in the Row Height dialog box (opened by choosing Format⇨Row⇨Height on the Menu bar) and occasionally hiding rows with sensitive or potentially confusing data. Follow these instructions for each type of action:

✦ **To adjust the height of a row with the mouse:** Position the mouse pointer on the lower edge of the row's border in the Row header and then drag up or down when the mouse pointer changes to a double-headed, vertical arrow. As you drag, a ToolTip appears to the side of the pointer, keeping you informed of the height in characters and also pixels (remember that 12.75 characters or 17 pixels is the default height of all rows in a new worksheet).

- **To change the height of a row in the Row Height dialog box:** Choose Format⇨Row⇨Height on the Menu bar and then enter the value for the new row height in the Row Height text box before you click OK or press Enter.
- **To hide a row:** Position the cell pointer in any one of the cells in that row and then choose Format⇨Row⇨Hide on the Menu bar. To then restore the rows that you currently have hidden in the worksheet, choose Format⇨Row⇨Unhide instead.

As with adjusting columns, you can change the height of more than one row and hide multiple rows at the same time by selecting the rows before you drag one of their lower borders, open the Row Height dialog box, or choose the Format⇨Row⇨Hide menu command.

Doing It with the Toolbars

The first line of spreadsheet formatting is literally the one shared by the Standard and Formatting toolbars. The Standard toolbar has the nifty Format Painter button as well as the highly useful Undo button (just in case you happen to apply some really ghastly formatting that demands immediate removal). The Formatting toolbar (as you can probably guess from its name), is chock-full of useful formatting tools — all of which you will find helpful at some time or other in beautifying your spreadsheets.

Doing it from the Formatting toolbar

Figure 2-6 shows the Formatting toolbar with captions identifying each of its many tools. In most cases, these are all the tools you'll need to successfully format most of the spreadsheets that you create with Excel.

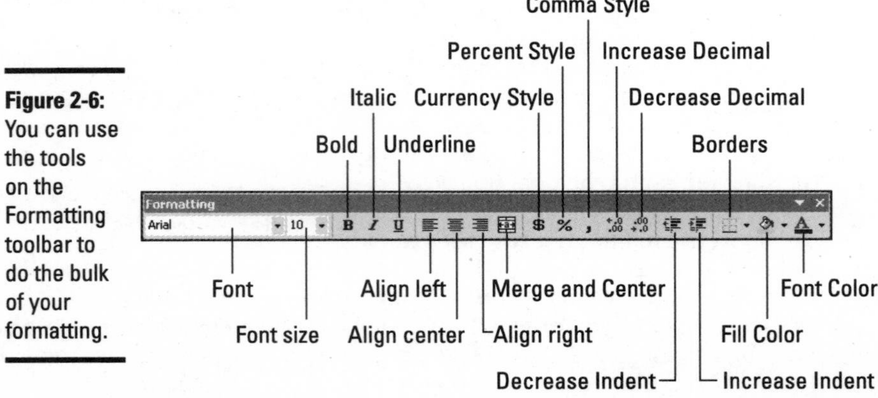

Figure 2-6: You can use the tools on the Formatting toolbar to do the bulk of your formatting.

The tools on the Formatting toolbar are organized into five different groups. The first group of buttons enables you to change fonts, font sizes, and apply or remove various text enhancements to the entries in the cells that you've selected:

- **Font** is a combo box that enables you to select a new font either by typing in its name or clicking it on the attached pop-up menu
- **Font Size** is a combo box that enables you to select a new font size either by typing in its point size or clicking it on the attached pop-up menu
- **Bold** is a toggle button that when clicked for the first time, emboldens the cell entries and when clicked the second time, removes the bold attribute
- **Italic** is a toggle button that when clicked for the first time, italicizes the cell entries and when clicked the second time, removes the italics
- **Underline** is a toggle button that when clicked for the first time, underlines the cell entries and when clicked the second time, removes the underlining

The second group of buttons enables you to change the alignment of the entries in the selected cells:

- **Align Left** button aligns all entries in the selected cells with their left borders
- **Center** button centers all entries in the selected cells between their left and right borders
- **Align Right** button aligns all entries in the selected cells with their right borders
- **Merge and Center** button merges all cells in the current selection into one big cell in which the leftmost entry is then centered (see "Merge and Center" in the section that immediately follows for details on how to use this button)

The third group of buttons enables you to apply the most commonly used number formatting to the numeric entries in the selected cells:

- **Currency Style** button applies the Currency format to all numbers in the cell selection, which adds a dollar sign, two decimal places, commas as the thousands separator, and encloses negative values in parentheses, as in $ 2,500.00 or ($ 409.25)
- **Percent Style** button applies the Percent format to all numbers in the cell selection, which multiplies the values by 100 and adds a percent sign
- **Comma Style** button applies the Comma format to all numbers in the cell selection, which adds two decimal places, commas as the thousands

separator, and encloses negative values in parentheses, as in 2,500.00 or (409.25)

- ✦ **Increase Decimal** button adds a decimal point to all numbers in the cell selection
- ✦ **Decrease Decimal** button removes a decimal point to all numbers in the cell selection

The fourth group of buttons enables you to increase or decrease the amount of indenting applied to the entries in the selected cells:

- ✦ **Decrease Indent** button removes a tab space from the entries in the cell selection (this only works if you've used the Increase Indent button and the columns are wide enough to accommodate indenting in the first place)
- ✦ **Increase Indent** button inserts a tab space into the entries in the cell selection (this only works if the columns are wide enough to accommodate indenting)

The fifth and final group of buttons on the Formatting toolbar enables you to add and remove borders and change the fill and text colors for the cells that you've selected:

- ✦ **Borders** button opens a palette where you can choose the type of border to draw around the cell selection. This palette also contains a Draw Borders item that, when clicked, displays a floating Borders toolbar that enables you to draw borders around any cell range in the worksheet.
- ✦ **Fill Color** button opens a palette from which you can choose a new fill color for the background of the selected cells.
- ✦ **Font Color** button opens a palette from which you can choose a new text color for the entries in the selected cells.

Note that the Borders, Fill Color, and Text Color palettes attached to their respective buttons on the Formatting toolbar are *tear-off palettes,* which is what they are called in the business. This means that you can drag off copies of each of these palettes and display them as floating palettes in the Excel window, as shown in Figure 2-7.

To tear off one of these palettes, click the drop-down button to the right of the Borders, Fill Color, or Text Color buttons on the Formatting toolbar to open its palette and then position the mouse pointer on the shaded bar at the top of the palette (refer to Figure 2-7). Then when the pointer becomes a four-headed arrow, drag the palette down until its title bar appears.

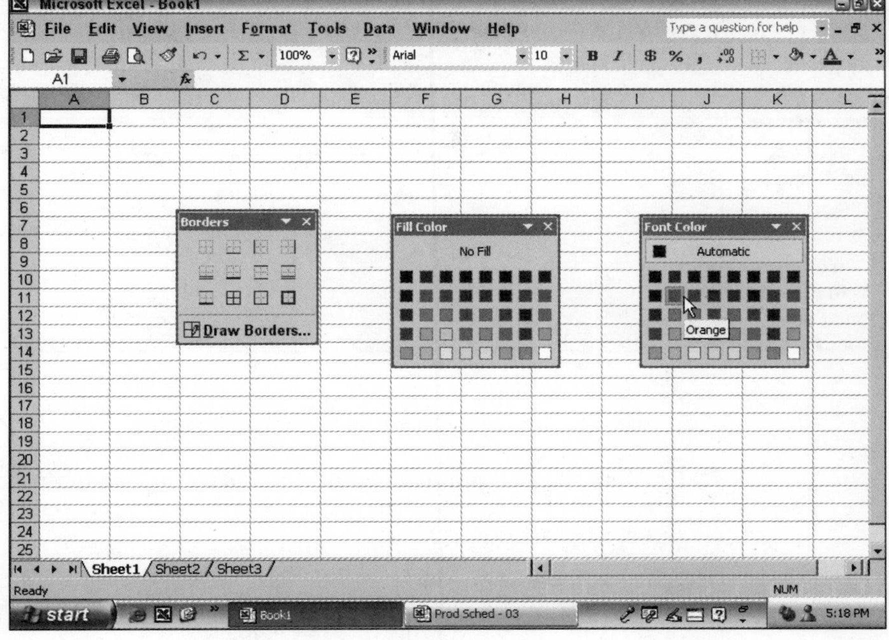

Figure 2-7: Worksheet with floating Borders, Fill Color, and Font Color palettes.

Tearing a palette off the Formatting toolbar gives you continuous, immediate access to their settings as you format your spreadsheet. You can move a floating palette out of the way as you work by dragging it by its title bar. After you finish using it, you can close the floating palette by clicking its Close button.

Merge and Center

At first glance, the Merge and Center button on the Formatting toolbar may not seem all that relevant to you, but believe it or not, this little baby is quite powerful and very useful when you need to center text over several columns of the worksheet as when centering the title of a table over all its columns of data.

Figure 2-8 illustrates this kind of use for Merge and Center. In this spreadsheet, I needed to center the title of the data table, "Production Schedule 2003," entered in cell A1 across all the columns of the table (that is, between column A and J).

	A	B	C	D	E	F	G	H	I	J
1	Production Schedule for 2003									
2		Apr-03	May-03	Jun-03	Jul-03	Aug-03	Sep-03	Oct-03	Nov-03	Dec-03
3	Part 100	500	485	437.5	505	482.5	540	441	550	345
4	Part 101	175	169.75	153.125	176.75	168.875	189	154.35	192.5	200
5	Part 102	350	339.5	306.25	353.5	337.75	378	308.7	385	350
6	Part 103	890	863.3	778.75	898.9	858.85	961.2	784.98	979	885
7	Total	1915	1857.55	1675.625	1934.15	1847.975	2068.2	1689.03	2106.5	1780

Figure 2-8: Centering a table's title over all its columns with Merge and Center.

To do this with Merge and Center, follow these steps:

1. **Position the cell pointer in cell A1 containing the table title, "Productions Schedule for 2003," and then drag through to cell J1 to select the cell range A1:J1.**

   When you click the Merge and Center button, the range of cells that you've selected is merged into one really wide cell and then simultaneously centered within this merged cell.

2. **Click the Merge and Center on the Formatting toolbar.**

As soon as you click the Merge and Center button, Excel makes the cell range A1:J1 into one cell that spans all ten columns and then centers the table title within this merged cell.

If you ever decide that you no longer need to have text centered across many columns with Merge and Center, you can return the worksheet to its original state by clicking the Align Left button on the Formatting toolbar and then choosing Format⇨Cells (Ctrl+1) to open the Format Cells dialog box. There, click the Alignment tab on which you then click the Merge Cells check box and then the OK button.

Hiring out the Format Painter

The Format Painter button is somewhat misplaced on the Standard toolbar (the one with the paintbrush icon) because its sole function is to take formatting from the current cell and apply it to cells that you "paint" by dragging its special thick-white-cross-plus-paintbrush mouse pointer through them. This tool, therefore, provides a quick-and-easy way to take a bunch of different formats (such as a new font, font size, bold, and italics) that you applied individually to a cell in the spreadsheet and then turn around and use it as the guide for formatting a new range of cells.

To use the Format Painter, follow these steps:

1. **Position the cell pointer in a cell that contains the formatting that you want copied to another range of cells in the spreadsheet.**

   This cell becomes the sample cell whose formatting is taken up by Format Painter and copied in the cells that "paint" with its special mouse pointer.

2. **Click the Format Painter button on the Standard toolbar.**

   As soon as you click this button, Excel adds a paintbrush icon to the standard thick white-cross mouse pointer, indicating that the Format Painter is ready to copy the formatting from the sample cell.

3. **Drag the mouse pointer through the range of cells that you want formatted identically to the sample cell.**

The moment that you release the mouse button, the cells in the range that you just selected with the Format Painter become formatted the same way as the sample cell.

Normally, using the Format Painter is a one-shot deal because as soon as you release the mouse button after selecting a range of cells with the Format Painter, it turns off and the mouse pointer reverts back to its normal function of just selecting cells in the worksheet (indicated by the return of the regular thick white-cross icon). If you ever want to keep the Format Painter turned on so that you can use it to format more than one range of cells in the worksheet, you need to double-click the Format Painter button on the Standard toolbar instead of just single-clicking it. When you do this, the Format Painter button remains depressed on the toolbar until you click the Format Painter again. During this time, you can "paint" as many different cell ranges in the worksheet as you desire.

All about Number Formats

When you enter numbers in a cell or a formula that returns a number, Excel automatically applies the General number format to your entry. The General format displays numeric entries more or less as you enter them. However, the format does make the following changes to your numeric entries:

- Drops any trailing zeros from decimal fractions so that **4.5** appears when you enter **4.500** in a cell
- Drops any leading zeros in whole numbers so that **4567** appears when you enter **04567** in a cell

- Inserts a zero before the decimal point in any decimal fraction without a whole number so that **0.123** appears when you enter **.123** in a cell
- Truncates decimal places in a number to display the whole numbers in a cell when the number contains too many digits to be displayed in the current column width. It also converts the number to scientific notation when the column width is too narrow to display all integers in the whole number — for example, **7890123** appears when you enter **7890123.45** in a cell using the default column width, but **7.89E+08** appears when you enter **789012345.67** in that cell.

Remember that you can always override the General number format when you enter a number by entering the characters used in recognized number formats. For example, to enter the value 2500 and assign it the Currency number format that displays two decimal places, you enter **$2,500.00** in the cell.

Note that although you can override the General number format and assign one of the others to any numeric value that you enter into a cell, you can't do this when you enter a formula into a cell. The only way to apply another format to a calculated result is to select its cell and then assign the Currency number format that displays two decimal places by clicking the Currency Style button in the Formatting toolbar or by selecting the Currency on the Number tab of the Format Cells dialog box (Ctrl+1).

Using one of the predefined number formats

Any time you apply a number format to a cell selection (even if you do so with a button on the Formatting toolbar instead of selecting the format directly from the Number tab of the Format Cells dialog box), you're telling Excel to apply a particular group of format codes to those cells. Figure 2-9 shows the Number tab of the Format Cells dialog box as it appears when you first open the dialog box. As you can see in this figure, when the Number tab is initially selected, the General category of number formats is highlighted in the Category list box with the words "General format cells have no specific number format" showing in the area to the right. Directly above this cryptic message (which is Excel-speak for "we don't care what you've put in your cell, we're not changing it!") is the Sample area that shows how the number in the active cell appears in whatever format you choose (this is blank if the active cell is blank or if it contains text instead of a number).

When you click the Number, Currency, Accounting, or Percentage category in the Category list box, more options appear in the area just to the right of the Category list box in the form of different check boxes, list boxes, and spinner buttons (Figure 2-10 shows the Format Cells dialog box when Currency is selected in the Category list box.) These options determine how you want items such as decimal places, dollar signs, comma separators, and negative numbers to be used in the format category that you've chosen.

What you see is *not* always what you get

The number format that you assign to cells with numeric entries in the worksheet affects *only* the way they are displayed in their cells, and not their underlying values. For example, if a formula returns the value **3.456789** in a cell and you apply a number format that displays only two decimal places, Excel will display the value **3.46** in the cell. If you then refer to the cell in a formula that multiplies its value by **2**, Excel returns the result **6.913578** instead of the result **6.92** which would be the result if Excel were actually multiplying **3.46** by **2**. If you want to modify the underlying value in a cell, you use ROUND function (see Book III, Chapter 5 for details).

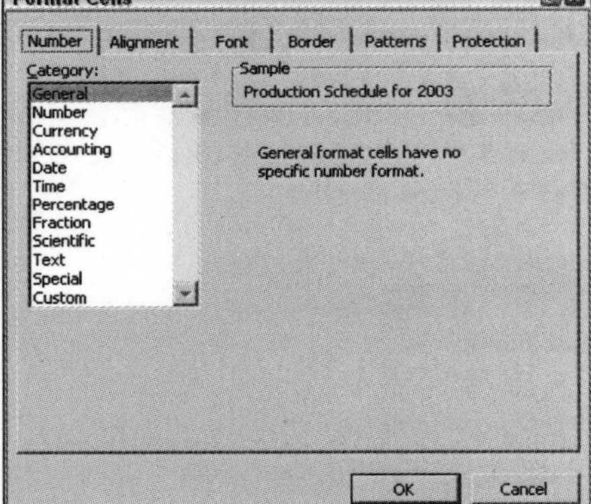

Figure 2-9: Opening the Number tab of the Format Cells dialog box to select a number format.

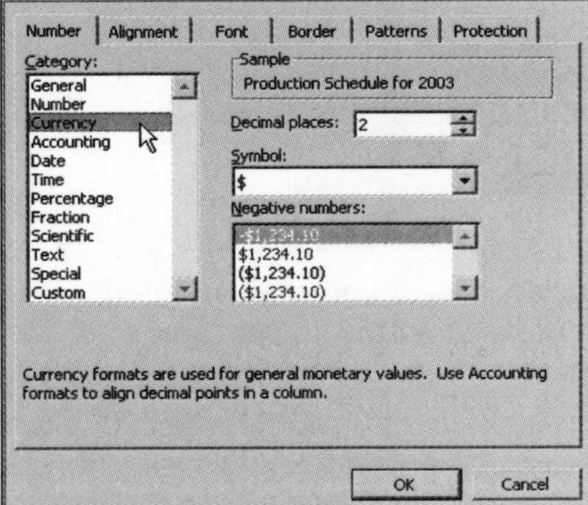

Figure 2-10: Selecting Currency in the Category list box of the Number tab.

When you choose the Date, Time, Fraction, Special, or Custom category, a large Type list box appears that contains handfuls of predefined category types, which you can apply to your value to change its appearance. Just like when you're selecting different formatting categories, the Sample area of the Format Cells dialog box shows you how the various category *types* will affect your selection. I should note here that Excel always tries to choose an appropriate format category in the Category list box based on the way you entered your value in the selected cell. If you enter 3:00 in a cell and then choose Format⇨Cells and the Number tab of the Format Cells dialog box, Excel highlights the h:mm time format in the Custom category in the Type list box.

Deciphering the Custom number formats

You probably noticed while clicking around the Category list box that for the most part, the different categories and their types are pretty easy — if not a breeze — to comprehend. For most people, that self-assured feeling goes right out the window as soon as they click the Custom category and get a load of its accompanying Type list box, shown in Figure 2-11. It starts off with the nice word *General,* then 0, then 0.00, and after that, all hell breaks loose! Codes with 0s and #s (and other junk) start to appear, and it only goes downhill from there.

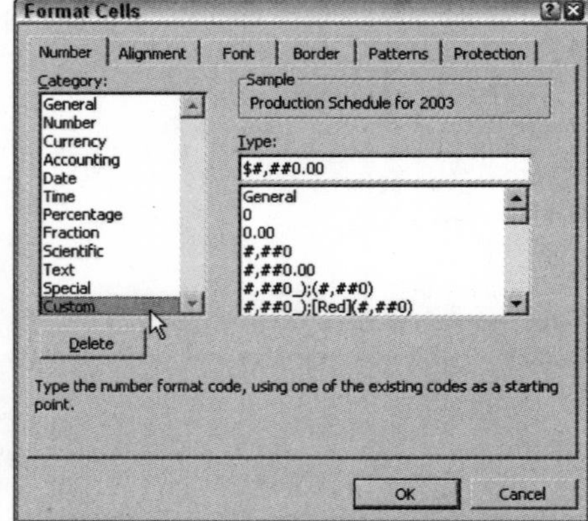

Figure 2-11: Selecting Custom in the Category list box of the Number tab.

As you move down the list, the longer codes are divided into sections separated by semicolons and enclosed within square brackets. Although at first glance these codes appear as so much gibberish, you'll actually find that they're quite understandable (well, would you believe *useful,* then?).

And these codes *can* be useful, especially after you understand them. You can use them to create number formats of your own design. The basic keys to understanding number format codes are as follows:

- Excel number formats use a combination of 0, ?, and # symbols with such punctuation as dollar signs, percent signs, and commas to stand for the formatted digits in the numbers that you format.
- The 0 is used to indicate how many decimal places (if any) are allowed in the format. The format code 0.00 indicates that two decimal places are used in the number. The format code 0 alone indicates that no decimal places appear (the display of all values is rounded up to whole numbers).
- The ? is used like the 0, except that it inserts spaces at the end as needed to make sure that values line up on the decimal point. For example, by selecting the number format 0.??, such values as 10.5 and 24.71 line up with each other in their cells because Excel adds an extra space after the 5 to push it over to the left so that it's in line with the 7 of 71. If you used the number format 0.00 instead, these two values would not line up on the decimal point when they are right-aligned in their cells.
- The # symbol is used with a comma to indicate that you want thousands, hundred thousands, millions, zillions, and so on in your numbers, with each group of three digits to be separated with a comma.
- The $ (dollar sign) symbol is added to the beginning of a number format if you want dollar signs to appear at the beginning of every formatted number.
- The % (percent sign) symbol is added to the end of the number format if you want Excel to actually transform the value into a percentage (multiplying it by 100 and adding a percent sign).

Number formats can specify one format for positive values, another for negative values, a third for zero values, and even a fourth format for text in the cells. In such complex formats, the format codes for positive values come first, followed by the codes for negative values, and a semicolon separates each group of codes. Any format codes for how to handle zeros and text in a cell come third and fourth, respectively, in the number format, again separated by semicolons. If the number format doesn't specify special formatting for negative or zero values, these values are automatically formatted like positive values. If the number format doesn't specify what to do with text, text is formatted according to Excel's default values. For example, look at the following number format:

```
#,##0_);(#,##0)
```

This particular number format specifies how to format positive values (the codes in front of the semicolon) and negative values (the codes after the semicolon). Because no further groups of codes exist, zeros are formatted like positive values, and no special formatting is applied to text.

If a number format puts negative values inside parentheses, the positive number format portion often pads the positive values with a space that is the same width as a right parenthesis. To indicate this, you add an underscore (by pressing Shift and the hyphen key) followed immediately by a closed parenthesis symbol. By padding positive numbers with a space equivalent to a right parenthesis, you ensure that digits of both positive and negative values line up in a column of cells.

You can assign different colors to a number format. For example, you can create a format that displays the values in green (the color of money!) by adding the code `[GREEN]` at the beginning of the format. A more common use of color is to display just the negative numbers in red (ergo the saying "in the red") by inserting the code `[RED]` right after the semicolon separating the format for positive numbers from the one for negative numbers. Color codes include `[BLACK]`, `[BLUE]`, `[CYAN]`, `[GREEN]`, `[MAGENTA]`, `[RED]`, `[WHITE]`, `[YELLOW]`, and `[COLOR n]` where *n* is the number of the Standard Color between 1 and 16 that you want to select from the Excel color palette. (To see the palette and its colors, choose Tools➪Options and then select the Color tab. When assigning a number to a color, count from left to right across each row: 1 to 8 across the top row and 9 to 16 across the second row and so on.)

Date number formats use a series of abbreviations for month, day, and year that are separated by characters, such as a dash (—) or a slash (/). The code `m` inserts the month as a number; `mmm` inserts the month as three-letter abbreviation, such as Apr or Oct; `mmmm` spells out the entire month, such as April or October. The code `d` inserts the date as a number; `dd` inserts the date as a number with a leading zero, such as 04 or 07; `ddd` inserts the date as a three-letter abbreviation of the day of the week, such as Mon or Tue; `dddd` inserts the full name of the day of the week, such as Monday or Tuesday. The code `yy` inserts the last two digits of the year, such as 05 or 07; `yyyy` inserts all four digits of the year, such as 2005, 2007, and so on.

Time number formats use a series of abbreviations for the hour, minutes, and seconds. The code `h` inserts the number of the hour; `hh` inserts the number of the hour with leading zeros, such as 02 or 06. The code `m` inserts the minutes; the code `mm` inserts the minutes with leading zeros, such as 01 or 09. The code `s` inserts the number of seconds; `ss` inserts the seconds with leading zeros, such as 03 or 08. Add `AM/PM` or `am/pm` to have Excel tell time on a 12-hour clock, and add either `AM` (or `am`) or `PM` (or `pm`) to the time number depending upon whether the date is before or after noon. Without these AM/PM codes, Excel displays the time number on a 24-hour clock, just like the military does. (For example, 2:00 PM on a 12-hour clock is expressed as 1400 on a 24-hour clock.)

So that's all you really need to know about making some sense of all those strange format codes that you see when you select the Custom category on the Number tab of the Format Cells dialog box.

Designing your own number formats

Armed with a little knowledge on the whys and wherefores of interpreting Excel number format codes, you are ready to see how to use these codes to create your own custom number formats. The reason for going through all that code business is that in order to create a custom number format, you have to type in your own codes.

To create a custom format, follow this series of steps:

1. **Open a worksheet and enter a sample of the values or text to which you will be applying the custom format.**

   If possible, apply the closest existing format to the sample value as you enter it in its cell (for example, if you're creating a derivative of a Currency format, enter it with the dollar sign, commas, and decimal points that you know you'll want in the custom format).

2. **Use the Format Cells dialog box to apply the closest existing number format to the sample cell.**

3. **Select Custom in the Category list box and then edit the codes applied by the existing number format that you chose in the Type list box until the value in the Sample section appears exactly as you want it.**

What could be simpler? Ah, but Step 3, there's the rub: editing weird format codes and getting them just right so that they produce exactly the kind of number formatting that you're looking for!

Actually, creating your own number format isn't as bad as it first sounds, because you "cheat" by selecting a number format that uses as many of the codes as possible that you need in the new custom number that you're creating. Then you use the Sample area to keep a careful eye on the results as you edit the codes in the existing number format. For example, suppose that you want to create a custom date format to use on the current date that you enter with Excel's built-in NOW function (see Book III, Chapter 3 for details). You want this date format to display the full name of the current month (January, February, and so on), followed by two digits for the date and four digits for the year, such as November 06, 2007.

To do this, use the Function Wizard to insert the current date into a worksheet cell; then with this cell selected, open the Format Cells dialog box and scroll down through the Custom category Type list box on the Number tab until you see the date codes m/d/yy h:mm. Highlight these codes and then edit them as follows in the Type text box directly above:

```
mmmm dd, yyyy
```

The mmmm format code inserts the full name of the month in the custom format; dd inserts two digits for the day (including a leading zero, like 02 and 03); the yyyy code inserts the year. The other elements in this custom format are the space between the mmmm and dd codes and a comma and a space between the dd and yyyy codes (these being purely "punctuational" considerations in the custom format).

What if you want to do something even fancier and create a custom format that tells you something like "Today is Saturday, January 11, 2007" when you format a cell containing the NOW function? Well, you select your first custom format and add a little bit to the front of it, as follows:

```
"Today is" dddd, mmmm dd, yyyy
```

In this custom format, you've added two more elements: Today is and dddd. The Today is code tells Excel to enter the text between the quotation marks verbatim; the dddd code tells the program to insert the whole name of the day of the week. And you thought this was going to be a hard section!

Next, suppose that you want to create a really colorful number format — one that displays positive values in blue, negative values in red (what else?), zero values in green, and text in cyan. Further suppose that you want commas to separate groups of thousands in the values, no decimal places to appear (whole numbers only, please), and negative values to appear inside parentheses (instead of using that tiny little minus sign at the start). Sound complex? Hah, this is a piece of cake.

Take four blanks cells in a new worksheet and enter **1200** in the first cell, **-8000** in the second cell, **0** in the third cell, and the text **Hello There!** in the fourth cell. Then select all four cells as a range (starting with the one containing 1200 as the first cell of the range). Open the Format Cells dialog box and select the Number tab and Number in the Category list. Then select the #,##0_);[Red](#,##0) codes in the Custom category Type list box (it's the seventh set down from the top of the list box) and edit them as follows:

```
[Blue]#,##0_);[Red](#,##0);[Green];[Cyan]
```

Click OK. That's all there is to that. When you return to the worksheet, the cell with 1200 appears in blue as 1,200, the -8000 appears in red as (8,000), the 0 appears in green, and the text "Hello There!" appears in a lovely cyan.

Before you move on, you should know about a particular custom format because it can come in really handy from time to time. I'm referring to the custom format that hides whatever has been entered in the cells. You can use this custom format to temporarily mask the display of confidential information used in calculating the worksheet before you print and distribute the worksheet. This custom format provides an easy way to avoid distributing confidential and sensitive information while protecting the integrity of the worksheet calculations at the same time.

To create a custom format that masks the display of the data in a cell selection, you simply create an "empty" format that contains just the semicolon separators in a row:

```
;;;
```

This is one custom format that you can probably type by yourself!

After creating this format, you can blank out a range of cells simply by selecting them and then selecting this three-semicolon custom format in the Format Cells dialog box. To bring back a cell range that's been blanked out with this custom format, simply select what now looks like blank cells and then select one of the other (visible) formats that are available. If the cell range contains text and values that normally should use a variety of different formats, first use General to make them visible. After the contents are back on display, format the cells in smaller groups or individually, as required.

All about Alignment

You can use Excel's Alignment options both on the Formatting toolbar and the Alignment tab of the Options to change the way cell entries are displayed within their cells. *Alignment* refers to both the horizontal and vertical placement of the characters in an entry with regard to its cell boundaries as well as the orientation of the characters and how they are read. Horizontally, Excel automatically right-aligns all numeric entries and left-aligns all text entries in their cells (referred to as General alignment). Vertically, Excel aligns all types of cell entries with the bottom of their cells.

Excel offers you the following Horizontal Text alignment choices:

- **General** (the default) to right-align a numeric entry and left-align a text entry in its cell.
- **Left (Indent)** to left-align the entry in its cell and indent the characters from the left edge of the cell by the number of characters entered in the Indent combo box (which is 0 by default).
- **Center** to center any type of cell entry in its cell.

- **Right (Indent)** to right-align the entry in its cell and indent the characters from the right edge of the cell by the number of characters entered in the Indent combo box (which is 0 by default).
- **Fill** to repeat the entry until its characters fill the entire cell display. When you use this option, Excel automatically increases or reduces the repetitions of the characters in the cell as you adjust the width of its column.
- **Justify** to spread out a text entry with spaces so that the text is aligned with the left and right edges of its cell. If necessary to justify the text, Excel automatically wraps the text onto more than one line in the cell and increases the height of its row. If you use the Justify option on numbers, Excel left-aligns the values in their cells just as if you had selected the Left align option.
- **Center Across Selection** to center a text entry over selected blank cells in columns to the right of the cell entry.

For text entries in the worksheet, you can also add the Wrap Text check box option to any of the horizontal alignment choices. When you select the Wrap Text option, Excel automatically wraps the text entry to multiple lines within its cells while maintaining the type of alignment that you've selected (something that automatically happens when you select the Justify alignment option).

Instead of wrapping text that naturally increases the row height to accommodate the additional lines, you can use the Shrink to Fit check box option to have Excel reduce the size of the text in the cell sufficiently, so that all of its characters fit within their current column widths.

In addition to all these horizontal alignment choices, Excel offers the following Vertical Text alignment options:

- **Top** (the default) to align any type of cell entry with the top edge of its cell
- **Center** to center any type of cell entry between the top and bottom edges of its cell
- **Bottom** to align any type of cell entry with the bottom edge of its cell
- **Justify** to wrap the text of a cell entry on different lines spread out with blank space so that they are vertically aligned between the top and bottom edges of the cell
- **Distributed** to wrap the text of the cell entry on different lines distributed evenly between the top and bottom edge of its cell

Finally, as part of its alignment options, Excel lets you alter the *orientation* or the angle of the characters in an entry in its cell and *text direction* or the way the characters are read (left-to-right being the way for European languages and right-to-left being the way for some languages, such as Hebrew and Arabic (Chinese characters can also sometimes be read from right-to-left, as well).

Using the Alignment tab

You must use the options on the Alignment tab of the Format Cells dialog box when you need to use any other horizontal text alignment besides left alignment, centering, right alignment, or centering over a group of cells, which are available on the Formatting toolbar by clicking the Left Align, Center, Right Align, and Merge and Center buttons, respectively. Figure 2-12 shows you the options on the Alignment tab of the Format Cells dialog box. Remember that you can get to this tab quickly by pressing Ctrl+1 to open the Format Cells dialog box and then clicking the Alignment tab with the mouse.

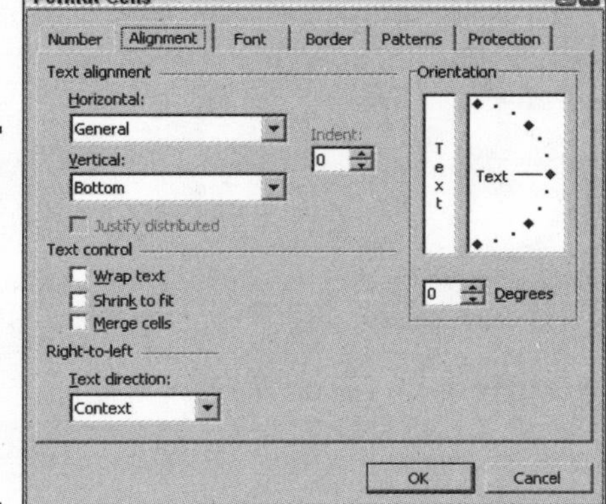

Figure 2-12: Using the alignment options on the Alignment tab of the Format Cells dialog box.

Wrapping text entries in their cells

You can use the Wrap Text check box in the Text Control section of the Alignment tab to have Excel create a multi-line entry from a long text entry that would otherwise spill over to blank cells to the right. In creating a multi-line entry in a cell, the program also automatically increases the height of its row if that is required to display all of the text.

To get an idea of how text wrap works in cells, compare Figures 2-13 and 2-14. Figure 2-13 shows you two long text entries that spill over to succeeding blank cells to the right. Figure 2-14 shows you these same entries after they have been formatted with the Wrap Text option. The first long text entry is in cell A2 and the second in cell A3. They both use General alignment (same as Left for text) with the Wrap Text option.

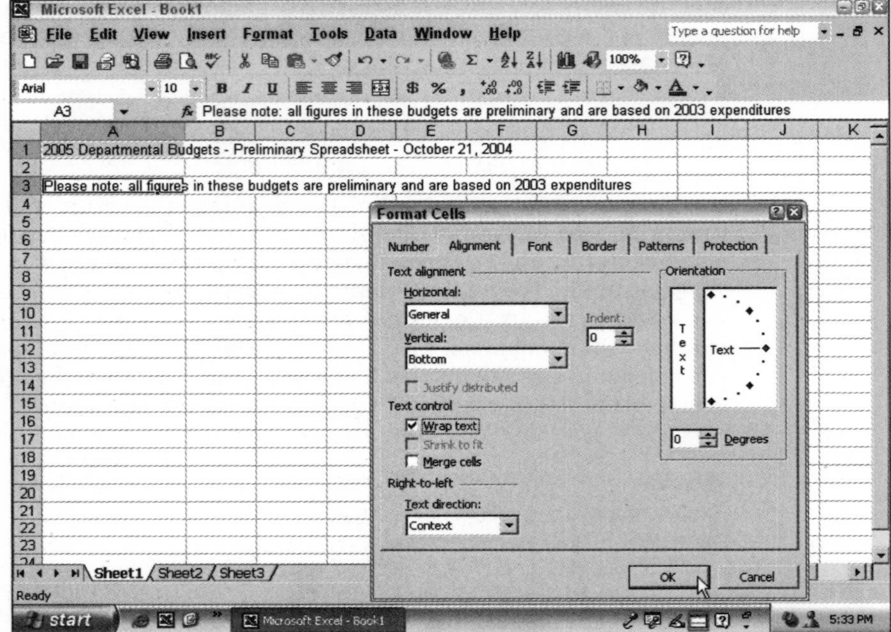

Figure 2-13: Spreadsheet with long text entries that spill over into blank cells on the right.

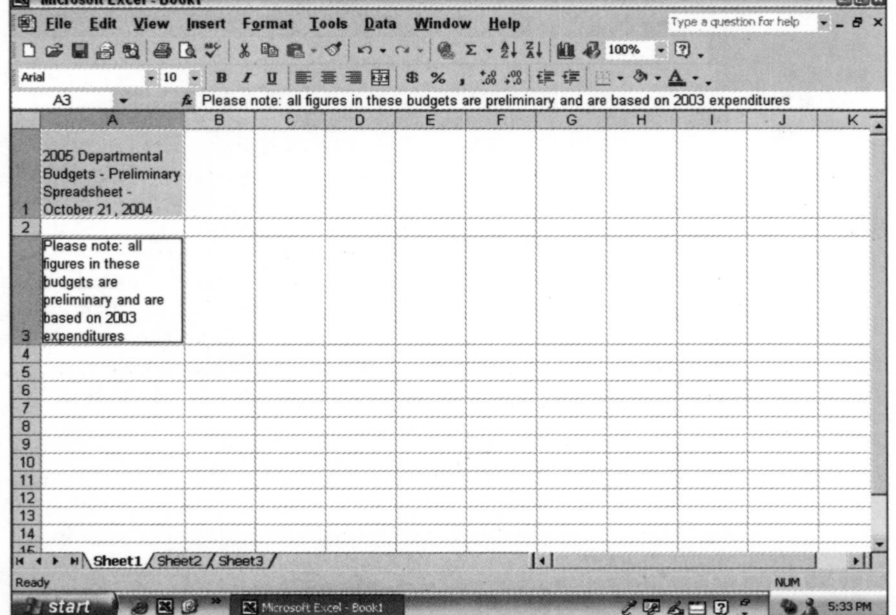

Figure 2-14: Spreadsheet after wrapping long text entries in their cells.

When you create multi-line text entries with the Wrap Text option, you can decide where each line breaks by inserting a new paragraph. To do this, you put Excel in Edit mode by clicking the insertion point in the formula bar at the place where a new line should start and press Alt+Enter. When you press the Enter key to return to Ready mode, Excel inserts an invisible paragraph marker at the insertion point that starts a new line both on the formula bar and within the cell with the wrapped text.

If you ever want to remove the paragraph marker and rejoin text split on different lines, click the insertion point at the beginning of the line that you want to join on the formula bar and press the Backspace key.

Reorienting your entries

Excel makes it easy to change the *orientation* (that is, the angle of the baseline on which the characters rest) of the characters in a cell entry. To change this orientation by rotating up or down the baseline of the characters, select the cells whose angle you want to change, open the Alignment tab on the Format Cells dialog box (Ctrl+1), and then do one of the following things in the Orientation area of this tab:

- Enter the value of the angle of rotation for the new orientation in the Degrees text box or click the Spin buttons to select this angle — enter a positive value (such as 45) to have the characters angled above the normal 90-degree line of orientation and a negative value (such as -45) to have them angled above this line.
- Click the point on the sample Text box on the right side of the Orientation area that corresponds to the angle of rotation that you want for the characters in the selected cells.
- Click the sample Text box on the left side of the Orientation area to have the characters stacked one on top of the other (as shown in the orientation of the word "Text" in this sample box).

After changing the orientation of entries in a selection in the Format Cells dialog box, Excel automatically adjusts the height of the rows in the cell selection to accommodate the rotation up or down of the cell entries. Figure 2-15 shows a spreadsheet after rotating the column headings of the data table up 45 degrees. Note how Excel increased the height of row 2 to accommodate this change.

	A	B	C	D	E	F	G	H	I	J
1	Production Schedule for 2003									
2		Apr-03	May-03	Jun-03	Jul-03	Aug-03	Sep-03	Oct-03	Nov-03	Dec-03
3	Part 100	500	485	437.5	505	482.5	540	441	550	345
4	Part 101	175	169.75	153.125	176.75	168.875	189	154.35	192.5	200
5	Part 102	350	339.5	306.25	353.5	337.75	378	308.7	385	350
6	Part 103	890	863.3	778.75	898.9	858.85	961.2	784.98	979	885
7	Total	1915	1857.55	1675.625	1934.15	1847.975	2068.2	1689.03	2106.5	1780

Figure 2-15: Spreadsheet after rotating the column headings up 45 degrees.

Fancy Fonts and Colors

You can assign any of the fonts that you've installed for your printer to cells in a worksheet. Along with selecting a new *font* (also known as a *typeface*), you can choose a new font size (in points), assign a font style (such as bold, italic, underline, or strikeout), as well as change the color of the font.

Note that you can always tell the font and font size of the cell entry in the active cell by looking at the font name displayed in the Font combo box and point size displayed in the Font Size combo box on the Formatting toolbar. You can also tell which, if any, text attributes are assigned to the entry by looking at the Bold, Italic, and Underline buttons on this toolbar. Excel indicates which of these attributes have been assigned to the cell by outlining the **B**, *I*, or U icons in a box.

Selecting fonts and colors from the Formatting toolbar

You can change the font, font size, font style, and font color from the Formatting toolbar. The only aspects you can't change or assign are the type of the underlining and special font styles including strikethrough, superscript, and subscript.

To change the font with the Formatting toolbar:

- ✦ Select the cell, cell range, or nonadjacent selection to which you want to assign the new font, size, style, or color
- ✦ To assign a new font to the selection, click the Font drop-down button and then click the font in the drop-down menu

- To assign a new point size to the selection, click the Font pop-up button and then click the size on the pop-up menu (you can also do this by clicking the Font text box, typing the point size, and pressing Enter)
- To assign a new font style to a selection, click the appropriate tool in the Formatting toolbar: click the Bold button (the one with **B**) to bold the selection, the Italic tool (the one with *I*) to italicize the selection, and the Underline tool (the one with the U) to underline the selection
- To assign a new font color, click the Font Color pop-up button and then click the new color in the pop-up palette

Note that you can immediately remove any font change that you make by clicking the Undo button on the Standard toolbar (or by pressing Ctrl+Z) and that you can also remove boldface, italics, and underlining assigned to a cell selection by clicking the appropriate button (Bold, Italic, and Underline) on the Formatting toolbar. This action removes the light gray box that outlines the button's **B**, *I*, or U icon.

Selecting fonts and colors in the Format Cells dialog box

You can also select a new font, font size, font styles, and, font color for your selection in the Font tab of the Format Cells dialog box (Ctrl+1). Figure 2-16 shows the Font tab of the Format Cells dialog box that appears when an empty cell that uses the Normal style is active. In this figure, the current Font is Arial, the Font Style is Regular, the Font Size is 10 (points), the Underline is None, and the Color is Automatic.

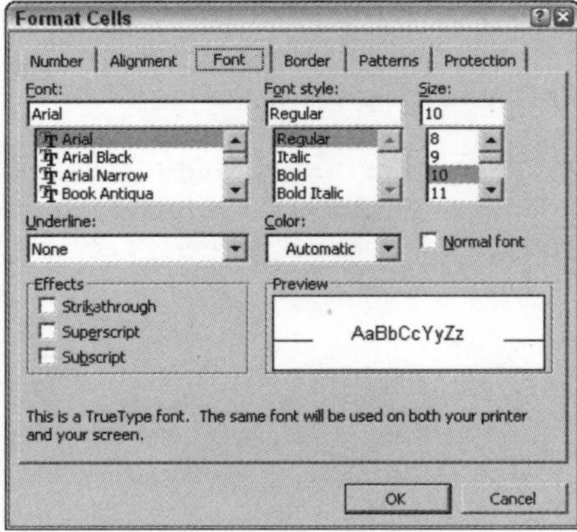

Figure 2-16: You can change fonts, font sizes, attributes, and colors on the Font tab.

The Automatic color in Excel always refers to the Window Font color that is currently selected in the Display Properties dialog box (Advanced Appearance in Windows XP). This color is black unless you change it in the Display Properties dialog box (done by right-clicking the Windows desktop and clicking Properties on the shortcut menu) and then specify a new Font color for the Window item. To do this in one of the versions of Windows 98, click Window in the Item pop-up menu on the Appearance tab and then click a new color in the Color pop-up palette next to the Font combo box right below. In Windows XP, you need to click the Advanced button on the Appearance tab and then click Window in the Item pop-up menu before you click a new color in the Color pop-up palette next to the Font drop-down box below in the Advanced Appearance dialog box.

Basic Borders and Patterns

Excel makes it easy to add borders and various shading patterns to cells in the worksheet. You can use the borders to outline tables of data — particularly important cells — or to underscore rows of key data. You can also apply various shading patterns to cells to draw attention to significant aspects of the spreadsheet.

When adding borders and shading, you can make your job a great deal easier by removing the light gray gridlines used in the Workbook document window to indicate the borders of the cells in worksheet. To remove these gridlines, click the Gridlines check box on the View tab of the Options dialog box (Tools⇨Options) to remove its checkmark. After you've dispensed with a worksheet's gridlines, you can immediately tell whether you've added the kind of borders that you want and better judge the effect of the color and shading changes that you make.

Note that removing the display of the gridlines in the Workbook window has no effect whatsoever on the appearance of gridlines in a printed copy of the spreadsheet. To remove gridlines from the printout of a worksheet as well, you must deselect the Gridlines check box on the Sheet tab of the Page Setup dialog box, which you open by choosing File⇨Page Setup on the Menu bar.

Right on the borderline

When applying borderlines to a cell selection, you have a choice between using the Borders palette that's attached to the Borders button on the Formatting toolbar (remember that this is one of those tear-off palettes that you can detach from the toolbar by dragging the bar at the top of the palette) and using the options on the Border tab of the Format Cells. You can compare the options offered by each in Figure 2-17, which shows the Format Cells dialog box with the Border tab selected next to a floating Borders palette.

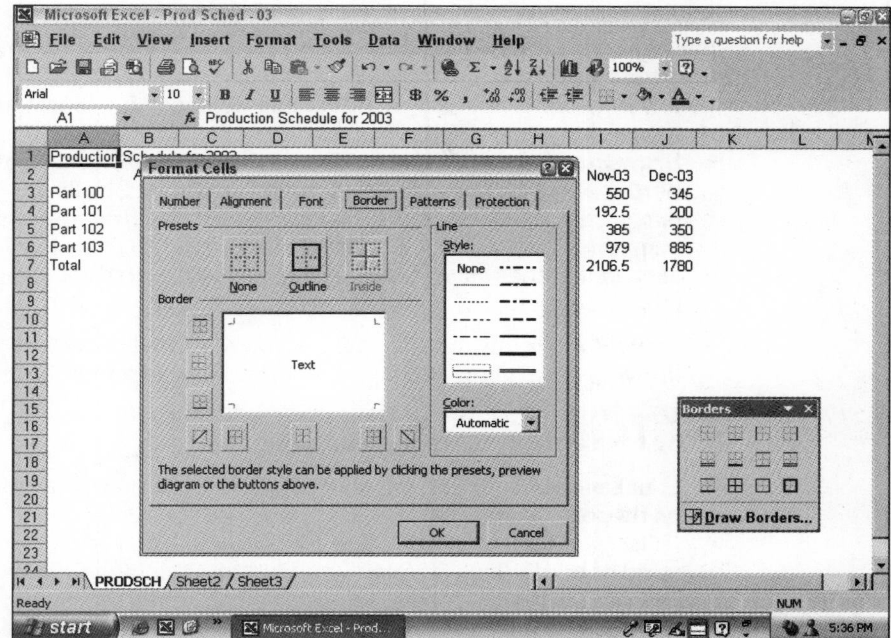

Figure 2-17: Comparing the options on the Border tab with those on the Borders tear-off palette.

To apply borders to a cell selection by using the options on the Border tab of the Format Cells dialog box, click the Preset or Border button for the particular type of border that you want to apply. As you click these buttons, the sample area (the list box that contains the word *text*) shows you what type of borderline will be drawn around or through the cells that you have selected in the worksheet. To remove a borderline that you select in error, simply click the same Preset or Border button that you used to apply the line.

While defining the borderlines to apply in the Border tab, you can select a new style for the borderlines by clicking the Line style in the Style sample area. To select a new color (besides boring old black) for the borderlines that you're about to apply, click the color in the Color pop-up palette.

When using the Borders palettes to assign borderlines to a cell selection, your options are limited to just the Border buttons displayed on the palette. This means that you don't have as much choice in terms of line style and type of borderlines (in other words, you can't be applying any dashed diagonal borderlines from this palette). You also can't change the color of the borderlines from the Borders palette.

What you can do, however (that you can't do from the Border tab), is draw your borders directly onto the cells by using the Draw Borders item located at the very bottom of the Borders palette. When you click this item, Excel opens a Borders dialog box that contains the following four items:

- **Draw Border** pop-up button that enables you to choose between Draw Border and Draw Border Grid items. Click Draw Border to draw an outline border only around the cell range that you drag through with the pencil mouse pointer. Click Draw Border Grid to draw borders around each cell in the range that you drag through with the pencil-plus-grid mouse pointer.
- **Erase Border** button that enables you to erase borderlines that you've drawn by dragging the eraser mouse pointer through those cells.
- **Line Style** drop-down list box that enables you to select a new line style by clicking it on its drop-down menu.
- **Line Color** button that enables you to select a new color by clicking it on its pop-up color palette.

To get rid of borderlines that you've added to a cell range, no matter which method you used to add them, select the range and then click the No Border button (the very first one) on the Border button's pop-up palette. Note that if this button was the last selected, you can select it simply by clicking the Border button on the Formatting toolbar — you don't have to click the Border pop-up button, open the palette, and then click the No Border button.

Pretty patterns

You can add shading patterns to your cells in addition to borders or instead of using them. To select a new pattern for a cell selection, click the Patterns tab in the Format Cells dialog box (Ctrl+1) and then click the Pattern pop-up button to open the Pattern pop-up palette (shown in Figure 2-18). On this palette, you then click the type of pattern to use at the top of the pop-up palette. If you want to change the color of the lines used in the pattern, click the Pattern pop-up button again and then click the color square that you want to use in the Pattern pop-up palette.

If you want to add a fill color or background color to the cell selection (a color that appears behind any shading that you apply), click the desired color in the Color section of the Patterns tab in the Format Cells dialog box. Note that you can also assign a new fill color to a cell selection by clicking the desired color square from the pop-up palette attached to the Fill Color button on the Formatting toolbar.

You can also get rid of all shading and any fill color in a cell selection by clicking the No Fill button at the top of the Fill Color button's pop-up palette.

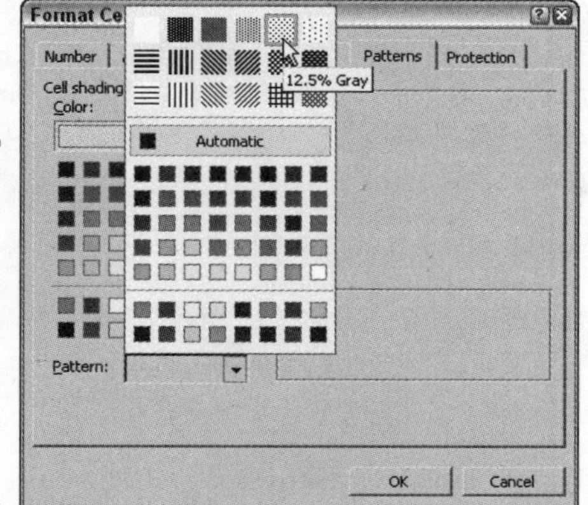

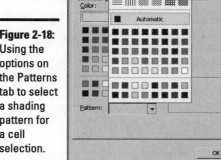

Figure 2-18: Using the options on the Patterns tab to select a shading pattern for a cell selection.

You AutoFormat It

AutoFormat has it hands-down when it comes to formatting a typical data table like the one shown in Figure 2-19. All you have to do when using AutoFormat is to position the cell pointer in some cell in the table, choose Format➪AutoFormat on the Menu bar, and then click the table format that you feel is best suited to the data in the AutoFormat dialog box before you click OK. That's all there is to it! Excel takes the raw, unformatted text and numbers in your table and applies to them the number, font, border, patterns, and alignment settings called for in the table format that you select. At the same time, it automatically adjusts both the column widths and row heights of the table to accommodate all these modifications to the table's cells.

The AutoFormat dialog box contains 16 different predefined table formats with descriptive names such as Accounting1, 2, and 3, and List1, 2, 3, and 4, that you can apply to any data table that has column headings in the top row, row headings in the first column, and numerical data entries in the rest of the cells of the table.

The 17th predefined format in the AutoFormat dialog box is called None. You select this table format only when you want to remove all the formatting applied earlier by selecting one of the other 16 table formats. Selecting None in the AutoFormat dialog box effectively puts your table back to square one.

Note that if your table has a title that you want formatted (like the one shown in Figure 2-2), be sure to place that title in the cell in the row immediately above the one with the column headings (don't leave a blank row) in the same column with the row headings (in the example shown in Figure 2-19, this cell happens to be cell A1).

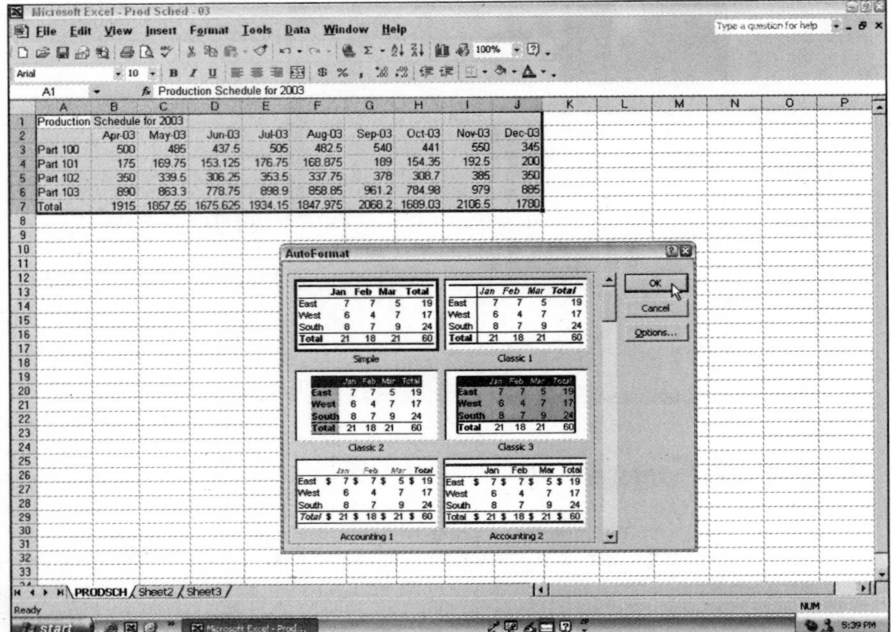

Figure 2-19: Selecting a table format in the AutoFormat dialog box.

All the predefined table formats automatically format a table's title (and many automatically center it over all the columns of the table by using the Merge and Center feature) even though this formatting change is not shown as part of the sample table format displayed in the AutoFormat dialog box. If your table uses a blank row to separate the table title from the table data, Excel displays an Alert dialog box indicating that the program can't determine the range of cells that you want to format. In such a case, after closing the Alert dialog box, you must select all the cells to be formatted and then open the AutoFormat dialog box again (Format⇨AutoFormat) and choose the table format to apply to the cell selection.

Although you can't create new table formats, you can modify which formats to apply when using any of the predefined table formats offered in the AutoFormat dialog box. To do this, open the AutoFormat dialog box and then click the Options button. This action expands the AutoFormat dialog box so that it includes a section called Formats to Apply at the very bottom of the dialog box (shown in Figure 2-19). You can then modify the selected table format by deselecting any of the formats (Number, Font, Alignment, Border, and so on) that you don't want used when you apply this particular table format to your selected cells (all check box format options in the Formats to Apply area are automatically selected for each predefined table format).

Conditionally Yours

Excel's Conditional Formatting feature enables you to set up formatting for a cell that is used only when the entry in that cell meets specific conditions that you set up. Perhaps the most common use for Conditional Formatting is in a projected income spreadsheet where the color and shading in the Net Income cell changes if the value in the cell falls below a certain target value. For example, you can set up a condition that says when the value in the cell is less than $500,000, display the value in a bold, red font with yellow shading enclosed in a red border. This way, the wild formatting in the Net Income cell immediately alerts you to the fact whenever you fail to meet your goal when playing around with different scenarios in the projected income statement.

To apply conditional formats to a cell selection, follow these general steps:

1. **Select the cell or cell range to which you want to Conditional Formatting applied.**
2. **Choose Format⇨Conditional Formatting on the Excel Menu bar.**

   This action opens the Conditional Formatting dialog box containing a Condition 1 area (you can set up to three different conditions in this dialog box) with the controls for setting the first condition and the ensuing formatting. This area also contains a sample box to give you an idea of how the conditional formats will affect your cell selection when the condition is TRUE.
3. **Use the drop-down list boxes in the Condition 1 area of the Conditional Formatting dialog box (similar to the one shown in Figure 2-20) to set up the condition that must be met before the formatting is applied.**

   The first drop-down list box contains the option Cell Value Is that enables Conditional Formatting to evaluate the value of the numbers in the cell selection, whether they are numbers you input directly (called *constants*) or numbers returned by formula calculation (*called expressions*). To have Excel apply conditional formats only when a Logical formula is TRUE (see Book III, Chapter 2 for details on Logical formulas), you select the Formula Is option on the pop-up menu that's attached to the first combo box. Note that when you select the Formula Is option, the criteria combo box disappears, leaving a single text box where you select the cell in the worksheet that contains the Logical formula or enter that formula directly.

The second drop-down list box establishes the operator used in evaluating the condition. By default, this box contains the operator, between, that enables you to set the range of values that numbers in the cell selection must fall within. You designate this range of values in the two text boxes to the right by selecting cells that contain these upper and lower values or by entering them into these combo boxes directly.

To use another operator, click the drop-drop button attached to the second drop-down list box and select Not Between, Equal To, Not Equal To, Greater Than, Less Than, Greater Than or Equal To, or Less Than or Equal To on its drop-down list. Then, designate the values to use when evaluating this new criteria in the accompanying combo box or boxes (only the Between and Not Between criteria require more than one value to establish the upper and lower limit of the range).

4. **Click the Format button and then select the formats that you want applied to the cell selection when Condition 1 is met by using the options on the Font, Border, and Patterns tabs in the Format Cells dialog box and then click OK.**

   The Format Cells dialog box that opens when you click the Format button is an abbreviated version of the normal Format Cells dialog box. This one contains only three tabs (Font, Border, and Patterns) that you can use in setting up the conditional formats for your cell selection. The options on these three tabs, however, are identical to those found on the corresponding tabs in the full-blown version of Format Cells dialog box, so you should have no trouble using them.

5. **To set up a second condition that applies a different set of formatting when TRUE, click the Add button and then use the controls in the Condition 2 area to set up the condition and formatting to be used.**

   When using the Cell Value Is option, you can set up three different conditions with different formats to be used. For example, you can set up a set of formatting to be used when a target cell contains a particular number, another set when the cell's value exceeds the number, and yet another set when it is below that number. So, you'd use the Equal To criteria in Condition 1 to establish the formatting when the target value is reached, the Greater Than criteria in Condition 2 to establish the formatting when the target value is exceeded, and the Less Than criteria in Condition 3 to establish the formatting when the target value is not met.

6. **To set up a third condition that applies yet a different set of formatting when TRUE, click the Add button and then use the controls in the Condition 3 area to set up the condition and formatting to be used.**
7. **Click OK to close the Conditional Formatting dialog box and have Excel format the cell selection based on whether the condition(s) that you set up are TRUE or FALSE.**

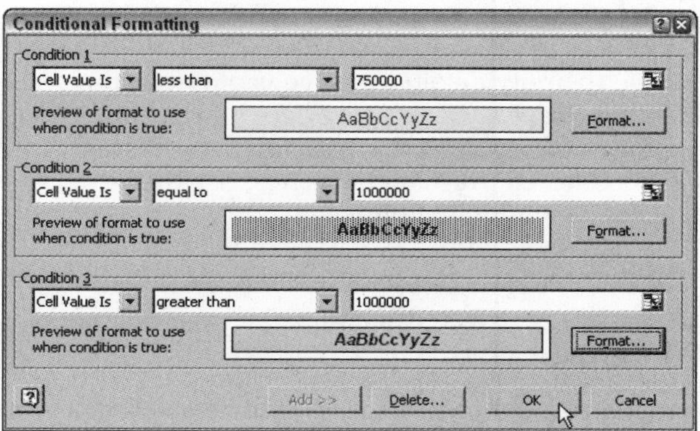

Figure 2-20: Setting up the formatting condition in the Conditional Formatting dialog box.

As soon as you close the Conditional Formatting dialog box, Excel applies the condition(s) to the current cell and formats it accordingly.

To copy Conditional Formatting that you've set up in a cell to another cell or cell range, use the Format Painter on the Standard toolbar (see "Hiring out the Format Painter" earlier in this chapter for details). To use different formatting with a condition, open the Conditional Formatting dialog box, click the Format button in area of the condition to be modified (Condition 1, 2, or 3), and then click the appropriate tab in the Format Cells dialog box and change the necessary format options. To get rid of all formatting on a particular tab, click the tab and then click its Clear button.

To get rid of a particular condition specified by the Conditional Formatting in a cell selection, open the Conditional Formatting dialog box, click the Delete button, and then click the check box for the condition or conditions (Condition 1, Condition 2, and/or Condition 3) in the Delete Conditions For dialog box that appears.

To get rid of Conditional Formatting applied to a cell selection, choose Edit⇨Clear⇨Formats on the menu bar. To find cells in the current worksheet that have Conditional Formatting applied to them, open the Go To dialog box (F5 or Ctrl+G), click the Special button and then click the Conditional

Formats radio button in the Go To Special dialog box. Leave the All radio button below the Data Validation selected when you click OK if you want to locate every cell that uses Conditional Formatting. Click the Same radio button before you click OK if you want Excel to find only those cells that use the same type of Conditional Formatting as the active cell in the current cell selection.

Doing It with Styles

As an alternative to applying different types of formatting to selected cell entries separately, Excel Style feature offers you the ability to apply a combination of attributes to any selection in a single operation. A style can include up to six different format characteristics that you can apply to a selection of cells, including the following:

- ✦ The number format to be applied to numeric entries
- ✦ The horizontal and vertical alignment and/or orientation to be applied to the cell entries
- ✦ The font, font size, font style, or color to be applied to the cell entries
- ✦ The type of border to be applied to the cells
- ✦ The shading patterns to be applied to the cells
- ✦ The protection status to be applied to the cells (cells can be locked or unlocked and the contents of locked cells can be hidden or unhidden on the formula bar — see Book IV, Chapter 3 for complete information on protecting a worksheet)

When creating a style for your worksheet, you can include any combination of these six formatting characteristics that provides the most effective formatting. Formatting your spreadsheet with styles offers the following advantages over formatting with it with separate Excel format commands:

- ✦ Styles allow you to apply many different types of formatting to a cell selection in a single operation.
- ✦ Styles ensure consistent formatting in every cell in the worksheet that uses a particular style.
- ✦ Changes that you make to a style are immediately and globally put into effect in every cell that uses that style.
- ✦ Styles that you use regularly don't have to be recreated in each new worksheet that you start — they can be merged (copied) from worksheets that you've already created.

Using the predefined styles

Each new workbook that you start comes with six predefined styles that you can use right away. These styles include:

- **Normal** — is the default style applied to all cells in a new worksheet. This style (shown in Figure 2-21) sets the number format to General, the font to 10-point Arial, horizontal alignment to General and vertical alignment to Bottom Aligned, No Borders, No Shading, and protection to Locked (preventing any changes to the cell's contents when the worksheet is protected).
- **Comma** — sets the number format to the Comma Style (same as clicking the Comma Style button on the Formatting toolbar).
- **Comma (0)** — sets the number format to the Comma Style format without any decimal places.
- **Currency** — sets the number format to the Currency style format (same as clicking the Currency Style button on the Formatting toolbar).
- **Currency (0)** — sets the number format to the Currency style format without any decimal places (making your financial figures all dollars and no cents).
- **Percent** — sets the number format to Percent style (same as clicking the Percent Style button on the Formatting toolbar).

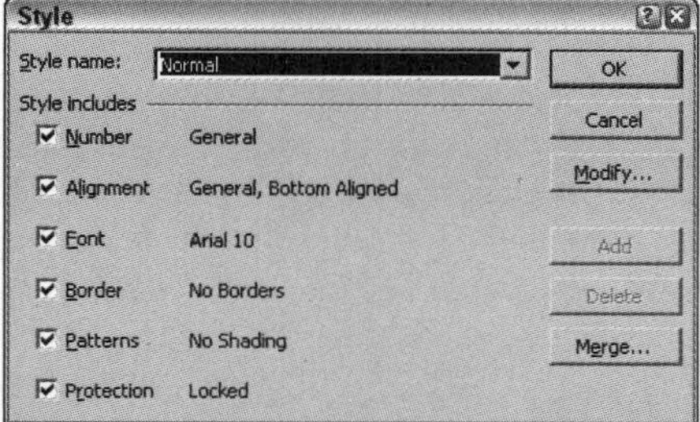

Figure 2-21: Selecting a cell style in the Style dialog box.

Keep in mind that you can modify the formatting applied by any of the six predefined styles. Simply open the Style dialog box (Format⇨Style), click the name of the style to modify in the Style Name pop-up menu, click the Modify button and then make changes to any of the formatting settings on the Number, Alignment, Font, Border, Patterns, or Protection tabs in the standard Format Cells dialog box that appears.

Defining a new style by example

By far the easiest way to create a new style is by example. When you create a style by example, you choose a cell that already displays all of the formatting attributes (applied separately using the techniques discussed previously in this chapter) that you want included in the new style. Then, you follow these simple steps to create the new style by using the formatting in sample cell:

1. **Position the cell pointer in the cell with the formatting that you want in the new style.**
2. **Choose Format⇨Style on the Excel Menu bar.**

   This action opens the Style dialog box with the Normal style selected in the Style Name combo box and the attributes for the Normal style are listed in Style Includes section of the dialog box (refer to Figure 2-21).
3. **Type the name for the new style in the Style Name text box (replacing Normal).**

   The settings displayed in the Style Includes area of the Style dialog box are immediately updated to reflect the formatting applied in the selected sample cell. Now, all that remains to do is to add the new style definition to the Style Name drop-down list before closing the dialog box.
4. **Click the Add button to add the style name to the Style Name drop-down list and then click OK to close the Style dialog box.**

When defining a style by example, select only one cell that you know contains all of the formatting characteristics that you want in the new style. This way, you avoid the potential problem of selecting cells that don't share the same formatting. If you select cells that use different formatting when defining a style by example, the new style will contain only the formatting that all cells share in common.

Creating a new style from scratch

You can also create styles from scratch by defining each of its formatting characteristics in the Style dialog box as follows:

1. **Position the cell pointer in a cell that doesn't have any formatting applied to it and then choose Format⇨Style on the Excel menu bar.**

   This action opens the Style dialog box with the Normal style selected in the Style Name combo box and the attributes for the Normal style are listed in Style Includes section of the dialog box (as shown in Figure 2-21).

2. **Type a name for the new style that you are defining in the Style Name combo box (replacing Normal in the Style Name combo box).**

   Now you need to select the formatting settings for the new style.

3. **Click the Modify button in the Style dialog box.**

   This action opens the standard Format Cells dialog box where you can use the options on its six tabs (Number, Alignment, Font, Border, Patterns, and Protection) to select all the formatting attributes that you want used when you apply the new style to a cell selection.

4. **After you finish assigning the formatting attributes that you want in the new style in the Format Cells, click OK to return to the Style dialog box.**

   Now all that's left to do is to add the new style to Style Name drop-down list before closing the Style dialog box.

5. **Click the Add button to add the style and then click OK to close the Style dialog box.**

As soon as you click OK, Excel applies the formatting in your newly defined style to the current cell.

Applying styles to a cell selection

To use any of the styles in your worksheet, select the cells to which you want to apply the style, open the Style dialog box (Format➪Style), click the name of the style in the Style Name drop-down box, and then click OK.

Sometimes after applying a style to a cell selection, you may find that you want to override the style's formatting attributes for just some of the cells. For example, after applying a style to all the column headings in a table that italicizes their text, you may want to apply shading and bold to just the last column heading that contains the label *YTD Totals*. When you need to override a style that you've applied to a cell, simply select the cell and then select the appropriate formatting attributes, as described previously in this chapter.

If you later modify a style that you've overridden in certain cells, Excel makes the necessary formatting changes in all cells that use the style (including those where the style has been overridden) while still retaining any attributes that you applied afterwards. For example, if you change the column heading style so that the font no longer uses the italic style, Excel will change all column headings to normal roman style while still retaining the light shading and bold in the label in the last column containing *YTD Totals*.

If you create a custom style that you use regularly, rather than having to go through the rigmarole of selecting it from the Style dialog box, record a macro that selects the style and then assign the macro to a custom button or shortcut keystroke that you can click or press whenever you need to apply the style to a cell selection (see Book I, Chapter 3 for information on creating custom buttons and Book IX, Chapter 1 for information on recording and assigning macros).

Merging styles into other workbooks

All styles that you create are saved, along with the data and formatting in the worksheet, when you save the file. The only styles, however, that are available when you begin a new worksheet are the six predefined styles provided by Excel. If you have created styles in another workbook that you want to use in a new workbook that you're building or an existing one that you've opened for editing, you can merge them into that workbook as follows:

1. **Open the workbook file containing the styles that you want to copy and use.**

   You must have the workbook containing the styles to merge open, along with the workbook into which these styles are to be copied.

2. **Click the button on the Windows taskbar for the workbook into which the styles will be merged.**

   This action makes the workbook into which the custom styles are to be copied the active one.

3. **Choose Format⇨Style on Excel menu bar.**

   This action opens the Style dialog box.

4. **Click the Merge button.**

   This action opens the Merge Styles dialog box with a list box that displays the file names of all the workbooks that are currently open in Excel.

5. **Click the name of the workbook that contains the styles you want merged into the active workbook and then click OK.**

   This action closes the Merge Styles dialog box. If the worksheet file that you selected contains styles with the same names as the styles defined in the active worksheet (other than the six predefined styles), Excel displays an alert box that asks if you want to merge the styles that have the same names.

6. **Click Yes to replace all styles in the active workbook with those that have the same name in the workbook file that you're copying from. Click No if you don't want the styles in the active workbook to be overwritten, in which case Excel merges the styles with unique names from the other worksheet.**
7. **Click the OK button in the Style dialog box.**

After merging styles from another open workbook, you can close that workbook by clicking its button on the Windows taskbar and then clicking its Close Window. You can then begin using the merged styles, which now appear on the Style Name drop-down list in the Style dialog box.

If you frequently use custom number formats in the worksheets that you work with, you should create custom styles for each of them. By creating styles for custom number formats, you not only make it easier to apply them in a worksheet (they are often difficult to locate on the Number tab of the Format Cells dialog box), but you can also make them available in a new workbook by merging them from an existing workbook.

Chapter 3: Editing Worksheets

In This Chapter

- Opening workbooks for editing
- Using basic cell editing techniques
- Zooming in and out on the worksheet
- Freezing columns and rows on the screen
- Deleting and inserting new data entries in a worksheet
- Copying and moving data entries
- Finding and replacing data entries
- Spell checking a worksheet
- Finding and eliminating errors with the Text to Speech feature

Creating a spreadsheet is almost never a one-time experience. Some of the spreadsheets that you will create with Excel will require routine changes on a regular basis, while others will require more radical changes only once in a while. Regardless of the extent of the changes and their frequency, you can be sure that sooner or later, most of the spreadsheets you create in Excel will require editing.

In this chapter, you find out how to make simple editing changes in a worksheet by modifying the contents of a cell as well as more complex editing changes in your worksheets. These techniques include how to use the Undo and Redo feature, zoom in and out on data, move and copy data; delete data entries and insert new ones, search and replace data entries, and spell check data entries in a worksheet.

However, before you can use any of these fine editing techniques, you have to open the workbook whose contents require editing. So, with that in mind, this chapter starts out by giving you the lowdown on finding and opening workbooks in Excel.

Opening a Workbook

One of the simplest ways to open a workbook for editing in Excel is to open its folder in Windows and then double-click the workbook file icon. If you haven't yet started Excel at the time you open the workbook, Windows automatically launches Excel at the same time that it opens the file. Remember that you can use the My Documents or My Computer desktop shortcuts to locate and then open your workbook files (Excel automatically saves workbook files in your My Documents folder unless you specifically select another folder).

If Excel is already running and you want to open a workbook file for editing from within Excel, you can use the File⇨New or the File⇨Open command to locate and open the file. If you can't remember where you saved the workbook that you need to edit (a common occurrence), you can use the File⇨Search command to locate it and then open it from the Search Results Task Pane.

Opening files from the New Workbook Task Pane

Excel automatically keeps track of the last four workbook files that you opened. If the workbook file that you need to edit is among these four or you know that you saved the file in your My Documents folder, the easiest way to open the file for editing is from the File pull-down menu or the New Workbook Task Pane. Remember that Excel automatically opens this Task pane when you first start Excel (and whenever this Task pane isn't displayed, you can open it by choosing File⇨New or View⇨Task Pane on the Excel Menu bar).

To open a workbook file that was among the last four that you opened, you click its name at the bottom of the File pull-down menu or click its link in the Open a Workbook section at the top of the New Workbook Task pane. To open a workbook file that isn't among the last four but is saved in the My Documents folder, click the More Workbooks link at the bottom of the Open a Workbook section.

This action opens My Documents in the Open dialog box, shown in Figure 3-1, just as if you had chosen the File⇨Open command. You can then open the workbook by double-clicking its file icon or by clicking it and then clicking the Open button.

Opening files with the Open dialog box

If the New Workbook Task Pane isn't open and you know that the file you want to work with is not among the last four that you opened, you can directly display the Open dialog box by choosing File⇨Open on the Menu bar or by pressing the Ctrl+O or Ctrl+F12 keyboard shortcuts.

If the workbook file that you need to edit isn't located in the My Documents folder, you can locate and then open the appropriate folder with the Look In drop-down list or various folder buttons (History, My Documents, Desktop, Favorites, or My Network Places) in the left pane of the Open dialog box.

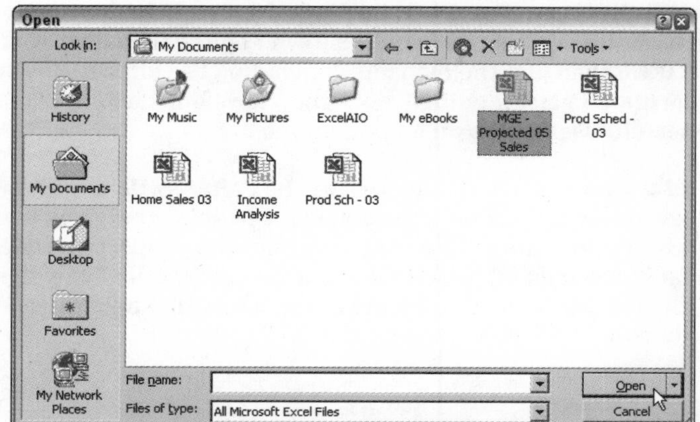

Figure 3-1: Selecting a workbook file to open in the My Documents folder.

If you want to work with a copy of workbook file rather than the original file, click the pop-up button on the right side of the Open button and then click Open as Copy on its pop-up menu. Excel opens a copy with the words "Copy (1) of" preceding the original filename. To rename this workbook after making your edits, choose the File⇨Save As command and then replace or edit the "Copy (1) of" filename in the File Name text box.

To open multiple workbook files in a single folder at the same time, Ctrl+click all their workbook file icons in the folder and after they're all selected, click the Open button in the Open dialog box. Excel opens all of the selected files in the order in which you clicked their icons (see Book II, Chapter 4 for information on working with multiple workbooks).

Changing the file view

The Open dialog box automatically filters the list of files in any folder that you select so that only the workbook files in that folder appear. This is the reason that a folder, which you know contains files, appears empty in the Open dialog box (it's only empty of Excel workbook and template files). If you want to see all the files in the folder — even those not created with Excel — you have to click the Files of Type drop-down list and then click All Files on its pop-up menu.

Most of the time, viewing just the Excel workbook and template files in the current folder is fine (although sometimes you may want to open a Web page that contains spreadsheet information — see Book VIII, Chapter 1 for more on this). As you're browsing through the Excel files in the folder, however, you may want to change the way the information on these files is displayed to help you find the one that you want to edit.

Normally, the Open dialog box displays the Excel file information in a simple list that shows the Excel file icon followed by the filename. To display more information than just the filenames, including the file size, file type, and date that the file was last modified, click the Views button in the Open dialog box and then choose Details on its pop-up menu.

Figure 3-2 shows a typical Open dialog box after switching from the normal List view to the Details view. As you can see, this view gives you four columns of information on each file: Name, Size, Type, and Date Modified. By default, the files in this view are sorted alphabetically by filename in ascending order (indicated by the triangle pointing upward next to the Name button at the top of the column).

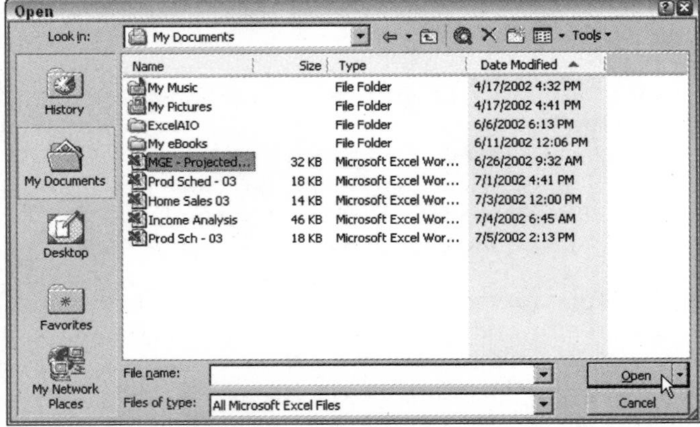

Figure 3-2: Switching to the Details view gives you more information on the files in the current folder.

You can change the way the files are sorted in this list by clicking the button with the name of the column. The first time you click a column name button, the files are sorted on that field in ascending order (indicated by a triangle pointing upward). If you click the same button a second time, the files are then sorted on that column in the opposite, descending order (and the upward-pointing triangle changes to a downward-pointing one). Because the files are automatically sorted by filename in ascending, A-to-Z order, clicking the Name column button re-sorts the list in descending, Z-to-A order and the triangle pointing up is replaced with one pointing down. To sort the files by their file size in ascending, smallest-to-largest order, click the Size column button. To resort them in descending, largest-to-smallest order, click the Size column button a second time.

If the Hide Extensions for Known File Types option is turned off in the Windows' Folder Options dialog box, the Excel filenames in the list and detail view don't include the `.xls` extension indicating workbook files and the `.xlt` extension indicating template files. The only way to differentiate an original workbook file from a template file is by their file icons. Remember that the workbook file icon shows the stylized green XL on a single sheet, whereas the template file icon shows a slightly smaller XL on a tablet with several sheets. Because these file icons can appear very similar (especially on a smaller monitor), you may want to reinstate the listing of filename extensions as well. To do this, open the My Documents or My Computer window by double-clicking their icons on the Windows desktop and then choose Tools⇨Folder Options on its menu bar. Finally, click the Hide Extensions for Known File Types check box on the View tab to remove its checkmark before clicking OK in the Folder Options dialog box.

Switch to the Properties view or the Preview view in the Open dialog box if you need more information on individual Excel files. When you choose Views⇨Properties from the Open dialog box menu bar, Excel splits the Open dialog box into two panes: the pane on the left shows the file list and the pane on the right shows a bunch of properties (such as the Author, Saved by, Created, Modified, and Size) for the file that is currently selected in the list on the left. When you choose Views⇨Preview, the dual left- and right-pane arrangement remains, except that this time, the right pane shows the first few columns and rows of the first worksheet in the workbook or template whose file is selected in the pane on the left.

Note that not all Excel files have previews available (especially those created with earlier versions of Excel). However, Excel will generate previews for the workbooks you save in the 2002 version if you click the Save Preview Picture check box on the Summary tab of a workbook's Properties dialog box (File⇨Properties). Note that file previews can be very helpful in identifying files — provided that their first worksheet has data entries in the first few columns and rows.

Variations on the Opening theme

Most of the time, you open the workbook file or files that you've selected in the current folder simply by clicking the Open button in the Open dialog box. As you may have noticed, the Open button contains its own pop-up button that, when clicked, offers you the following additional variations on the standard Open command:

- **Open Read Only** to open the files in a special read-only mode that prevents you from saving editing changes with the Save command. The only way you can save changes in this mode is by choosing File⇨Save As and then renaming, relocating, or replacing the original workbook or template file.
- **Open as Copy** to open copies of the original files so that the changes you save in them with the Save command are not saved in the original files. Excel prefaces the original filenames with the text "Copy (1) of", which you can change by using the File⇨Save As command.

- **Open in Browser** to open copies of the files with your default Internet browser (Internet Explorer in most cases) instead of Excel. This Open option is available only when you select files that Excel identifies as Web pages saved in the HTML or XML file format (see Book VIII, Chapter 1 for information on saving spreadsheets as Web pages).
- **Open and Repair** to have Excel attempt to repair corrupted files before opening them. When you choose this option, an Alert dialog box appears, giving you a choice between trying to repair the files by clicking the Repair button and extracting their data, or saving them in new workbook files by clicking the Extract Data button.

Use the Open and Repair option on any workbook file that Excel can't open normally. If you choose the Extract Data button in the first Alert dialog box that appears when you choose Open and Repair, another Alert dialog box appears, giving you a choice between converting the formulas in the corrupted file to their calculated values and attempting to salvage the formulas. Click the Convert to Values button to convert all formulas to their current calculated values. Click the Recover Formulas button to have Excel recover as many of the formulas in the spreadsheet as possible. Excel then displays yet another Alert dialog box, letting you know how successful (or unsuccessful) its formula recovery operation was.

Searching for files in the Search Task Pane

Sometimes, like it or not (and you won't like it, trust me on that), you won't remember where you saved the spreadsheet that you desperately need to edit or print. In such cases, you need to call upon Excel's Search feature to help you locate the missing workbook file. Of course, you do have to remember *something* about the file (and thankfully, it doesn't have to be its filename) in order to give Excel something to go on when searching for it!

What's the difference between Search and Find?

You use the Search feature to find errant workbook files that you need to open for editing or printing. When doing a search, you specify what part of your computer system to search as well as some piece of information about the file, such as its filename, its creation date, author, or some text that it contains, to use as the basis of the search. You use the Find feature to search for cells in an open workbook whose contents you need to review or edit. In Excel, the Find feature is combined with Replace (so that its dialog box is actually called Find and Replace). When you use Replace, you can have Excel automatically make a specified replacement for the text for which you are searching (see the "Find and Replace This Disgrace!" section later in this chapter for details).

To search for a file, open the Basic Search Task Pane. You can access the Basic Search Task Pane from the Excel Menu bar by choosing File➪Search. If another Task Pane is open, such as New Workbook or Clipboard, you can open the Basic Search Task Pane by clicking the Task Pane pop-up button and then clicking Search on the pop-up menu.

Figure 3-3 shows the Basic Search Task Pane as it appears when you first open it. As you can see, this Task Pane contains three types of information that you specify when doing a file search:

- **Search Text** — in this text box, you enter one or more words contained in the file that you want to find. When entering the search text, you can use the wildcard characters "?" and "*" if you are unsure of how certain words are spelled. The "?" wildcard stands for a single character so that entering "t?m" finds files that contain "Tim" and "Tom," but not "team" and "trim." The "*" wildcard characters stand for any number of characters so that entering "t*m" finds files that contain all four words.
- **Search In** — in this combo box, you specify the place on your computer system to search. By default, Excel searches everywhere on your computer (including the Desktop, My Documents folder, all local hard drives, and all shared document folders). To restrict the search to just your local hard drive, click the Search In drop-down button, click the My Computer Expand button (with the +) and then remove checkmarks from all the elements except for Local Drive (C:) — in other words, all the things that you *don't* want searched. To restrict the search on your hard drive to just certain folders, click the Local Drive (C:) Expand button and then remove checkmarks from all the folders that you *don't* want searched. If you're part of a network and think that the workbook may be saved on a networked drive, click the check box in front of My Network Places (note that some networks don't support searching, in which case, you'll receive a message telling you that it is an unavailable location when you perform the search).
- **Results Should Be** — in this drop-down list box, you specify what type or types of files to find. To restrict this list to only Excel workbook and template files, click the Office Files check box to remove the checkmarks from all of the Office file types and then click the Excel Files check box so that it alone has a checkmark.

When you do a basic search, Excel finds workbook files that contain any form of the words that you enter as the search text. For example, if you enter "invest" in the Search Text field, Excel finds files that contain "invest," "investing," "invested," "investor," and "investments." The program also searches for an occurrence of the words in the cells in all the worksheets in the workbook, as well as any in the Keywords and other fields entered on the Summary tab of the file's Properties dialog box, shown in Figure 3-4.

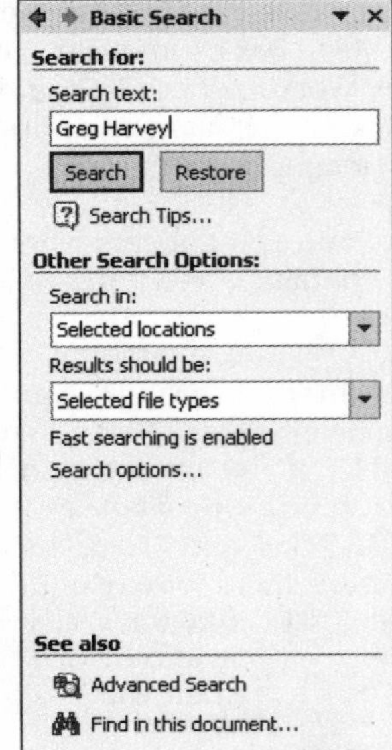

Figure 3-3: Using the Basic Search Task Pane to find a file for editing.

Figure 3-4: Excel searches the body of the file as well as the fields of the file's Summary tab.

If you create a lot of spreadsheets, especially those of a similar type or from the same template, you can help yourself to differentiate the workbooks when it comes time to open them for editing or printing by filling in the fields on the Summary tab of the file's Properties dialog box (which you open by choosing File➪Properties on the Menu bar). Because you know that Excel uses this information when doing a search, you can enter information in various fields on the Summary tab that clearly identify both its generic and individual characteristics, thus making it a great deal easier to locate the file that you need when you pull it up and use it.

Doing a search and using the results

After you finish specifying the search text, the location to search, and the results to return, you begin the search by clicking the Search button. When you click this button, the Basic Search Task Pane becomes a Search Results Task Pane, where Excel shows you all the files that contain your search text. If the workbook that you want to open appears in the Search Results Task Pane, you can click the Stop button to prevent Excel from doing any further searching.

To open a workbook file displayed in the Search Results Task Pane, click its file icon or position the mouse pointer on the icon and then, when a pop-up button appears, click this button followed by the Edit with Microsoft Excel item on the pop-up menu (shown in Figure 3-5).

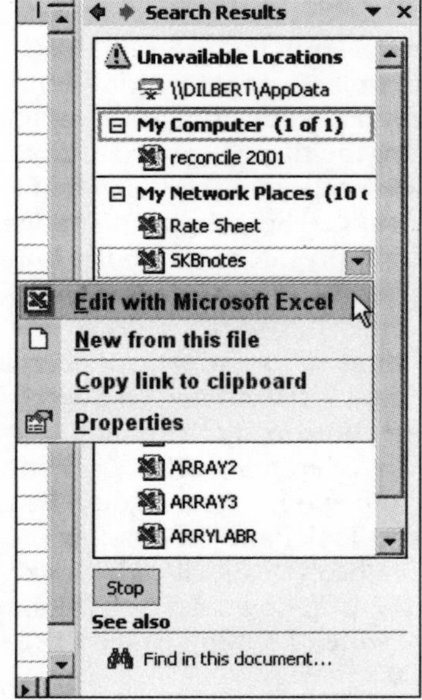

Figure 3-5: Opening a workbook file in the Search Results Task Pane.

If you're not sure from viewing the filenames alone which of the files displayed in the Search Results Task Pane is the one that you want to open, position the mouse pointer on the file icon for a few seconds. A ToolTip showing the complete path to the file, along with the date that it was last modified, appears below the file icon. If this information alone isn't enough, click the file's pop-up button and then click Properties at the bottom of the pop-up menu. This action opens a Properties dialog box containing a General, Custom, and Summary tab that give you all sorts of information about the file (note that the Summary tab will be empty except for the Author if you didn't fill in this information prior to saving the workbook file).

If your search returned more files that can be displayed together in the Search Results Task Pane, a Next *x* Results link (where *x* is the actual number of results) appears when you scroll down to the end of the list. Click this link to display the next group of ten results. If you find that you're not getting the results that you expected, click the Stop button at the bottom of the Search Results Task Pane and then click the Modify button (this button immediately replaces Stop when you click it) to return to the Basic Search Task Pane, where you can tweak your search criteria or even try narrowing the search by using the Advanced Search feature.

Using the Advanced Search Task Pane

Excel supports a so-called Advanced Search feature, which enables you to add more specific search criteria than just simple words (although it uses exactly the same Search In and Search Results Should Be options). To open the Advanced Search Task Pane from the Basic Search Task Pane, click the Advanced Search link in the See Also section at the bottom of the Basic Search Task Pane. Note that the Advanced Search link disappears after you do a basic search. To bring it back, simply click the Modify button at the bottom of the Search Results Task Pane.

When you click this link, Excel switches to the Advanced Search Task Pane, shown in Figure 3-6. As this figure shows, the Advanced Search Task Pane contains a Search For section where you specify the conditions that must be met in order for a file to appear in the Search Results Task Pane. Below this section, you find a Search button (to begin the Search) and Restore button (to take you back to the Basic Search Task Pane) and below these buttons, you find the Search In drop-down list box (to specify which drives and folders to search) and Results Should Be drop-down list box (to specify which types of files to search for), both of which function exactly the same as their counterparts in the Basic Search Task Pane.

The Search For section of the Advanced Search Task Pane contains the following items for specifying the condition or conditions to be applied in the search:

- **Property** — in this combo box, you specify the property to search for. The pop-up menu attached to this box contains a complete list of things that you can specify, including the author, keywords, date last saved or printed, file size, and total editing time, as well as the more mundane default of "Text or property."
- **Condition** — in this drop-down list box, you select the type of limitation set on the property during the search. The conditions available in the drop-down list box vary according to the type of property that you select in the Property combo box. For text properties, you can specify "is (exactly)" for exact matches or "includes" for partial matches. For date properties, you can specify "on," "on or after," "on or before," along with a variety of time-specific conditions. For numeric properties, you can specify "equals," "not equal to," "more than," "less than," "at least," and "at most."
- **Value** — in this text box, you enter the text or value that is used in judging whether the condition that you set up for the property you specified is TRUE or FALSE. You enter the label or number that you want used in the Value text box just as you would enter it in your spreadsheet.

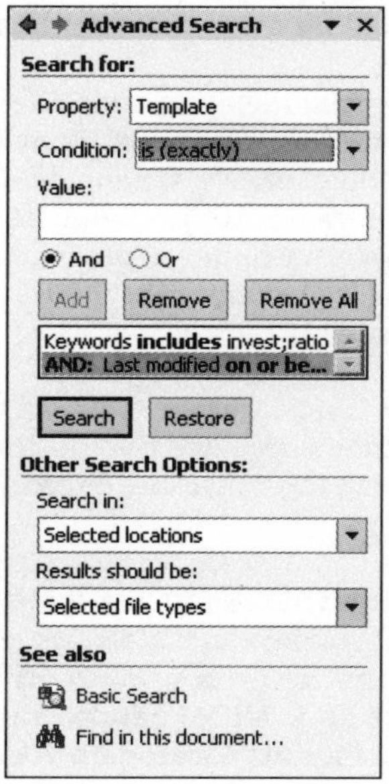

Figure 3-6: Using the Advanced Search Task Pane to find a file for editing.

After using these three boxes to specify your search criteria, click the Add button to add it to the list box that appears in the middle of the Advanced Search Task Pane. When specifying search criteria in the Advanced Search

Task Pane, you can apply more than a single set of criteria. After specifying the second set of criteria in the Property, Condition, and Value boxes, choose between the "And" and the "Or" radio button before you click the Add button. When you click the And button, a file matches only when all the criteria applied to it are TRUE. When you click the Or button, a file matches when any one of the criteria applied to it is TRUE.

After you finish adding criteria in the Search For section, the place to search in the Search In combo box, and the files to search for in the Results Should Be drop-down list box, you begin the advanced searching by clicking the Search button. As when doing a basic search, the Advanced Search Task Pane becomes a Search Results Task Pane where the files that meet your criteria appear. You can then open them for editing by clicking their file icons.

Enabling the Fast Search feature

Excel supports an indexing utility called Fast Search that can significantly speed up file searching when dealing with lots and lots of rather large spreadsheet files. When you first start using Excel's Search feature, Fast Search is turned off. To enable Fast Search, you need to click the Search Options link that appears under the text, "Fast Searching is Currently Disabled" right under the Results Should Be drop-down list box.

When you click this link, Excel displays an Indexing Service Settings dialog box where you click the Yes, Enable Indexing Service and Run When My Computer Is Idle radio button before you click OK. When you do this, the Indexing Service closes the Indexing Service Settings dialog box and then begins indexing all the files on your system whenever the computer is idle. You will notice that the "Fast Searching is Currently Disabled" message is now replaced by "Fast Searching is Enabled."

After enabling the Indexing Service for fast searching, you can open the Indexing Service dialog box from which you manage the indexing by clicking the Search Options link and then clicking the Advanced button in the Indexing Service Settings dialog box.

Fast Search may not even be installed on your computer. If it isn't, instead of "Fast Searching is Currently Disabled," you see an Install link. Click this link and follow the prompts to install this service on your hard drive. Keep in mind that you have to have your Office XP CD-ROM handy or be able to tell the Windows Installer where the Office files are located on your network in order to be able to successfully install this service.

Doing a search from within the Open dialog box

The Basic Search and Advanced Search Task Panes aren't the only place from which you can do searches for the workbooks that you need to open.

You can also perform a basic or advanced search from within the Open dialog box itself.

If you find that you're unable to locate the workbook that you want to work with in the Open dialog box on your own, click the Tools button on the Open dialog box toolbar and then click Search. This action opens a Search dialog box with a Basic and Advanced tab. Each of these tabs contains the same search options as the Basic Search and Advanced Search Task Panes. Figure 3-7 shows you the Search dialog box that opens when you click the Search item at the very top of the Tools pop-up menu within the Open dialog box.

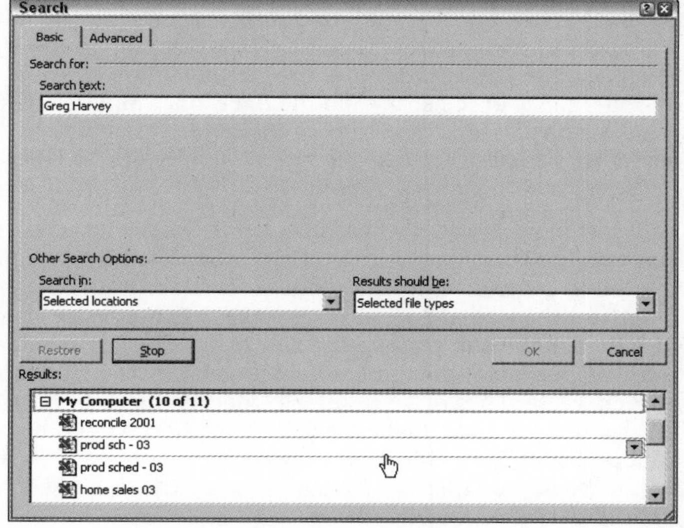

Figure 3-7: Searching for workbook files in the Search dialog box.

Searching for files in the Search dialog box is just like doing a search from the Basic Search or Advanced Search Task Panes (it just presents the information in a little different format). In fact, the Search dialog box actually inherits any basic and advanced search criteria that you specify in the Basic Search and Advanced Search Task Panes.

Cell Editing 101

The biggest thing to remember about basic cell editing is that you have to put the cell pointer in the cell whose contents you want to modify. When modifying a cell's contents, you can replace the entry entirely, delete characters from the entry, and/or insert new characters into the entry:

- To replace a cell's contents, position the cell pointer in the cell and just start inputting your new entry over it (remember you can do this by typing from the keyboard, speaking the new entry with the Dictation function of the Speech Recognition feature, or writing it by hand with the Handwriting Recognition feature). The moment you start inputting the new entry, the first characters that are input entirely replace the existing data entry. To finish replacing the original entry, complete the new cell entry by using whatever technique you like (such as pressing an arrow key or Enter, or clicking the Enter button on the Formula bar). To abort the replacement and restore the original cell entry, click the Cancel button on the Formula bar or press the Escape key on your keyboard.
- To delete characters in a cell entry, click the insertion point in the entry on the Formula bar, press F2, or double-click the mouse pointer in the cell to get Excel into Edit mode (indicated by Edit on the Status bar). Then, use the Home, End, or ← or → keys to move the insertion point to a proper place in the entry and the Backspace and Delete keys to remove unnecessary or incorrect characters. (Backspace deletes characters to the left of the insertion point and Delete removes characters to the right of the insertion point.)
- To insert new characters in a cell entry, click the insertion point in the entry on the Formula bar, press F2, or double-click the mouse pointer in the cell to get Excel into Edit mode (indicated by Edit on the Status bar). Then, use the Home, End, or ← or → keys to move the insertion point to the place in the entry where the new characters are needed and if OVR is *not* displayed on the right side of the Status bar, start inputting the new characters. Excel automatically inserts the new characters at the insertion point, thus pushing existing text to the right. If you do see the OVR indicator, press the Insert key to get out of overtype mode (in which the new characters you input eat up the existing ones on the right) before you start inputting.

When you edit the contents of a cell by inserting and/or deleting characters in it, you need to remember to click the Enter button on the Formula bar or press the Enter key to complete the editing change and switch the program from Edit back to Ready mode (indicated by the reappearance of Ready on the Status bar). If you're editing a cell with a simple text or number entry, you can also do this by clicking the mouse pointer in another cell to make it current (this doesn't work, however, when editing a formula because Excel will just include the address of the cell that you click as part of the edited formula). Also, you can't use any of the keystrokes that normally complete a new cell entry except for the Tab and Shift+Tab keystrokes for moving to the next and previous column in the worksheet (all the rest including the arrow keys, Home, and End just move the insertion point within the cell entry).

Editing in the cell versus on the Formula bar

When doing simple editing to a cell's contents, the question arises as to whether it's better to edit the contents in the cell directly or edit the contents on the Formula bar. When editing short entries that fit entirely within the current column width, it really is a matter of personal choice. Some people prefer editing on the Formula bar because it's out of the way of other cells in the same region of the worksheet. Other people prefer editing on the Formula bar because they find it easier to click the insertion point with the I-beam mouse pointer at precisely the place in the entry that needs editing (when you press F2 to edit in the cell, Excel always positions the insertion point at the very end of the entry and when you double-click the thick white mouse pointer in the cell, you really can't tell exactly where you're putting the insertion point).

When it comes to editing longer cell entries (that is, text entries that spill over into empty neighboring cells, and numbers that, if their digits weren't truncated by the number format assigned, wouldn't fit within the current cell width), you probably will want to edit their contents on the Formula bar because that way, you can see the entire entry without having to scroll characters back and forth with the ← and → keys. When it comes to editing long formulas, you sometimes want to edit them on the Formula bar and other times in the cell depending upon how long they are. Really long formulas often require several lines on the Formula bar that then obscure the upper part of the worksheet, thus making it impossible to see the cells in those first visible rows of the worksheet.

Undo and Redo

Excel supports multiple levels of undo that you can use to recover from potentially costly editing mistakes that would require data re-entry or extensive repair operations. The most important thing to remember about the Undo command is that it is cumulative, meaning that you don't use it right away after making a boo-boo. In fact, you may have to select it multiple times to reverse several actions that you've taken before you get to the one that sets your spreadsheet right again.

You can select the Undo command either by clicking the Undo button on the Standard toolbar, choosing Edit⇨Undo on the Menu bar, or by pressing Alt+Backspace or Ctrl+Z. Excel will then reverse the effect of the last edit you made in the worksheet. For example, if you edit a cell entry and erase some of its text in error, selecting Undo will restore the characters that you just erased to the entry. Likewise, if you delete a group of cells by mistake, selecting Undo will restore both their contents and formatting to the worksheet.

On the Standard toolbar, you can click the drop-down button attached to the Undo button to display a pop-up menu that shows a brief menu of the actions that you've recently taken in the spreadsheet. Instead of undoing one action at a time, you undo multiple actions by dragging through them in the pop-up menu. As soon as you release the mouse button, Excel then restores the spreadsheet to the state that it was in before you took all the actions that you selected on this pop-up menu.

When you make an editing change in a spreadsheet, the Undo item on the Edit pull-down menu actually changes to reflect the action that you just took. For example, if you delete a group of cells with one of the items on the Edit⇨Clear cascading menu (or by pressing the Delete key) and then open the Edit menu, the Undo command will appear as follows:

```
Undo Clear      Ctrl+Z
```

If you then apply new formatting to a cell selection, such as assigning a new alignment, and then open the Edit menu, the Undo command will now appear as follows:

```
Undo Alignment  Ctrl+Z
```

You need to be aware that not all Excel commands can be reversed with the Undo command. For example, commands that make changes on the hard drive, such as File⇨Save, can't be reversed. If you select an Excel command whose effects are irreversible, the command name changes to Can't Undo, which appears dimmed on the Edit menu.

The Undo feature works by storing a "snapshot" of the worksheet in the memory of your computer at each stage in its editing. Sometimes, if you attempt a large-scale edit in a worksheet, Excel will determine that sufficient free memory doesn't exist to hold a snapshot of the worksheet in its current state and complete the planned editing change as well. For example, this can happen if you try to cut and paste a really large range in a big worksheet. In such a case, Excel displays an Alert dialog box that indicates a lack of enough memory and asks if you want to continue without Undo. If you then select the Yes option, Excel completes the planned edit but without the possibility of you being able to reverse its effects with Undo. Before you take such an action, consider how much time and effort would be required to manually restore the worksheet to its previous state if you make a mistake in carrying out your editing change.

After you use the Undo feature to reverse an editing change, a Redo menu item joins Undo on the Edit menu and the Redo button on the Standard toolbar becomes active. The Redo command item on the Edit menu has the name of the latest type of editing that you just reversed with the Undo command, such as Redo Clear when the last action you took was to restore a cell entry that you just deleted.

You use the Redo command to restore the worksheet to the condition that it was in before you last selected the Undo command. As with using the Undo button on the Standard toolbar, when you click the pop-up button attached to the Redo button, you can drag through a series of actions that you want repeated (assuming that you used the Undo command multiple times). You can also restore edits that you've undone one at a time by choosing Edit⇨Redo on the Menu bar, clicking the Redo button, or by pressing Ctrl+Y.

You can use Undo and Redo to toggle between a "before and after" view of your spreadsheet. For example, suppose that you update an entry in a cell that was used in formulas throughout a data table. As soon as you enter the new number in this cell, Excel recalculates the table and displays the new results. To once again view the original version of the table before you made this latest change, you use Undo (Ctrl+Z). After checking some values in the original table, you then restore the latest change to its numbers by selecting the Redo command (Ctrl+Y). You can then continue in this manner as long as you want, switching between "before" and "after" versions by holding down the Ctrl key as you type Z and then type Y, alternating between Undo and then Redo.

Get that out of here!

Sometimes you need to delete an entry that you made in a cell of the spreadsheet without replacing it with any other contents. Excel refers to this kind of deletion as *clearing* the cell. This is actually more correct than referring to it as "emptying" the cell because although the cell may appear empty when you delete its contents, it may still retain the formatting assigned to it, and therefore not truly be empty.

For this reason, choosing the Edit⇨Clear command on the Menu bar opens the following cascading menu of further menu items:

- ✦ **All** — Use this to get rid of both the contents and the formatting assigned to the current cell selection.
- ✦ **Formats** — Use this to get rid of just formatting assigned to the current cell selection without getting rid of the contents.
- ✦ **Contents** — Use this to get rid of just the contents in the current cell selection without getting rid of the formatting assigned to it (this is the equivalent of pressing the Delete key).
- ✦ **Comments** — Use this to get rid of just the comments assigned to the cells in the selection without touching either the contents or the formatting (see Book IV, Chapter 1 for information on assigning comments to cells).

The Edit⇨Clear⇨All command is great when you need to truly empty a cell of all formatting and contents while at the same time retaining that empty cell in the worksheet. However, what about the times when you need to get rid of the cell as well as all its contents? For example, suppose that you entered a column of numbers that you've totaled with a summing formula only to discover that midway in the list, you entered the same number twice, in one cell above the other. You don't want to just delete the duplicate number in one of the two cells, thus leaving a single empty cell in the middle of your list of values (although having an empty cell in the middle of the list won't skew the total, it just won't look professional!).

In this case, you want to delete both the duplicate entry and remove the newly emptied cell while at the same time pulling up the cells with the rest of the numbers in the list below along with the cell at the end that contains the formula that sums the values together. Excel offers just such a command on the Menu bar, Edit⇨Delete. When you choose Edit⇨Delete, a Delete dialog box appears, similar to the one shown in Figure 3-8. This dialog box lets you choose how you want the remaining cells to be shifted when the selected cell (or cells) is removed from the worksheet. Keep in mind that when you use Edit⇨Delete, Excel zaps everything, including the contents, formatting, and any and all attached comments (just don't forget about Edit⇨Undo in case you ever zap something you shouldn't have!).

Figures 3-8 and 3-9 illustrate how Edit⇨Delete works in the example where a duplicate entry has been mistakenly entered in a column of numbers that is totaled by a summing formula. In Figure 3-8, I selected cell B5 containing the duplicate $175,000 entry before choosing the Edit⇨Delete command and displaying the Delete dialog box.

As this figure shows, when the Delete dialog box opens, the Shift Cells Up radio button is automatically selected. Figure 3-9 shows the same worksheet after clicking the OK button in the Delete dialog box. Notice how Excel pulled up the entries in the cells below when it deleted the duplicate in cell B5, while at the same time automatically recalculating the sum formula to reflect the total of the remaining entries.

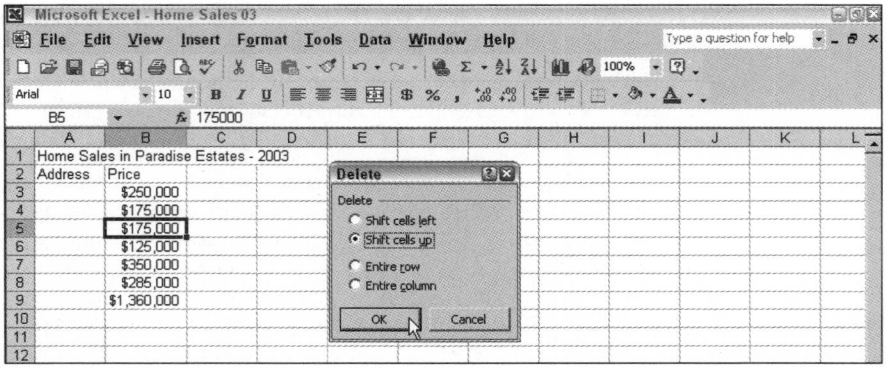

Figure 3-8: Deleting a cell with a duplicate entry.

	A	B	C	D	E	F	G	H	I	J	K	L
1	Home Sales in Paradise Estates - 2003											
2	Address	Price										
3		$250,000										
4		$175,000										
5		$125,000										
6		$350,000										
7		$285,000										
8		$1,185,000										
9												
10												
11												
12												

Figure 3-9: Worksheet after deleting the cell with the duplicate entry.

Don't confuse the use of the Delete key and the Edit⇨Delete command. When you press the Delete key, Excel automatically deletes just the contents of the cells that are selected (keeping whatever formatting is used intact), leaving seemingly blank cells in the worksheet. When you choose Edit⇨Delete on the Menu bar, Excel displays the Delete dialog box, which deletes the selected cells and then shifts the remaining cells in the direction that you designate (up or to the left) to fill in what would otherwise be blank cells.

Can I just squeeze this in here?

The Insert⇨Cells menu command is the polar opposite of Edit⇨Delete. You use Insert⇨Cells to insert blank cells in places where data entries that were somehow left out need to be squeezed in. For example, suppose that you discover that you've left out three numbers from a column of summed numbers and that these values should have appeared in the middle of the column. To make this edit, position the cell pointer in the first cell of those cells whose values need to be shifted down to make room for the three missing entries and then drag the cell pointer down two rows so that you have selected the three cells with entries that you want to retain but also need to have moved down.

Figures 3-10 and 3-11 illustrate this situation. In Figure 3-10, I selected the cell range B5:B7 where cells for the three missing entries are to be inserted. I then selected Insert⇨Cells on the Excel Menu bar. This action opens the Insert dialog box with the Shift Cells Right radio button selected. Because I needed to have the cells in the selected range moved down to make room for the missing entries, I clicked the Shift Cells Down radio button.

Figure 3-11 shows the spreadsheet after clicking OK in the Insert dialog box to insert three new blank cells in the cell range B5:B7 and move down the existing $125,000, $350,000, and $285,000 entries to the cell range B8:B10, and then entering the missing entries in the newly inserted and blank range B5:B7. As you can see, the sum formula in the last cell in this column (now shifted down to cell B11 from cell B8) has automatically been recalculated so that the total reflects the addition of the missing values that I entered in the newly inserted cells.

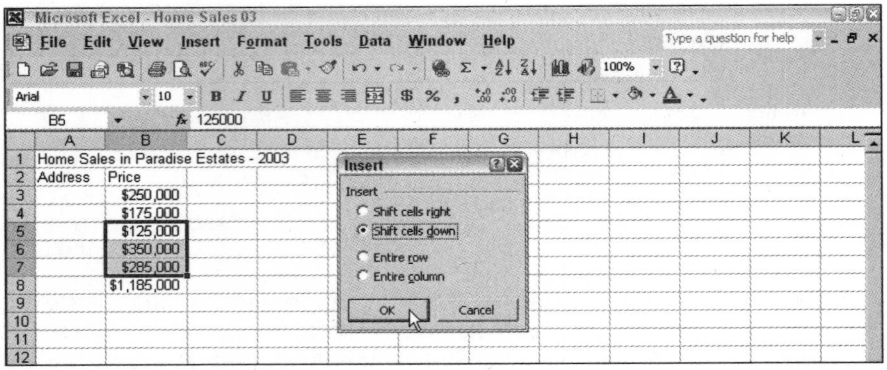

Figure 3-10: Inserting three blank cells for missing entries in a column of summed numbers.

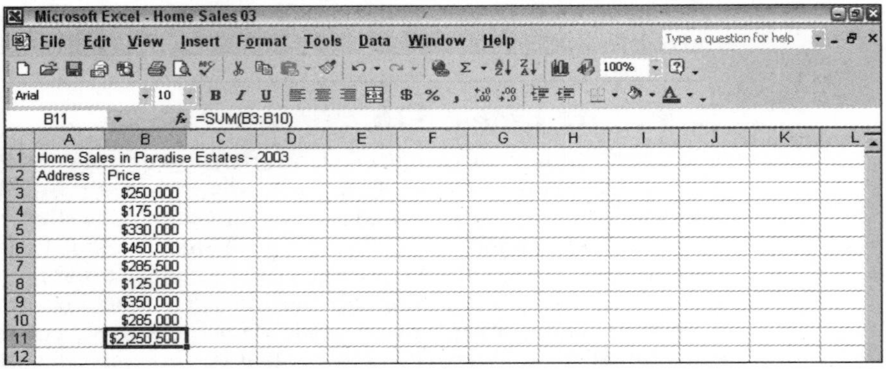

Figure 3-11: Worksheet after entering the missing values in the newly inserted cells.

A Spreadsheet with a View

The biggest problem with editing is finding and getting to the place in the worksheet that needs modification and then keeping your place in the worksheet as you make the changes. This problem is exacerbated by the fact that you probably often work with really large spreadsheets of which only a small portion can be displayed at any one time on your screen.

Excel provides a number of features that can help you find your way and keep your place in the spreadsheet that needs editing. Among these are its Zoom feature that enables you to increase or decrease the magnification of the worksheet window, thus making it possible to switch from a really up-close view to a really far-away view in seconds, and its Freeze Panes feature that enables you to keep pertinent information, such as column and row headings on the worksheet window, as you scroll other columns and rows of data into view.

"Zoom, zoom, zoom"

Excel makes it easy to see more data in the active worksheet window with its Zoom feature. You can access Excel's Zoom feature in one of two ways: the Zoom combo box on the Standard toolbar or the Zoom dialog box, which you can open by choosing View⇨Zoom on the Menu bar.

You can click the menu items on the Zoom button's drop-down list or the radio buttons in the Zoom dialog box to select the preset magnification percentages 200%, 100%, 75%, 50%, and 25%, with 100% being the default settings for all worksheets (of course, the size of the cells at the 100% setting can vary, depending on the overall size of your monitor's screen).

The Zoom combo box and Zoom dialog box also enable you to set any percentage between a minimum of 10% and a maximum of 400%. To set a custom percentage in the Zoom combo box, click its text box, type the new percentage, and press Enter. To set a custom percentage in the Zoom dialog box, open the Zoom dialog box (View⇨Zoom), click the Custom text box, type a new percentage, and click OK.

You can also have Excel change the magnification to suit the cell range that you have selected. To do this, select your cell range, click Selection on the Zoom box's pop-up menu or open the Zoom dialog box (View⇨Zoom), click the Fit Selection radio button, and click OK.

If you own a version of Microsoft's IntelliMouse (that is, a mouse with a wheel in between the two mouse buttons, you can set it up in Excel so that rolling the wheel back and forth zooms out and in on the current worksheet. To do this, click the Zoom on Roll with IntelliMouse check box, which is located on the General tab of the Options dialog box (Tools⇨Options). After you select this check box, rolling the wheel backward increases the magnification by 15% until you reach the maximum 400%, whereas rolling the wheel forward decreases the magnification by 15% until you reach the minimum 10% value.

Figures 3-12 and 3-13 illustrate how you can use the Zoom feature to first zoom out to locate a region in a large spreadsheet that needs editing and then zoom in on the region to do the editing. In Figure 3-12, I zoomed out on the Income Analysis to display all of its data by selecting a 35% magnification setting (I actually did this by first selecting the 25% preset magnification, and then manually adjusting it up to 35% after finding that 25% was too much. At the 35% setting, I could just barely make out the headings and read the numbers in the cells. I then located the cells that needed editing and selected their cell range (J20:L25) in the worksheet.

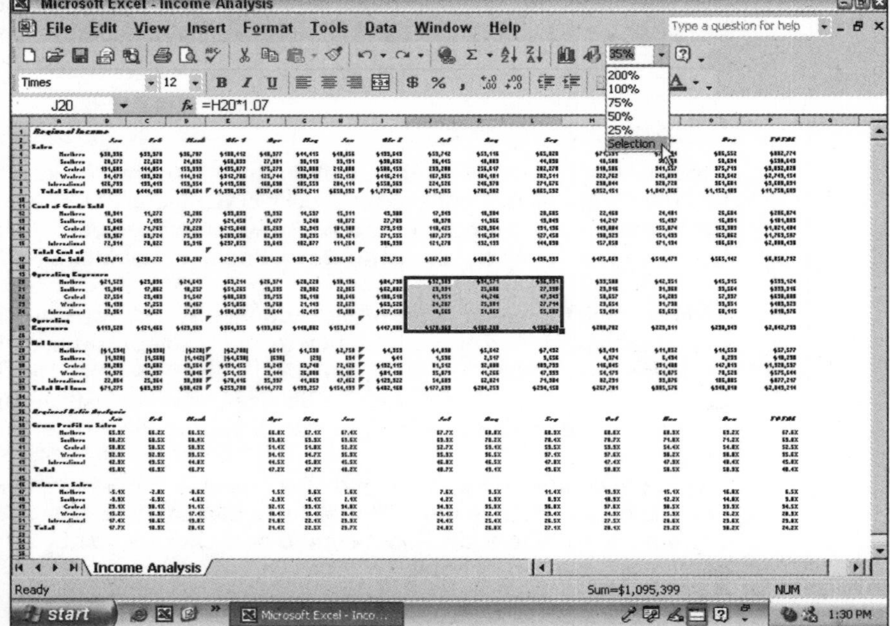

Figure 3-12: Income Analysis spreadsheet after zooming out to a 35% magnification setting.

After selecting the range of cells to be edited, I then clicked the Selection item on the Zoom button's pop-up menu. You can see the result in Figure 3-13. As you can see in the Zoom combo box, Excel boosted the magnification from 35% up to 179% when I clicked Selection on the Zoom button's pop-up menu: a comfortable size for editing these cells on even one of the smaller computer monitors.

Freezing window panes

Figure 3-13 could be the poster-boy for the Freeze Panes feature. Although zooming in on the range of cells that needs editing has made their data entries easy to read, it has also removed all the column and headings that give you any clue as to what kind of data you're looking at. If I had used the Freeze Panes command to freeze column A with the row headings and row 2 with the column headings, they would remain displayed on the screen — regardless of the magnification settings you select or how you scroll through the cells.

To use the Freeze Panes feature in this manner, you first position the cell pointer in the cell that's located to the immediate left of the column or columns that you want to freeze and immediately beneath the row or rows that you want to freeze before you choose Window⇨Freeze Panes. If want to bisect the entire worksheet horizontally by freezing just a row or two, position the cell pointer in column A in the row immediately beneath the ones that you want to freeze before you choose Window⇨Freeze Panes. If you want to bisect the entire worksheet vertically by freezing just a column or two, position the cell pointer in row 1 of the column to the immediate right of the column or columns that you want to freeze on the display before you choose this command.

Figures 3-14 and 3-15 illustrate how this works. Figure 3-14 shows the Income Analysis spreadsheet after freezing column A and rows 1 and 2. To do this, I positioned the cell pointer in cell B3 before choosing Window⇨Freeze Panes. Notice the thin black line that runs down column A and across row 2, marking which column and rows of worksheet are frozen on the display and that will now remain in view — regardless of how far you scroll to the right to new columns or scroll down to new rows.

As Figure 3-15 shows, frozen panes stay on the screen even when you zoom in and out on the worksheet. For Figure 3-15, I repeated the steps I took in changing the magnification for Figures 3-12 and 3-13 (only this time with the frozen panes in place). First, I zoomed out on the Income Analysis spreadsheet by using the 35% magnification setting; second, I selected the range J20:L25 and then clicked Selection on the Zoom button's pop-up menu.

Figure 3-15 shows the result. Note that with the frozen panes in place, this time Excel only selected a 133% magnification setting instead of the original 179% setting. This lower magnification setting is worth it because of all of the important information that has been added to the cell range.

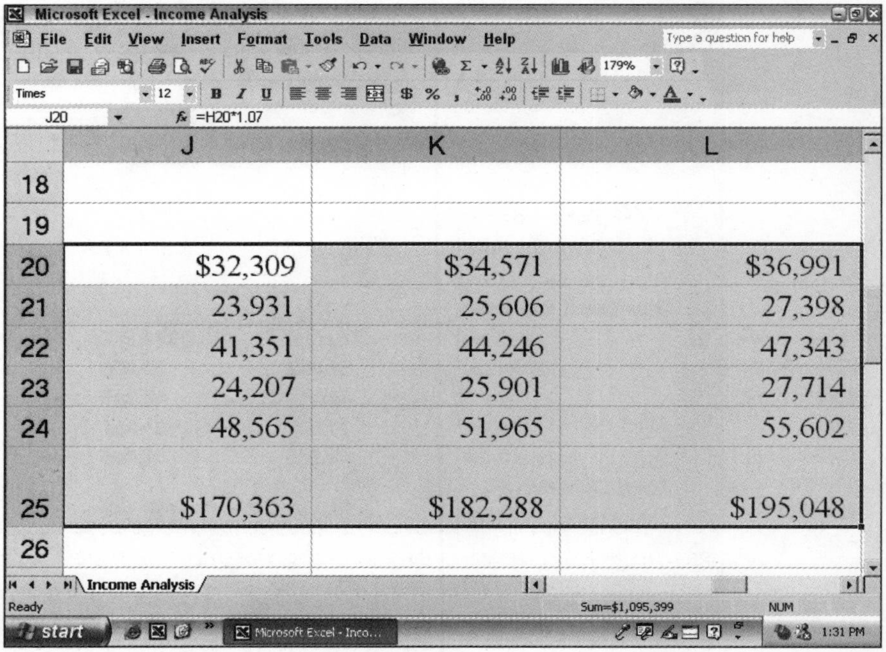

Figure 3-13: Spreadsheet after zooming in on a cell selection.

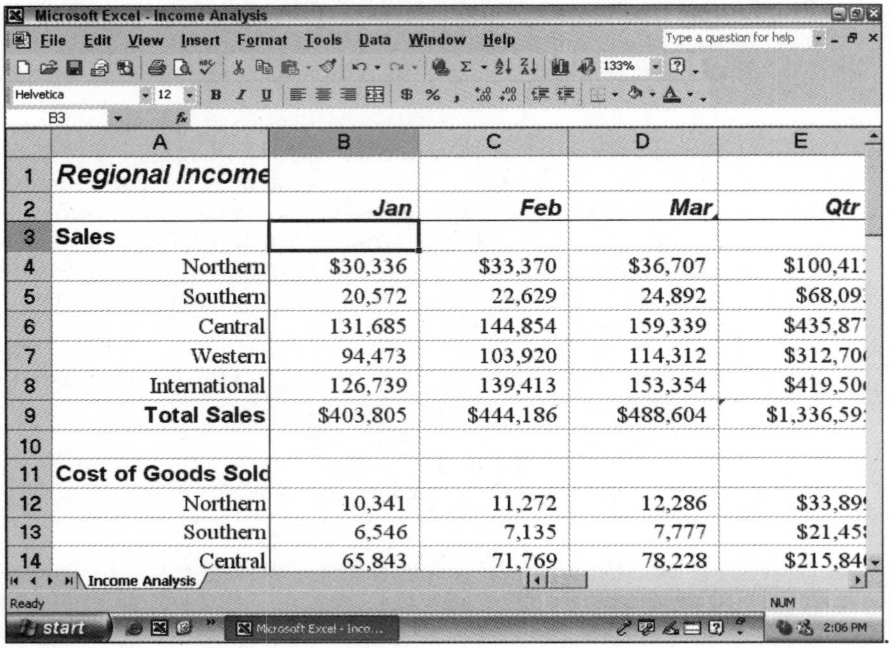

Microsoft Excel - Income Analysis

B3

	A	B	C	D	E
1	*Regional Income*				
2		*Jan*	*Feb*	*Mar*	*Qtr*
3	**Sales**				
4	Northern	$30,336	$33,370	$36,707	$100,41
5	Southern	20,572	22,629	24,892	$68,09
6	Central	131,685	144,854	159,339	$435,87
7	Western	94,473	103,920	114,312	$312,70
8	International	126,739	139,413	153,354	$419,50
9	**Total Sales**	$403,805	$444,186	$488,604	$1,336,59
10					
11	**Cost of Goods Sold**				
12	Northern	10,341	11,272	12,286	$33,89
13	Southern	6,546	7,135	7,777	$21,45
14	Central	65,843	71,769	78,228	$215,84

Figure 3-14: Income Analysis spreadsheet after freezing column A and rows 1:2 on-screen.

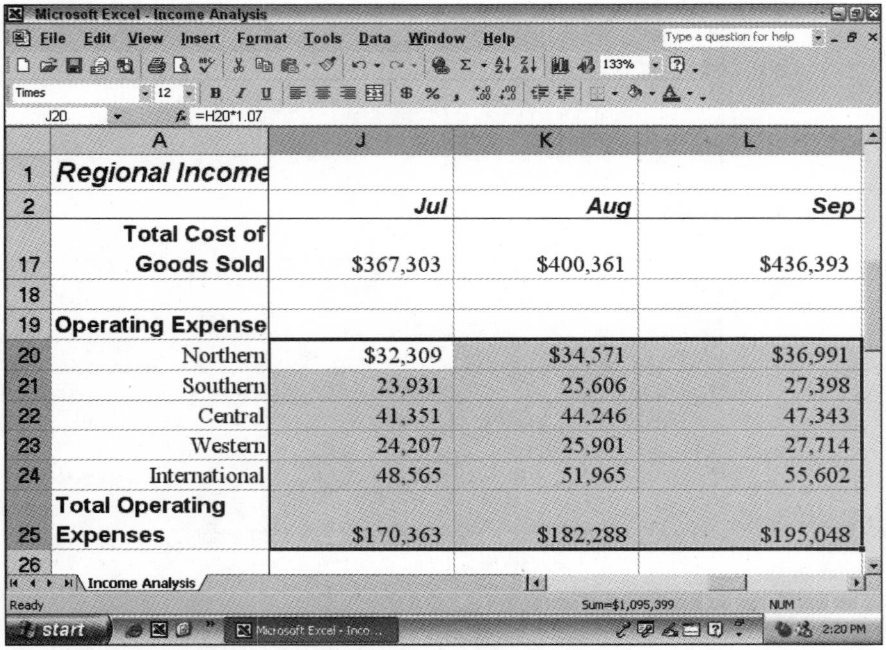

Microsoft Excel - Income Analysis

J20 =H20*1.07

	A	J	K	L
1	*Regional Income*			
2		*Jul*	*Aug*	*Sep*
17	**Total Cost of Goods Sold**	$367,303	$400,361	$436,393
18				
19	**Operating Expense**			
20	Northern	$32,309	$34,571	$36,991
21	Southern	23,931	25,606	27,398
22	Central	41,351	44,246	47,343
23	Western	24,207	25,901	27,714
24	International	48,565	51,965	55,602
25	**Total Operating Expenses**	$170,363	$182,288	$195,048
26				

Sum=$1,095,399

Figure 3-15: Spreadsheet after zooming in on a cell selection after freezing panes.

When you press the Ctrl+Home shortcut key when you've frozen panes in a worksheet, instead of positioning the cell pointer in cell A1 as normal, Excel positions the cell pointer in the first unfrozen cell. In the example illustrated in Figure 3-14, pressing Ctrl+Home from anywhere in the worksheet puts the cell pointer in B3. From there, you can position the cell pointer in A1 either by clicking the cell or by pressing the arrow keys.

To unfreeze the panes after you've finished editing, choose Window⇨Unfreeze Panes on the Excel Menu bar (which replaces Freeze Panes on the Window menu). Note that when Excel unfreezes a pane, it automatically takes you back to the cell from which you defined the panes — regardless of where the cell pointer is located in the worksheet at the time you choose the Window⇨Unfreeze Panes command.

Frozen Panes in the worksheet display have a parallel feature when printing a spreadsheet called Print Titles. When you use Print Titles in a report, the columns and rows that you define as the titles are printed at the top and to left of all data on each page of the report (see Book II, Chapter 5 for details).

Saving custom views

In the course of creating and editing a worksheet, you may find that you need to modify the worksheet display many times as you work with the document. For example, you may find at some point that you need to reduce the magnification of the worksheet display to 75% magnification. At another point, you may need to return to 100% magnification and hide different columns in the worksheet. At some later point, you may have to redisplay the hidden columns and then freeze panes in the worksheet.

With Excel's View⇨Custom Views command, you can save any of these types of changes to the worksheet display. This way, instead of taking the time to manually set up the worksheet display that you want, you can have Excel recreate it for you simply by selecting the view. When you create a view, Excel can save any of the following settings: the current cell selection, print settings (including different page setups), column widths and row heights (including hidden columns), display settings on the View tab of the Options dialog box, as well as the current position and size of the document window and the window pane arrangement (including frozen panes).

To create a custom view of your worksheet, follow these steps:

1. **Make all of the necessary changes to the worksheet display so that the worksheet window appears exactly as you want it to appear each time you select the view. Also select all of the print settings in the Page Setup dialog box that you want used in printing the view (see Book II, Chapter 5 for details).**
2. **Choose the View⇨Custom Views on the Excel menu bar.**

This action opens the Custom Views dialog box, shown in Figure 3-16, where you add the view that you've just set up in the worksheet.

3. **Click the Add button.**

   This action opens the Add View dialog box, where you type a name for your new view.

4. **Enter a unique descriptive name for your view in the Name text box.**

   Make sure that the name you give the view reflects all of its pertinent settings.

5. **To include print settings and hidden columns and rows in your view, leave the Print Settings and Hidden Rows, Columns and Filter Settings check boxes selected when you click the OK button. If you don't want to include these setting, clear the checkmark from either one or both of these check boxes before you click OK.**

   When you click OK, Excel closes the Add View dialog box and returns you to the Custom Views dialog box, where the name of your new view now appears in the Views list box.

6. **Click the Close button to close the Custom Views dialog box.**

   Custom views are saved as part of the workbook file. To be able to use them whenever you open the spreadsheet for editing, you need to save the workbook with the new view.

7. **Click the Save button on the Standard toolbar or press Ctrl+S to save the new view as part of the workbook file.**

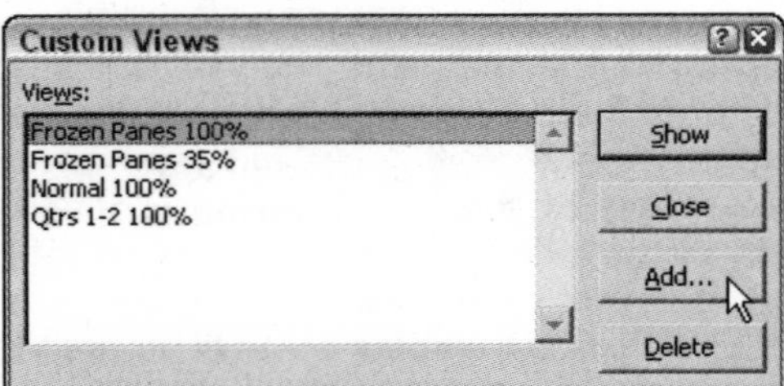

Figure 3-16: Adding a new view in the Custom Views dialog box.

After you create your views, you can display the worksheet in that view at any time while working with the spreadsheet. To display a view, follow these steps:

1. **Choose View⇨Custom Views on the Excel Menu bar.**
2. **Double-click the name of the view that you want to use in displaying your worksheet in the Views list box or click the name and then click the Show button.**

Always start by defining a Normal 100% view in the Custom Views dialog box that represents the standard view of the worksheet before you go abo defining custom views that hide columns, freeze panes, and mess with the worksheet's magnification. This way, you can recover from a special view (especially one that you only use in printing part of the spreadsheet but never use when editing it) simply by double-clicking Normal 100% in the Views list box of the Custom Views dialog box.

Copying and Moving Stuff Around

Moving and copying worksheet data are among the most common editing tasks that you perform when editing a typical spreadsheet. Excel offers two basic methods for moving and copying a cell selection in a worksheet: First, you can use drag-and-drop to drag the cells to a new location or second, you can cut or copy the contents to the Clipboard and then past them into the desired area. Moving and copying data to new areas in a spreadsheet are basically very straightforward procedures. You need to keep a few things in mind, however, when rearranging cell entries in a worksheet:

- When you move or copy a cell, Excel moves everything in the cell, including the contents, formatting, and any comment assigned to the cell (see Book IV, Chapter 1 for information on adding comments to cells).
- If you move or copy a cell so that it overlays an existing entry, Excel replaces the existing entry with the contents and formatting of the cell that you're moving or copying. This means that you can replace existing data in a range without having to first clear the range before moving or copying the replacement entries. It also means that you must be careful not to overlay any part of an existing range that you don't want replaced with the relocated or copied cell entries.
- When you move cells referred to in formulas in a worksheet, Excel automatically adjusts the cell references in the formulas to reflect their new locations in the worksheet.
- When you copy formulas that contain cell references, Excel automatically adjusts the cell references in the copies relative to the change in their position in the worksheet (see Book III, Chapter 1 for details on copying formulas in a spreadsheet).

For situations in which you only need to copy a single data entry to cells in a single row or to cells in a single column of the worksheet, keep in mind that you can use the AutoFill to extend the selection left or right or up or down by dragging the Fill handle (see Book II, Chapter 1 for information about using AutoFill to extend and copy a cell entry).

...ith drag-and-drop

...rovides the newest and quickest way to move or copy a ... single worksheet. To move a range, simply select the cells, ...r on any one of the edges of the range, and then drag the ...position in the worksheet and release the mouse button.

...ly thing that you need to be mindful of when using drag-and-drop is that you must position the pointer on one of the edges of the cell range and *wait* until the pointer changes shape from a thick white cross to an outlined arrowhead pointing to the center of a black cross comprised of double-headed arrows (shown in the margin) before you begin dragging the range to its new position in the worksheet. Also, when positioning the pointer on an edge of the range, avoid the lower-right corner because locating the pointer there transforms it into the Fill handle (a simple black cross) used by the AutoFill feature to extend the cell range rather than move the range.

As you drag a cell range using drag-and-drop, Excel displays only the outline of the range with a ToolTip that keeps you informed of its new cell or range address. When you have positioned the outline of the range so that it surrounds the appropriate cells in a new area of the worksheet, simply release the mouse button. Excel moves the selected cells (including the entries, formatting, and comments) to this area.

If the outline of the cell selection that you're dropping encloses any cells with existing data entries, Excel displays an Alert dialog box asking if you want to replace the contents of the destination cells. If you click OK in this dialog box, the overlaid data entries will be completely zapped when they're replaced by the incoming entries.

You can use drag-and-drop to copy cell ranges as well as to move them. To modify drag-and-drop so that the feature copies the selected cells rather than relocating them, hold down the Ctrl key when you position the pointer on one of the edges of the selected range (remember to avoid that lower-right corner!). Excel indicates that drag-and-drop is ready to copy rather than move the cell selection by changing the mouse pointer to an outline pointer with a small plus sign on the upper-right (shown in the margin). When the pointer assumes this shape, you simply drag the outline of the selected cell range to the desired position and release both the Ctrl key and mouse button.

Note that you can't use drag-and-drop to copy or move a cell selection unless the first cell of the range into which the cells are being copied or moved is visible in the Excel work area. This means that you can't use drag-and-drop to copy or move cells between different worksheets in the same workbook or between different workbook files *unless* you first set up windows in the Excel work area that display both the cells that you're moving or copying and the cells into which they're being moved or copied (see Book II, Chapter 4 for information on setting up windows that enable this). Use the cut-and-paste method (as described in the following section) to move and copy cell selections beyond the current worksheet when you don't have such windows set up.

Carried away with cut-and-paste

Given the convenience of using drag-and-drop, you may still prefer to use the more traditional cut-and-paste method when moving or copying cells in a worksheet. Cut-and-paste uses the Clipboard (a special area of memory shared by all Windows programs), which provides a temporary storage area for the data in your cell selection until you paste the selection into its new position in the worksheet.

To move a cell selection, click the Cut button on the Standard toolbar or choose Edit⇨Cut on the Menu bar (or the press the shortcuts, Ctrl+X or Shift+Delete). To copy the selection, click the Copy button on the Standard toolbar or choose Edit⇨Copy (or press the shortcuts, Ctrl+C or Ctrl+Insert). When you cut or copy a selection to the Clipboard, Excel displays a marquee around the cell selection (sometimes called *marching ants*), and the following message appears on the Status bar:

```
Select destination and press ENTER or choose Paste
```


To complete the move or copy operation, simply select the first cell in the range where you want the relocated or copied selection to appear and press the Enter key or click the Paste button on the Standard toolbar or choose Edit⇨Paste (or press the shortcuts, Ctrl+V or Shift+Insert). Excel then completes the move or copy operation, pasting the range as required, starting with the active cell. When selecting the first cell of a paste range, be sure that you have sufficient blank cells below and to the right of the active cell so that the range you're pasting doesn't overlay any existing data that you don't want Excel to replace.

Keep in mind that you don't have to select the entire paste range before you select the Paste command to complete a move or copy operation. If, when moving a cell selection with cut-and-paste, you do select the paste range rather than just its first cell, you must select a range that is identical in size and shape to the one that you cut or copied to the Clipboard. If you don't, Excel displays an Alert dialog box with the following message:

```
The information cannot be pasted because the Cut and paste
   areas are not the same size and shape
```

You then have to clear the Alert dialog box and then reselect the paste range before you can complete the move. Note that you don't get this warning when you're copying a cell selection with cut-and-paste: Excel just goes ahead and completes the copy operation by using the first cell that you selected as the anchor point and laying down the rest of the copied cells to suit.

Unlike when moving and copying a cell selection with drag-and-drop, the cut-and-paste method doesn't warn you when it's about to replace existing cell entries in cells that are overlaid by the incoming cell range — it just goes ahead and replaces them with nary a beep or an alert! If you find that you moved the selection to the wrong area or replaced cells in error, immediately choose the Edit⇨Undo Paste or press Ctrl+Z to restore the range to its previous position in the worksheet.

"Paste it again, Sam"

When you complete a copy operation with cut-and-paste by clicking the Paste button or by choosing Edit⇨Paste instead of pressing the Enter key, Excel copies the selected cell range to the paste area in the worksheet without removing the marquee from the original range. This allows you to continue to paste the selection to other areas in the worksheet without having to open the Clipboard Task Pane to recopy the cell range to the Clipboard. If you don't need to paste the cell range in any other place in the worksheet, you can press Enter to complete the copy operation. If you don't need to make further copies but you choose the Paste command, you can remove the marquee from the original selection simply by pressing the Escape key.

Also, when you paste a cell selection that you've copied to the Clipboard (this doesn't apply when pasting cells that you've cut to the Clipboard), Excel displays the Paste Options button in the lower-right corner of the cell selection (shown in the margin). When you position the mouse pointer over this Paste Options button, a pop-up button appears that, when clicked, displays a pop-up menu with the following options:

- **Keep Source Formatting** to use the formatting applied to the cell selection that you're copying.
- **Match Destination Formatting** to use the formatting applied to the cells where the selection is being copied.
- **Values and Number Formatting** to copy only the number formatting applied to the cell selection that you copied to the Clipboard.
- **Keep Source Column Widths** to adjust the columns in the cells where the selection is being copied to match the widths of the columns in the cell selection that you copied to the Clipboard.
- **Formatting Only** to copy all the formatting (and only the formatting) applied to the cell selection that you copied to the Clipboard.

✦ **Link Cells** to create linking formulas that bring the data entries in the copied cell selection forward to the destination cells (rather than actually copying the contents to these cells). When you link cells, any changes that you make to the original cell entries are automatically applied to the linked copies.

By default, Excel selects the Keep Source Formatting item to copy the entries along with its formatting. To switch to one of the other options, click its item on the Paste Options pop-up menu.

Taking it out of the Clipboard Task pane

As soon as you cut or copy a cell selection with cut-and-paste, Excel puts the contents of the cell selection into the Clipboard. In fact, as you edit your spreadsheet, the Clipboard stores the contents of up to the last 24 cell selections that you cut or copy (before replacing them with new selections that you cut or copy). Up to that time, you can examine the contents of the Clipboard and even paste your cell selections in other places in your spreadsheet or even in documents open in other programs that you're running (see Book IV, Chapter 3 for information about pasting Excel data from the Clipboard into other applications).

To open the Clipboard Task Pane when another pane is displayed, click the Task Pane drop-down button and then click Clipboard on the pop-up menu. To open the Clipboard Task Pane when no Task Pane is displayed in the Excel Work area, press Ctrl+CC (that is, hold the Ctrl key and then type two Cs in a row).

When the Clipboard Task Pane is displayed, it shows all the individual items that have been cut or copied there (up to a maximum of 24). To paste an item into a cell of one of your worksheets, click the cell, and then position the mouse pointer over the item in the Clipboard Task Pane. When the item's pop-up button appears, click this button and then click Paste on the pop-up menu, shown in Figure 3-17.

Inserting rather than replacing copied cells

When you use cut-and-paste to move or copy a cell selection, you can have Excel paste the data into the worksheet without replacing existing entries in overlaid cells by choosing Insert⇨Copied Cells on the Menu bar instead of using the normal Paste command. When you choose Insert⇨Copied Cells, Excel displays the Insert Paste dialog box, where you can choose between a Shift Cells Right or a Shift Cells Down radio button. Select Shift Cells Right to have existing cells moved to columns on the right to make room for the moved or copied cells. Select Shift Cells Down to have the existing cells moved to lower rows to make room for them.

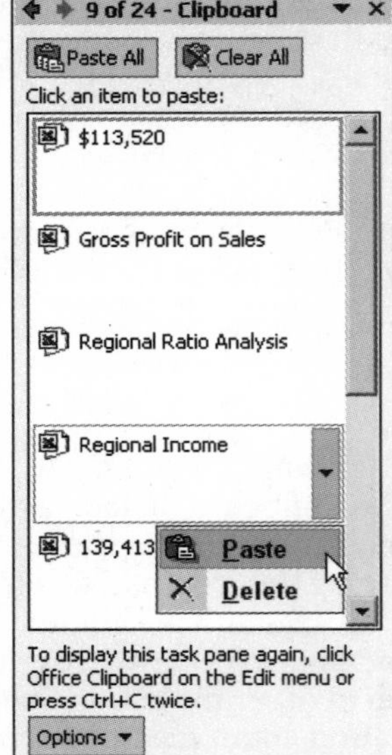

Figure 3-17: Pasting an entry into a new cell from the Clipboard Task Pane.

Pasting just the good parts with Paste Special

Normally, when you paste worksheet data from the Clipboard, Excel pastes all of the information (entries, formatting, and comments) from the cell selection into the designated paste area, thus replacing any existing entries in the cells that are overlaid. You can, however, use the Edit⇨Paste Special command to control what information is pasted into the paste range and/or have Excel perform simple mathematical computations between the number of cell entries that overlay each other.

When you choose Edit⇨Paste Special after selecting the first cell of the destination range, Excel opens the Paste Special dialog box that contains two areas: Paste and Operation. The Paste radio buttons enable you to specify which components of the copied cell selection that you want copied; see Table 3-1 for a list of paste options. The Operation option buttons enable you to specify which mathematical operation, if any, should be performed between the overlaying values in copy and paste ranges. You select the Skip Blanks check box when you don't want Excel to replace existing entries in the paste range with overlaying blank cells in the copy range. You select the Transpose check box when you want to invert the copy range so that its orientation is reversed in the paste range.

Table 3-1 The Paste Options in the Paste Special Dialog Box

Paste Option	*What It Does*
All	Pastes all types of entries (numbers, formulas, and text), their formats, and comments from the selection in the paste area
Formulas	Pastes only the entries (numbers, formulas, and text) from the selection in the paste area
Values	Pastes only numbers and text from the selection in the paste area, converting all formulas to their current calculated values so they're pasted into the worksheet as numbers
Formats	Pastes only the formats from the selection into the paste area
Comments	Pastes only the comments from the selection into the paste area
Validation	Pastes only the entries in cells that use data validation in the paste area (see Book II, Chapter 1 for info on Data Validation)
All Except Borders	Pastes everything but the borders assigned to the cell selection into the paste area
Column Widths	Pastes everything into the paste area and adjusts the columns widths in this area to match those of the original cell selection
Formulas and Number Formats	Pastes only the formulas and number formatting (omitting all text and numeric entries) from the cell selection into the paste area
Values and Number Formats	Pastes only the numbers and number formatting (omitting all text and converting all formulas to their calculated values) from the cell selection into the paste area

The Transpose check box in the Paste Special dialog box is particularly helpful when you have a row of column headings that you want to convert into a column of row headings or when you have a column of row headings that you want to convert into a row of column headings. You can also use this dialog box to pivot an entire table of data so that the data that runs across the rows now runs down the columns and vice versa.

Figure 3-18 illustrates just such a situation. Here, I selected the data and headings in the cell range A2:J7, clicked the Copy button on the Standard toolbar, and then moved the cell pointer to cell A9. After that, I chose Edit⇨Paste Special and clicked the Transpose check box before clicking OK.

2003 Production Schedule

	Apr-03	May-03	Jun-03	Jul-03	Aug-03	Sep-03	Oct-03	Nov-03	Dec-03
Part 100	500	485	438	505	483	540	441	550	345
Part 101	175	170	153	177	169	189	154	193	200
Part 102	350	340	306	354	338	378	309	385	350
Part 103	890	863	779	899	859	961	785	979	885
Total	1,915	1,858	1,676	1,934	1,848	2,068	1,689	2,107	1,780

	Part 100	Part 101	Part 102	Part 103	Total
Apr-03	500	175	350	890	1,915
May-03	485	170	340	863	1,858
Jun-03	438	153	306	779	1,676
Jul-03	505	177	354	899	1,934
Aug-03	483	169	338	859	1,848
Sep-03	540	189	378	961	2,068
Oct-03	441	154	309	785	1,689
Nov-03	550	193	385	979	2,107
Dec-03	345	200	350	885	1,780

Figure 3-18: Transposing a row of column headings into a column of row headings.

The results of this transposition appear in the cell range A9:F18 in Figure 3-18. As you can see, transposing a table that uses borders can present you with some cleanup work (the borders applied to the bottom of the last row with the Part 103 production units need to be removed from the cell range E9:E18 in the transposed table), but otherwise, everything else — including the formulas that total the units produced each month — turned out just fine.

You click the Paste Link button when you want to create a formula that links to the values in the cell selection rather than copying them verbatim. Linking formulas are automatically updated when you change the original values to which they refer.

To convert a cell range that contains formulas to its calculated values (as though you had input them as numbers), select the cell range, choose Edit⇨Copy and then choose Edit⇨Paste Special, click the Values radio button, and then click OK *without* moving the cell pointer. This causes Excel to paste the calculated values on top of the formulas that created them, thus zapping the overlaid formulas and leaving you only with the computed values!

Find and Replace This Disgrace!

No discussion of spreadsheet editing would be complete without including the Find and Replace features in Excel. You can use the Find feature to quickly locate each and every occurrence of a specific *string* (a series of characters) in a worksheet. You can use the Replace feature to have Excel actually update the cells that it finds with new text or numbers.

Both the Find and the Replace features share the same dialog box (aptly called the Find and Replace dialog box). If you only want to find a cell's particular contents, you just use the options on the Find tab (which is automatically selected when you open the Find and Replace dialog box with Edit⇨Find or Ctrl+F). If you want to update the contents of some or all of the cells that you find, use the options on the Replace tab (which is automatically selected when you open the Search and Replace dialog box with Edit⇨Replace or Ctrl+H).

The Find and Replace tabs in the Find and Replace dialog box contain a bunch of search options that you can use in finding and replacing stuff in your spreadsheet. The only problem is that these options are hidden when you first open the Find and Replace dialog box. To expand the Search and Replace dialog box to display the extra search options on the Find and Replace tab, click the Options> button.

Finding stuff

To use the Find command to locate information in your worksheet, follow these steps:

1. **To search the entire worksheet, select a single cell. To restrict the search to a specific cell range or nonadjacent selection, select all the cells to be searched.**
2. **Choose Edit⇨Find on Menu bar or press Ctrl+F.**

   Excel opens the Find and Replace dialog box with the Find tab selected, containing the options shown in Figure 3-19.
3. **Type the search string that you want to locate in the Find What combo box.**

   When entering the search string, you can use the question mark (?) or asterisk (*) wildcards to stand in for any characters that you're unsure of. Use the question mark to stand for a single character as in "Sm?th", which will match either *Smith* or *Smyth*. Use the asterisk to stand for multiple characters as in "9*1", which will locate *91*, *94901*, or even *9553 1st Street*. To search for a wildcard character, precede the character with a tilde (~), as in "~*2.5", to locate formulas that are multiplied by the number 2.5 (the asterisk is the multiplication operator in Excel).

If the cell holding the search string that you're looking for is formatted in a particular way, you can narrow the search by specifying what formatting to search for.

4. **Click the Format drop-down button to specify the formatting to search for in addition to your search string, and then click the Format item to select the formatting from the Find Format dialog box or click Choose Format from Cell to select the formatting directly from a cell in the worksheet.**

   When you click the Format item, Excel opens a Find Format dialog box with the same tabs and options as the standard Format Cells dialog box. You then select the formatting that you want to search for in this dialog box and then click OK.

   When you click the Choose Format from Cell item on the Format button pop-up menu, the Find and Replace dialog box temporarily disappears until you click the cell in the worksheet that contains the formatting that you want to search for with the thick, white-cross mouse pointer with eyedropper icon.

   Note that when using the Find feature to locate a search string, by default, Excel searches only the current worksheet for your search string. If you want Excel to search all the cells of all worksheets in the workbook, you need to follow Step 5.

5. **Click Workbook on the Within pop-up menu to have Excel search all worksheets in the workbook.**

   If the Within drop-down list box doesn't appear at the bottom of your Find and Replace dialog box, click the Options> button to expand it and add the Within, Search, and Look In drop-down list boxes along with the Match Case and Match Entire Cell Contents check boxes.

   By default, Excel searches across the rows in the worksheet or current selection (that is, to the right and then down from the active cell). If you want to have the program search down the columns and then across the rows, you need to follow Step 6.

6. **Click By Columns on the Search pop-up menu to have Excel search down the columns (that is, down and then to the right from the active cell).**

   By default, Excel locates the search string in the contents of each cell as entered on the Formula bar. This means that if you're looking for a cell that contains 1,250 and the spreadsheet contains the formula, =750+500, whose calculated value as displayed in the cell is 1,250, Excel won't consider this cell to be a match because in searching the Formula bar, it finds =750+500 instead of 1,250.

To have Excel search the contents of each cell (and thus, consider a cell that displays your value to be a match even when its contents on the Formula bar don't contain the search string), you need to change the Look In setting from Formulas to Values. If you want Excel to search for the search string in the comments you've added to cells, you need to change the Look In setting to Comments.

7. **Click Values on the Look In pop-up menu to have Excel locate the search string in the contents of each cell as it's displayed in the worksheet. Click Comments on this pop-up menu instead to have Excel locate the search string in the comments that you've added to cells.**

   Note that when you select Comments to search the comments you've added to the spreadsheet, you can't specify any formatting to search for as the Format button in the Find and Replace dialog box becomes grayed out.

   By default, Excel ignores case differences between search string and the contents of the cells being searched so that *Assets*, *ASSETS*, and *assets* all match the search string, Assets. To find only exact matches, follow Step 8.

8. **Click the Match Case check box to find occurrences of the search string when it matches the case that you entered.**

   By default, Excel considers any occurrence of the search string to be a match — even when it occurs as part of another part of the cell entry so that when the search string is 25, cells containing 25, 15.25, 25 Main Street, and 250,000 are all considered matches. To find only complete occurrences of your search string in a cell, follow Step 9.

9. **Click the Match Entire Cell Contents check box to find occurrences of the search string only when it's the entire cell entry.**

   After you have the search string and search options entered as you want them, you're ready to start searching the spreadsheet.

10. **Click the Find All button to find all occurrences of the search string. Click the Find Next button to find just the first occurrence of the search string.**

    When you click Find All, Excel lists all the cells containing the search string in a list box at the bottom of the Find and Replace dialog box, as shown in Figure 3-19. You can then have Excel select the cell with a particular occurrence by clicking its link in this list box. You may have to drag the Find and Replace dialog box out of the way to see the selected cell.

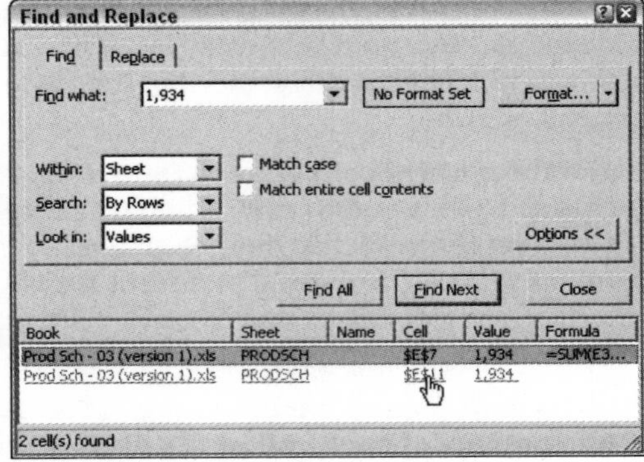

Figure 3-19: Finding a value in a spreadsheet by using the options on the Find tab.

When you click Find Next, Excel selects the next cell in the spreadsheet (using the designated search direction). To find subsequent occurrences of the search string, you need to continue to click Find Next until you reach the cell that you're looking for. Again, you may have to drag the Find and Replace dialog box out of the way to see the cell that Excel has located and selected in the worksheet.

11. **After you finish searching the spreadsheet for the search string, click the Close button.**

Note that Excel retains your search string and search option conditions even after closing the Find and Replace dialog box. To repeat a search, just press Ctrl+F and then click Find All or Find Next. You can also reinstate a search string that you used earlier in your work session by clicking it on the Find What pop-up menu.

Finding and replacing stuff

The Find feature is sufficient if all that you want to do is locate an occurrence of a search string in your worksheet. Many times, however, you will also want to change some or all of the cells that match the search string. For those situations, you use the Replace feature to locate the search string and replace it with some other string.

To search and replace information in your worksheet, follow these steps:

1. **To search and replace the entire worksheet, select a single cell. To restrict the search and replace operation to a specific cell range or nonadjacent selection, select all the cells to be edited.**
2. **Choose Edit⇨Replace on the Menu bar or press Ctrl+H.**

Excel opens the Find and Replace dialog box with the Replace tab selected (similar to the one shown in Figure 3-20). Note that if the Find and Replace dialog box is already open from selecting Edit⇨Find or pressing Ctrl+F, all you have to do is click the Replace tab.

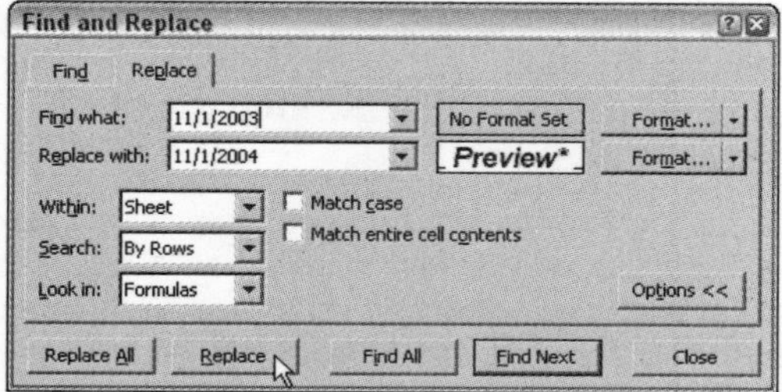

Figure 3-20: Replacing dates in a spreadsheet by using the options on the Replace tab.

3. **Type the search string that you want to locate in the Find What combo box and specify any formatting to be searched by using its Format button.**

   Refer back to the previous steps on finding a search string for details on specifying the search string in the Find What combo box and specifying the formatting to be searched for.

4. **Type the replacement string in the Replace With combo box.**

   Enter this string *exactly* as you want it to appear in the cells of the worksheet. Use uppercase letters where uppercase is to appear, lowercase letters where lowercase is to appear, and the question mark and asterisk only where they are to appear (they don't act as wildcard characters in a replacement string).

5. **Click the Format drop-down button and select Format to select the formatting to be added to your replacement string from the Find Format dialog box, or click Choose Format from Cell and select the formatting directly from a cell in the worksheet.**

   When you click the Format item, Excel opens a Find Format dialog box with the same tabs and options as the standard Format Cells dialog box. You may then select the formatting that you want to replacement string to have in this dialog box and then click OK.

   When you click the Choose Format from Cell item on the Format button pop-up menu, the Find and Replace dialog box temporarily disappears until you click the cell in the worksheet that contains the formatting that you want the replacement string to have with the thick, white-cross mouse pointer with eyedropper icon.

6. **Make any necessary changes to the Within, Search, Look In, Match Case, and Match Entire Contents options for the search string.**

   These options work just as they do on the Find tab. If these options aren't displayed on the Replace tab of your Find and Replace dialog box, click its Options>> button to expand the dialog box.

7. **Click the Find Next button to locate the first occurrence of the search string. Then, click the Replace button to replace the first occurrence with the replacement string or click the Find Next button again to skip this occurrence.**

   Using the Find Next and Replace buttons to search and replace on a case-by-case basis is by far the safest way to use the Find and Replace feature. If you're certain (really certain) that you won't mess anything up by replacing all occurrences throughout the spreadsheet, you can click the Replace All button to have Excel make the replacements globally without stopping to show you which cells are updated.

8. **When you finish replacing entries on a case-by-case basis, click the Close button.**

   This action abandons the Find and Replace operation and closes the Find and Replace dialog box. When you globally replace the search string, Excel automatically closes the Find and Replace dialog box after replacing the last search string match.

Remember that you can use Edit⇨Undo (Ctrl+Z) or the Undo button on the Standard toolbar to restore any replacements that you made in error.

Spell Checking Heaven

You can use Excel's Spell Check feature to catch all the spelling mistakes that AutoCorrect lets slip through. To spell check your spreadsheet, click the Spelling button on the Standard toolbar, click F7, or choose Tools⇨Spelling on the Excel Menu bar.

When you spell check a spreadsheet, Excel looks up each word in the Excel Dictionary. If the word is not found (as is often the case with less-common last names, abbreviations, acronyms, and technical terms), Excel selects the cell with the unknown spelling and then displays a Spelling dialog box showing the unknown word in the Not in Dictionary text box with suggested correct spellings shown in a Suggestions list box below, which is similar to the one shown in Figure 3-21.

You can then take any of the following actions to take care of the unknown word:

- ✦ Click one of the words in the Suggestions list box and then click the Change button to have Excel replace the unknown word with the selected suggestion and continue spell checking the rest of the spreadsheet
- ✦ Click one of the words in the Suggestions list box and then click the Change All button to have Excel replace all occurrences of the unknown word with the selected suggestion throughout the entire spreadsheet and then continue spell checking
- ✦ Click the Ignore Once button to let the misspelling slide just this once and continue spell checking the rest of the spreadsheet
- ✦ Click the Ignore All button to ignore all occurrences of the unknown word in the spreadsheet and continue spell checking
- ✦ Click the Add to Dictionary button to add the unknown word to a custom dictionary so that Excel will know the word the next time you spell check the worksheet
- ✦ Click the AutoCorrect button to have Excel add the unknown word to the AutoCorrect list with the selected suggestion as its automatic replacement

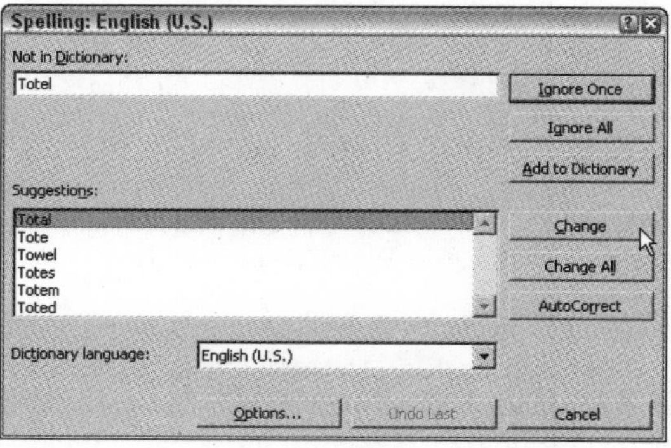

Figure 3-21: Spell checking the spreadsheet with the Spelling dialog box.

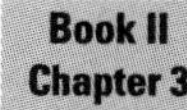

Keep in mind that Excel checks the spelling of the cells only in the current worksheet (and not all the sheets in the workbook). If you want Excel to spell check another worksheet, you need to click its sheet tab to make it active and then choose Tools⇨Spelling (F7). If you want to spell check just a portion of the worksheet, select the range or nonadjacent cell selection before you start the spell check.

When Excel finishes checking the current worksheet or cell selection, the program displays an Alert dialog box that indicates that the spell checking has been completed.

Changing the Spelling options

When you use Spell Check feature, you can change certain spelling options to better suit the spreadsheet that you're checking. To change the spelling options, click the Options button at the bottom of the Spelling dialog box. This action opens the Options dialog box with the single Spelling tab shown in Figure 3-22.

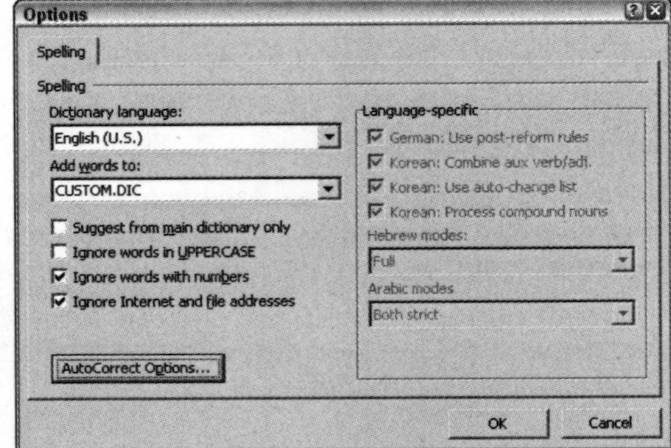

Figure 3-22: Changing the Spelling options.

In the Spelling Options dialog box, you can select a new dictionary language in the Dictionary Language drop-down list box (this is especially useful if your spreadsheet contains British English spellings or French or Spanish terms). If you have created a different custom dictionary for various types of technical terms, you can also select it as the custom dictionary to which all new terms are added in the Add Word To combo box.

To have Excel only use the main dictionary when doing a spell check (thus, ignoring all words that you've added to the custom dictionary) click the Suggest from Main Dictionary Only check box. To have Excel ignore acronyms that use all capital letters in your spreadsheet, click the Ignore Words in UPPERCASE check box.

By default, Excel doesn't flag words that contain numbers as unknown (such as B52). If you would like to have such words checked, click the Ignore Words with Numbers check box to remove its checkmark. Also, Excel ignores all entries that it identifies as an Internet address and file path (you know, stuff like `www.dummies.com` and `c:\mydocuments\finance`). To have Excel spell check these types of entries, click the Ignore Internet and File Addresses check box to remove its checkmark.

Note that Language Specific check boxes and drop-down list boxes on the right side of the Options dialog box remain grayed out until you select a dictionary in the Dictionary Language drop-down list box either for German, Korean, Hebrew, or Arabic. Then, you can use them (depending on the language selected) to determine how their words are treated during spell checking.

Adding words to the Custom Dictionary

You use the Add to Dictionary button in the Spelling dialog box to add unknown words to a custom dictionary. By default, Excel adds words to a custom dictionary file named `custom.dic`. This file is located in the Proof Folder, which is located within the Microsoft folder inside the Application Data folder. The Application Data folder is either inside the Windows folder on your C: hard drive or, if you're on a network, this file may be located in your username folder inside the Profiles folder that lies within the Windows folder on your C: hard drive.

If you want, you can create other custom dictionaries to use when spell checking your worksheets (although you can only use one custom dictionary at a time). To create a new custom dictionary, follow these steps:

1. **Choose Tools⇨Spelling on the Menu bar, click the Spelling button on the Standard toolbar, or press F7 to begin spell-checking your spreadsheet.**

   You can't start adding words to a new custom dictionary until you spell check a spreadsheet and Excel starts flagging some unknown words.

2. **When Excel locates an unknown word that you want to add to a new custom dictionary, click the Options button at the bottom of the Spelling dialog box.**

   This action opens the Options dialog box, where you can select a new custom dictionary to use.

3. **Click Add Word To combo box and then edit the `custom` part of the dictionary filename before you click OK or press Enter.**

   When editing the `custom.dic` filename to create a name for your new custom dictionary, be sure not to delete the `.dic` filename extension in the Add Words To combo box. As soon as you click OK or press Enter, Excel adds the unknown word to your new custom dictionary.

4. **Continue spell checking your spreadsheet, using the Add to Dictionary button to add all unknown words that you want to be part of your new custom dictionary.**

Note that Excel continues to add all unknown words to your new custom dictionary until you change back to the original custom dictionary (or another custom one that you've created). To change back and start adding unknown words to the original custom dictionary, click the Options button in the Spelling dialog box and then click `custom.dic` in the Add Words To pop-up menu.

You can directly edit the words that you add to your custom dictionary with the Notepad text editor that comes with Windows. Simply open the CUSTOM.DIC on your hard drive (located in the Proof folder inside the Microsoft folder within the Application Data folder) and then make any changes to the entries in this file (to delete an entry, select it with the I-beam mouse pointer and then press the Delete key). Choose File➪Save on 90Notepad pull-down menus to save your changes.

Eliminating Errors with Text to Speech

Find and Replace is a great tool for eliminating errors that you've flagged in the worksheet. Likewise, the Spell Check feature is great for eliminating input errors that result from typos. Unfortunately, neither of these features can help you to identify data input errors that result from inaccuracies stemming from actions, such as mistyping the entry (without misspelling it) or transposing one entry with another. The only way that you can flag and then correct these errors is by checking and verifying the accuracy of each and every data entry in the worksheet. Usually, you do this by checking the columns and rows of data in a spreadsheet against the original documents from which you generated the spreadsheet.

Excel 2002 introduces a powerful feature known as Text to Speech that can help you through the drudgery of checking and verifying the data input in your spreadsheets. When you use Text to Speech, the computer speaks the contents of each cell in the range that you select. As the computer speaks each data entry in the range, you can be checking the hard copy to make sure that you (or a coworker) correctly input the data. If you discover a discrepancy between the spoken data entry and what should have been entered from the printed copy, you can stop Text to Speech and then edit the cell and make the correction on the spot before continuing reading aloud of the other cells in the range.

To use the Text to Speech feature, choose Tools➪Speech➪Show Text to Speech Toolbar on the Excel pull-down menus. The first time you do this, if the Text to Speech feature isn't installed on your computer, Excel asks if you want to install Text to Speech. You then follow the prompts to install this feature (make sure that you have the Office XP CD-ROM handy when you do this or make sure that you can provide the Windows Installer with the path to the Office program files on your network).

After Text to Speech is installed, choose Tools➪Speech➪Show Text to Speech Toolbar command to open the Text to Speech toolbar, shown in Figure 3-23. To then use its buttons to verify the data entries in a particular range of your worksheet, simply select the cells and then click the Speak Cells button. Text to Speech then speaks all the data entries in the selected cell range, moving left to right from column to column across and then down the rows in this selection.

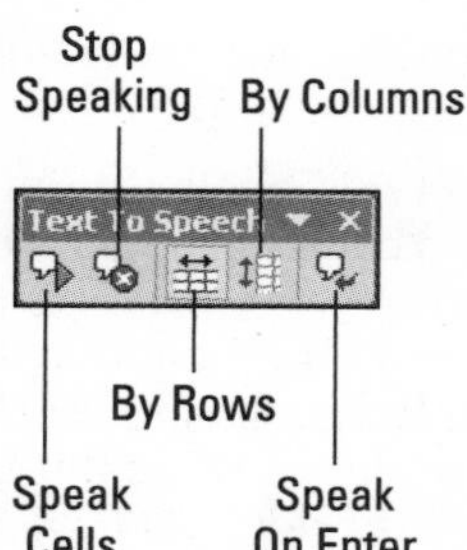

Figure 3-23: Use the Text to Speech toolbar to verify data input and locate and eliminate errors.

If the entry being spoken for a cell doesn't match the one in your printed copy, you can temporarily stop Text to Speech by clicking the Stop Speaking button. You can then edit the entry by clicking its contents on the Formula bar and then clicking the Enter button to complete the edit and update the cell's contents.

If Excel moves the cell pointer after editing the entry in such a way that it skips one or more cells in the selected range that should be verified by Text to Speech, use the Tab or Shift+Tab key to move the cell pointer to the cell that next needs to be verified with Text to Speech (don't use the arrow keys or click the cell because this immediately de-selects the cell range that Text to Speech is reading aloud).

When using Text to Speech, you can change the direction in which the cells are read. Instead of having Text to Speech read across the columns and then down the rows, you can have it read down the rows and across the columns by clicking the By Columns button on the Text to Speech toolbar before you have it start reading aloud the entries in the selected range.

You can also modify the voice that the Text to Speech feature uses to read aloud the entries in a cell range. To do this, follow these steps:

1. **Click Start on the Windows Taskbar and then highlight Settings on the Start menu and click Control Panel on the cascading menu.**

   If you're using Windows XP, click Control Panel directly on the Start menu.

This action opens the Control Panel window.

2. **Double-click the Speech icon in the Control Panel window to open the Speech Properties dialog box.**

   If you're using Windows XP and the Control Panel is in Category view, you can click the Switch to Classic View link and then double-click the Speech icon, or you can click the Sounds, Speech, and Audio Devices link followed by the Speech link.

3. **Click the Text to Speech tab in the Speech Properties dialog box.**
4. **Click the name of the voice that you want to use from the Voice Selection drop-down list.**

   You can select between LH Michael and LH Michelle as the voice on Windows 98, and between LH Michael, LH Michelle, and Microsoft Sam as the voice on Windows XP. LH stands for Lerned and Hauspie (the creator of Michael and Michelle's voice). LH Michael sounds like the voice used by the eminent physicist, Stephen Hawking, and LH Michelle sounds like the female equivalent of that voice. Microsoft Sam sounds to me like the voice of HAL 9000 in Stanley Kubrick's *2001: A Space Odyssey*, when Dave was disconnecting his memory circuits!

5. **Click the Use the Following Text to Preview the Voice text box and then edit the text that you want the voice you selected to say to you.**

   For example, when previewing the Microsoft Sam voice, you can enter the text, "I'm afraid Dave. Dave, I'm afraid" to see if you think this voice sounds like HAL 9000 as well.

6. **Click the Preview Voice button to have the voice that you selected read back the text shown in the Use the Following Text to Preview the Voice text box.**
7. **If you want to adjust the voice speed, drag the Voice Speed slider toward Slow or Fast to either slow down the speaking or speed it up.**

   After adjusting the speed, be sure to click the Preview Voice button again to make sure that you haven't slowed or sped up the rate of speaking too much.

   If you drag the slider toward Slow when the Microsoft Sam voice is selected, you definitely have a dead ringer for HAL 9000 in his famous disconnection scene.

8. **Click OK to close the Speech Properties dialog box.**

   If you're using Windows XP, you also need to click the Close button in the Control Panel window or the Sounds, Speech, and Audio Devices window to close it.

After changing the voice in the Windows' Speech Properties dialog box, Excel's Text to Speech feature uses that voice the next time you employ it in validating the accuracy of the data input in your spreadsheet.

Click the Speak On Enter button to have Text to Speech read each data entry back to you as you complete its entry in the cell. That way, you can verify the accuracy of the data entries as you make them and not have to worry about editing them later on. Just keep in mind when using Text to Speech in Speak on Enter mode that you must press the Enter key in order to have the entry read aloud to you: this verbal feedback doesn't happen when you use any other method to complete a data entry, including clicking the Enter button on the Formula bar (in this case, "Enter" means only pressing the Enter key).

Note that the Speak on Enter button is a toggle so that you turn off this speaking mode by clicking the button a second time. The Text to Speech feature is great because it tells you exactly when clicking the Speak On Enter button turns on and off the mode. When you click the button to turn it on, Text to Speech says, "Cells will now be spoken on Enter." So too, when you click the button to turn this Speak-on-Enter mode off, Text to Speech says, "Turn off Speak on Enter."

Chapter 4: Managing Worksheets

In This Chapter

- **Inserting and deleting columns and rows in a worksheet**
- **Splitting the worksheet into separate panes**
- **Outlining data in a worksheet**
- **Inserting, deleting, and reordering worksheets in a workbook**
- **Opening windows on different worksheets in a workbook**
- **Working with multiple workbooks**
- **Opening windows on different workbooks**
- **Creating and using custom workspaces**
- **Consolidating worksheet data**

Being able to manage and reorganize the information in your spreadsheet is almost as important as being able to input data and edit it. As part of these skills, you need to know how to manipulate the columns and rows of a single worksheet, the various worksheets within a single workbook, and, at times, other workbooks that contain supporting or relevant data.

This chapter examines how to reorganize information in a single worksheet by inserting and deleting columns and rows, as well as how to apply outlining to data tables that enables you expand and collapse details by showing and hiding columns and rows. It also covers how to reorganize and manipulate the actual worksheets in a workbook and discusses strategies for visually comparing and transferring data between the different workbooks that you have open for editing.

Reorganizing the Worksheet

Every worksheet that you work with has 256 columns and 65,536 rows, no more, no less, regardless of how many or how few of its cells you use. As your spreadsheet grows, you may find it beneficial to rearrange the data so that it doesn't creep. Many times, this involves deleting unnecessary columns and rows to bring the various data tables and lists in closer proximity to each other. At other times, you may need to insert new columns and rows in the worksheet so as to put a minimum of space between the groups of data.

Within the confines of the large worksheet space, your main challenge is often keeping tabs on all the information spread out throughout the sheet. At times, you may find that you need to split the worksheet window into panes so that you can view two disparate regions of the spreadsheet together in the same window and compare their data. For large data tables and lists, you may want to outline the worksheet data so that you can immediately collapse the information down to the summary or essential data and then just as quickly expand the information to show some or all of the supporting data.

Inserting and deleting columns and rows

The first thing to keep in mind when inserting or deleting columns and rows in a worksheet is that these operations affect all 65,536 rows in those columns and all 256 columns in those rows. As a result, you have to be sure that you're not about to adversely affect data in unseen rows and columns of the sheet before you undertake these operations. Note that in this regard, inserting columns or rows can be almost as detrimental as deleting them if, by inserting them, you split apart existing data tables or lists whose data should always remain together.

One way to guard against inadvertently deleting existing data or splitting apart a single range is to use the Zoom feature to zoom out on the sheet and then check visually for intersecting groups of data in the hinterlands of the worksheet. You can do this quickly by selecting the 25 percent setting on the Zoom button's pop-up menu or in the Zoom dialog box (View➪Zoom). Of course, even at the smallest zoom setting of 10 percent, you can see neither all the columns nor all the rows in the worksheet, and because everything's so tiny at that setting, you can't always tell whether or not the column or row you intend to fiddle with intersects those data ranges that you can identify.

Another way to check is to use the Ctrl key with the → or ↓ key to move the cell pointer from data range to data range across the column or row affected by your column or row deletion. Remember that pressing Ctrl plus and arrow key when the cell pointer is in a blank cell jumps the cell pointer to the next occupied cell in its row or column. That means if you press Ctrl+→ when the cell pointer is in row 52 and the pointer jumps to cell IV52 (the end of the worksheet in that row), you know that there isn't any data in that row that would be eliminated by your deleting that row or shifted up or down by your inserting a new row. So too, if you press Ctrl+↓ when the cell pointer is in column D and the cell pointer jumps down to cell D65536, you're assured that no data is about to be purged or shifted left or right by that column's deletion or a new column's insertion at that point.

When you're sure that you aren't about to make any problems for yourself in other, unseen parts of the worksheet by deleting or inserting columns, you're ready to make these structural changes to the worksheet.

Eradicating columns and rows

To delete columns or rows of the worksheet, you select them by clicking their column letters or row numbers in the column or row header and then choose Edit⇨Delete on the Excel Menu bar. Remember that you can select groups of columns and rows by dragging through their letters and numbers in the column or row header. You can also select nonadjacent columns and rows by holding down the Ctrl key as you click them.

When you delete a column, all the data entries within the cells of that column are immediately zapped. At the same, all remaining data entries in succeeding columns to the right move left to fill the blank left by the now-missing column. When you delete a row, all the data entries within the cells of that row are immediately eliminated, and the remaining data entries in rows below move up to fill in the gap left by the missing row.

Remember that pressing the Delete key is *not* the same as selecting Edit⇨Delete on the Menu bar. When you press the Delete key after selecting columns or rows in the worksheet, Excel simply clears the data entries in their cells without adjusting any of the existing data entries in neighboring columns and rows. Use Edit⇨Delete when your purpose is *both* to delete the data in the selected columns or rows *and* to fill in the gap by adjusting the position of entries to the right and below the ones you eliminate.

Should your column or row deletions remove data entries referenced to in formulas, the #REF! error value replaces the calculated values in the cells of the formulas affected by the elimination of the original cell references. You must then recreate the original formula and then recopy it to get rid of these nasty formula errors. (See Book III, Chapter 2 for more on error values in formulas.)

Adding new columns and rows

To insert a new column or row into the worksheet, you select the column or row where you want the new blank column or row to appear (again by clicking its column letter or row number in the column or row header) and then choose Insert⇨Columns or Insert⇨Rows on the Excel Menu bar. In inserting a blank column, Excel moves the existing data in the selected column to the column to the immediate right, while simultaneously adjusting any other columns of data on the right over one. In inserting the blank row, Excel moves the existing data in the selected row down to the row immediately underneath, while simultaneously adjusting any other rows of existing data that fall below it, down by one.

To insert multiple columns or rows at one time in the worksheet, you select the columns or rows where you want the new blank columns or rows to appear (by dragging through their column letters and row numbers in the column and row header) before you choose Insert➪Columns or Insert➪Rows from the Menu bar.

If you find that you can't safely take out or insert an entire column or row, you can delete or insert cells in the particular region of the worksheet instead. You may also be able to make space between tables or lists by just moving some of the data down or to the right. (See Book II, Chapter 3 for more on moving data and deleting and inserting cells in a worksheet.)

Whenever your column or row insertions reposition data entries that are referenced to in other formulas in the worksheet, Excel automatically adjusts the cell references in the formulas affected to reflect the movement of their columns left or right, or rows up or down.

Splitting the worksheet into panes

Excel enables you to split the active worksheet window into two or four panes, each of which is equipped with its own scroll bars. After splitting up the window into panes, you can then use the pane's scroll bars to bring different parts of the same worksheet into view. This is great for comparing the data in different sections of a table that would otherwise not be legible if you zoomed out far enough to have both sections displayed in the worksheet window.

To split the worksheet window into panes, you can use any of the following methods:

- ✦ To split the window horizontally into two panes (upper and lower), drag the horizontal split bar (the thin bar located above the up scroll arrow on the vertical scroll bar) down until you reach the row border in the worksheet where you want the window divided.
- ✦ To split the window vertically into two panes (left and right), drag the vertical split bar (the thin bar located behind the right scroll arrow on the horizontal scroll bar) to the left until you reach the column border in the worksheet where you want the window divided.
- ✦ To split the window both horizontally and vertically into four panes (upper-left, upper-right, lower-left, and lower-right), drag the horizontal split bar down to the desired row and then the vertical split bar left to the desired column (or vice versa).

Note that you can also split the window by positioning the cell pointer position in the worksheet in the cell whose top border marks the place where you want the horizontal division to take place and whose left border marks the place where you want the vertical division to take place before choosing Window⇨Split on the Menu bar.

Excel displays the borders of the window panes you create in the document window with a gray bar that ends with the vertical or horizontal split bar. To modify the size of a pane, you position the white-cross pointer on the appropriate dividing bar, then, as soon as the pointer changes to a double-headed arrow, drag the bar until the pane is the correct size and release the mouse button.

When you split a window into panes, Excel automatically synchronizes the scrolling, depending upon how you split the worksheet. When you split a window into two horizontal panes, as shown in Figure 4-1, the worksheet window contains a single horizontal scroll bar and two separate vertical scroll bars. This means that all horizontal scrolling of the two panes is synchronized, while vertically scrolling of each pane remains independent.

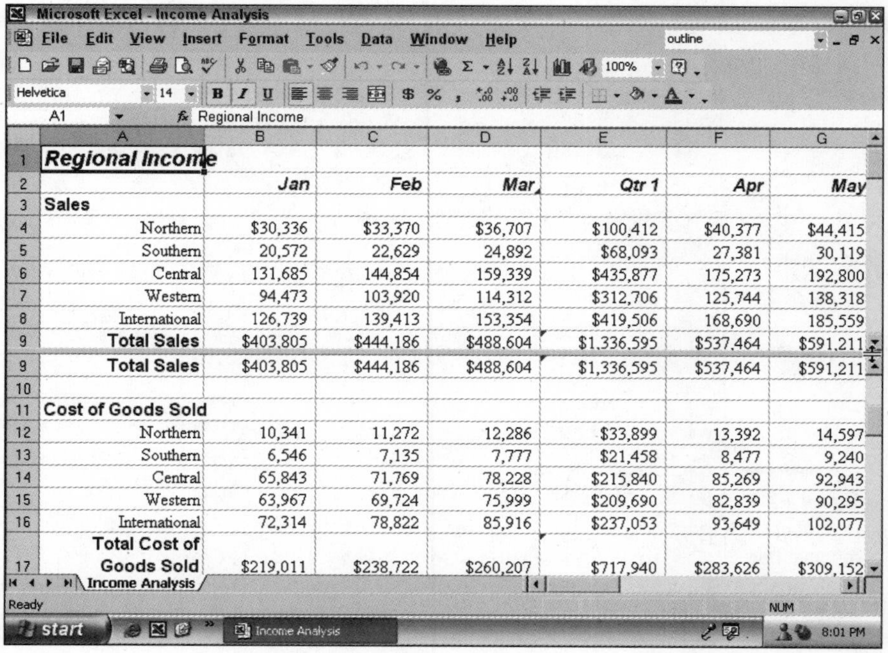

Microsoft Excel - Income Analysis

	A	B	C	D	E	F	G
1	Regional Income						
2		Jan	Feb	Mar	Qtr 1	Apr	May
3	Sales						
4	Northern	$30,336	$33,370	$36,707	$100,412	$40,377	$44,415
5	Southern	20,572	22,629	24,892	$68,093	27,381	30,119
6	Central	131,685	144,854	159,339	$435,877	175,273	192,800
7	Western	94,473	103,920	114,312	$312,706	125,744	138,318
8	International	126,739	139,413	153,354	$419,506	168,690	185,559
9	Total Sales	$403,805	$444,186	$488,604	$1,336,595	$537,464	$591,211
9	Total Sales	$403,805	$444,186	$488,604	$1,336,595	$537,464	$591,211
10							
11	Cost of Goods Sold						
12	Northern	10,341	11,272	12,286	$33,899	13,392	14,597
13	Southern	6,546	7,135	7,777	$21,458	8,477	9,240
14	Central	65,843	71,769	78,228	$215,840	85,269	92,943
15	Western	63,967	69,724	75,999	$209,690	82,839	90,295
16	International	72,314	78,822	85,916	$237,053	93,649	102,077
17	Total Cost of Goods Sold	$219,011	$238,722	$260,207	$717,940	$283,626	$309,152

Figure 4-1: Dragging the split bar to divide the worksheet window into two horizontal panes.

When you split a window into two vertical panes, as shown in Figure 4-2, the situation is reversed. The worksheet window contains a single vertical scroll bar and two separate horizontal scroll bars. This means that all vertical scrolling of the two panes is synchronized, while horizontal scrolling of each pane remains independent.

When you split a window into two horizontal and two vertical panes, as shown in Figure 4-3, the worksheet window contains two horizontal scroll bars and two separate vertical scroll bars. This means that vertical scrolling is synchronized in the top two window panes when you use the top vertical scroll bar and synchronized for the bottom two window panes when you use the bottom vertical scroll bar. Likewise, horizontal scrolling is synchronized for the left two window panes when you use the horizontal scroll bar on the left and synchronized for the right two window panes when you use the horizontal scroll bar on the right.

To move the cell pointer from pane to pane after splitting the worksheet window from the keyboard, you can press F6 to move the cell pointer to the first cell in each pane in a clockwise direction or press Shift+F6 to move the cell pointer to the first cell in each pane in a counterclockwise manner. (When you've divided the window into just two panes, it just looks like pressing F6 jumps the cell pointer back and forth or up and down.)

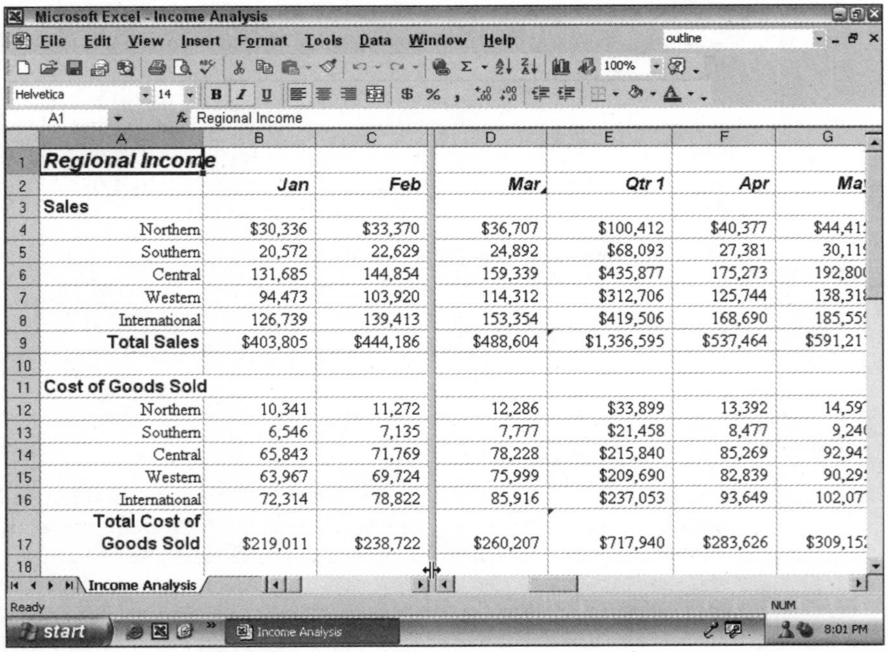

	A	B	C	D	E	F	G
1	Regional Income						
2		Jan	Feb	Mar	Qtr 1	Apr	Ma
3	Sales						
4	Northern	$30,336	$33,370	$36,707	$100,412	$40,377	$44,41
5	Southern	20,572	22,629	24,892	$68,093	27,381	30,11
6	Central	131,685	144,854	159,339	$435,877	175,273	192,80
7	Western	94,473	103,920	114,312	$312,706	125,744	138,31
8	International	126,739	139,413	153,354	$419,506	168,690	185,55
9	Total Sales	$403,805	$444,186	$488,604	$1,336,595	$537,464	$591,21
10							
11	Cost of Goods Sold						
12	Northern	10,341	11,272	12,286	$33,899	13,392	14,59
13	Southern	6,546	7,135	7,777	$21,458	8,477	9,24
14	Central	65,843	71,769	78,228	$215,840	85,269	92,94
15	Western	63,967	69,724	75,999	$209,690	82,839	90,29
16	International	72,314	78,822	85,916	$237,053	93,649	102,07
17	Total Cost of Goods Sold	$219,011	$238,722	$260,207	$717,940	$283,626	$309,15

Figure 4-2: Dragging the split bar to divide the worksheet window into two vertical panes.

Microsoft Excel - Income Analysis

A1 Regional Income

	A	B	C	D	E	F	G
1	Regional Income						
2		Jan	Feb	Mar	Qtr 1	Apr	Ma
3	Sales						
4	Northern	$30,336	$33,370	$36,707	$100,412	$40,377	$44,41
5	Southern	20,572	22,629	24,892	$68,093	27,381	30,11
6	Central	131,685	144,854	159,339	$435,877	175,273	192,80
7	Western	94,473	103,920	114,312	$312,706	125,744	138,31
8	International	126,739	139,413	153,354	$419,506	168,690	185,55
9	Total Sales	$403,805	$444,186	$488,604	$1,336,595	$537,464	$591,21
10							
11	Cost of Goods Sold						
12	Northern	10,341	11,272	12,286	$33,899	13,392	14,59
13	Southern	6,546	7,135	7,777	$21,458	8,477	9,24
14	Central	65,843	71,769	78,228	$215,840	85,269	92,94
15	Western	63,967	69,724	75,999	$209,690	82,839	90,29
16	International	72,314	78,822	85,916	$237,053	93,649	102,07
17	Total Cost of Goods Sold	$219,011	$238,722	$260,207	$717,940	$283,626	$309,15

Income Analysis

Figure 4-3: Splitting the worksheet window into four panes: two horizontal and two vertical.

To remove all panes from a window when you no longer need them, you simply choose Window⇨Remove Split on the Excel Menu bar, or you can also remove individual panes by dragging the gray dividing bar either for the horizontal or vertical pane until you reach one of the edges of the worksheet window. You can also remove a pane by positioning the mouse pointer on a pane-dividing bar and then, when it changes to a double-header arrow, double-click it.

Keep in mind that you can freeze panes in the window so that information in the upper pane and/or in the leftmost pane remains in the worksheet window at all times, no matter what other columns and rows you scroll to or how much you zoom in and out on the data. (See Book II, Chapter 3 for more on freezing panes.)

Outlining worksheets

The Outline feature enables you to control the level of detail displayed in a data table or list in a worksheet. After outlining a table or list, you can condense the table's display when you only want to use certain levels of summary information, and you can just as easily expand the outlined table or list to display various levels of detail data as needed. Being able to control which outline level is displayed in the worksheet makes it easy to print summary reports with various levels of data (see Book II, Chapter 5) as well as to chart just the summary data (see Book V, Chapter 1).

Spreadsheet outlines are a little different from the outlines you created in high school and college. In those outlines, you placed the headings at the highest levels (I.) at the top of the outline with the intermediate headings indented below. Most worksheet outlines, however, are backwards in the sense that the highest level summary row and column are located at the bottom and far right of the table or list of data, with the columns and rows of intermediate supporting data located above and to the left of the summary row and column.

The reason that worksheet outlines often seem "backwards" when compared to word processing outlines is that, most often, to calculate your summary totals in the worksheet, you naturally place the detail levels of data above the summary rows and to the left of the summary columns that total them. When creating a word processing outline, however, you place the major headings above subordinate headings, while at the same time indenting each subordinate level, reflecting the way we read words from left to right and down the page.

Outlines for data tables (as opposed to data lists) are also different from regular word-processed outlines because they outline the data in not one, but two hierarchies: a vertical hierarchy that summarizes the row data, and horizontal hierarchy that summarizes the column data. (You don't get much of that in your regular term paper!)

Creating the outline

To create an outline from a table of data, you select the table cells to be included in the outline, and then choose Data➪Group and Outline➪Auto Outline on the Excel Menu bar.

By default, Excel assumes that summary rows in the selected data table are below their detail data and summary columns are to the right of their detail data, which is normally the case. If, however, the summary rows are above the detail data and summary columns to the left of the detail data, Excel can still build the outline.

Simply start by choosing Data➪Group and then Outline➪Settings to open the Settings dialog box. In this dialog box, clear the checkmarks from the Summary Rows Below Detail and/or Summary Columns to Right of Detail check boxes in the Direction section. Also, you can have Excel automatically apply styles to different levels of the outline by selecting the Automatic Styles check box. (For more information on these styles, see the "Applying outline styles" section, later in this chapter.) To have Excel create the outline, click the Create button — if you select the OK button, the program simply closes the dialog box without outlining the selected worksheet data.

Figure 4-4 shows you the first part of the outline created by Excel for the CG Media sales worksheet. Note the various outline symbols that Excel added to the worksheet when it created the outline. Figure 4-4 identifies most of these outline symbols (the Show Detail button with the plus sign is not displayed in this figure), and Table 4-1 explains their function.

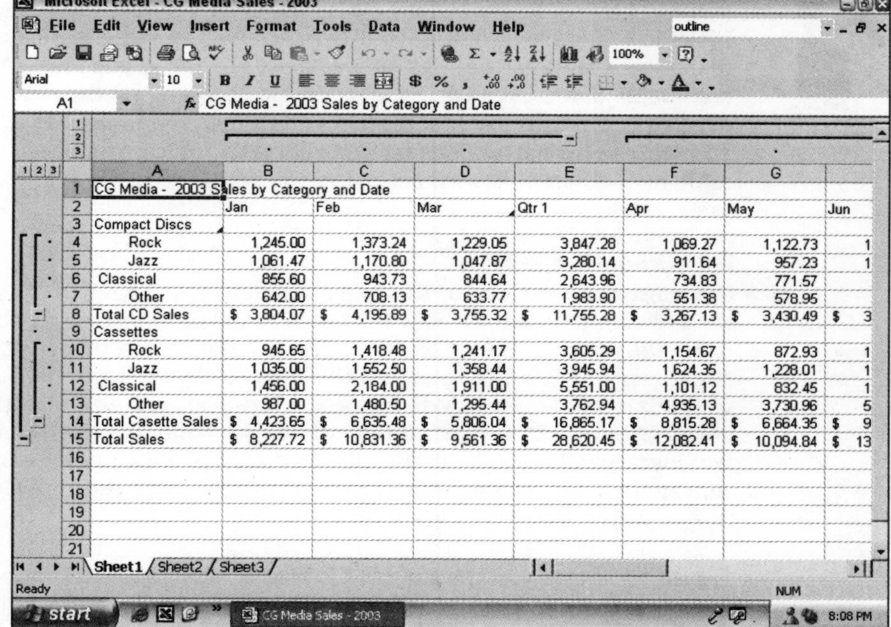

Figure 4-4: Outlining the 2003 CG Media Sales table arranged by category and date.

Table 4-1 Outline Symbols

Symbol	*Function*
Row and column level symbol (1, 2, 3, and so on up to 8)	Displays a desired level of detail throughout the outline. When you click a row or column level symbol, Excel displays the level and all levels above it in the worksheet display.
Row and column level bar	Hides the display of the detail rows or columns the level bar includes, which is the same as clicking the collapse symbol — see below.
Expand (+) symbol	Expands the display to show the detail rows or columns that have been collapsed.
Collapse (–) symbol	Condenses the display to hide the detail rows or columns that are included in its row or column level bar.

If you don't see any of the outline symbols identified in Figure 4-4 and Table 4-1, this means that Outline Symbols check box on the View tab in the Options dialog box (Tools⇨Options) is not checked. All you have to do is open the Options dialog box and click the Outline Symbols check box before you click OK to have Excel display the various outline symbols specific to your worksheet outline.

You can have only one outline per worksheet. If you've already outlined one table and then try to outline another table on the same worksheet, Excel will display the Modify Existing Outline? alert box when you choose the Outline command. If you click OK, Excel adds the outlining for the new table to the existing outline for the first table (even though the tables are nonadjacent). To create separate outlines for different data tables, you need to place each table on a different worksheet of the workbook.

Applying outline styles

You can apply predefined row and column outline styles to the table or list data. To apply these styles when creating the outline, be sure to select the Automatic Styles check box in the Settings dialog box before you click its Create button (Data⇨Group and Outline⇨Settings). If you didn't select this check box in the Settings dialog box before you created the outline with the Data⇨Group and Outline⇨Auto Outline command, you can do so afterwards by selecting all the cells in the outlined table of data, opening the Settings dialog box (Data⇨Group and Outline⇨Settings), and then clicking the Apply Styles button before you click OK.

Figure 4-5 shows you the sample CG Media Sales table after applying the automatic row and column styles to the outlined table data. In this example, Excel applied two row styles (RowLevel_1 and RowLevel_2) and two column styles (ColLevel_1 and ColLevel_2) to the worksheet table.

The RowLevel_1 style is applied to the entries in the first-level summary row (row 15) and makes the font appear in bold. The ColLevel_1 style is applied to the data in the first-level summary column (column R, which isn't shown in the figure), and it, too, simply makes the font bold. The RowLevel_2 style is applied to the data in the second-level rows (rows 8 and 14) and this style adds italics to the font. The ColLevel_2 style is applied to all second-level summary columns (columns E, I, M, and Q), and it also italicizes the font.

After applying the automatic outline styles to your outlined data, you can modify the formatting of the row and column level styles in the Style dialog box (Format⇨Style). As when redefining built-in styles such as the Normal, Comma, Currency, or Percent styles, Excel automatically updates the formatting of the data that currently use a particular outline style. This means that you don't need to manually reapply each redefined outline style to the cell entries in the outline level to have your changes take effect. (See Book II, Chapter 2 for more on modifying styles.)

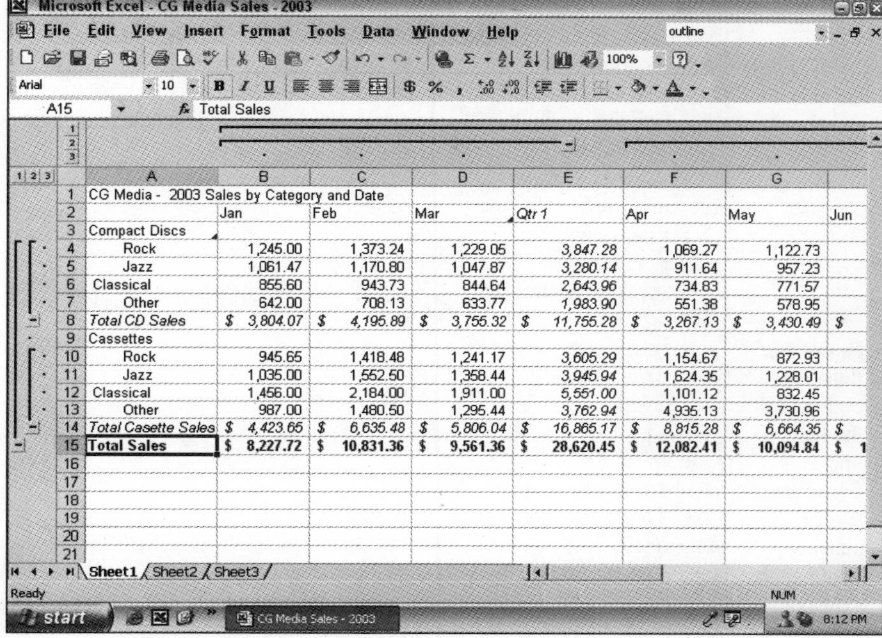

	A	B	C	D	E	F	G	
1	CG Media - 2003 Sales by Category and Date							
2		Jan	Feb	Mar	Qtr 1	Apr	May	Jun
3	Compact Discs							
4	Rock	1,245.00	1,373.24	1,229.05	3,847.28	1,069.27	1,122.73	
5	Jazz	1,061.47	1,170.80	1,047.87	3,280.14	911.64	957.23	
6	Classical	855.60	943.73	844.64	2,643.96	734.83	771.57	
7	Other	642.00	708.13	633.77	1,983.90	551.38	578.95	
8	Total CD Sales	$ 3,804.07	$ 4,195.89	$ 3,755.32	$ 11,755.28	$ 3,267.13	$ 3,430.49	$
9	Cassettes							
10	Rock	945.65	1,418.48	1,241.17	3,605.29	1,154.67	872.93	
11	Jazz	1,035.00	1,552.50	1,358.44	3,945.94	1,624.35	1,228.01	
12	Classical	1,456.00	2,184.00	1,911.00	5,551.00	1,101.12	832.45	
13	Other	987.00	1,480.50	1,295.44	3,762.94	4,935.13	3,730.96	
14	Total Casette Sales	$ 4,423.65	$ 6,635.48	$ 5,806.04	$ 16,865.17	$ 8,815.28	$ 6,664.35	$
15	Total Sales	$ 8,227.72	$ 10,831.36	$ 9,561.36	$ 28,620.45	$ 12,082.41	$ 10,094.84	$ 1

Figure 4-5: Applying outline styles to the outlined data table.

Displaying and hiding different outline levels

The real effectiveness of outlining worksheet data only becomes apparent when you start using the various outline symbols to change the way the table data are displayed in the worksheet. By clicking the appropriate row or column level symbol, you can immediately hide detail rows and columns to display just the summary information in the table. For example, Figure 4-6 shows you the CG Media Sales table after clicking the number 2 row level button and number 2 column level buttons. Here, you see only the first and second-level summary information, that is, the totals for the quarterly and annual totals for the two types of media.

Figure 4-7 shows you the same table, this time after clicking the number 1 row level button and number 1 column level button. Here, you see only the first-level summary for the column and the row, that is, the grand total of the annual CG Media sales. To expand this view horizontally to see the totals sales for each quarter, you would simply click the number 2 column level button. To expand this view even further horizontally to display each monthly total in the worksheet, you would click the number 3 column level button. So too, to expand the outline vertically to see totals for each type of media, you would click the number 2 row level button. To expand the outline one more level vertically so that you can see the sales for each type of music as well as each type of media, you would click the number 3 row level button.

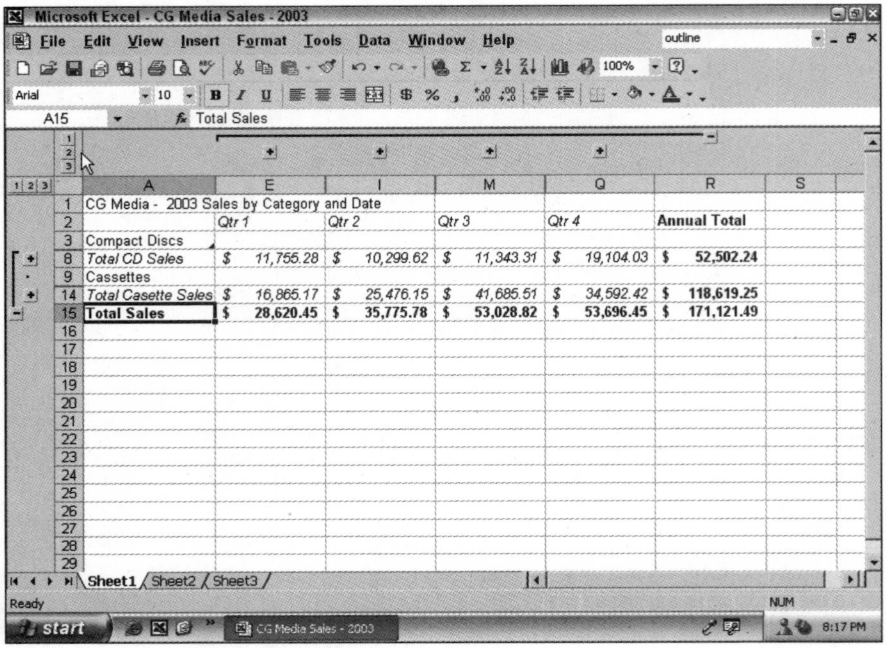

Figure 4-6: Collapsed outline with the first- and secondary-level summary information displayed.

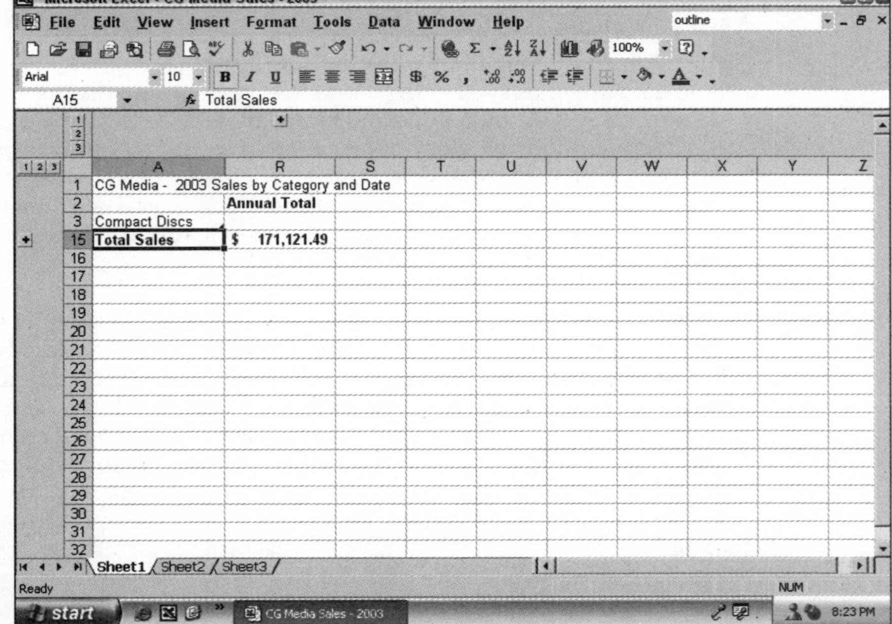

Figure 4-7: Collapsed outline with only the first-level summary information displayed.

When displaying different levels of detail in a worksheet outline, you can use the collapse or expand symbols along with the row level and column level buttons. For example, Figure 4-8 shows you another view of the CG Media outlined sales table. Here, in the horizontal dimension, you see all three column levels have been expanded, including the monthly detail columns for each quarter. In the vertical dimension, however, only the detail rows for the CD sales have been expanded. The detail rows for cassette tape sales are still collapsed. To create this view of the outline, you simply click the number 2 row level button, then click the expand symbol (+) located to the left of the Total CD Sales row heading. When you want to view only the summary-level rows for each media type, you can click the collapse symbol (–) to the left of the Total CD Sales heading or you can click its level bar (drawn from the collapse symbol up to the first music type to indicate all the details rows included in that level).

Excel adjusts the outline levels displayed on the screen by hiding and redisplaying entire columns and rows in the worksheet. Therefore, keep in mind that changes that you make that reduce the number of levels displayed in outlined table also hide the display of all data outside of the outlined table that are in the affected rows and columns.

Microsoft Excel - CG Media Sales - 2003

	A	E	I	M	Q	R
1	CG Media - 2003 Sales by Category and Date					
2		Qtr 1	Qtr 2	Qtr 3	Qtr 4	Annual Total
3	Compact Discs					
4	Rock	3,847.28	3,370.87	3,712.45	6,252.39	$ 17,182.99
5	Jazz	3,280.14	2,873.96	3,165.18	5,330.70	$ 14,649.98
6	Classical	2,643.96	2,316.56	2,551.30	4,296.82	$ 11,808.65
7	Other	1,983.90	1,738.23	1,914.37	3,224.12	$ 8,860.62
8	Total CD Sales	$ 11,755.28	$ 10,299.62	$ 11,343.31	$ 19,104.03	$ 52,502.24
9	Cassettes					
14	Total Casette Sales	$ 16,865.17	$ 25,476.15	$ 41,685.51	$ 34,592.42	$ 118,619.25
15	Total Sales	$ 28,620.45	$ 35,775.78	$ 53,028.82	$ 53,696.45	$ 171,121.49

Figure 4-8: Outline expanded to show only CD sales details for all four quarters.

After selecting the rows and columns you want displayed, you can then remove the outline symbols from the worksheet display to maximize the amount of data displayed onscreen. To do this without having to open the Options dialog box and fool around with the Outline Symbols check box on the View tab, press Ctrl+8 (the number eight on the top row of the standard keyboard). Ctrl+8 is an old toggle key combination that switches between showing and hiding all the outline symbols in a worksheet.

Manually adjusting the outline levels

Most of the time, Excel correctly outlines the data in your table. Every once in a while, however, you will have to manually adjust one or more of the outline levels so that the outline's summary rows and columns include the right detail rows and columns. To adjust levels of a worksheet outline, you must select the rows or columns that you want to promote to a higher level (that is, one with a lower level number) in the outline and then choose the Data⇨Group and Outline⇨Group command on the Menu bar. If you want to demote selected rows or columns to a lower level in the outline, select the rows or columns with a higher level number and choose Data⇨Group and Outline⇨Ungroup instead.

Before you use the Group and Ungroup menu items to change an outline level, you must select the rows or columns that you want to promote or demote. To select a particular outline level and all the rows and columns included in that level, you need to display the outline symbols (Ctrl+8), and then hold down the Shift key as you click its collapse or expand symbol. Note that when you click an expand symbol, Excel selects not only the rows or columns visible at that level, but all the hidden rows and columns included in that level as well. If you want to select only a particular detail or summary row or column in the outline, you can click that row number or column letter in the worksheet window, or you can hold down the Shift key and click the dot (period) to the left of the row number or above the column letter in the outline symbols area.

If you only select a range of cells in the rows or columns (as opposed to entire rows and columns) before you choose the Group and Ungroup menu items, Excel displays the Group or Ungroup dialog box which contains a Rows and Columns radio button (with the Rows button selected by default). To promote or demote columns instead of rows, click the Columns radio button before you select OK. To close the dialog box without promoting or demoting any part of the outline, click Cancel.

To see how you can use the Group and Ungroup menu items on the Data⇨Group and Outline cascading menu to adjust outline levels, consider once again the CG Media sales table outline. When Excel created this outline, the program did not include row 3 (which contains only the row heading,

Compact Discs) in the outline. As a result, when you collapse the rows by selecting the number 1 row level button to display only the first-level Total Sales summary row (refer to Figure 4-7), this row heading remains visible in the table, even though it should have been included and thereby hidden along with the other summary and detail rows.

You can use the Group menu item to move this row (3) down a level so that it is included in the first level of the outline. You simply click the row number 3 to select the row and then choose Data⇨Group and Outline⇨Group on the Excel Menu bar. Figure 4-9 shows you the result of doing this. Notice how the outside level bar (for level 1) now includes this row. Now, when you collapse the outline by clicking the number 1 row level button, the heading in row 3 is hidden as well (see Figure 4-10).

Removing an outline

To delete an outline from your worksheet, you choose Data⇨Group and Outline⇨Clear Outline on the Excel Menu bar. Note that removing the outline does not affect the data in any way — Excel merely removes the outline structure. Also note that it doesn't matter what state the outline is in at the time you select this command. If the outline is partially or totally collapsed, deleting the outline automatically displays all the hidden rows and columns in the data table or list.

Keep in mind that restoring an outline that you've deleted is not one of the commands that you can undo (Ctrl+Z). If you delete an outline by mistake, you must recreate it all over again. For this reason, most often you'll want to expand all the outline levels (by clicking the lowest number column and row level button) and then hide all the outline symbols by pressing Ctrl+8 rather than permanently remove the outline with the Data⇨Group and Outline⇨Clear Outline command.

Creating different custom views of the outline

After you've created an outline for your worksheet table, you can create custom views that display the table in various levels of detail. Then, instead of having to display the outline symbols and manually click the appropriate row level buttons and/or column level buttons to view a particular level of detail, you simply select the appropriate outline view in the Custom Views dialog box (View⇨Custom Views).

When creating custom views of outlined worksheet data, be sure that you leave the Hidden Rows, Columns, and Filter Settings check box selected in the Include in View section of the Add View dialog box. (See Book II, Chapter 3 for details on creating and using custom views in a worksheet.)

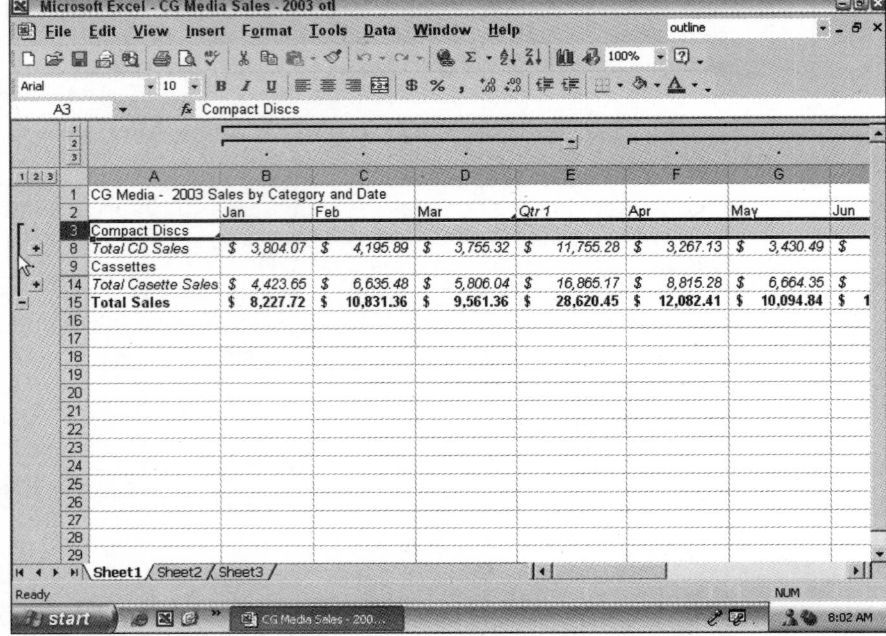

Figure 4-9: Manually adjusting the Level 1 rows in the outlined sales table.

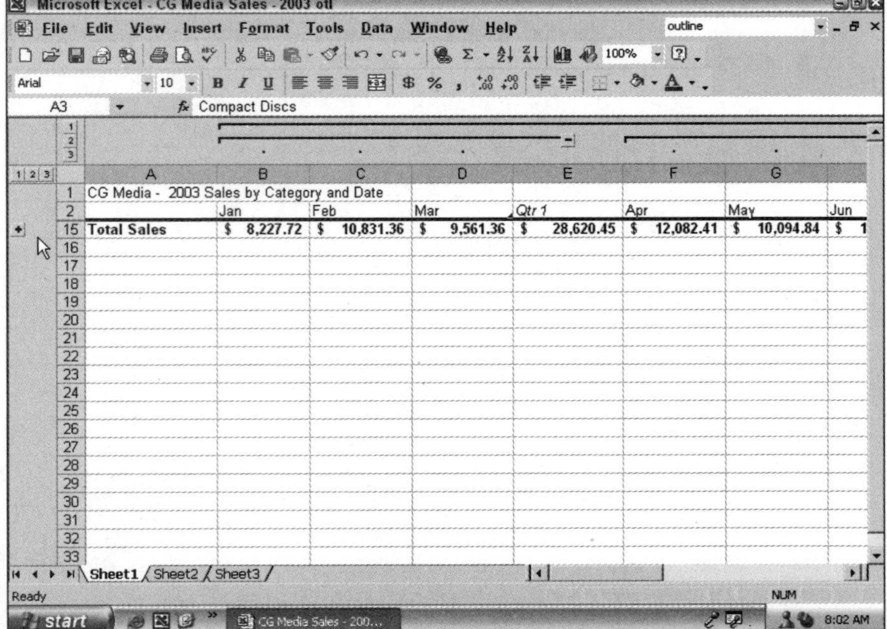

Figure 4-10: Collapsing the adjusted outline down to row level 1.

Reorganizing the Workbook

Any new workbook that you open comes already equipped with three blank worksheets. Although most of the spreadsheets you create and work with may never wander beyond the confines of the first of these three sheets, you do need to know how to organize your spreadsheet information three-dimensionally for those rare occasions when spreading all the information out in one humongous worksheet is not practical. However, the normal everyday problems related to keeping on top of the information in a single worksheet can easily go off the scale when you begin to use multiple worksheets in a workbook. For this reason, you need to be sure that you are fully versed in the basics of using more than one worksheet in a workbook.

To move between the sheets in a workbook, you can click the sheet tab for that worksheet or press Ctrl+PgDn (next sheet) or Ctrl+PgUp (preceding sheet) until the sheet is selected. If the sheet tab for the worksheet you want is not displayed on the scroll bar at the bottom of the document window, use the tab scrolling buttons (the buttons with the left- and right-pointing triangles) to bring it into view.

To use the tab scrolling buttons, click the one with the right-pointing triangle to bring the next sheet into view and click the one with the left-pointing triangle to bring the preceding sheet into view. The tab scrolling buttons with the directional triangles pointing to vertical lines display the very first or very last group of sheet tabs in a workbook. The button with the triangle pointing left to a vertical line brings the first group of sheet tabs into view; the button with the triangle pointing right to a vertical line brings the last group of sheet tabs into view. When you scroll sheet tabs to find the one you're looking for, for heaven's sake, don't forget to click the desired sheet tab to make the worksheet current.

Renaming sheets

The sheet tabs shown at the bottom of each workbook are the keys to keeping your place in a workbook. To tell which sheet is current, you have only to look at which sheet tab appears on the top and matches the background of the other cells in the worksheet. Typically, this means that the active sheet tab's background appears in white in contrast to the non-active sheet tabs, which sport a light gray background.

When you start a new workbook, the sheet tabs are all the same width because they all have the default sheet names (Sheet1, Sheet2, and so on). As you assign your own names to the sheets, the tabs appear either longer or shorter, depending on the length of the sheet tab name. Just keep in mind that the longer the sheet tabs, the fewer you can see at one time, and the more sheet tab scrolling you'll have to do to find the worksheet you want.

To rename a worksheet, you take these steps:

1. **Press Ctrl+PgDn until the sheet you want to rename is active or click its sheet tab if it's displayed at the bottom of the workbook window.**

   Don't forget that you have to select and activate the sheet you want to rename or you end up renaming whatever sheet happens to be current at the time you perform the next step.

2. **Choose Format⇨Sheet⇨Rename on the Menu bar or right-click the sheet tab and then click Rename on its shortcut menu.**

   When you choose this command, Excel selects the current name of the tab and positions the insertion point at the end of the name.

3. **Replace or edit the name on sheet tab and then press the Enter key.**

When you rename a worksheet in this manner, keep in mind that Excel then uses that sheet name in any formulas that refer to cells in that worksheet. So, for instance, if you rename Sheet2 to 2003 Sales and then create a formula in cell A10 of Sheet1 that adds its cell B10 to cell C34 in Sheet2, the formula in cell A10 becomes:

```
=B10+'2003 Sales'!C34
```

This is in place of the more obscure, `=B10+Sheet2!C34`. For this reason, keep your sheets names short and to the point so that you can easily and quickly identify the sheet and its data without creating excessively long formula references.

Designer sheets

Excel 2002 now enables you to color code the worksheets in your workbook. This enables you to create a color scheme that helps either identify or prioritize the sheets and the information they contain (as you might with different colored folder tabs in a filing cabinet).

When you color a sheet tab, note that the tab appears in that color only when it's not the active sheet. The moment you select a color-coded sheet tab, it becomes white with just a bar of the assigned color appearing under the sheet name. Note too, that when you assign darker colors to a sheet tab, Excel automatically reverses out the sheet name text to white when the worksheet is not active.

Color coding sheet tabs

To assign a new color to a sheet tab, follow these three steps:

1. **Press Ctrl+PgDn until the sheet whose tab you want to color is active or click its sheet tab if it's displayed at the bottom of the workbook window.**

   Don't forget that you have to select and activate the sheet whose tab you want to color or you end up coloring the tab of whatever sheet happens to be current at the time you perform the next step.

2. **Choose Format⇨Sheet⇨Tab Color or right-click the tab and then click Tab Color on the shortcut menu.**

   Doing this opens the Format Tab Color dialog box, as shown in Figure 4-11.

3. **Click the color square in the Format Tab Color dialog box that you want to assign and then click OK.**

To remove color coding from a sheet tab, click the No Color option at the top of the Format Tab Color dialog box (Format⇨Sheet⇨Tab Color) after making the worksheet active.

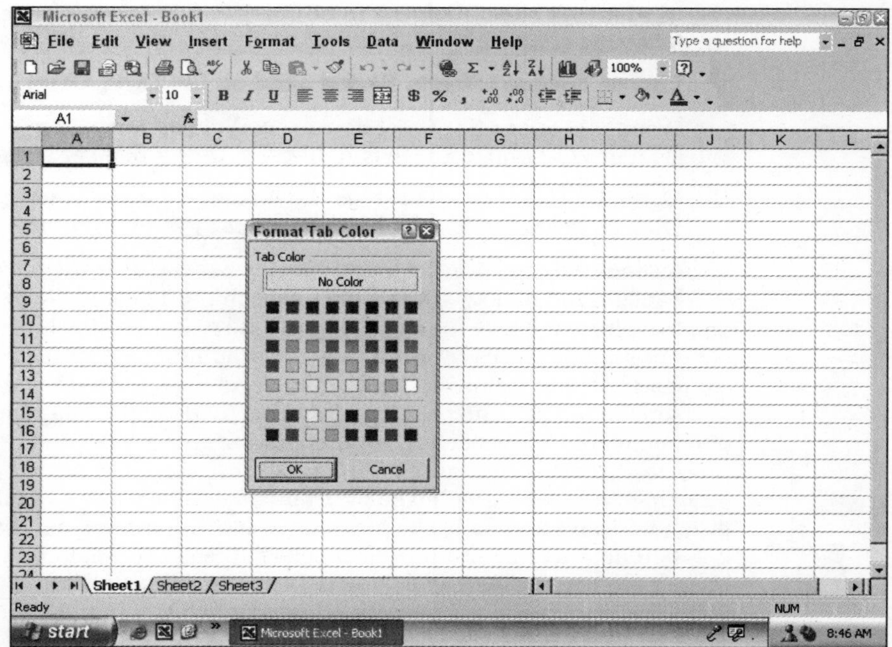

Figure 4-11: Assigning a new color to a tab in the Format Tab Color dialog box.

Assigning graphic sheet backgrounds

If coloring the sheet tabs isn't enough for you, you can also assign a graphic image to be used as the background for all the cells in the entire worksheet. Just be aware that background image must either be very light in color or use a greatly reduced opacity in order for your worksheet data to be read over the image. This probably makes most graphics that you have readily available unusable as worksheet background images. It can, however, be quite effective if you have a special corporate watermark graphic (as with the company's logo at extremely low opacity) that adds just a hint of a background without obscuring the data being presented in its cells.

To add a graphic file as the background for your worksheet, take these steps:

1. **Press Ctrl+PgDn until the sheet to which you want to assign the graphic as the background is active or click its sheet tab if it's displayed at the bottom of the workbook window.**

   Don't forget that you have to select and activate the sheet to which the graphic file will act as the background or you end up assigning the file to whatever sheet happens to be current at the time you perform the following steps.

2. **Choose Format⇨Sheet⇨Background on the Excel Menu bar.**

   Doing this opens the Sheet Background dialog box where you select the graphics file whose image is to become the worksheet background.

3. **Open the folder that contains the image you want to use and then click its graphic file icon before you click the Insert button.**

   As soon as you click the Insert button, Excel closes the Sheet Background dialog box and the image in the selected file becomes the background image for all cells in the current worksheet. (Usually, the program does this by stretching the graphic so that it takes up all the cells that are visible in the Workbook window. In the case of some smaller images, the program does this by tiling the image so that it's duplicated across and down the viewing area.)

Keep in mind that a graphic image that you assign as the worksheet background doesn't appear in the printout, unlike the pattern and background colors that you assign to ranges of cells in the sheet. Also, background images are not retained when you publish the worksheet as a single Web page. Backgrounds are, however, retained when you publish the entire workbook as a Web page. (See Book VIII, Chapter 1 for details on publishing worksheets as Web pages.)

To remove a background image, you simply choose Format⇨Sheets⇨Delete Background on the Excel Menu bar, and Excel immediately clears the image from the entire worksheet.

Adding and deleting sheets

Although you only start out with three worksheets, you can have as many worksheets as you need in building and remodeling your spreadsheet. To add a new worksheet, choose Insert⇨Worksheet on the Excel Menu bar. Excel then inserts a new sheet in front of whatever sheet is active when you choose this command, and the program assigns it the next available sheet number (as in Sheet4, Sheet5, Sheet6, and so on).

You can also insert a new worksheet by right-clicking a sheet tab and then clicking Insert at the top of the tab's shortcut menu. When you do this, however, Excel opens the Insert dialog box, which resembles the Templates dialog box except that in addition to the templates you usually use, the General tab also contains Chart, MS Excel 4.0 Macro, and a MS Excel 5.0 Dialog file icons that enable you to insert a blank chart sheet (see Book V, Chapter 1) or a blank macro or dialog sheet (see Book IX, Chapter 1), rather than just a blank worksheet. Note that if you select a template file icon rather than the standard Worksheet icon, Excel inserts a new worksheet based on that template's design, rather than just your plain, vanilla-flavored blank worksheet, when you click OK.

If you find that three worksheets just never seems to be enough for the kind of spreadsheets you normally create, you can change the default number of sheets that are automatically available in all new workbook files that you open. To do this, enter a number in the Sheets in a New Workbook text box (up to a maximum of 255 — that's a lotta sheets!) on the General tab of the Options dialog box (Tools⇨Options). Of course, if you find that three sheets are always too much (because you only use one), you can reduce the default number from three by entering 1 or 2 in this text box (remember you can't go lower than 1 because a workbook with no worksheet is no workbook at all).

To remove a worksheet, make the sheet active and then choose Edit⇨Delete Sheet on the Menu bar or right-click its tab and then click Delete on its shortcut menu. If Excel detects that worksheet contains some data, the program then displays an alert dialog box cautioning you that data may exist in the worksheet you're just about to zap. To go ahead and delete the sheet (data and all), you click the Delete button. To preserve the worksheet, click Cancel or press the Escape key.

Deleting a sheet is one of those actions that you can't undo with Edit⇨Undo. This means that after you click the Delete button, you've kissed your worksheet goodbye, so please don't do this unless you're *certain* that you aren't dumping needed data. Also, keep in mind that you can't delete a worksheet if that sheet is the only one in the workbook until you've inserted another blank worksheet: Excel won't allow a workbook file to be completely sheetless.

Changing the sheets

A worksheet that you add to a workbook is always inserted in front of whichever worksheet is active at the time you choose Insert⇨Worksheet. Because of this positioning, the first thing you may have to do with the new worksheet is move it to a different position in the workbook.

To move the worksheet, click its sheet tab and drag it to the new position in the row of tabs. As you drag, the pointer changes shape to an arrowhead on a dog-eared piece of paper, and you see a black triangle pointing downward above the sheet tabs. When this triangle is positioned over the tab of the sheet that is to follow the one you're moving, release the mouse button.

If you need to copy a worksheet to another position in the workbook, hold down the Ctrl key as you click and drag the sheet tab. When you release the mouse button, Excel creates a copy with a new sheet tab name based on the number of the copy and the original sheet name. For example, if you copy Sheet1 to a new place in the workbook, the copy is renamed Sheet1 (2). You can then rename the worksheet whatever you want.

Group editing

One of the nice things about a workbook is that it enables you to edit more than one worksheet at a time. Of course, you should be concerned with group editing only when you're working on a bunch of worksheets that share essentially the same layout and require the same type of formatting.

For example, suppose that you have a workbook that contains annual sales worksheets (named YTD04, YTD05, and YTD06) for three consecutive years. The worksheets share the same layout (with months across the columns and quarterly and annual totals, locations, and types of sales down the rows) but lack standard formatting.

To format any part of these three worksheets in a single operation, you simply resort to group editing, which requires selecting the three sales worksheets. Simply click the YTD04, YTD05, and YTD06 sheet tabs as you hold down the Ctrl key, or click the YTD04 tab and then hold down the Shift key as you click the YTD06 tab.

After you select the last sheet, the message [GROUP] appears in the title bar of the active document window (with the YTD04 worksheet, in this case).

The [GROUP] message indicates that any editing change you make to the current worksheet will affect all the sheets that are currently selected. For example, if you select a row of column headings and add bold and italics to the headings in the current worksheet, the same formatting is applied to the same cell selection in all three sales sheets. All headings in the same cell range in the other worksheets are now in bold and italics. Keep in mind that you can apply not only formatting changes to a cell range, but also editing changes, such as replacing a cell entry, deleting a cell's contents, or moving a cell selection to a new place in the worksheet. These changes also affect all the worksheets you have selected as long as they're grouped together.

After you are finished making editing changes that affect all the grouped worksheets, you can break up the group by right-clicking one of the sheet tabs and then clicking Ungroup Sheets at the top of the shortcut menu. As soon as you break up the group, the [GROUP] message disappears from the title bar, and thereafter, any editing changes that you make affect only the cells in the active worksheet.

TIP

To select all the worksheets in the workbook for group editing in one operation, right-click the tab of the sheet where you want to make the editing changes that affect all the other sheets and then click Select All Sheets on its shortcut menu.

"Now you see them; now you don't"

Another technique that comes in handy when working with multiple worksheets is hiding particular worksheets in the workbook. Just as you can hide particular columns, rows, and cell ranges in a worksheet, you can also hide particular worksheets in the workbook. For example, you may want to hide a worksheet that contains sensitive (for-your-eyes-only) material, such as the one with all the employee salaries in the company or the one that contains all the macros used in the workbook.

As with hiding columns and rows, hiding worksheets enables you to print the contents of the workbook without the data in worksheets that you consider either unnecessary in the report or too classified for widespread distribution but which, nonetheless, are required in the workbook. Then after the report is printed, you can redisplay the worksheets by unhiding them.

To hide a worksheet, make it active by selecting its sheet tab, and then choose the Format⇨Sheet⇨Hide command. Excel removes this sheet's tab from the row of sheet tabs, making it impossible for anyone to select and display the worksheet in the document window.

To redisplay any of the sheets you've hidden, choose the Format⇨Sheet⇨Unhide command, which displays the Unhide dialog box. In the Unhide Sheet list box, click the name of the sheet that you want to display once again in the workbook. As soon as you click OK, Excel redisplays the sheet tab of the previously hidden worksheet — as simple as that! Unfortunately, although you can hide multiple worksheets in one hide operation, you can select only one sheet at a time to redisplay with the Unhide command.

Opening windows on different sheets

The biggest problem with keeping your spreadsheet data on different worksheets rather than keeping it all together on the same sheet is being able to compare the information on the different sheets. When you use a single worksheet, you can split the workbook window into horizontal or vertical panes and then scroll different sections of the sheet into view. The only way to do this when the spreadsheet data are located on different worksheets is open a second window on a second worksheet and then arrange the windows with the different worksheets so that data from desired regions are both displayed on the screen.

Figure 4-12 helps illustrate how this works. This figure contains two windows showing parts of two different worksheets. These windows are arranged horizontally so that they fit one above the other. The top window shows the upper-left portion of the first worksheet with the 2003 sales data, while the lower window shows the upper-left portion of the second worksheet with the 2004 sales data. Note that both windows contain the same sheet tabs (although different tabs are active in the different windows) and that both windows are equipped with horizontal and vertical scroll bars, enabling you to bring different sections of the two sheets into view.

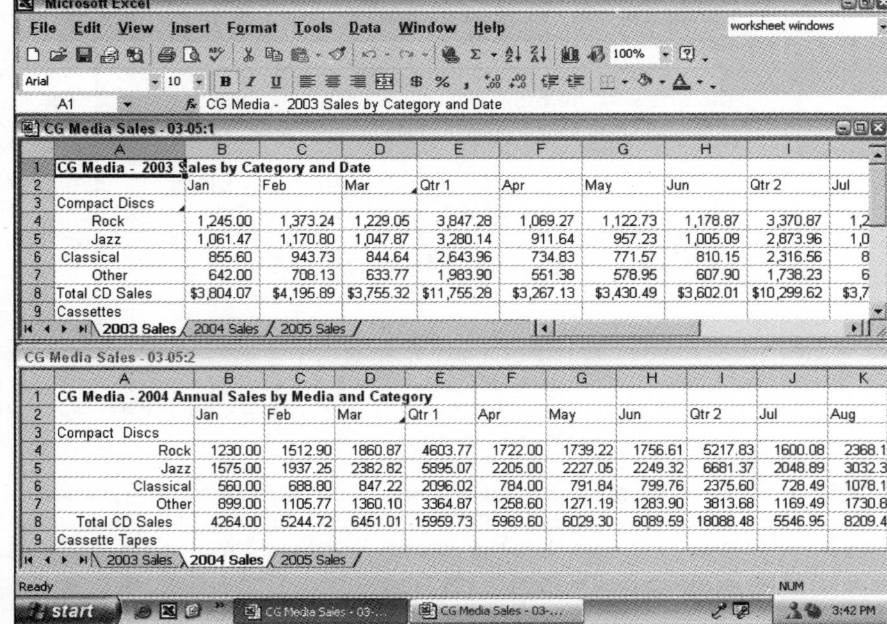

Figure 4-12: Using windows to compare data stored on two different sheets in the same workbook.

Here is the procedure I followed to create and arrange these windows in the CG Media Sales 03-05 workbook:

1. **Open the workbook file for editing and then create a new window by choosing Window⇨New Window on the Excel Menu bar.**
2. **Arrange the windows one on top of the other by choosing Window⇨Arrange on the Menu bar, and then clicking the Horizontal radio button and the Windows of Active Workbook check box before clicking the OK button in the Arrange Windows dialog box.**
3. **Click the second (lower) window (indicated by the ":2" after the filename on its Title bar) to activate the window and then click the 2004 Sales sheet tab to activate it.**
4. **Click the first (upper) window (indicated by the ":1" following the filename on its Title bar) to activate the window.**

After you've added a second window to a workbook, you can then vary the arrangement of the two windows by selecting different arrangement options in the Windows Arrange dialog box (Tiled or Vertical to set them side by side or Cascade to slightly offset them one over the other). You can also select different sheets to display in either window by clicking their sheet tabs and different parts of the sheet to display by using the window's scroll bars.

TIP

To activate different windows on the workbook so that you can activate a different worksheet by selecting its sheet tab and/or use the scroll bars to bring new data into view, click the window's title bar or press Ctrl+F6 until its title bar is selected.

When you want to resume normal full-screen viewing in the workbook window, click the Maximize button in one of the windows. To get rid of a second window, click its button on the Taskbar and then click its Close Window button on the far right side of the Menu bar. (Be sure that you don't click the Close button on the far-right of the Excel Title bar, because doing this closes your workbook file and exits you from Excel!)

Working with Multiple Workbooks

Working with more than one worksheet in a single workbook is bad enough, but working with worksheets in different workbooks can be really wicked. The key to doing this successfully is just keeping track of "who's on first," and you do this by opening and using windows on the individual workbook files you have open.

With the different workbook windows in place, you can then compare the data in different workbooks, use the drag-and-drop method to copy or move data between workbooks, or even copy or move entire worksheets.

Arranging windows on different workbooks

To work with sheets from different workbook files you have open, you arrange their workbook windows in the Excel Work area. You do this simply by arranging their windows with the same Arrange options (Tiled, Horizontal, Vertical, or Cascading) as you use when arranging the windows that you've opened in a single workbook. The big difference is that when arranging windows on different workbook files in the Arrange Windows dialog box (Window⇨Arrange), you must make sure that the Windows of Active Workbook check box is not selected (in other words, is empty of its checkmark).

After these windows are arranged on-screen the way you want them, you can compare or transfer information between them as you need. To compare data in different workbooks, you switch between the different windows, activating and bringing the regions of the different worksheets you want to compare into view.

To move data between workbook windows, arrange the worksheets in these windows so that both the cells with the data entries you want to move and the cell range into which you want to move them are both displayed in their respective windows. Then, select the cell selection to be moved, drag it to the other window to the first cell of the range in the worksheet where it is to be moved to, and release the mouse button. To copy data between workbooks, you follow the exact same procedure, except that you hold down the Ctrl key as you drag the selected range from one window to another. (See Book II, Chapter 3 for information on using drag-and-drop to copy and move data entries.)

When you're finished working with workbook windows arranged in some manner in the Excel Work area, you can return to the normal full-screen view by clicking the Maximize button on one of the windows. As soon as you maximize one workbook window, all the rest of the arranged workbook windows are made full size as well.

Transferring sheets from one workbook to another

Instead of copying cell ranges from one workbook to another, you can move (or copy) entire worksheets between workbooks. You can do this with drag-and-drop or by using a variation on the standard cut-and-paste method, the Edit⇨Move or Copy menu command.

To use drag-and-drop to move a sheet between open windows, you simply drag its sheet tab from its window to the place on the sheet tabs in the other window where the sheet is to be moved to. As soon as you release the mouse button, the entire worksheet is moved from one file to the other and its sheet tab now appears among the others in that workbook. To copy a sheet rather than move it, you perform the same procedure, except that you hold down the Ctrl key as you drag the sheet tab from one window to the next.

To use the Edit⇨Move or Copy Sheets command on the Excel Menu bar to copy or move entire worksheets, you follow these steps:

1. **Open both the workbook containing the sheets to be moved or copied and the workbook where the sheets will be moved or copied to.**

   Both the source and destination workbooks must be open in order to copy or move sheets between them.

2. **Click the workbook window with sheets to be moved or copied.**

   Doing this activates the source workbook so that you can select the sheet or sheets you want to move or copy.

3. **Select the sheet tab of the worksheet or worksheets to be moved or copied.**

   To select more than one worksheet, hold down the Ctrl key as you click the individual sheet tabs.

4. **Choose Edit⇨Move or Copy Sheets on the Excel Menu bar.**

   Doing this opens the Move or Copy dialog box, as shown in Figure 4-13.

5. **Click the filename of the workbook into which the selected sheets are to be moved or copied in the To Book pop-up menu.**

   If you want to move or copy the selected worksheets into a new workbook file, click the (New Book) item at the very top of this pop-up menu.

6. **Click the name of the sheet that should immediately follow the sheet(s) that you're about to move or copy into this workbook in the Before Sheet list box.**

   If you want to move or copy the selected sheet(s) to the very end of the destination workbook, click (Move to End) at the bottom of this list box.

7. **If you want to copy the selected sheet(s) rather than move them, click the Create a Copy check box.**

   If you don't select this check box, Excel automatically moves the selected sheet(s) from one workbook to the other rather than copying them.

8. **Click OK to close the Move or Copy dialog box and complete the move or copy operation.**

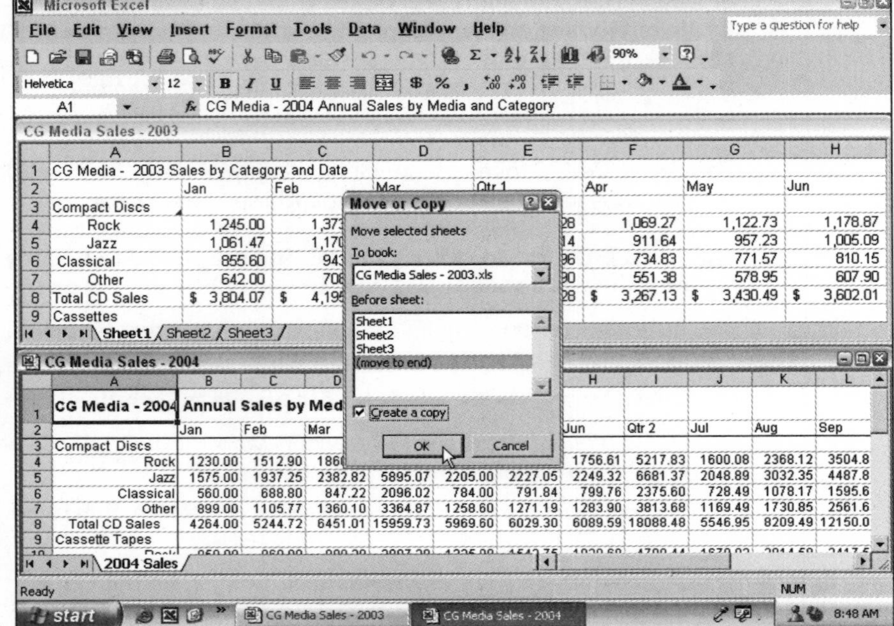

Figure 4-13: Copying a worksheet to another workbook in the Move or Copy dialog box.

Saving a workspace

Excel's Workspace feature enables you to save the window arrangement that you've set up in a special workspace file (given the filename extension, .XLW, which stands for Excel workspace). In a workspace file, Excel saves all the information about the open workbooks, including the window arrangement, magnification settings, and display settings. (The workspace file also saves the print areas defined in the open workbooks — see Book II, Chapter 5 for information on printing.)

Note that workspace files only contain such information about the open workbooks, not the workbook files themselves. This means that you can't send a workspace file to a co-worker and expect him or her to be able to successfully open the file without also sending the associated workbook files.

To save a workspace, you take the following steps:

1. **Open all the workbooks you want opened when you open the workspace file.**

2. **Arrange the windows for these workbooks as you want them to appear when you first open the workspace file.**

   To arrange the windows, choose the Window⇨Arrange menu command and then select the type of arrangement in the Arrange Windows dialog box (be sure that the Windows of Active Workbook check box is not selected).

3. **Select any display settings and magnification settings that you want used in the individual workbook windows when you first open the workspace file.**

   To change the display settings for a workbook, activate its window and then change the settings on the View tab of the Options dialog box (Tools⇨Options). To change the magnification, select or enter the desired percentage in the combo box attached to the Zoom button on the Standard toolbar.

4. **Choose File⇨Save Workspace on the Excel Menu bar.**

   Doing this opens the Save Workspace dialog box, which is just like the Save As dialog box, except that Workspaces (`*.xlw`) is selected as the default file type in the Save as Type combo box.

5. **Select the folder in which you want the workspace file saved in the Save In drop-down list box and then edit the desired filename in the File Name combo box.**

   If you want the workspace file to open automatically each time you start Excel, save the file in the XLStart folder in your Office10 folder. This folder is located within the Microsoft Office folder inside the Programs Folder on your hard drive (usually `C:`).

6. **Click the Save button to save the workspace and to close the Save workspaces dialog box.**

After saving your workspace file, you can then open it as you would any other Excel workbook or template file: Choose File⇨Open and then open the folder with the `.XLW` file you want to use, click its file icon and then click the Open button. (See Book II, Chapter 3 for details on opening Excel files.)

Consolidating Worksheets

Excel allows you to consolidate data from different worksheets into a single worksheet. Using the program's Data⇨Consolidate command, you can easily combine data from multiple spreadsheets. For example, you can use the Consolidate command to total all budget spreadsheets prepared by each department in the company or to create summary totals for income statements for a period of several years. If you used a template to create each worksheet you're consolidating or an identical layout, Excel can quickly consolidate the values by virtue of their common position in their respective worksheets. However, even when the data entries are laid out differently in each spreadsheet, Excel can still consolidate them provided that you've used the same labels to describe the data entries in their respective worksheets.

Most of the time, you want to total the data that you're consolidating from the various worksheets. By default, Excel uses the SUM function to total all of the cells in the worksheets that share the same cell references (when you consolidate by position) or use the same labels (when you consolidate by category). You can, however, have Excel use any of other following statistical functions when doing a consolidation: AVERAGE, COUNT, COUNTA, MAX, MIN, PRODUCT, STDEV, STDEVP, VAR, or VARP (see Book III, Chapter 5 for more information on these functions).

To begin consolidating the sheets in the same workbook, you select a new worksheet to hold the consolidated data (if need be insert a new sheet in the workbook by choosing Insert⇨Worksheet). To begin consolidating sheets in different workbooks, open a new workbook. If the sheets in the various workbooks are generated from a template, open the new workbook for the consolidated data from that template.

Before you begin the consolidation process on the new worksheet, you choose the cell or cell range in this worksheet where the consolidated data is to appear (this range is called the *destination area*). If you select a single cell, Excel expands the destination area to columns to the right and rows below as needed to accommodate the consolidated data. If you select a single row, the program expands the destination area down subsequent rows of the worksheet, if required to accommodate the data. If you select a single column, Excel expands the destination area across columns to the right, if required to accommodate the data. If, however, you select a multi-cell range as the destination area, the program does not expand the destination area and restricts the consolidated data just to the cell selection.

If you want Excel to use a particular range in the worksheet for all consolidations you perform in a worksheet, assign the range name Consolidate_Area to this cell range. Excel then consolidates data into this range whenever you use the Data⇨Consolidate command.

When consolidating data, you can select data in sheets in workbooks that you've opened in Excel or in sheets in unopened workbooks stored on disk. The cells that you specify for consolidation are referred to as the *source area* and the worksheets that contain the source areas are known as the *source worksheets*.

If the source worksheets are open in Excel, you can specify the references of the source areas by pointing to the cell references (even when the Consolidate dialog box is open, Excel will allow you to activate different worksheets and scroll through them as you select the cell references for the source area). If the source worksheets are not open in Excel, you must type in the cell references as external references, following the same guidelines you use when typing a linking formula with an external reference (except that you don't type =). For example, to specify the data in range B4:R21 on Sheet1 in a workbook named "CG Media - 2000 Sales.xls" as a source area, you enter the following external reference:

```
'[CG Media - 2000 Sales.xls]Sheet1'!$b$4:$r$21
```

Note that if you want to consolidate the same data range in all of the worksheets that use a similar file name (for example, CG Media - 2000 Sales, CG Media - 2001 Sales, CG Media - 2002 Sales, and so on), you can use the asterisk (*) or the question mark (?) as a wildcard character to stand for missing characters as in

```
'[CG Media - 20?? Sales.xls]Sheet1'!$b$4:$r$21
```

In this example, Excel consolidates the range A2:R21 in Sheet1 of all versions of the workbooks that use "CG - Media - 20" in the main file when this name is followed by another two characters (be they, 00, 01, 02, 03, and so on).

When you consolidate data, Excel uses only the cells in the source areas that contain values. If the cells contain formulas, Excel uses their calculated values, but if the cells contain text, Excel ignores them and treats them as though they were blank (except in the case of category labels when you're consolidating your data by category as described later in this chapter).

Consolidating by position

You consolidate worksheets by position when they use the same layout (such as those created from a template). When you consolidate data by position, Excel does not copy the labels from the source areas to the destination area, only values. To consolidate worksheets by position, you follow these steps:

1. **Open all the workbooks with the worksheets you want to consolidate. If the sheets are all in one workbook, open it in Excel.**

   Now you need to activate a new worksheet to hold the consolidated data. If you're consolidating the data in a new workbook, you need to open it (File⇨New). If you're consolidating worksheets generated from a template, use the template to create the new workbook in which you are to consolidate the spreadsheet data.

2. **Open a new worksheet to hold the consolidated data.**

   Next, you need to select destination area in the new worksheet that is to hold the consolidated data.

3. **Click the cell at the beginning of the destination area in the consolidation worksheet or, select the cell range if you want to limit the destination area to a particular region.**

   If you want Excel to be expand the size of the destination area as needed to accommodate the source areas, just select the first cell of this range.

4. **Choose Data⇨Consolidate from the Excel menu bar.**

   Doing this opens the Consolidate dialog box similar to the one shown in Figure 4-14. By default, Excel uses the SUM function to total the values in the source areas. If you want to use another statistical function such as AVERAGE or COUNT, select the desired function in the Function drop-down list box.

5. **(Optional) Click the function you want to use in the Function drop-down list box if you don't want the values in the source areas summed together.**

   Now, you need to specify the various source ranges to be consolidated and add them to the All References list box in the Consolidate dialog box. To do this, you specify each range to be used as the source data in the Reference text box and then click the Add button to add it to the All References list box.

6. **Select the cell range or type the cell references for the first source area in the Reference text box.**

   When you select the cell range by pointing, Excel minimizes the Consolidate dialog box to the Reference text box so that you can see what you're selecting. If the workbook window is not visible, choose it on the Window pull-down menu, then select the cell selection as you normally would (remember that you can move the Consolidate dialog box minimized to the Reference text box by dragging it by the title bar).

   If the source worksheets are not open, you can click the Browse command button to select the file name in the Browse dialog box to enter it (plus an exclamation point) into Reference text box, whereupon you can type in the range name or cell references you want to use. If you prefer, you can type in the entire cell reference including the file name. Remember that you can use the asterisk (*) and question mark (?) wildcard characters when typing in the references for the source area.

7. **Click the Add command button to add this reference to the first source area to the All References list box.**

8. **Repeat steps 6 and 7 until you have added all of the references for all of the source areas that you want to consolidate.**

9. **Click the OK button in the Consolidate dialog box.**

   Excel closes the Consolidate dialog box and then consolidates all the values in the source areas in the place in the active worksheet designated as the destination area. Note that you can use the Edit⇨Undo Consolidate command (Ctrl+Z) to undo the effects of a consolidation if you find that you defined the destination and/or the source areas incorrectly.

Figure 4-15 shows you the first part of a consolidation for three years (2000, 2001, and 2002) of record store sales in the “CG Media - 2000-02 Consolidated Sales.xls” in the workbook window in the lower-right corner. The Consolidated worksheet in this file totals the source area B4:R21 from the Sales worksheets in the “CG Media - 2000 Sales.xls” workbook with the 2000 annual sales, the “CG Media - 2001 Sales.xls” workbook with the 2001 annual sales, and the “CG Media - 2000 Sales.xls” workbook with the 2002 annual sales. These sales figures are consolidated in the destination area, B4:R21, in Consolidated sheet in the “CG Media - 2000-02 Consolidated Sales.xls” workbook (however, because all of these worksheets use the same layout, only cell B4, the first cell in this range, was designated at the destination area).

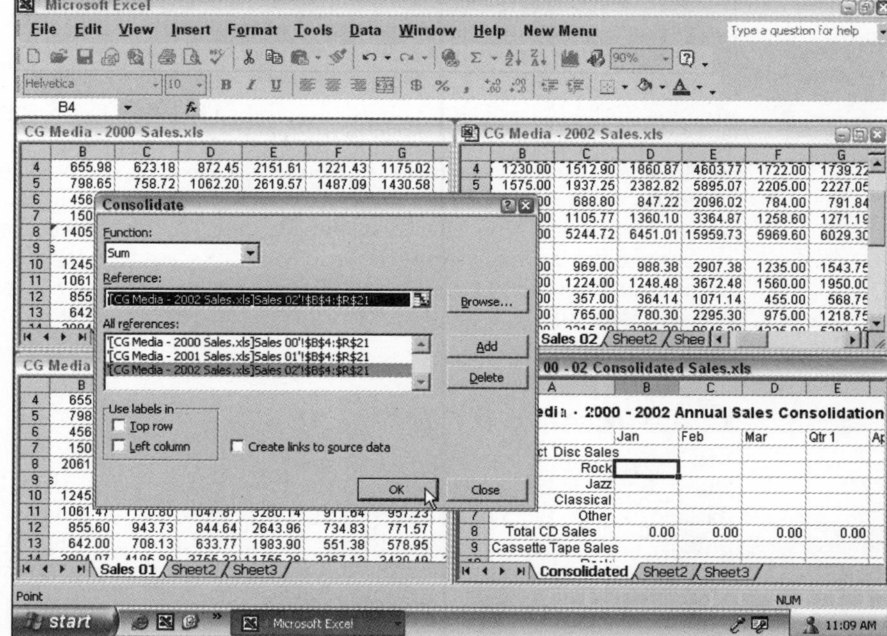

Figure 4-14: Using the Consolidate dialog box to sum together sales data from three years.

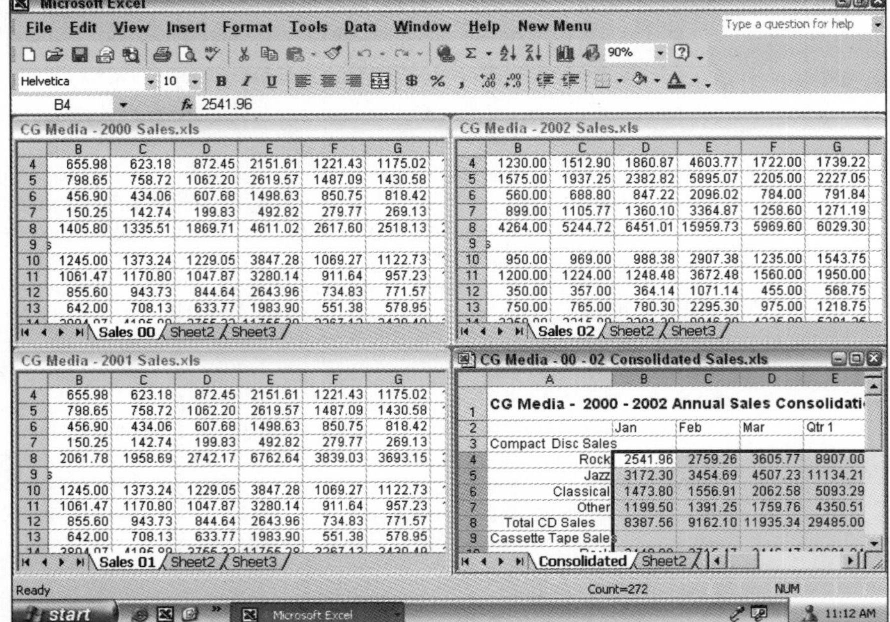

Figure 4-15: Consolidated worksheet after having Excel total the sales data from three years.

Excel allows only one consolidation per worksheet at one time. You can, however, add to or remove source areas and repeat a consolidation. To add new source areas, open the Consolidate dialog box, then specify the cell references in the Reference text box and choose the Add button. To remove a source area, click its references in the All References list box and then click the Delete button. To perform the consolidation with the new source areas, click OK. To perform a second consolidation in the same worksheet, choose a new destination area, then open the Consolidate dialog box, clear all the source areas you don't want to use in the All References list box with the Delete button, then redefine all of the new source areas in Reference text box with the Add button before you perform the consolidation by clicking the OK button.

Consolidating by category

You consolidate worksheets by category when their source areas do not share the same cell coordinates in their respective worksheets but their data entries do use common column and/or row labels. When you consolidate by category, you include these identifying labels as part of the source areas. Unlike when consolidating by position, Excel copies the row labels and/or column labels when you specify that they should be used in the consolidation.

When consolidating spreadsheet data by category, you must specify whether to use top row of column labels and/or the left column of row labels in determining which data to consolidate. To use the top row of column labels, you click the Top Row check box in the Use Labels In section of the Consolidate dialog box. To use the left column of row labels, you click the Left Column check box in this area. Then, once you've specified all the source areas (including the cells that contain these column and row labels), you perform the consolidation in the destination area by clicking the Consolidate dialog box's OK button.

Linking consolidated data

Excel allows you to link the data in the source areas to destination areas during a consolidation. That way, any changes that you make to the values in the source area will be automatically updated in the destination area of the consolidation worksheet. To create links between the source worksheets and the destination worksheet, you simply click the Create Links to Source Data check box in the Consolidate dialog box to put a checkmark in it when defining the settings for the upcoming consolidation.

When you perform a consolidation with linking, Excel creates the links between the source areas and the destination area by outlining the destination area (see "Outlining worksheets" earlier in this chapter for details). Each outline level created in the destination area holds rows or columns that contain the linking formulas to the consolidated data.

Figure 4-16 shows an outline created during consolidation after expanding only the level of the outline showing the consolidation of the Rock music CD sales. Here, you can see that during consolidation, Excel created three detail rows for each of the three years of sales (2000, 2001, and 2002) used in the linked consolidation. These rows contain the external reference formulas that link to the source data. For example, the formula in cell B4 contains the following formula:

```
='[CG Media - 2000 Sales.xls]Sales00'!$B$4
```

This formula links value in cell B4 in the Sales 00 sheet of the "CG Media - 2000 Sales.xls" workbook. If you change this value in that worksheet, the new value is automatically updated in cell B4 in the "CG Media - 2000-2002 Consolidated Sales" workbook, which, in turn, changes the subtotal for the January Rock music CD sales in its cell B7.

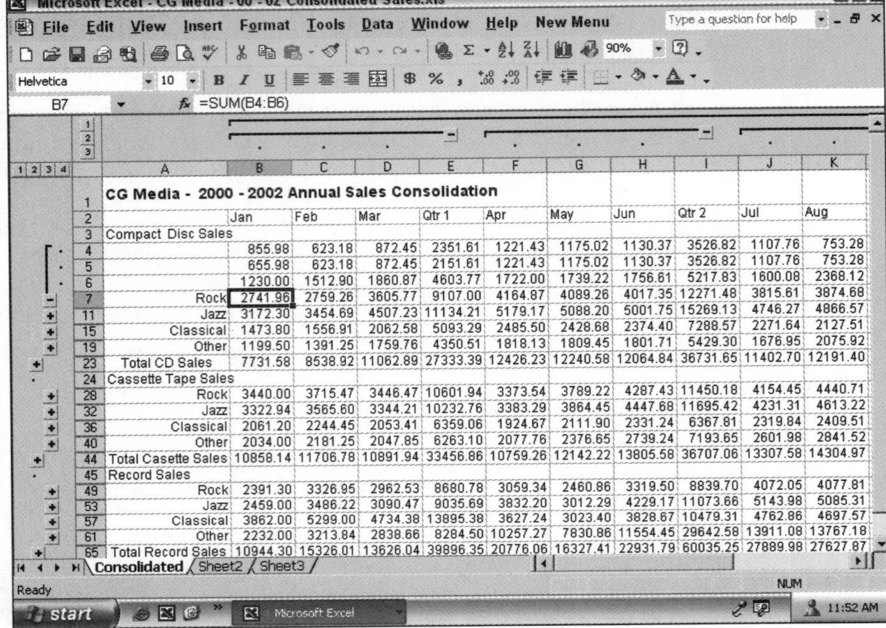

Figure 4-16: Consolidated worksheet with links to the sales data from three years.

Chapter 5: Printing Worksheets

In This Chapter

- Using Print Preview and Page Break Preview
- Printing the basic worksheet
- Printing a range of pages or part of the worksheet
- Printing the formulas in a worksheet
- Modifying the page and margin settings
- Adding headers and footers to a report
- Modifying the sheet options and adding print titles
- Changing the printer-specific options

Printing the spreadsheet is one of the most important tasks that you do in Excel (second only to saving your spreadsheet in the first place). Fortunately, Excel makes it easy to produce professional-looking reports from your worksheets. This chapter covers how to select the printer that you want to use; print all or just selected parts of the worksheet; change your page layout and print settings, including the orientation, paper size, print quality, number of copies, and range of pages; set up reports using the correct margin settings, headers and footers, titles, and page breaks; and how to use the Print Preview and Page Break Preview features to make sure that the pages of your report are the way you want them to appear before you print them.

The printing techniques covered in this chapter focus primarily on printing the data in your spreadsheets. Of course in Excel, you can also print your charts in chart sheets. Not surprisingly, you will find that most of the printing techniques that you learn for printing worksheet data in this chapter also apply to printing charts in their respective sheets. (For specific information on printing charts, see Book V, Chapter 1.)

Selecting the Printer

Windows allows you to install more than one printer for use with your applications. If you have installed multiple printers, the first one installed becomes the default printer, which is used by all Windows applications, including Excel. If you get a new printer, you must first install it in the Windows Printers dialog box (called Printers and Faxes in Windows XP) before you can select and use the printer in Excel.

To select a new printer to use in printing the current worksheet, follow these steps:

1. **Open the workbook with the worksheet that you want to print, activate that worksheet, and then choose File⇨Print on the Excel Menu bar or press Ctrl+P.**

   The Print dialog box opens (similar to the one shown in Figure 5-1). Be sure that you don't click the Print button on the Standard toolbar because doing so sends the active worksheet directly to the default printer (without giving you an opportunity to change the printer!).

2. **Click the name of the new printer that you want to use in the Name drop-down list box.**

   If the printer that you want to use isn't listed on the drop-down list, you can try to find the printer with the Find Printer button. When you click this button, Excel opens the Find Printers dialog box, where you specify the location for the program to search for the printer that you want to use. Note that if you don't have a printer connected to your computer, clicking the Find Printer button and opening the Find Printers dialog box results in opening a Find in the Directory alert dialog box with the message, "The Directory Service is Currently Unavailable." When you click OK in this alert dialog box, Excel closes it as well as the Find Printers dialog box.

3. **To change any of the default settings for the printer that you've selected, click the Properties button to the right of the Name drop-down list box and then select the new settings in the Properties dialog box for the printer that you selected.**

4. **Make any other required changes to the Print Range, Copies, or Collate settings in the Print dialog box.**

5. **Click OK to print the worksheet using the newly selected printer.**

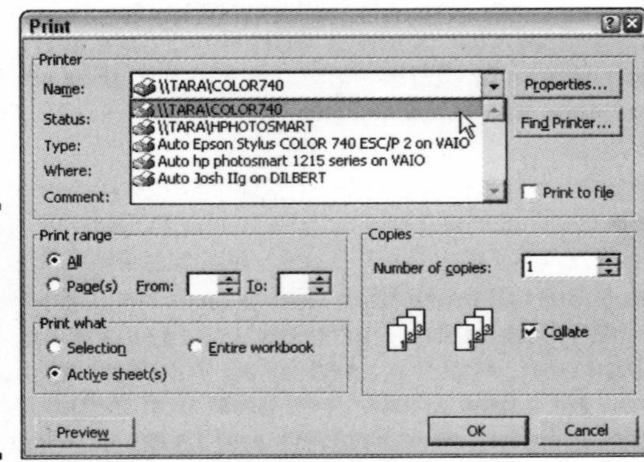

Figure 5-1: Selecting a new printer to use in the Print dialog box.

Keep in mind that the printer you select and use in printing the current worksheet remains the selected printer in Excel until you change back to the original printer (or some other printer).

Previewing the Printout and Its Page Breaks

Excel's Print Preview and Page Break Preview can save you countless trips to the printer — not to mention piles of wasted paper that result from printing errors that you didn't catch before you sent your report to the printer. By previewing selected pages of a report, you can usually spot any trouble areas that need fixing before you send the print job to the printer.

In Print Preview, text as well as graphics elements that are assigned to the cells in the *Print Area* (that is, the section of the current worksheet included in the printout) appear exactly as they will print. Unlike the standard on-screen view of the worksheet, Print Preview shows you the headers and footers that you've defined for the report and allows you to page through the report one page at a time so that you can check the page breaks. If you find any data errors when previewing a report, you can then edit them before you send the job to the printer by clicking the Close button to exit Print Preview and return to the normal worksheet view. If you don't find any problems, you can then send the job on to the printer directly from the Print Preview window.

In Page Break Preview, Excel displays the Workbook window at a reduced magnification that shows the page breaks and identifies which cells are printed on what pages of the report. This window also enables you to adjust the page breaks by dragging the page borders with the mouse.

Using Print Preview

You can open the Print Preview window from the normal Worksheet window, the Page Setup dialog box, or the Print dialog box:

- ✦ To open Print Preview from the worksheet, click the Print Preview button on the Standard toolbar or choose File⇨Print Preview on the Excel Menu bar.
- ✦ To open the Print Preview window from the Page Setup dialog box, click File⇨Page Setup on the Excel Menu bar and then click its Print Preview button on the right side of the dialog box beneath the Print button.
- ✦ To open the Print Preview window from the Print dialog box, click File⇨Print on the Menu bar or press Ctrl+P and then click the Preview button, located in the lower-left corner of the dialog box.

When you first open the Print Preview window, the window displays a full-page view of the first page of the report (similar to the one shown in Figure 5-2). To increase the page size to 100 percent, click the Zoom mouse pointer on the section of the page that you want to see in detail.

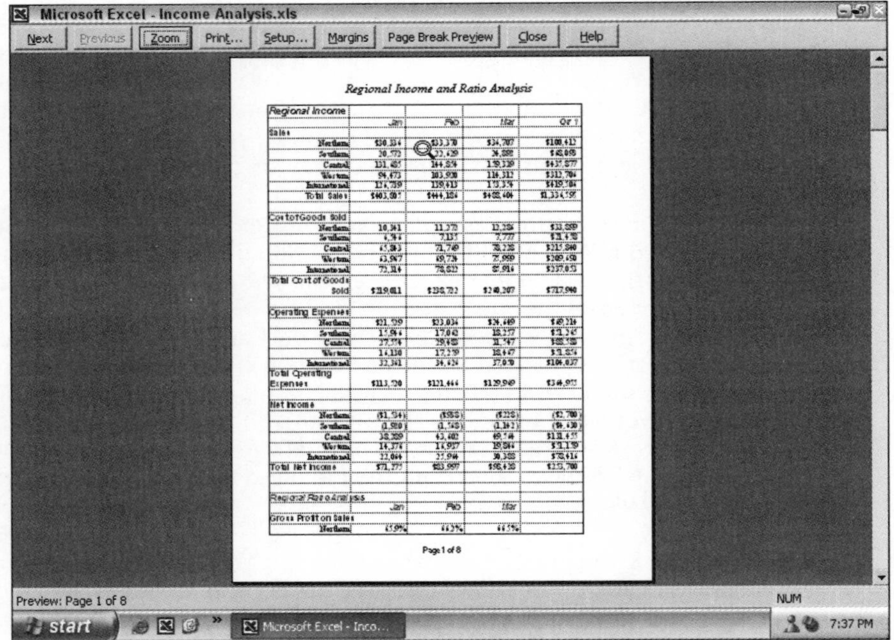

Figure 5-2: Viewing the first page of a report in the Print Preview window.

When the page is enlarged to 100 percent, you can use the scroll bars to bring new parts of the page into view in the Print Preview window. If you prefer using the keyboard, you can press the ↑ and ↓ keys or Page Up and Page Down to scroll up or down the page and ← and → or Ctrl+Page Up and Ctrl+Page Down to scroll left and right.

You can also press the Home key to position the left edge of the page on the screen and the End key to position the right edge. Press Ctrl+Home to position the upper-left corner of the page on the screen, press Ctrl+End to position the lower-right corner on the screen, and press Ctrl+ an arrow key (←, →, ↑, or ↓) to position the left, right, top, or bottom corner of the page on the screen from whatever part of the page is displayed.

To return to the full-page view in the Print Preview window, click the outlined arrowhead pointer, located somewhere on the page, or click the Zoom button, located at the top of the Print Preview window. If your report consists of more than one page, you can view succeeding pages by clicking the

Next button, located at the top of the window, or by pressing the Page Down key. To review pages that you've already seen, click the Previous button or press Page Up.

To exit the Print Preview window and return to the normal Worksheet window to make any necessary last minute changes, click the Close button. To go ahead and send the report to the printer, click the Print button. If you need to adjust the page breaks in the report before printing it, click the Page Break Preview button.

Changing Setup Options from Print Preview

If you identify a problem with the page settings while previewing the pages of a report, you can open the Page Setup dialog box by selecting the Setup button and then fix the problem without having to close the Print Preview window. For example, if you notice in Print Preview that the report will print the cell gridlines and the row and column headings (neither of which you want printed), you can remove these elements on the Sheet tab in the Page Setup dialog box.

To do this, click the Setup button to open the Page Setup dialog box, click the Sheet tab, and then deselect the Row and Column Headings and the Cell Gridlines check boxes. Then, when you click OK, Excel closes the Page Setup dialog box and returns you to the Print Preview window where the program redraws the current page of the report without either cell gridlines or column and row headings.

Changing the margins in Print Preview

If you detect problems with the margin settings for your report, you can change them by clicking the Margins button to add top, bottom, left, and right margin indicators along column indicators in the Print Preview window, as shown in Figure 5-3.

You can then change the margins and adjust the column widths by positioning the pointer on the margin or column indicator and then, when the mouse pointer changes to a double-headed arrow, by dragging the indicator in the appropriate direction. As soon as you release the mouse button, Excel redraws the data on the page that you're previewing to suit the new margin settings (note that changing the margins has no effect on the positioning of the header or footer text — only the data in the body of the report).

To change a column width in the Print Preview window, position the mouse pointer on the indicator of the column border that you want to increase or decrease, and then drag it with the double-headed mouse pointer in the appropriate direction. After you finish modifying the margins or column widths, you can remove the on-screen markers by clicking the Margins button again.

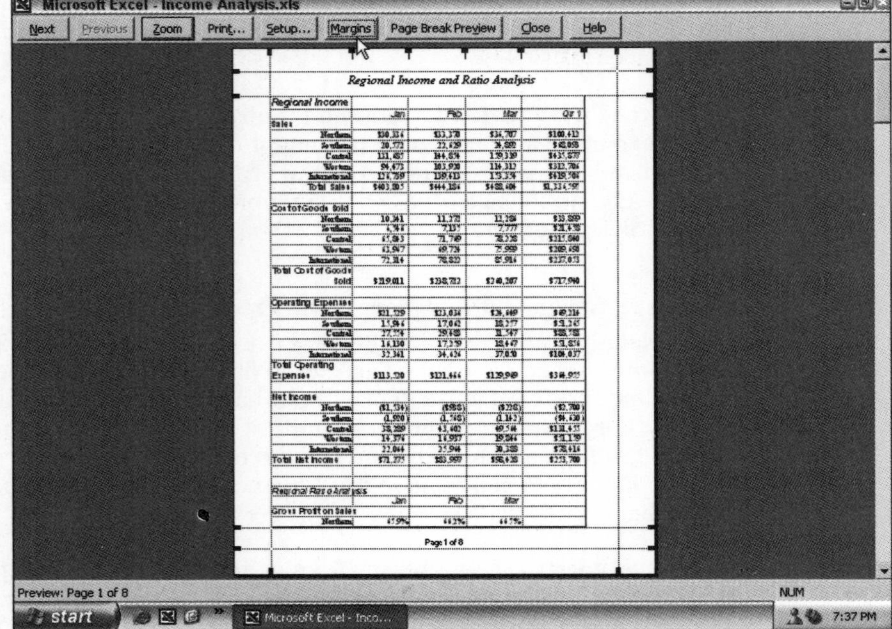

Figure 5-3: Manually adjusting the margins and column widths in the Print Preview window.

Using Page Break Preview

You can use the Page Break Preview feature to manually adjust bad page breaks in the report that would otherwise split up important information by printing it on separate pages. You can access Page Break Preview from the normal Worksheet window or the Print Preview window:

- ✦ To open Page Break Preview from the normal worksheet, choose View⇨Page Break Preview on the Excel Menu bar.
- ✦ To open Page Break Preview from the Print Preview window, click the Page Break Preview button on its toolbar, located at the top of the window.

When you choose Page Break Preview, Excel displays the worksheet at a smaller magnification with the page breaks clearly defined and identified in the Worksheet window — similar to one shown in Figure 5-4. The first time you choose Page Break Preview, Excel displays a Page Break Preview Welcome information dialog box, which informs you that you can adjust the page breaks displayed on the screen by dragging them.

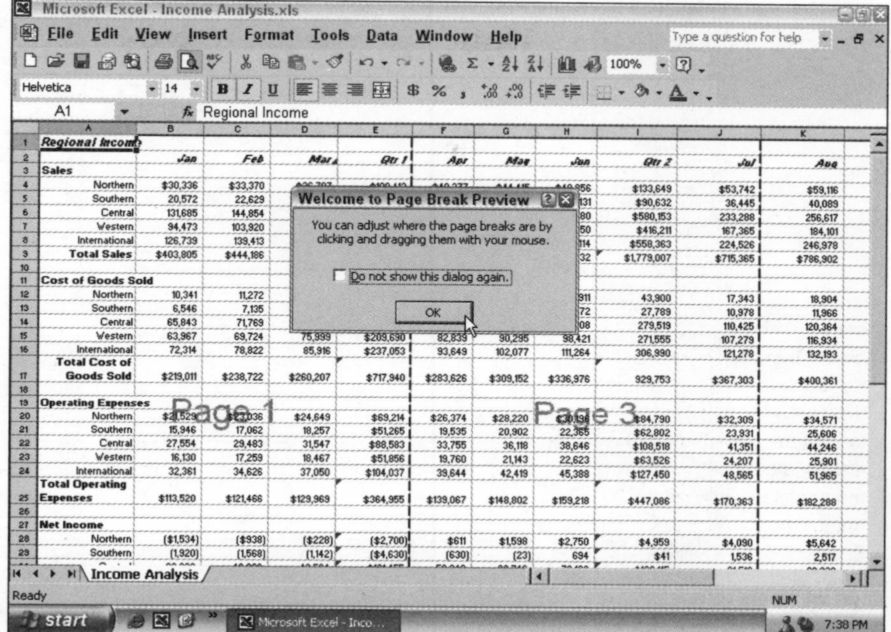

Figure 5-4: Manually adjusting the page breaks in the Print Break Preview display.

After clearing the Page Break Preview Welcome information dialog box, you can examine the page breaks (indicated by the dotted lines) by scrolling through the worksheet. Note that you can use the Zoom button on the Standard toolbar to reduce the magnification on the worksheet even further so that you can see all the pages as well as the order in which they will be printed (indicated by the page numbers shown in light gray in the middle of the previewed page).

Figure 5-5 shows the Page Break Preview display shown in Figure 5-4 after reducing the magnification setting in the Zoom control to 35% of normal. At this reduced magnification setting (Excel originally chose a 60% setting for Page Break Preview), the breaks for all eight pages of the report are now visible. In the Page Break Preview display at this Zoom setting, you can also see clearly how Excel pages the data in your worksheet proceeding down the rows of data before going across the columns (so that all the even-numbered pages are below rather than to the right of odd-numbered pages of the report).

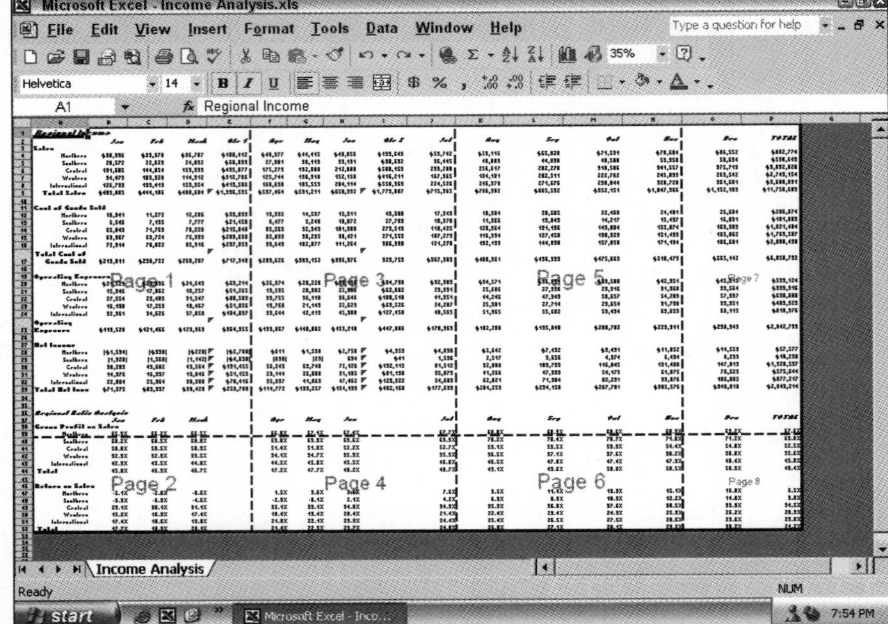

Figure 5-5: Reducing the Zoom setting to display all the pages in the Print Break Preview display.

After you've looked over all the pages in the Page Break Preview display, you can then decide whether to manually adjust the page breaks, and, if so, which breaks to adjust. Keep in mind when deciding how to adjust page breaks that Excel won't allow you to drag the page breaks to include more columns to the right or more rows lower in the worksheet because these represent the limit of columns and rows that fit on the page, given the current page and printing settings. (To be able to include more of these columns or rows on a page, you'd have to adjust the margin settings, column widths, or the scaling of the printing.)

To adjust a page break, drag it to the column or row in the reduced view of the worksheet where you want the page to break. Note that Excel distinguishes the page breaks that you adjusted manually from the page breaks that it put in by displaying them as solid blue lines (rather than dotted blue lines) in the Page Break Preview display. If you move a page break in error, use Edit➪Undo (Ctrl+Z) to restore the previous break.

After you finish examining and adjusting page breaks in the Page Break Preview display, you can return to the normal worksheet display by choosing View➪Normal on the Excel Menu bar.

Many times you can deal with bad page breaks more effectively by changing the page setup settings (especially the orientation and/or scaling of the printing) rather than trying to manually adjust the page breaks in the Page Break Preview display.

Spreadsheet Printing 101

Excel uses a number of default printing and page settings (all of which you can override) whenever you print your spreadsheet. Some of these settings vary according to the printer that you use, although most are not printer dependent. In most cases, the following printing and page settings are in effect when you first start printing in Excel:

- ✦ Print Quality is set to Normal (some types of printers can switch between High, Normal, and Draft printing quality, controlling how much ink is used, with Normal being in the middle of the two).
- ✦ Color printing is turned on (when using a color printer!).
- ✦ Print Range is set to All so that all pages of the report are printed.
- ✦ Print What is set to Active Sheet(s) so that all the data on all the selected worksheets are printed. If only the current worksheet tab is selected, Excel prints only the data on that active sheet.
- ✦ Copies are set to 1 (one) so that you get one copy of the report.
- ✦ Collated is turned so that each copy of the report (when printing more than one copy) is printed in ascending page order.
- ✦ Orientation is set to portrait (that is, printing runs parallel to the short edge of the paper).
- ✦ Scaling is set to 100% (actual size).
- ✦ Paper Size is set to Letter (8½ x 11 inches).
- ✦ Starting Page Number is 1.
- ✦ Margins are set to 0.75 inch in from the left and right edge of the paper, and 1 inch in from the top and bottom edge.
- ✦ Header and Footer is set to None.
- ✦ Order is set to Down, Then Over so that lower sections of the print range are printed before sections to the right.
- ✦ Cell gridlines are printed in the report.

Printing the worksheet

When you want to print all the information in the active worksheet by using the current printing and page settings, you can simply click the Print button on the Standard toolbar or open the Print dialog box (File➪Print) and click OK. Because Excel is automatically programmed to print all the data in the current worksheet, your only concern is to be sure that the sheet you want to print is active before you choose the Print command.

Excel only prints the data entries in the cells that are displayed in the worksheet. If you want to omit certain data from the printed report, you need to remember to hide their columns or rows in the worksheet (by selecting the columns or rows and then choosing Format➪Column➪Hide or Format➪Row➪Hide) before you click the Print button or open the Print dialog box and click OK.

If you need to print the data on multiple worksheets in the workbook, you need to select their sheet tabs (see Book II, Chapter 4 for details) prior to clicking the Print button on the Standard toolbar or opening the Print dialog box and clicking OK.

When you need to print the data on every worksheet in the workbook, you can either select all the sheet tabs in the workbook (by right-clicking a sheet tab and then clicking Select All Sheets on it shortcut menu) before you click the Print button, or you can open the Print dialog box (Ctrl+P) and then click the Entire Workbook radio button before clicking OK.

Click the Preview button in the Print dialog box to check and make sure that all the data on all the selected worksheets is going to be printed, as well as to check the page count and page breaks. If everything looks okay, click the Print button in the Print Preview window to send the print job to the printer. If you need to adjust the page breaks before printing, click the Page Break Preview button and make your adjustments in the Page Break Preview display. If you need to reselect or deselect some worksheets, click the Close button in the Print Preview window and make your changes in the normal worksheet view.

Printing a range of pages

When printing a report generated from the worksheet, you don't have to print all the pages. To print just a range of pages, follow these steps:

1. **Choose View➪Page Break Preview on the Excel Menu bar.**

   The active worksheet in the Page Break Preview display appears so that you can determine which pages you want to print. If you already know the numbers of the range of pages that you want to print, you can skip Step 1.

2. **Choose File⇨Print on the Excel Menu bar or press Ctrl+P.**

   The Print dialog box opens.

3. **Click the Page(s) radio button and then enter the number of the first page to print in the From text box and the number of the last page to print in the To text box.**

   You can also select the numbers of the pages in the page range by clicking the Spin buttons attached to the From and To text boxes.

4. **Click the OK button to send the print job to the printer.**

Printing part of the worksheet

Sometimes, you don't need to print all the data in the active worksheet. If you only need to print a particular part of the active worksheet, follow these steps:

1. **Select the cell range or ranges to print.**

   Remember that you can select more than one cell range by holding down the Ctrl key as you drag through succeeding cell ranges.

2. **Choose File⇨Print on the Excel Menu bar or press Ctrl+P.**

   You need to open the Print dialog box so that you can click the Selection radio button.

3. **Click the Selection radio button in the Print What section of the Print dialog box.**

   You must select the Selection option in the Print dialog box or Excel will simply ignore your current cell selection and go ahead and print the entire worksheet.

4. **Click the OK button to send the print job to the printer.**

   To make sure that only the cells that you have selected in the active worksheet will print, click the Preview button rather than OK to view the data in the Print Preview window. If everything looks okay, click the Print button on the Print Preview toolbar to send the job to the printer.

If you have a particular area in the worksheet that you routinely need to print, you can use the Print Area feature to designate that particular cell selection as the one to print anytime Excel prints the worksheet. This means that you don't have to open the Print dialog box and click the Selection radio button to print only the cell selection — instead, you can simply click the Print button to do this.

The steps for setting up the Print Area are simple:

1. **Choose the View⇨Page Break Preview on the Menu bar.**

   By turning on the Page Break Preview display before you set the Print Area, you can tell right away that the Print Area includes only the cell selection that you habitually need to print.

2. **Select the cell range or nonadjacent selection that you routinely want included in the Print Area.**

3. **Choose File⇨Print Area⇨Set Print Area on the Excel Menu bar.**

   As soon as you choose this command, Excel resets the Page Break Preview display so that it now includes only the current cell selection.

4. **Choose View⇨Normal to return the worksheet to Normal view and click any cell in the worksheet to deselect the cell selection.**

After you're back in Normal view, Excel indicates the boundaries of the Print Area with dotted lines along the column and row borders that make up the pages. To remove this display, click the Page Breaks check box to remove its checkmark on the View tab of the Options dialog box (Tools⇨Options).

To print the cells in the Print Area, you simply click the Print button on the Standard toolbar or choose File⇨Print (Ctrl+P) and then click OK (there's no need to fool around with the radio buttons in the Print What section of the Print dialog box).

If your worksheet has more than one section of data that you reprint frequently, assign a range name to its cells (see Book II, Chapter 2 for details on naming ranges). Then, whenever you need to print this section, follow these steps:

1. **Click the range name in the Name box on the Formula bar to select the cells.**

2. **Choose File⇨Print Area⇨ Set Print Area to set this cell selection as the new Print Area.**

3. **Click the Print button on the Standard toolbar to print the new Print Area.**

Keep in mind that after you define a cell selection as the Print Area, if you then need to print the entire worksheet, you first have to clear the Print Area (by choosing File⇨Print Area⇨Clear Print Area) before you click the Print button. Of course, after you've cleared the Print Area, you then have to go through the steps for setting up the Print Area before you can use it to print only a portion of the worksheet.

Sending a job to the printer

When you start printing a spreadsheet, Excel sends the print job using the current printing and page setting to your printer. During the time Excel is sending the print job to the printer, the program displays a Printing dialog box that keeps you informed of its progress by displaying the current page being sent, as well as the total number of pages in the print job (as in "Page 2 of 3"). Windows continues to display the Printing dialog box until the entire print job has been sent off to the printer, at which point the Printing dialog box closes and you're once again free to resume your work in Excel.

To terminate the printing before the entire print job has been sent to the printer, simply click the Cancel button in the Printing dialog box. If you aren't able to cancel the printing before the Printing dialog box closes, you must open the printer on the Windows taskbar (by double-clicking its icon on the System tray or right-clicking it and then clicking Open on the pop-up menu) and then cancel the printing from the printer's window. To do this, make sure that your print job is the one currently being printed and then choose Document⇨Cancel on the printer's Menu bar. If your spreadsheet is the only print job listed in the printer's window, you can also do this by choosing Printer⇨Cancel All Documents.

If you only want to pause the printing of the current print job, choose Document⇨Pause on the printer's Menu bar. Then, when you're ready to resume the printing, choose Document⇨Resume. If your spreadsheet is the only print job listed, you can also do this by choosing Printer⇨Pause Printing and Printer⇨Resume Printing. Note that if you're printing a fairly small spreadsheet on a fast computer and with a new printer, you may not have time to use these procedures to cancel or pause the printing as the print job may be entirely in the hands of the printer before you get a chance to open your printer's dialog box from the Windows taskbar.

Printing formulas in the worksheet

When you print a worksheet, Excel prints the entries exactly as they appear in their cells of the worksheet. As a result, when you print a section of worksheet that contains formulas, the printout shows only the results of the calculations performed by the formulas, and not the contents of the formulas themselves. In addition to a printout showing the results, you may also want to print a copy of the worksheet showing the formulas by which these results were derived. You can then use this printout of the formulas when double-checking the formulas in the worksheet to make sure that they are designed correctly.

To print a copy of the worksheet with the formulas displayed in the cells, follow these steps:

1. **Choose Tools⇨Options on the Excel menu bar.**

   The Options dialog box opens.

2. **Click the View tab and then click the Formulas check box in the Window Options section before you click OK.**

   When the Formulas check box is selected, Excel displays the entry in each cell in the worksheet as it appears on the formula. This means that not only do formulas appear as entered in the worksheet, but also that all values (text and numeric) appear without their formatting.

3. **Click the Print button on the Standard toolbar to send the print job to the printer.**

   If you only need to print an area of the worksheet, designate that section as the Print Area (following the steps outlined earlier) before you click the Print button.

   After printing the formulas in the worksheet, you can return the worksheet to its Normal view without the formulas displayed in the cells.

4. **Click Tools⇨Options and then click the Formulas check box on the View tab (to remove the checkmark) before you click OK.**

Excel returns the worksheet display to normal so that only the results of formulas are displayed in the cells and all entries are displayed with their formatting.

To help you identify the cell reference of each formula in your printout, print the version of the worksheet that displays the formulas in the cells with the column letters and row numbers on the top row and leftmost column of each page. To do this, you need to open the Page Setup dialog box (File⇨Page Setup), click the Sheet tab, and then click the Row and Column Headings check box (to put a checkmark in it). Then you can print the worksheet by clicking the Print button in the Page Setup dialog box. If you need to return to the worksheet to display the formulas in the worksheet before sending the job to printer, click the Close button instead.

Modifying the Page Setup

Excel's Page Setup dialog box contains four tabs full of printing options that you can modify prior to sending a print job to the printer. You can access this dialog box in the regular Worksheet window by choosing File⇨Page Setup on the Excel Menu bar or in the Print Preview window by clicking the Setup button on the window's toolbar.

Page tab settings

The Page tab of the Page Setup dialog box, shown in Figure 5-6, contains the following options that you can modify:

- **Orientation** to choose between Portrait in which the printing runs with the short edge of the paper and Landscape printing in which the printing runs with the long edge.
- **Scaling** to change the proportional size of the printing either by adjusting the percentage of normal size in the Adjust To text box or entering values in the Fit To Pages Wide By and Tall text boxes.
- **Paper Size** to select a new paper size for your printer in its drop-down list box.
- **Print Quality** to select a new value (in dpi or *dots per inch*) for the printing resolution in its drop-down list box (note that the values vary with the capabilities of the currently selected printer).
- **First Page Number** to enter the starting page number for the report in its text box (which is automatically 1 unless you replace Auto with a new number).

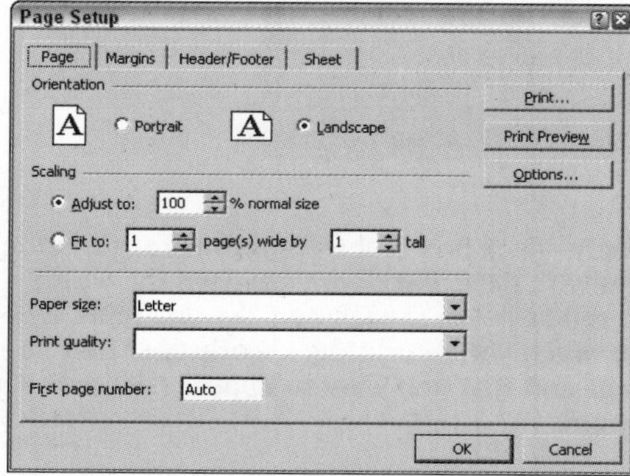

Figure 5-6: Changing the options on the Page tab of the Page Setup dialog box.

You can sometimes use the Orientation and/or Scaling options on the Page tab to deal with paging problems. By switching to the Landscape orientation, you can often fit all of the columns in the data table or list across a single page, which usually makes for much better paging in the report. If you find that almost all — but not quite all — of the columns fit across a single page, try adjusting down the percentage of normal size in the Adjust To text box until they all fit. If you're printing a small data table or list that almost all fits on a single page, use the Fit To radio button and then enter 1 as the number in both the Pages Wide and Tall text boxes.

Margins tab settings

The Margins tab of the Page Setup dialog box, shown in Figure 5-7, enables you to change the four page margins (Top, Bottom, Left, and Right) by entering values (instead of dragging the margin indicators as when you click the Margins button in the Print Preview window). It also enables you to set new margins for the Headers and Footers used in the report (see the "Headers and Footers" section that follows for more details), as well as to center the printing horizontally (between the left and right margins) or vertically (between the top and bottom margins). Note that any changes you make to the margin and page centering options on this tab are immediately reflected in the sample page that appears in the middle of the page.

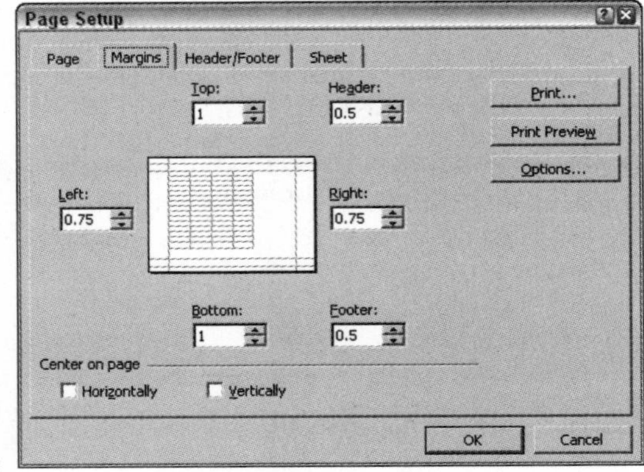

Figure 5-7: Changing the options on the Margins tab of the Page Setup dialog box.

Select the Horizontally check box in the Center on Page section when you're printing a worksheet with data that doesn't exceed the width of page and that you want centered between the left and right margins. Select the Vertically check box when you're printing a worksheet that doesn't exceed the length of the page and that you want to appear centered between the top and bottom margins.

Headers and Footers

The Header/Footer tab of the Page Setup dialog box, shown in Figure 5-8, enables you to define or to remove a header and footer from the printed report. The header contains the information that you want printed at the top of every page of the report, whereas the footer contains the information that you want printed at the bottom of each page. Excel doesn't assign either a header or footer when you first print a report from a workbook.

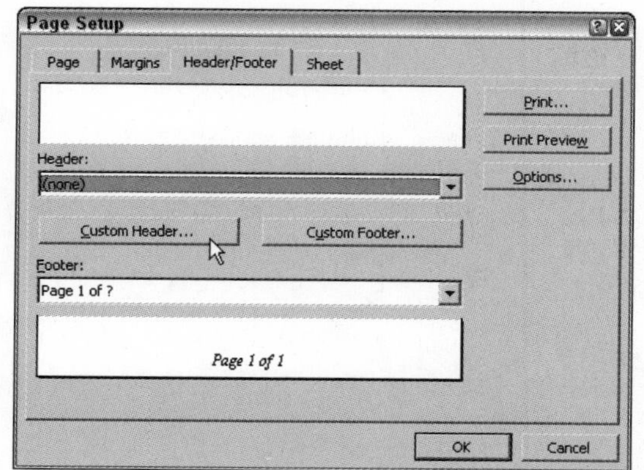

Figure 5-8: Changing the options on the Header/ Footer tab of the Page Setup dialog box.

When assigning a header or footer for your report, you can either select one of the stock headings (such as those that print the current page number or date, or those that print the name of the workbook or worksheet, and so forth) or create a custom heading of your own. To select a stock heading on the Header/Footer tab, click the heading in the Header and/or Footer drop-down list box to replace the default setting of (none).

For example, to display the current page along with the total number of pages in the report in the bottom margin as a footer using the form Page 1 of 10, click the following stock heading in the Footer drop-down list:

```
Page 1 of ?
```

Note that when you select a stock heading from the Header or Footer drop-down list, Excel automatically centers the heading between the left and right margins if the heading consists of a single piece of information (such as the page numbers or worksheet name). If the stock heading consists of two pieces of information, Excel centers the first piece and right-justifies the second piece. In any case, the program shows you a preview of how the stock heading actually appears in the header and footer for your workbook in the preview list boxes at the top and bottom of the Header/Footer tab.

To create a custom heading for the header and/or footer, click the Custom Header or Custom Footer button on this tab to open the respective Header or Footer dialog boxes. Figure 5-9 shows the Header dialog box (the Footer dialog box is just like this). As you can see, a custom header and footer can consist of up to three parts: a Left Section in which all the items are left-justified, a Center Section in which they are centered between the left and right margins, and a Right Section in which they are right-justified.

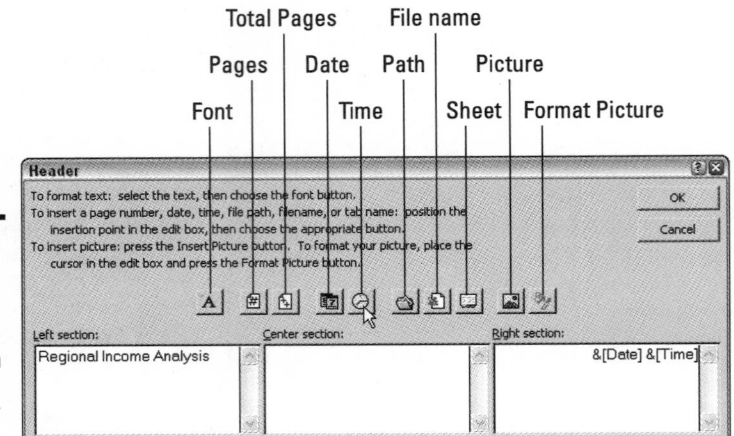

Figure 5-9: Creating a custom header for the report in the Header dialog box.

When you create a custom header or footer, you can mix your text with stock information, such as the current page number, total number of pages, date, path to the folder containing the file, workbook filename, and worksheet name. To do this, click the insertion point in the section where you want to add text and then type your text interspersed with the stock information whose code you insert. To insert the code for a piece of stock information, click the appropriate button in the Header or Footer dialog box (see Figure 5-9).

Table 5-1 shows you the codes that Excel inserts into the text of your custom header or footer when you click the various buttons in the Header or Footer dialog box. Note that when you click the Font button, Excel opens the Font dialog box where you can select a new font, font size, or font style for the selected text without inserting any codes into the current section of the custom header or footer.

Table 5-1 Header and Footer Codes

Button	*Code*	*Function*
Page Number	&[Page]	Inserts current page number
Total Pages	&[Pages]	Inserts the total number of pages
Date	&[Date]	Inserts current date in the form 7/14/04
Time	&[Time]	Inserts current time in the form 9:05 AM
Path	&[Path]	Inserts the complete pathname for the file in the form C:\mydocuments\finances\budget04

Button	*Code*	*Function*
Filename	&[File]	Inserts the workbook filename
Sheet	&[Tab]	Inserts the worksheet name
Picture	&[Picture]	Inserts the graphic image you select

Also, when you click the Picture button, Excel opens the Insert Picture dialog box, where you choose the graphics file whose image you want to appear in the header or footer (normally a logo or other mark that fits well within the top or bottom margin), represented by the &[Picture] code in the header or footer. When you click the Format Picture button (available only after you've inserted the &[Picture] code in the header or footer), Excel opens the Format Picture dialog box, which enables you to modify the size and the appearance of the graphic image.

Sheet tab settings

The Sheet tab of the Page Setup dialog box, shown in Figure 5-10, enables you to change various and sundry options related to the worksheet. These options include:

- **Print Area** to reset the Print Area by selecting a cell range or nonadjacent selection. Remember that when you set the Print Area, Excel prints only the cell selection in this area instead of the entire worksheet (as when you click the Print button on the Standard toolbar).
- **Print Titles** to print the range of rows displayed in the Rows to Repeat at Top text box and the range of columns displayed in the Columns to Repeat at Left text box on each page of the printed report.
- **Gridlines** check box to turn off and on the printing of the worksheet gridlines in the printed report.
- **Row and Column Headings** check box to turn on and off the printing of the worksheet column letters and row numbers in the printed report.
- **Black and White** check box to turn on and off color printing (when using a color printer!).
- **Comments** drop-down list box to print comments appended to the cells in the printout either at the end of the report or as they are displayed in the worksheet.
- **Draft Quality** check box to turn on and off draft quality printing to save on ink (if your computer is capable of changing).
- **Cell Errors As** drop-down list box to determine how formula errors (see Book III, Chapter 2) are displayed in the printed report. You can choose between putting blanks in cells with error values, putting a double dash, and putting in the #NA (Not Available) value.

✦ **Page Order** to determine how the worksheet is paged. When the default Down, Then Over radio button is selected, Excel pages the worksheet by moving down the rows of the first set of columns before moving over (so that Page 2 is comprised of cell entries in rows under the ones in Page 1). When you select the Over, Then Down radio button, Excel pages the worksheet in just the opposite manner — over to columns on the right before moving down (so that Page 2 is comprised of cell entries in columns to the right of the ones in Page 1).

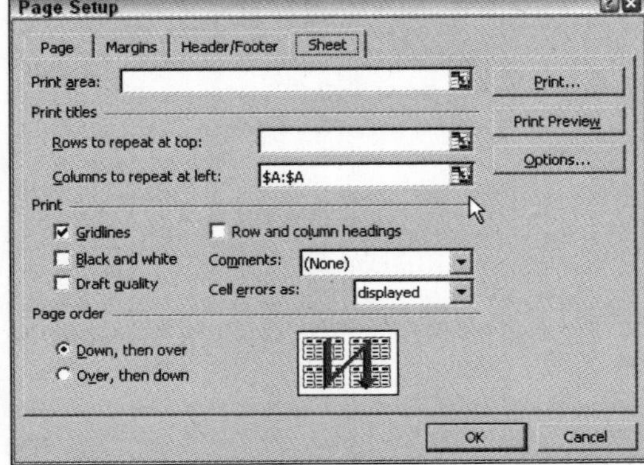

Figure 5-10: Changing the options on the Sheet tab of the Page Setup dialog box.

Adding Print Titles to a report is analogous to freezing panes on the worksheet display in that the information in the designated rows and columns is repeated in the same position (row titles at the very top of the page underneath the header, if the report has one and Column titles at the very left of the page).

Note that when you print a graph that's saved on a separate Chart sheet in the workbook, instead of a Sheet tab, the Page Setup dialog box has a Chart tab that enables you to change the way the chart is printed (see Book V, Chapter 1 for details).

Printer options

You can click the Options button in the Page Setup dialog box to open the printer dialog box for the particular printer that's currently selected in the Print dialog box. This printer-specific dialog box enables you to change options that are unique to your brand or type of printer. For example, if your laser printer has more than one paper tray, you can select the Paper Source option in the Paper/Quality tab to use a different tray, and if you're using an inkjet printer, your printer may provide a nozzle check or head-cleaning utility that you can select from its Utilities tab to improve the print quality of your report.

Book III

Formulas and Functions

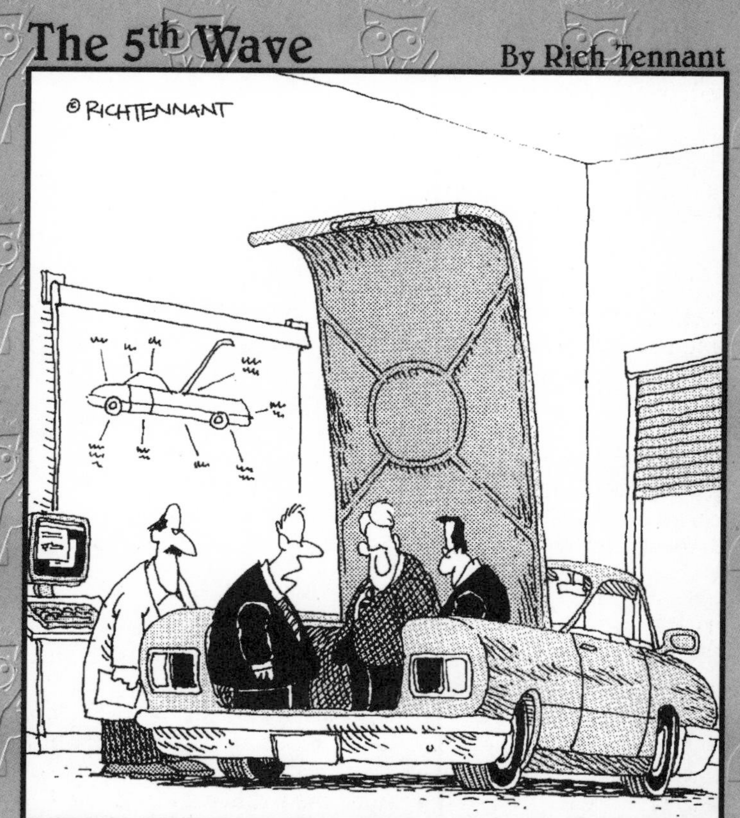

"Unless there's a corrupt cell in our spreadsheet analysis concerning the importance of trunk space, this should be a big seller next year."

Contents at a Glance

Chapter 1: Building Basic Formulas

In This Chapter

- **Summing data ranges with the AutoSum button**
- **Creating simple formulas with operators**
- **Understanding the operators and their precedence in the formula**
- **Using the Insert Function button on the Formula bar**
- **Copying formulas and changing the type of cell references**
- **Building array formulas**
- **Using range names in formulas**
- **Creating linking formulas that bring values forward**
- **Controlling formula recalculation**
- **Dealing with circular references in formulas**

Formulas, to put it mildly, are the very "bread and butter" of the worksheet. Without formulas, the electronic spreadsheet would be little better than its green-sheet paper equivalent. Fortunately, Excel gives you the ability to do all your calculations right within the cells of the worksheet without any need for a separate calculator.

The formulas that you build in a spreadsheet can run the gamut from very simple to extremely complex. Formulas can rely totally upon the use of simple *operators* or the use of built-in *functions*, both of which describe the type of operation or calculation to perform and the order in which to perform it, or they can blend the use of operators and functions together. When you use Excel functions in your formulas, you need to learn what particular type of information that particular function uses in performing its calculations. The information that you supply a function and that it uses in its computation is referred to as the *argument(s)* of the function.

Formulas 101

From the simple addition formula to the most complex ANOVA statistical variation, all formulas in Excel have one thing in common: They all begin with the equal sign (=). This doesn't mean that you always have to type in the equal sign — although if you do, Excel expects that a formula of some type is to follow. When building a formula that uses a built-in function, oftentimes you use the Insert Function button on the Formula bar to select and insert the function, in which case, Excel adds the opening equal sign for you (also, if you're an old Lotus 1-2-3 user and you type @ to start a function, Excel automatically converts the @ sign into the equal sign the moment that you complete the formula entry). It does mean, however, that each and every completed formula that appears on the Formula bar starts with the equal sign.

When building your formulas, you can use *constants* that actually contain the number that you want used in the calculation (such as "4.5%," "$25.00," or "–78.35") or you can use cell addresses between the operators or as the arguments of functions. When you create a formula that uses cell addresses, Excel then uses the values that you've input in those cells in calculating the formula. Unlike when using constants in formulas, when you use cell addresses, Excel automatically updates the results calculated by a formula whenever you edit the values in the cells to which it refers.

Formula building methods

When building formulas manually, you can either type in the cell addresses or you can point to them in the worksheet. Using the Pointing method to supply the cell addresses for formulas is often easier and is always a much more foolproof method of formula building; when you type in a cell address, you are less apt to notice that you've just designated the wrong cell than when pointing directly to it. For this reason, stick to pointing when building original formulas and restrict typing cell addresses to the odd occasion when you need to edit a cell address in a formula and pointing to it is either not practical or just too much trouble.

When you use the Pointing method to build a simple formula that defines a sequence of operations, you stop and click the cell or drag through the cell range after typing each operator in the formula. When using the method to build a formula that uses a built-in function, you click the cell or drag through the cell range that you want used when defining the function's arguments in the Function Arguments dialog box.

As with the other types of cell entries, you must take some action to complete a formula and enter it into the current cell (such as clicking the Enter button on the Formula bar, pressing the Enter key, or pressing an arrow key). Unlike when entering numeric or text entries, however, you will want to stay clear of clicking another cell to complete the data entry. This is because when you click a cell when building or editing a formula on the Formula bar, more often than not, you end up not just selecting the new cell but also adding its address to the otherwise complete formula.

Formulas and formatting

When defining a formula that uses only operators, Excel picks up the number formatting of the cells that are referenced in the formula (with the exception of the Percent style number format). For example, if you add cell A2 to B3, as in =A2+B3, and cell B3 is formatted with the Currency Style format, the result will inherit this format and be displayed in its cell using the Currency Style. This is not true, however, when you define a formula that uses a built-in function. If you sum cells A2 and B3 with the SUM function, as in =SUM(A2:B3), the result appears in its cell using the normal General number, even if cell B3 uses the Currency Style format.

As soon as you complete a formula entry, Excel calculates the result, which is then displayed inside the cell within the worksheet (the contents of the formula, however, continue to be visible on the Formula bar anytime the cell is active). If you make an error in the formula that prevents Excel from being able to calculate the formula at all, Excel displays an Alert dialog box suggesting how to fix the problem. If, however, you make an error that prevents Excel from being able to display a proper result when it calculates the formula, the program displays an Error value rather than the expected computed value (see Chapter 2 in this book for details on dealing with both of these types of errors in formulas).

Editing formulas

As with numeric and text entries, you can edit the contents of formulas either in their cells or on the Formula bar. To edit a formula in its cell, double-click the cell or press F2 to position the pointer in that cell (double-clicking positions the insertion pointer in the middle of the formula, whereas pressing F2 positions it at the end of the formula). To edit a formula on the Formula bar, use the I-beam pointer to click the insertion point at the place in the formula that needs editing first.

As soon as you put the Excel program into Edit mode, Excel displays each of the cell references in the formula in a different color and uses this color to outline the cell or cell range in the worksheet itself. This enables you to quickly identify the cells and their values that are referred to in your formula and, if necessary modify them as well. You can use any of the four sizing handles that appear around the cell or cell range to modify the cell selection in the worksheet and consequently update the cell references in the formula.

Using Excel like a handheld calculator

Sometimes, you may need to actually calculate the number that you need to input in a cell as a constant. Instead of reaching for your pocket calculator to compute the needed value and then manually entering it into a cell of your spreadsheet, you can set up a formula in the cell that returns the number that you need to input and then convert the formula into a constant value. You convert the formula into a constant by pressing F2 to edit the cell, and then immediately pressing F9 to recalculate the formula and display the result on the Formula bar, and then clicking the Enter button on the Formula bar or pressing the Enter key to input the calculated result into the cell (as though you had manually input the result in the cell).

When you AutoSum numbers in a spreadsheet

The easiest, and often the most used formula that you will create is the one that totals rows and columns of numbers in your spreadsheet. Most often, to total a row or column of numbers, you can use the AutoSum button on the Standard toolbar. When you click this button, Excel inserts the built-in SUM function into the active cell, while at the same time selecting what the program thinks is the most likely range of numbers that you want summed.

Figure 1-1 demonstrates how this works. For this figure, I positioned the cell pointer in cell B7, which is the first cell where I need to build a formula that totals the various parts produced in April. I then clicked the AutoSum button on the Standard toolbar (the one with the Sigma icon). As Figure 1-1 shows, Excel then inserted an equal sign followed by the SUM function, while at the same time correctly suggesting the cell range B3:B6 as the argument to this function (that is, the range to be summed). Because Excel correctly selected the range to be summed (leaving out the date value in cell B2), all I have to do to have the April total calculated is to click the Enter button on the Formula bar.

Figure 1-2 shows another example of using the AutoSum button to instantly build a SUM formula, this time to total the monthly production numbers for the Part 100 in cell K3. Again, all I did to create the formula shown in Figure 1-2 was to select cell K3 and then click the AutoSum button on the Standard toolbar. Again, Excel correctly selected B3:J3 as the range to be summed (rightly ignoring cell A3 with the row title) and input this range as the argument of the SUM function. All that remains to be done is to click the Enter button on the Formula bar to compute the monthly totals for Part 100.

Microsoft Excel - Prod Sch - 03.xls

SUM =SUM(B3:B6)

	A	B	C	D	E	F	G	H	I	J	K
1	2003 Production Schedule										
2		Apr-03	May-03	Jun-03	Jul-03	Aug-03	Sep-03	Oct-03	Nov-03	Dec-03	Total
3	Part 100	500	485	438	505	483	540	441	550	345	
4	Part 101	175	170	153	177	169	189	154	193	200	
5	Part 102	350	340	306	354	338	378	309	385	350	
6	Part 103	890	863	779	899	859	961	785	979	885	
7	Total	=SUM(B3:B6)									

Figure 1-1: Using the AutoSum button to create a SUM formula that totals a column of numbers.

Microsoft Excel - Prod Sch - 03.xls

SUM =SUM(B3:J3)

	A	B	C	D	E	F	G	H	I	J	K
1	2003 Production Schedule										
2		Apr-03	May-03	Jun-03	Jul-03	Aug-03	Sep-03	Oct-03	Nov-03	Dec-03	Total
3	Part 100	500	485	438	505	483	540	441	550	345	=SUM(B3:J3)
4	Part 101	175	170	153	177	169	189	154	193	200	
5	Part 102	350	340	306	354	338	378	309	385	350	
6	Part 103	890	863	779	899	859	961	785	979	885	
7	Total	1,915									

Figure 1-2: Using the AutoSum button to create a SUM formula that totals a row of numbers.

If for some reason AutoSum doesn't select the entire or correct range that you want summed, you can adjust the range by dragging the cell pointer through the cell range or by clicking the marquee around the cell range, which turns the marching ants into a solid colored outline, and then positioning the mouse pointer on one of the sizing handles at the four corners and dragging the outline until it includes all the cells you want included in the total.

Keep in mind that all Excel functions enclose their argument(s) in a closed pair of parentheses as shown in the examples with the SUM function. Even those rare functions that don't require any arguments at all still require the use of a closed pair of parentheses (even when you don't put anything inside of them).

Building formulas with operators

Many of the simpler formulas that you build require the sole use of Excel's operators, which are the symbols that indicate the type of computation that is to take place between the cells and/or constants interspersed between them. Excel uses four different types of operators: arithmetic, comparison, text, and reference. Table 1-1 shows all of these operators arranged by type and accompanied by an example.

Table 1-1 The Different Types of Operators in Excel

Type	*Character*	*Operation*	*Example*
Arithmetic	+ (plus sign)	Addition	=A2+B3
	- (minus sign)	Subtraction or negation	=A3-A2 or -C4
	* (asterisk)	Multiplication	=A2*B3
	/	Division	=B3/A2
	%	Percent (dividing by 100)	=B3%
	^	Exponentiation	=A2^3
Comparison	=	Equal to	=A2=B3
	>	Greater than	=B3>A2
	<	Less than	=A2<B3
	>=	Greater than or equal to	=B3>=A2
	<=	Less than or equal to	=A2<=B3
	<>	Not equal to	=A2<>B3
Text	&	Concatenates (connects) entries to produce one continuous entry	=A2&" "&B3
Reference	: (colon)	Range operator that includes	=SUM(C4:D17)
	, (comma)	Union operator that combines multiple references into one reference	=SUM(A2,C4:D17,B3)
	(space)	Intersection operator that produces one reference to cells in common with two references	=SUM(C3:C6 C3:E6)

"Smooth operator"

Most of the time, you'll rely on the arithmetic operators when building formulas in your spreadsheets that don't require functions because these operators actually perform computations between the numbers in the various cell references and produce new mathematical results.

When AutoSum doesn't sum

Although the AutoSum button's primary function is to build formulas with the SUM function that totals ranges of numbers, that's not its only function (pun intended). Indeed, you can have the AutoSum button build formulas that compute the average value, count the number of values, or return the highest or lowest value in a range — all you have to do is click the pop-up button that's attached to AutoSum and then click Average, Count, Max, or Min on its pop-up menu.

Also, don't forget about the AutoSum indicator on the Status bar. This indicator automatically shows you the sum of all numbers in the current cell selection. You can use this feature to preview the total that's to be returned by the SUM formula that you create with the AutoSum button by selecting the cell range that contains the numbers to be summed. Just as with the AutoSum button, you can have the AutoSum indicator show you the average, count, highest, or lowest number in the cell selection; to do so, just right-click the indicator and then click Average, Count, Max, or Min before you select the cell range or nonadjacent cell selection.

The comparison operators, on the other hand, produce only the logical value TRUE or the logical value FALSE, depending upon whether the comparison is accurate. For example, if you enter the following formula in cell A10:

```
=B10<>C10
```

If B10 contains the number 15 and C10 contains the number 20, the formula in A10 returns the logical value TRUE. If, however, both cell B10 and C10 contain the value 12, the formula returns the logical value FALSE.

The single text operator (the so-called Ampersand) is used in formulas to join together two or more text entries (an operation with the highfalutin' name *concatenation*). For example, suppose that you enter the following formula in cell C2:

```
=A2&B2
```

If cell A2 contains "John" and cell B2 contains "Smith", the formula returns the new (squashed together) text entry, "JohnSmith." To have the formula insert a space between the first and last name, you have to include the space as part of the concatenation as follows:

```
=A2&" "&B2
```

You most often use the comparison operators with the IF function when building more complex formulas that perform one type of operation when the IF condition is TRUE and another when it is FALSE. You use the concatenating operator (&) when you need to join text entries that come to you entered in separate cells but that need to be entered in single cells (like the first and last names in separate columns). See Chapter 2 in this book for more on logical formulas and Chapter 6 in this book for more on text formulas.

Order of operator precedence

When you build a formula that combines different operators, Excel follows the set order of operator precedence, as shown in Table 1-2. When you use operators that share the same level of precedence, Excel evaluates each element in the equation by using a strictly left-to-right order.

Table 1-2 Natural Order of Operator Precedence in Formulas

Precedence	*Operator*	*Type/Function*
1	–	Negation
2	%	Percent
3	^	Exponentiation
4	* and /	Multiplication and Division
5	+ and –	Addition and Subtraction
6	&	Concatenation
7	=, <, >, <=, >=, <>	All Comparison Operators

Suppose that you enter the following formula in cell A4:

```
=B4+C4/D4
```

Because multiplication has a higher level of precedence than addition (4 versus 5), Excel evaluates the division between cells C4 and D4 and then adds that result to the value in cell B4. If, for example, cell B4 contains 2, C4 contains 9, and D4 contains 3, Excel would essentially be evaluating this equation in cell A4:

```
=2+9/3
```

In this example, the calculated result displayed in cell A4 is 5 because the program first performs the division (9/3) that returns the result 3 and then adds it to the 2 to get the final result of 5.

If you had wanted Excel to evaluate this formula in a strictly left-to-right manner, you could get it to do so by enclosing the leftmost operation (the addition between B4 and C4) in a closed pair of parentheses. Parentheses alter the natural order of precedence so that any operation enclosed within a pair is performed before the other operations in the formula, regardless of level in the order (after that, the natural order is once again used).

To have Excel perform the addition between the first two terms (B4 and C4) and then divide the result by the third term (cell D4), you modify the original formula by enclosing the addition operation in parentheses as follows:

```
=(B4+C4)/D4
```

Assuming that cells B4, C4, and D4 still contain the same numbers (2, 9, and 3, respectively), the formula now calculates the result as 3.666667 and returns it to cell A4 (2+9=11 and 11/3=3.66667).

If necessary, you can *nest* parentheses in your formulas by putting one set of parentheses within another (within another, within another, and so on). When you nest parentheses, Excel performs the calculation in the inmost pair of parentheses first before anything else and then starts performing the operations in the outer parentheses.

Consider the following sample formula:

```
=B5+(C5-D5)/E5
```


In this formula, the parentheses around the subtraction (C5-D5) ensure that it is the first operation performed. However, after that the natural order of precedence takes over so that the result of the subtraction is then divided by the value in E5 and that result is then added to the value in B5. If you want the addition to be performed before the division, you need to nest the first set of parentheses within another set as follows:

```
=(B5+(C5-D5))/E5
```

In this revised formula, Excel performs the subtraction between the values in C5 and D5, and then adds the result to the value in cell B5, and then divides that result by the value in cell E5.

WARNING!

Of course, the biggest problem with parentheses is that you have to remember to enter them in pairs. If you forget to balance each set of nested parentheses by having a right parenthesis for every left parenthesis, Excel displays an Alert dialog box, informing you that it has located an error in the formula. It will also suggest a correction that would balance the parentheses used in the formula. Although the suggested correction corrects the imbalance in the formula, unfortunately it doesn't give you the calculation order that you wanted, and — if accepted — would give you what you consider an incorrect result. For this reason, be very careful before you click the Yes button in this kind of Alert dialog box. Do so only when you're certain that the corrected parentheses give you the calculation order that you want. Otherwise, click No and balance the parentheses in the formula by adding the missing parenthesis or parentheses yourself.

Using the Insert Function button

Excel supports a wide variety of built-in functions that you can use when building your formulas. Of course, the most popular built-in function is by far the SUM function, which is automatically inserted when you click the AutoSum button on the Standard toolbar (keep in mind that you can also use this button to insert the AVERAGE, COUNT, MAX, and MIN functions — see the "When you AutoSum numbers in a spreadsheet" section previously in this chapter for details). To use other Excel functions, you can use the Insert Function button on the Formula bar.

When you click the Insert Function button, Excel displays the Insert Function dialog box, similar to the one shown in Figure 1-3. You can then use its options to find and select the function that you want to use and to define the argument or arguments that the function requires in order to perform its calculation.

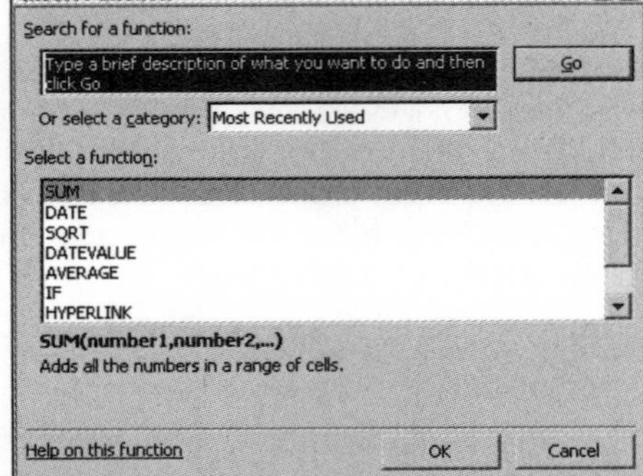

Figure 1-3: Selecting a function to use in the Insert Function dialog box.

To select the function that you want to use, you can use any of the following methods:

- Click the function name if it's one that you've used lately and is therefore already listed in the Select a Function list box.
- Click the name of the category of the function that you want to use in the Or Select a Category drop-down list box (Most Recently Used is the default category) and then select the function that you want to use in that category in the Select a Function list box.

✦ Replace the text "Type a brief description of what you want to do and then click Go" in the Search for a Function text box with keywords or a phrase about the type of calculation that you want to do (such as "return on investment"), and then click the Go button and click the function that you want to use in the Recommended category displayed in the Select a Function list box.

When selecting the function to use in the Select a Function list box, click the function name to have Excel give you a short description of what the function does, displayed underneath the name of the function with its argument(s) shown in parentheses (referred to as the function's *syntax*). To get help on using the function, click the Help on This Function link displayed in the lower-left corner of the Insert Function dialog box to open the Help window in its own pane on the right. When you finish reading and/or printing out this help topic, click the Close button to close the Help window and return to the Insert Function dialog box.

When you click OK after selecting the function that you want to use in the current cell, Excel inserts the function name followed by a closed set of parentheses on the Formula bar. At the same time, the program closes the Insert Function dialog box and then opens the Function Arguments dialog box, similar to the one shown in Figure 1-4. You then use the argument text box or boxes displayed in the Function Arguments dialog box to specify what numbers and other information are to be used when the function calculates its result.

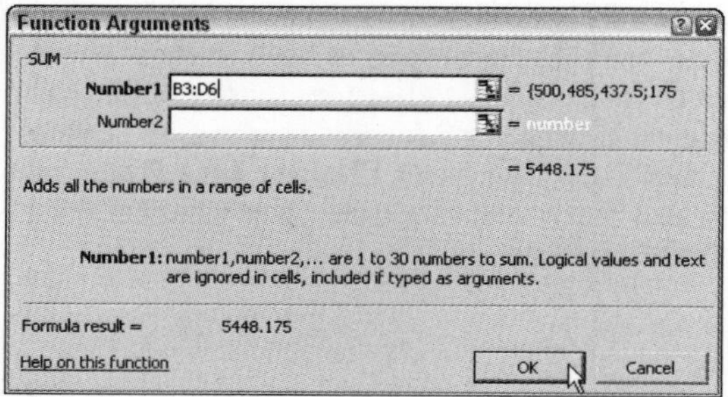

Figure 1-4: Selecting the arguments for a function in the Function Arguments dialog box.

All functions — even those that don't take any arguments, such as the TODAY function — follow the function name by a closed set of parentheses, as in =TODAY(). If the function requires arguments (and almost all require at least one), these arguments must appear within the parentheses following the function name. When a function requires multiple arguments, such as the DATE function, the various arguments are entered in the required order (as in *year*, *month*, *day* for the DATE function) within the parentheses separated by commas, as in DATE(33,7,23).

When you use the text boxes in the Function Arguments dialog box to input the arguments for a function, you can select the cell or cell range in the worksheet that contains the entries that you want used. Click the text box for the argument that you want to define, and then either start dragging the cell pointer through the cells or, if the Function Arguments dialog box is obscuring the first cell in the range that you want to select, click the Collapse Dialog Box button located to the immediate right of the text box (shown in the left margin). Dragging or clicking this button reduces the Function Arguments dialog box to just the currently selected argument text box, thus enabling you to drag through the rest of the cells in the range.

If you started dragging without first clicking the Collapse Dialog Box button, Excel automatically expands the Function Arguments dialog box as soon as you release the mouse button. If you clicked the Collapse Dialog Box button, you have to click the Expand Dialog Box button (which replaces the Collapse Dialog Box button located to the right of the argument text box — shown in the left margin) in order to restore the Function Arguments dialog box to its original size.

As you define arguments for a function in the Function Arguments dialog box, Excel shows you the calculated result following the heading, "Formula result =" near the bottom of the Function Arguments dialog box. When you finish entering the required argument(s) for your function (and any optional arguments that may pertain to your particular calculation), click OK to have Excel close the Function Arguments dialog box and replace the formula in the current cell display with the calculated result.

For details on how to use different types of built-in functions for your spreadsheets, refer to the following chapters in this book that discuss the use of various categories: Chapter 2 for information on Logical functions, Chapter 3 for Date and Time functions, Chapter 4 for Financial functions, Chapter 5 for Math and Statistical functions, and Chapter 6 for Lookup, Information, and Text functions.

Copying Formulas

Copying formulas is one of the most common tasks that you do in a typical spreadsheet that relies primarily on formulas. When a formula uses cell references rather than constant values (as most should), Excel makes the task of copying an original formula to every place that requires a similar location a piece of cake. The program does this by automatically adjusting the cell references in the original formula to suit the position of the copies that you make. It does this through a system known as *relative cell addresses,* whereby the column references in the cell address in the formula change to suit their new column position and the row references change to suit their new row position.

Figures 1-5 and 1-6 illustrate how this works. For Figure 1-5, I used the AutoSum button in cell B7 to build the original formula that uses the SUM function that totals the April 2003 sales. This formula in cell B7 reads:

```
=SUM(B3:B6)
```

I then used the AutoFill feature to copy this formula by dragging the Fill handle to include the cell range B7:K7 (copying the formula with the cut-and-paste method would work just as well, although it's a little more work). Note in the cell range C7:K7 that Excel did not copy the original formula to the other cells verbatim (otherwise each of the copied formulas would return the same result, 1,915 as the original in cell B7). If you look at the Formula bar in Figure 1-5, you see that in the copy of the original formula in cell C7 reads:

```
=SUM(C3:C6)
```

In this copy, Excel adjusted the column reference of the range being summed from B to C to suit the new position of the copy. Figure 1-6 shows how this works when copying an original formula in the other direction, this time down a column. For this figure, I used the AutoSum button to create a SUM formula that totals all the monthly sales for Part 100 in row 3. This formula in cell K3 reads:

```
=SUM(B3:J3)
```


I then used the Fill handle to copy this formula down the last column of the table to include the cell range K3:K6. You can see on the Formula bar in Figure 1-6 that when Excel copied the original formula in cell K3 down to cell K4, it automatically adjusted the row reference to suit its new position so that the formula in cell K4 reads:

```
=SUM(B4:J4)
```

Microsoft Excel - Prod Sch - 03.xls

C7 =SUM(C3:C6)

2003 Production Schedule

	Apr-03	May-03	Jun-03	Jul-03	Aug-03	Sep-03	Oct-03	Nov-03	Dec-03	Total
Part 100	500	485	438	505	483	540	441	550	345	4,286
Part 101	175	170	153	177	169	189	154	193	200	
Part 102	350	340	306	354	338	378	309	385	350	
Part 103	890	863	779	899	859	961	785	979	885	
Total	1,915	1,858	1,676	1,934	1,848	2,068	1,689	2,107	1,780	4,286

Figure 1-5: Copying an original formula with the Fill handle across the last row of the data table.

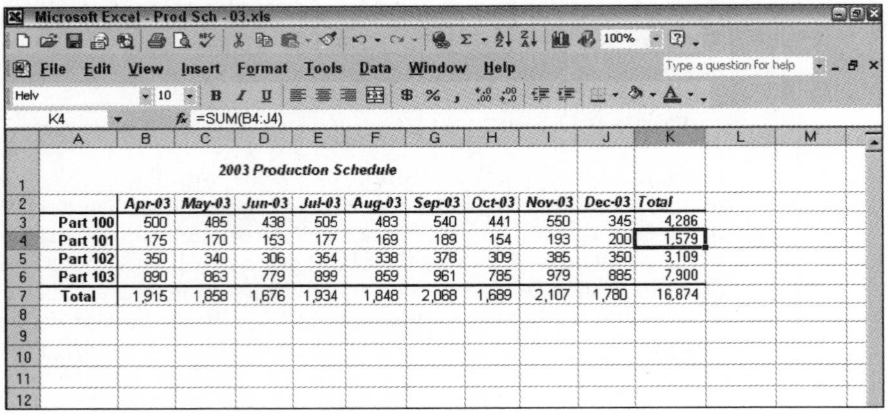

Microsoft Excel - Prod Sch - 03.xls

K4 =SUM(B4:J4)

2003 Production Schedule

	Apr-03	May-03	Jun-03	Jul-03	Aug-03	Sep-03	Oct-03	Nov-03	Dec-03	Total
Part 100	500	485	438	505	483	540	441	550	345	4,286
Part 101	175	170	153	177	169	189	154	193	200	1,579
Part 102	350	340	306	354	338	378	309	385	350	3,109
Part 103	890	863	779	899	859	961	785	979	885	7,900
Total	1,915	1,858	1,676	1,934	1,848	2,068	1,689	2,107	1,780	16,874

Figure 1-6: Copying an original formula with the Fill handle down the last column of the data table.

Although at first glance it appears that Excel isn't making exact copies of the original formula when it uses the relative cell addressing, that isn't technically true. Although the cell column references in the first example in Figure 1-5 and the row references in the second example in Figure 1-6 appear to be adjusted to suit the new column and row position where you view the worksheet by using the R1C1 cell notation system, you'd actually see that in R1C1 notation (unlike the default A1 system) each and every copy of the original formula is *exactly* the same.

For example, the original formula that I input into cell B7 (known as cell R7C2 in the R1C1 system) to sum the April 2003 sales for all the different part numbers reads as follows when you switch to R1C1 notation:

```
=SUM(R[-4]C:R[-1]C)
```

In this notation, the SUM formula is more difficult to decipher, so I will explain and then translate it for you. In R1C1 notation, the cell range in the SUM argument is expressed in terms completely relative to the position of the cell containing the formula. The row portion of the cell range expresses how many rows above or below the one with the formula the rows are (negative integers indicate rows above, while positive integers indicate rows below). The column portion of the cell range in the SUM argument expresses how many columns to the left or right of the one with the formula the columns are (positive integers indicate columns to the right and negative integers columns to the left). When a column or row in the cell range is not followed by an integer in square brackets, this means that there is no change in the column or row.

Armed with this information, my translation R1C1 form of this formula may just make sense; it says, "sum the values in the range of the cells that is four rows (R[-4]) above the current cell in the same column (C) down through the cell that is just one row (R[-1]) above the current cell in the same column (C)." When this original formula is copied over to the columns in the rest of the table, it doesn't need to be changed because each copy of the formula performs this exact calculation (when expressed in such relative terms).

The original formula in cell K3 (R3C11 in R1C1-speak) appears as follows when you switch over to the R1C1 notation:

```
=SUM(RC[-9]:RC[-1])
```

It says, "sum the range of values in the cell nine columns to the left (C[-9]) in the same row through the cell that is one column to the left (C[-1]) in the same row." This is exactly what all the copies of this formula in the three rows below it do so that when Excel copies this formula it doesn't change.

You can use the R1C1 notation to check that you've copied all the formulas in a spreadsheet table correctly. Just switch to the R1C1 system, and then move the cell pointer through all the cells with copied formulas in the table. When this notation is in effect, all copies of an original formula across an entire row or down an entire column of the table should be identical when displayed on the Formula bar as you make their cells current.

Absolute references

Most of the time, relative cell references are exactly what you need in the formulas that you build, thus allowing Excel to adjust the row and/or column references as required in the copies that you make. You will encounter some circumstances, however, where Excel should not adjust one or more parts of the cell reference in the copied formula. This occurs, for example, whenever you want to use a value in a cell as a constant in all of the copies that you make of a formula.

Figure 1-7 illustrates just such a situation. In this situation, you want to build a formula in cell B9 that calculates what percentage April's part production total (B7) is of the total nine-month production (cell K7). Normally, you would create the following formula in cell B9 with all its relative cell references:

```
=B7/K7
```

However, because you want to copy this formula across to the range C9:J9 to calculate the percentages for the eight months (May through December), you need to alter the relative cell references in the last part of the formula in cell K7 so that this cell reference with the nine-month production total remains unchanged in all your copies.

2003 Production Schedule

	Apr-03	May-03	Jun-03	Jul-03	Aug-03	Sep-03	Oct-03	Nov-03	Dec-03	Total
Part 100	500	485	438	505	483	540	441	550	345	4,286
Part 101	175	170	153	177	169	189	154	193	200	1,579
Part 102	350	340	306	354	338	378	309	385	350	3,109
Part 103	890	863	779	899	859	961	785	979	885	7,900
Total	1,915	1,858	1,676	1,934	1,848	2,068	1,689	2,107	1,780	16,874
% Total	11.35%	11.01%	9.93%	11.46%	10.95%	12.26%	10.01%	12.48%	10.55%	

Figure 1-7: Using an absolute address in the formula to calculate monthly percentage of the total.

You can start to understand the problem caused by adjusting a relative cell reference that should remain unchanged by just thinking about copying the original formula from cell B9 to C9 to calculate the percentage for May. In this cell, you want the following formula that divides the May production total in cell C7 by the nine-month total in cell K7:

```
=C7/K7
```

However, if you don't indicate otherwise, Excel adjusts both parts of the formula in the copies so that C9 incorrectly contains the following formula:

```
=C7/L7
```

Because cell L7 is currently blank and blank cells have the equivalent of the value 0, this formula returns the #DIV/0 formula error as the result, thus indicating that Excel can't properly perform this arithmetic operation (see Chapter 2 in this book for details on this error message).

To indicate that you don't want a particular cell reference (such as cell K7 in the example) to be adjusted in the copies that you make of a formula, you change the cell reference from a relative cell reference to an *absolute cell reference*. In the A1 system of cell references, an absolute cell reference contains dollar signs before the column letter and the row number, as in $K$7. In the R1C1 notation, you simply list the actual row and column number in the cell reference, as in R7C11, without placing the row and column numbers in square brackets.

If you realize that you need to convert a relative cell reference to an absolute reference as you're building the original formula, you can convert the relative reference to absolute by selecting the cell and then pressing F4. To get an idea of how this works, follow along with these steps for creating the correct formula =B7/$K$7 in B9:

1. **Click cell B9 to make it active.**
2. **Type = to start the formula and then click cell B7 and type / (the sign for division).**

   The Formula bar now reads =B7/.
3. **Click K7 to select this cell and add it to the formula.**

   The formula bar now reads =B7/K7.
4. **Press F4 once to change the cell reference from relative (K7) to absolute ($K$7).**

   The formula bar now reads =B7/$K$7. You're now ready to enter the formula and then make the copies.
5. **Click the Enter button on the Formula bar and then drag the Fill handle to cell J9 before you release the mouse button.**

Like it or not, you won't always anticipate the need for an absolute value until after you've built the formula and copied it to a range. When this happens, you have to edit the original formula, change the relative reference to absolute, and then make the copies again.

When editing the cell reference in the formula, you can change its reference by positioning the insertion point anywhere in its address and then pressing F4. You can also do this by inserting dollar signs in front of the column letter(s) and row number when editing the formula, although doing that isn't nearly as easy as pressing F4.

You can make an exact copy of a formula in another cell without using absolute references. To do this, make the cell with the formula that you want to copy the active one, use the I-beam pointer to select the entire formula in the Formula bar by dragging through it, and then choose the Edit⇨Copy on the Menu bar (Ctrl+C). Next, click the Cancel button to deactivate the Formula bar, select the cell where you want the exact copy to appear, and then choose Edit⇨Paste command on the Menu bar (Ctrl+V). Excel then pastes an exact duplicate of the original formula into the active cell without adjusting any of its cell references (even if they are all relative cell references).

A mixed bag of references

Some formulas don't require you to change the entire cell reference from relative to absolute in order to copy them correctly. In some situations, you only need to indicate that the column letter or the row number remains unchanged in all copies of the original formula. A cell reference that is part relative and part absolute is called a *mixed cell reference*.

In the A1 notation, a mixed cell reference has a dollar sign just in front the column letter or row number that should not be adjusted in the copies, as in $C10, which adjusts row 10 in copies down the rows but leaves column C unchanged in all copies across columns to its right or C$10, which adjusts column C in copies to columns to the right but leaves row 10 unchanged in all copies down the rows. (For an example of using mixed cell references in a master formula, refer to the information on using the PMT Function in Chapter 4 of this book.)

To change a cell reference from relative to mixed, continue to press F4 until the type of mixed reference appears on the Formula bar. When the formula bar is active and the insertion point is somewhere in the cell reference (either when building or editing the formula), pressing F4 cycles through each cell reference possibility in the following order:

- ✦ The first time you press F4, Excel changes relative cell reference to absolute (C10 to $C$10)
- ✦ The second time you press F4, Excel changes the absolute reference to a mixed reference where the column is relative and the row is absolute ($C$10 to C$10)
- ✦ The third time you select the Reference command, Excel changes the mixed reference where the column is relative and the row is absolute to a mixed reference where the row is relative and the column is absolute (C$10 to $C10)
- ✦ The fourth time you press F4, Excel changes the mixed reference where the row is relative and the column is absolute back to a relative reference ($C10 to C10).

If you bypass the type of cell reference that you want to use, you can return to it by continuing to press F4 until you cycle through the variations again to reach the one that you need.

Adding Array Formulas

As noted previously in this chapter, many spreadsheet tables use an original formula that you copy to adjacent cells by using relative cell references (sometimes referred to as a *one-to-many copy*). In some cases, you can build the original formula so that Excel performs the desired calculation not only in the active cell, but also in all the other cells to which you would normally copy the formula. You do this by creating an *array formula*. An array formula is a special formula that operates on a range of values. If a cell range supplies this range (as is often the case), it is referred to as an *array range*. If this range is supplied by a list of numerical values, they are known as an *array constant*.

Although the array concept may seem foreign at first, you are really quite familiar with arrays because the Excel worksheet grid with its column-and-row structure naturally organizes your data ranges into one-dimensional and two-dimensional arrays (1-D arrays take up a single row or column while 2-D arrays take up multiple rows and columns).

Figure 1-8 illustrates a couple of two-dimensional arrays with numerical entries of two different sizes. The first array is a 3 x 2 array in the cell range B2:C4. This array is a 3 x 2 array because it occupies three rows and two columns. The second array is a 2 x 3 array in the cell range F2:H3. This array is a 2 x 3 array because it uses two rows in three columns. If you were to list the values in the first 3 x 2 array as an array constant in a formula, they would appear as follows:

```
{1,4;2,5;3,6}
```

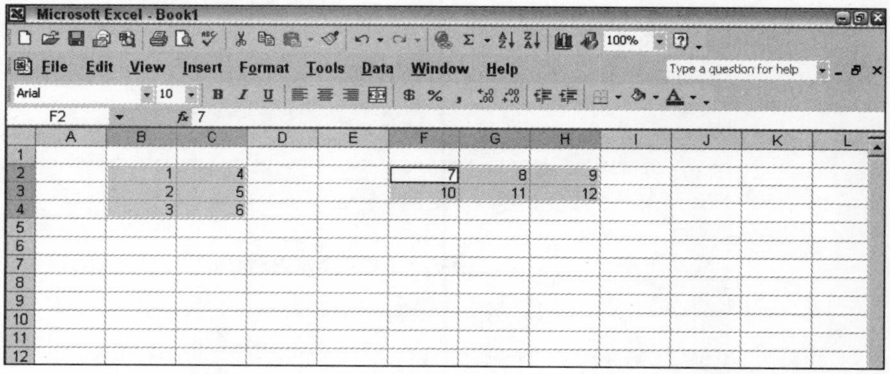

Figure 1-8: Worksheet with two different sized arrays.

Several things in this expression are noteworthy. First, the array constant is enclosed in a pair of braces ({}). Second, columns within each row are separated by commas (,) and rows within the array are separated by semicolons (;). Third, the constants in the array are listed across each row and then down each column, and *not* down each column and across each row.

The second 2 x 3 array expressed as an array constant appears as follows:

```
{7,8,9;10,11,12}
```

Note again that you list the values across each row and then down each column, separating the values in different columns with commas and the values in different rows with a semicolon.

The use of array formulas can significantly reduce the amount of formula copying that you have to do in a worksheet by producing multiple results throughout the array range in a single operation. In addition, array formulas use less computer memory than standard formulas copied in a range. This can be important when creating a large worksheet with many tables because it may mean the difference between fitting all of your calculations on one worksheet and having to split your model into several worksheet files.

Building an array formula

To get an idea of how you build and use array formulas in a worksheet, consider the sample worksheet shown in Figure 1-9. This worksheet is designed to compute the bi-weekly wages for each employee. It will do this by multiplying each employee's hourly rate by the number of hours worked in each pay period. Instead of creating the following formula in cell R10, you must copy down the cells R11 through R13:

```
=A4*R4
```

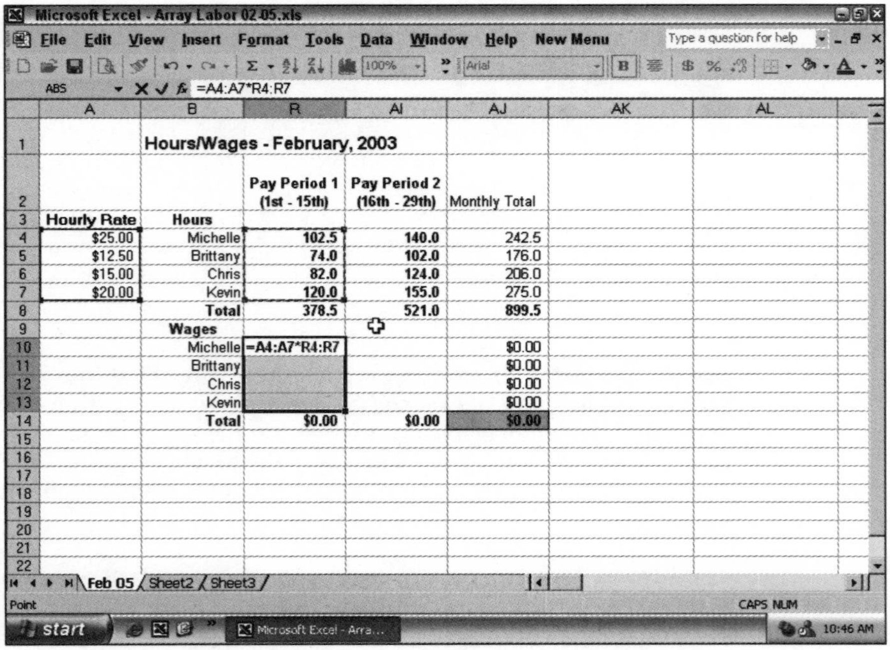

Figure 1-9: Building an array formula to calculate hourly wages for the first pay period.

You can create the following array formula in the array range:

```
={A4:A7*R4:R7}
```

This array formula multiplies each of the hourly rates in the 4 x 1 array in the range A4:A7 with each of the hours worked in the 4 x 1 array in the range R4:R7. This same formula is entered into all cells of the array range (R10:R13) as soon as you complete the formula in the active cell R10. To see how this is done, follow along with the steps required to build this array formula:

1. **Make cell R10 the active cell, and then select the array range R10:R13 and type = (equal sign) to start the array formula.**

   You always start an array formula by selecting the cell or cell range where the results are to appear. Note that array formulas, like standard formulas, begin with the equal sign.

2. **Select the range A4:A7 that contains the hourly rate for each employee as shown, and then type an * (asterisk for multiplication), and then select the range R4:R7 that contains the total number of hours worked during the first pay period.**

3. **Press Ctrl+Shift+Enter to insert an array formula in the array range.**

   When you press Ctrl+Shift+Enter to complete the formula, Excel inserts braces around the formula and copies the array formula {=A4:A7*R4:R7} into each of the cells in the array range R10:R13.

Book III Chapter 1

Building Basic Formulas

REMEMBER

When entering an array formula, you must remember to press Ctrl+Shift+Enter instead of just the Enter key because it is this special key combination that tells Excel that you are building an array formula, so that the program encloses the formula in braces and copies it to every cell in the array range. Also, don't try to create an array formula by editing it on the Formula bar and then inserting curly braces because this doesn't cut it. The only way to create an array formula is by pressing Ctrl+Shift+Enter to complete the formula entry.

Figure 1-10 shows you the February wage table after completing all of the array formulas in three ranges: R10:R13, AI10:AI13, and AJ10:AJ13. In the second cell range, AI10:AI13, I entered the following array formula to calculate the hourly wages for the second pay period in February:

```
{=A4:A7*AI4:AI7}
```

In the third cell range, AJ10:AJ13, I entered the following array formula to calculate the total wages paid to each employee in February 2003:

```
{=R10:R13+AI10:AI13}
```

Microsoft Excel - Array Labor 02-05.xls

AJ10 = {=R10:R13+AI10:AI13}

	A	B	R	AI	AJ
1		Hours/Wages - February, 2003			
2			Pay Period 1 (1st - 15th)	Pay Period 2 (16th - 29th)	Monthly Total
3	Hourly Rate	Hours			
4	$25.00	Michelle	102.5	140.0	242.5
5	$12.50	Brittany	74.0	102.0	176.0
6	$15.00	Chris	82.0	124.0	206.0
7	$20.00	Kevin	120.0	155.0	275.0
8		Total	378.5	521.0	899.5
9		Wages			
10		Michelle	2,562.50	3,500.00	$6,062.50
11		Brittany	925.00	1,275.00	$2,200.00
12		Chris	1,230.00	1,860.00	$3,090.00
13		Kevin	2,400.00	3,100.00	$5,500.00
14		Total	$7,117.50	$9,735.00	$16,852.50

Feb 05 / Sheet2 / Sheet3 — Ready — Sum=$16,852.50 — NUM

Figure 1-10: Hourly wage spreadsheet after entering all three array formulas.

When you enter an array formula, the formula should produce an array with the same dimensions as the array range that you selected. If the resulting array returned by the formula is smaller than the array range, Excel expands the resulting array to fill the range. If the resulting array is larger than the array range, Excel doesn't display all of the results. When expanding the results in an array range, Excel considers the dimensions of all the arrays used in the arguments of the operation. Each argument must have the same number of rows as the array with the most rows and the same number of columns as the array with the most columns.

Editing an array formula

Editing array formulas differs somewhat from editing normal formulas. In editing an array range, you must treat the range as a single unit and edit it in one operation (corresponding to the way in which the array formula was entered). This means that you can't edit, clear, move, insert, or delete individual cells in the array range. If you try, Excel will display an Alert dialog box stating "You cannot change part of an array."

To edit the contents of an array formula, select a cell in the array range and then activate the Formula bar. When you do this, Excel displays the contents of the array formula without the customary braces. The program also outlines the ranges referred to in the array formula in the cells of the worksheet in different colors that match those assigned to the range addresses in the edited formula on the Formula bar. After you make your changes to the formula contents, you must remember to press Ctrl+Shift+Enter to enter your changes and have Excel enclose the array formula in braces once again.

If you want to convert the results in an array range to their calculated values, select the array range, choose Edit⇨Copy on the Menu bar, and then, without changing the selection, choose Edit⇨Paste Special and click the Values radio button in the Paste Special dialog box before you click OK. As soon as you convert an array range to its calculated values, Excel no longer treats the cell range as an array.

Range Names in Formulas

Thus far, all the example formulas in this chapter have used a combination of numerical constants and cell references (both relative and absolute and using the A1 and R1C1 notation). Although cell references provide a convenient method for pointing out the cell location in the worksheet grid, they are not at all descriptive of their function when used in formulas. Fortunately, Excel makes it easy to assign descriptive names to the cells, cell ranges, constants, and even formulas that make their function in the worksheet much more understandable.

To get an idea of how names can help to document the purpose of a formula, consider the following formula for computing the sale price of an item that uses standard cell references:

```
=B4*B2
```

Now consider the following formula that performs the same calculation but this time with the use of range names:

```
=Retail_Price*Discount_Rate
```

Obviously, the function of the second formula is much more comprehensible, not only to you as the creator of the worksheet but also to anyone else who has to use it.

Range names are not only extremely useful for documenting the function of the formulas in your worksheet but they also enable you to quickly and easily find and select cell ranges. This is especially helpful in a large worksheet that you aren't very familiar with or only use intermittently. After you assign a name to a cell range, you can locate and select all the cells in that range with the Go To dialog box. Simply choose the Edit⇨Go To on the Menu bar (or press Ctrl+G or F5) and then double-click the range name in the Go To list box or click and select OK. Excel then selects the entire range and, if necessary, shifts the worksheet display so that you can see the first cell in that range on the screen.

Defining range names

You can define a name for the selected cell range or nonadjacent selection by typing its range name into the Name box on the Formula bar and then pressing Enter. You can also name a cell, cell range, or nonadjacent selection by choosing Insert➪Name➪Define on the Excel Menu bar. This action opens the Define Name dialog box where you can input its name in the Names in Workbook text box. If Excel can identify a label in the cell immediately above or to the left of the active one, the program inserts this label as the suggested name in the Names in Workbook text box. The program also displays the cell reference of the active cell or the range address of the range or nonadjacent selection that is currently marked (by using absolute references) in the Refers To text box below. To accept the suggested name and assign it to the cell references displayed in the Define Name dialog box, click the Add button, shown in Figure 1-11.

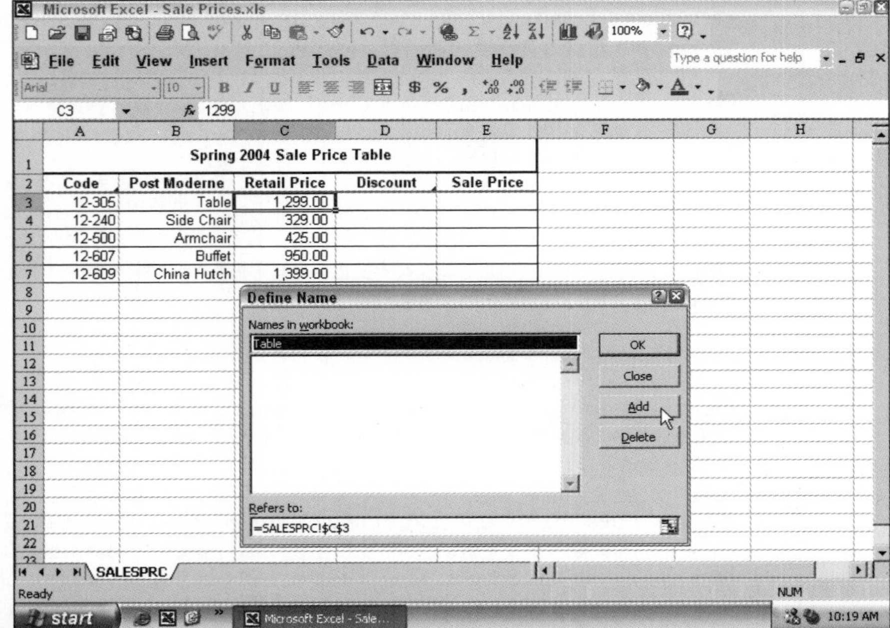

Figure 1-11: Adding a new range name in the Define Name dialog box.

If Excel is unable to suggest a name or you don't want to use the suggested name, type a new range name in the Name in Workbook text box (it's automatically selected when you open the Define Name dialog box). If you need to, you can also modify the cell references in the Refers To text box by selecting this box and editing the cell addresses. When editing the contents of the Refers To text box, be very careful not to delete the equal sign (=) at the beginning of this text box. If you do, you must retype this sign before you click the Add button to add its name to the Names in Workbook list box.

When naming a range in the Define Name dialog box, you need to follow the same naming conventions as when defining a name in the Name box on the Formula bar. Basically, this means that the name must begin with a letter rather than a number, contain no spaces, and not duplicate any other name in the workbook (see Book II, Chapter 2 for more on naming ranges).

If you want to assign the same range name to similar ranges on different worksheets in the workbook, preface the range name with the sheet name followed by an exclamation point and then the descriptive name. For example, if you want to give the name Costs to the cell range A2:A10 on both Sheet1 and Sheet2, you name the range Sheet1!Costs on Sheet1 and Sheet2!Costs on Sheet2. If you have renamed the worksheet to something more descriptive than Sheet1, you need to enclose the name in single quotes if it contains a space when you enter the range. For example, if you rename Sheet1 to Inc. Statement 04, you enter the range name including the worksheet reference for the Costs cell range as follows:

```
'Inc. Statement 04'!Costs
```

When you preface a range name with the sheet name as shown in this example, you don't have to use the sheet name part of the range name in the formulas that you create on the same worksheet. In other words, if you create a SUM formula that totals the values in the 'Inc. Statement 04'!Costs range somewhere on the Inc. Statement 04 worksheet, you can enter the formulas as follows:

```
=SUM(Costs)
```

However, if you were to create this formula on any another worksheet in the workbook, you would have to include the full range name in the formula, as in:

```
=SUM('Inc. Statement 04'!Costs)
```

Naming constants and formulas

In addition to naming cells in your worksheet, you can also assign range names to the constants and formulas that you use often. For example, if you are creating a spreadsheet table that calculates sales prices, you can assign the discount percentage rate to the range name discount_rate. Then, you can supply this range name as a constant in any formula that calculates the sale discount used in determining the sale price for merchandise.

Figure 1-12 illustrates how you would assign a constant value to the range name discount_rate. Here, you see the Define Name dialog box after I entered discount_rate as the name in the Names in Workbook text box and =15% as the discount rate in the Refers To text box. After assigning this constant percentage rate to the range name discount_rate in this manner, you can apply it to any formula by typing or pasting in the name (see the "Using names in building formulas" section that follows in this chapter for details).

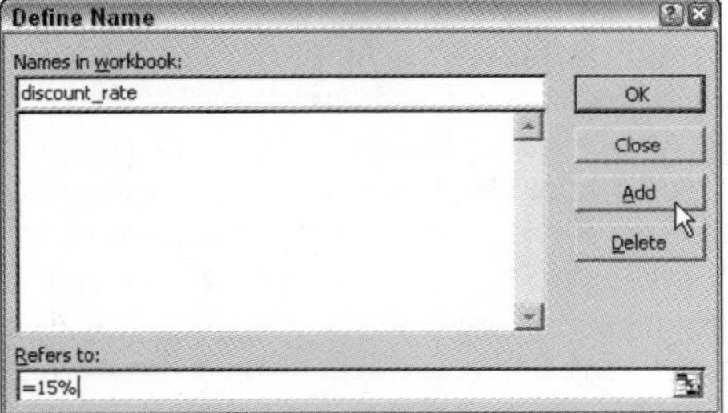

Figure 1-12: Defining the discount rate constant as a range name in the Define Name dialog box.

In addition to naming constants, you can also give a range name to a formula that you use repeatedly. When building a formula in the Refers To text box of the Define Name dialog box, keep in mind that Excel automatically applies absolute references to any cells that you point to in the worksheet. If you want to create a formula with relative cell references that Excel adjusts when you enter or paste the range name in a new cell, you must press F4 to convert the current cell reference to relative or type the cell address in without dollar signs.

Using names in building formulas

After you assign a name to a cell or cell range in your worksheet, you can then choose Insert⇨Name⇨Paste on the Menu bar to paste them into the formulas that you build. For example, in the sample Sales Price table shown in Figure 1-13, after assigning the discount rate of 15% to the range name, discount_rate, you can create the formulas that calculate the amount of the sale discount. To do this, you multiply the retail price of each item by the discount_rate constant using the Paste Name command by following these steps:

1. **Make cell D3 active.**
2. **Type = (equal sign) to start the formula.**
3. **Click cell C3 to select the retail price for the first item.**

   The formula on the Formula bar now reads, =C3*.
4. **Choose Insert⇨Name⇨Paste on the Excel Menu bar.**

   This action opens the Paste Name dialog box where you can select the discount_rate range name.
5. **Click the name discount_rate in the Paste Name list box or click it and then click OK.**

   The formula now reads =C3*discount_rate on the Formula bar.
6. **Click the Enter button on the Formula bar to input the formula in cell D3.**

   Now, all that remains is to copy the original formula down column D.
7. **Drag the Fill handle in cell D3 down to cell D7 and release the mouse button to copy the formula and calculate the discount for the entire table.**

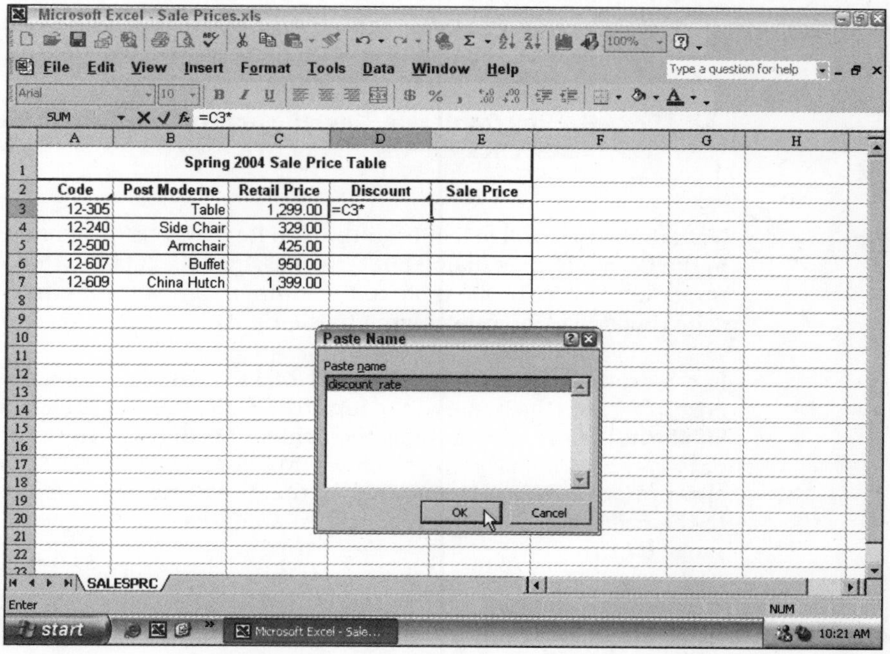

Figure 1-13: Pasting the range name for the discount_rate constant into a formula.

Creating names from column and row headings

You can use the Insert⇨Name⇨Create command to assign existing column and row headings in a table of data to the cells in that table. When using this command, you can have Excel assign the labels used as column headings in the top or bottom row of the table, the labels used as row headings in the leftmost or rightmost column, or even a combination of these headings.

For example, the sample worksheet in Figure 1-14 illustrates a typical table layout that uses column headings in the top row of the table and row headings in the first column of the table. You can assign these labels to the cells in the table by using the Create Names command as follows:

1. **Select the cells in the table, including those with the column and row labels that you want to use as range names.**

   For the example shown in Figure 1-14, you select the range B2:E7.

2. **Choose Insert⇨Name⇨Create from the Excel Menu bar.**

   This action opens the Create Names dialog box that contains four check boxes: Top Row, Left Column, Bottom Row, and Right Column. The program selects the check box or boxes in this dialog box based on the arrangement of the labels in your table. In the example shown in Figure 1-14, Excel selects both the Top Row and Left Column check boxes because the table contains both column headings in the top row and row headings in the left column.

3. **After selecting (or deselecting) the appropriate Create Names in check boxes, click the OK button to assign the range names to your table.**

Note that when you select both the Top Row and Left Column check boxes in the Create Names dialog box, Excel assigns the label in the cell in the upper-left corner of the table to the entire range of values in the table (one row down and one column to the right).

In the example illustrated in Figure 1-14, Excel assigns the name *Post_Moderne* (the name of the furniture collection) to the cell range C3:E7. Similarly, the program assigns the column headings to the appropriate data in the table in the rows below and the row headings to the data in the appropriate columns to the right so that the name *Retail_Price* is assigned to the cell range C3:C7 and the name *China_Hutch* is assigned to the cell range C7:E7.

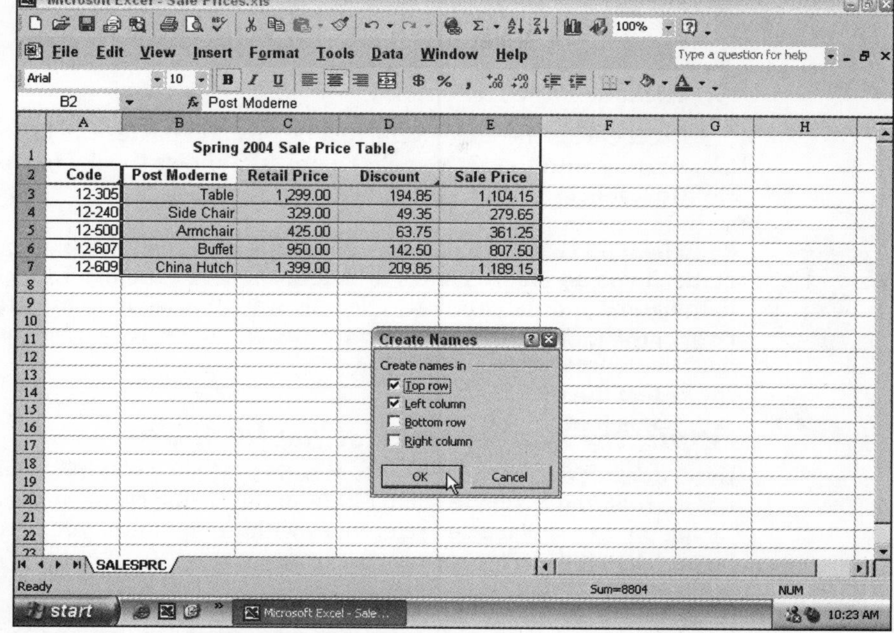

Figure 1-14: Creating range names from the row and column headings in a spreadsheet table.

Pasting a list of names

After assigning existing labels as range names, all of the new names appear in the Names in Workbook list box when you next open the Define Name dialog box (Insert⇨Name⇨Define) and the Paste Name list box when you open the Paste Name dialog box (Insert⇨Name⇨Paste). If you need to verify the extent of the cell selection assigned to a name or want to select the named range, open the Go To dialog box by choosing Edit⇨Go To on the Menu bar or pressing F5 and double-click the name in the Go To list box. Excel then selects all the cells in the worksheet to which that name is assigned.

To obtain a complete list of the names used in your worksheet and their locations, you use the Paste List button in the Paste Name dialog box as follows:

1. **Select a blank cell of the worksheet where you want the list of names to begin.**

   This cell will form the upper-left corner of the table listing the names. When selecting this cell, make sure that you choose one in an area where there is no danger of replacing existing data in the column to the right or rows below. The list of names uses two columns (one for the name and one immediately to the right for range address) and as many rows as there are names in the worksheet.

2. **Choose Insert➪Name➪Paste on the Excel Menu bar.**

   This action opens the Paste Name dialog box.

3. **Click the Paste List button.**

   Excel closes the Paste Name dialog box and pastes the list of names, starting with the active cell (Figure 1-15 shows the list for the sample worksheet with the sale prices).

Keep in mind that the list created by Excel with the Paste List button is static. If you add more names or delete names on the list, Excel doesn't automatically update the list. The only way to bring it up to date is by replacing the list in the worksheet by using the Paste List button as described previously.

Applying names to existing formulas

Excel doesn't automatically replace cell references with the descriptive names that you assign to them either in the Define Name or Create Names dialog box. To replace cell references with their names, you need to use the Insert➪Name➪Apply command.

Microsoft Excel - Sale Prices.xls

A9 Armchair

	A	B	C	D	E
1	Spring 2004 Sale Price Table				
2	Code	Post Moderne	Retail Price	Discount	Sale Price
3	12-305	Table	1,299.00	194.85	1,104.15
4	12-240	Side Chair	329.00	49.35	279.65
5	12-500	Armchair	425.00	63.75	361.25
6	12-607	Buffet	950.00	142.50	807.50
7	12-609	China Hutch	1,399.00	209.85	1,189.15
8					
9	Armchair	LESPRC!$C$5:$E$5			
10	Buffet	=SALESPRC!$C$6	E$6		
11	China_Hutch	=SALESPRC!$C$7	E$7		
12	Discount	=SALESPRC!$D$3	D$7		
13	discount_rate	=15%			
14	Post_Moderne	=SALESPRC!$C$3	E$7		
15	Retail_Price	=SALESPRC!$C$3	C$7		
16	Sale_Price	=SALESPRC!$E$3	E$7		
17	Side_Chair	=SALESPRC!$C$4	E$4		
18	Table	=SALESPRC!$C$3	E$3		

SALESPRC

Figure 1-15: Pasting in a list of all the range names defined in the workbook.

When you choose this command, Excel opens the Apply Names dialog box where you select the range names that you want applied in formulas used in your worksheet by selecting them in the Apply Names list box.

Note that when you first open this dialog box, it contains just two check boxes: Ignore Relative/Absolute and Use Row and Column Names (both of which are checked). You can click the Options>> button to expand the Apply Names dialog box and display other options that you can use when applying your range names, shown in Figure 1-16. The Apply Names options include:

- **Ignore Relative/Absolute** check box to have the program replace cell references with the names that you've selected in the Apply Names list box regardless of the type of reference used in their formulas. If you want Excel to replace only those cell references that use the same type of references as are used in your names (absolute for absolute, mixed for mixed, and relative for relative), deselect this check box. Most of the time, you will want to leave this option check box selected because Excel automatically assigns absolute cell references to the names that you define and relative cell references in the formulas that you build.
- **Use Row and Column Names** check box to have the names created from row and column headings with the Create Names command appear in your formulas. Deselect this option if you don't want these row and column names to appear in the formulas in your worksheet.
- **Omit Column Name If Same Column** check box to prevent Excel from repeating the column name when the formula is in the same column. Deselect this check box when you want the program to display the column name even in formulas in the same column as the heading used to create the column name.
- **Omit Row Name If Same Row** check box to prevent Excel from repeating the row name when the formula is in the same row. Deselect this check box when you want the program to display the row name even in formulas in the same row as the heading used to create the row name.
- **Name Order** to choose between the Row Column radio button (the default) in which the row name precedes the column name when both names are displayed in the formulas and the Column Row radio button in which the column name precedes the row name.

After applying all the range names by using the default Apply Names options (that is, Ignore Relative/Absolute, Use Row and Column Names, Omit Column Name If Same Column, Omit Row Name If Same Row, and Row Column options selected), Excel replaces all of the cell references in the formulas in the Sale Price table. In cell E3, for example, in place of the original formula =C3-D3, the cell now contains the formula:

```
=Retail_Price-Discount
```

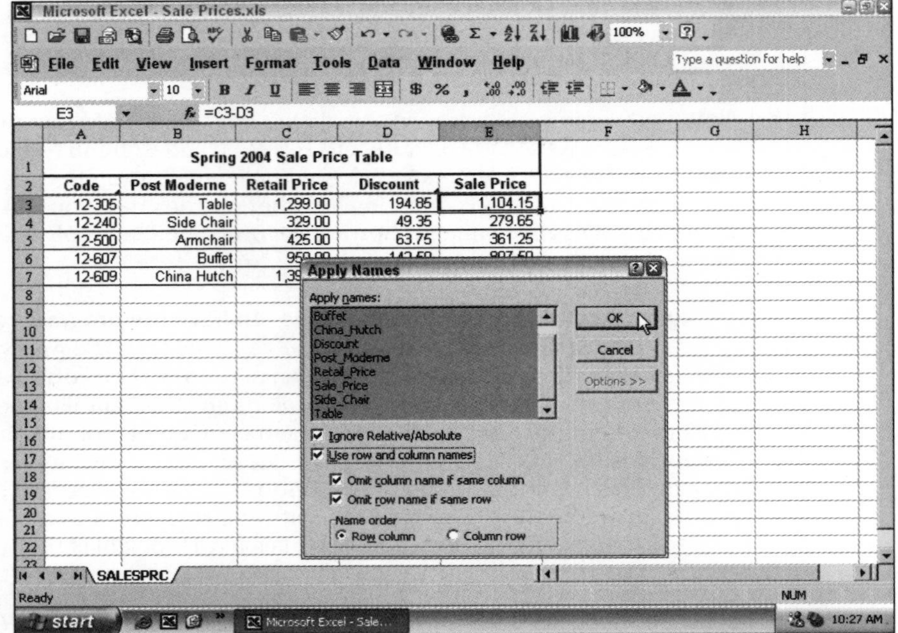

Figure 1-16: Using the options in the Apply Names dialog box to assign range names to formulas.

Cell D3, to the immediate left, instead of =C3*discount_rate now contains:

```
=Retail_Price*discount_rate
```

Only one problem occurs with applying names by using the default settings. This problem begins to show up as soon as you select cell E4. Although this formula subtracts cell D4 from C4, its contents now also appear as

```
=Retail_Price-Discount
```

This is identical in appearance to the contents of cell E3 above (and, in fact, identical in appearance to cells E5, E6, and E7 in the cells below).

The reason that the formulas all appear identical (although they're really not) is because I selected the Omit Column Name if Same Column and Omit Row Name if Same Row check boxes. When you use these settings, Excel doesn't bother to repeat the row name when the formula is in the same row, or repeats the column name when the formula is in the same column.

If you were to deselect the Omit Row Name if Same Row check box while still selecting the Use Row and Column Name check box in the Apply Names dialog box, the formula in cell E3 would appear as follows:

```
=Table  Retail_Price-Table  Discount
```

If you were then to select cell E4 below, the formula would now appear quite differently in this form:

```
=Side_Chair  Retail_Price-Side_Chair  Discount
```

Now Excel displays both the row and column name separated by a space for each cell reference in the formulas in this column. Remember that the space between the row name and column name is called the intersection operator (see Table 1-1). You can interpret the formula in E3 as saying, "Take the cell at the intersection of the Table row and Retail_Price column and subtract it from the cell at the intersection of the Table row and Discount column." The formula in E4 is similar except that it says, "Take the cell at the intersection of the Side_chair row and Retail_Price column and subtract it from the cell at the intersection of the Side_chair row and Discount column."

Editing range names

You can edit the names that you assign to your worksheet with the Define Name command or Change Name command. The Define Name command enables you to modify the cell references assigned to the name or to delete the name altogether. The Change Name command enables you to assign a new name to the same cell selection or delete it as well. The Change Name Command, unlike the Define Name command, always warns you if the name that you are about to delete is currently in use in formulas in the worksheet.

WARNING!

Be careful that you don't delete a range name that is already used in formulas in the worksheet. If you do, Excel will return the #NAME! error value to any formula that refers to the name you deleted!

Adding Linking Formulas

Linking formulas are formulas that transfer a constant or other formula to a new place in the same worksheet, same workbook, or even a different workbook without copying it to its new location. When you create a linking formula, it brings forward the constant or original formula to a new location so that the result in the linking formula remains dynamically tied to the original. If you change the original constant or any of the cells referred to in the original formula, the result in the cell containing the linking formula is updated at the same time as the cell containing the original constant or formula.

You can create a linking formula in one of two ways:

- Select the cell where you want the linking formula, type = (equal sign), and then click the cell with the constant (text or number) or the formula that you want to bring forward to that cell. Complete the cell entry by clicking the Enter button on the Formula bar or pressing the Enter key.
- Select the cell with the constant or formula that you want to bring forward to a new location, choose Edit⇨Copy (Ctrl+C), click the cell where the linking formula is to appear, and then choose Paste⇨Special from the Menu bar and click the Paste Link button in the Paste Special dialog box.

When you create a linking formula in a new location on the same worksheet, Excel simply inserts the cell address with the original constant or formula (by using absolute references) followed by the equal sign. For example, if you bring forward a formula in cell A10 to cell D4 in the same sheet, cell D4 contains the following linking formula:

```
=$A$10
```

When you create a linking formula to a cell on a different sheet of the same workbook, Excel inserts the worksheet name (followed by an exclamation point) in front of the cell address. So, if you bring forward a formula in cell A10 on a different worksheet called Income 05, Excel inserts the following linking formula:

```
='Income 05'!$A$10
```

When you create a linking formula to a cell in a different workbook, Excel inserts the workbook filename enclosed in square brackets before the name of the worksheet, which precedes the cell address. So, if you bring forward a formula in cell A10 on a worksheet called Cost Analysis in the Projected Income 06 workbook, Excel inserts this linking formula:

```
='[Projected Income 06.xls]Cost Analysis'!$A$10
```

If you ever need to sever a link between the one containing the original value or formula and the cell to which it's been brought forward, you can do so by editing the linking formula by pressing F2, and then immediately recalculating it by pressing F9, and then clicking the Enter button on the Formula bar or pressing Enter. This replaces the linking formula with the currently calculated result. Because you've converted the dynamic formula into a constant, changes to the original cell no longer affect the one to which it was originally brought forward.

For more on linking data in different workbook files, see Book IV, Chapter 3.

Controlling Formula Recalculation

Normally, Excel recalculates your worksheet automatically as soon you change any entries, formulas, or names on which your formulas depend. This system works fine as long as the worksheet is not too large or doesn't contain tables whose formulas depend upon several values.

When Excel does calculate your worksheet, the program recalculates only those cells that are affected by the change that you've made. Nevertheless, in a complex worksheet that contains many formulas, recalculation may take several seconds (during which time, the pointer will change to an hourglass and the word "Recalc" followed by the number of cells left to be recalculated appears on the left side of the formula bar).

Because Excel recalculates dependent formulas in the background, you can always interrupt this process and make a cell entry or choose a command even when the pointer assumes the hourglass shape during the recalculation process. As soon as you stop making entries or selecting commands, Excel resumes recalculating the worksheet.

To control when Excel calculates your worksheet, you choose the Manual radio button on the Calculation tab in the Options dialog box (Tools⇨Options). After switching to manual recalculation in this manner, when you make a change in a value, formula, or name that would usually cause Excel to recalculate the worksheet, the program displays the message "Calculate" on the status bar.

When you're ready to have Excel recalculate the worksheet, you then press F9 or Ctrl+=, whereupon the program recalculates all dependent formulas and open charts and the Calculate status indicator disappears from the status bar.

After switching to manual recalculation, Excel still automatically recalculates the worksheet whenever you save the file. When you are working with a really large and complex worksheet, recalculating the worksheet each time you want to save your changes can make this process quite time-consuming. If you want to save the worksheet without first updating dependent formulas and charts, you need to deselect the Recalculate Before Save check box under the Manual radio button on the Calculation tab of the Options dialog box.

Sometimes, you may want to switch recalculation from automatic to manual even when a worksheet is not very large. For example, you may want to switch to manual recalculation when performing what-if scenarios so that you can change a number of variables before having the formulas in the scenario or data table updated (see Book VII, Chapter 1 for more on performing what-if analysis).

Automatic and manual are by no means the only recalculation options available in Excel. Table 1-3 explains each of the options that appear on the Calculation tab of the Options dialog box.

Table 1-3 The Calculation Options in Excel

Option	*Purpose*
Automatic	Calculates all dependent formulas and updates open or embedded charts every time you make a change to a value, formula, or name. This is the default setting for each new worksheet that you start.
Automatic Except Tables	Calculates all dependent formulas and updates open or embedded charts but does not calculate data tables created with the Data Table feature (see Book VII, Chapter 1 for information on creating data tables). To recalculate data tables when this option button is selected, click the Calc Now (F9) command button on the Calculation tab in the Options dialog box or press F9 in the worksheet.
Manual	Calculates open worksheets and updates open or embedded charts only when you click the Calc Now (F9) button on the Calculation tab in the Options dialog box or press F9 or Ctrl+= in the worksheet.
Recalculate Before Save	When this check box is selected, Excel calculates open worksheets and updates open or embedded charts when you save them even when the Manual radio button is selected.
Calc Now (F9)	Calculates all open worksheets (including data tables) and updates all open or embedded charts.
Calc Sheet	Calculates only the active worksheet (including data tables) and updates only charts on the worksheet or open charts that are linked to the active worksheet.
Iteration	When this check box is selected, Excel sets the iterations, that is, the number of times that a worksheet is recalculated, when performing goal seeking (see Book VII, Chapter 1) or resolving circular references to the number displayed in the Maximum Iterations text box.
Maximum Iterations	Sets the maximum number of iterations (100 by default) when the Iteration check box is selected.
Maximum Change	Sets the maximum amount of change to the values during each iteration (0.001 by default) when the Iteration check box is selected.
Update Remote References	Calculates formulas that include references to other applications (see Book IV, Chapter 3). When this check box is deselected, these formulas use the last value received from the other program.

Option	Purpose
Precision as Displayed	When this check box is selected, Excel changes the values in cells from full precision (15 digits) to whatever number format is displayed so that the displayed value is used in calculations.
1904 Date System	When this check box is selected, Excel changes the starting date from which all serial numbers in dates are calculated from January 1, 1900 to January 2, 1904.
Save External Link Values	When this check box is selected, Excel saves copies of values contained in an external file that is linked to your Excel worksheet. To reduce the amount of drive space required for this copy or to reduce the amount of time that it takes to open this external document, deselect this check box.
Accept Labels In Formulas	Enables you to use label names in formulas if your data table has row and column headings (label). When this check box is activated, you can use the Insert⇨Name⇨Labels command to assign the label names to your formulas.

Circular References

A *circular reference* in a formula is one that depends, directly or indirectly, upon its own value. The most common type of circular reference occurs when you mistakenly refer in the formula to the cell in which you're building the formula itself. For example, suppose that cell B10 is active when you build the formula

```
=A10+B10
```

As soon as you press Enter or an arrow key to insert this formula in cell B10 (assuming the program is in Automatic recalc mode), Excel displays an Alert dialog box, stating that it cannot calculate the formula due to the circular reference. As soon as you press Enter or click OK to close this Alert dialog box, the program inserts 0 in the cell with the circular reference and the indicator Circular followed by the cell address with the circular reference appears on the status bar.

Excel is not able to resolve the circular reference in cell B10 because the formula's calculation depends directly upon the formula's result — each time the formula returns a new result, this result is fed into the formula, thus creating a new result. This type of circular reference sets up an endless loop that continuously requires recalculating and can never be resolved.

Not all circular references are impossible for Excel to resolve. Some formulas contain a circular reference that can eventually be resolved after many recalculations of its formula. Each time the formula is recalculated with a new value in the circular reference, the results in each cell get closer and closer to the correct results.

Figure 1-17 illustrates the classic example of a formula that uses a circular reference, which ultimately can be resolved. Here, you have an income statement that includes bonuses equal to 20 percent of the net earnings entered as an expense in cell B15 with the formula

```
=-B21*0.2
```

This formula contains a circular reference because it refers to the value in B21, which itself indirectly depends upon the amount of bonuses (the bonuses being used as an expense in the formulas that determine the amount of net earnings in cell B21).

To resolve the circular reference in cell B15 and calculate the bonuses based on net earnings in B21, you simply need to select the Iteration check box on the Calculation tab in the Options dialog box (unless the Manual option button is selected, in which case you must click the Calc Now (F9) button command or press F9 or Ctrl+= as well).

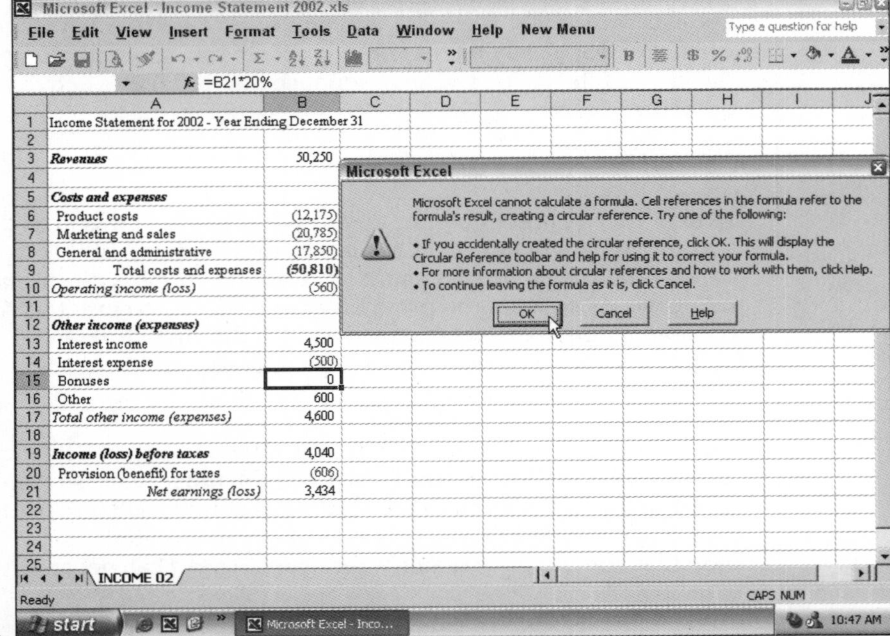

Figure 1-17: Income statement with a resolvable circular reference.

Chapter 2: Logical Functions and Error Trapping

In This Chapter

- Understanding formula Error Values
- Understanding the logical functions
- Creating IF formulas that trap errors
- Tracing formula errors
- Changing the Error Checking options
- Masking Error Values in your printouts

Troubleshooting the formula errors in a worksheet is the main topic of this chapter. Here, you see how to locate the source of all those vexing formula errors so that you can shoot them down and set things right! The biggest problem with errors in your formulas — besides how ugly such values as #REF! and #DIV/0! are — is that they spread like wildfire through the workbook to other cells containing formulas that refer to their error-laden cells. If you're dealing with a large worksheet in a really big workbook, you may not be able to tell which cell actually contains the formula that's causing all the hubbub. And if you can't apprehend the cell that is the cause of all this unpleasantness, you really have no way of restoring law and order to your workbook.

Keeping in mind that the best defense is a good offense, you also find out in this chapter how to trap potential errors at their source and thereby keep them there. This technique, known affectionately as *error trapping* (just think of yourself as being on a spreadsheet safari), is easily accomplished by skillfully combining the IF function to the workings of the original formula.

Understanding Error Values

If Excel can't properly calculate a formula that you enter in a cell, the program displays an *error value* in the cell as soon as you complete the formula entry. Excel uses several error values, all of which begin with the number sign (#). Table 2-1 shows you the error values in Excel along with the meaning and the most probable cause for its display. To remove an error value from a cell, you must discover what caused the value to appear and then edit the formula so that Excel can complete the desired calculation.

Table 2-1	Error Values in Excel
Error Value	***Meaning***
#DIV/0	Division by zero — this error value appears if the division operation in your formula refers to a cell that contains the value 0 or is *blank.*
#N/A	No value is available — technically this is not an error value but a special value that you can manually enter into a cell to indicate that you don't yet have a necessary value.
#NAME?	You used a name that Excel doesn't recognize: this error value appears when you incorrectly type the range name, refer to a deleted range name, or forget to put quotation marks around a text string in a formula (causing Excel to think that you're referring to a range name).
#NULL!	This error value appears when you specify an intersection of two ranges whose cells don't actually intersect; because the space is the intersection operator, this error will occur if you insert a space instead of a comma (the union operator) between ranges used in function arguments.
#NUM!	Problem with a number in the formula; this error can be caused by an invalid argument in an Excel function or a formula that produces a number too large or too small to be represented in the worksheet.
#REF!	Invalid cell reference; this error occurs when you delete a cell referred to in the formula or if you paste cells over the ones referred to in the formula.
#VALUE!	This error value appears when you use the wrong type of argument in a function or the wrong type of operator; this is most often the result of specifying a mathematical operation with one or more cells that contain text.

If a formula in your worksheet contains a reference to a cell that returns an error value, that formula returns that error value as well. This can cause error values to appear throughout the worksheet, thus making it very difficult for you to discover which cell contains the formula that caused the original error value so that you can fix the problem.

Using Logical Functions

Excel uses the following six logical functions, all of which return either the logical TRUE or logical FALSE to their cells when their functions are evaluated:

- TRUE() — takes no argument and simply enters logical TRUE in its cell
- FALSE() — takes no argument and simply enters logical FALSE in its cell
- IF(*logical_test,value_if_true,value_if_false*) — tests whether the *logical_test* expression is TRUE or FALSE. If TRUE, the IF function uses the *value_if_true* argument and returns it to the cell. If FALSE, the IF function uses the *value_if_false* argument and returns it to the cell.

- NOT(*logical*) — tests whether the *logical* argument is TRUE or FALSE. If TRUE, the NOT function returns FALSE to the cell. If FALSE, the NOT function returns TRUE to the cell.
- AND(*logical1, logical2,...*) — tests whether the *logical* arguments are TRUE or FALSE. If they are all TRUE, the AND function returns TRUE to the cell. If any are FALSE, the AND function returns FALSE.
- OR(*logical1,logical2,...*) — tests whether the *logical* arguments are TRUE or FALSE. If any are TRUE, the OR function returns TRUE. If all are FALSE, the OR function returns FALSE.

The *logical_test* and *logical* arguments that you specify for these logical functions usually employ the comparison operators (=, <, >, <=, >=, or <>), which themselves return logical TRUE or logical FALSE values. For example, suppose that you enter the following formula in your worksheet:

```
=AND(B5=D10,C15>=500)
```

In this formula, Excel first evaluates the first *logical* argument to determine whether the contents in cell B5 and D10 are equal to each other. If they are, the first comparison returns TRUE. If they are not equal to each other, this comparison returns FALSE. The program then evaluates the second *logical* argument to determine whether the contents of cell C15 is greater than or equal to 500. If it is, the second comparison returns TRUE. If it is not greater than or equal to 500, this comparison returns FALSE.

After evaluating the comparisons in the two *logical* arguments, the AND function compares the results: if *logical* argument 1 and *logical* argument 2 are both found to be TRUE, then the AND function returns logical TRUE to the cell. If, however, either argument is found to be FALSE, then the AND function returns FALSE to the cell.

When you use the IF function, you specify what's called a *logical_test* argument whose outcome determines whether the *value_if_true* or *value_if_false* argument is evaluated and returned to the cell. The *logical_test* argument normally uses comparison operators, which return either the logical TRUE or logical FALSE value. When the argument returns TRUE, the entry or expression in the *value_if_true* argument is used and returned to the cell. When the argument returns FALSE, the entry or expression in the *value_if_false* argument is used.

Consider the following formula that uses the IF function to determine whether to charge tax on an item:

```
=IF(E5="Yes",D5+D5*7.5%,D5)
```

If cell E5 (the first cell in the column where you indicate whether the item being sold is taxable or not) contains "Yes," the IF function uses the *value_if_true* argument that tells Excel to add the extended price entered in cell D5, multiply it by a tax rate of 7.5% and then add the computed tax to the extended price. If, however, cell D5 is blank or contains anything other than the text "Yes" then the IF function uses the *value_if_false* argument, which tells Excel to just return the extended price to cell D5 without adding any tax to it.

As you can see, the *value_if_true* and *value_if_false* arguments of the IF function can contain constants or expressions whose results are returned to the cell that holds the IF formula.

Error-Trapping Formulas

Sometimes, you know ahead of time that certain error values are unavoidable in a worksheet as long as it's missing certain data. The most common error value that gets you into this kind of trouble is our old friend, the #DIV/0! error value. Suppose, for example, that you're creating a new sales workbook from your sales template, and one of the rows in this template contains formulas that calculate the percentage that each monthly total is of the quarterly total. To work correctly, the formulas must divide the value in the cell that contains the monthly total by the value in the cell that contains the quarterly total. When you start a new sales workbook from its template, the cells that contain the formulas for determining the quarterly totals contain zeros, and these zeros put #DIV/0! errors in the cells with formulas that calculate the monthly/quarterly percentages.

These particular #DIV/0! error values in the new workbook don't really represent mistakes as such because they automatically disappear as soon as you enter some of the monthly sales for each quarter (so that the calculated quarterly totals are no longer 0). The problem that you may have is convincing your non–spreadsheet-savvy coworkers (especially the boss) that despite the presence of all these error values in your worksheet, the formulas are hunky-dory. All that your coworkers see is a worksheet riddled with error values, and these error values undermine your coworkers' confidence in the correctness of your worksheet.

Well, I have the answer for just such "perception" problems. Rather than risk having your boss freak out over the display of a few little #DIV/0! errors here and there, you can set up these formulas so that whenever they're tempted to return any type of error value (including #DIV/0!), they instead return zeros in their cells. Only when absolutely no danger exists of cooking up error values will Excel actually do the original calculations called for in the formulas.

This sleight of hand in an original formula not only effectively eliminates errors from the formula but also prevents their spread to any of its dependents. To create such a formula, you use the IF function, which operates one way when a certain condition exists and another when it doesn't.

To see how you can use the IF function in a formula that sometimes gives you a #DIV/0! error, consider the sample worksheet shown in Figure 2-1. This figure shows a blank Production Schedule worksheet for storing the 2004 production figures arranged by month and part number. Because you haven't yet had a chance to input any data into this table, the SUM formulas in the last row and column contain 0 values. Because cell K7 with the grand total currently also contains 0, all the percent-of-total formulas in the cell range B9:J9 contain #DIV/0! error values.

	A	B	C	D	E	F	G	H	I	J	K
1				2004 Production Schedule							
2		Jan-04	Feb-04	Mar-04	Apr-04	May-04	Jun-04	Jul-04	Aug-04	Sep-04	Total
3	Part 101										0
4	Part 101										0
5	Part 102										0
6	Part 103										0
7	Total	0	0	0	0	0	0	0	0	0	0
8											
9	% To	#DIV/0!	#DIV/0!	#DIV/0!	#DIV/0!	#DIV/0!	#DIV/0!	#DIV/0!	#DIV/0!	#DIV/0!	

Figure 2-1: Blank 2004 Production Schedule spreadsheet that's full of #DIV/0! errors.

The first percent-of-total formula in cell B9 contains the following:

```
=B7/$K$7
```

Because cell K7 with the grand total contains 0, the formula returns the #DIV/0! error value. Now, I show you how to set a trap for the error in the *logical_test* argument inside an IF function. After the *logical_test* argument, you enter the *value_if_true* argument (which is 0 in this example) and the *value_if_false* argument (which is the division of B7/$K$7). With the addition of the IF function, the final formula looks like this:

```
=IF($K$7=0,0,B7/$K$7)
```

This formula then inputs 0 into cell B9, as shown in Figure 2-2, when the formula actually returns the #DIV/0! error value (because cell K7 is still empty or has a 0 in it) and returns the percentage of total production when the formula doesn't return the #DIV/0! error value (because cell K7 with the total production divisor is no longer empty or contains any other value besides 0). Next, all you have to do is copy this error-trapping formula in cell B9 over to J9 to remove all the #DIV/0! errors from this worksheet.

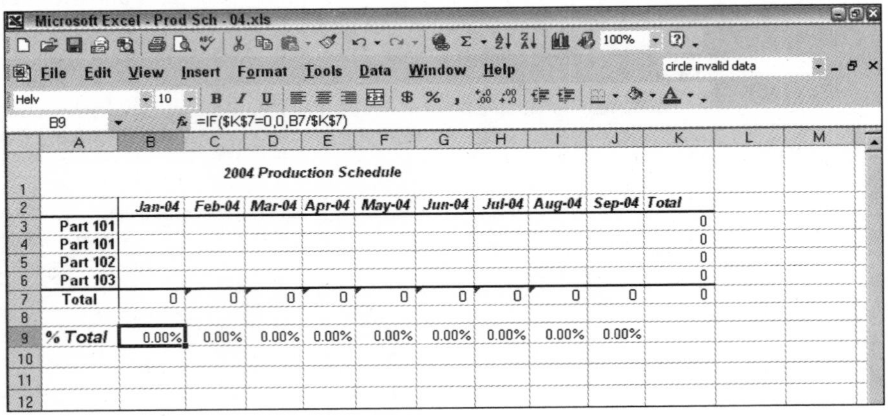

Microsoft Excel - Prod Sch - 04.xls

B9 =IF($K$7=0,0,B7/$K$7)

	A	B	C	D	E	F	G	H	I	J	K
1				*2004 Production Schedule*							
2		*Jan-04*	*Feb-04*	*Mar-04*	*Apr-04*	*May-04*	*Jun-04*	*Jul-04*	*Aug-04*	*Sep-04*	*Total*
3	Part 101										0
4	Part 101										0
5	Part 102										0
6	Part 103										0
7	Total	0	0	0	0	0	0	0	0	0	0
8											
9	*% Total*	0.00%	0.00%	0.00%	0.00%	0.00%	0.00%	0.00%	0.00%	0.00%	

Figure 2-2: 2004 Production Schedule spreadsheet after trapping all the #DIV/0! errors.

The error-trapping formula created with the IF function in cell B9 works fine as long as you know that the grand total in cell K7 will contain either 0 or some other numerical value. It does not, however, trap any of the various error values, such as #REF! and #NAME?, nor does it account for the special #NA (Not Available) value. If, for some reason, one of the formulas feeding into the SUM formula in K7 returns one of these beauties, they will suddenly cascade throughout all the cells with the percent-of-total formulas (cell range B9:J9).

To trap all error values in the grand total cell K7 and prevent them from spreading to the percent-to-total formulas, you need to add the ISERROR function to the basic IF formula. The ISERROR function returns the logical value TRUE if the cell specified as its argument contains any type of error value, including the special #N/A value (if you use ISERR instead of ISERROR, it checks for all types of error values except for #N/A).

To add the ISERROR function, place it in the IF function as the *logical_test* argument. If, indeed, K7 does contain an error value or the #N/A value at the time the IF function is evaluated, you specify 0 as the *value_if_true* argument so that Excel inputs 0 in cell B9 rather than error value or #N/A. For the *value_if_false* argument, you specify the original IF function that inputs 0 if the cell K7 contains 0; otherwise, it performs the division that computes what percentage the January production figure is of the total production.

This amended formula with the ISERROR and two IF functions in cell B9 looks like this:

```
=IF(ISERROR($K$7),0,IF($K$7=0,0,B7/$K$7))
```

As soon as you copy this original formula to the cell range C9:J9, you've protected all the cells with the percent-of-total formulas from displaying and spreading any of those ugly error values.

Some people prefer to remove the display of zero values from any template that contains error-trapping formulas so that no one interprets the zeros as the correct value for the formula. To remove the display of zeros from a worksheet, deselect the Zero Values check box on the View tab of the Options dialog box (Tools➪Options). By this action, the cells with error-trapping formulas remain blank until you give them the data that they need to return the correct answers!

Error Tracing

If you don't happen to trap those pesky error values before they get out into the spreadsheet, then you end up having to track down the original cell that caused all the commotion and set it right. Fortunately, Excel offers some very effective tools for tracking down the cell that's causing your error woes by tracing the relationships between the formulas in the cells of your worksheet. By tracing the relationships, you can test formulas to see which cells, called *direct precedents* in spreadsheet jargon, directly feed the formulas and which cells, called *dependents* (nondeductible, of course), depend upon the results of the formulas. Excel even offers a way to visually backtrack the potential sources of an error value in the formula of a particular cell.

The easiest method for tracing the relationship between cells is offered by the tools on the Formula Auditing toolbar, shown in Figure 2-3. To display the Formula Auditing toolbar, choose Tools➪Formula Auditing➪Show Formula Auditing Toolbar on the pull-down menu or choose Auditing on the shortcut menu of one of the displayed toolbars. When you first display the Formula Auditing toolbar, Excel automatically makes it a floating toolbar, which you can dock or not, as you see fit.

If you prefer choosing commands from the pull-down menus rather than clicking toolbar tools, you can select pull-down commands equivalent to most of the buttons found on the Formula Auditing toolbar. These commands are available on a submenu that appears after you choose Tools➪Formula Auditing.

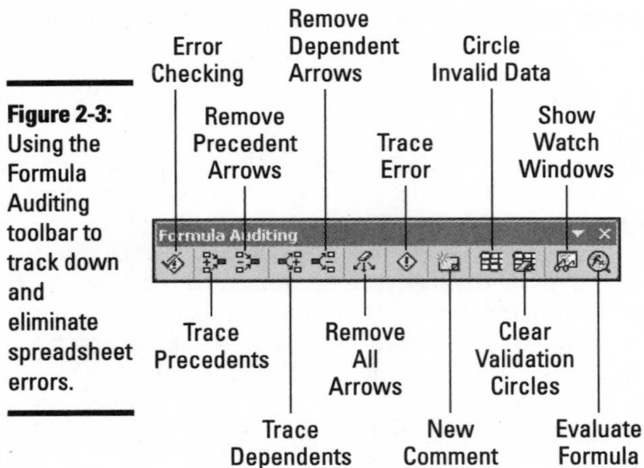

Figure 2-3: Using the Formula Auditing toolbar to track down and eliminate spreadsheet errors.

This nifty toolbar contains the following tools (from left to right) that you can put to good use in your never-ending struggle for truth, justice, and perfection in your Excel workbooks:

- **Trace Precedents:** When you click this button, Excel draws arrows to the cells (the so-called *direct precedents*) that are referred to in the formula inside the selected cell. When you click this button again, Excel adds "tracer" arrows that show the cells (the so-called indirect precedents) that are referred to in the formulas in the direct precedents.
- **Remove Precedent Arrows:** Clicking this button gets rid of the arrows that were drawn when you clicked the Trace Precedents button.
- **Trace Dependents:** When you click this button, Excel draws arrows from the selected cell to the cells (the so-called *direct dependents*) that use, or depend on, the results of the formula in the selected cell. When you click this button again, Excel adds tracer arrows identifying the cells (the so-called *indirect dependents*) that refer to formulas found in the direct dependents.
- **Remove Dependent Arrows:** Clicking this button gets rid of the arrows that were drawn when you clicked the Trace Dependents button.
- **Remove All Arrows:** Clicking this button removes all the arrows drawn, no matter what button or pull-down command you used to put them there.
- **Trace Error:** When you click this button, Excel attempts to locate the cell that contains the original formula that has an error. If Excel can find this cell, it selects it and then draws arrows to the cells feeding it (the direct precedents) and the cells infected with its error value (the direct dependents). Note that you can use this button only on a cell that contains an error value.

- **New Comment:** Clicking this button opens a comment box attached to the current cell where you can add a text note (see Book IV, Chapter 1).
- **Circle Invalid Data:** Clicking this button draws red circles around all of the data entries in the worksheet that don't currently contain valid data (as defined with the Data Validation feature — see Book II, Chapter 1 for information on using Data Validation to restrict input in a cell).
- **Clear Validation Circles:** Clicking this button removes all circles drawn by clicking the Circle Invalid Data button (to remove individual circles, select the cell and then enter the data that's required by the Data Validation assigned to the cell).
- **Show Watch Window:** Clicking this button opens the Watch Window dialog box, which displays the workbook, sheet, and cell location, range name, current value, and formula in any cells that you add to the watch list. To add a cell to the watch list, click the cell in the worksheet and then click the Add Watch button in the Watch Window, and then click Add in the Add Watch dialog box that appears.
- **Evaluate Formula:** Clicking this button opens the Evaluate Formula dialog box, where you can have Excel evaluate each part of the formula in the current cell. This can be quite useful in formulas that nest many functions within them.

Clicking the Trace Precedents and Trace Dependents buttons on the Formula Auditing toolbar (or choosing the Trace Precedents and Trace Dependents on the Tools⇨Formula Auditing cascading menus) lets you see the relationship between a formula and the cells that directly and indirectly feed it, as well as those cells that directly and indirectly depend upon its calculation. Excel establishes this relationship by drawing arrows from the precedent cells to the active cell and from the active cell to its dependent cells.

If these cells are on the same worksheet, Excel draws solid red or blue arrows (on a color monitor) extending from each of the precedent cells to the active cell and from the active cell to the dependent cells. If the cells are not located locally on the same worksheet (they may be on another sheet in the same workbook or even on a sheet in a different workbook), Excel draws a black dotted arrow. This arrow comes from or goes to an icon picturing a miniature worksheet that sits to one side, with the direction of the arrowheads indicating whether the cells on the other sheet feed the active formula or are fed by it.

Setting precedents

You can use the Trace Precedents button on the Formula Auditing toolbar to trace all the generations of cells that contribute to the formula in the selected cell (kinda like tracing all the ancestors in your family tree). Figures 2-4 and

2-5 illustrate how you can use the Trace Precedents button to quickly locate the cells that contribute, directly and indirectly, to the simple addition formula in cell B9.

Figure 2-4 shows the worksheet after I clicked the Trace Precedents button the first time. As you can see, Excel draws trace arrows from cells A5 and C5 to indicate that they are the direct precedents of the addition formula in cell B9. In Figure 2-5, you see what happened when I clicked this button a second time to display the indirect precedents of this formula (think of them as being a generation earlier in the family tree). The new tracer arrows show that cells A2, A3, and A4 are the direct precedents of the formula in cell A5 — indicated by a border around the three cells. (Remember that cell A5 is the first direct precedent of the formula in cell B9.) Likewise, cells B2 and B3 as well as cell C4 are the direct precedents of the formula in cell C5. (Cell C5 is the second direct precedent of the formula in cell B9.)

Figure 2-6 shows what happened after I clicked the Trace Precedents button (after clicking it twice before, as shown in Figures 2-4 and 2-5). Clicking the button reveals both the indirect precedents for cell C5. The formulas in cells C2 and C3 are the direct precedents of the formula in cell C5. The direct precedent of the formula in cell C2 (and, consequently, the indirect precedent of the one in cell C5) is not located on this worksheet. This fact is indicated by the dotted tracer arrow coming from that cute miniature worksheet icon sitting on top of cell A3.

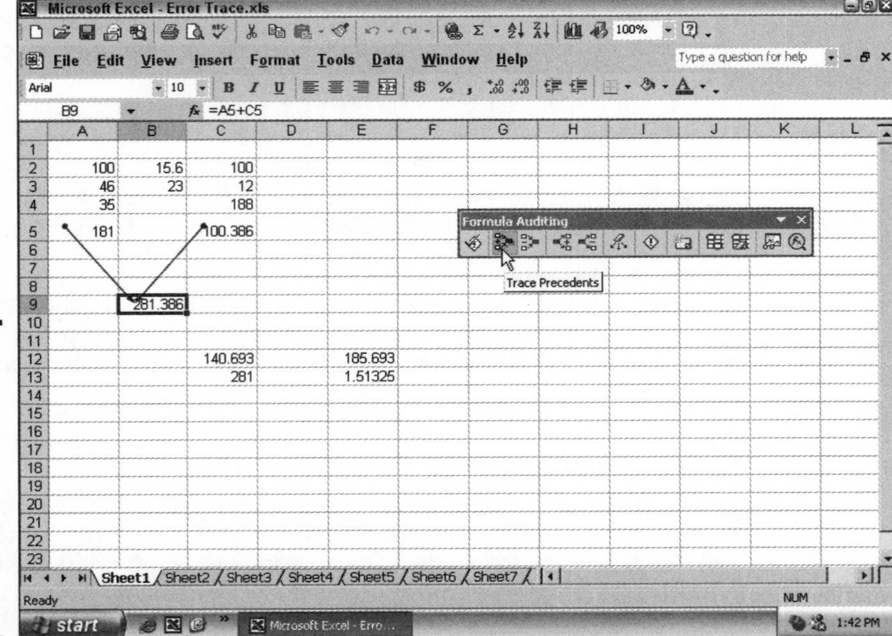

Figure 2-4: Clicking the Trace Precedents button shows the direct precedents of the formula.

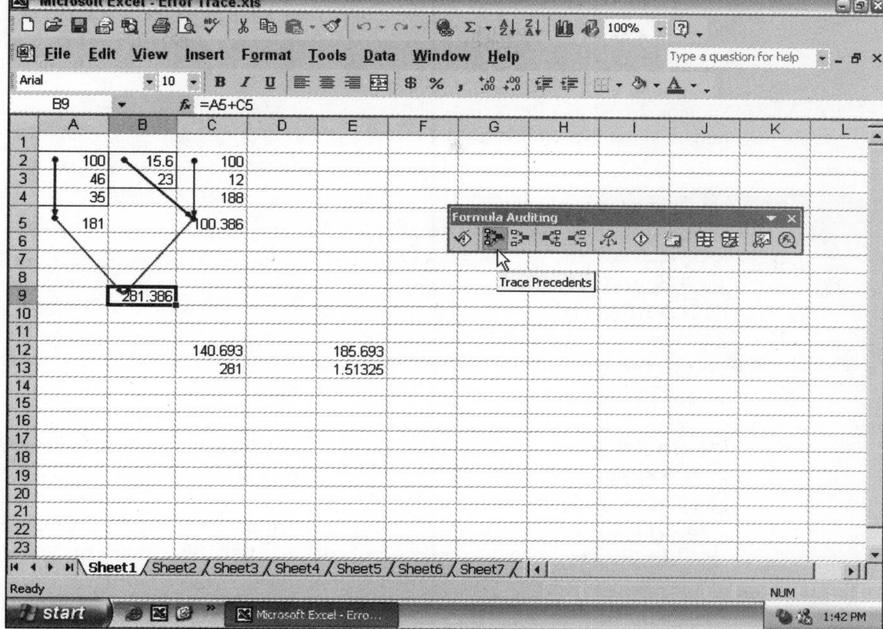

Figure 2-5: Clicking the Trace Precedents button again shows the indirect precedents of the formula.

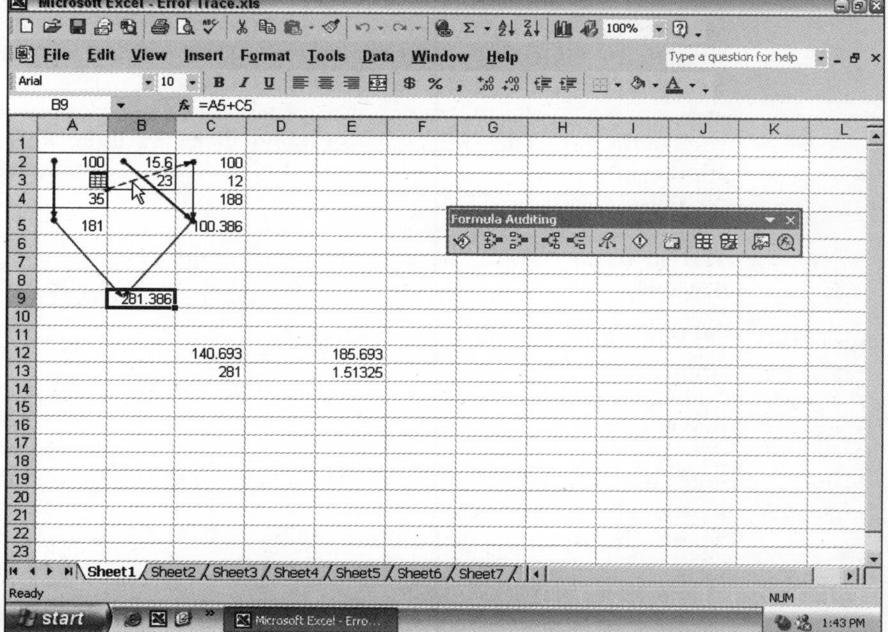

Figure 2-6: Clicking Trace Precedents button a third time shows a precedent on another worksheet.

When Trace Error loses the trail

Trace Error finds errors along the path of a formula's precedents and dependents until it finds either the source of the error or one of the following problems:

- ✦ It encounters a branch point with more than one error source. In this case, Excel doesn't make a determination on its own as to which path to pursue.
- ✦ It encounters existing tracer arrows. Therefore, *always* click the Remove All Arrows button to get rid of trace arrows before you click the Trace Error button.
- ✦ It encounters a formula with a circular reference (see Book III, Chapter 1 for more on circular references).

Each time you click the Trace Precedents button, Excel displays another (earlier) set of precedents (until no more generations exist). If you are in a hurry (as most of us are most of the time), you can speed up the process and display both the direct and indirect precedents in one operation by double-clicking the Trace Precedents button. To clear the worksheet of tracer arrows, click the Remove Precedent Arrows button on the Formula Auditing toolbar.

To find out exactly which workbook, worksheet, and cell(s) hold the direct precedents of cell C2, I double-clicked somewhere on the dotted arrow (clicking the icon with the worksheet miniature doesn't do a thing). Double-clicking the dotted tracer arrow opens the Go To dialog box, which shows a list of all the precedents (including the workbook, worksheet, and cell references). To go to a precedent on another worksheet, double-click the reference in the Go To list box, or select it and click OK. (If the worksheet is in another workbook, this workbook file must already be open before you can go to it.)

The Go To dialog box, shown in Figure 2-7, displays the following direct precedent of cell C2, which is cell B4 on Sheet2 of the same workbook:

```
'[Error Tracer.xls]Sheet2'!$B$4
```

To jump directly to this cell, double-click the cell reference in the Go To dialog box.

You can also select precedent cells that are on the same worksheet as the active cell by double-clicking somewhere on the cell's tracer arrow. Excel selects the precedent cell without bothering to open up the Go To dialog box.

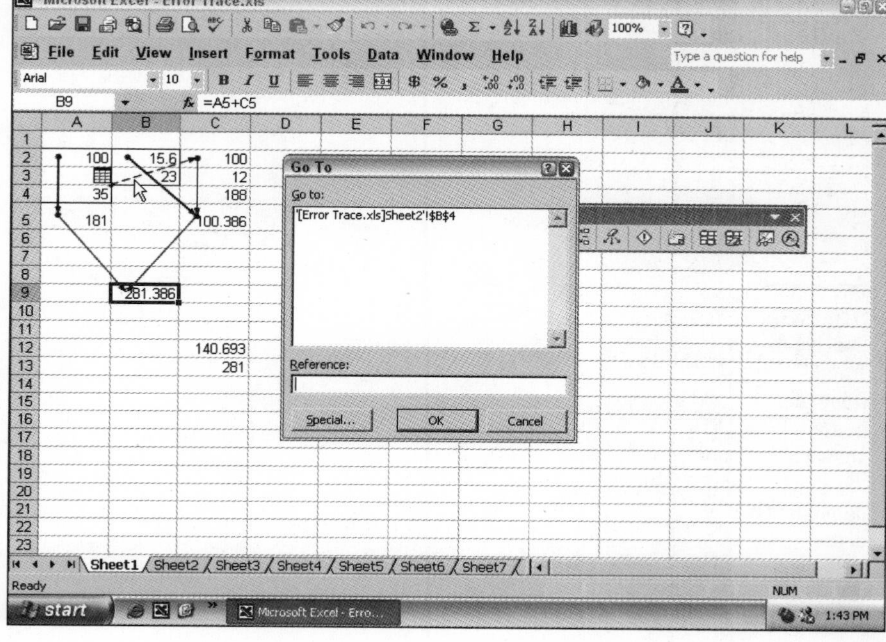

Figure 2-7: Double-clicking the dotted tracer arrow opens the Go To dialog box showing the location.

You can use the Special button in the Go To dialog box (see Figure 2-7) to select all the direct or indirect precedents or the direct or indirect dependents that are on the same sheet as the formula in the selected cell. After opening the Go To dialog box (Ctrl+G or F5) and clicking the Special button, you simply click the Precedents or Dependents radio button and then choose between the Direct Only or All Levels radio button before you click OK.

Knowing your dependents

You can use the Trace Dependents button on the Formula Auditing toolbar to trace all the generations of cells that either directly or indirectly utilize the formula in the selected cell (kind of like tracing the genealogy of all your progeny). Tracing dependents with the Trace Dependents button is much like tracing precedents with the Trace Precedents button. Each time you click this button, Excel draws another set of arrows that show a generation of dependents further removed. To display both the direct and indirect dependents of a cell in one fell swoop, double-click the Trace Dependents button.

Figure 2-8 shows what happened after I selected cell B9 and then double-clicked the Trace Dependents button to display both the direct and indirect dependents and then clicked it a third time to display the dependents on another worksheet.

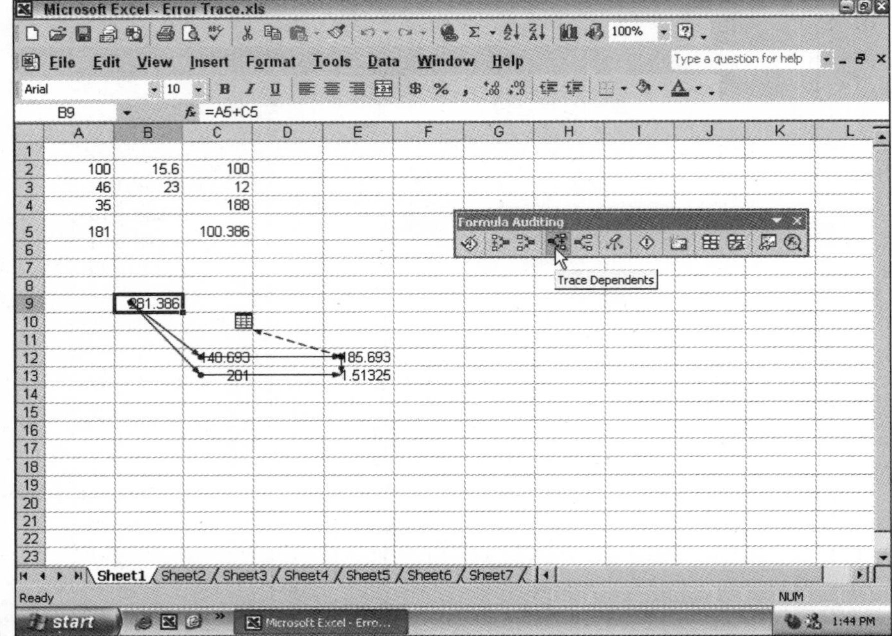

Figure 2-8: Clicking the Traced Dependents button shows all the dependents of the formula in B9.

As Figure 2-8 shows, Excel first draws tracer arrows from cell B9 to cells C12 and C13, indicating that C12 and C13 are the direct dependents of cell B9. Then, it draws tracer arrows from cells C12 and C13 to E12 and E13, respectively, the direct dependents of C12 and C13 and the indirect dependents of B9. Finally, it draws a tracer arrow from cell E12 to another sheet in the workbook (indicated by the dotted tracer arrow pointing to the worksheet icon).

Using the Trace Error button

Tracing a formula's family tree, so to speak, with the Trace Precedents and Trace Dependents buttons is fine, as far as it goes. However, when it comes to a formula that returns a hideous error value, such as #VALUE! or #NAME!, you need to turn to the trusty Trace Error button on the Formula Auditing toolbar (the one with an exclamation point in a diamond).

Using the Trace Error button is a lot like using both the Trace Precedents and the Trace Dependents tools, except that the Trace Error button works only when the active cell contains some sort of error value returned by either a bogus formula or a reference to a bogus formula. In tracking down the actual cause of the error value in the active cell (remember that these error values spread to all direct and indirect dependents of a formula), Excel draws blue tracer arrows from the precedents for the original bogus formula and then draws red tracer arrows to all the dependents that contain error values as a result.

Figure 2-9 shows the sample worksheet after I made some damaging changes that left three cells — C12, E12, and E13 — with #DIV/0! errors (meaning that somewhere, somehow, I ended up creating a formula that is trying to divide by zero, which is a real no-no in the wonderful world of math). To find the origin of these error values and identify its cause, I clicked the Trace Error button on the Formula Auditing toolbar while cell E12 was the active cell to engage the use of Excel's faithful old Trace Error feature.

Figure 2-9 shows the results (unfortunately without color, so you can't tell which trace arrows were drawn in blue or red). Note that Excel has selected cell C12, although cell E12 was active when I clicked the Trace Error button. To cell C12, Excel has drawn two blue tracer arrows (you'll have to take my word for it) that identify cells B5 and B9 as its direct precedents. From cell C12, the program has drawn a single red tracer arrow (again, you have to trust me on this) from cell C12 to cell E12 that identifies its direct dependent.

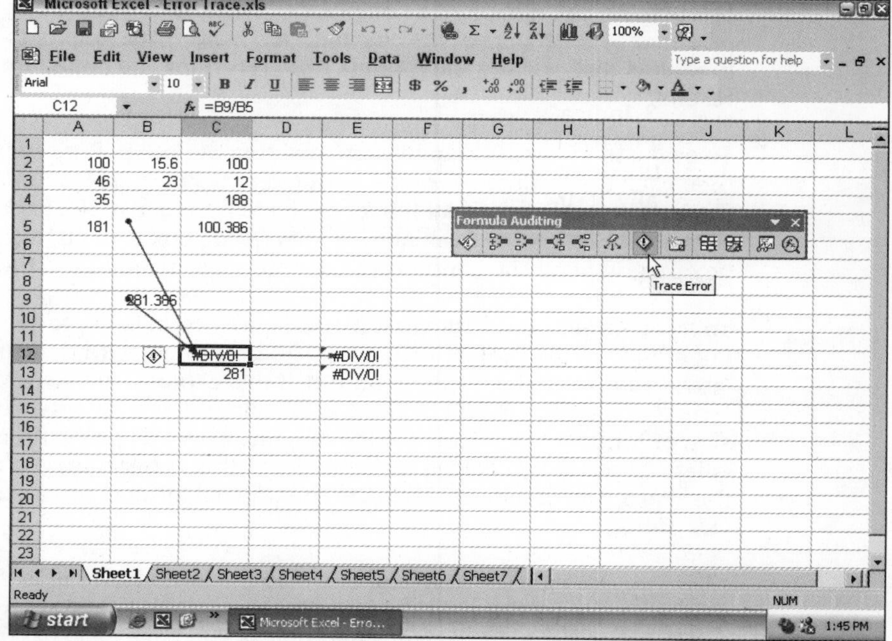

Figure 2-9: Clicking the Trace Error button to show the precedents and dependents of the formula.

As it turns out, Excel's Trace Error button is right on the money because the formula in cell C12 contains the bad apple rotting the whole barrel. I had revised the formula in cell C12 so that it divided the value in cell B9 by the value in cell B5 without making sure that cell B5 first contained the SUM formula that totaled the values in the cell range B2:B4. The #DIV/0! error value showed up — remember that an empty cell contains a zero value as if you had actually entered 0 in the cell — and immediately spread to cells E12 and E13 which, in turn, use the value returned in C12 in their own calculations. Thus, these cells were infected with #DIV/0! error values as well.

As soon as you correct the problem in the original formula and thus get rid of all the error values in the other cells, Excel automatically converts the red tracer arrows (showing the proliferation trail of the original error) to regular blue tracer arrows, indicating merely that these restored cells are dependents of the formula that once contained the original sin. You can then remove all the tracer arrows from the sheet by clicking the Remove All Arrows button on the Formula Auditing toolbar.

"Evaluate this!"

The last button on the Formula Auditing toolbar is the Evaluate Formula button, which opens the Evaluate Formula window, where you can step through the calculation of a complicated formula to see the current value returned by each part of the calculation. This is often helpful in locating problems that prevent the formula from returning the hoped for or expected results.

To evaluate a formula step-by-step, position the cell pointer in that cell and then click the Evaluate Formula button on the Formula Auditing toolbar (or choose Tools⇨Formula Auditing⇨Evaluate Formula on the Excel menus). This action opens the Evaluate Formula dialog box with an Evaluation list box that displays the contents of the entire formula that's in the current cell.

To have Excel evaluate the first expression or term in the formula (shown underlined in the Evaluation list box) and replace it with the currently calculated value, click the Evaluate button. If this expression uses an argument or term that is itself a result of another calculation, you can display its expression or formula by clicking the Step In button (see Figure 2-10) and then calculate its result by clicking the Evaluate button. After that, you can return to the evaluation of the expression in the original formula by clicking the Step Out button.

After you evaluate the first expression in the formula, Excel underlines the next expression or term in the formula (by using the natural order of precedence and a strict left-to-right order unless you have used parentheses to override this order), which you can then replace with its calculated value by clicking the Evaluate button. When you finish evaluating all the expressions and terms of the current formula, you can close the Evaluate Formula window by clicking its Close button in the upper-right corner of the window.

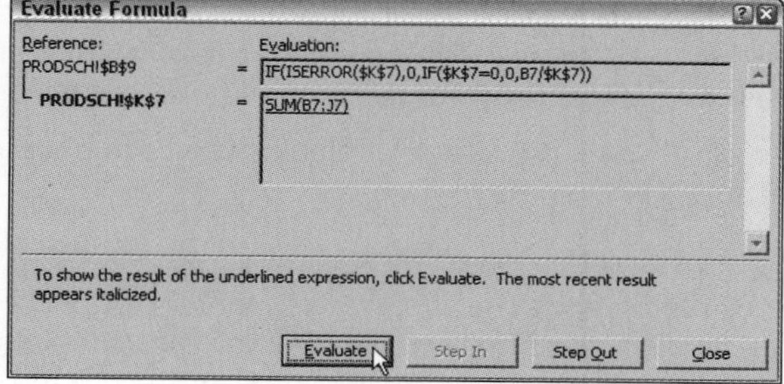

Figure 2-10: Calculating each part of a formula in the Evaluate Formula dialog box.

Instead of the Evaluate Formula dialog box, open the Watch Window dialog box and add formulas to it when all you need to do is to keep an eye on the current value returned by a mixture of related formulas in the workbook. This enables you to see the effect that changing various input values has on their calculations (even when they're located on different sheets of the workbook).

Error Checking Options

Whenever a formula yields an error value other than #N/A (refer to Table 2-1 for a list of all the error values) in a cell, Excel displays a tiny error indicator (in the form of the triangle) in the upper-left corner of the cell and an alert options button appears to the left of that cell when you make it active. If you position the mouse pointer on that options button, a pop-up button appears to its right that you can click to display a pop-up menu and a ToolTip appears below describing the nature of the error value.

When you click the pop-up button, a menu appears, containing an item with the name of the error value followed by the following items:

- **Help on This Error** to open a Help window with information on the type of error value in the active cell
- **Show Calculations Steps** to open the Evaluate Formula dialog box where you can step through the calculation of each expression and term in the formula

- **Ignore Error** to bypass error checking for this cell and remove the error alert and Error options button from it
- **Edit in Formula Bar** to activate Edit mode and put the insertion at the end of the formula on the Formula bar
- **Error Checking Options** to open the Options dialog box with only the Error Checking tab displayed where you can modify the options used in checking the worksheet for formula errors
- **Show Formula Auditing Toolbar** to display the Formula Auditing toolbar so that you have access to its tools

When you click the Error Checking Options item on the pop-up menu or open the Options dialog box (Tools⇨Options) and click the Error Checking tab, Excel displays the Error Checking options that are currently in effect in Excel (see Figure 2-11). You can use the options on this tab to control when the worksheet is checked for errors and what cells are flagged:

- **Enable Background Error Checking** check box to have Excel check your worksheets for errors when the computer is idle. When this check box is selected, you can change the color of the error indicator that appears as a tiny triangle in the upper-left corner of the cell (normally this indicator is green) by clicking a new color on the Error Indicator Color's pop-up palette.
- **Reset Ignored Errors** button to restore the error indicator and alert options button to all cells that you previously told Excel to ignore by choosing the Ignore Error item on the alert options' pop-up menu attached to the cell.
- **Evaluates to Error Value** check box to have Excel insert the error indicator and add the alert options button to all cells that return error values.
- **Text Date with 2 Digit Years** to have Excel flag all dates entered as text with just the last two digits of the year errors by adding an error indicator and alert options button to their cells.
- **Number Stored as Text** check box to have Excel flag all numbers entered as text as errors by adding an error indicator and alert options button to their cells.
- **Inconsistent Formula in Region** check box to have Excel flag any formula that differs from the others in the same area of the worksheet as an error by adding an error indicator and alert options button to its cell.
- **Formula Omits Cells in Region** check box to have Excel flag any formula that omits cells from the range that it refers to as an error by adding an error indicator and alert options button to its cell.

+ **Unlocked Cells Contain Formulas** check box to have Excel flag any formula whose cell is unlocked when the worksheet is protected as an error by adding an error indicator and alert options button to its cell (see Book IV, Chapter 3 for information on protecting worksheets).
+ **Formulas Referring to Empty Cells** check box to have Excel flag any formula that refers to blank cells as an error by adding an error indicator and alert options button to its cell.

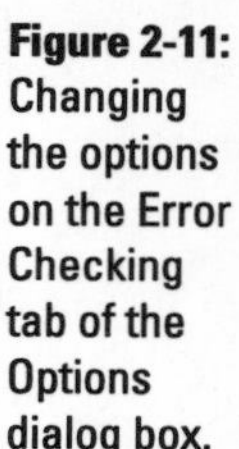

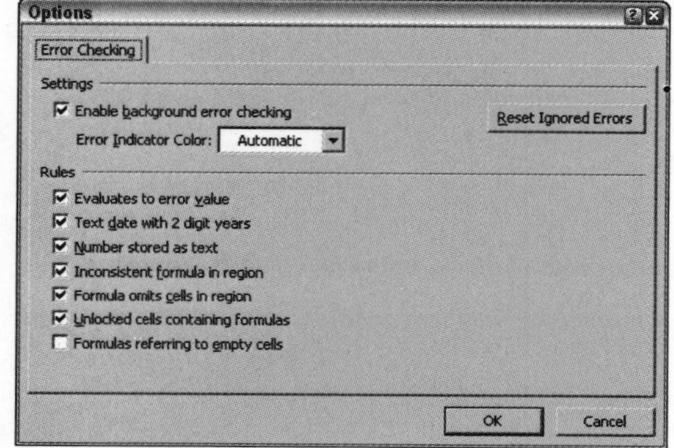

Figure 2-11: Changing the options on the Error Checking tab of the Options dialog box.

Removing Errors from the Printout

What if you don't have the time to trap all the potential formula errors or track them down and eliminate them before you have to print out and distribute the spreadsheet? In that case, you may just have to remove the display of all the error values before you print the report.

To do this, click the Sheet tab in the Page Setup dialog box opened by choosing File⇨Page Setup on the Excel menu or by clicking the Setup button in the Print Preview window (File⇨Print Preview) and then clicking the drop-down button attached to the Cell Errors As drop-down list box. The default value for this drop-down list box is "displayed," meaning that all error values are displayed in the printout exactly as they currently appear in the worksheet. This pop-up menu also contains the following items that you can click to remove the display of error values from the printed report:

+ Click the <blank> option to replace all error values with blank cells
+ Click the -- option to replace all error values with two dashes
+ Click the #N/A option to replace all error values (except for #N/A entries, of course) with the special #N/A value (which is considered an error value when you select the <blank> or – options)

Keep in mind that blanking out error values or replacing them with dashes or #N/A values has no effect on them in the worksheet itself, only in any printout you make of the worksheet. This means that you need to view the pages in the Print Preview window (File⇨Print Preview) before you can see the effect of selecting an option besides "displayed" in the Cell Errors As drop-down list box. Also, remember to reset the Cell Errors As option on the Sheet tab of the Page Setup back to "displayed" when you want to print a version of the worksheet that shows the error values in all their cells in the worksheet printout.

Chapter 3: Date and Time Formulas

In This Chapter

- Understanding dates and times in Excel
- Creating formulas that calculate elapsed dates and times
- Using the Date functions
- Using the Time functions

Creating formulas that use dates and times can be a little confusing if you don't have a good understanding of how Excel treats these types of values. After you're equipped with this understanding, you can begin to make good use of the many Date and Time functions offered by the program.

This chapter begins with a quick overview of date and time numbers in Excel and how you can use them to build simple formulas that calculate differences between elapsed dates and times. The chapter goes on to survey Excel built-in Date and Time functions, including the Date functions that are available after you've installed and activated the Analysis ToolPak add-in.

Understanding Dates and Times

Excel doesn't treat the dates and times that you enter in the cells of your worksheet as simple text entries (for more information on inputting numbers in a spreadsheet, see Book II, Chapter 1). Any entry with a format that resembles one of the data and time number formats utilized by Excel is automatically converted, behind the scenes, into a serial number. In the case of dates, this serial number represents the number of days that have elapsed since the beginning of the twentieth century so that January 1, 1900 is serial number 1; January 2, 1900, is serial number 2; and so forth. In the case of times, this serial number is a fraction that represents the number of hours, minutes, and seconds that have elapsed since midnight, which is serial number 0.00000000, so that 12:00:00 p.m. (noon) is serial number 0.50000000; 11:00:00 p.m. is 0.95833333; and so forth.

As long as you format a numeric entry so that it conforms to a recognized date or time format, Excel enters it as a date or time serial number. Only when you enter a formatted date or time as a text entry (by prefacing it with an apostrophe) or import dates and times as text entries into a worksheet do you have to worry about converting them into date and time serial numbers, so you can build spreadsheet formulas that perform calculations on them.

Changing the Regional date settings

Excel isn't set up to automatically recognize European date formats in which the number of the day precedes the number of the month and year; for example, so that 6/11/1969 represents November 6, 1969 rather than June 11, 1969. If you're working with a spreadsheet that uses this type of European date system, you have to customize Windows' Regional settings for the United States so that the Short Date format in Windows programs, such as Excel and Word, use the D/m/yyyy (day, month, year) format rather than the default M/d/yyyy (month, day, year) format.

If you're running a version of Windows 98, you can do this by following these steps:

1. **Click the Start button on the Windows Taskbar and then highlight Settings on the Start menu and click Control Panel on the Settings submenu.**

   The Control Panel window opens.

2. **Double-click Regional Settings in the Control Panel window.**

   The Regional Settings Properties dialog box opens.

3. **Click the Date tab in the Regional Setting Properties dialog box.**

4. **Click the Short Date Style combo box and then type in the new European date format,** D/m/yyyy, **in its text box.**

   You have to type this European date format because the United States regional settings don't automatically include this format in its Short Date Style drop-down list. After manually entering this format, the European date format becomes part of the list that you can then select from in the future.

5. **Click OK to close the Regional Settings dialog box and then click the Close button in the upper-right corner of the Control Panel window to close it.**

If you're running Windows XP, make this date format change by following these steps:

1. **Click the Start button on the Windows Taskbar and then click Control Panel.**

   The Control Panel window opens in Category view.

2. **Click the Date, Time, and Regional Options link.**

   The Date, Time, Language, and Regional Options window opens.

3. **Click the Change the Format of Numbers, Dates, and Times link.**

   The Regional and Language Options dialog box opens. Note that if the Control Panel dialog box opens in Classic view (in which all the control panels are represented by individual file icons), you can open this dialog box in one step by double-clicking the Regional and Language Options icon.

4. **Click the Customize button, located to the right of the current format setting, which is English (United States) for most of you.**

   The Customize Regional Options dialog box opens.

5. **Click the Date tab in the Customize Regional Options dialog box.**
6. **Click the Short Date Format and then type** D/m/yyyy, **the new date format.**

   You have to type this European date format because the United States regional settings don't automatically include this format in its Short Date Style drop-down list. After manually entering this format, the European date format becomes part of the list that you can then select from in the future.

7. **Click OK twice, once to close the Customize Regional Options and then a second time to close the Regional and Language Options dialog box.**
8. **Click the Close button in the upper-right corner of the Control Panel window to close it.**

After changing the Short Date format in the Windows Control Panel, the next time you open Excel, it automatically interprets short dates using the D/m/yyyy form; so that, for example, 3/5/02 is May 3, 2002 rather than March 5, 2002.

Don't forget to change the Short Date format back to its original M/d/yyyy format in the Regional Settings Properties dialog box (Windows 98.*x*) or the Customize Regional Options dialog box (Windows XP) when working with spreadsheets that follow the "month-day-year" Short Date format preferred in the United States. Also, don't forget that you have to restart Excel to get it to pick up on the changes that you make in the Windows Control Panel to the Regional settings.

Building formulas that calculate elapsed dates

Most of the date formulas that you build are designed to calculate the number of days or years that have elapsed between two dates. To do this, you build a simple formula that subtracts the later date from the earlier date.

For example, if you input the date 4/25/75 in cell B11 and 6/3/02 in cell C11 and you want to calculate the number of days that have elapsed between April 25, 1975 and June 3, 2002 in cell D11, you would enter the following subtraction formula in that cell:

```
=C11-B11
```

Excel then inputs the number of days between these dates in cell D5. The only problem is that the program will also apply the Date format used by these two dates so that the result in cell D5 appears as the date:

```
2/8/1927
```

To display this result as a whole number, as you'd expect, you still have to format the result with another number format. If, for example, you apply the General number format to the cell D5 (you can do this quickly by pressing Ctrl+Shift+~), the calculated result in this cell becomes the much more sensible number of days:

```
9901
```

If you want the result between two dates expressed in the number of years rather than the number of days, divide the result of your subtraction by the number of days in a year. In this example, you can enter the formula =D11/365 in cell E11 to return the result 27.12603, which you can then round off to 27 by clicking Decrease Decimal button on the Formatting toolbar until only 27 remains displayed in the cell.

Building formulas that calculate elapsed times

Some spreadsheets require that formulas calculate the amount of elapsed time between a starting and ending time. For example, suppose that you keep a worksheet that records the starting and stopping times for your hourly employees and you need to calculate the number of hours and minutes that elapses between these two times in order to figure their daily and monthly wages.

To build a formula that calculates how much time has elapsed between two different times of the day, subtract the ending time of day from the starting time of day. For example, suppose that you enter a person's starting time in cell B14 and ending time in C14. In cell D14, you would enter the following subtraction formula:

```
=C14-B14
```

Excel then returns the difference in cell D14 as a decimal value representing what fraction that difference represents of an entire day (that is, a 24-hour period). If, for example, cell B14 contains a starting time of 9:15 a.m. and cell C14 contains an ending time of 3:45 p.m., Excel returns the following decimal value to cell D14:

```
6:30 AM
```

To convert this time of day into its equivalent decimal number, you convert the time format automatically given to it to the General format (Ctrl+Shift+~), which gives the following result in cell D14:

```
0.270833
```

To convert this decimal number representing the fraction of an entire day into the number of hours that have elapsed, you simply multiply this result by 24 as in =D14*24, which gives you a result of 6.5 hours when you apply the General format (Ctrl+Shift+~) to it.

Using Date Functions

Excel contains a number of built-in date functions that you can use in your spreadsheets. When you install and activate the Analysis ToolPak add-in (see Book I, Chapter 3 for details), you have access to a number of additional Date functions — many of which are specially designed to deal with the normal Monday through Friday, five-day workweek (excluding, of course, your precious weekend days from the calculation).

TODAY

The easiest Date function has to be `TODAY`. This function takes no arguments and is always entered as follows:

```
=TODAY()
```

When you enter the TODAY function in a cell, Excel returns the current date by using the following Date format:

```
7/23/2003
```

Keep in mind that the date inserted into a cell with the TODAY function is not static. Whenever you open a worksheet that contains this function, Excel recalculates the function and updates its contents to the current date. This means that you don't usually use TODAY to input the current date when you're doing it for historical purposes (an invoice, for example) and never want it to change.

If you do use TODAY and then want to make the current date static in the spreadsheet, you need to convert the function into its serial number. You can do this for individual cells: First, select the cell, press F2 to activate Edit mode, press F9 to replace the TODAY function with today's serial number on the Formula bar, and click the Enter button to insert this serial number into the cell. You can do this conversion on a range of cells by selecting the range, copying it to the Clipboard (by pressing Ctrl+C), and then immediately pasting the calculated values into the same range (by choosing Edit⇨Paste Special to open the Paste Special dialog box and then clicking the Values radio button before you click OK).

DATE and DATEVALUE

The DATE function returns a date serial number for the date specified by the *year, month,* and *day* argument. This function uses the following syntax:

```
DATE(year,month,day)
```

This function comes in handy when you have a worksheet that contains the different parts of the date in separate columns, similar to the one shown in Figure 3-1. You can use it to combine the three columns of date information into a single date cell that you can use in sorting and filtering (see Book VI, Chapters 1 and 2 to find out how to sort and filter data).

D3 =DATE(C3,A3,B3)

	A	B	C	D
1				
2	Month	Day	Year	Date
3	2	15	1967	2/15/1967
4	7	23	1938	7/23/1938
5	11	6	1969	11/6/1969
6	1	6	1954	1/6/1954
7	3	13	1998	3/13/1998
8	7	30	1995	7/30/1995
9	5	14	2000	5/14/2000
10	12	12	2002	12/12/2002

Figure 3-1: Using the DATE function to combine separate date information into a single entry.

The DATEVALUE function returns the date serial number for a date that's been entered into the spreadsheet as text so that you can use it in date calculations. This function takes a single argument:

```
DATEVALUE(date_text)
```

Suppose, for example, that you've made the following text entry in cell B12:

```
'5/21/2003
```

You can then convert this text entry into a date serial number by entering the following formula in cell C12 next door:

```
=DATEVALUE(B12)
```

Excel then returns the date serial number, 37762 to cell C12, which you can convert into a more intelligible date by formatting it with one of Excel's Date number formats (Ctrl+1).

You must convert the DATE and DATEVALUE functions into their calculated date serial numbers in order to sort and filter them. To convert these functions individually, select a cell, press F2 to activate Edit mode, and then press F9 to replace the function with the calculated date serial number; finally, click the Enter button on the Formula bar to insert this serial number into the cell. To do this conversion on a range of cells, select the range, copy it to the Clipboard by pressing Ctrl+C, and then immediately paste the calculated serial numbers into the same range by choosing Edit⇨Paste Special to open the Paste Special dialog box and then clicking the Values radio button before you click OK.

DAY, WEEKDAY, MONTH, and YEAR

The DAY, WEEKDAY, MONTH, and YEAR date functions all return just parts of the date serial number that you specify as their argument:

- DAY(*serial_number*) to return the day of the month in the date (as a number between 1 and 31)
- WEEKDAY(*serial_number*,[*return-type*]) to return the day of the week (as a number between 1 and 7 or 0 and 6). The optional *return_type* argument is a number between 1 and 3; 1 (or no *return_type* argument) specifies the first type where 1 equals Sunday and 7 equals Saturday; 2 specifies the second type where 1 equals Monday and 7 equals Sunday; and 3 specifies the third type where 0 equals Monday and 6 equals Sunday.
- MONTH(*serial_number*) to return the number of the month in the date serial number (from 1 to 12).
- YEAR(*serial_number*) to return the number of the year (as an integer between 1900 and 9999) in the date serial number.

For example, if you enter the following DAY function in a cell as follows:

```
DAY(DATE(04,4,15))
```

Excel returns the value 15 to that cell. If, instead, you use the WEEKDAY function as follows:

```
WEEKDAY(DATE(04,4,15))
```

Excel returns the value 6, which represents Friday (using the first return_type where Sunday is 1 and Saturday is 7) because the optional *return_type* argument isn't specified. If you use the MONTH function on this date as in the following:

```
MONTH(DATE(04,4,15))
```

Excel returns 4 to the cell. If, however, you use the YEAR function on this date as in the following:

```
YEAR(DATE(04,4,15))
```

Excel returns 1904 to the cell (instead of 2004).

This means that if you want to enter a year in the twenty-first century as the *year* argument of the DATE function, you need to enter all four digits of the date, as in the following:

```
DATE(2004,4,15)
```

Note that you can use the YEAR function to calculate the difference in years between two dates. For example, if cell B12 contains 7/23/1938 and cell C12 contains 7/23/2003, you can enter the following formula using the YEAR function to determine the difference in years:

```
=YEAR(C12)-YEAR(B12)
```

Excel then returns 3/5/1900 to the cell containing this formula, which becomes 65 as soon as you apply the General number format to it (by pressing Ctrl+Shift+~).

Don't use these functions on dates entered as text entries. Always use the DATEVALUE function to convert these text dates and then use the DAY, WEEKDAY, MONTH, or YEAR functions on the serial numbers returned by the DATEVALUE function to ensure accurate results.

DAYS360

The DAYS360 function returns the number of days between two dates based on a 360-day year (that is, one in which there are 12 equal months of 30 days each). The DAYS360 function takes the following arguments:

```
DAYS360(start_date,end_date,[method])
```

The *start_date* and *end_date* arguments are date serial numbers or references to cells that contain such serial numbers. The optional *method* argument is either TRUE or FALSE, where FALSE specifies the use of the U.S. calculation method and TRUE specifies the use of the European calculation method:

- ✦ **U.S. (NASD) method** (FALSE or *method* argument omitted). In this method, if the starting date is equal to the 31st of the month, it becomes equal to the 30th of the same month; if the ending date is the 31st of a month and the starting date is earlier than the 30th of the month, the ending date becomes the 1st of the next month; otherwise, the ending date becomes equal to the 30th of the same month.
- ✦ **European method** (TRUE). In this method, starting and ending dates that occur on the 31st of a month become equal to the 30th of the same month.

Analysis ToolPak Date Functions

When you activate the Analysis ToolPak add-in, Excel adds six new Date functions to the Date and Time category in the Insert Function dialog box (see Book I, Chapter 3 for details on installing and activating the Analysis ToolPak add-ins). These Date functions expand your abilities to do date calculations in the worksheet — especially those that only work with normal, Monday through Friday workdays.

Note that when typing in functions included in the Analysis ToolPak, Excel does not display the arguments that each function requires as a ToolTip (this only occurs when typing in built-in Excel functions). For that reason, you may want to insert them into your formulas with the Insert Function button on the Formula bar. This way, you find out what arguments are required when you open the function's Function Arguments dialog box.

EDATE

The EDATE (for Elapsed Date) function calculates a future or past date that is so many months ahead or behind the date that you specify as its *start_date* argument. You can use the EDATE function to quickly determine the particular date at a particular interval in the future or past (for example, three months ahead or one month ago).

The EDATE function takes two arguments:

```
EDATE(start_date,months)
```

The *start_date* argument is the date serial number that you want used as the base date. The *months* argument is a positive (for future dates) or negative (for past dates) integer that represents the number of months ahead or months past to calculate.

For example, suppose that you enter the following EDATE function in a cell:

```
=EDATE(DATE(2004,1, 31),1)
```

Excel returns the date serial number, 38046, which becomes 2/29/2004 when you apply the first Date format to its cell.

EOMONTH

The EOMONTH (for End of Month) function calculates the last day of the month that is so many months ahead or behind the date that you specify as its *start_date* argument. You can use the EOMONTH function to quickly determine the end of the month at a set interval in the future or past.

For example, suppose that you enter the following EOMONTH function in a cell:

```
=EOMONTH(DATE(2000,1,1),1)
```

Excel returns the date serial number, 36585, which becomes 2/29/2000 when you apply the first Date format to its cell.

NETWORKDAYS

The NETWORKDAYS function returns the number of workdays that exist between a starting date and ending date that you specify as arguments:

```
NETWORKDAYS(start_date,end_date,[holidays])
```

When using this function, you can also specify a cell range in the worksheet or array constant to use as an optional *holidays* argument that lists the state, federal, and floating holidays observed by your company. Excel then excludes any dates listed in the *holidays* argument when they occur in between *start_date* and *end_date* arguments.

Figure 3-2 illustrates how this function works. In this worksheet, I created a list in the cell range B3:B13 with all the observed holidays in the calendar year 2003. I then entered the following NETWORKDAYS function in cell E4:

```
NETWORKDAYS(DATE(2002,12,31),DATE(2003,12,31),B3:B13)
```

The preceding function calculates the number of workdays between December 31, 2002 and December 31, 2003 (262 total work days) and then subtracts the dates listed in the cell range B3:B13 if they fall on a week day. As all 11 holidays in the cell the range B3:B13 happen to fall on a weekday in the year 2003, the number of work days between December 31, 2002 and December 31, 2003 is calculated as 251 in cell E14 (262 – 11 = 251)

Microsoft Excel - Work Days 2003.xls

E4 =NETWORKDAYS(DATE(2002,12,31),DATE(2003,12,31),B3:B13)

	A	B	C	D	E
1	**2003 List of Observed Holidays**				
2	**Holiday**	**Date**			
3	New Year's Day	1/1/2003		Work Days in 2003	262
4	Martin Luther King Day	1/20/2003		Work Days minus week day holidays	251
5	President's Day	2/17/2003			
6	Memorial Day	5/26/2003			
7	Independence Day	7/4/2003			
8	Labor Day	9/1/2003			
9	Veteran's Day	11/11/2003			
10	Thanksgiving Day	11/27/2003			
11	Day after Thanksgiving	11/28/2003			
12	Christmas Day	12/25/2003			
13	Day after Christmas	12/26/2003			

Figure 3-2: Using the NETWORKDAYS function to find the number of workdays between two dates.

WEEKNUM

The WEEKNUM function returns a number indicating where the week in a particular date falls within the year. This function takes the following arguments:

```
WEEKNUM(serial_number,[return_type])
```

In this function, the *serial_number* argument is the date whose week in the year you want to determine. The optional *return_type* argument is number 1 or 2, where number 1 (or omitted) indicates that the new week begins on Sunday and weekdays are numbered from 1 to 7, and number 2 indicates that the new week begins on Monday and weekdays are also numbered from 1 to 7.

For example, if you enter the following WEEKNUM function in a cell:

```
=WEEKNUM(DATE(2003,1,19))
```

Excel returns the number 4, indicating that the week containing the date January 19, 2003 is the fourth week in the year when the Sunday is considered to be the first day of the week (January 19, 2003 is a Sunday). Note that if I had added 2 as the optional *return-type* argument, Excel would return 3 as the result because January 19, 2003 is deemed to fall on the last day of the third week of the year when Monday is considered the first day of the week.

WORKDAY

You can use the WORKDAY function to find out the date that is so many workdays before or after a particular date. This function takes the following arguments:

```
WORKDAY(start_date,days,[holidays])
```

The *start_date* argument is the initial date that you want used in calculating the date of the workday that falls so many day before or after it. The *days* argument is the number of workdays ahead (positive integer) or behind (negative integer) the *start_date*. The optional *holidays* argument is an array constant or cell range that contains the dates of the holidays that should be excluded (when they fall on a weekday) in calculating the new date.

For example, suppose that you want to determine a due date for a report that is 30 workdays after February 2, 2003 (Groundhog Day) by using the same holiday schedule entered in the cell range B3:B11 in the Work Days 2003 workbook, shown in Figure 3-2. To do this, you enter the following formula:

```
=WORKDAY(DATE(2003,2,1),30,B3:B11)
```

Excel then returns the serial number 37697 to the cell, which then appears as March 17, 2003 (St. Patrick's Day) when you format it with the first Date format.

YEARFRAC

The YEARFRAC (for Year Fraction) function enables you to calculate the fraction of the year, which is computed from the number of days between two dates. You can use the YEARFRAC function to determine the proportion of a whole year's benefits or obligations to assign to a specific period.

The YEARFRAC function uses the following arguments:

```
YEARFRAC(start_date,end_date,[basis])
```

The optional *basis* argument in the YEARFRAC is a number between 0 and 4 that determines the day count basis to use in determining the fractional part of the year:

- 0 (or omitted) to base it on the U.S. (NASD) method of 30/360 (see DAYS360 earlier in the chapter for details on the U.S. method)
- 1 to base the fraction on actual days/actual days
- 2 to base the fraction on actual days/360
- 3 to base the fraction on actual days/365
- 4 to base the fraction on the European method of 30/360 (see DAYS360 earlier in the chapter for details on the European method)

For example, if you enter the following YEARFRAC formula in a cell to find what percentage of the year remains as of October 15, 2003:

```
=YEARFRAC(DATE(2003,10,15),DATE(2003,12,31),2)
```

Excel returns the decimal value 0.213889 to the cell, indicating that just over 21 percent of the year remains.

Using Time Functions

Excel offers much fewer Time functions when compared to the wide array of Date functions. Like the Date functions, however, the Time functions enable you to convert text entries representing times of day into time serial numbers so that you can use them in calculations. The Time functions also include functions for combining different parts of a time into a single serial time number, as well as those for extracting the hours, minutes, and seconds from a single time serial number.

NOW

The NOW function gives you the current time and date based on your computer's internal clock. You can use the NOW function to date- and time-stamp the worksheet. Like the TODAY function, NOW takes no arguments and is automatically recalculated every time you open the spreadsheet:

```
=NOW()
```

When you enter the NOW function in a cell, Excel puts the date before the current time. It also formats the date with the first Date format and the time with 24-hour Time format. So, if the current date were July 23, 2004 and the current time were 1:44 p.m. at the moment when Excel calculates the NOW function, your cell would contain the following entry:

```
7/23/2004 13:44
```

Note that the combination date/time format that the NOW function uses is a custom number format. If you want to assign a different date/time to the date and time serial numbers returned by this function, you have to create your own custom number format and then assign it to the cell that contains the NOW function (see Book II, Chapter 2 for information on creating custom number formats).

TIME and TIMEVALUE

The TIME function enables you to create a decimal number representing a time serial number, ranging from 0 (zero) to 0.99999999, representing time 0:00:00 (12:00:00 AM) to 23:59:59 (11:59:59 PM). You can use the TIME function to combine the hours, minutes, and seconds of a time into a single time serial number when these parts are stored in separate cells.

The TIME function takes the following arguments:

```
TIME(hour,minute,second)
```

When specifying the *hour* argument, you use a number between 0 and 23 (any number greater than 23 is divided by 24 and the remainder is used as the hour value). When specifying the *minute* and *second* arguments, you use a number between 0 and 59 (any *minute* argument greater than 59 is converted into hours and minutes, just as any *second* argument greater than 59 is converted into hours, minutes, and seconds).

For example, if cell A3 contains 4, cell B3 contains 37, and cell C3 contains 0 and you enter the following TIME function in cell D3:

```
=TIME(A3,B3,C3)
```

Excel enters 4:37 a.m. in cell D3. If you then assign the General number format to this cell (Ctrl+Shift+~), it would then contain the time serial number, 0.192361.

The TIMEVALUE function converts a time entered or imported into the spreadsheet as a text entry into its equivalent time serial number so that you can use it in time calculations. The TIMEVALUE function uses a single *time_text* argument as follows:

```
TIMEVALUE(time_text)
```

So, for example, if you put the following TIMEVALUE function in a cell to determine the time serial number for 10:35:25:

```
=TIMEVALUE("10:35:25")
```

Excel returns the time serial number 0.441262 to the cell. If you then assign the first Time number format to this cell, the decimal number appears as 10:35:25 a.m. in the cell.

HOUR, MINUTE, and SECOND

The HOUR, MINUTE, and SECOND functions enable you to extract specific parts of a time value in the spreadsheet. Each of these three Time functions takes a single *serial_number* argument that contains the hour, minute, or second that you want to extract.

So, for example, if cell B5 contains the time 1:30:10 p.m. (otherwise known as serial number 0.5626157) and you enter the following HOUR function in cell C5:

```
=HOUR(B5)
```

Excel returns 13 as the hour to cell C5 (hours are always returned in 24-hour time). If you then enter the following MINUTE function in cell D5:

```
=MINUTE(B5)
```

Excel returns 30 as the number of minutes to cell D5. Finally, if you enter the following SECOND function in cell E5:

```
=SECOND(B5)
```

Excel returns 10 as the number of seconds to cell E5.

Chapter 4: Financial Formulas

In This Chapter

- **Understanding how Excel rounds up values**
- **Using basic investment functions**
- **Using basic depreciation functions**
- **Using basic currency conversion functions**

Money! There's nothing quite like it: you can't live with it and you certainly can't live without it, and many of the spreadsheets that you work with exist only to let you know how much of it you can expect to come in or how much of it you can expect to pay out. Excel contains a fair number of sophisticated financial functions for determining such things as the present, future, or net present value of an investment; the payment, number of periods, or the principal or interest part of a payment on an amortized loan; the rate of return on an investment; or the depreciation of your favorite assets.

By activating the Analysis ToolPak add-in, you add over 30 specialized financial functions that run the gamut from those that calculate the accrued interest for a security paying interest periodically and only at maturity, all the way to those that calculate the internal rate of return and the net present value for a schedule of non-periodic cash flows.

Financial Functions 101

The key to using any of Excel's financial functions is to understand the terminology used by their arguments. Many of the most common financial functions, such as PV (Present Value), NPV (Net Present Value), FV (Future Value), and PMT (Payment), take similar arguments:

- **PV** is the present value that is the principal amount of the annuity.
- **FV** is the future value that represents the principal plus interest on the annuity.
- **PMT** is the payment made each period in the annuity. Normally, the payment is set over the life of the annuity and includes principal plus interest without any other fees.

- **RATE** is the interest rate per period. Normally, the rate is expressed as an annual percentage.
- **NPER** is the total number of payment periods in the life of the annuity. You calculate this number by taking the Term (the amount of time that interest is paid) and multiplying it by the Period (the point in time when interest is paid or earned) so that a loan with a three-year term with 12 monthly interest payments has 3 × 12, or 36 payment periods.

When using financial functions, keep in mind that the `fv`, `pv`, or `pmt` arguments can be positive or negative, depending on whether you're receiving the money (as in the case of an investment) or paying out the money (as in the case of a loan). Also keep in mind that you want to express the `rate` argument in the same units as the `nper` argument, so that if you make monthly payments on a loan and you express the `nper` as the total number of monthly payments, as in 360 (30 × 12) for a 30-year mortgage, you need to express the annual interest rate in monthly terms as well. For example, if you pay an annual interest rate of 7.5 percent on the loan, you express the `rate` argument as 0.075/12 so that it is monthly as well.

The PV, NPV, and FV functions

The PV (Present Value), NPV (Net Present Value), and FV (Future Value) functions enable you to determine the profitability of an investment.

Calculating the Present Value

The PV, or present value, function returns the present value of an investment, which is the total amount that a series of future payments is worth presently. The syntax of the PV function is as follows:

```
=PV(rate,nper,pmt,[fv],[type])
```

The *fv* and *type* arguments are optional arguments in the function (indicated by the square brackets). The *fv* argument is the future value or cash balance that you want to have after making your last payment. If you omit the *fv* argument, Excel assumes a future value of zero (0). The *type* argument indicates whether the payment is made at the beginning or end of the period: Enter 0 (or omit the *type* argument) when the payment is made at the end of the period and use 1 when it is made at the beginning of the period.

Figure 4-1 contains several examples using the PV function. All three PV functions use the same annual percentage rate of 7¼ percent and term of 10 years. Because payments are made monthly, each function converts these annual figures into monthly ones. For example, in the PV function in cell E3, the annual interest rate in cell A3 is converted into a monthly rate by dividing by 12 (A3/12), and the annual term in cell B3 is converted into equivalent monthly periods by multiplying by 12 (B3×12).

Microsoft Excel - PVSHEET.XLS [Read-Only]

E3 =PV(A3/12,B3*12,C3)

	A	B	C	D	E	F
1						
2	Annual Interest Rate	Term in years	Payment	Future Value	Present Value	Formula
3	7.25%	10	($218.46)		$18,608.01	=PV(A3/12,B3*12,C3)
4						
5	7.25%	10	($218.46)		$18,607.53	=PV(A5/12,B5*12,C5,1)
6						
7	7.25%	10		$8,000.00	($3,883.06)	=PV(A7/12,B7*12,,D7)

Figure 4-1: Using the PV function to calculate the present value of various investments.

Note that although the PV functions in cells E3 and E5 use the `rate`, `nper`, and `pmt` ($218.46) arguments, their results are slightly different. This is caused by the difference in the `type` argument in the two functions: the PV function in cell E3 assumes that each payment is made at the end of the period (the `type` argument is 0 whenever it is omitted), while the PV function in cell E5 assumes that each payment is made at the beginning of the period (indicated by a `type` argument of 1). When the payment is made at the beginning of the period, the present value of this investment is $0.49 higher than when the payment is made at the end of the period, reflecting the interest accrued during the last period.

The third example in cell E7 (shown in Figure 4-1) uses the PV function with an `fv` argument instead of the `pmt` argument. In this example, the PV function states that you would have to make monthly payments of $3,883.06 for a 10-year period to realize a cash balance of $8,000, assuming that the investment returned a constant annual interest rate of 7¼ percent. Note that when you use the PV function with the `fv` argument instead of the `pmt` argument, you must still indicate the position of the `pmt` argument in the function with a comma (thus the two commas in a row in the function) so that Excel doesn't mistake your `fv` argument for the `pmt` argument.

Calculating the Net Present Value

The NPV function calculates the net present value based on a series of cash flows. The syntax of this function is

```
=NPV(rate,value1,[value2],[...])
```

where `value1`, `value2`, and so on are between 1 to 13 value arguments representing a series of payments (negative values) and income (positive values), each of which is equally spaced in time and occurs at the end of the period. The NPV investment begins one period before the period of the `value1` cash flow and ends with the last cash flow in the argument list. If your first cash flow occurs at the beginning of the period, you must add it to the result of the NPV function rather than include it as one of the arguments.

Figure 4-2 illustrates the use of the NPV function to evaluate the attractiveness of a five-year investment that requires an initial investment of $30,000 (the value in cell G3). The first year, you expect a loss of $22,000 (cell B3); the second year, a profit of $15,000 (cell C3); the third year, a profit of $25,000 (cell D3); the fourth year, a profit of $32,000 (cell E3); and the fifth year, a profit of $38,000 (cell F3). Note that these cell references are used as the `value` arguments of the NPV function.

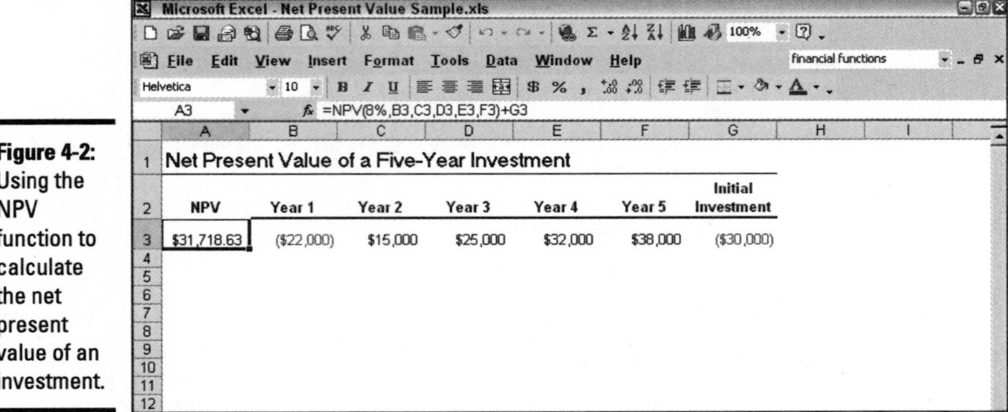

Figure 4-2: Using the NPV function to calculate the net present value of an investment.

Unlike when using the PV function, the NPV function doesn't require an even stream of cash flows. The `rate` argument in the function is set at 8 percent. In this example, this represents the discount rate of the investment; that is, the interest rate that you may expect to get during the five-year period if you put your money into some other type of investment, such as a high-yield money-market account. This NPV function in cell A3 returns a net present value of $31,718.63, indicating that you can expect to realize about $1,719 more from investing your $30,000 in this investment than you would from investing the money in a money-market account at an interest rate of 8 percent.

Calculating the Future Value

The FV function calculates the future value of an investment. The syntax of this function is

```
=FV(rate,nper,pmt,[pv],[type])
```

The *rate*, *nper*, *pmt*, and *type* arguments are the same as those used by the PV function. The *pv* argument is the present value or lump-sum amount for which you want to calculate the future value. As with the *fv* and *type* arguments in the PV function, both the *pv* and *type* arguments are optional in the FV function. If you omit these arguments, Excel assumes their values to be zero (0) in the function.

You can use the FV function to calculate the future value of an investment like IRA (Individual Retirement Account). For example, suppose that you establish an IRA at age 43 and will retire 22 years hence at age 65 and that you plan to make annual payments into the IRA at the beginning of each year. If you assume a rate of return of 8.5 percent a year, you would enter the following FV function in your worksheet:

```
=FV(8.5%,22,-1000,,1)
```

Excel then indicates that you can expect a future value of $64,053.66 for your IRA when you retire at age 65. If you had established the IRA a year prior and the account already has a present value of $1,085, you would amend the FV function as follows:

```
=FV(8.5%,22,-1000,-1085,1)
```

In this case, Excel indicates that you can expect a future value of $70,583.22 for your IRA at retirement.

The PMT function

The PMT function calculates the periodic payment for an annuity, assuming a stream of equal payments and a constant rate of interest. The PMT function uses the following syntax:

```
=PMT(rate,nper,pv,[fv],[type])
```

As with the other common financial functions, *rate* is the interest rate per period, *nper* is the number of periods, *pv* is the present value or the amount the future payments are worth presently, *fv* is the future value or cash balance that you want after the last payment is made (Excel assumes a future value of zero when you omit this optional argument as you would when calculating loan payments), and *type* is the value 0 for payments made at the end of the period or the value 1 for payments made at the beginning of the period (if you omit the optional *type* argument, Excel assumes that the payment is made at the end of the period).

The PMT function is often used to calculate the payment for mortgage loans that have a fixed rate of interest. Figure 4-3 shows you a sample worksheet that contains a table using the PMT function to calculate loan payments for a range of interest rates (from 6½ percent to 7¾ percent) and principals ($350,000 to $359,000). The table uses the initial principal that you enter in cell B2 and copies it to cell A7 and then increases it by $1,000 in the range A8:A16. The table uses the initial interest rate that you enter in cell B3 and copies to cell B6 and then increases this initial rate by ¼ of a percent in the range C6:G6. The term in years in cell B4 is a constant factor that is used in the entire loan payment table.

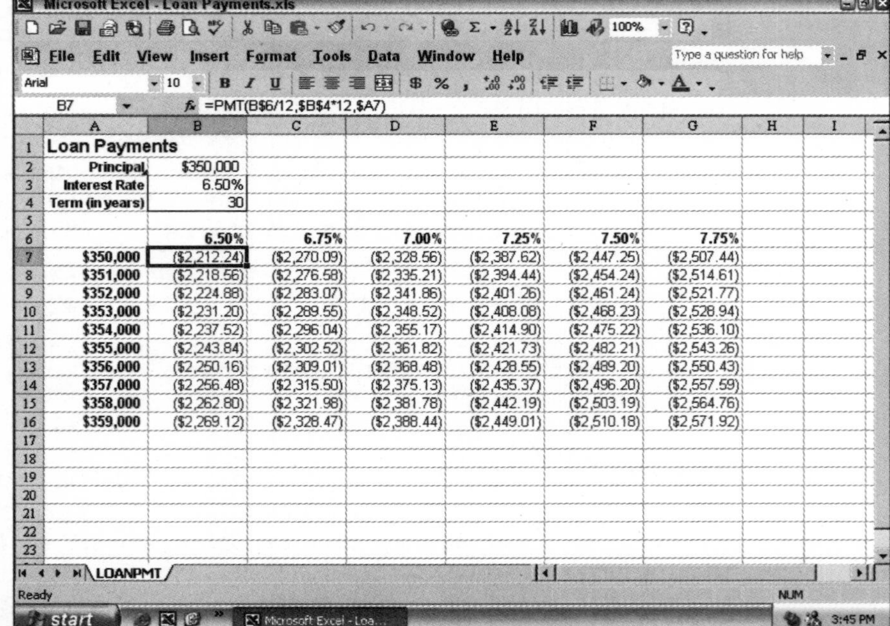

	A	B	C	D	E	F	G
1	Loan Payments						
2	Principal	$350,000					
3	Interest Rate	6.50%					
4	Term (in years)	30					
5							
6		6.50%	6.75%	7.00%	7.25%	7.50%	7.75%
7	$350,000	($2,212.24)	($2,270.09)	($2,328.56)	($2,387.62)	($2,447.25)	($2,507.44)
8	$351,000	($2,218.56)	($2,276.58)	($2,335.21)	($2,394.44)	($2,454.24)	($2,514.61)
9	$352,000	($2,224.88)	($2,283.07)	($2,341.86)	($2,401.26)	($2,461.24)	($2,521.77)
10	$353,000	($2,231.20)	($2,289.55)	($2,348.52)	($2,408.08)	($2,468.23)	($2,528.94)
11	$354,000	($2,237.52)	($2,296.04)	($2,355.17)	($2,414.90)	($2,475.22)	($2,536.10)
12	$355,000	($2,243.84)	($2,302.52)	($2,361.82)	($2,421.73)	($2,482.21)	($2,543.26)
13	$356,000	($2,250.16)	($2,309.01)	($2,368.48)	($2,428.55)	($2,489.20)	($2,550.43)
14	$357,000	($2,256.48)	($2,315.50)	($2,375.13)	($2,435.37)	($2,496.20)	($2,557.59)
15	$358,000	($2,262.80)	($2,321.98)	($2,381.78)	($2,442.19)	($2,503.19)	($2,564.76)
16	$359,000	($2,269.12)	($2,328.47)	($2,388.44)	($2,449.01)	($2,510.18)	($2,571.92)

Figure 4-3: Loan Payments table using the PMT function to calculate various loan payments.

To get an idea of how easy it is to build this type of loan payment table with the PMT function, follow these steps for creating it in a new worksheet:

1. **Enter the titles** Loan Payments **in cell A1,** Principal **in cell A2,** Interest Rate **in cell A3, and** Term (in years) **in cell A4.**

2. **Enter** $350,000 **in cell B2, enter** 6.50% **in cell B3, and enter** 30 **in B4.**

   These are the starting values with which you build the Loan Payments table.

3. **Position the cell pointer in B6 and then build the formula =B3.**

   By creating a linking formula that brings forward the value in B3 with the formula, you ensure that the value in B6 will immediately reflect any change that you make in cell B3.

4. **Position the cell pointer in cell C6 and then build the formula =B6+.25%.**

   By adding ¼ of a percent to the interest rate to the value in B6 with the formula =B6+.25% in C6 rather than creating a series with the AutoFill handle, you ensure that the value in cell C6 will always be ¼ of a percent larger than any value entered in cell B6.

5. **Drag the Fill handle in cell C6 to extend the selection to the right to cell G6 and then release the mouse button.**

6. **Position the cell pointer in cell A7 and then build the formula =B2.**

   Again, by using the formula =B2 to bring the initial principal forward to cell A7, you ensure that A7 always has the same value as cell B2.

7. **Position the cell pointer in A8 active and then build the formula =A7+1000.**

   Here too, you use the formula =A7+1000 rather than create a series with the AutoFill feature so that the value in A8 will always be 1000 greater than any value placed in cell A7.

8. **Drag the Fill handle in cell A8 down until you extend the selection to cell A16 and then release the mouse button.**

9. **In cell B7, click the Insert Function button on the Formula bar, and then Financial in the Or Select a Category drop-down list, and then double-click the PMT function in the Select a Function list box.**

   The Function Arguments dialog box opens, where you specify the `rate`, `nper`, and `pv` arguments. Be sure to move the Function Arguments dialog box to the right so that no part of it obscures the data in column A and B of your worksheet before proceeding with the following steps for filling in the arguments.

10. **Click cell B6 to insert B6 in the Rate text box and then press F4 twice to convert the relative reference B6 to the mixed reference B$6 (column relative, row absolute) before you type** /12.

    You convert the relative cell reference B6 to the mixed reference B$6 so that Excel does *not* adjust the row number when you copy the PMT formula down each row of the table, but *does* adjust the column letter when you copy the formula across its columns. Because the initial interest rate entered in B3 (and then brought forward to cell B6) is an *annual* interest rate, but you want to know the *monthly* loan payment, you need to convert the annual rate to a monthly rate by dividing the value in cell B6 by 12.

11. **Click the Nper text box, click cell B4 to insert this cell reference in this text box, and then press F4 once to convert the relative reference B4 to the absolute reference $B$4 before you type** *12.

    You need to convert the relative cell reference B4 to the absolute reference $B$4 so that Excel adjusts neither the row number nor the column letter when you copy the PMT formula down the rows and across the columns of the table. Because the term in B3 (which is then brought forward to cell B6) is an *annual* period, but you want to know the *monthly* loan payment, you need to convert the yearly periods to monthly periods by multiplying the value in cell B4 by 12.

12. **Click the Pv text box, then click A7 to insert this cell reference in this text box, and then press F4 three times to convert the relative reference A7 to the mixed reference $A7 (column absolute, row relative).**

    You need to convert the relative cell reference A7 to the mixed reference $A7 so that Excel won't adjust the column letter when you copy the PMT formula across each column of the table, but will adjust the row number when you copy the formula down across its rows.

13. **Click OK to insert the formula =PMT(B$6/12,$B$4*12,$A7) in cell B7.**

    Now you're ready to copy this original PMT formula down and then over to fill in the entire Loan Payments table.

14. **Drag the Fill handle on cell B7 down until you extend the fill range to cell B16 and then release the mouse button.**

    After you've copied the original PMT formula down to cell B16, you're ready to copy it to the right to G16.

15. **Drag the Fill handle to the right until you extend the fill range B7:B16 to cell G16 and then release the mouse button.**

After copying the original formula with the Fill handle, be sure to widen columns B through G sufficiently to display their results (you can do this in one step by dragging through the headers of these columns and then double-clicking the right border of column G).

After you've created a loan table like this, you can then change the beginning principal or interest rate, as well as the term to see what the payments would be under various other scenarios. You can also turn on the Manual Recalculation so that you can control when the Loan Payments table is recalculated.

For information on how to switch to Manual Recalculation and use this mode to control when formulas are recalculated, see Chapter 1 in this book. For information on how to protect the worksheet so that users can input new values only into the three input cells (B2, B3, and B4) to change the starting loan amount, interest rate, and the term of the loan, see Book IV, Chapter 2.

Depreciation functions

Excel lets you choose between four different Depreciation functions, each of which uses a slightly different method for depreciating an asset over time. These built-in Depreciation functions include:

- SLN(*cost,salvage,life*) to calculate straight-line depreciation
- SYD(*cost,salvage,life,period*) to calculate sum-of-years-digits depreciation
- DB(*cost,salvage,life,period,*[*month*]) to calculate declining balance depreciation
- DDB(*cost,salvage,life,period,*[*factor*]) to calculate double-declining balance depreciation

As you can see, with the exception of the optional `month` argument in the DB function and the optional `factor` argument in the DDB function, all of the Depreciation functions require the `cost`, `salvage` and `life` arguments and all but the SLN function require a `period` argument as well:

- `Cost` is the initial cost of the asset that you're depreciating.
- `Salvage` is the value of the asset at the end of the depreciation (also known as the salvage value of the asset).
- `Life` is the number of periods over which the asset is depreciating (also known as the useful life of the asset).
- `Period` is the period over which the asset is being depreciated. The units that you use in the period argument must be the same as those used in the `life` argument of the Depreciation function so that if you express the `life` argument in years, you must also express the `period` argument in years.

Note that DB function accepts an optional `month` argument. This argument is the number of months that the asset is in use in the first year. If you omit the `month` argument from your DB function, Excel assumes the number of months of service to be 12.

When using the DDB function to calculate double-declining balance method of depreciation, you can add an optional `factor` argument. This argument is the rate at which the balance declines in the depreciation schedule. If you omit this optional `factor` argument, Excel assumes the rate to be 2 (thus, the name *double-declining balance*).

Figure 4-4 contains a Depreciation table that uses all four depreciation methods to calculate the depreciation of office furniture originally costing $50,000 to be depreciated over a 10-year period, assuming a salvage value of $1,000 at the end of this depreciation period.

The Formula bar shown in Figure 4-4 shows the SLN formula that I entered into cell B9:

```
=B8-SLN($B$3,$B$5,$B$4)
```

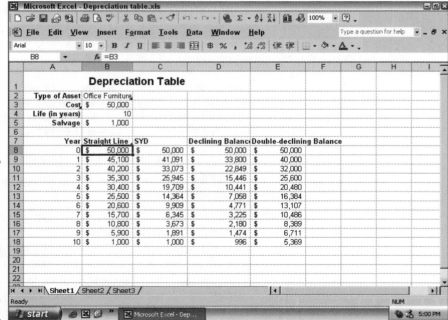

Microsoft Excel - Depreciation table.xls

B8 =B3

Depreciation Table

Type of Asset	Office Furniture			
Cost	$ 50,000			
Life (in years)	10			
Salvage	$ 1,000			
Year	**Straight Line**	**SYD**	**Declining Balanc**	**Double-declining Balance**
0	$ 50,000	$ 50,000	$ 50,000	$ 50,000
1	$ 45,100	$ 41,091	$ 33,800	$ 40,000
2	$ 40,200	$ 33,073	$ 22,849	$ 32,000
3	$ 35,300	$ 25,945	$ 15,446	$ 25,600
4	$ 30,400	$ 19,709	$ 10,441	$ 20,480
5	$ 25,500	$ 14,364	$ 7,058	$ 16,384
6	$ 20,600	$ 9,909	$ 4,771	$ 13,107
7	$ 15,700	$ 6,345	$ 3,225	$ 10,486
8	$ 10,800	$ 3,673	$ 2,180	$ 8,389
9	$ 5,900	$ 1,891	$ 1,474	$ 6,711
10	$ 1,000	$ 1,000	$ 996	$ 5,369

Figure 4-4: Depreciation Table showing 10-year depreciation of an asset using various methods.

This formula subtracts the amount of straight-line depreciation to be taken in the first year of service from the original cost of $50,000 (this value is brought forward from cell B3 by the formula =B3). After creating this original formula in cell B9, I then used the Fill handle to copy it down to cell B18, which contains the final salvage value of the asset in the 10th year of service.

Cell C9 contains a similar formula for calculating the sum-of-years-digits depreciation for the office furniture. This cell contains the following formula:

```
=C8-SYD($B$3,$B$5,$B$4,$A9)
```

This formula subtracts the amount of sum-of-years-digits depreciation to be taken at the end of the first year from the original cost of $50,000 in cell C8 (also brought forward from cell B3 by the formula =B3). After creating this original formula in cell C9, I again used the Fill handle to copy it down to cell C18, which also contains the final salvage value of the asset in the 10th year of service.

I used the same basic procedure to create the formulas using the DB and DDB depreciation methods in the cell ranges D8:D18 and E8:E18, respectively. Cell D9 contains the following DB formula:

```
=D8-DB($B$3,$B$5,$B$4,$A9)
```

Cell E9 contains the following DDB formula:

```
=E8-DDB($B$3,$B$5,$B$4,$A9)
```

Note that like the SYD function, both of these depreciation functions require the use of a *period* argument, which is supplied by the list of years in the cell range A9:A18. Note also, that the values in cell B4 that supplies the *life* argument to the SYD, DB, and DDB functions matches the year units used in this cell range.

Analysis ToolPak financial functions

By activating the Analysis ToolPak add-in (Tools⇨Add-Ins), you add a whole bunch of powerful financial functions to Excel. Table 4-1 shows all the financial functions that are added to the Insert Function dialog box when the Analysis ToolPak is activated. As you can see from this table, the Analysis ToolPak financial functions are varied and quite sophisticated.

Table 4-1 The Financial Functions Included in the Analysis ToolPak

Function	*What It Calculates*
ACCRINT(*issue,first_interest,settlement, rate,*[*par*],*frequency,*[*basis*])	Calculates the accrued interest for a security that pays periodic interest.
ACCRINTM(*issue,maturity,rate,* [*par*],[*basis*])	Calculates the accrued interest for a security that pays interest at maturity.
AMORDEGRC(*cost,date_purchased, first_period,salvage,period,rate,basis*) and AMORLINC(*cost,date_purchased, first_period,salvage,period,rate,basis*)	Used in French accounting systems for calculating depreciation. AMORDEGRC and AMORLINC return the depreciation for each accounting period. AMORDEGRC works like AMORLINC except that it applies a depreciation coefficient in the calculation that depends upon the life of the assets.
COUPDAYBS(*settlement,maturity, frequency,*[*basis*])	Calculates the number of days from the beginning of a coupon period to the settlement date.
COUPDAYS(*settlement,maturity, frequency,*[*basis*])	Calculates the number of days in the coupon period.
COUPDAYSNC(*settlement,maturity, frequency,*[*basis*])	Calculates the number of days from the settlement date to the next coupon date.
COUPNCD(*settlement,maturity, frequency,*[*basis*])	Calculates a number that represents the next coupon date after a settlement date.
COUPNUM(*settlement,maturity, frequency,*[*basis*])	Calculates the number of coupons payable between the settlement date and maturity date, rounded up to the nearest whole coupon.
COUPPCD(*settlement,maturity, frequency,*[*basis*])	Calculates a number that represents the previous coupon date before the settlement date.
CUMIPMT(*rate,nper,pv,start_period, end_period,type*)	Calculates the cumulative interest paid on a loan between the start_period and end_period. The type argument is 0 when the payment is made at the end of the period and 1 when it's made at the beginning of the period.
CUMPRINC(*rate,nper,pv,start_period, end_period,type*)	Calculates the cumulative principal paid on a loan between the start_period and end_period. The type argument is 0 when the payment is made at the end of the period and 1 when it's made at the beginning of the period.
DISC(*settlement,maturity,pr, redemption,*[*basis*])	Calculates the discount rate for a security.

Function	What It Calculates
DOLLARDE(*fractional_dollar,fraction*)	Converts a dollar price expressed as a fraction into a dollar price expressed as a decimal number.
DOLLARFR(*decimal_dollar,fraction*)	Converts a dollar price expressed as a decimal number into a dollar price expressed as a fraction.
DURATION(*settlement,maturity,coupon, yld,frequency,*[*basis*])	Calculates the Macauley duration for an assumed par value of $100 (duration is defined as the weighted average of the present value of the cash flows and is used as a measure of the response of a bond price to changes in yield).
EFFECT(*nominal_rate,npery*)	Calculates the effective annual interest rate given the nominal interest rate and the number of compounding periods per year.
INTRATE(*settlement,maturity, investment,redemption,*[*basis*])	Calculates the interest rate for a fully invested security.
MDURATION(*settlement,maturity, coupon,yld,frequency,*[*basis*])	Calculates the modified Macauley duration for a security with an assumed part value of $100.
NOMINAL(*effect_rate,npery*)	Calculates the nominal annual interest rate given the effect rate and the number of compounding periods per year.
ODDPRICE(*settlement,maturity,issue, first_coupon,rate,yld,redemption, frequency,*[*basis*])	Calculates the price per $100 face value of a security having an odd (short or long) first period.
ODDFYYIELD(*settlement,maturity, issue,first_coupon,rate,pr,redemption, frequency,*[*basis*])	Calculates the yield of a security that has an odd (short or long) first period.
ODDLPRICE(*settlement,maturity, last_interest,rate,yld,redemption, frequency,*[*basis*])	Calculates the price per $100 face value of a security having an odd (short or long) last coupon period.
ODDLYIELD(*settlement,maturity, last_interest,rate,pr,redemption, frequency,*[*basis*])	Calculates the yield of a security that has an odd (short or long) last period.
PRICE(*settlement,maturity,rate,yld, redemption,frequency,*[*basis*])	Calculates the price per $100 face value of a security that pays periodic interest.
PRICEDISC(*settlement,maturity, discount,redemption,*[*basis*])	Calculates the price per $100 face value of a discounted security.
PRICEMAT(*settlement,maturity,issue, rate,yld,*[*basis*])	Calculates the price per $100 face value of a security that pays interest at maturity.

(continued)

Table 4-1 (continued)

Function	*What It Calculates*
RECEIVED(*settlement,maturity, investment,discount,*[*basis*])	Calculates the amount received at maturity for a fully invested security.
TBILLEQ(*settlement,maturity,discount*)	Calculates the bond-equivalent yield for a Treasury bill.
TBILLPRICE(*settlement,maturity, discount*)	Calculates the price per $100 face value for a Treasury bill.
TBILLYIELD(*settlement,maturity,pr*)	Calculates the yield for a Treasury bill.
XIRR(*values,dates,*[*guess*])	Calculates the internal rate of return for a schedule of cash flows that are not periodic.
XNPV(*rate,values,dates*)	Calculates the net present value for a schedule of cash flows that are not periodic.
YIELD(*settlement,maturity,rate,pr, redemption,frequency,*[*basis*])	Calculates the yield on a security that pays periodic interest (used to calculate bond yield).
YIELDDISC(*settlement,maturity,pr, redemption,*[*basis*])	Calculates the annual yield for a discounted security.
YIELDMAT(*settlement,maturity,issue, rate,pr,*[*basis*])	Calculates the annual yield of a security that pays interest at maturity.

You may note in Table 4-1 that many of the Analysis ToolPak financial functions make use of an optional `basis` argument. This optional `basis` argument is a number between 0 and 4 that determines the day count basis to use in determining the fractional part of the year:

- 0 (or omitted) to base it on the U.S. (NASD) method of 30/360 (see the DAYS360 function in Chapter 3 in this book for details on the U.S. method)
- 1 to base the fraction on actual days/actual days
- 2 to base the fraction on actual days/360
- 3 to base the fraction on actual days/365
- 4 to base the fraction on the European method of 30/360 (see the DAYS360 function in Chapter 3 in this book for details on the European method)

For detailed information on other required arguments in the Analysis ToolPak financial functions shown in this table, refer to the Function Reference on the Contents tab in the Excel Help window (see Book I, Chapter 3 for information on using the Contents tab and printing out help topics).

Chapter 5: Math and Statistical Formulas

In This Chapter

- **Rounding off numbers**
- **Raising numbers to powers and finding square roots**
- **Conditional summing**
- **Using basic statistical functions, such as AVERAGE, MIN, and MAX**
- **Building formulas that count**
- **Using specialized statistical functions**

This chapter examines two larger categories of Excel functions: math and statistical functions. Math functions include all of the specialized trigonometric functions (such as those that return the sine, cosine, or tangents of various angles) and logarithmic functions (for finding the base-10 and natural logarithms of a number), along with the more common math functions for summing numbers, rounding numbers up or down, raising a number to a certain power, and finding the square root of numbers.

The statistical functions include the more common functions that return the average, highest, and lowest value in a cell range all the way to the very sophisticated and specialized functions that calculate such things as the chi-squared distribution, binomial distribution probability, frequency, standard deviation, variance, and — my personal favorite — the skewness of a distribution in a particular population.

Math Functions

The mathematical functions are technically known as the Math & Trig category when you encounter them in the Insert Function dialog box or look for them in the Function Reference on the Contents tab in the Excel Help window. This category groups together all the specialized trigonometric functions with the more common arithmetic functions. Although the trigonometric functions are primarily of use to engineers and scientists, the mathematical functions provide you with the ability to manipulate any type of values. This category of functions includes SUM, the most commonly used of all functions;

functions such as INT, EVEN, ODD, ROUND, and TRUNC that round off the values in your worksheet; functions such as PRODUCT, SUMPRODUCT, and SUMSQ that you can use to calculate the products of various values in the worksheet; and the SQRT function that you can use to calculate the square root of a value.

Rounding off numbers

You use the ROUND function to round up or down fractional values in the worksheet. Unlike when applying a number format to a cell, which affects only the number's display, the ROUND function actually changes the way Excel stores the number in the cell that contains the function. ROUND uses the following syntax:

```
ROUND(number,num_digits)
```

In this function, the *number* argument is the value that you want to round off and *num_digits* is the number of digits to which you want the number rounded. If you enter 0 (zero) as the *num_digits* argument, Excel rounds the number to the nearest integer. If you make the *num_digits* argument a positive value, Excel rounds the number to the specified number of decimal places. If you enter the *num_digits* argument as a negative number, Excel rounds the number to the left of the decimal point.

Instead of the ROUND function, you can use the ROUNDUP or ROUNDDOWN functions. Both ROUNDUP and ROUNDDOWN take the same number and *num_digits* arguments as the ROUND function. The difference is that the ROUNDUP function always rounds up the value specified by the number argument, whereas the ROUNDDOWN function always rounds the value down.

Figure 5-1 illustrates the use of the ROUND, ROUNDUP, and ROUNDDOWN functions in rounding off the value of the mathematical constant pi (_). In cell A3, I entered the value of this constant (with just nine places of non-repeating fraction displayed when the column is widened) into this cell, using Excel's PI function in the following formula:

```
=PI()
```

I then used the ROUND, ROUNDUP, and ROUNDDOWN functions in the cell range B3 through B10 to round this number up and down to various decimal places.

Cell B3, the first cell that uses one of the ROUND functions to round off the value of pi, rounds this value to 3 because I used 0 (zero) as the *num_digits* argument of its ROUND function (causing Excel to round the value to the nearest whole number).

Microsoft Excel - Round Samples.xls

B3 =ROUND($A$3,0)

	A	B	C
1	ROUND Examples		
2	Value of pi	Rounding pi	ROUND Function
3	3.141592654	3	=ROUND($A$3,0)
4		3.1	=ROUND($A$3,1)
5		3.14	=ROUND($A$3,2)
6		3.142	=ROUND($A$3,3)
7		3.15	=ROUNDUP($A$3,2)
8		3.1416	=ROUNDUP($A$3,4)
9		3.14	=ROUNDDOWN$A$3,2)
10		3.1415	=ROUNDDOWN$A$3,4)
11			
12			

Figure 5-1: Rounding off the value of pi with the ROUND, ROUNDUP, and ROUND-DOWN functions.

In Figure 5-1, note the difference between using the ROUND and ROUNDUP functions both with 2 as their *num_digits* arguments in cells B5 and B7, respectively. In cell B5, Excel rounds the value of pi off to 3.14, whereas in cell B7, the program rounds its value up to 3.15. Note that using the ROUND-DOWN function with 2 as its *num_digits* argument yields the same result, 3.14, as does using the ROUND function with 2 as its second argument.

The whole number and nothing but the whole number

You can also use the INT (for Integer) and TRUNC (for Truncate) functions to round off values in your spreadsheets. When you use the INT function, which requires only a single *number* argument, Excel rounds the value down to the nearest integer (whole number). For example, cell A3 contains the value of pi as shown in Figure 5-1, and you enter the following INT function formula in the worksheet:

```
=INT($A$3)
```

Excel returns the value 3 to the cell, the same as when you use 0 (zero) as the *num_digits* argument of the ROUND function in cell B3.

The TRUNC function uses the same number and *num_digits* arguments as the ROUND, ROUNDUP, and ROUNDDOWN functions, except that in the TRUNC function, the *num_digits* argument is purely optional. This argument is required in the ROUND, ROUNDUP, and ROUNDDOWN functions.

The TRUNC function doesn't round off the number in question; it simply truncates the number to the nearest integer by removing the fractional part of the number. However, if you specify a *num_digits* argument, Excel uses that value to determine the precision of the truncation. So, going back to the example illustrated in Figure 5-1, if you enter the following TRUNC function, omitting the optional *num_digits* argument as in:

```
=TRUNC($A$3)
```

Excel returns 3 to the cell just like the formula, =ROUND($A$3,0) does in cell B3. However, if you modify this TRUNC function by using 2 as its *num_digits* argument as in:

```
=TRUNC($A$3,2)
```

Excel then returns 3.14 (by cutting rest of the fraction) just as the formula, =ROUND($A$3,2) does in cell B5.

The only time you notice a difference between the INT and TRUNC functions is when you use them with negative numbers. For example, if you use the TRUNC function to truncate the value -5.4 in the following formula:

```
=TRUNC(-5.4)
```

Excel returns the -5 to the cell. If, however, you use the INT function with the same negative value as in:

```
=INT(-5.4)
```

Excel returns -6 to the cell. This is because the INT function rounds numbers down to the nearest integer using the fractional part of the number.

Let's call it even or odd

Excel's EVEN and ODD functions also round off numbers. The EVEN function rounds the value specified as its *number* argument up to the nearest even integer. The ODD function, of course, does just the opposite: rounding the value up to the nearest odd integer. So, for example, if cell C18 in a worksheet contains the value 345.25 and you use the EVEN function in the following formula:

```
=EVEN(C18)
```

Excel rounds the value up to the next whole even number and returns 346 to the cell. If, however, you use the ODD function on this cell as in:

```
=ODD(C18)
```

Excel rounds the value up to the next odd whole number and returns 347 to the cell instead.

Building in a ceiling

The CEILING function enables you to not only round up a number, but also to set the multiple of significance to be used when doing the rounding. This function can be very useful when dealing with figures that need rounding to particular units.

For example, suppose that you're working on a spreadsheet that lists the retail prices for the various products that you sell, all based upon a particular markup over wholesale, and that many of these calculations result in many prices with cents below 50. If you don't want to have any prices in the list that aren't rounded to nearest 50 cents or whole dollar, you can use the CEILING function to round up all these calculated retail prices to the nearest half dollar.

The CEILING uses the following syntax:

```
CEILING(number,significance)
```

The *number* argument specifies the number you want to round up and the *significance* argument specifies the multiple to which you want to round. For the half-dollar example, suppose that you have the calculated number $12.35 in cell B3 and you enter the following formula in cell C3:

```
=CEILING(B3,0.5)
```

Excel then returns $12.50 to cell C3. Further, suppose that cell B4 contains the calculated value $13.67 and you copy this formula down to cell C4 so that it contains:

```
=CEILING(B4,0.5)
```

Excel then returns $14.00 to that cell.

POWER and SQRT

Although you can use the caret (^) operator to build a formula that raises a number to any power, you also need to be aware that Excel includes a math function called POWER that accomplishes the same thing. For example, to build a formula that raises 5.9 to the third power (that is, cubes the number), you can use the exponentiation operator as in:

```
=5.9^3
```

You can have Excel perform the same calculation with the POWER function by entering this formula:

```
=POWER(5.9,3)
```

In either case, Excel returns the same result, 205.379. The only difference between using the exponentiation operator and the POWER function occurs on that rare, rare occasion when you have to raise a number by a fractional power. In that case, you need to use the POWER function instead of the caret (^) operator to get the correct result. For example, suppose that you need to raise 20 by the fraction ¾; to do this, you build the following formula with the POWER function:

```
=POWER(20,3/4)
```

To use the exponentiation operator to calculate the result of raising 20 by the fraction ¾, you can convert the fraction into decimal form as in:

```
=20^0.75
```

The SQRT function enables you to calculate the square root of any number that you specify as its sole *number* argument. For example, if you use the SQRT function to build the following formula in a cell:

```
=SQRT(144)
```

Excel returns 12 to that cell.

The SQRT function can't deal with negative numbers, so if you try to find the square root of a negative value, Excel returns a nice #NUM! error value to that cell. To avoid such a nuisance, you need to use the ABS (for absolute) math function that returns the absolute value of a number (that is, the number without a sign). For example, suppose that cell A15 contains ($49.00), showing that it's something you owe and you want to return the square root of this number in cell A16. To avoid the dreaded #NUM! error, you nest the ABS function inside the SQRT function. The ABS function returns the absolute value of the number you specify as its sole argument, that is, the value without its sign. To nest this function inside the SQRT function, you create the following formula:

```
=SQRT(ABS(A15))
```

Excel then returns 7 instead of #NUM! to cell A16 because the ABS function removes the negative sign from the 49.00 before the SQRT function calculates its square root (remember that Excel always performs the calculations in the inmost pair of parentheses first).

The SUM of the parts

No function in the entire galaxy of Excel functions comes anywhere close to the popularity of the SUM function in the spreadsheets that you build. So popular is this function, in fact, that Excel has its own AutoSum button that you most often use to build your SUM formulas. You should, however, be aware of the workings of the basic SUM function that the AutoSum button makes so easy to use.

For the record, the syntax of the SUM is as follows:

```
SUM(number1,[number2],[...])
```

When using the SUM function, only the *number1* argument is required; this is the range of numbers in a cell range or array constant that you want added together. Be aware that you can enter up to a total of 29 other optional *number* arguments in a single SUM formula, all of which are separated from each other with a comma (,). For example, you can build a SUM formula that totals numbers in several different ranges as in:

```
=SUM(B3:B10,Sheet2!B3:B10,Sheet3!B3:B10)
```

In this example, Excel sums the values in the cell range B3:B10 on Sheet1, Sheet2, and Sheet3 of the workbook, giving you the grand total of all these values in whatever cell you build this SUM formula.

Conditional summing

The SUM function is perfect when you want to get the totals for all the numbers in a particular range or set of ranges. But what about those times when you only want the total of certain items within a cell range? For those situations, you can use the SUMIF function. The SUMIF function enables you to tell Excel to add together the numbers in a particular range *only* when those numbers meet the criteria that you specify. The syntax of the SUMIF function is as follows:

```
SUMIF(range,criteria,[sum_range])
```

In the SUMIF function, the *range* argument specifies the range of cells that you want Excel to evaluate when doing the summing; the *criteria* argument specifies the criteria to be used in evaluating whether to include certain values in the range in the summing; and finally, the optional *sum_range* argument is the range of all the cells to be summed together. If you omit the *sum_range* argument, Excel sums only the cells specified in the *range* argument (and, of course, only if they meet the criteria specified in the *criteria* argument).

Summing only certain cells with SUMIF

Figure 5-2 illustrates how you can use the SUMIF function to total sales by the items sold. This figure shows a Sales data list sorted by the store location (there are three locations: Mission Street, Anderson Rd., and Curtis Way, of which only Mission Street and one sale on Anderson Rd. are visible) and then the item sold. To total the sales of Lemon tarts at all three locations, I created the following SUMIF formula in cell I3:

```
=SUMIF(item_sold,"=Lemon tarts",daily_sales)
```

In this example, item_sold is the range name given to the cell range C3:C62 that contains the list of each item that has been sold in the first five days of January, 2005 (Lemon tarts, Blueberry muffins, Lots of chips cookies, or Strawberry pie) and daily_sales is the range name assigned to the cell range G3:G62 that contains the extended sales made at each store for each item.

The SUMIF formula in cell I3 then looks for each occurrence of "Lemon tarts" in the item_sold range (the *criteria* argument for the SUMIF function) in the Item column of the Cookie Sales list and then adds its extended sales price from the daily_sales range in the Daily Sales column to the total.

Microsoft Excel - Chris Cookies - Jan05 Sales.xls

I3 =SUMIF(Item_sold,"=Lemon tarts",daily_sales)

	A	B	C	D	E	F	G	H	I	J
1	Chris' Cookies - Daily Sales by Store for January, 2005									
2	No.	Store	Item	Date	Dozens	Price/Doz	Daily Sales			
3	1	Mission Street	Lemon tarts	1/1/2005	35	2.50	87.50		$ 815.00	Lemon tarts
4	2	Mission Street	Blueberry muffins	1/1/2005	28	3.75	105.00		$1,305.00	Blueberry muffins
5	3	Mission Street	Strawberry pie	1/1/2005	42	8.99	377.58		$ 771.12	Lots of chips cookies
6	4	Mission Street	Lots of chips cookies	1/1/2005	18	1.89	34.02		$2,256.49	Strawberry pie
7	5	Mission Street	Lemon tarts	1/2/2005	19	2.50	47.50			
8	6	Mission Street	Blueberry muffins	1/2/2005	25	3.75	93.75		$2,891.12	All but Strawberry pie
9	7	Mission Street	Strawberry pie	1/2/2005	35	8.99	314.65			
10	8	Mission Street	Lots of chips cookies	1/2/2005	47	1.89	88.83			
11	9	Mission Street	Lemon tarts	1/3/2005	28	2.50	70.00			
12	10	Mission Street	Blueberry muffins	1/3/2005	36	3.75	135.00			
13	11	Mission Street	Strawberry pie	1/3/2005	18	8.99	161.82			
14	12	Mission Street	Lots of chips cookies	1/3/2005	23	1.89	43.47			
15	13	Mission Street	Lemon tarts	1/4/2005	14	2.50	35.00			
16	14	Mission Street	Blueberry muffins	1/4/2005	24	3.75	90.00			
17	15	Mission Street	Strawberry pie	1/4/2005	16	8.99	143.84			
18	16	Mission Street	Lots of chips cookies	1/4/2005	45	1.89	85.05			
19	17	Mission Street	Lemon tarts	1/5/2005	32	2.50	80.00			
20	18	Mission Street	Blueberry muffins	1/5/2005	32	3.75	120.00			
21	19	Mission Street	Strawberry pie	1/5/2005	15	8.99	134.85			
22	20	Mission Street	Lots of chips cookies	1/5/2005	25	1.89	47.25			

Jan, 05 Sales / Sheet2 / Sheet3

Figure 5-2: Using SUMIF to total sales by items sold.

The formulas in cells I4, I5, and I6 contain SUMIF functions very similar to the one in cell I3, except that they substitute the name of the dessert goodie in question in place of the =Lemon tarts *criteria* argument. The formula in cell I8, however, is slightly different: This formula sums the sales for all items except for Strawberry pies. It does this with the SUMIF function in the following formula:

```
=SUMIF(item_sold,"<>Strawberry pie",daily_sales)
```

Because I prefaced the item Strawberry pie with the not (<>) operator (which can be placed before or after the open double quotation mark), Excel sums the daily sale for every item except for Strawberry pie.

Using the Conditional Sum Wizard

The SUMIF function is just great when you have only one criterion that you want to apply in doing the summing. It does not, however, work when you have multiple criteria that you need to use in determining which numbers get added to the total and which don't. For those situations, you can turn to the Conditional Sum Wizard, a nifty little Excel add-in tool that walks you through the steps of building more complex SUM formulas that utilize IF conditions that can include multiple criteria.

For example, harkening back to the Chris' Cookies Daily Sales spreadsheet shown in Figure 5-2, suppose that you need the sum of all the sales made in the Anderson Rd. store location for all items except for Strawberry pie but only for dates after January 1, 2005. You can use the Conditional Sum Wizard to create the SUM formula that calculates this special subtotal in no time flat.

Before you can use the Conditional Sum Wizard, however, you have to add its menu item to the Tools pull-down menu. To do this, activate the Conditional Sum Wizard by taking these steps:

1. **Choose Tools⇨Add-Ins on the Excel Menu bar.**

   The Add-Ins dialog box opens; it contains a list of all the add-in programs installed on your computer.

2. **Click the Conditional Sum Wizard check box in the Add-Ins dialog box and then click the OK button.**

After you put a checkmark in the Conditional Sum Wizard check box in the Add-Ins dialog box, Excel adds the Conditional Sum item to the Tools menu. When you choose Tools⇨Conditional Sum on the Excel pull-down menu,

Excel opens the Conditional Sum Wizard — Step 1 of 4 dialog box (similar to the one shown in Figure 5-3). You then follow these steps to build a SUM formula by using multiple criteria:

1. **Enter the address or name of the cell range that contains the values to sum, including the column headings, or drag through the range in the current worksheet.**

   If you drag through the cells rather than type their range address or range name, Excel automatically reduces the Conditional Sum Wizard — Step 1 of 4 dialog box to the Where is the List text box until you release the mouse button.

   For this example, in which you want to sum the daily sales for the store location in Anderson Rd., the item is anything but Strawberry pie, and the date is any date after January 1, 2005, select the entire range of data (including the column headings in row 2) except for column A that tracks only the record number.

2. **Click the Next> button.**

   The Conditional Sum Wizard — Step 2 of 4 dialog box displays (similar to the one shown in Figure 5-4). Here, you specify which column to sum and what criteria to apply when doing the summing.

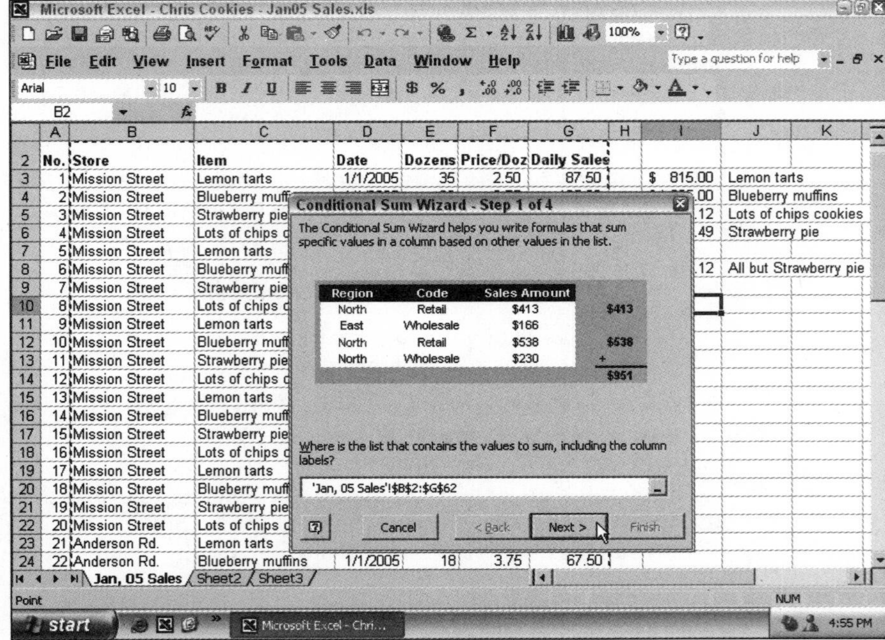

Figure 5-3: Specifying the values to sum in the Conditional Sum Wizard — Step 1 of 4 dialog box.

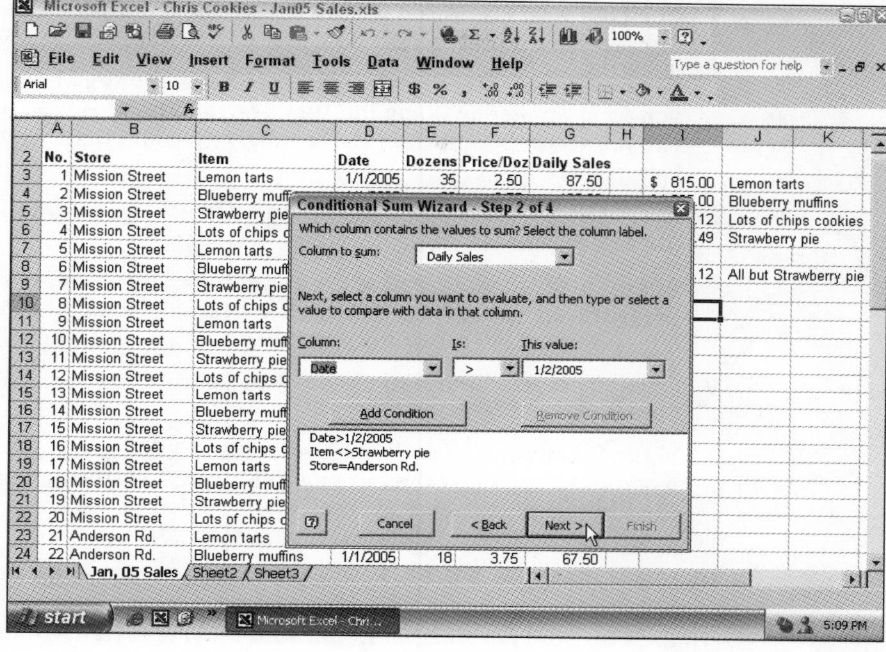

Figure 5-4: Adding the criteria to use in the Conditional Sum Wizard — Step 2 of 4 dialog box.

3. **Click the name of the column that you want summed in the Column to Sum drop-down list box.**

   For this example, select the Daily Sales column as the column to sum.

   After you specify the column to sum, you're ready to build and then add the various conditions (criteria) to be applied when doing the summing.

4. **Click the name of the column to be included in the first condition in the Column drop-down list box.**

   For the first condition in this example, click Store in the Column drop-down list.

5. **Click the comparison operator that you want to use in the condition in the Is drop-down list box.**

   For this example, you want to leave the default equal to (=) operator selected in the Is drop-down list box.

6. **Click the name of the number or label that you want used as the value of the condition in the This Value drop-down list box.**

   For this example, click Anderson Rd. in the This Value drop-down list so that the condition reads Store = Anderson Rd.

7. **Click the Add Condition button to add the condition that you just built to the Conditions list box.**

   You now repeat Steps 5 through 7 for all the additional conditions that you want applied in doing the sum. For this example, you build and add two more conditions: Item <> Strawberry pie and Date > 1/1/2005 (see Figure 5-4).

8. **Repeat Steps 5 through 7 to add any and all additional conditions to the Conditions list box.**

   After you finish adding all of the conditions that you want applied in doing the summing, click the Next> button to display the Conditional Sum Wizard — Step 3 of 4 dialog box.

9. **Click the Next> button to display the Conditional Sum Wizard — Step 3 of 4 dialog box.**

   In the Conditional Sum Wizard — Step 3 of 4 dialog box, you indicate whether to copy just the formula to a single cell (the default) or to copy the formula plus the values that you specified in the This Value drop-down list for each condition that you created.

10. **Leave the Copy Just the Formula to a Single Cell radio button selected to just insert to the new SUM formula in the worksheet. Click the Copy the Formula and Conditioned Values radio button to copy the values and formula in the worksheet.**

    If you elect to copy only the formula to a cell, you have only one more step to complete in the Conditional Sum Wizard — Step 4 of 4 dialog box, and that is to designate the cell in the worksheet where the SUM formula is to go.

    If you elect to copy the conditional values plus the formula, the Conditional Sum Wizard adds as many wizard dialog boxes as necessary to individually specify the cell location for each conditional value, as well as the one for the SUM formula.

    For this example, the Conditional Sum Wizard would add three more dialog boxes if you were to click the Copy the Formula and Conditioned Values radio button, making a total of 7 steps in the Conditional Sum Wizard. This is to accommodate specifying a cell for copying the conditional value, Anderson Rd. in Step 4 of 7, another for copying Strawberry pie in Step 5 of 7, another for copying 1/1/2005 in Step 6 of 7, and finally, a cell to hold the SUM formula in Step 7 of 7.

11. **Click the Next> button to display the Conditional Sum Wizard — Step 4 of 4 dialog box.**

    If you selected the Copy Just the Formula to a Single Cell option back in Step 10, you now designate the address of the cell to hold the formula in Step 12. If, however, you selected the Copy the Formula and Conditioned

Values option, you need to specify the cell address for each conditional value plus the conditional SUM formula in however many Conditional Sum Wizard dialog boxes remain.

12. **Click the cell in the worksheet where you want the conditional SUM formula or the first conditional value in the worksheet to appear.**

    If you're designating conditional values, click the Next> button and continue on in this manner until you reach the final wizard dialog box and have designated the location of the conditional SUM formula.

13. **Click the Finish button in the final wizard dialog box to close the Conditional Sum Wizard and calculate the total based on your condition(s).**

Figure 5-5 shows the resulting SUM formula in cell I10 created by the Conditional Sum Wizard, which calculates the total where the store location is Anderson Rd., the sales item is anything but Strawberry pie, and the date of the sale is after January 1, 2005. As you can see in this figure, in order to accomplish conditional summing, the Conditional Sum Wizard used no less than three IF functions nested within each other within a SUM function all entered as an array formula (indicated by the pair of curly braces surrounding the entire formula).

Microsoft Excel - Chris Cookies - Jan05 Sales.xls

I10 {=SUM(IF(store="Anderson Rd.",IF(item<>"Strawberry pie",IF(date_sold>DATEVALUE("1/1/2005"), daily_sales,0),0),0))}

Chris' Cookies - Daily Sales by Store for January, 2005

	No.	Store	Item	Date	Dozens	Price/Doz	Daily Sales		
3	1	Mission Street	Lemon tarts	1/1/2005	35	2.50	87.50	$ 815.00	Lemon tarts
4	2	Mission Street	Blueberry muffins	1/1/2005	28	3.75	105.00	$1,305.00	Blueberry muffins
5	3	Mission Street	Strawberry pie	1/1/2005	42	8.99	377.58	$ 771.12	Lots of chips cookies
6	4	Mission Street	Lots of chips cookies	1/1/2005	18	1.89	34.02	$2,256.49	Strawberry pie
7	5	Mission Street	Lemon tarts	1/2/2005	19	2.50	47.50		
8	6	Mission Street	Blueberry muffins	1/2/2005	25	3.75	93.75	$2,891.12	All but Strawberry pie
9	7	Mission Street	Strawberry pie	1/2/2005	35	8.99	314.65		
10	8	Mission Street	Lots of chips cookies	1/2/2005	47	1.89	88.83	$ 727.17	Multiple conditions
11	9	Mission Street	Lemon tarts	1/3/2005	28	2.50	70.00		
12	10	Mission Street	Blueberry muffins	1/3/2005	36	3.75	135.00		
13	11	Mission Street	Strawberry pie	1/3/2005	18	8.99	161.82		
14	12	Mission Street	Lots of chips cookies	1/3/2005	23	1.89	43.47		
15	13	Mission Street	Lemon tarts	1/4/2005	14	2.50	35.00		
16	14	Mission Street	Blueberry muffins	1/4/2005	24	3.75	90.00		
17	15	Mission Street	Strawberry pie	1/4/2005	16	8.99	143.84		
18	16	Mission Street	Lots of chips cookies	1/4/2005	45	1.89	85.05		
19	17	Mission Street	Lemon tarts	1/5/2005	32	2.50	80.00		
20	18	Mission Street	Blueberry muffins	1/5/2005	32	3.75	120.00		
21	19	Mission Street	Strawberry pie	1/5/2005	15	8.99	134.85		
22	20	Mission Street	Lots of chips cookies	1/5/2005	25	1.89	47.25		

Jan, 05 Sales / Sheet2 / Sheet3

Figure 5-5: Daily Sales spreadsheet with SUM formula that totals values based on multiple conditions.

Statistical Functions

Excel includes one of the most complete sets of statistical functions available outside of a dedicated statistics software program. These functions run the gamut from the more mundane AVERAGE, MAX, and MIN functions to the more exotic and much more specialized CHITEST, POISSON, and PERCENTILE statistical functions.

In addition to the more specialized statistical functions, Excel offers an assortment of counting functions that enable you to count the number of cells that contain values, are nonblank (and thus contain entries of any kind), or count only the cells in a given range that meet the criteria that you specify.

AVERAGE, MAX, and MIN

The AVERAGE, MAX (for maximum), and MIN (for minimum) functions are the most commonly used of the statistical functions because they are of use to both the average number cruncher as well as the dedicated statistician. All three functions follow the same syntax as the good old SUM function. For example, the syntax of the AVERAGE function uses the following arguments just as the SUM, MAX, and MIN functions do:

```
AVERAGE(number1,[number2],[...])
```

Just as in the SUM function, the *number* arguments are between 1 and 30 numeric arguments for which you want the average. Figure 5-6 illustrates how you can use the AVERAGE, MAX, MIN, and MEDIAN functions in a worksheet. This example uses these functions to compute a few statistics on the selling prices of homes in a particular neighborhood. These statistics include the average, highest, lowest, and median selling price for the homes sold in April and May of 2003. All of the statistical functions in this worksheet use the same *number* argument; that is, the cell range C4:C8.

The AVERAGE function computes the arithmetic mean of the values in this range by summing them and then dividing them by the number of values in the range. This AVERAGE function is equivalent to the following formula:

```
=SUM(C4:C8)/COUNT(C4:C8)
```

Note that this formula uses the SUM function to total the values and another statistical function called COUNT to determine the number of values in the list. The MAX and MIN functions simply compute the highest and lowest values in the cell range used as the *number* argument. The MEDIAN function computes the value that is in the middle of the range of values; that is, the one where half the values are greater and half are less. This is the reason that the median sales price (in cell C16) differs from the average sales price (in cell C10) in this worksheet.

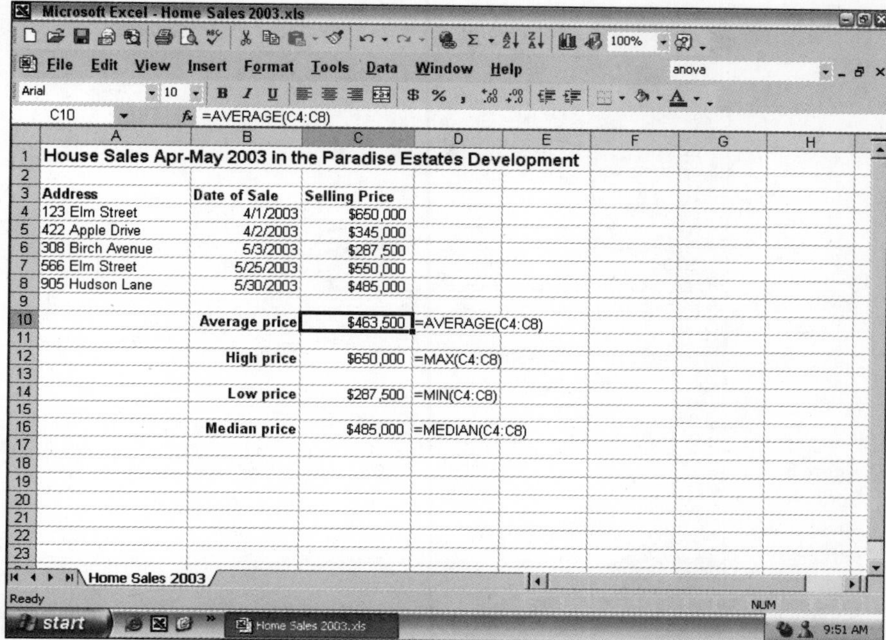

Figure 5-6: Spreadsheet using common statistical functions.

Counting cells

Sometimes you need to know how many cells in a particular cell range, column or row, or even worksheet in your spreadsheet have cell entries and how many are still blank. Other times, you need to know just how many of the occupied cells have text entries and how many have numeric entries. Excel includes a number of counting functions that you can use in building formulas that calculate the number of cells in a particular region or worksheet that are occupied and can tell you what general type of entry they contain.

Building counting formulas

Figure 5-7 illustrates the different types of counting formulas that you can build to return such basic statistics as the total number of cells in a particular range, the number of occupied cells in that range, as well as the number of numeric and text entries in the occupied range. In this example spreadsheet, I gave the name sales_data to the cell range A1:C8 (shown selected in Figure 5-7).

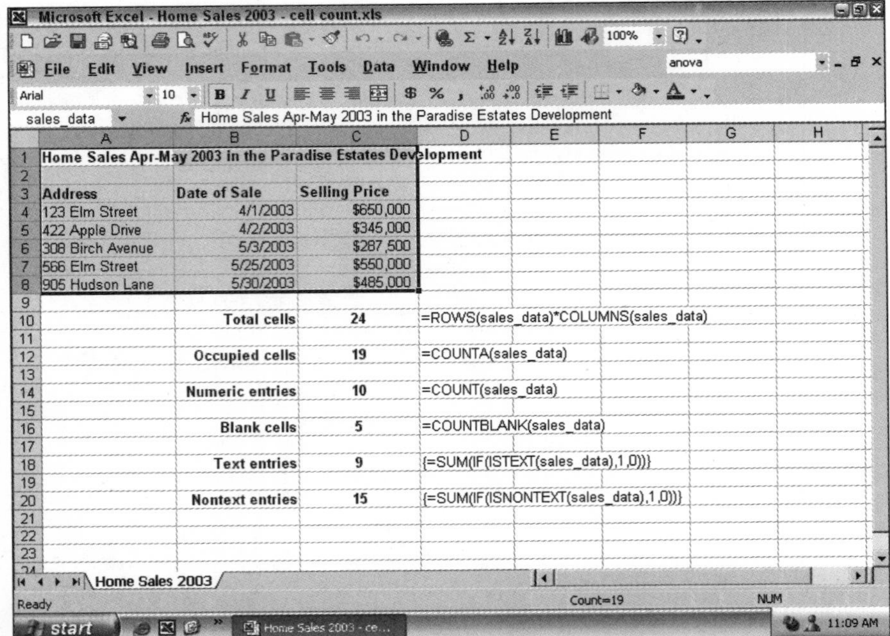

Figure 5-7: Spreadsheet with various counting formulas.

I then used the sales_data range name in a number of formulas that count its different aspects. The most basic formula is the one that returns the total number of cells in the sales_data range. To build this formula in cell C10, I used the ROWS and COLUMNS information functions (see Chapter 6 in this book for more on these types of functions) to return the number of rows and columns in the range, and then I created the following formula that multiplies these two values together:

```
=ROWS(sales_data)*COLUMNS(sales_data)
```

This formula, of course, returns 24 to cell C10. In the next formula, I calculated the number of these 24 cells that contain data entries (of whatever type) using the COUNTA function. This function counts the number of cells that are not empty in the ranges that you specify. The COUNTA function uses the following the following syntax:

```
COUNTA(value1,[value2],[...])
```

The *value* arguments (all of which are optional except for value1) are up to 30 different values or cell ranges that you want counted. Note that the COUNTA function counts a cell as long it has some entry, even if the entry is empty text set off by a single apostrophe ('). In the example shown in Figure 5-7, cell C12 contains the following COUNTA function:

```
=COUNTA(sales_data)
```

This formula returns 19 to cell C12. The next formula in the sample spreadsheet calculates the number of numeric entries in the cell range called sales_data. To do this, you use the COUNT function. The COUNT function takes the same arguments as COUNTA, the only difference being that COUNT only counts a value or cell specified in its *value* arguments if they contain numeric entries.

Cell C14 contains the following formula for calculating the number of numeric entries in the Home Sales table range called sales_data:

```
=COUNT(sales_data)
```

Excel returns 10 to cell C12. Note that in calculating this result, Excel counts the five date entries (with the date of each sale) in the cell range B4:B8 as well as the five numeric data entries (with the selling prices of each home) in the cell range C4:C8.

The next formula in the sample spreadsheet shown in Figure 5-7 uses the COUNTBLANK function to calculate the number of blank cells in the sales_data range. The COUNTBLANK function works just like the COUNTA and COUNT functions except that it returns the number of non-occupied cells in the range. For this example, I entered the following COUNTBLANK function in cell C16:

```
=COUNTBLANK(sales_data)
```

Excel then returns 5 to cell C16 (which makes sense because you know that of the 24 total cells in this range, Excel already said that 19 of them have entries of some kind).

The last two counting formulas in the sample spreadsheet shown in Figure 5-7 return the number of text and nontext entries in the sales_data cell range. To do this, instead of counting functions, they use the ISTEXT and ISNONTEXT information functions as part of the IF conditions used with the good old SUM function.

The first formula for returning the number of text entries in the sales_data range in cell C18 is:

{=SUM(IF(ISTEXT(sales_data),1,0))}

The second formula for returning the number of nontext entries in the sales_data range in cell C20 is just like the one in cell C18 except that it uses the ISNONTEXT function instead of ISTEXT, as follows:

```
{=SUM(IF(ISNONTEXT(sales_data),1,0))}
```

The ISTEXT function in the formula in cell C18 returns logical TRUE when a cell in the sales_data range contains a text entry and FALSE when it does not. The ISNONTEXT function in the formula in cell C20 returns logical TRUE when a cell is blank or contains a numeric entry (in other words, anything but text) and FALSE when it contains text.

In both these formulas, the ISTEXT and ISNONTEXT functions are used as the *logical_test* arguments of an IF function with 1 as the *value_if_true* argument and 0 as the *value_if_false* argument (so that the cells are counted only when the ISTEXT or ISNONTEXT functions return the logical TRUE values). These IF functions are then nested within SUM functions, and these SUM functions, in turn, are then entered as array formulas.

Note that you must enter these formulas in the worksheet as array formulas (by pressing Ctrl+Shift+Enter) so that Excel performs its counting calculations on each and every cell in the sales_data cell range. If you just enter the SUM formula with the nested IF and ISTEXT and ISNONTEXT functions as regular formulas, they would return 0 as the count for both text and nontext entries in the sales_data cell range (see Chapter 1 in this book for details on building array formulas).

Counting occupied cells in entire rows, columns, and worksheet

You can use the COUNTA function to count the number of occupied cells in an entire row or column of a worksheet or even an entire worksheet in your workbook. For example, to count all the occupied cells in row 17 of a worksheet, you enter the following COUNTA formula:

```
=COUNTA(17:17)
```

If you want to find the number of nonblank cells in column B of the worksheet, you enter the following COUNTA formula:

```
=COUNTA(B:B)
```

To find out the number of occupied cells in the entire second worksheet of your workbook (assuming that it's still called Sheet2), you enter this COUNTA formula:

```
=COUNTA(Sheet2!1:65536)
```

Note that you can also enter the argument for this COUNTA function by designating the entire range of column letters (rather than the range of row numbers) as in:

```
=COUNTA(Sheet2!A:IV)
```

However, Excel automatically converts the *column range* argument to rows, using absolute references ($1:$65536) as soon as you enter the COUNTA function in its cell.

When entering COUNTA functions that return the number of occupied cells in an entire row, column, or worksheet, you must be sure that you do *not* enter the formula in a cell within that row, column, or worksheet. If you do, Excel displays a Circular Reference Alert dialog box when you try to enter the formula in the worksheet. This is because you are asking Excel to use the cell with the formula that does the counting in the count itself (definitely the type of circular logic that the program doesn't allow).

Conditional counting

Excel includes a COUNTIF function that you can use to count cells in a range only when they meet a certain condition. The COUNTIF function takes two arguments and uses the following syntax:

```
COUNTIF(range,criteria)
```


The *range* argument specifies the range of cells from which the conditional count is to be calculated. The *criteria* argument specifies the condition to use. You can express this argument as a number, expression, or text that indicates which cells to count. When specifying a number for the *criteria* argument, you don't have to enclose the number in quotes. For example, to count the number of entries in a cell range named table_data that contain the number 5, you enter the following COUNTIF formula:

```
=COUNTIF(table_data,5)
```

However, when specifying an expression or text as the *criteria* argument, you must enclose the expression or text in closed quotes as in "=5,", ">20.", or "New York". So, if you want to use COUNTIF to find out how many cells in the table_data range have values greater than 5, you enter this version of the COUNTIF function:

```
=COUNTIF(table_data,">5")
```

When you want to use the COUNTIF function to find out the number of cells whose contents are equal to the contents of a particular cell in the worksheet, you just add the cell reference as the function's *criteria* argument. For example, if you want to count the number of cells in the table_data range that are equal to the contents of cell B3 in the worksheet, you enter this formula:

```
=COUNTIF(table_data,B3)
```

However, when you want to specify an expression other than equality that refers to the contents of a cell in the worksheet, you must enclose the operator in a pair of double quotation marks and then add the ampersand (&) concatenation operator before the cell reference. For example, if you want to count how many cells in the table_data range have a value greater than the contents of cell B3, you enter this form of the COUNTIF function:

```
=COUNTIF(table_data,">"&B3)
```

Note that when specifying text as the condition, you can use the two wildcard characters: the asterisk (*) to represent an unspecified amount of characters and the question mark (?) to represent single characters in the COUNTIF function's *criteria* argument. For example, to count all the cells in the table_data range whose text entries end with the word *Street,* you use the asterisk in the COUNTIF *criteria* argument as follows:

```
=COUNTIF(table_data,"*Street")
```

To count the cells in the table_data range whose text entries contain the word *discount* anywhere in the entry, you sandwich discount between two asterisks in the COUNTIF *criteria* argument as follows:

```
=COUNTIF(table_data,"*discount*")
```

To count the cells in the table_data range whose cell entries consist of any two characters followed by the letter *y* (as in *day, say, pay,* and so on), you use two question marks to stand in for the nonspecific characters followed by a *y* in the COUNTIF *criteria* argument as in:

```
=COUNTIF(table_data,"??y")
```

When using the COUNTIF function to find the number of cells, you can include other statistical functions as the *criteria* argument. For example, suppose that you want to know the number of cells in the table_data range whose values are less than the average value in the range. To do this, you insert the AVERAGE function in the COUNTIF *criteria* argument as follows:

```
=COUNTIF(table_data,"<"&AVERAGE(table_data))
```

Using specialized statistical functions

As mentioned at the beginning of this chapter, Excel is rich in specialized statistical functions that enable you to do complex statistical analysis. In addition to the built-in statistical functions found in the Statistical category in Or Select a Category drop-down list in the Insert Function dialog box, Excel offers a complete set of special analysis tools as part of the Analysis ToolPak add-in.

The tools included in the Analysis ToolPak enable you to analyze worksheet data by using such things as Anova, F-Test, rank and percentile, t-Test, and Fourier analysis. Before you can use the statistical functions added by the Analysis ToolPak, you must activate this add-in by opening the Add-Ins dialog box (Tools⇨Add Ins) and then putting a checkmark in the Analysis ToolPak check box in the Available Add-Ins list box before clicking OK.

After you activate the Analysis ToolPak in this manner, you then access the statistical analysis tools that it adds by choosing Tools⇨Data Analysis on the Excel Menu bar (the addition of the Data Analysis item at the bottom of the Tools pull-down menu is your signal that the Analysis ToolPak has been successfully activated). When you choose this command, Excel opens the Data Analysis dialog box, as shown in Figure 5-8.

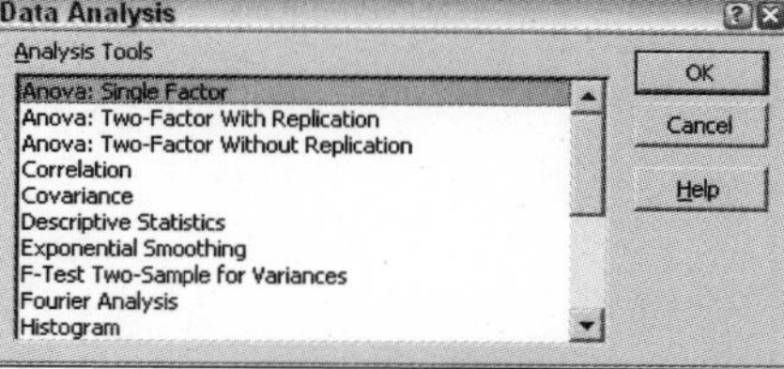

Figure 5-8: Selecting a statistical analysis tool added by the Analysis ToolPak.

The Data Analysis dialog box lists all the statistical analysis tools added by the Analysis ToolPak from ANOVA: Single Factor at the very top down to z-Test Two Sample for Means at the bottom of list. To use one of these tools in your spreadsheet, click its name in the Analysis Tools list box and then click OK. Excel then opens another dialog box specific to the tool that you select, where you can specify the data and the options that you want used in the analysis.

For general help with the function and use of the various statistical analysis tools added by the Analysis ToolPak, click the Help button in the Data Analysis dialog box.

Chapter 6: Lookup, Information, and Text Formulas

In This Chapter

- **Looking up data in a table and adding it to a list**
- **Using the Lookup Wizard to perform two-way lookups**
- **Transposing vertical cell ranges to horizontal and vice versa**
- **Getting information about a cell's contents**
- **Evaluating a cell's type with the IS information functions**
- **Using text functions to manipulate text entries**
- **Creating formulas that combine text entries**

This chapter covers three categories of Excel functions: the lookup and reference functions that return values and cell addresses from the spreadsheet, the information functions that return particular types of information about cells in the spreadsheet, and the text functions that enable you to manipulate strings of text in the spreadsheet.

In these three different categories of Excel functions, perhaps none are as handy as the lookup functions that enable you to have Excel look up certain data in a table and then return other related data from that same table based on the results of that lookup. In fact, this type of procedure is considered of such great importance that Excel includes a Lookup Wizard add-in that walks you through the steps for building Lookup formulas that perform a special type of two-way table lookup.

Lookup and Reference

The lookup functions in Excel make it easy to perform table lookups that either return information about entries in the table or actually return related data to other data lists in the spreadsheet. By using Lookup tables to input information into a data list, you not only reduce the amount data input that you have to do but you also eliminate the possibility of data entry errors. Using Lookup tables also makes it a snap to update your data lists: All you have to do is make the edits to the entries in the original Lookup table or schedule to have all of their data entries in the list updated as well.

The reference functions in Excel enable you to return specific information about particular cells or parts of the worksheet; create hyperlinks to different documents on your computer, network, or the Internet; and transpose ranges of vertical cells so that they run horizontally and vice versa.

Looking up a single value with VLOOKUP and HLOOKUP

The most popular of the lookup functions are HLOOKUP (for Horizontal Lookup) and VLOOKUP (for Vertical Lookup) functions. These functions are located in the Lookup & Reference category in the Insert Function dialog box. They are part of a powerful group of functions that can return values by looking them up in data tables.

The VLOOKUP function searches vertically (top to bottom) the leftmost column of a Lookup table until the program locates a value that matches or exceeds the one you are looking up. The HLOOKUP function searches horizontally (left to right) the topmost row of a Lookup table until it locates a value that matches or exceeds the one that you're looking up.

The VLOOKUP function uses the following syntax:

```
VLOOKUP(lookup_value,table_array,col_index_num,[range_lookup])
```

The HLOOKUP follows the nearly identical syntax:

```
HLOOKUP(lookup_value,table_array,row_index_num,[range_lookup])
```

In both functions, the *lookup_value* argument is the value that you want to look up in the Lookup table, table_array is the cell range or name of the Lookup table that contains both the value to look up and the related value to return.

The *col_index_num* argument in the VLOOKUP function is the number of the column whose values are compared to the *lookup_value* argument in a vertical table. The *row_index_num* argument in the HLOOKUP function is the number of the row whose values are compared to the *lookup_value* in a horizontal table.

When entering the *col_index_num* or *row_index_num* arguments in the VLOOKUP and HLOOKUP functions, you must enter a value greater than zero that does not exceed the total number of columns or rows in the Lookup table.

The optional *range_lookup* argument in both the VLOOKUP and the HLOOKUP functions is the logical TRUE or FALSE that specifies whether you want Excel to find an exact or approximate match for the *lookup_value* in the table_array. When you specify TRUE or omit the *range_lookup* argument in the VLOOKUP or HLOOKUP function, Excel finds an approximate match. When you specify FALSE as the *range_lookup* argument, Excel finds only exact matches.

Finding approximate matches pertains only when you're looking up numeric entries (rather than text) in the first column or row of the vertical or horizontal Lookup table. When Excel doesn't find an exact match in this Lookup column or row, it locates the next highest value that doesn't exceed the *lookup_value* argument and then returns the value in the column or row designated by the *col_index_num* or *row_index_num* arguments.

When using the VLOOKUP and HLOOKUP functions, the text or numeric entries in the Lookup column or row (that is, the leftmost column of a vertical Lookup table or the top row of a horizontal Lookup table) must be unique. These entries must also be arranged or sorted in ascending order; that is, alphabetical order for text entries, and lowest-to-highest order for numeric entries (see Book VI, Chapter 1 for detailed information on sorting data in a spreadsheet).

Figure 6-1 shows an example of using the VLOOKUP function to return either a 15% or 20% tip from a tip table, depending upon the pretax total of the check. Cell F5 contains the VLOOKUP function:

```
=VLOOKUP(Pretax_Total,Tip_Table,IF(Tip_Percentage=0.15,2,3))
```

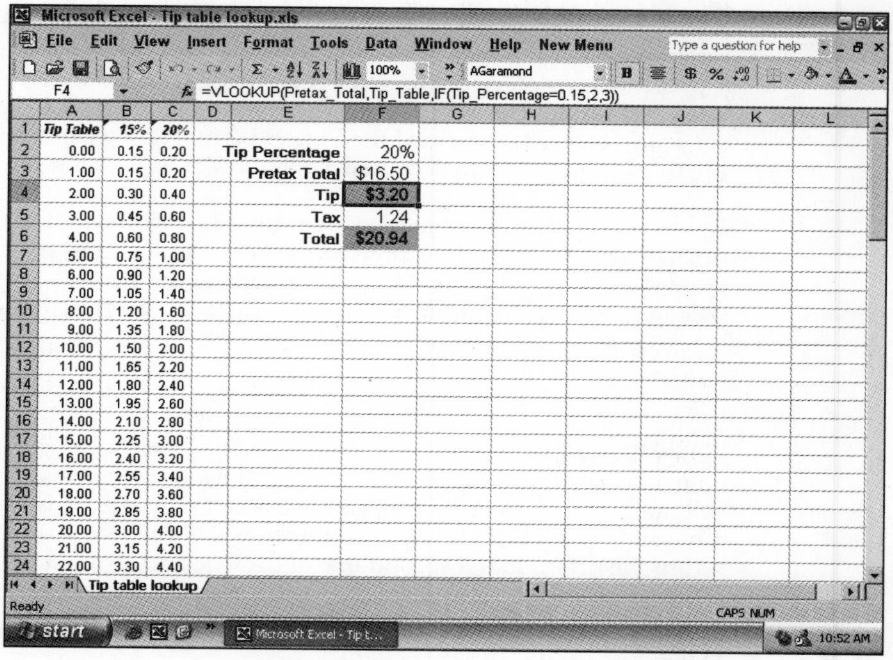

Figure 6-1: Using the VLOOKUP function to return the amount of the tip to add from a Lookup table.

This formula returns the amount of the tip based on the tip percentage in cell F3 and the pretax amount of the check in cell F4.

To use this tip table, enter the percentage of the tip (15% or 20%) in cell F2 (named Tip_Percentage) and the amount of the check before tax in cell F3 (named Pretax_Total). Excel then looks up the value that you enter in the Pretax_Total cell in the first column of the Lookup table, which includes the cell range A2:C101 and is named Tip_Table.

Excel then moves down the values in the first column of Tip_Table until it finds a match, whereupon the program uses the *col_index_num* argument in the VLOOKUP function to determine which tip amount from that row of the table to return to cell F4. If Excel finds that the value entered in the Pretax_Total cell ($16.50 in this example) doesn't exactly match one of the values in the first column of Tip_Table, the program continues to search down the comparison range until it encounters the first value that exceeds the pretax total (17.00 in cell A19 in this example). Excel then moves back up to the previous row in the table and returns the value in the column that matches the *col_index_num* argument of the VLOOKUP function (this is because the optional *range_lookup* argument has been omitted from the function).

Note that the tip table example in Figure 6-1 uses an IF function to determine the *col_index_num* argument for the VLOOKUP function in cell F4. The IF function determines the number of the column to be used in the tip table by matching the percentage entered in Tip_Percentage (cell F2) with 0.15. If they match, the function returns 2 as the *col_index_num* argument and the VLOOKUP function returns a value from the second column (the 15% column B) in the Tip_Table range. Otherwise, the IF function returns 3 as the *col_index_num* argument and the VLOOKUP function returns a value from the third column (the 20% column C) in the Tip_Table range.

Figure 6-2 shows an example that uses the HLOOKUP function to look up the price of each bakery item stored in a separate price Lookup table and then to return that price to the Price/Doz column of the Daily Sales list. Cell F7 contains the original formula with the HLOOKUP function that is then copied down column F:

```
=HLOOKUP(item,prices,2,FALSE)
```

In this HLOOKUP function, the range name Item that's given to the Item column in the range C7:C66 is defined as the *lookup_value* argument and the cell range name Prices that's given to the cell range D3:G4 is the *table_array* argument. The *row_index_num* argument is 2 because you want Excel to return the prices in the second row of the Prices Lookup table, and the optional *range_lookup* argument is FALSE because the item name in the Daily Sales list must match exactly the item name in the Prices Lookup table.

Microsoft Excel - Chris Cookies - HLookup.xls

F7 =HLOOKUP(item,prices,2,FALSE)

Chris' Cookies - Daily Sales by Store for January, 2005

Price Table	Pastry	Blueberry muffins	Lemon tarts	Lots of chips cookies	Strawberry pie
	Price/Doz	3.75	2.50	1.89	8.99

No.	Store	Item	Date	Dozens	Price/Doz	Daily Sales
1	Mission Street	Lemon tarts	1/1/2005	35	2.50	87.50
2	Mission Street	Blueberry muffins	1/1/2005	28	3.75	105.00
3	Mission Street	Strawberry pie	1/1/2005	42	8.99	377.58
4	Mission Street	Lots of chips cookies	1/1/2005	18	1.89	34.02
5	Mission Street	Lemon tarts	1/2/2005	19	2.50	47.50
6	Mission Street	Blueberry muffins	1/2/2005	25	3.75	93.75
7	Mission Street	Strawberry pie	1/2/2005	35	8.99	314.65
8	Mission Street	Lots of chips cookies	1/2/2005	47	1.89	88.83
9	Mission Street	Lemon tarts	1/3/2005	28	2.50	70.00
10	Mission Street	Blueberry muffins	1/3/2005	36	3.75	135.00
11	Mission Street	Strawberry pie	1/3/2005	18	8.99	161.82
12	Mission Street	Lots of chips cookies	1/3/2005	23	1.89	43.47
13	Mission Street	Lemon tarts	1/4/2005	14	2.50	35.00
14	Mission Street	Blueberry muffins	1/4/2005	24	3.75	90.00
15	Mission Street	Strawberry pie	1/4/2005	16	8.99	143.84
16	Mission Street	Lots of chips cookies	1/4/2005	45	1.89	85.05
17	Mission Street	Lemon tarts	1/5/2005	32	2.50	80.00

Jan, 05 Sales / Sheet2 / Sheet3

Figure 6-2: Using the HLOOKUP function to return the price of a bakery item from a Lookup table.

By having the HLOOKUP function use the Prices Lookup table to input the price per dozen for each bakery goods item in the Daily Sales list, you make it a very simple matter to update any of the sales in the list. All you have to do is change its Price/Doz cost in the Prices Lookup table and the HLOOKUP function immediately updates the new price in the Daily Sales list wherever the item is sold.

Performing a two-way lookup

In both the VLOOKUP and HLOOKUP examples, Excel only compares a single value in the data list to a single value in the vertical or horizontal Lookup table. Sometimes, however, you may have a table in which you need to perform a two-way lookup whereby a piece of data is retrieved from the Lookup table based on looking up a value in the top row (with the table's column headings) and a value in the first column (with the table's row headings).

Figure 6-3 illustrates a situation in which you would use two values, the production date and the part number, to look up the expected production. In the 2003 Production Schedule table, the production dates for each part form the column headings in the first row of the table, and the part numbers form the row headings in its first column of the table.

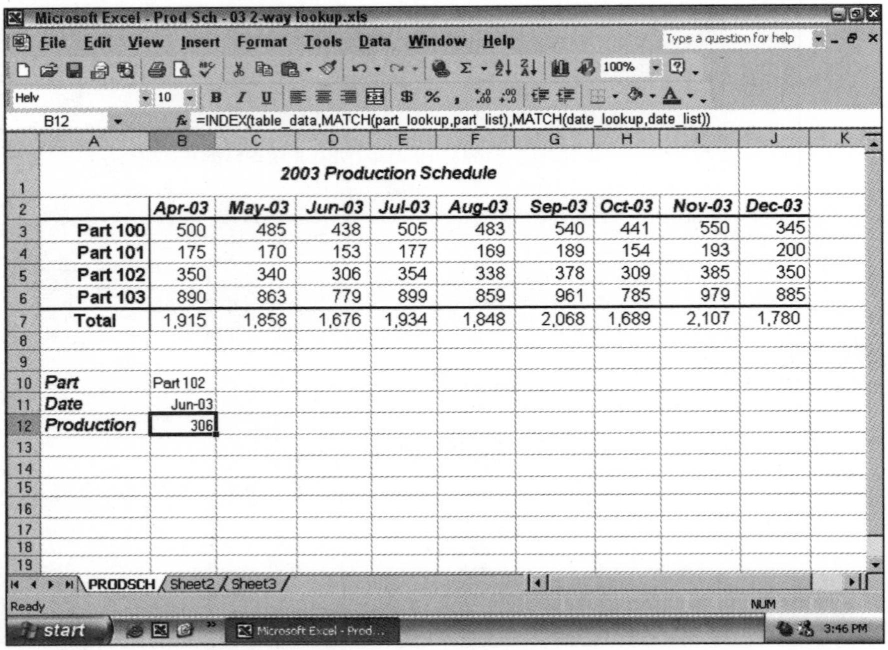
Microsoft Excel - Prod Sch - 03 2-way lookup.xls
File Edit View Insert Format Tools Data Window Help
Type a question for help
B12
=INDEX(table_data,MATCH(part_lookup,part_list),MATCH(date_lookup,date_list))
2003 Production Schedule
Apr-03 May-03 Jun-03 Jul-03 Aug-03 Sep-03 Oct-03 Nov-03 Dec-03
Part 100 500 485 438 505 483 540 441 550 345
Part 101 175 170 153 177 169 189 154 193 200
Part 102 350 340 306 354 338 378 309 385 350
Part 103 890 863 779 899 859 961 785 979 885
Total 1,915 1,858 1,676 1,934 1,848 2,068 1,689 2,107 1,780
Part Part 102
Date Jun-03
Production 306
PRODSCH Sheet2 Sheet3
Ready
NUM
start
Microsoft Excel - Prod...
3:46 PM

Figure 6-3: Doing a two-way lookup in the Production Schedule table.

To look up the number of parts to be produced for a particular month, you need to the use the MATCH function, which returns the relative position of a particular value in a cell range or array. The syntax of the MATCH function is as follows:

```
MATCH(lookup_value,lookup_array,[match_type])
```

The *lookup_value* argument is, of course, the value whose position you want returned when a match is found, and the *lookup_array* is the cell range or array containing the values that you want to match. The optional *match_type* argument is the number 1, 0, or -1, which specifies how Excel matches the value specified by the *lookup_value* argument in the range specified by the *lookup_array* argument:

- Use *match_type 1* to find the largest value that is less than or equal to the *lookup_value*. Note that the values in the *lookup_array* must be placed in ascending order when you use the 1 *match_type* argument (Excel uses this type of matching when the *match_type* argument is omitted from the MATCH function).
- Use *match_type 0* to find the first value that is exactly equal to the *lookup_value*. Note that the values in the *lookup_array* can be in an order when you use the 0 *match_type* argument.

✦ Use *match_type -1* to find the smallest value that is greater than or equal to the *lookup_value*. Note that the values in the *lookup_array* must be placed in descending order when you use the -1 *match_type* argument.

In addition to looking up the position of the production date and part number in the column and row headings in the Production Schedule table, you need to use an INDEX function, which uses the relative row and column number position to return the number to be produced from the table itself. The INDEX function follows two different syntax forms: array and reference. You use the array form when you want a value returned from the table (as you do in this example), and you use the reference form when you want a reference returned from the table.

The syntax of the array form of the INDEX function is as follows:

```
INDEX(array,[row_num],[col_num])
```

The syntax of the reference form of the INDEX function is as follows:

```
INDEX(reference,[row_num],[col_num],[area_num])
```

The *array* argument of the array form of the INDEX function is a range of cells or array constant that you want Excel to use in the lookup. If this range or constant contains only one row or column, the corresponding *row_num* or *col_num* arguments are optional. If the range or array constant has more than one row or more than one column, and you specify both the *row_num* and the *col_num* arguments, Excel returns the value in the *array* argument that is located at the intersection of the *row_num* argument and the *col_num* argument.

For the MATCH and INDEX functions in the example shown in Figure 6-3, I assigned the following range names to the following cell ranges:

✦ Table_data to the cell range A2:J6 with the production data plus column and row headings

✦ Part_list to the cell range A2:A6 with the row headings in the first column of the table

✦ Date_list to the cell range A2:J2 with the column headings in the first row of the table

✦ Part_lookup to cell B10 that contains the name of the part to look up in the table

✦ Date_lookup to cell B11 that contains the name of the production date to look up in the table

As Figure 6-3 shows, cell B12 contains a rather long and — at first glance — complex formula using the range names outlined previously and combining the INDEX and MATCH functions:

```
=INDEX(table_data,MATCH(part_lookup,part_list),MATCH(date_loo
    kup,date_list))
```

So you better understand how this formula works, I break the formula down into its three major components: the first MATCH function that returns the *row_num* argument for the INDEX function, the second MATCH function that returns the *col_num* argument for the INDEX function, and the INDEX function itself that uses the values returned by the two MATCH functions to return the number of parts produced.

The first MATCH function that returns the *row_num* argument for the INDEX function is:

```
MATCH(part_lookup,part_list)
```

This MATCH function uses the value input into cell B10 (named part_lookup) and looks up its position in the cell range A2:A6 (named part_list). It then returns this row number to the INDEX function as its *row_num* argument. In the case of the example shown in Figure 6-3 where Part 102 is entered in the part_lookup cell in B10, Excel returns 4 as the *row_num* argument to the INDEX function.

The second MATCH function that returns the *col_num* argument for the INDEX function is:

```
MATCH(date_lookup,date_list)
```

This second MATCH function uses the value input into cell B11 (named date_lookup) and looks up its position in the cell range A2:J2 (named date_list). It then returns this column number to the INDEX function as its *col_num* argument. In the case of the example shown in Figure 6-3 where June 1, 2003 (formatted as Jun-03) is entered in the date_lookup cell in B11, Excel returns 4 as the *col_num* argument to the INDEX function.

This means that for all its supposed complexity, the INDEX function shown on the Formula bar in Figure 6-3 contains the equivalent of the following formula:

```
=INDEX(table_data,4,4)
```

As Figure 6-3 shows, Excel returns 306 as the planned production value for Part 102 in June, 2003. You can verify that this is correct by manually counting the rows and the columns in the table_data range (cell range A2:J6). If you count down four rows (including row 2, the first row of this range), you come to Part 102 in column A. If you then count four columns over (including column A with Part 102), you come to cell D5 in the Jun-03 column with the value 306.

Using the Lookup Wizard

Instead of using the INDEX and MATCH lookup functions to do a two-way lookup, you can use the Lookup Wizard add-in to build the necessary formulas. After you activate the Lookup Wizard add-in by clicking the Lookup Wizard check box in the Add Ins dialog box (Tools⇨Add-Ins), Excel adds a Lookup menu item to the Tools pull-down menu.

To better understand how this works, follow these steps for using the Lookup Wizard to extract the number of items produced for a particular part number and date in the Production Schedule table shown in Figure 6-3:

1. **Choose Tools⇨Lookup from the Excel menu bar.**

   When you choose Tools⇨Lookup from the Excel menu bar after activating the Lookup Wizard add-in, the program opens the Lookup Wizard — Step 1 of 4 dialog box (similar to the one shown in Figure 6-4), where you select the range of cells that contains the values to be used in the lookup. In the example shown in Figure 6-4, I selected the cell range A2:J6 as the range on which to perform the lookup (and because this range is named table_data, I could have entered it in the Where Is the Range to Search, Including the Row and Column Labels combo box instead of selecting the cell range).

2. **Click the Next> button in the Lookup Wizard - Step 1 of 4 dialog box.**

   After you click the Next> button, the Lookup Wizard — Step 2 of 4 dialog box appears (similar to the one shown in Figure 6-5), where you select first the column and then the row that contains the value you want looked up in the cell range that you just designated in the Step 1 of 4 dialog box.

3. **Click the name of the column on Which Column Contains the Value to Find drop-down list that you open by clicking its drop-down button.**

   For this example, I designate Oct-03 as the column to use by clicking its name on this column drop-down list.

4. **Click the name of the row on the Which Row Contains the Value to Find drop-down list that you open by clicking its drop-down button.**

   For this example, I designate Part 100 as the row to use by clicking its name on this row drop-down list.

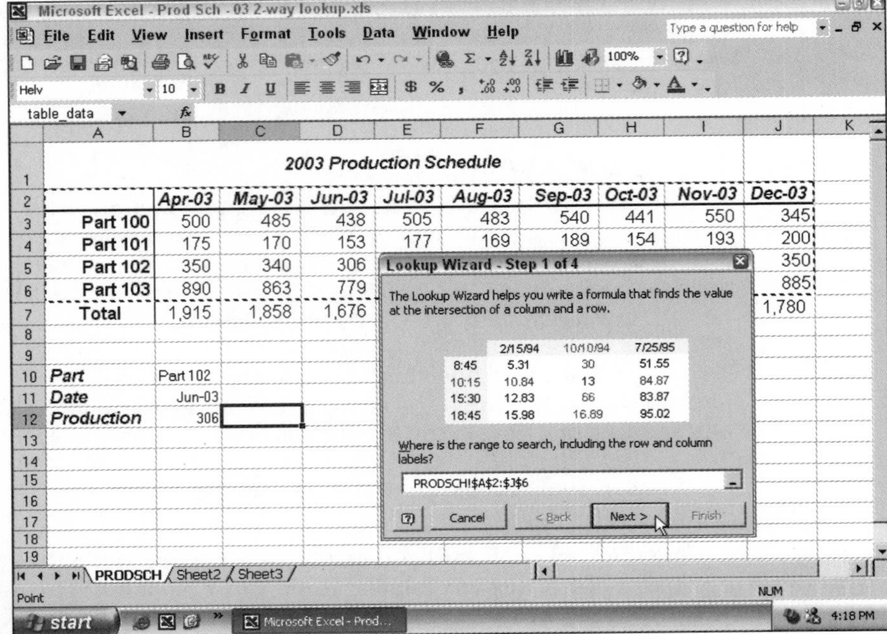

Figure 6-4: Selecting the cell range to search in the Step 1 of 4 dialog box.

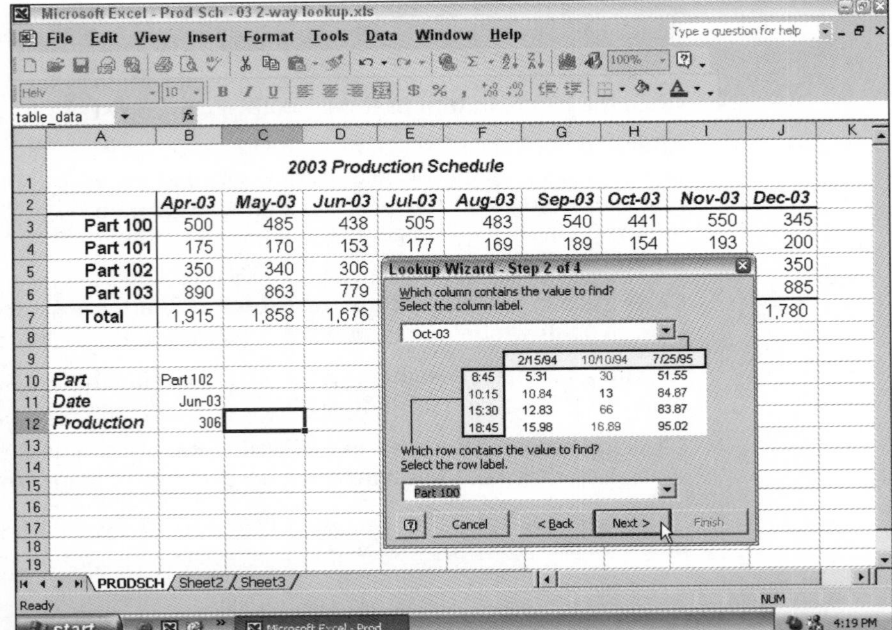

Figure 6-5: Selecting the column and rows with the values to find in the Step 2 of 4 dialog box.

5. **Click the Next> button in the Lookup Wizard - Step 2 of 4 dialog box.**

   Excel displays the Lookup Wizard — Step 3 of 4 dialog box, where you select between the Copy Just the Formula to a Single Cell radio button and the Copy the Formula and Lookup Parameters radio button.

6. **Leave the Copy Just the Formula to a Single Cell radio button selected to have only the formula inserted a cell. Click the Copy the Formula and Lookup Pararmeters radio button to have the column and row information copied along with the formula.**

   For this example, I clicked the Copy the Formula and Lookup Parameters radio button to have Excel copy both the date and the part number into the worksheet above the lookup formula that it creates (see Figure 6-6).

7. **Click the Next> button in the Lookup Wizard - Step 3 of 4 dialog box.**

   When you leave the Copy Just the Formula to a Single Cell radio button selected, Excel displays the Lookup Wizard - Step 4 of 4 dialog box where you indicate the cell where the formula is to be copied (see Step 10).

   When you click the Copy the Formula and Lookup Parameters radio button, the Lookup Wizard - Step 4 of 6 dialog box appears. In this dialog box, you designate the address of the cell into which to copy the column parameter (Oct-03 in this example).

8. **Type the address of the cell where you want column parameter copied or click the cell directly in the spreadsheet and then click the Next> button.**

   Excel displays the Lookup Wizard - Step 5 of 6 dialog box where you indicate the address of the cell into which to copy the row parameter (Part 100 in this example).

9. **Type the address of the cell where you want the row parameter copied or click the cell directly in the spreadsheet and then click the Next> button.**

   Excel displays the Lookup Wizard - Step 6 of 6 dialog box where you indicate the address of the cell into which to copy the formula that looks up the value at the intersection of the column and row parameter.

10. **Type the address of the cell where you want lookup formula or click the cell directly in the spreadsheet and then click the Finish button.**

Figure 6-6 shows what happened when I clicked the Finish button in the Lookup Wizard — Step 6 of 6 dialog box. As you can see, the final formula created and inserted into cell C12 by the Lookup Wizard uses the INDEX function to look up the column and row numbers returned by the following two MATCH functions:

```
=INDEX(table_data,MATCH(C10,part_list),MATCH(C11,date_list))
```

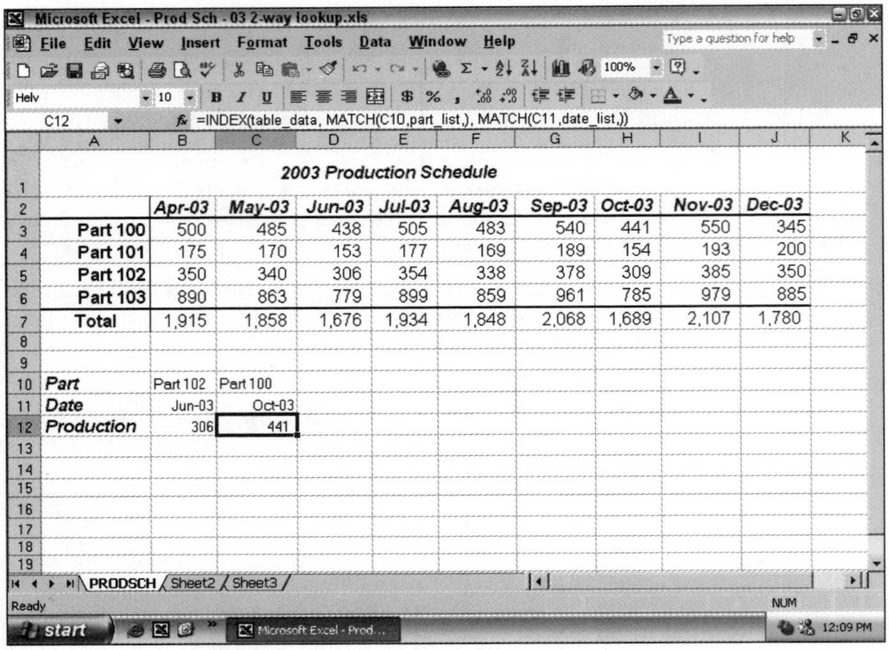

Microsoft Excel - Prod Sch - 03 2-way lookup.xls

C12 =INDEX(table_data, MATCH(C10,part_list,), MATCH(C11,date_list,))

	A	B	C	D	E	F	G	H	I	J
1	2003 Production Schedule									
2		Apr-03	May-03	Jun-03	Jul-03	Aug-03	Sep-03	Oct-03	Nov-03	Dec-03
3	Part 100	500	485	438	505	483	540	441	550	345
4	Part 101	175	170	153	177	169	189	154	193	200
5	Part 102	350	340	306	354	338	378	309	385	350
6	Part 103	890	863	779	899	859	961	785	979	885
7	Total	1,915	1,858	1,676	1,934	1,848	2,068	1,689	2,107	1,780
10	Part	Part 102	Part 100							
11	Date	Jun-03	Oct-03							
12	Production	306	441							

Figure 6-6: Spreadsheet after inserting the lookup formula with parameters in the cell range C10:C12.

So there you have it — a foolproof way to create a sophisticated two-way lookup formula without having to go through all the trouble of correctly nesting the MATCH functions within an INDEX function, not to mention entering in all of the necessary arguments and properly pairing parentheses yourself!

Reference functions

The reference functions, as their name implies, are designed to deal specifically with different aspects of cell references in the worksheet. This group of functions includes:

- ADDRESS to return a cell reference as a text entry in a cell of the worksheet
- AREAS to return the number of areas in a list of values (*areas* are defined as a range of contiguous cells or a single cell in the cell reference)
- COLUMN to return the number representing the column position of a cell reference
- COLUMNS to return the number of columns in a reference

- HYPERLINK to create a link that opens another document stored on your computer, network, or the Internet (you can also do this with the Insert➪Hyperlink command — see Book VIII, Chapter 2 for details)
- INDIRECT to return a cell reference specified by a text string and bring the contents in the cell to which it refers to that cell
- ROW to return the row number of a cell reference
- ROWS to return the number of rows in a cell range or array
- TRANSPOSE to return a vertical array as a horizontal array and vice versa

Get the skinny on columns and rows

The COLUMNS and ROWS function return the number of columns and rows in a particular cell range or array. For example, if you have a cell range in the spreadsheet named product_mix, you can find out how many columns it contains by entering this formula:

```
=COLUMNS(product_mix)
```

If you want to know how many rows this range uses, you then enter this formula:

```
=ROWS(product_mix)
```


As indicated in the previous chapter, you can use the COLUMNS and ROWS functions together to calculate the total number of cells in a particular range. For example, if you want to know the exact number of cells used in the product_mix cell range, you create the following simple multiplication formula by using the COLUMNS and ROWS functions:

```
=COLUMNS(product_mix)*ROWS(product_mix)
```

Don't confuse the COLUMNS (plural) function with the COLUMN (singular) function and the ROWS (plural) function with the ROW (singular) function. The COLUMN function returns the number of the column (as though Excel were using the R1C1 reference system) for the cell reference that you specify as its sole argument. Likewise, the ROW function returns the number of the row for the cell reference that you specify as its argument.

Transposing cell ranges

The TRANSPOSE function enables you to change the orientation of a cell range. You can use this function to transpose a vertical cell range where the data runs down the rows of adjacent columns to one where the data runs across the columns of adjacent rows and vice versa. To successfully use the TRANSPOSE function, not only must you select a range that has an opposite number of columns and row, but you must also enter it as an array formula.

For example, if you're using the TRANSPOSE function to transpose a 2 x 5 cell range (that is, a range that takes up two adjacent rows and five adjacent columns), you must select a blank 5 x 2 cell range (that is, a range that takes five adjacent rows and two adjacent columns) in the worksheet before you use the Insert Function button to insert the TRANSPOSE function in the first cell. Then, after selecting the 2 x 5 cell range that contains the data that you want to transpose in the Array text box of the Function Arguments dialog box, you need to press Ctrl+Shift+Enter to close this dialog box and enter the TRANSPOSE function into the entire selected cell range as an array formula (enclosed in curly braces).

Suppose that you want to transpose the data entered into the cell range A10:C11 (a 2 x 3 array) to the blank cell range E10:F12 (a 3 x 2 array) of the worksheet. When you press Ctrl+Shift+Enter to complete the array formula, after selecting the cell range A10:A11 as the *array* argument, Excel puts the following array formula in every cell of the range:

```
{=TRANSPOSE(A10:C11)}
```

Clicking the OK button in the Function Arguments dialog box only results in inserting the TRANSPOSE function into the active cell of the current cell selection, which in turn returns the #VALUE! error value to the cell — you must remember to press Ctrl+Shift+Enter to put the formula into the entire cell range.

Information, Please . . .

The information functions consist of a number of functions designed to test the contents of a cell or cell range and give you information on its current contents. Such information functions are often combined with IF functions, which determine what type of calculation, if any, to perform. The information function then becomes the *logical_test* argument of the IF function, and the outcome of the test, expressed as the logical TRUE or logical FALSE value, decides whether its *value_if_true* or its *value_if_false* argument is executed (see Chapter 2 in this book for information on using information functions that test for error values to trap errors in a spreadsheet).

In addition to the many information functions that test whether the contents of a cell are of a certain type, Excel offers a smaller set of functions that return coded information about a cell contents or formatting and about the current operating environment in which the workbook is functioning. The program also offers an N (for Number) function that returns the value in a cell and an NA function (for Not Available) that inserts the #NA error value in the cell.

Getting specific information about a cell

The CELL function is the basic information function for getting all sorts of data about the current contents and formatting of a cell. The syntax of the CELL function is:

```
CELL(info_type,[reference])
```

The *info_type* argument is a text value that specifies the type of cell information you want returned. The optional *reference* argument is the reference of the cell range for which you want information. When you omit this argument, Excel specifies the type of information specified by the *info_type* argument for the last cell that was changed in the worksheet. When you specify a cell range as the *reference* argument, Excel returns the type of information specified by the *info_type* argument for the first cell in the range (that is, the one in the upper-left corner, which may or may not be the active cell of the range).

Table 6-1 shows the various *info_type* arguments that you can specify when using the CELL function. Remember that you must enclose each *info_type* argument in the CELL function in double-quotes (to enter them as text values) to prevent Excel from returning the #NAME? error value to the cell containing the CELL function formula. So, for example, if you want to return the contents of the first cell in the range B10:E80, you enter the following formula:

```
=CELL("contents",B10:E80)
```


Table 6-1 The *info_type* Arguments of the CELL Function

Info_type	*Returns*
"address"	Cell address of the first cell in the reference as text using absolute cell references
"col"	Column number of the first cell in the reference
"color"	1 when the cell is formatted in color for negative values; otherwise returns 0 (zero)
"contents"	Value of the upper-left cell in the reference
"filename"	Filename (including the full pathname) of the file containing the cell reference: returns empty text,"", when the workbook containing the reference has not yet been saved

(continued)

Table 6-1 *(continued)*	
Info_type	*Returns*
"format"	Text value of the number format of the cell (see Table 6-2): returns "-" at the end of the text value when the cell is formatted in color for negative values and "()" when the value is formatted with parentheses for positive values or for all values
"parentheses"	1 when the cell is formatted with parentheses for positive values or for all values
"prefix"	Text value of the label prefix used in the cell: single quote (') when text is left-aligned; double quote (") when text is right-aligned; caret (^) when text is centered; backslash (\) when text is fill-aligned; and empty text ("") when cell contains any other type of entry
"protect"	0 when the cell is unlocked and 1 when the cell is locked (see Book IV, Chapter 2 for details on protecting cells in a worksheet)
"row"	Row number of the first cell in the reference
"type"	Text value of the type of data in the cell: "b" for blank when cell is empty; "l" for label when cell contains text constant; and "v" for value when cell contains any other entry
"width"	Column width of the cell rounded off to the next highest integer (each unit of column width is equal to the width of one character in Excel's default font size)

Table 6-2 shows the different text values along with their number formats (codes) that can be returned when you specify "format" as the *info_type* argument in a CELL function (refer to Book II, Chapter 3 for details on number formats and the meaning of the various number format codes).

Table 6-2	Text Values Returned by the "format" *info_type*
Text Value	*Number Formatting*
"G"	General
"F0"	0
",0"	#,##0
"F2"	0.00
",2"	#,##0.00
"C0"	$#,##0_);($#,##0)
"C0-"	$#,##0_);[Red]($#,##0)
"C2"	$#,##0.00_);($#,##0.00)
"C2-"	$#,##0.00_);[Red]($#,##0.00)
"P0"	0%
"P2"	0.00%
"S2"	0.00E+00

Text Value	*Number Formatting*
"G"	# ?/? or # ??/??
"D4"	m/d/yy or m/d/yy h:mm or mm/dd/yy
"D1"	d-mmm-yy or dd-mmm-yy
"D2"	d-mmm or dd-mmm
"D3"	mmm-yy
"D5"	mm/dd
"D7"	h:mm AM/PM
"D6"	h:mm:ss AM/PM
"D9"	h:mm
"D8"	h:mm:ss

For example, if you use the CELL function that specifies "format" as the *info_type* argument on cell range A10:C28 (that you've formatted with the Comma style button on the Formula bar), as in the following formula:

```
=CELL("format",A10:C28)
```

Excel returns the text value ",2-" (sans quotes) in the cell where you enter this formula signifying that the first cell uses the Comma style format with two decimal places and that negative values are displayed in color (red) and enclosed in parentheses.

Are you my type?

Excel provides another information function that returns the type of value in a cell. Aptly named, the TYPE function enables you to build formulas with the IF function that execute one type of behavior when the cell being tested contains a value and another when it contains text. The syntax of the TYPE function is:

```
TYPE(value)
```

The *value* argument of the TYPE function can be any Excel entry: text, number, logical value, or even an Error value or a cell reference that contains such a value. The TYPE function returns on the following values, indicating the type of contents:

- 1 for numbers
- 2 for text
- 3 for logical value (TRUE or FALSE)
- 4 for an array range or constant (see Chapter 1 in this book)

The following formula combines the CELL and TYPE function nested within an IF function. This formula returns the type of the number formatting used in cell D11 only when the cell contains a value: Otherwise, it assumes that D11 contains a text entry and it evaluates the type of alignment assigned to the text in that cell:

```
=IF(TYPE(D11)=1,CELL("format",D11),CELL("prefix",D11))
```

Using the IS functions

The IS information functions (as in ISBLANK, ISERR, and so on) are a large group of functions that perform essentially the same task. They evaluate a value or cell reference and return the logical TRUE or FALSE, depending upon whether the value is or isn't the type for which the IS function tests. For example, if you use the ISBLANK function to test the contents of cell A1 as in:

```
=ISBLANK(A1)
```

Excel returns TRUE to the cell containing the formula when A1 is empty and FALSE when it's occupied by any type of entry.

Excel offers 9 built-in IS information functions:

- ISBLANK(*value*) to evaluate whether the value or cell reference is empty
- ISERR(*value*) to evaluate whether the value or cell reference contains an Error value (except for #NA)
- ISERROR(*value*) to evaluate whether the value or cell reference contains an Error value (including #NA)
- ISLOGICAL(*value*) to evaluate whether the value or cell reference contains the logical TRUE or FALSE value
- ISNA(*value*) to evaluate whether the value or cell reference contains the special #NA Error value
- ISNONTEXT(*value*) to evaluate whether the value or cell reference contains any type of entry other than text
- ISNUMBER(*value*) to evaluate whether the value or cell reference contains a number
- ISREF(*value*) to evaluate whether the value or cell reference is itself a cell reference
- ISTEXT(*value*) to evaluate whether the value or cell reference contains a text entry

In addition to these nine IS functions, Excel adds two more, ISEVEN and ISODD, when you activate the Analysis ToolPak add-in. The ISEVEN function evaluates whether the number or reference to a cell containing a number is even, whereas the ISODD function evaluates whether it is odd.

Much Ado about Text

Normally, when you think of doing calculations in a spreadsheet, you think of performing operations on its numeric entries. You can, however, use the text functions as well as the concatenation operator (&) to perform operations on its text entries as well (referred to collectively as *string operations*).

Using text functions

Text functions include two types of functions: functions such as VALUE, TEXT, and DOLLAR that convert numeric text entries into numbers and numeric entries into text, and functions such as UPPER, LOWER, and PROPER that manipulate the strings of text themselves.

Many times, you need to use the text functions when you work with data from other programs. For example, suppose that you purchase a target client list on disk, only to discover that all the information has been entered in all uppercase letters. In order to use this data with your word processor's Mail merge feature, you would use Excel's PROPER function to convert the entries so that only the initial letters of each word is in uppercase.

Text functions such as the UPPER, LOWER, and PROPER functions all take a single *text* argument that indicates the text that should be manipulated. The UPPER function converts all letters in the *text* argument to uppercase. The LOWER function converts all letters in the *text* argument to lowercase. The PROPER function capitalizes the first letter of each word as well as any other letters in the *text* argument that don't follow another letter — all other letters in the *text* argument are changed to lowercase.

Figure 6-7 illustrates a situation in which you would use the PROPER function. Here, both last and first name text entries have been made in all uppercase letters. Follow along with these steps for using the PROPER function to convert text entries to the proper capitalization:

1. **Position the cell pointer in cell C3 and then click the Insert Function button on the Formula bar.**

   The Insert Function dialog box opens. Next, you need to select Text as the function category.

2. **Click Test in the Or Select a Category drop-down list box, and then double-click PROPER in the Select a Function list box.**

   The Function Arguments dialog box opens, where you need to specify the cell reference A3 as the *text* argument in the Text box.

3. **Click cell A3 in the worksheet to insert A3 in the Text box and then click OK to insert the PROPER function into cell C3.**

   Excel closes the Insert Function dialog box and inserts the formula =PROPER(A3) in cell C3, which now contains the proper capitalization of the last name Aiken.

4. **Drag the Fill handle in the lower-right corner of cell C3 to the right to cell D3 and then release the mouse button to copy the formula with the PROPER function to this cell.**

   Excel now copies the formula =PROPER(B3) to cell D3, which now contains the proper capitalization of the first name, Christopher. Now you're ready to copy these formulas with the PROPER function down to row 17.

5. **Drag the Fill handle in the lower-right corner of cell D3 down to cell D17, and then release the mouse button to copy the formulas with the PROPER function down.**

   The cell range C3:D17 now contains first and last name text entries with the proper capitalization. Before replacing all the uppercase entries in A3:B17 with these proper entries, you convert them to their calculated values. This action replaces the formulas with the text as though you had typed each name in the worksheet.

6. **With the cell range A3:D17 still selected, choose Edit⇨Copy on the Excel Menu bar.**

7. **Immediately choose Edit⇨Paste Special on the Excel Menu bar and then click the Values option button in the Paste Special dialog box before you click OK.**

   You've now replaced the formulas with the appropriate text. Now you're ready to move this range on top of the original range with the all-uppercase entries. This action will replace the uppercase entries with the ones using the proper capitalization.

8. **With the cell range A3:D17 still selected, position the white-cross pointer on the bottom of the range and then when the pointer changes to an arrowhead, drag the cell range until its outline encloses the range A3:B7, and then release the mouse button.**

   Excel displays an alert box asking if you want the program to replace the contents of the destination's cells.

9. **Click OK in the Alert dialog box to replace the cells with the all-uppercase text entries with the entries with proper capitalization.**

Your worksheet now looks like the one shown in Figure 6-8. Everything is fine in the worksheet with the exception of the two last names, Mcavoy and Mcclinton. You have to manually edit cells A11 and A12 to capitalize the *A* in McAvoy and the second *C* in McClinton.

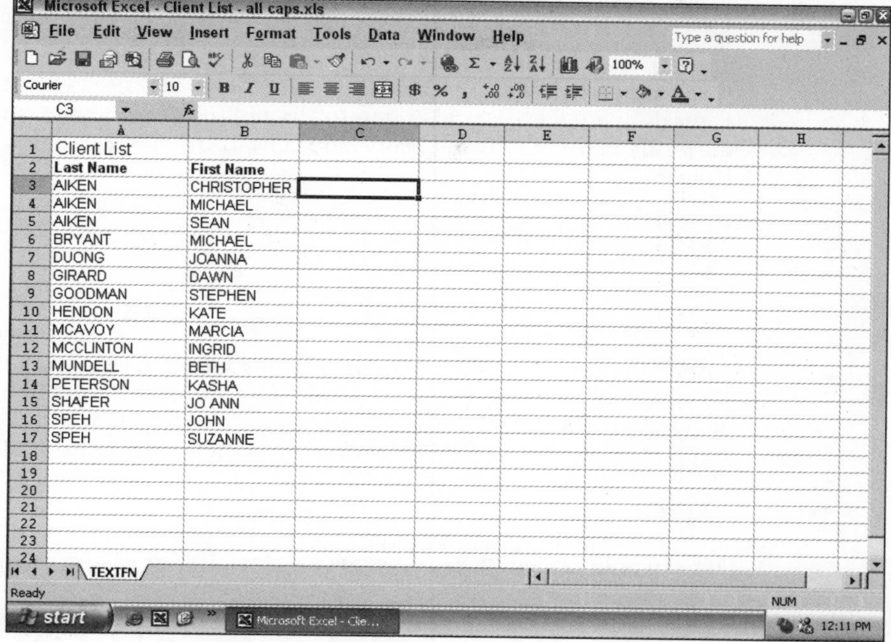

	A	B
1	Client List	
2	**Last Name**	**First Name**
3	AIKEN	CHRISTOPHER
4	AIKEN	MICHAEL
5	AIKEN	SEAN
6	BRYANT	MICHAEL
7	DUONG	JOANNA
8	GIRARD	DAWN
9	GOODMAN	STEPHEN
10	HENDON	KATE
11	MCAVOY	MARCIA
12	MCCLINTON	INGRID
13	MUNDELL	BETH
14	PETERSON	KASHA
15	SHAFER	JO ANN
16	SPEH	JOHN
17	SPEH	SUZANNE

Figure 6-7: Spreadsheet with names in all uppercase letters.

	A	B
1	Client List	
2	**Last Name**	**First Name**
3	Aiken	Christopher
4	Aiken	Michael
5	Aiken	Sean
6	Bryant	Michael
7	Duong	Joanna
8	Girard	Dawn
9	Goodman	Stephen
10	Hendon	Kate
11	Mcavoy	Marcia
12	Mcclinton	Ingrid
13	Mundell	Beth
14	Peterson	Kasha
15	Shafer	Jo Ann
16	Speh	John
17	Speh	Suzanne

Figure 6-8: Spreadsheet after converting the names to initial caps with the PROPER function.

Concatenating text

You can use the ampersand (&) operator to concatenate (or join) separate text strings together. For example, in the Client list spreadsheet shown in Figure 6-8, you can use this operator to join together the first and last names currently entered in two side-by-side cells into a single entry, as shown in Figure 6-9.

To join the first name entry in cell B3 with the last name entry in cell A3, I entered the following formula in cell C3:

```
=B3&" "&A3
```

Notice the use of the double quotes in this formula. They enclose a blank space that is placed between the first and last name joined to them with the two concatenation operators. If I didn't include this space in the formula, but just joined the first and last name together with this formula:

```
=B3&A3
```

Excel would return ChristopherAiken to cell C3, all as one word.

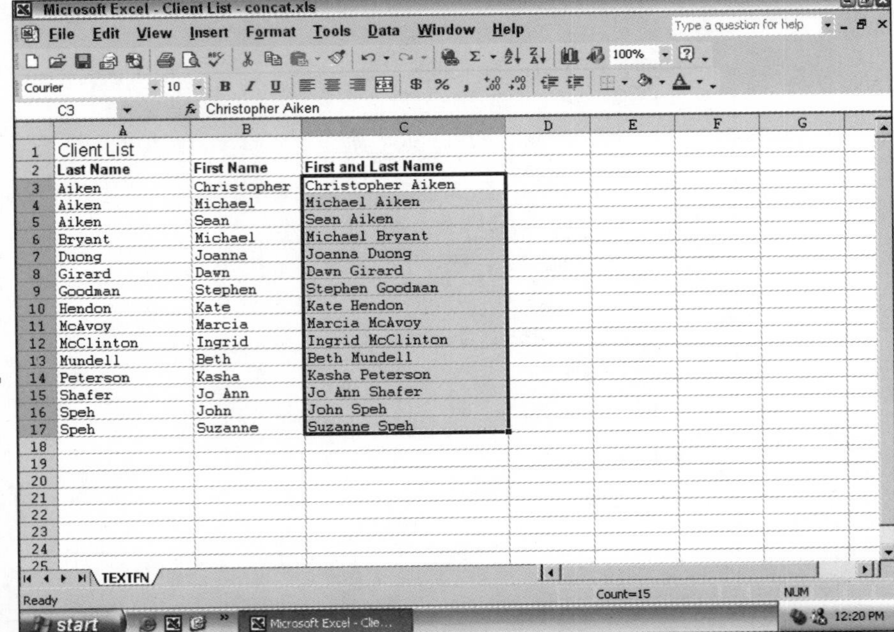

Figure 6-9: Spreadsheet after concatenating the first and last names in column C.

After entering the concatenation formula that joins the first and last names in cell C3 separated by a single space, I then dragged the Fill handle in cell C3 down to C17 to join all of the other client names in a single cell in column C.

After the original concatenation formula is copied down the rows of column C, I then copied the selected cell range C3:C17 to the Clipboard (Ctrl+C) and then used the Values option in the Paste Special dialog box (Edit⇨Paste Special) to paste calculated text values over the concatenation formulas, thereby replacing the original formulas. The result, as evidenced by cell C3 in Figure 6-9, is a list of first and last names together in the same cell in the range C3:C17, as though I had manually input each one.

Book IV

Worksheet Collaboration

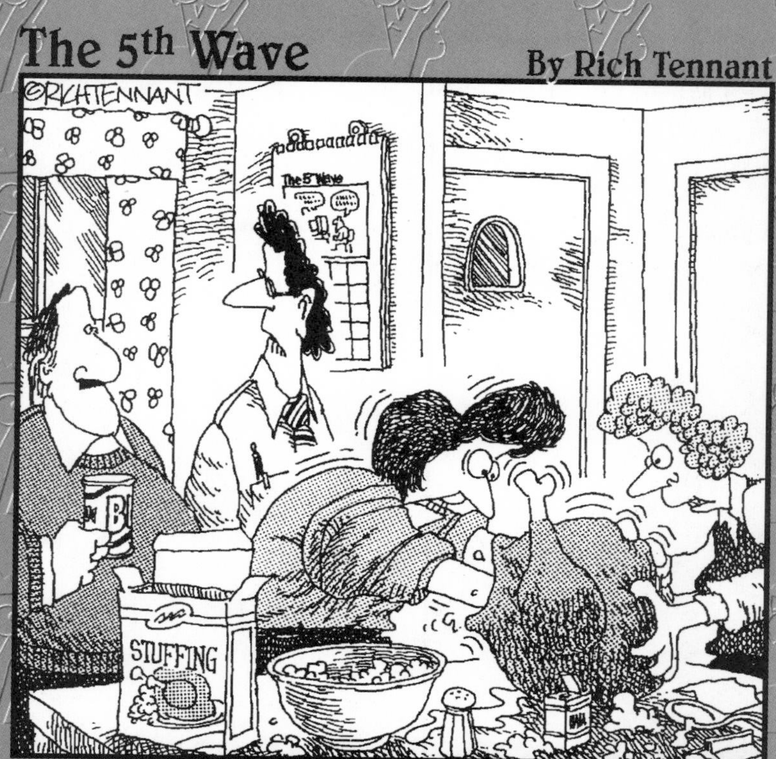

"That reminds me – I have to fill in customized data in my Excel Spreadsheet."

Contents at a Glance

Chapter 1: Sharing and Reviewing Workbooks

In This Chapter

- Sharing workbooks on a network
- Using Change tracking to share a workbook
- Merging changes in different copies of a workbook back into the original
- Adding and reviewing comments in a workbook
- Sending a workbook out for review
- Routing a workbook to a series of reviewers
- Posting a workbook to a public Exchange folder

In this day and age of networked personal computers and high-speed Internet access, Excel offers you the capability of not only sharing your Excel spreadsheets with co-workers and clients, but also tracking and managing your collective editing changes, in effect, enabling you to create spreadsheets by committee.

In this chapter, you discover how to track the changes you make to a shared workbook and enable co-workers to simultaneously edit them. You also find out how to merge changes that different workers independently make to the contents of the workbook so you end up with a single, updated version that you can distribute within and without the company.

As part of the review process, you may want to just comment on aspects of the spreadsheet and suggest possible changes rather than make these changes yourself. In this chapter, you find out how to get your two cents in by annotating a spreadsheet with text notes that indicate suggested improvements or corrections.

Workbook Sharing 101

If you use Excel on a computer that's connected to a network, you can share the spreadsheets that you create with the others who have network access. Workbook sharing is perfect for spreadsheets that require frequent or regular data updates, especially for those whose data comes from several different departments, such as spreadsheets that track budgets or schedule projects that rely on input from many departments.

By sharing a workbook, you enable several people to edit its contents at the same time. Most often, you facilitate this process by saving the workbook file in a folder on network drive to which everyone who needs to edit the spreadsheet has access.

You can share an Excel workbook on a network in one of two ways:

- ✦ Set up file sharing for the workbook by choosing the Tools⇨Share Workbook command.
- ✦ Turn on Change tracking for the workbook by choosing the Tools⇨Track Changes⇨Highlight Changes command.

Whenever you share a workbook using either of these two methods, Excel automatically saves your workbook under the same filename with the shared information. The program then indicates that the workbook can now be shared by appending [Shared] to the workbook's filename as it appears on the title bar of the Excel program window. When a second person on another computer on the network opens the shared workbook file, Excel opens a copy of the workbook file and the [Shared] indicator also appears on the title bar of his or her Excel program window, appended to its filename.

This is in stark contrast to what happens when you try to open an unshared workbook on your computer that's already open on another computer on the network. In that case, Excel displays a File in Use alert dialog box, informing you that the workbook you want to open is already open. You can then choose between clicking the Read Only button to open the file in read-only mode (in which you can't save your changes under the original filename) and clicking the Notify button to have the program open the file in read-only mode and then notify you when the other person closes the workbook so you can save your changes.

If you click the Notify button, as soon as the other person who was editing the workbook closes the file, Excel then displays a File Now Available alert dialog box, letting you know that the file is now available to save your editing. You then click its Read-Write button to close this alert dialog box, and after that you're free to save your editing changes to the original filename with the File⇨Save command.

Note that you don't have to be running Excel 2002 on your computer in order to open and edit a shared workbook. Workbook sharing is supported by all versions of Excel, from Excel 97 through Excel 2002. You can't, however, save changes to a shared workbook if you're using an earlier version of Excel.

Also note that when you make changes to a shared workbook, Excel uses your user name to identify the modifications that you made. To modify your user name, you edit the contents of the User Name text box on the General tab of the Options dialog box (Tools⇨Options).

Keep in mind that when you share a workbook, Excel disables some of the program's editing features so they can't be used in editing the shared spreadsheet. The following tasks are not enabled in a shared workbook:

- ✦ Deleting worksheets from the workbook
- ✦ Merging cells in the worksheets of a workbook
- ✦ Applying conditional formats to the cells of the worksheets (although all conditional formats in effect before you share the workbook remain in effect)
- ✦ Setting up or applying data validation to cells of the worksheets (although all data validations, restrictions, and messages remain in effect in the shared workbook)
- ✦ Inserting or deleting blocks of cells in a worksheet (although you can insert or delete entire columns and rows from the sheet)
- ✦ Drawing shapes and adding text boxes with the tools on the Drawing toolbar (see Book V, Chapter 2 for details)
- ✦ Assigning passwords for protecting individual worksheets or the entire workbook (although all protection and passwords defined prior to sharing the workbook remain in effect — see Book IV, Chapter 2 for details on protecting worksheets)
- ✦ Grouping or outlining data in a worksheet (see Book II, Chapter 4 for details)
- ✦ Inserting automatic subtotals in a worksheet (see Book VI, Chapter 1 for details)
- ✦ Creating data tables or pivot tables in a worksheet (see Book VII, Chapters 1 and 2 for details)
- ✦ Creating, revising, or assigning macros (although you can run macros that were created in the worksheet before it was shared, provided that they don't perform any operations that aren't supported by a shared workbook — see Book IX, Chapter 1 for details)

Turning on file sharing

The first way to share a workbook is by turning on file sharing as follows:

1. **Open the workbook to be shared and then make any last-minute edits to the file, especially those that are not supported in a shared workbook.**

   Keep in mind, when making these last-minute changes, that when you share a workbook, some of Excel's editing features become unavailable to you and any others working in the file. (Refer to the list in the previous section for exactly which features are unavailable.)

   Before turning on file sharing, you may want to save the workbook in a special folder on a network drive to which everyone who is to edit the file has access.

2. **(Optional) Choose File➪Save As and then select the network drive and the folder in which you want to the make the shared version of this file available.**

3. **Choose Tools➪Share Workbook from the Excel Menu bar.**

   Excel opens a Share Workbook dialog box (similar to the one shown in Figure 1-1). This dialog box contains two tabs: an Editing tab that enables you to turn on file sharing for all the users who have the file open, and an Advanced tab where you control the amount of time that changes are tracked and how updates are handled.

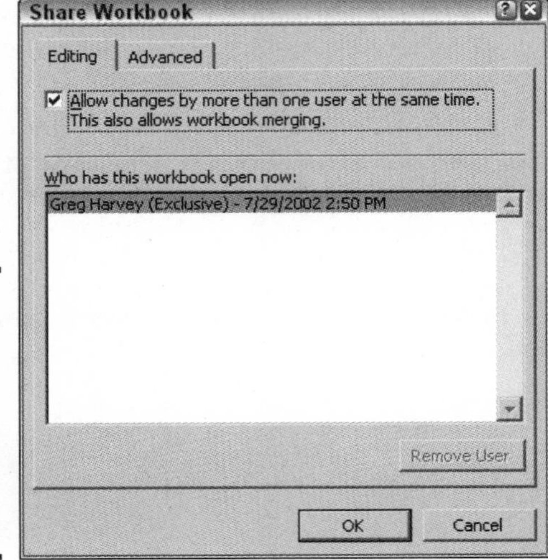

Figure 1-1: Turning on file sharing on the Editing tab of the Share Workbook dialog box.

4. **Click the Allow Changes by More Than One User at the Same Time check box on the Editing tab.**

By default, Excel maintains a Change History log for 30 days. If you wish, you can use the Advanced tab settings to modify whether Excel maintains this Change History log (necessary if you want to reconcile and merge changes) or to change how long the program saves this log. You can also change when changes are updated, how conflicts are handled, and whether or not your print settings and data filtering settings are shared.

5. **(Optional) Click the Advanced tab and then change options on this tab that affect how long a change log is maintained and how editing conflicts are handled.**

   See the following section, "Modifying the Workbook Share options," for details on changing these settings.

6. **Click the OK button to close the Share Workbook dialog box.**

   As soon as Excel closes the Share Workbook dialog box, an alert dialog box appears, telling you that Excel will now save the workbook and asking you if you want to continue.

7. **Click the OK button in the Microsoft Excel alert dialog box to save the workbook with the file sharing settings.**

Immediately after you click OK and close the alert dialog box, Excel saves the workbook and the [Shared] indicator appears at the end of the filename on the Excel program window's title bar.

Modifying the Workbook Share options

As soon as you turn on file sharing for a workbook, Excel also turns on a Change History log that records all changes made by different individuals to the same workbook file. You can use the Change History log to view information about the various changes made to a shared workbook and to determine which of the changes to retain in the event that conflicting changes are made by different people to the same cells of a workbook. You can also use the Change History log when merging changes from different copies of the same workbook into a single file.

By default, Excel maintains the Change History log for a period of thirty days from the date that you first share the workbook. If you wish, you can change length of time that Excel maintains the Change History or, in rare circumstances, elect not to keep the log.

To make changes to length of time that Excel maintains the Change History log, you click the Advanced tab in the Share Workbook dialog box, as shown in Figure 1-2. This tab contains the following sections, with options for not only changing how long the Change History log is maintained, but also for controlling when and how updates are handled:

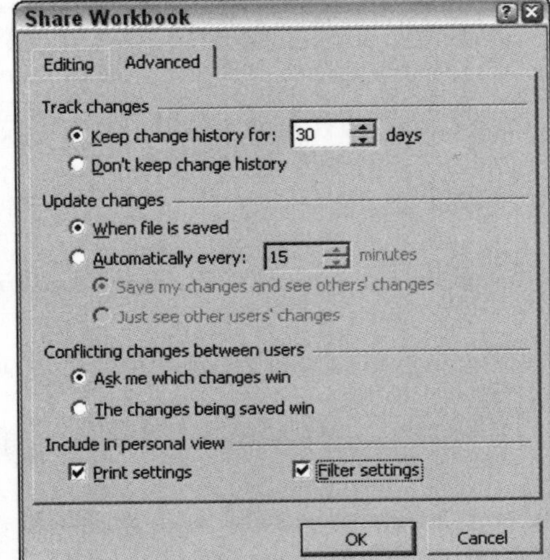

Figure 1-2: Modifying the sharing options on the Advanced tab of the Share Workbook dialog box.

- **Track Changes:** Enables you to modify how long Excel keeps the Change History log by entering a new value in the Keep Change History For text box or selecting a new value with the spinner buttons. Click the Don't Keep Change History radio button should you ever decide that you don't need the Change History log.
- **Update Changes:** Enables you to select when changes made by different users are saved. By default, Excel saves changes when the file is saved. To have the program save changes every so many minutes, click the Automatically Every radio button and then enter the number of minutes for the save interval in the Minutes text box (or select this interval value with its spinner buttons). When automatically saving changes every so many minutes, by default, Excel saves only your changes while showing you changes made to the workbook by others. To have the program just display the changes made to file by others when the save interval is reached (without saving your changes), click the Just See Other Users' Changes radio button.
- **Conflicting Changes Between Users:** Enables you to select how changes made to the same cells of a shared workbook by different users are treated. By default, Excel is set to ask you which users' changes to accept and which to deny. If you want Excel to accept the changes made by any user at the time she or he saves the workbook, click the The Changes Being Saved Win radio button.

- **Include in Personal View:** Enables you to determine which of your personal settings are saved when you save the workbook. By default, Excel saves both your personal print settings (including such things as page breaks, changes to the print area, and changes to the printing settings in the Page Setup dialog box — see Book II, Chapter 5 for details) and the filtering settings you select with Filter submenu on the Data pull-down menu (see Book VI, Chapter 2 for details). Deselect the Print Settings and/or Filter Settings check boxes at the bottom of the Advanced tab if you decide that you don't want these settings saved as part of the shared workbook.

Turning on Change tracking

The second way to share a workbook on a network is by turning on Change tracking. When you do this, Excel tracks all changes you make to the contents of the cells in the shared workbook, highlighting their cells and adding comments that summarize the type of change you make. When you turn on Change tracking, Excel automatically turns on file sharing along with the workbook's Change History log.

To turn on Change tracking in a workbook, you take these steps:

1. **Open the workbook for which you want to track changes and you wish to share and then make any last minute edits to the file, especially those that are not supported in a shared workbook.**

   Keep in mind, when making these last-minute changes, that when you share a workbook, some of Excel's editing features become unavailable to you and any others working in the file. (Refer to the list in the "Workbook Sharing 101" section, earlier in this chapter, for exactly which features are unavailable.)

   Before turning on file sharing, you may want to save the workbook in a special folder on a network drive to which everyone who is to edit the file has access.

2. **(Optional) Choose File⇨Save As and then select the network drive and the folder in which you want to the make the Change tracking version of this file available.**

3. **Choose Tools⇨Track Changes⇨Highlight Changes on the Excel Menu bar.**

   Doing this opens the Highlight Changes dialog box, shown in Figure 1-3, where you turn on Change tracking and indicate which changes to highlight.

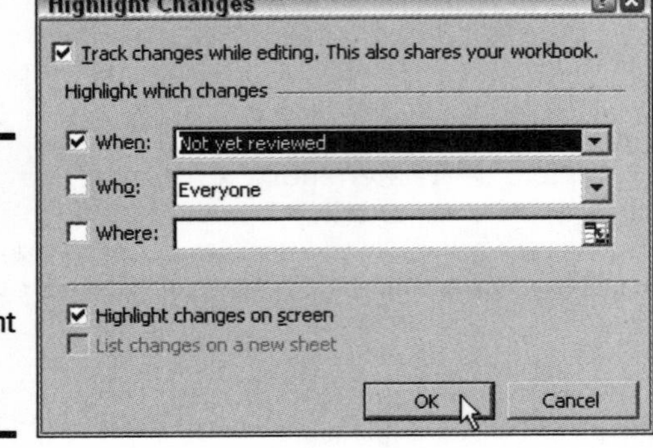

Figure 1-3: Turning on Change tracking in the Highlight Changes dialog box.

4. **Click the Track Changes While Editing check box.**

   Doing this turns on Change tracking and automatically turns on file sharing for the workbook.

   By default, Excel selects the When combo box and chooses the All option from its pop-up menu to have all changes made to workbook tracked. To track the changes only from the time you last saved the workbook, you click the Since I Last Saved item on the When pop-up menu. To track all changes that you've not yet reviewed (and decided whether or not to accept), you click the Not Yet Reviewed item on the When pop-up menu (most often, you want this option so that you can use the Tools⇨Track Changes⇨Accept or Reject Changes command to go through each person's changes and decide whether or not to keep them). To track changes from a particular date, click Since Date on the When pop-up menu: Excel then inserts the current date into the When combo box, which you can then edit, if necessary.

5. **(Optional) If you don't want to track all changes in the workbook, click the When pop-up button and then click the menu item on its pop-up menu (Since I Last Saved, Not Yet Reviewed, or Since Date).**

   By default, Excel tracks the changes made by anybody who opens and edits the workbook (including you). If you want to exempt yourself from Change tracking or restrict it to a particular user, you click the Who check box and then click Everyone But Me or the user's name on the Who pop-up menu.

6. **(Optional) If you want to restrict Change tracking, click the name of the person to whom you want to restrict Change tracking in the Who pop-up list.**

   Note that selecting any option on the Who pop-up menu automatically selects the Who check box by putting a checkmark in it.

   By default, Change Tracking tracks changes made to any and all cells in every sheet in the workbook. To restrict the Change tracking to a particular range or nonadjacent cell selection, click the Where check box and then select the cells.

7. **(Optional) If you want to restrict Change tracking to a particular cell range or cell selection in the workbook, click the Where combo box and then select the cell range or nonadjacent cell selection in the workbook.**

   Clicking the Where combo box and selecting a cell range in the workbook automatically selects the Where check box by putting a checkmark in it.

   By default, Excel highlights all editing changes in the cells of the worksheet on the screen by selecting the Highlight Changes on Screen check box. If you don't want the changes marked in the cells, you need to deselect this check box.

8. **(Optional) If you don't want changes displayed in the cells on screen, click the Highlight Changes on Screen check box to remove its checkmark.**

   Note that after you finish saving the workbook as a shared file, you can return to the Highlight Changes dialog box and then select its List Changes on a New Sheet check box to have all your changes listed on a new worksheet added to the workbook. Note, too, that if you select this check box when the Highlight Changes on Screen check box is selected, Excel both marks the changes in their cells and lists them on a new sheet. If you deselect the Highlight Changes on Screen check box while the List Changes on a New Sheet check box is selected, Excel just lists the changes on a new worksheet without marking them in the cells of the worksheet.

9. **Click the OK button to close the Highlight Changes dialog box.**

   As soon as Excel closes the Highlight Changes dialog box, an alert dialog box appears, telling you that Excel will now save the workbook and asking you if you want to continue.

10. **Click the OK button in the Microsoft Excel alert dialog box to save the workbook with the Change tracking and file sharing settings.**

After you turn on Change tracking in a shared workbook, Excel highlights the following changes:

- ✦ Changes to the cell contents, including moving and copying the contents to new cells in the worksheet
- ✦ Deletion of the cell contents
- ✦ Insertion of new rows, columns, or cells in a worksheet

When Change tracking is turned on in a workbook, the program does *not*, however, highlight any of these changes:

- Formatting changes made to the cells
- Hidden or unhidden rows and columns in the worksheet
- Renamed sheet tabs in the workbook
- Insertion or deletion of worksheet in the workbook
- Comments added to the cells
- Changes to cell values resulting from the recalculation of formulas (or in cells whose values depend upon those formulas)

In highlighting changes you make to the shared workbook, Excel draws a thin line (in another color — usually blue) around the borders of the cell, while at the same time placing a triangle of the same color in the cell's upper-left corner. When you position the thick white-cross mouse pointer on a highlighted cell, Excel displays a comment indicating the change made to the cell, along with the date and time it was made and who it was made by, as shown in Figure 1-4.

When you turn on Change tracking, you also necessarily turn on file sharing, and when file sharing is in effect, you can't make certain kinds of editing changes. For a complete list of these changes, refer to the section, "Workbook Sharing 101," earlier in this chapter.

	A	B	C	D	E	F	G
1	CG Media - 2003 Sales by Category and Date						
2		Jan	Feb	Mar	Qtr 1	Apr	May
3	Compact Discs						
4	Rock	1,245.00	1,373.24	1,229.05	3,847.28	1,069.27	1,122.73
5	Jazz	1,500.00	1,170.80	1,047.87	3,718.67	911.64	957.23
6	Classical	855.60	943.73	844.64	2,643.96	734.83	771.57
7	Other	642.00	708.13	633.77	1,983.90	551.38	578.95
8	Total CD Sales	$ 4,242.60	$ 4,195.89	$ 3,755.32	$ 12,193.81	$ 3,267.13	$ 3,430.49
9	Cassettes						
10	Rock	945.65	1,418.48	1,241.17	3,605.29	1,154.67	872.93
11	Jazz	1,035.00	1,552.50	1,358.44	3,945.94	1,624.35	1,228.01
12	Classical	1,456.00			61.00	1,101.12	832.45
13	Other				75.94	4,935.13	3,730.96
14	Total Casette Sales	$ 3,436.65	$		78.17	$ 8,815.28	$ 6,664.35
15	Total Sales	$ 7,679.25	$		71.98	$ 12,082.41	$ 10,094.84

Greg Harvey, 7/30/2002 10:03 AM:
Changed cell B13 from ' $987.00 ' to '<blank>'.

Figure 1-4: Displaying the comment added to cell highlighted by Change tracking.

Merging changes from different users

At some point after sharing a workbook, you'll want to update the workbook to incorporate the changes made by different users. When merging changes, you may also have to deal with conflicting changes made to the same cells and decide which changes to accept and which to reject. After you've merged all the input and decided how to deal with all the conflicting changes, you may even want to turn off file sharing to prevent users from doing any further editing.

Resolving conflicts

When you turn on file sharing for a workbook, Excel automatically updates the changes made to the shared workbook whenever anybody who's editing the file saves his or her changes. Should the program identify cells in the workbook that contain conflicting changes (that is, different values placed in the same cell by different users), it flags the cell in the workbook and then displays the conflict in the Resolve Conflicts dialog box, as shown in Figure 1-5. To accept your change to the cell in question, you click the Accept Mine button. To accept the change made by another user, you click the Accept Other button instead.

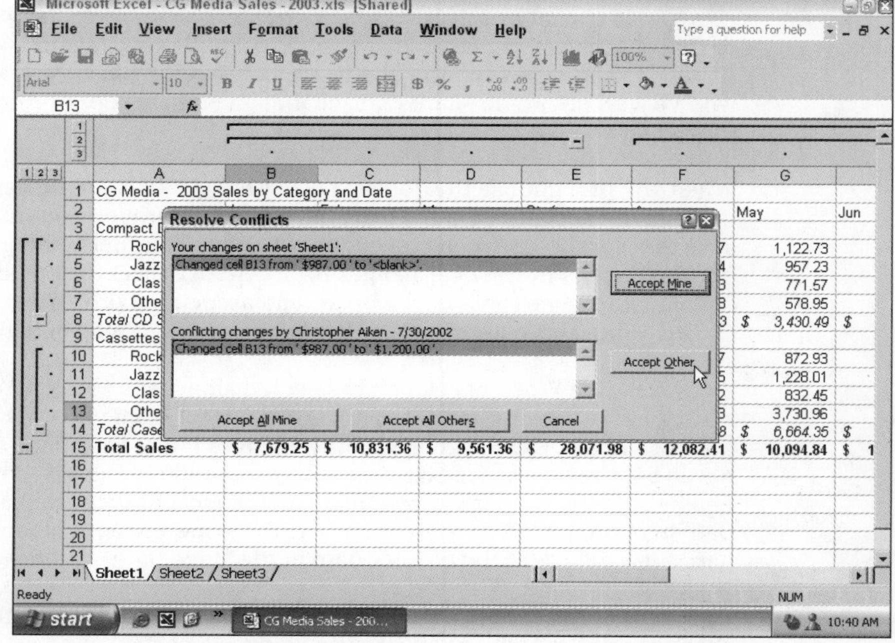

Figure 1-5: Deciding which change to accept in the Resolve Conflicts dialog box.

After you accept your change or the other user's change in the case of the first conflict, Excel flags the next case and displays a description of the conflicting values in the Resolve Conflicts dialog box. When you finish accepting or rejecting your change or the one made by another user for the last conflicting value, Excel automatically closes the Resolve Conflicts dialog box, and you can save your changes to the workbook with the File⇨Save command.

If want Excel to accept only your changes in all cases of conflicting values, click the Accept All Mine button. To have Excel reject all your changes and accepts all those made by others, click the Accept All Others button instead.

If you know that you always want all your changes to be accepted in the case of conflicting values, open the Share Workbook dialog box (Tools⇨Share Workbook) and then click The Changes Being Saved radio button on the Advanced tab before you click OK. If you prefer to have your changes (including conflicting ones) automatically saved at set intervals, click the Automatically radio button, set the number of minutes between saves in the Minutes text box before you click OK.

Accepting or rejecting highlighted changes

When you turn on Change tracking for a workbook, you can decide which changes to accept or reject by selecting the Tools⇨Track Changes⇨Accept or Reject Changes command from the Excel pull-down menus. When you do this, Excel reviews all the highlighted changes made by you and others who've worked on the shared file, enabling you to accept or reject individual changes.

When you first choose the Tools⇨Track Changes⇨Accept or Reject Changes command, Excel displays the alert dialog box, informing you that Excel will save the workbook. When you click OK to close this alert dialog box, the program opens the Select Changes to Accept or Reject dialog box, which contains the same three check boxes and associated drop-down items (When, Who, and Where) as the Highlight Changes dialog box in Figure 1-3.

By default, the When check box is selected along with the Not Yet Reviewed setting in the Select Changes to Accept or Reject dialog box. When this setting is selected, Excel displays all the changes in the workbook that you haven't yet reviewed for everyone who has modified the shared file. To review only those changes you made on the current date, click the Since Date item on the When drop-down list. To review changes made since a particular date, edit the current date in the Since Date drop-down list.

To review only changes that everyone has made except you, only those changes you've made, or only those changes a particular co-worker has made, click the appropriate item (Everyone But Me, your name, or another user's name) on the Who drop-down list. If you want to restrict the review to particular range or region of a worksheet, click the Where combo box and then select the range or nonadjacent cell ranges with the cells to review.

After you select which changes to review in the Select Changes to Accept or Reject dialog box, click the OK button. Excel then closes this dialog box, highlights the cell in the worksheet that contains the first change to review, and opens the Accept or Reject Changes dialog box (similar to the one shown in Figure 1-6) where you indicate whether to accept or reject the change. To accept the change, you click the Accept button. To reject the change and keep the original value, you click the Reject button instead. Excel then highlights the next cell in worksheet that needs reviewing, while at the same time displaying a description of the change in the Accept or Reject Changes dialog box.

If you know ahead of time that you want to accept or reject all the changes that have been made since you last reviewed the workbook (or the date you specified), click the Accept All button or the Reject All button, respectively. When you accept or reject the last change identified in the workbook, the Accept or Reject Changes dialog box automatically closes, and you can then save the workbook (Ctrl+S) with the editing changes made as a result of this review.

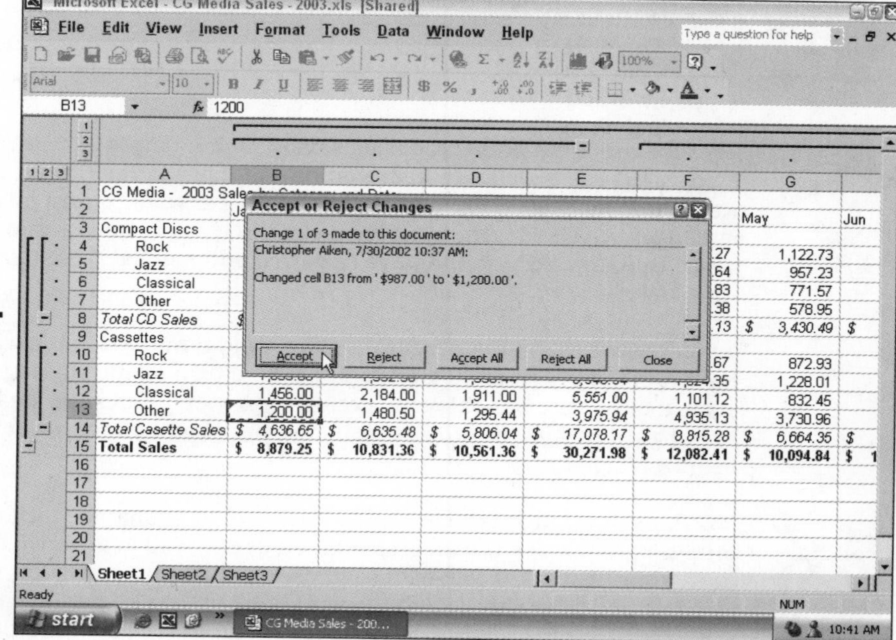

Figure 1-6: Deciding whether or not to accept a change in the Accept or Reject Changes dialog box.

How to stop sharing a workbook

If you decide that you no longer want to share a particular workbook, you can turn off the file sharing. To do this, open the Share Workbook dialog box (Tools➪Share Workbook), remove the checkmark from the Allow Changes by More Than One User at the Same Time check box on the Editing tab before you click OK.

As soon as you click OK, Excel displays an Information alert dialog box (see Figure 1-7), indicating that your action is about to remove the workbook from shared use and (at the same time) erase the Change History log. It also informs you that users who are currently editing this workbook will be unable to save their changes, even if you should later change your mind and turn the file sharing back again.

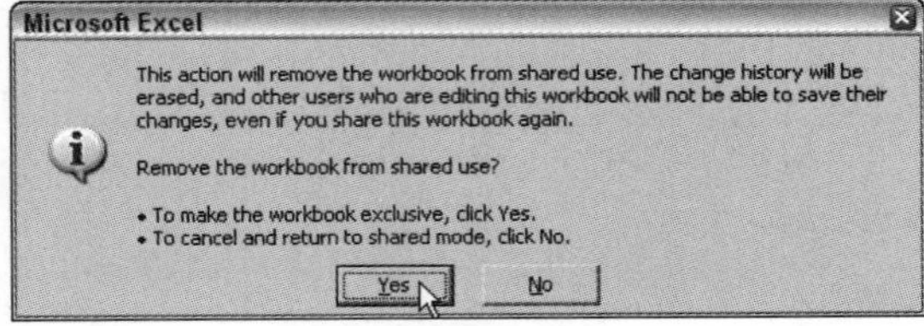

Figure 1-7: Information alert dialog box that appears when you're about to stop sharing a workbook.

Because users are prevented from saving their changes and the Change History log is erased as soon as you turn off file sharing (and make the workbook once again exclusive), you don't *ever* want to turn off file sharing until *after* you're sure that you have everybody's comments and changes saved to the workbook and have reviewed and merged the changes you want to keep.

If you're sure that you've met these two conditions, you can click the Yes button in the Information alert dialog box to turn off file sharing and once again make the workbook your exclusive property. Click the No button, however, to abort this procedure if you have any doubt about having all of your users' changes.

It's always a good idea to inform the users of your shared workbook of your intention to remove the file from shared use — well in advance of the actual date. Your best bet is to e-mail each user and let him or her know exactly the date and time after which the workbook will no longer be shared and open to their edits. That way, each person on the team knows the exact time after which his or her changes and comments will no longer be accepted (which is often a good inducement for the procrastinators on the team to send you their last-minute suggestions and changes).

Removing a user from the shared workbook

Sometimes, rather than preventing everyone from sharing a particular workbook, you may only need to stop particular users from being able to edit it. To remove a specific user from sharing in the editing, you open the Share Workbook dialog box (Tools⇨Share Workbook), click the name of the person you want to remove in the Who Has the Workbook Open Now list box, and then click the Remove User button.

As soon as you click this button, Excel displays an alert dialog box, informing you that if the user you selected is currently editing the workbook, your action will prevent him or her from saving the workbook; all unsaved work is automatically lost. To proceed with removing the user, click the OK button in this alert dialog box. To abandon the removal until after you've verified that the user isn't currently editing the file, click the Cancel button instead.

Merging different copies of a shared workbook

Instead of sharing a single workbook with other users on the network and then doing a review in which you accept or reject their changes when you save the file (or at some predefined time interval), you can distribute copies of a shared workbook and then merge the changes made by different people into one version. The key to merging different copies of a shared workbook is that each copy must have the Change History log turned on and be saved under a different filename.

This means that before you create and distribute copies of the workbook, you must turn on the Change History log by opening the Share Workbook dialog box (Tools⇨Share Workbook) and then clicking the Allow Changes by More Than One User at the Same Time check box to put a checkmark in it. Then you can save copies of the original shared workbook under slightly different filenames (perhaps by appending numbers or the initials of the people doing the review to the filename) before you distribute these different copies to the intended users. These users then make their edits and save their changes to the shared copy of the original workbook that they receive from you.

The only catch is that they must do this editing before the time period set for keeping the Change History log expires (30 days by default). To lengthen this period, increase the number of days in the Keep Change History For text box on the Advanced tab of the Share Workbook dialog box (Tools⇨Share Workbook) before you save copies of the original workbook and distribute them to other users.

When you're ready to merge the copies of the shared workbook into one version, you follow these steps:

1. **Open the original shared workbook into which you want to merge changes from another copy in Excel.**

   Note that this copy or copies of the original workbook (whose changes are to be merged into the workbook you now have open in Excel) must *not* also be open in Excel, and they must have different filenames.

2. **Choose Tools⇨Compare and Merge Workbooks on the Excel Menu bar.**

   Doing this opens the Select Files to Merge Into Current Workbook dialog box, where you indicate the workbook file or files to merge.

3. **Select the folder that contains the workbook(s) to be merged and then click the file icon, or Ctrl+click the file icon to select more than one file.**

4. **Click the OK button to close the Select Files to Merge Into Current Workbook.**

As soon as you click OK, Excel merges the version(s) of the selected workbook(s) into the version you have open in Excel (without prompting you to review or accept or reject any of the updates). All changes in the different version(s) are merged to the one open on your screen. You can then save this single, updated version of the workbook under the same name (Ctrl+S) or under a new filename (File⇨Save As).

Workbooks on Review

Even if you don't use Excel on a network, you still can add your comments to the cells of a workbook; you can ask for clarification or suggest changes, and then distribute copies of the workbook by e-mail to other people who need to review and, perhaps, respond to your remarks. Excel makes it easy to annotate the cells of a worksheet. It also provides a Reviewing toolbar that makes it easy to review these notes, e-mail the workbook to others who have to review the comments, and even reply to suggested changes.

Figure 1-8 identifies the various buttons on the Reviewing toolbar that you can open by choosing View⇨Toolbars⇨Reviewing from the Excel Menu bar or by right-clicking one of the other displayed toolbars (or the Excel Menu bar) and then clicking Reviewing on the shortcut menu.

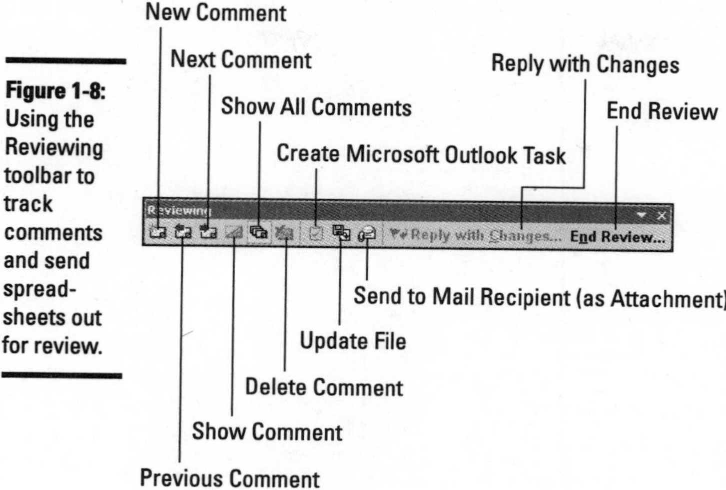

Figure 1-8: Using the Reviewing toolbar to track comments and send spreadsheets out for review.

Adding comments

You can add comments to the current cell either by clicking the New Comment button on the Reviewing toolbar or by choosing Insert Comment on the Excel Menu bar. Excel responds by adding a comment box (similar to the one shown in Figure 1-9) with your name listed at the top (or the name of the person who shows up in the User Name text box on the General tab of the Options dialog box). You can then type the text of your comment in this box. When you finish typing the text of the note, click the cell to which you're attaching the note (or any other cell in the worksheet) to close the Comment box.

Excel indicates that you've attached a comment to a worksheet cell by adding a red triangle to its upper-right corner. To display the Comment box with its text, you position the thick, white-cross mouse pointer on this red triangle, or you position the cell pointer in its cell and then click the Show Comment button on the Reviewing toolbar.

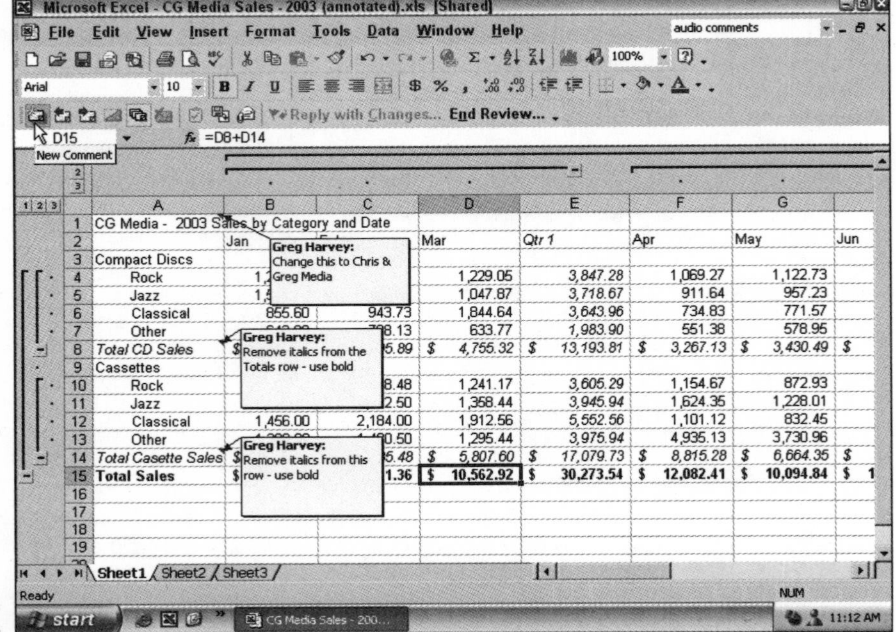

Figure 1-9: Adding comments to the cells of a spreadsheet.

Displaying and hiding comments

When you display a comment by positioning the mouse pointer on the cell's red triangle, the comment disappears as soon as you move the pointer outside the cell. When you display a comment by clicking the Show Comment button, you must click the Show Comment button a second time before Excel closes the comment box.

To display all the comments you've added to cells in the worksheet, click the Show All Comments button on the Reviewing toolbar or choose View➪Comments on the Excel Menu bar. The Comment boxes for all your cell notes appear in the worksheet until you click the Show All Comments button or choose View➪Comment again.

Editing and formatting comments

When you first add a comment to a cell, its Comment box appears to the right of the cell with an arrow pointing to the red triangle in the cell's upper-right corner. If you need to, you can reposition a cell's Comment box and/or resize it so that it doesn't obscure certain cells in the immediate region. You can also edit the text of a comment and change the formatting of the text font.

To reposition or resize a Comment box or edit the note text or its font, you position the cell pointer in the cell and then click the Edit Comment button, which replaces the Add Comment button as the first button on the Reviewing toolbar. If the Reviewing toolbar is not displayed, you can also do this by right-clicking the cell and then clicking Edit Comment on the cell's shortcut menu.

Whichever method you use to choose Edit Comment, Excel then displays the cell's Comment box and positions the insertion point at the end of the comment text. To reposition the Comment box, position the mouse pointer on the edge of the Comment box (indicated with cross-hatching and open circles around the perimeter). When the mouse pointer assumes the shape of a white arrowhead pointing to a black double-cross, you can then drag the outline of the Comment box to a new position in the worksheet. After you release the mouse button, Excel draws a new line (ending in an arrowhead) from the repositioned Comment box to the red triangle in the cell's upper-right corner.

To resize the Comment box, you position the mouse pointer on one of the open circles at the corners, as well as in the middle of each edge on the box's perimeter. When the mouse pointer changes into a double-headed arrow, you drag the dotted outline of the Comment box until it's the size and shape you want. (Excel automatically reflows the comment text to suit the new size and shape of the box.)

To edit the text of the comment (when the insertion point is positioned somewhere in it), drag the I-beam mouse pointer through text that needs to be replaced or press the Backspace key (to remove characters to the left of the insertion point) or Delete key (to remove characters to the right). You can insert new characters in the comment to the right at the insertion by simply typing them.

To change the formatting of the comment text, select the text by dragging the I-beam mouse pointer through it, then right-click the text and click Format Comment on the shortcut menu. Doing this opens the Format Comment dialog box (with the same options as the Font tab of the Format Cells dialog box) where you can change the font, font style, font size, font color, or add special effects that include underlining and strikethrough, as well as super- and subscripting.

When you finish making your changes to the Comment box and text, close the Comment box by clicking its cell or any of the other cells in the worksheet.

Deleting comments

When you no longer need a comment, you can delete it by selecting its cell and then doing any of the following:

- Choose Edit⇨Clear⇨Comments on the Excel Menu bar.
- Click the Delete Comment button on the Reviewing toolbar.
- Right-click the cell and then click Delete Comment on its shortcut menu.

If you delete a comment in error, you can restore it to its cell by choosing Edit⇨Undo Comment or pressing Ctrl+Z.

Sending and reviewing workbooks

Excel makes it easy to send out workbooks that you've annotated for review to clients, co-workers, and managers. You have a choice between sending the spreadsheet embedded within the body of the e-mail message or attaching the workbook to an e-mail message. If you're part of a Microsoft Exchange Server system, you can place a copy of the workbook in a public folder so that all users who have permission to access the contents of that folder can open the workbook for review.

Sending a worksheet in the body of a message

If you just want the recipient to be able to look over the numbers in a spreadsheet and read over your comments to give you an okay — without actually making any changes to the cells or responding to any specific comments — you can send the current worksheet as the body of an e-mail message (that way, they don't even have to have a copy of Excel running on their computers in order to go over the figures in your worksheet). To do this, you select File⇨Send To⇨Mail Recipient. Excel then displays an E-mail dialog box that enables you to choose between sending the workbook as an e-mail attachment and sending the current worksheet as the body of a new message.

To do the latter, you click the Send the Current Sheet as the Message Body radio button and then click OK button on the E-mail dialog box. When you do this, Excel adds a message header along with an E-mail toolbar to the Excel window, as shown in Figure 1-10. You can then fill in the header with the recipient's e-mail address in the To text box, others who are to get copies of the worksheet in the Cc text box, the subject of the message in the Subject text box, and overall instructions and general comments in the Introduction text box. After you fill in this information (or, at the very least, the recipient's e-mail address in the To text box), you're ready to send the message by clicking the Send This Sheet button at the beginning of the E-mail toolbar. When Excel finishes sending the worksheet, the E-mail toolbar and message header automatically disappear from the Excel window.

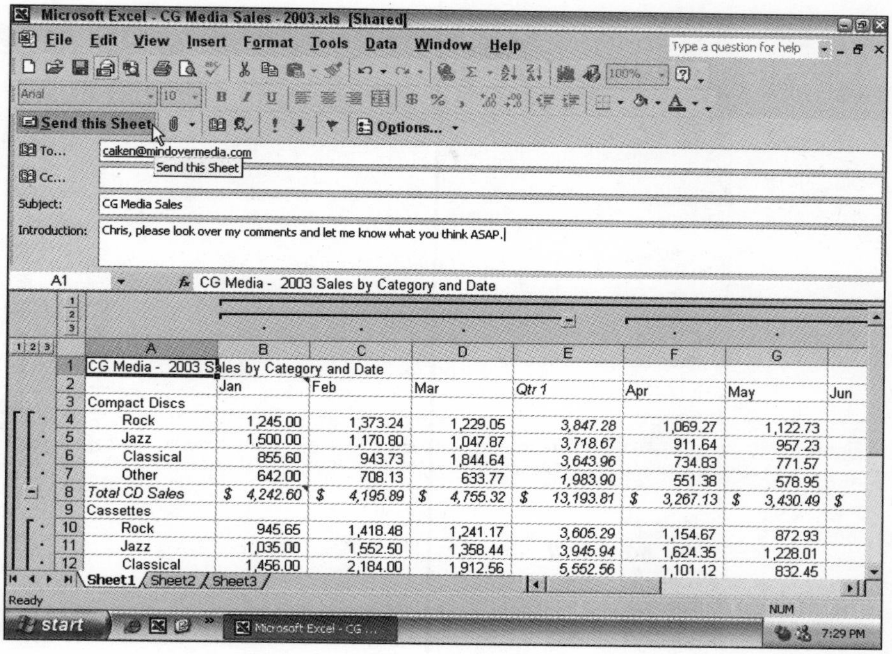

Figure 1-10: Sending the current worksheet as the body of an e-mail message.

Figure 1-11 shows how an e-mail message that contains a spreadsheet in the body appears when opened in Microsoft Outlook. As you can see in this figure, Outlook not only shows all the text and numbers in the spreadsheet as a table set up in columns and rows, but also shows the text of all comments added to the worksheet as electronic footnotes. The program also places a note reference number next to the spreadsheet entry to which the note is attached and then displays the text of the note as a numbered footnote at the bottom of the table. Note that both the reference number in the worksheet and the corresponding footnote number at the bottom of the table are hyperlinks that you can click. When you click a note number in the worksheet, it jumps to and displays the text of the footnote at the bottom of the table. When you click a footnote number at the bottom of the table, Excel jumps you to the corresponding note number in the table and displays the entry that's being referred to in the text of the note.

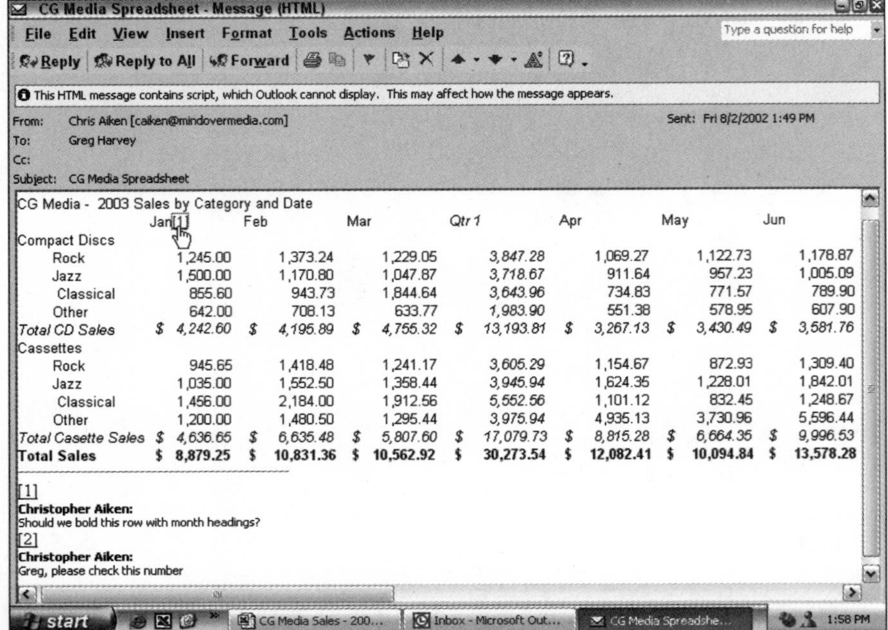

CG Media - 2003 Sales by Category and Date

	Jan[1]	Feb	Mar	Qtr 1	Apr	May	Jun
Compact Discs							
Rock	1,245.00	1,373.24	1,229.05	*3,847.28*	1,069.27	1,122.73	1,178.87
Jazz	1,500.00	1,170.80	1,047.87	*3,718.67*	911.64	957.23	1,005.09
Classical	855.60	943.73	1,844.64	*3,643.96*	734.83	771.57	789.90
Other	642.00	708.13	633.77	*1,983.90*	551.38	578.95	607.90
Total CD Sales	*$ 4,242.60*	*$ 4,195.89*	*$ 4,755.32*	*$ 13,193.81*	*$ 3,267.13*	*$ 3,430.49*	*$ 3,581.76*
Cassettes							
Rock	945.65	1,418.48	1,241.17	*3,605.29*	1,154.67	872.93	1,309.40
Jazz	1,035.00	1,552.50	1,358.44	*3,945.94*	1,624.35	1,228.01	1,842.01
Classical	1,456.00	2,184.00	1,912.56	*5,552.56*	1,101.12	832.45	1,248.67
Other	1,200.00	1,480.50	1,295.44	*3,975.94*	4,935.13	3,730.96	5,596.44
Total Casette Sales	*$ 4,636.65*	*$ 6,635.48*	*$ 5,807.60*	*$ 17,079.73*	*$ 8,815.28*	*$ 6,664.35*	*$ 9,996.53*
Total Sales	**$ 8,879.25**	**$ 10,831.36**	**$ 10,562.92**	**$ 30,273.54**	**$ 12,082.41**	**$ 10,094.84**	**$ 13,578.28**

[1]
Christopher Aiken:
Should we bold this row with month headings?
[2]
Christopher Aiken:
Greg, please check this number

Figure 1-11: Reviewing the e-mail message with the worksheet in the body.

Sending a workbook as an e-mail attachment

If you want your recipients to be able to open the workbook in Excel and be able to review and to respond to specific comments with the program, you can click the Send to Mail Recipient (as Attachment) button on the Reviewing toolbar or choose the File⇨Send To⇨Mail Recipient (as Attachment) command to simply send a copy of the workbook you have open in Excel as an e-mail attachment.

When you do this, Excel opens your e-mail program (such as Outlook or Outlook Express), starts a new e-mail message, and automatically fills in the Subject line of the message and attaches a copy of the current workbook to this new message. You can fill in the recipient's e-mail address in the To text box, type in the body of the message, and then click the Send button to send it off to your recipient or recipients.

When the e-mail recipients open the e-mail message with an attached workbook file, they can save the file to disk and then open it as they would any other Excel workbook.

To save a workbook attached to an e-mail message, right-click the filename of the attached workbook that appears on the message's header and then click Save As on the shortcut menu. If you want to open the workbook directly in Excel, you click Open on the attachment's shortcut menu instead. If your e-mail program is Outlook or Outlook Express, you may receive an Opening Mail Attachment alert dialog box, warning that the file may contain potentially damaging viruses and suggesting that you first save the workbook to disk. If you're sure of the source of the e-mail and aren't worried about a virus, click the Open It radio button in this alert dialog box and then click OK.

Sending a workbook out for review

You can also choose the File➪Send To➪Mail Recipient (for Review) command to send a copy of the current workbook to an e-mail recipient for him or her to review. When you choose this command, Excel opens your e-mail program (such as Outlook or Outlook Express), starts a new e-mail message, and attaches the current workbook as an e-mail attachment. This time, Excel also automatically fills in the Subject line of the message asking the recipient to review the attached file (see Figure 1-12), and inserts the following text into the body of the message:

```
Please review the attached document.
```

All you have to do then is fill in the recipient's e-mail address in the To text box (and those of any other people you want to copy in the Cc text box), and then click the Send button send it off to your recipient or recipients.

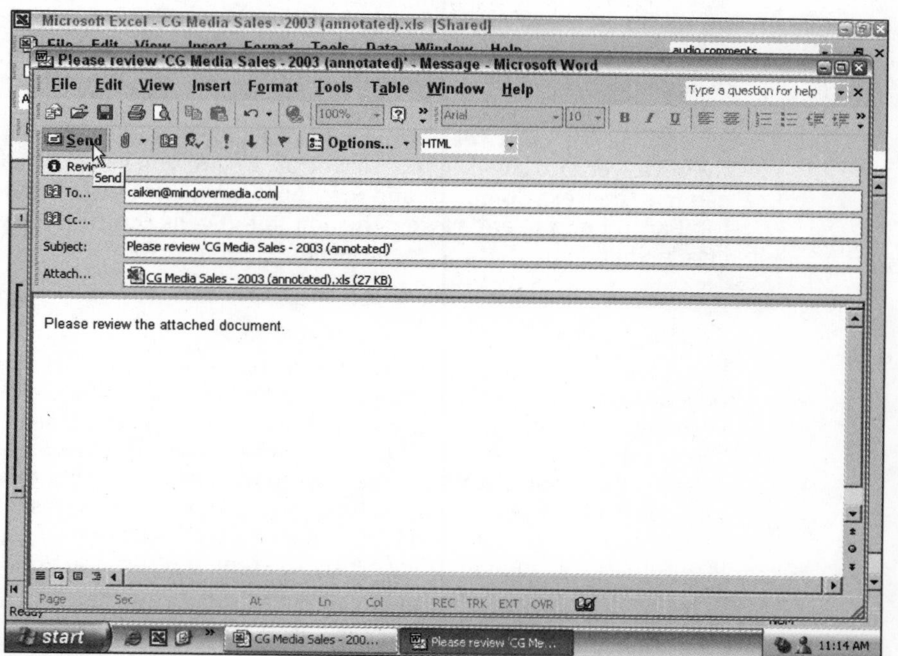

Figure 1-12: Sending out a workbook for review attached to an e-mail message.

Reviewing and then replying with changes

When you (or your recipients) receive the e-mail message and then open the attached workbook file in Excel, the program automatically opens the Reviewing toolbar (if it's not already displayed in the Excel window) at the same as it opens the workbook. You can then use the Next Comment and Previous Comment buttons to jump to the comments. You can then respond to the comments by making changes to cells that have been flagged or by adding comments of your own.

When you're ready to send your changes and responses back to the person who sent the workbook, you click the Reply with Changes button on the Reviewing toolbar. When you do this, Excel opens your e-mail program with a new message, to which your modified version of the workbook has automatically been attached. This new message also has the Subject field filled in and a short message in the body stating that you have reviewed the attached workbook. All you have to do is fill in the e-mail address of the original sender in the To field and then click the Send button to send the modified workbook back to the person who originally sent you the file to review.

Merging review changes back into the original workbook

When the original sender of the workbook opens the modified workbook attached to the response e-mail in Excel, the program immediately displays a Microsoft Excel alert dialog box informing you that the workbook was sent for review and asking you if you want to merge the changes in this workbook back into the original workbook file. To do this, click Yes button in the alert dialog box.

As soon as you click Yes, Excel automatically merges all changes made by the reviewer into the original workbook. Before you save the changes, you can use the Next Comment and Previous Comment button on the Reviewing toolbar to jump to and review the annotated cells (both those you originally attached and any that the reviewer attached in response).

Routing a workbook to different reviewers

If you and all your recipients use Microsoft Outlook as your e-mail program on a network running the Microsoft Exchange Server, you can use the File⇨Send To⇨Routing Recipient command in Excel to create a routing slip. The routing slip indicates all the people you want to review the workbook, as well as the order in which they are to receive the workbook and have an opportunity to comment on its contents. You can use this command to have a group of people give their input and feedback to a workbook, which is automatically merged together by the time it returns to you.

To set up the routing slip, you choose File⇨Send To⇨Routing Recipient on the Excel Menu bar. Excel then opens the Routing Slip dialog box where you can add all the people who are to get the workbook in the order in which the file is to be routed to them. To do this, you follow these steps:

1. **Click the Address button in the Routing Slip dialog box.**

   Doing this opens the Address Book dialog box where you can select the names of all the recipients in the order in which they are to receive the workbook.

2. **Click the name of the first recipient in the Name list box on left side of the Address Book dialog box and then click the To button to add the name to the list box on the right side of the dialog box.**

   You can select names for the routing slip from two sources: your Contacts list (made up of all the people you've e-mailed) and your Outlook Address book. If the name of the person does not show up in the source you're using, click the Show Names From drop-down button and select the other source on the pop-up menu.

3. **Repeat Step 2, selecting the name of the next person in the Address book to whom the workbook should be sent.**

   You repeat Step 2 until you've added all the people whose names are to appear on the routing slip.

4. **Click the OK button.**

   Doing this closes the Address Book dialog box and returns you to the Routing Slip dialog box where the names (and possibly the e-mail addresses, depending upon how your address book is set up) appear in the To: list box (as shown in Figure 1-13).

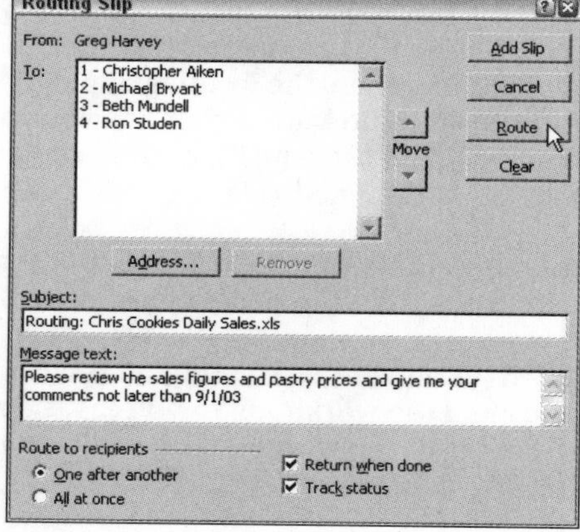

Figure 1-13: Setting up the routing slip for sending out a workbook for review.

After you've added all the recipients to the Routing Slip dialog box, you can click the Route button to begin sending the workbook to the first person listed in the routing slip. Because the One after Another radio button is automatically selected in the Route to Recipients section of the Routing Slip dialog box, Excel sends the workbook to the first recipient shown in To: list box. Because the Return When Done and Track Status check boxes are both selected, Excel keeps track of the progress of the workbook from recipient to recipient and ultimately returns the workbook to you.

When the first recipient listed on the routing slip receives the e-mail with the workbook to be reviewed attached, the text that you entered in the Message Text list box in the Routing Slip dialog box appears at the top of the e-mail message, followed by these routing instructions:

```
The enclosed document has a routing slip. When you are done
reviewing this document, choose Send To from the Microsoft
Excel File menu. Then select Next Recipient to continue
routing.
```

After the first recipient finishes responding to your comments and saving any changes made in Excel, he or she then chooses the File➪Send To➪Next Recipient command from the Excel Menu bar. Excel responds by opening a Routing Slip dialog box that contains a radio button option that offers "Route document" followed by the name of the next recipient on the original routing list, already selected.

When this first recipient then clicks the OK button in this Routing Slip dialog box, Excel closes the dialog box and sends the current workbook to the next recipient on the list. Excel then generates a status report that is sent to your Inbox (as the workbook's creator), informing of you that the first recipient has now routed the file to the next person on the list.

This process continues until the last recipient makes his or her changes to the workbook and then chooses the File➪Send To➪Next Recipient command from the Excel Menu bar. This time, the Routing Slip dialog box contains a selected "Route document" radio button that has your name. When the last recipient clicks OK, Excel and the e-mail program send the reviewed workbook back to you with everyone's feedback and modifications.

Click the All at Once radio button in the Route to Recipients section of the Routing Slip when you need to expedite the review process by having all the recipients receive the workbook as soon as possible. When you choose this option, Excel sends the workbook to everybody on the list, along with routing instructions for returning the workbook to you (as the sole Next Recipient). As you receive copies of the workbooks back from each recipient, you can use the Tools⇨Compare and Merge Workbooks command to merge the changes from each of their copies back into the original. (See the "Merging different copies of a shared workbook" section, earlier in this chapter, for details on merging workbooks.)

Posting a copy of a workbook to an Exchange folder

If you use Outlook as your e-mail program along with the Microsoft Exchange Server, you can post Excel workbooks into public folders to which you have access and over which you have permission to grant co-workers access. That way, your co-workers can open the workbooks, review them, and even send copies of them to others, all within Microsoft Outlook (assuming that they too have permission to both view and alter the workbook).

To post the current workbook into an Exchange folder (over which you have permission to make changes), you choose the File⇨Send To⇨Exchange Folder from the Excel Menu bar. Doing this opens the Send to Exchange dialog box, where you locate and select the public folder in which a copy of the current workbook is to be stored. You do this by expanding the outline of the Folder List displayed in the Select a Folder list until the Public Folders folder and all its subfolders are displayed.

To create a new folder for the workbook, click the Public Folders icon (or subfolder within the Public Folders folder in which the new public folder is to reside) and then click the New Folder button. Excel then displays a New Folder dialog box, in which you type the folder name. When you click OK, the program closes the New Folder dialog box and returns you to the Send to Exchange Folder dialog box, where the name of the new folder is automatically selected.

You then click the OK button to have Excel copy the file and post it to the designated pubic folder. You can then create a shortcut to the public folder that contains your Excel workbook by right-clicking its folder icon in the Outlook Folder list and then clicking Add to Outlook Bar on the shortcut menu.

After you post an Excel workbook to a public folder, all the co-workers to whom you (or your IT administrator) have given permission can open the workbook by opening the public folder into which you copied the workbook in the Folder List in their copy of Microsoft Outlook and double-clicking the workbook file icon or by right-clicking it and then clicking Open on the file's shortcut menu. Note that each of your co-workers must have Excel installed on his or her computer in order to be able to open the workbook from the Exchange folder within Microsoft Outlook.

Chapter 2: Protecting Worksheets

In This Chapter

- Assigning a password to open a workbook
- Assigning a password to make changes in a workbook
- Understanding how to use the Locked and Hidden Protection formats
- Protecting a worksheet and selecting what actions are allowed
- Enabling cell range editing by particular users in protected sheet
- Protecting a workbook
- Protecting and sharing a workbook

Security in Excel exists on two levels: Protecting the workbook file (so that only people entrusted with the password can open the file to view, print, or edit the data) and protecting the worksheets in a workbook from unwarranted changes (so that only people entrusted with that password can make modifications to the contents and design of the spreadsheet).

When it comes to securing the integrity of your spreadsheets, you can decide which aspects of the sheets in the workbook your users can and cannot change. For example, you might prevent changes to all formulas and headings in a spreadsheet, while still enabling users to make entries in the cells referenced to in the formulas themselves.

Password-Protecting the File

In password-protecting the workbook, you can prevent unauthorized users from opening the workbook and/or editing the workbook. You set a password for opening the workbook file when you're dealing with a spreadsheet whose data is of a sufficiently sensitive nature that only a certain group of people in the company should have access to it (such as spreadsheets dealing with personal information and salaries). Of course, after you set the password required to open the workbook, you must supply this password to those people who need access so they can open the workbook file.

You set a password for modifying the workbook when you're dealing with a spreadsheet whose data needs to be viewed and printed by different users, none of whom are authorized to make changes to any of the entries. For example, you might assign a password for modifying to a workbook before distributing it company-wide, after the workbook's been through a complete editing and review cycle and all suggested changes have been merged (see Book IV, Chapter 1 for details).

If you're dealing with a spreadsheet whose data is of a sensitive nature and should not be modified by any of those authorized to open it, you need to set both a password for opening and a password for modifying the workbook file. You assign either one or both of these types of passwords to a workbook file at the time you save it with the File⇨Save As command on the Excel Menu bar.

When you select this command (or select the File⇨Save command for a new file that's never been saved before), Excel opens the Save As dialog box. You can then set the password to open and/or the password to modify the file by taking these steps:

1. **Click the Tools pop-up button in the Save As dialog box and then click General Options on the pop-up menu.**

   Doing this opens the Save Options dialog box, similar to the one shown in Figure 2-1, where you can enter a password to open and/or a password to modify. When entering a password, it can be up to 255 characters long and consist of a combination of letters and numbers with spaces. Keep in mind, when using letters, that passwords are case-sensitive, so opensesame and OpenSesame are not the same password because of the different use of upper- and lowercase letters.

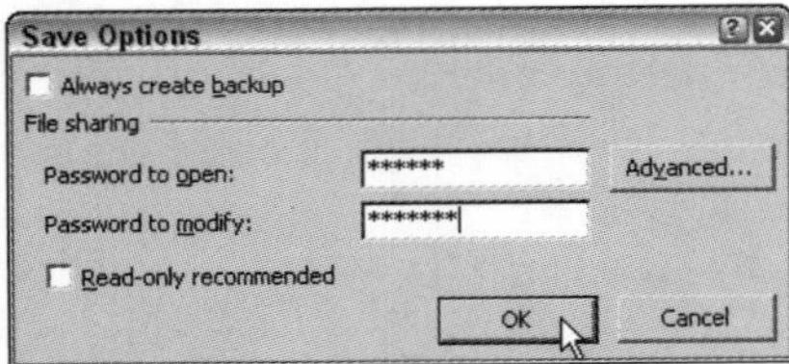

Figure 2-1: Setting a password to open and modify in the Save Options dialog box.

   When entering a password, make sure that you don't enter something that you can't easily reproduce and, for heaven's sake, that you can't remember. You must be able to immediately reproduce the password in order to assign it, and you must be able to reproduce it later on if you ever want to be able to open or change the darned workbook ever again.

2. **(Optional) If you want to assign a password to open the file, type the password (up to 255 characters maximum) in Password to Open text box.**

As you type the password, Excel masks the actual characters you type by rendering them as asterisks (*) in the text box.

By default, Excel assigns an Office 97/2000 Compatible type encryption when you assign a password to open the file. You can use the Advanced button to assign another type of encryption for password-protecting the opening of the file. You should not, however, fool with these options unless you know what you're doing or have been instructed to use another type by someone in your IT department.

If you decide to assign a password for opening and modifying the workbook at the same time, proceed to Step 3. Otherwise, skip to Step 4.

When entering the password for modifying the workbook, be sure that you assign a different password from the one you just assigned for opening the file (if you did assign a password for opening the file in this step).

3. **(Optional) If you want to assign a password for modifying the workbook, click the Password to Modify text box and then type the password for modifying the workbook there.**

   Before you can assign a password to open the file and/or to modify the file, you must confirm the password by reproducing it in a Confirm Password dialog box, exactly as you originally entered it.

4. **Click the OK button.**

   Doing this closes the Save Options dialog box and opens a Confirm Password dialog box where you need to exactly reproduce the password. If you just entered a password in the Password to Open text box, you need to reenter this password in the Confirm Password dialog box. If you just entered a password in the Password to Modify text box, you need only reproduce this password in the Confirm Password dialog box. However, if you entered a password in both the Password to Open text box and the Password to Modify text box, you must reproduce the password entered in the Password to Open text box in the first Confirm Password dialog box and then reproduce the password you entered in the Password to Modify text box in the second Confirm Password dialog box (which appears immediately after you click OK in the first Confirm Password dialog box).

5. **Type the password exactly as you entered it in the Password to Open text box (or Password to Modify text box, if you didn't use the Password to Open text box), and then click OK.**

   If your password does not match exactly (in both characters and case) the one you originally entered, Excel displays an alert dialog box, indicating that the confirmation password is not identical. When you click OK in this alert dialog box, Excel returns you to the original Save Options dialog box, where you can either reenter the password in the original text box or click its OK button to redisplay the Confirm Password dialog box, where you can try again to reproduce the original. (Make sure that you've not engaged the Caps Lock key by accident.)

If you assigned both a password to open the workbook and one to modify it, Excel displays a second Confirm Password dialog box as soon as you click OK in the first one and successfully reproduce the password to open the file. You then repeat Step 5, this time exactly reproducing the password to modify the workbook, before you click OK.

When you finish confirming the original password(s), you are ready to save the workbook in the Save As dialog box.

6. **(Optional) If you want to save the password-protected version under a new filename or in a different folder, edit the name in the File Name text box and then select the new folder on the Save In drop-down list.**
7. **Click the Save button to save the workbook with the password to open and/or password to modify.**

   As soon as you do this, Excel saves the file — if this is the first time you've saved it. If not, the program displays an alert dialog box, indicating that the file you're saving already exists, and asking you if you want to replace the existing file.
8. **Click the Yes button if the alert dialog box asking you if you want to replace the existing file appears.**

Entering the password to gain access

After you save a workbook file to which you've assigned a password for opening it, you must thereafter be able to faithfully reproduce the password in order to open the file (at least until such time as you change or delete the password). When you next try to open the workbook, Excel opens Password dialog box like the one shown in Figure 2-2, where you must enter the password exactly as it was assigned to the file.

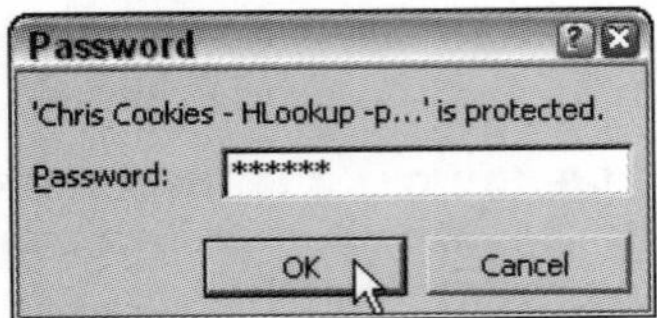

Figure 2-2: Entering the password required to open a protected workbook file.

If you mess up and type the wrong password, Excel displays an alert dialog box, letting you know that the password you entered is incorrect. When you click OK to clear the alert, you are returned to original Excel window where you must repeat the entire file-opening procedure (hoping that this time you're able to enter the correct password). When you supply the correct password, Excel immediately opens the workbook for viewing and printing (and editing as well, unless you've also assigned a password for modifying the file). If you're unable to successfully reproduce the password, you are unable to open the file and put it to any use!

The last chance you have to chicken out of password-protecting the opening of the file is before you close the file during the work session in which you originally assign the password. If, for whatever reason, you decide that you don't want to go through the hassle of having to reproduce the password each and every time you open this file, you can get rid of it by choosing File—Save As, clicking General Options on Tools pop-up menu, and then deleting the password in the Password to Open text box before clicking OK in the Save Options dialog box and the Save button in the Save As dialog box. Doing this re-saves the workbook file without a password to open it, so that you don't have to worry about reproducing the password the next time you open the workbook for editing or printing.

A password-protected workbook file for which you can't reproduce the correct password is the ultimate nightmare (especially if you're talking about a really important spreadsheet with loads and loads of vital data), so for heaven's sake, don't forget your password, or you'll be stuck. Excel does not provide any sort of command for overriding the password and opening a protected workbook, nor does Microsoft offer any such utility. If you think that you might forget the workbook's password, be sure to write it down somewhere and then keep that piece of paper in a secure place, preferably under lock and key. It's always better to be safe than sorry when it comes to passwords for opening files.

Entering the password to make changes

If you've protected your workbook from modifications, as soon as you attempt to open the workbook (and have entered the password to open the file, if one has been assigned), Excel immediately displays the Password dialog box similar to the one shown in Figure 2-3, where you must accurately reproduce the password assigned for modifying the file.

Figure 2-3: Entering the password required to modify a protected workbook file.

As when supplying the password to open a protected file, if you type the wrong password, Excel displays the alert dialog box, letting you know that the password you entered is incorrect. When you click OK to clear the alert, you are returned to the Password dialog box, where you can try reentering the password in the Password text box.

When you supply the correct password, Excel immediately closes the Password dialog box and you are free to edit the workbook in any way you wish (unless certain cell ranges or worksheets are protected). If you're unable to successfully reproduce the password, you can click the Read Only button, which opens a copy of the workbook file into which you can't save your changes unless you use the File➪Save As command and then rename the workbook and/or locate the copy in a different folder.

When you click this button, Excel opens the file with a [Read-Only] indicator appended to the filename as it appears on the Excel title bar. If you then try to save changes with the File➪Save command, the program displays an alert dialog box, indicating that the file is read-only and that you must save a copy by renaming the file in the Save As dialog box. As soon as you click OK to clear the alert dialog box, Excel displays the Save As dialog box, where you can save the copy under a new filename and/or location. Note that the program automatically removes the password for modifying from the copy so that you can modify its contents any way you like.

Because password-protecting a workbook against modification does not prevent you from opening the workbook and then saving a unprotected version under a new filename (with the File➪Save As command), you can assign passwords for modifying files without nearly as much trepidation as assigning them for opening files. Assigning a password for modifying the file assures you that you'll always have an intact original of the spreadsheet, from which you can open and save a copy, even if you can never remember the password to modify the original itself.

Changing or deleting a password

Before you can change or delete a password for opening a workbook, you must first be able to supply the current password you want to change to get the darned thing open. Assuming you can do this, all you have to do to change or get rid of the password is open the Save As dialog box (File⇨Save As), and then click the General Options item on Tools pop-up menu to open the Save Options dialog box, which opens with the password in the Password to Open text box selected.

To delete the password, simply press the Delete key to remove all the asterisks from this text box. To reassign the password, replace the current password with the new one you want to assign by typing it over the original one. Then, when you click OK in the Save Options dialog box, reenter the new password in the Confirm Password dialog box and then click its OK button.

Finally, after closing the Save Options dialog box, you simply click the Save button in the Save As dialog box and then click Yes in the alert dialog box, which asks you if you want to replace the existing file.

To change or delete the password for modifying the workbook, you follow the same procedure, except that you have to be able to successfully reproduce the password for modifying the workbook after opening it, and then change or delete the password that's entered into the Password to Modify text box in the Save Options dialog box.

Protecting the Spreadsheet

After you've got the spreadsheet the way you want it, you often need the help of Excel's Protection feature to keep it that way. Nothing's worse than having an inexperienced data-entry operator doing major damage to the formulas and functions that you've worked so hard to build and validate. To keep the formulas and standard text in a spreadsheet safe from any unwarranted changes, you need to protect its worksheet.

Before you start using the Tools⇨Protection⇨Protect Sheet command, you need to understand how protection works in Excel. All cells in the workbook can have one of two different protection formats: locked or unlocked, and hidden or unhidden.

Whenever you begin a new spreadsheet, all the cells in the workbook have the locked and unhidden status. However, this status in and of itself means nothing until you turn on protection in the worksheet by choosing Tools⇨Protection⇨Protect Sheet. At that time, you are then prevented from making any editing changes to all locked cells — and from viewing the contents of all hidden cells on the Formula bar when they contain the cell pointer.

What this means in practice is that prior to turning on worksheet protection, you go through the spreadsheet removing the Locked protection format from all cell ranges in which you or your users need to do data entry and editing even when the worksheet is protected. You also assign the Hidden protection format to all cell ranges in the spreadsheet where you don't want the contents of the cell displayed when protection is turned on in the worksheet. Then, when that formatting is done, you use the Tools⇨Protection⇨Protect Sheet command to activate protection for all remaining Locked cells and block the Formula bar from displaying the Hidden cells in the sheet.

When setting up your own spreadsheet templates, you will want to unlock all the cells where users need to input new data — and keep locked all the cells that contain headings and formulas that never change. You may also want to hide cells with formulas if you're concerned that their display might tempt users to waste time trying to fiddle with or finesse them. Then, turn on worksheet protection prior to saving the file in the template file format (see Book II, Chapter 1 for details). You are then assured that all spreadsheets generated from that template automatically inherit the same level and type of protection you assigned in the original spreadsheet.

Changing the Locked and Hidden cell formatting

To change the status of cells from locked to unlocked or from unhidden to hidden, you use the Locked and Hidden check boxes found on the Protection tab of the Format Cells dialog box (Ctrl+1).

To remove the Locked protection status from a cell range or nonadjacent selection, you follow these steps:

1. **Select the range or ranges to be unlocked.**

   To select multiple ranges to create a nonadjacent cell selection, hold down the Ctrl key as you drag through each range.

2. **Choose Format⇨Cells on the Excel Menu bar or press Ctrl+1.**

   Doing this opens the Format Cells dialog box.

3. **Click the Protection tab.**

   The Protection tab contains two check box options: Locked and Hidden (see Figure 2-4). By default, the Locked check box is selected (indicated by the checkmark) and the Hidden check box is not (indicated by the lack of a checkmark).

4. **Click the Locked check box.**

   Doing this removes the checkmark from the check box.

5. **Click the OK button to close the Format Cells dialog box.**

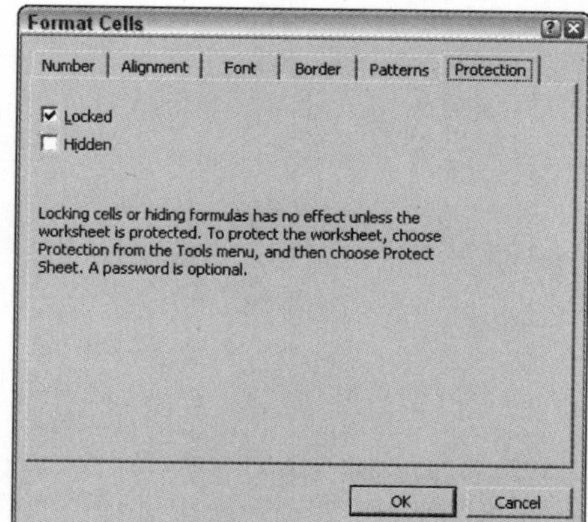

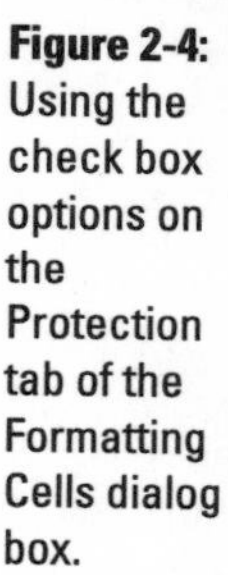

Figure 2-4: Using the check box options on the Protection tab of the Formatting Cells dialog box.

To hide the display of the contents of a range of cells or nonadjacent cell selection, you follow the foregoing steps, except that you click the Hidden check box in Step 4 (to put a checkmark in the box) instead.

Changing the protection formatting of cell ranges in the worksheet (as outlined above) does nothing in and of itself. It's not until you turn on the protection for your worksheet (as outlined in the next section) that your unlocked and hidden cells work — or appear — any differently from the locked and unhidden cells. At that time, only unlocked cells accept edits, and only unhidden cells display their contents on the Formula bar when they contain the cell pointer.

Protecting the worksheet

When you've gotten all cell ranges that you want unlocked and hidden correctly formatted in the worksheet, you're ready to turn on protection. To do this, you choose Tools⇨Protection⇨Protect Sheet on the Excel Menu bar to open the Protect Sheet dialog box, as shown in Figure 2-5.

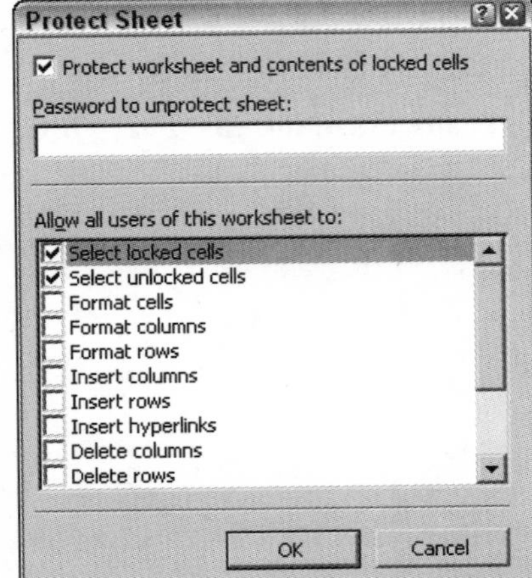

Figure 2-5: Selecting the protection options in the Protect Sheet dialog box.

When you first open this dialog box, only the Protect Worksheet and Contents of Locked Cells check box at the very top and the Select Locked Cells and Select Unlocked Cells check boxes in the Allow All Users of This Worksheet To list box are selected. All the other check box options (including a number that are not visible without scrolling up the Allow All Users of This Worksheet To list box) are unselected.

This means that if you click OK at this point, the *only* things that you'll be permitted to do in the worksheet is edit *unlocked* cells and to select cell ranges (of any type: both locked and unlocked alike).

If you really want to keep other users out of all the locked cells in a worksheet, click the Select Locked Cells check box in the Allow All Users of This Worksheet To list box to remove its checkmark. That way, your users are completely restricted to just those unlocked ranges where you permit data input and contents editing.

Don't deselect the Select Unlocked Cells check box as well as the Select Locked Cells check box, because doing this makes the cell pointer disappear from the worksheet, making the cell address in the Name Box on the Formula bar the sole way for you and your users to keep track of their position in the worksheet (which is, believe me, the quickest way to drive you and your users stark raving mad).

Selecting what actions are allowed in a protected sheet

In addition to enable users to select locked and unlocked cells in the worksheet, you can enable the following actions in the protected worksheet by selecting their check boxes in the Allow All Users of This Worksheet To list box of the Protect Sheet dialog box:

- **Format Cells:** Enables the formatting of cells (with the exception of changing the locked and hidden status on the Protection tab of the Format Cells dialog box).
- **Format Columns:** Enables formatting so that users can modify the column widths and hide and unhide columns.
- **Format Rows:** Enables formatting so that users can modify the row heights and hide and unhide rows.
- **Insert Columns:** Enables the insertion of new columns in the worksheet.
- **Insert Rows:** Enables the insertion of new rows in the worksheet.
- **Insert Hyperlinks:** Enables the insertion of new hyperlinks to other documents, both local and on the Web. (See Book VII, Chapter 2 for details.)
- **Delete Columns:** Enables the deletion of columns in the worksheet.
- **Delete Rows:** Enables the deletion of rows in the worksheet.
- **Sort:** Enables the sorting of data in unlocked cells in the worksheet. (See Book VI, Chapter 1 for details.)
- **Use AutoFilter:** Enables the filtering of data in the worksheet. (See Book VI, Chapter 2 for more information.)
- **Use Pivot Table Reports:** Enables the manipulation of pivot tables in the worksheet. (For more about pivot tables, see Book VII, Chapter 2.)
- **Edit Objects:** Enables the editing of graphic objects, such as text boxes, embedded images, and the like, in the worksheet. (See Book V, Chapter 2 for details.)
- **Edit Scenarios:** Enables the editing of what-if scenarios, including modifying and deleting them. (For details of what-if scenarios, see Book VII, Chapter 1.)

Assigning a password to unprotect the sheet

In addition to enabling particular actions in the protected worksheet, you can also assign a password that's required in order to remove the protections from the protected worksheet. When entering a password in the Password to Unprotect Sheet text box of the Protect Sheet dialog box, you observe the same guidelines as when assigning a password to open or to make changes in the workbook (255 characters maximum that can consist of a combination of letters, numbers, and spaces, with the letters being case sensitive).

As with assigning a password to open or make changes to a workbook, when you enter a password (whose characters are masked with asterisks) in the Password to Unprotect Sheet text box and then click OK, Excel displays the Confirm Password dialog box, where you must accurately reproduce the password you just entered (including upper- and lowercase letters) before Excel turns on sheet protection and assigns the password to its removal.

If you don't successfully reproduce the password, when you click OK in the Confirm Password dialog box, Excel replaces it with an alert dialog box indicating that the confirmation password is not identical to the one you entered in the Protect Sheet dialog box. When you click OK to clear this alert dialog box, you are returned to the Protect Sheet dialog box where you may modify the password in the Password to Unprotect Sheet text box before you click OK and try confirming the password again.

As soon as you accurately reproduce the password in the Confirm Password dialog box, Excel closes the Protect Sheet dialog box and enables protection for that sheet, using whatever settings you designated in that dialog box.

If you don't assign a password to unprotect the sheet, any user with a modicum of Excel knowledge can lift the worksheet protection and make any manner of changes to its contents, including wreaking havoc on its computational abilities by corrupting its formulas. Keep in mind that it makes little sense to turn on the protection in a worksheet if you're going to permit anybody to turn it off by simply choosing Tools⇨Protection⇨Unprotect Sheet command.

Removing protection from a worksheet

When you assign protection to a sheet, your input and editing are restricted solely to unlocked cells in the worksheet, and you can only perform those additional actions that you enabled in the Allow Users of this Worksheet To list box. If you try to replace, delete, or otherwise modify a locked cell in the protected worksheet, Excel displays an alert dialog box with the following message:

```
The cell or chart you are trying to change is protected
and therefore read-only
```

The message then goes on to tell you that to modify a protected worksheet, you must first remove the protection by choosing the Tools⇨Protection⇨Unprotect Sheet command. If you've assigned a password to unprotect the sheet, the program displays the Unprotect Sheet dialog box where you must enter the password exactly as you assigned it. As soon as you remove the protection by entering the correct password in this dialog box and clicking OK, Excel turns off the protection in the sheet and you can once again make any kinds of modifications to its structure and contents, in both the locked and unlocked cells.

Keep in mind that when you protect a worksheet, only the data and graphics on that particular worksheet are protected. This means that you can modify the data and graphics on other sheets of the same workbook without removing protection. If you have data or graphics on other sheets of the same workbook that need protecting as well, you need to activate that sheet and then repeat the entire procedure for protecting it as well (including unlocking cells that need to be edited and then selecting which other actions — if any — to enable in the worksheet, and whether to assign a password to unprotect the sheet) before distributing the workbook. When assigning passwords to unprotect the various sheets of the workbook, you may want to stick with a single password rather than worry about remembering a different password for each sheet (which is a bit much, don't you think?).

Enabling cell range editing by certain users

If you're running Excel 2002 under the Windows 2000 operating system (Windows XP doesn't count), you can use the Tools⇨Protection⇨Allow Users to Edit Ranges command to enable the editing of particular ranges in the protected worksheet by certain users. When you use this feature, you give certain users permission to edit particular cell ranges, provided they can correctly provide the password you assign to that range.

To give access to particular ranges in a protected worksheet, you follow these steps:

1. **Choose Tools⇨Protection⇨Allow Users to Edit Ranges from the Excel Menu bar.**

   Note that the Allow Users to Edit Ranges menu item is grayed out and unavailable if the worksheet is currently protected. In that case, you must remove protection with the Tools⇨Protection⇨Unprotect Sheet command before you retry Step 1.

   When you choose the Tools⇨Protection⇨Allow Users to Edit Ranges command, Excel opens the Allow Users to Edit Ranges dialog box where you can add the ranges you want to assign, as shown in Figure 2-6.

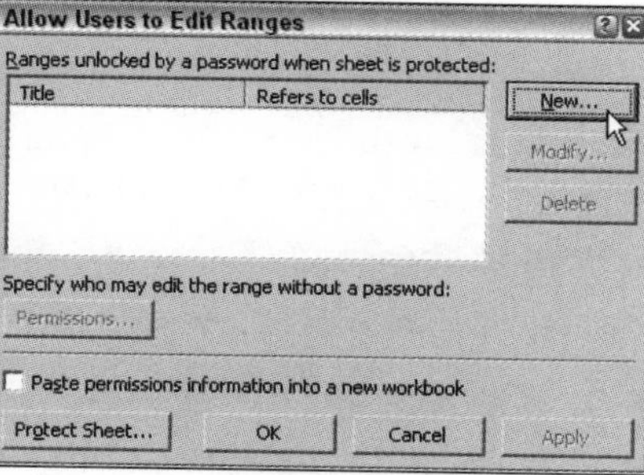

Figure 2-6: Designating the range to be unlocked by password in a protected worksheet.

2. **Click the New button.**

   Doing this opens the New Range dialog box where you give the range a title, define its cell selection, and provide the range password, as shown in Figure 2-7.

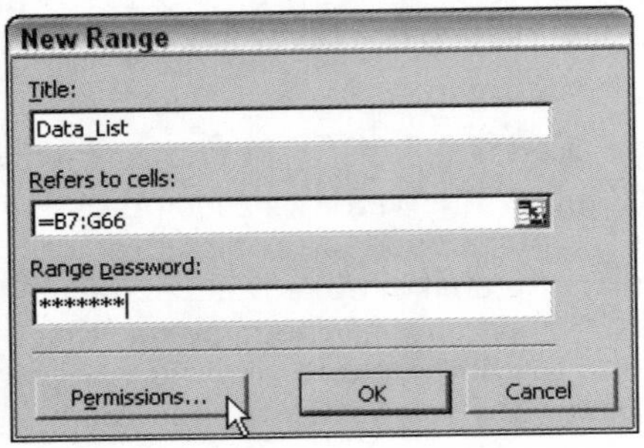

Figure 2-7: Assigning the range title, address, and password in New Range dialog box.

3. **If you wish, type a name for the range in the Title text box (otherwise, Excel assigns a name such as Range1, Range2, and so on).**

   Next, you designate the cell range or nonadjacent cell selection to which access is restricted.

4. **Click the Refers to Cells text box and then type in the address of the cell range (without removing the = sign) or select the range or ranges in the worksheet.**

   Next, you need to enter a password that's required to get access to the range. Like all other passwords in Excel, this one can be up to 255 characters long, mixing letters, numbers, and spaces. Pay attention to the use of upper- and lowercase letters, because the range password is case-sensitive.

5. **Type in the password for accessing the range in the Range Password dialog box.**

   You need to use the Permissions button in the New Range dialog box to open the Permissions dialog box for the range you're setting.

6. **Click the Permissions button in the Range Password dialog box.**

   Next, you need to add the users who are to have access to this range.

7. **Click the Add button in the Permissions dialog box.**

   Doing this opens the Select Users or Groups dialog box where you designate the names of the users to have access to the range.

8. **Click the name of the user in the Enter the Object Names to Select list box at the bottom of the Select Users or Groups dialog box. To select multiple users from this list, hold down the Ctrl key as you click each user name.**

   If this list box is empty, click the Advanced button to expand the Select Users or Groups dialog box and then click Find Now button to locate all users for your location. You can then click the name or Ctrl+click the names you want to add from this list, and then when you click OK, Excel returns you to the original form of Select Users or Groups dialog box and adds these names to its Enter the Object Names to Select list box.

9. **Click OK in the Select Users or Groups dialog box.**

   Doing this returns you to the Permissions dialog box where the names you've selected are now listed in the Group of User Names list box. Now you need to set the permissions for each user. When you first add users, each one is permitted to edit the range without a password. To restrict the editing to only those who have the range password, you need to click each name and then click the Deny check box.

10. **Click the name of the first user who must know the password and then click the Deny check box in the Permissions For list box.**

    You need to repeat Step 10 for each person in the Group or Users Names list box that you want to restrict in this manner (see Figure 2-8).

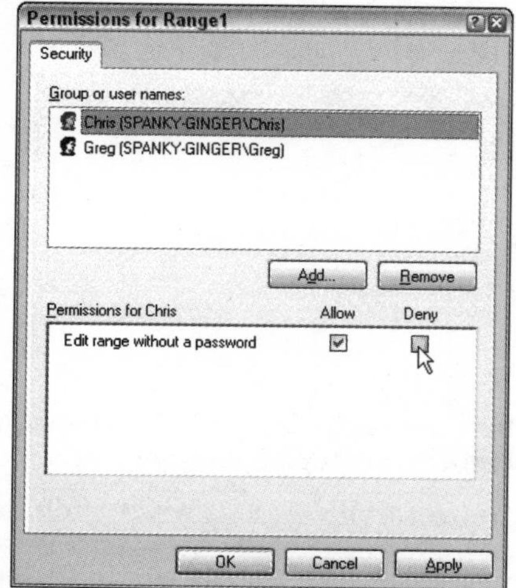

Figure 2-8: Setting the permissions for each user in the Permissions dialog box.

11. **Repeat Step 10 for each user who must know the password and then click OK in the Permissions dialog box.**

    As soon as you click OK, Excel displays a warning alert dialog, letting you know that you are setting a deny permission that takes precedence over any allows entries; if the person is a member of two groups, one with an allow entry and the other with a deny entry, the deny entry permission rules (meaning that they have to know the range password).

12. **Click the Yes button in the Security alert dialog box.**

    Doing this closes this dialog box and returns you to the New Range dialog box.

13. **Click OK in the New Range dialog box.**

    Doing this opens the Confirm Range text box where you must accurately reproduce the range password.

14. **Type the range password in the Reenter Password to Proceed text box and then click the OK button.**

    Doing this returns you to the Allow Users to Edit Ranges dialog box where the title and cell reference of the new range is displayed in the Ranges Unlocked by a Password When Sheet Is Protected list box, as shown in Figure 2-9.

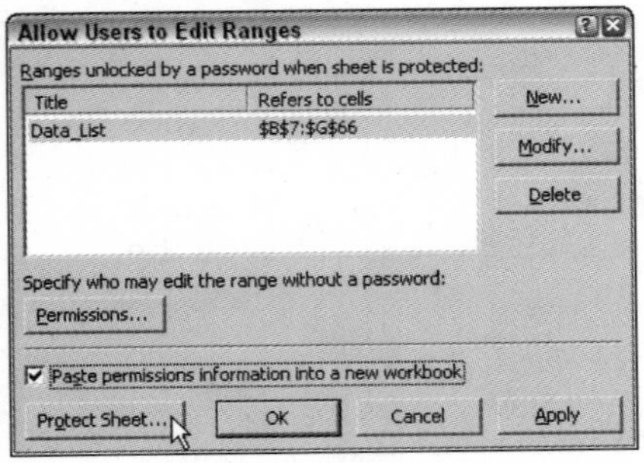

Figure 2-9: Getting ready to protect the sheet in Allow Users to Edit Ranges dialog box.

If you need to define other ranges available to other users in the worksheet, you can do so by repeating Steps 2 through 14.

When you finish adding ranges to the Allow Users to Edit Ranges dialog box, you're ready protect the worksheet. If you want to retain a record of the ranges you've defined, take Step 15. Otherwise, skip to Step 16.

15. **(Optional) Click the Paste Permissions Information Into a New Workbook check box to put a checkmark in it if you want create a new workbook that contains all the permissions information.**

When you select this check box, Excel creates a new workbook whose first worksheet lists all the ranges you've assigned, along with the users who may gain access by providing the range password. You can then save this workbook for your records. Note that the range password is not listed on this worksheet — if you want to add it, be sure that you password-protect the workbook so that only you can open it.

Now, you're ready to protect the worksheet. If you want to do this from within the Allow Users to Edit Ranges dialog box, you click the Protect Sheet button to open the Protect Sheet dialog box. If you want to protect the worksheet later on, you click OK to close the Allow Users to Edit Ranges dialog box and then choose the Tools⇨Protection⇨Protect Sheet on the Excel pull-down menus when you're ready to activate the worksheet protection.

16. **Click the Protect Sheet button to protect the worksheet; otherwise, click the OK button to close the Allow Users to Edit Ranges dialog box.**

If you click the Protect Sheet button, Excel opens the Protect Sheet dialog box where you can set a password to unprotect the sheet, as well as to select the actions that you permit all users to perform in the protected worksheet (as outlined earlier in this chapter).

After you turn on protection in the worksheet, only the users you've designated are able to edit the cell range or ranges you've defined. Of course, you need to supply the range password to all the users allowed to do editing in the range or ranges at the time you distribute the workbook to them.

Be sure to assign a password to unprotect the worksheet at the time you protect the worksheet if you want to prevent unauthorized users from being able to make changes to the designated editing ranges in the worksheet. If you don't, any user can make changes by turning off the worksheet protection, thereby gaining access to the Allow Users to Edit Ranges command by choosing Tools⇨Protection⇨Unprotect Sheet.

Doing data entry in the unlocked cells of a protected worksheet

The best part of protecting a worksheet is that you and your users can jump right to unlocked cells and avoid even dealing with the locked ones (which you can't change anyway) by using the Tab and Shift+Tab keys to navigate the worksheet. When you press the Tab key in a protected worksheet, Excel jumps the cell pointer to the next unlocked cell to the right of the current one in that same row. When you reach the last unlocked cell in that row, the program then jumps to the first unlocked cell in the rows below. To move back to a previous unlocked cell, you press Shift+Tab. When Excel reaches the last unlocked cell in the spreadsheet, it automatically jumps back to the very first unlocked cell on the sheet.

Of course, provided you haven't changed the behavior of the Enter key on the Edit tab of the Options dialog box (Tools⇨Options), you can also use the Enter key to move down the columns instead of across the rows, although pressing the Enter key to progress down a column will select locked cells in that column as well as the unlocked ones, whereas pressing the Tab key skips all cells with the Locked protection format.

Figure 2-10 illustrates how you can put the Tab key to good use in filling out and navigating a protected worksheet. This figure shows a new invoice for Spa Holiday Hot Tubs that's been generated from a template. Because the SPHT Invoice sheet in the original template is protected, this sheet is protected as well in the SPA Holiday Invoice1 workbook created from it. The only cells that are unlocked in this sheet are C3, C4, C5, C6, G4, G5, E6, and the cell range B8:C18. All the rest of the cells in this worksheet are locked and off limits.

To fill in the data for this new invoice, you can press the Tab key to complete the data entry in each field such as Name, Street, Date, City, Invoice, and so on. By pressing Tab, you don't have to waste time moving through the locked cells that contain headings that you can't modify anyway. If you need to back up and return to the previous field in the invoice, you just press Shift+Tab to go back to the previous unlocked cell.

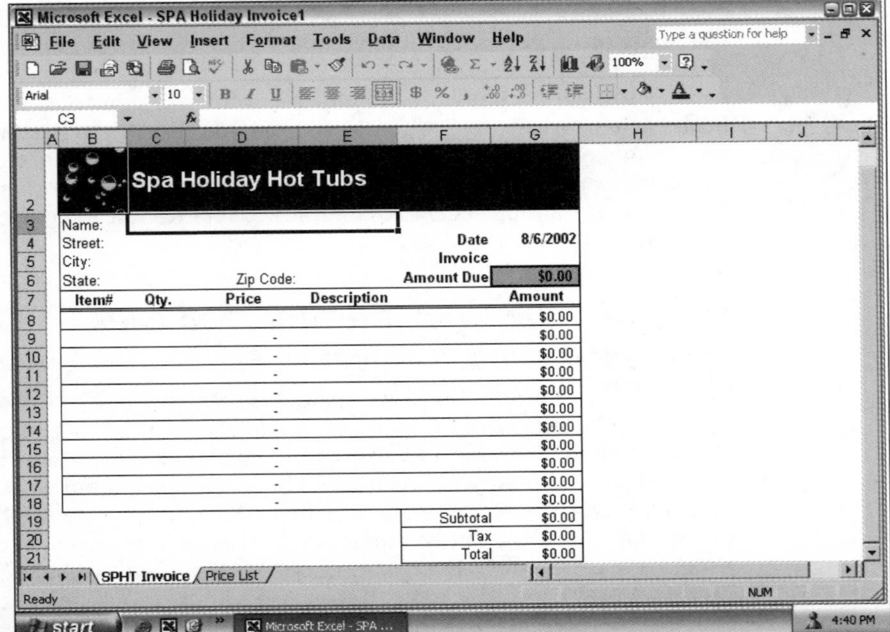

Figure 2-10: Using the Tab key to move from unlocked cell to unlocked cell in a protected worksheet.

If you want to make it impossible for the user to select anything but the unlocked cells in the protected worksheet, you can do so by removing the checkmark from the Selected Locked Cells check box in the Allow All Users of This Worksheet To list box of the Protect Sheet dialog box.

Protecting the workbook

There is one last level of protection that you can apply to your spreadsheet files, and that is protecting the entire workbook. When you protect the workbook, you ensure that its users can't change the structure of the file by adding, deleting, or even moving and renaming any of its worksheets. To protect your workbook, you choose Tools⇨Protection⇨Protect Workbook from the Excel Menu bar.

When you choose this command, Excel displays a Protect Workbook dialog box like the one shown in Figure 2-11. This dialog box contains two check boxes: Structure (which is automatically checked) and Windows (which is not selected). This dialog box also contains a Password (Optional) text box where you can enter a password that must be supplied before you can unprotect the workbook. Like every other password in Excel, the password to unprotect the workbook can be up to 255 characters maximum, consisting of a combination of letters, numbers, and spaces, with all the letters being case-sensitive.

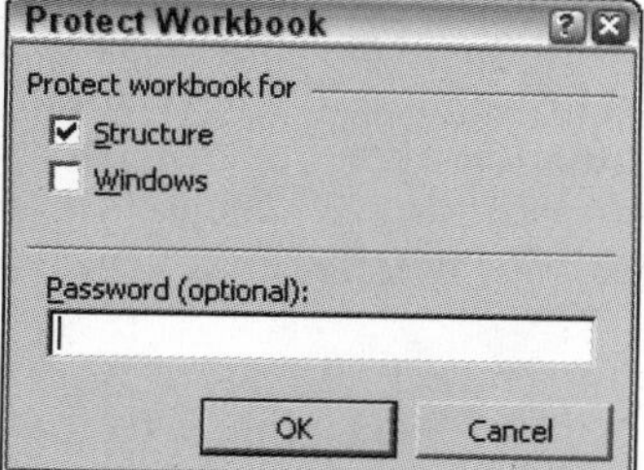

Figure 2-11: Protecting a workbook in the Protect Workbook dialog box.

When you protect a workbook with the Structure check box selected, Excel prevents you or your users from doing any of the following tasks to the file:

- ✦ Inserting new worksheets
- ✦ Deleting existing worksheets
- ✦ Renaming worksheets
- ✦ Hiding or viewing hidden worksheets
- ✦ Moving or copying worksheets to another workbook

- Displaying the source data for a cell in a pivot table or display a table's page fields on separate worksheets (see Book VII, Chapter 2 for details)
- Creating a summary report with the Scenario Manager (see Book VII, Chapter 1 for details)

When you turn on protection for a workbook after checking the Windows check box in the Protect Workbook dialog box, Excel prevents you from changing the size or position of the workbook's windows (not usually something you need to control).

After you've enabled protection in a workbook, you can then turn it off by choosing the Tools⇨Protection⇨Unprotect Workbook on the Excel menus. If you've assigned a password to unprotect the workbook, you must accurately reproduce it in the Password text box in the Unprotect Workbook dialog box that then appears.

Protecting a shared workbook

Many times you will want to protect a workbook that you intend to share on a network. That way, you can allow simultaneous editing of its contents of its worksheets (assuming that you don't also protect individual sheets), while at the same time preventing anybody but you from removing the Change tracking (and thus deleting the Change History log — see Book IV, Chapter 1).

If the workbook is not currently shared, you can both protect the workbook and share it by choosing the Tools⇨Protection⇨Protect and Share Workbook command on the Excel pull-down menus. Note that if the workbook is already shared, you must stop sharing the file before you can use this command (see Book IV, Chapter 1 for details on how to do this).

When you choose Tools⇨Protection⇨Protect and Share Workbook, Excel opens the Protect Shared Workbook dialog box, similar to the one shown in Figure 2-12. In this dialog box, you click the Sharing with Track Changes check box to enable file sharing and to turn on the Change tracking. As soon as you click this check box to put a checkmark in it, Excel makes available the Password (Optional) text box, where you can enter a password that must be supplied before you can stop sharing the workbook.

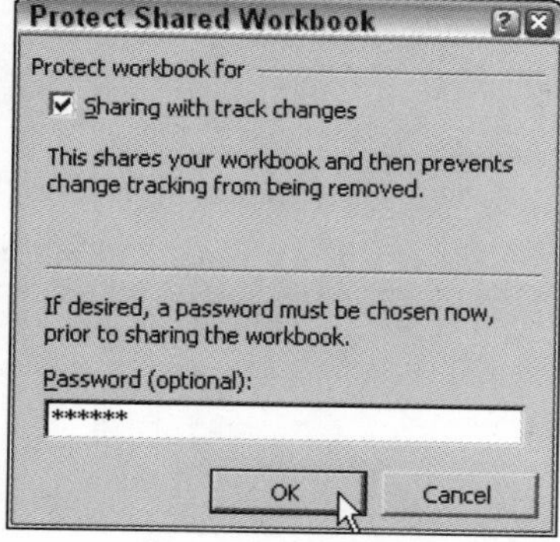

Figure 2-12: Setting up protection for a shared workbook in the Protect Shared Workbook dialog box.

If you enter a password in this text box (and you should, otherwise, there's little reason to use this option, because anyone can remove the protection from the shared workbook and thus stop the file sharing), Excel immediately displays the Confirm Password dialog box where you must accurately reproduce the password.

When you do this, Excel displays an alert dialog box that informs you that it will now save the workbook. When you click the Yes button, the program saves the workbook as a shared file and protects it from being made exclusive without the password.

To remove the protection from the shared workbook and (at the same time) stop sharing it, you choose the Tools➪Protection➪Unprotect Shared Workbook on the Excel Menu bar. After you enter the password to unprotect the file in the Unprotect Sharing dialog box and click OK, Excel displays an alert dialog box, informing you that your action is about to remove the file from shared use and erase the Change History log file, thus preventing users who are currently editing the workbook from saving their changes. If you're sure that no else is using the workbook, you can continue and remove the file sharing by clicking the Yes button.

Chapter 3: Sharing Data with Other Programs

In This Chapter

- **Understanding the basics of data sharing between Windows programs**
- **Importing text files into Excel worksheets**
- **Getting Excel data and charts into a Word document**
- **Getting Excel data and charts into the slides of a PowerPoint presentation**
- **Exporting your Outlook Contacts into an Excel worksheet**
- **Using Smart Tags to share online information**

Sharing data between Excel and other Windows programs that you use is the topic of this chapter. In many cases, data sharing involves getting Excel data tables, data lists, and charts into other Office programs that you use, especially Microsoft Word documents and PowerPoint presentations. In other cases, data sharing involves getting data generated in other programs, such as in tables and lists created in Microsoft Word and contacts maintained in Microsoft Outlook, into an Excel worksheet.

In a few cases, data sharing involves importing text files into Excel worksheets. As part of this process, you tell Excel how to split up items in each line of the text file so that these items are entered into separate cells (making it possible to sort and filter the list by various data items).

In addition to data sharing that involves bringing data stored in different types of documents into Excel worksheets, Excel 2002 introduces a new kind of data sharing in the form of *Smart Tags* that can bring information into the spreadsheet that's related to a particular type of data entry — such as a person's name, a company's stock symbol, or the name of a city. Information imported through the use of Smart Tags can come from local sources, such as your Outlook Contacts file, as well as from online sources such as MSN MoneyCentral on the Web.

Data Sharing 101

You share information between Excel and other Windows programs in two major ways: You either copy or move discrete objects or blocks of data from one program's file to another, or you open an entire file created with one program in the other program.

The key to sharing blocks of data or discrete objects in Excel is the Windows Clipboard. Remember that Excel always gives you access to contents of the Clipboard in the form of the Clipboard Task Pane, which you can quickly open by pressing Ctrl+CC (that's two Cs in a row while holding down the Ctrl key). When the Clipboard Task Pane is open, you can then copy its objects or blocks of text into cells of the open worksheet simply by clicking the item in this Task Pane.

The key to data sharing on the file level is to use the Files of Type pop-up menu in the Open (Ctrl+F12) and the Save As (F12) dialog boxes. The Files of Type pop-up menus in these two dialog boxes list all the file types that Excel recognizes and can therefore import into Excel or export from Excel.

This list includes other compatible data processing programs, such as Lotus 1-2-3, Quattro Pro, Paradox, and dBASE, as well as text files and Web Pages. In the case of exporting an Excel workbook file in the Save As dialog box, this list also includes earlier versions of Excel files (so the spreadsheet data that you generate in Excel 2002 can be read and opened by much earlier versions, such as Excel 4.0 and 3.0).

Excel 2002 is very good at opening Web pages in Excel and saving spreadsheet files as Web pages for distribution on your company intranet or corporate Web site. However, because this is such an important and specialized topic, you can find all the information on doing this kind of Web-related data sharing in Book VIII, Chapter 1.

Importing Text Files

Text files used to be the *lingua franca* (that's *common tongue* to you) of data sharing on personal computers — that was way back before the universal adoption of Microsoft Windows on the PC platform and the widespread use of the Internet — so it should come as no surprise to learn that Excel is totally prepared to import data from almost any text file. Excel is so prepared, in fact, that the program has a special Text Import Wizard that enables you to tell Excel exactly how to split up the data on each line of the text file into separate cells in the worksheet (a process technically known as *parsing* the text file).

Most text files containing lists of related data use some sort of standard character to separate each data item (such as a comma or tab) in every line, just as it uses the character for the Enter key to mark the separation of each line of data within the file. Those text files that use the comma to separate data items are known as *CSV files* (for Comma Separated Values). Those that use tabs to separate the individual data items are known as *Tab delimited* files. Note that some programs use the generic term, *delimited files*, to refer to any text file that uses a standard character, such as a comma or tab, to separate its individual data items.

The Text Import Wizard uses these facts about text files to analyze the structure of incoming text files to help you to determine how to parse the data in the text file. Because the Text Import Wizard always imports the parsed text data into the current worksheet starting at the active cell and then using as many subsequent columns and rows as necessary, you should always select an empty cell at the beginning of a blank region in the worksheet (or better yet, in a blank worksheet) before you invoke the Text Import Wizard. That way, you never run the risk of the incoming text file data wiping out existing data in the worksheet.

Figure 3-1 illustrates how the Text Import Wizard works and can help you to successfully import a text file that consists of a data list into an Excel worksheet. This figure shows the Text Import Wizard — Step 1 of 3 dialog box that first appears when you try to open a text file from the Open dialog box (File⇨Open).

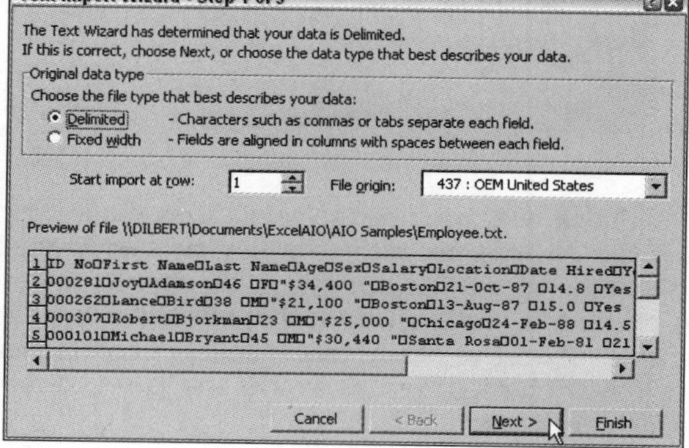

Figure 3-1: First of three Text Import Wizard dialog boxes for parsing a text file.

As this figure shows, Excel has analyzed the data and determined that it uses some sort of delimiting character (represented by the open square between the lines of data shown in the preview list box at the bottom of the Step 1 of 3 dialog box). If you're dealing with a text file in which the data items all use the same number of characters (such as 11 spaces for SSN and 10 spaces for ID number), click the Fixed Width radio button.

The Text Import Wizard always assumes that you want to start importing the data from the first to the very last line in the text file. If you don't need the first line or lines imported (because they contain data, such as titles, that you'd only have to eliminate from the worksheet if you did bring them in), use the preview list box to determine the number of the first line to import and then enter that number in the Start Import Row text box or use its Spin buttons to select this number.

Figure 3-2 shows the second Text Import Wizard dialog box that appears when you click the Next> button in the Step 1 of 3 dialog box. As you can see, the Text Import Wizard — Step 2 of 3 dialog box contains a Data Preview section that shows your text data aligned (simulating their column arrangement in your Excel worksheet).

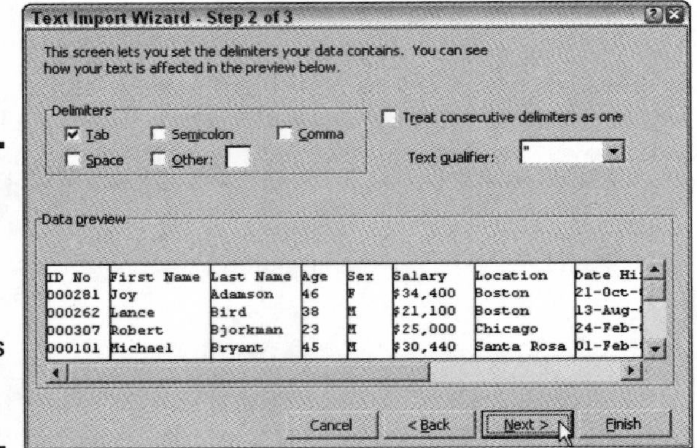

Figure 3-2: Second of three Text Import Wizard dialog boxes for parsing the text file.

In the Step 2 of 3 dialog box, you need to select the delimiting character in the event that the wizard selects the wrong character in the Delimiters section. If your text file uses a custom delimiting character, you need to click the Other check box and then enter that character in its text box. If your file uses two consecutive characters (such as a comma and a space), you need to click their check boxes, as well as the Treat Consecutive Delimiters As One check box.

By default, the Text Import Wizard treats any characters enclosed in a pair of double quotes as text entries (as opposed to numbers). If your text file uses a single quote, click the single quote (') character in the Text Qualifier drop-down list box.

Figure 3-3 shows you the third Text Import Wizard that appears when you click the Next button in the Step 2 of 3 dialog box. In the Step 3 of 3 dialog box, you get to assign a data format to the various columns of text data or indicate that a particular column of data should be skipped and therefore not imported into your Excel worksheet.

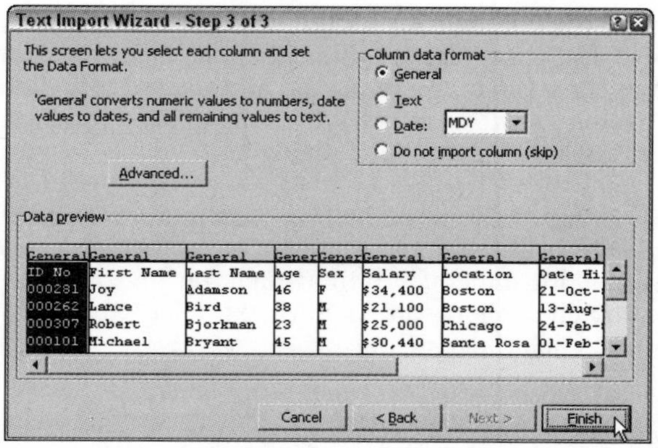

Figure 3-3: Third of three Text Import Wizard dialog boxes for parsing the text file.

When setting data formats for the columns of the text file, you can choose among the following three data types:

- **General** (the default) to convert all numeric values to number, entries recognized as date values to dates, and everything else in the column to text
- **Text** to convert all the entries in the column to text
- **Date** to convert all the entries to dates by using the date format shown in the associated drop-down list box

To assign one of these data types to a column, click its column in the Data Preview section and then click the appropriate radio button (General, Text, or Date) in the Column Data Format section in the upper-right corner.

In determining values when using the General data format, Excel uses the period (.) as the decimal separator and the comma (,) as the thousands separator. If you're dealing with data that uses these two symbols in just the opposite way (the comma for the decimal and the period for the thousands separator), as is the case in many European countries, click the Advanced button in the Step 3 of 3 dialog box to open the Advanced Text Import Settings dialog box. There, click the comma (,) in the Decimal Separator drop-down list box and the period (.) in the Thousands Separator drop-down list box before you click OK. If your text file uses trailing minus signs (as in 100–) to represent negative numbers (as in –100), make sure that the Traling Minus for Negatvie Numbers check box contains a checkmark.

If you want to change the date format for a column to which you've assigned the Date data format, click its M-D-Y code in the Date drop-down list box (where *M* stands for the month, *D* for the day, and *Y* for the year). To skip the importing of a particular column, click it in the Data Preview and then click the Do Not Import Column (Skip) radio button at the bottom of the Column Data Format section.

After you have all the columns formatted as you want, click the Finish button to import and parse the text file data starting at the current cell. Figure 3-4 shows the rows of the imported and parsed text data that appear in the new worksheet starting at cell A1 when I clicked the Finish button in the Text Import Wizard — Step 3 of 3 dialog box.

Don't forget to change the type of file from text to Microsoft Excel Workbook when you first save your imported text file. To do this, choose File⇨Save As from the Excel pull-down menu and then click the Save as Type drop-down list box where you click Microsoft Excel Workbook (*.xls) at the very top of the list before you click the Save button.

	A	B	C	D	E	F	G	H	I	J
1	ID No	First Name	Last Name	Age	Sex	Salary	Location	Date Hired	Years of S	Profit Sharing
2	281	Joy	Adamson	46	F	$34,400	Boston	21-Oct-87	14.8	Yes
3	262	Lance	Bird	38	M	$21,100	Boston	13-Aug-87	15	Yes
4	307	Robert	Bjorkman	23	M	$25,000	Chicago	24-Feb-88	14.5	Yes
5	101	Michael	Bryant	45	M	$30,440	Santa Ros	1-Feb-81	21.5	Yes
6	159	Sherry	Caulfield	40	F	$24,100	Boston	19-Mar-84	18.4	No
7	139	William	Cobb	42	M	$27,500	Boston	########	20.2	Yes
8	141	Angela	Dickinson	33	F	$23,900	Detroit	13-Nov-86	15.7	No
9	174	Cindy	Edwards	27	F	$21,500	San Franc	15-Aug-85	17	No
10	220	Jack	Edwards	44	M	$32,200	Atlanta	14-Feb-87	15.5	Yes
11	367	Amanda	Fletcher	22	F	$16,500	Boston	3-Jan-89	13.6	No
12	315	Dave	Grogan	26	M	$17,500	Seattle	3-Apr-88	14.4	No
13	185	Rebecca	Johnson	35	F	$20,200	Boston	4-Feb-86	16.5	No
14	211	Stuart	Johnson	37	M	$21,000	Seattle	29-Dec-86	15.6	No
15	118	Janet	Kaplan	44	F	$34,000	Boston	22-Jun-81	21.1	Yes
16	222	Mary	King	24	F	$18,100	Detroit	10-Mar-87	15.4	No
17	146	Edward	Krauss	41	M	$26,200	Chicago	13-Jul-83	19.1	Yes
18	162	Kimberly	Lerner	29	F	$24,900	Chicago	28-Jun-84	18.1	No
19	210	Victoria	Morin	31	F	$20,700	Seattle	20-Dec-86	15.6	No
20	284	Miriam	Morse	23	F	$19,600	Chicago	2-Nov-87	14.8	No
21	192	Deborah	Mosley	34	F	$20,800	Detroit	23-Aug-86	16	No
22	297	James	Percival	36	M	$19,200	Atlanta	18-Dec-87	14.6	Yes
23	348	Carl	Reese	23	M	$15,800	Atlanta	13-Sep-88	13.9	No

Figure 3-4: New worksheet with data after opening the parsed text file.

Sharing Data with Other Office Programs

Because very few people purchase Excel as a separate program outside of the Office suite, it should be no surprise that most of the file sharing that takes place between Excel and other programs are between Excel and one of the other major applications included in Microsoft Office (such as Word, PowerPoint, and Access).

However, before you rush off and start wildly throwing Excel worksheets into Word documents and Excel charts into PowerPoint presentations, you need to realize that Microsoft offers you a choice in the way you exchange data between your various Office programs. Namely, you can either embed the worksheet or chart in the other program or set up a link between the Excel-generated object in the other program and Excel itself:

- *Embedding* means that the Excel object (whether it's a worksheet or a chart) actually becomes part of the Word document or PowerPoint presentation. Any changes that you then need to make to the worksheet or chart must be made within the Word document or PowerPoint presentation. This presupposes, however, that you have Excel on the same computer as Word or PowerPoint and that your computer has enough memory to run them both.
- *Linking* means that the Excel object (worksheet or chart) is only referred to in the Word document or PowerPoint presentation. Any changes that you make to the worksheet or chart must be made in Excel itself and then updated in the Word document or PowerPoint presentation to which it is linked.

Use the embedding method when the Excel object (worksheet or chart) is not apt to change very often, if at all. Use the linking method when the Excel object (worksheet or chart) changes fairly often, when you always need the latest and greatest version of the object to appear in your Word document or PowerPoint presentation, or when you don't want to make the Word or PowerPoint document any bigger by adding the Excel data to it.

Be aware that when you link an Excel worksheet or chart to another Office document and you want to show that document (or print it on a different computer), you must copy both the Excel workbook with the linked worksheet/chart and the Word or PowerPoint file to that computer. Also be aware that when you embed an Excel worksheet or chart in another Office document and then want to edit it on another computer, that computer must have both Excel and the other Microsoft Office program (Word or PowerPoint) installed on it.

Use the embedding or linking techniques only when you have a pretty good suspicion that the Excel stuff is far from final and that you want to be able to update the Excel data either manually (with embedding) or automatically (with linking). If your Excel stuff will remain unchanged, just use the old standby method of copying the Excel data to the Clipboard with Edit⇨Copy (Ctrl+C) and then switching to the Word or PowerPoint document and pasting it in place with the Edit⇨Paste (Ctrl+V) command.

Excel maintains a very close relationship with Microsoft Access, thus making it easy to import data from anyone of the tables or queries set up for a database into your Excel worksheet. For details on how to bring in data from Access, see Book VI, Chapter 2.

Excel and Word

Of all the Office programs (besides our beloved Excel), Microsoft Word is the one that you are most apt to use. You will probably find yourself using Word to type up any memos, letters, and reports that you need in the course of your daily work (even if you really don't understand how the program works). From time to time, you may need to bring some worksheet data or charts that you've created in your Excel workbooks into a Word document that you're creating. When those occasions arise, check out the information in the next section.

Although Word has a Table feature that supports calculations through a kind of mini-spreadsheet operation, you probably will be more productive if you create the data (formulas, formatting, and all) in an Excel workbook and then bring that data into your Word document by following the steps outlined in the next section. Likewise, although you can keep, create, and manage the data records that you use in mail merge operations within Word, you probably will find it more expedient to create and maintain them in Excel — considering that you are already familiar with how to create, sort, and filter database records in Excel — and then select them as described in the mail merge section.

Getting Excel data into a Word document

As with all the other Office programs, you have two choices when bringing Excel data (worksheet cell data or charts) into a Word document: You can embed the data in the Word document, or you can link the data that you bring into Word to its original Excel worksheet. Embed the data or charts when you want to be able to edit right within Word. Link the data or charts when you want to be able to edit in Excel and have the changes automatically updated when you open the Word document.

Happily embedded after

The easiest way to embed a table of worksheet data or a chart is to use the good old drag-and-drop method: Simply drag the selected cells or chart between the Excel and Word program windows rather than to a new place in a worksheet. The only trick to dragging and dropping between programs is the sizing and maneuvering of the Excel and Word program windows themselves. Figures 3-5 and 3-6 illustrate the procedure for dragging a table of worksheet data (with first January sales for the Mission Street store) from its worksheet (named Mission Street) into a memo started in Word.

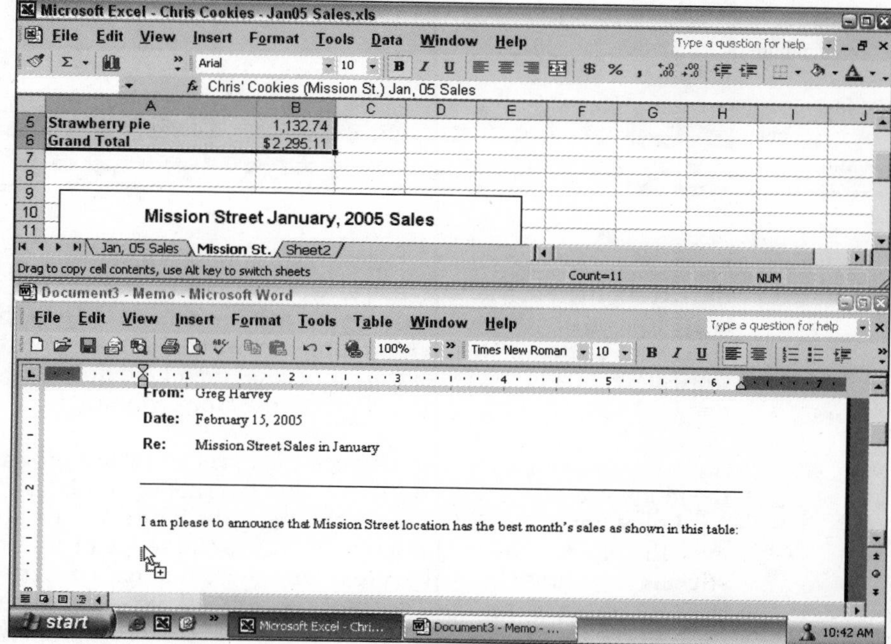

Figure 3-5: Dragging the cell range A1:B6 from the sales workbook to the Word memo.

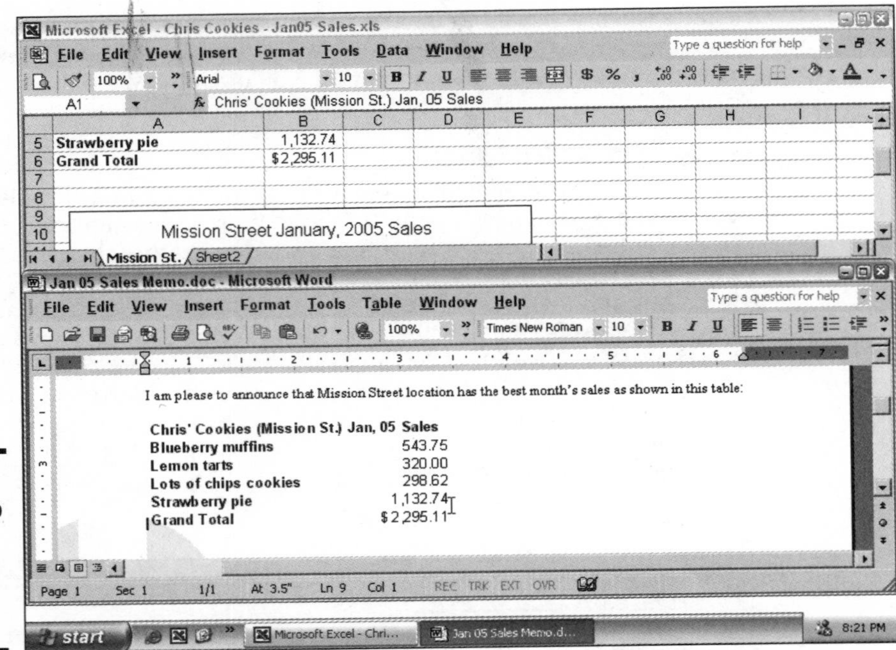

Figure 3-6: Word memo after copying the worksheet data.

Before I could drag the selected worksheet data, I had to size and position the Excel program window. In Figure 3-5, you can see that the Excel window is positioned above the Word window and sized to about half the full-screen size. After futzing with these two program windows, I had only to select the worksheet data in the Excel worksheet and then hold down the Ctrl key (to copy) as I dragged the outline down to the Word window.

As I passed over the border between the Excel and Word program windows, the mouse pointer changed shape to the international "oh-no-you-don't" symbol. When I reached the safe havens of the Word document area, however, the pointer changed again, this time to the shape of an arrowhead sticking up from a box with a plus sign (how's that for a description?). To indicate where in the Word document to embed the selected data, I simply positioned the arrowhead-sticking-up-from-a-box-with-a-plus-sign pointer at the place in the document where the Excel stuff is to appear. Then I released the mouse button. Figure 3-6 shows you the embedded worksheet table that appeared after I released the mouse button.

You can also use the cut-and-paste method to embed worksheet data into a Word document. Simply select the cells in Excel and then copy them to the Clipboard (Ctrl+C). Then open the Word document, position the cursor at the place where the spreadsheet table is to appear, and then select Edit⇨Paste Special from the Word Menu bar. Click Microsoft Excel Worksheet

Object in the As list box and then click OK. Word then embeds the data in the body of the Word document just as though you had Ctrl+dragged the data from the Excel window over to the Word window.

Editing embedded stuff

The great thing about embedding Excel stuff (as opposed to linking, which I get to in a later section) is that you can edit the data right from within Word. Figure 3-7 shows the table after I centered it with the Center button on Word's Formatting toolbar. Notice what happens when I double-click the embedded table (or click the table once and then choose Worksheet Object⇨Edit on the table's shortcut menu): A frame with columns and rows, scroll bars, and sheet tabs miraculously appears around the table. Notice, also, that the pull-down menus and toolbars in the Word window have changed to Excel's pull-down menus and Excel's Standard and Formatting toolbars (it's like being at home when you're still on the road). At this point, you can edit any of the table's contents by using the Excel commands that you already know.

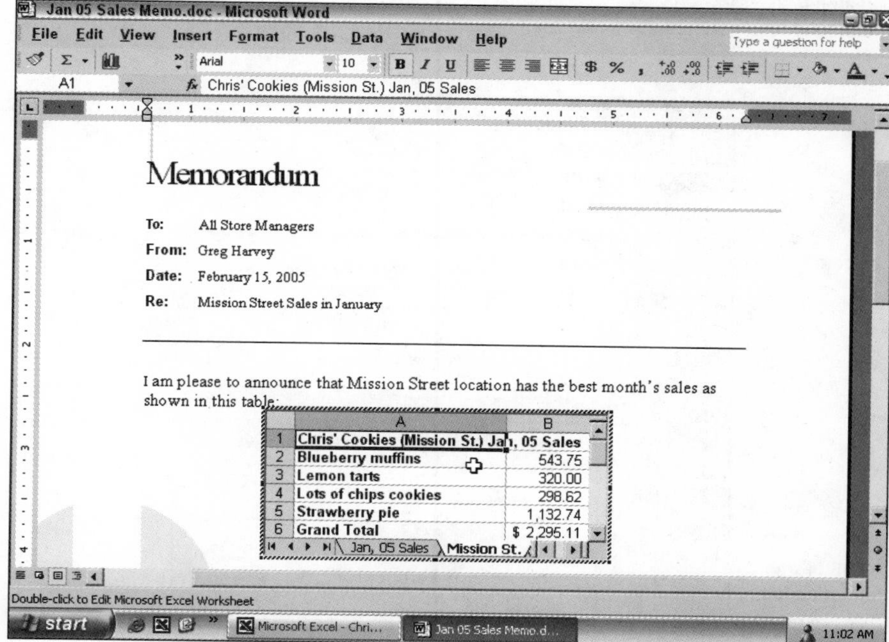

Figure 3-7: Editing the embedded worksheet data in the Sales memo.

The links that bind

Of course, as nice as embedding is, you will encounter occasions when linking the Excel data to the Word document is the preferred method (and, in fact, even easier to do). Figures 3-8 and 3-9 illustrate the linking process. First, I selected a chart that I created in the worksheet by *single*-clicking it, not double-clicking it, as I would do to edit the chart in the worksheet. I was about to select the Copy command on its shortcut menu (Edit➪Copy or Ctrl+C) to send a copy of it to the Clipboard.

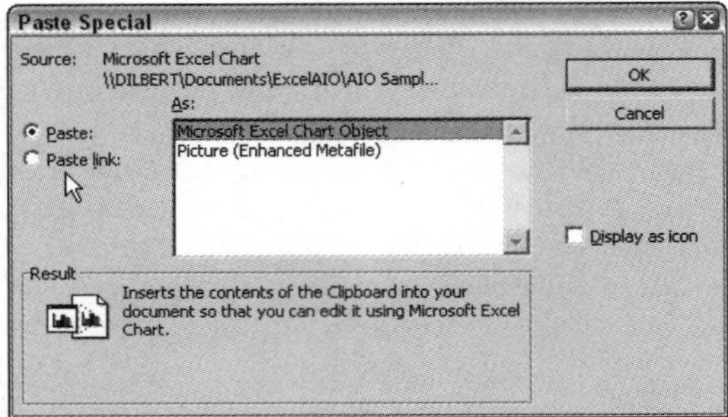

Figure 3-8: Selecting the Paste Link option in Word's Paste Special dialog box.

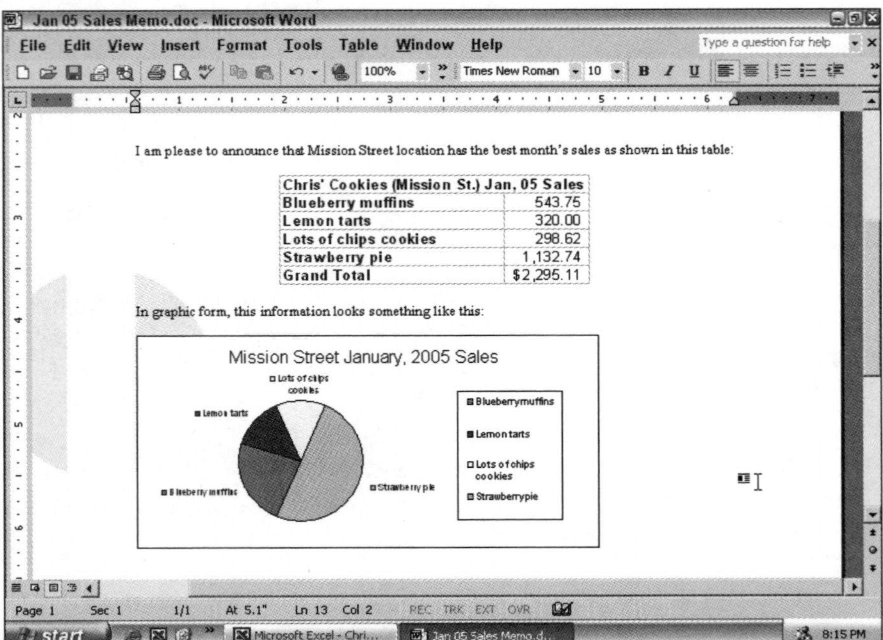

Figure 3-9: Pasting the linked chart into the Word memo.

After copying the chart (or selected data) to the Clipboard, I switched over to Word and my memo to all store managers. After positioning the insertion point at the beginning of the paragraph where the chart needs to be, I chose Edit⇨Paste Special from the Word Menu bar. Figure 3-8 shows the Paste Special dialog box that appears. In this dialog box, the crucial thing is to select the Paste Link radio button before clicking OK. Figure 3-9 shows the Word memo after I clicked OK and pasted the Excel chart into place.

Editing linked data

Editing data linked to Excel (as a chart or cells) is not quite as delightful as editing embedded worksheet data. For one thing, you first have to go back to Excel and make your changes — although you can easily open Excel and its workbook just by double-clicking the linked chart. The nice thing is that any changes that you make to the original data or chart immediately crop up in the Word document when you open it.

Figures 3-10 illustrates how this works. In this figure, changes I made to the title and the legend of the linked chart were automatically updated, as well as the change in the pie sections due to my increasing the sales of Blueberry muffins from $543.75 to $843.75. Unfortunately, because the worksheet data in the table is embedded instead of linked, I must manually correct the Blueberry muffin sales in cell B2 in the embedded table by increasing it as well (in this case, I should have linked both elements; worksheet data along with the chart generated from the data).

Excel and PowerPoint

The process of embedding and linking worksheet data and charts in the slides of your Microsoft PowerPoint presentations is very similar to the techniques outlined for Word. To embed a cell selection or chart, drag the data or chart object from the Excel worksheet to the PowerPoint slide. If you prefer using the cut-and-paste method, copy the data or chart to the Clipboard (Ctrl+C), switch to PowerPoint and choose Edit⇨Paste Special from the PowerPoint Menu bar. Then, make sure that the Microsoft Excel Worksheet Object is selected in the As list box and the Paste radio button are both selected in the Paste Special dialog box before you click OK.

If you want to link Excel data or a chart that you pasted into a PowerPoint presentation slide to its source Excel workbook, the only thing you do differently is to click the Paste Link radio button in the Paste Special dialog box before you click OK.

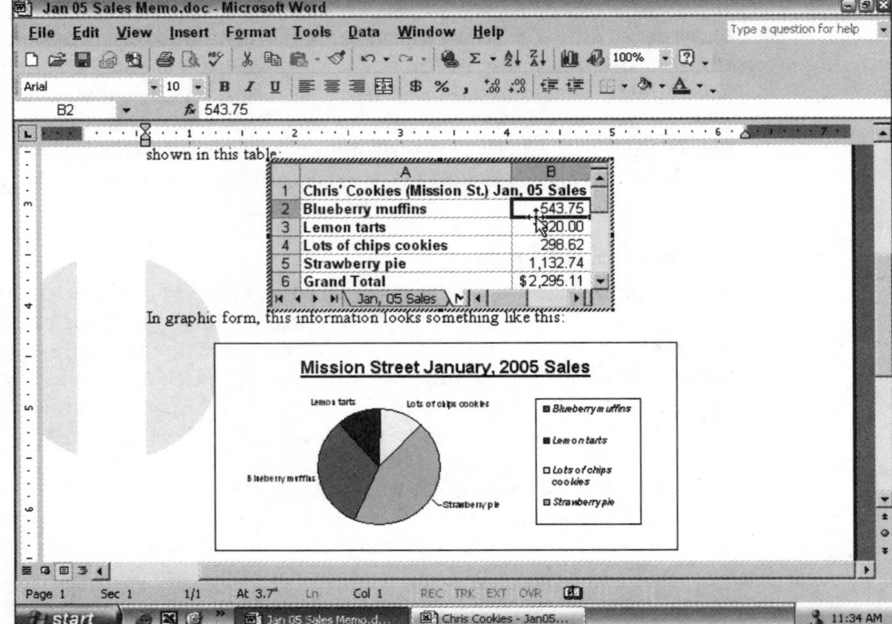

Figure 3-10: Changes to the linked chart in Excel are immediately updated in the Word memo.

Sometimes, after making changes to the linked data or chart in Excel, you need to manually update the link in the PowerPoint presentation slide to ensure that your presentation has the latest and greatest version of the Excel data. To manually update a linked table of Excel spreadsheet data or a linked chart, go to the slide in question, right-click the table or chart, and then click Update Link on its shortcut menu.

Excel and Outlook

Microsoft Outlook is a group of powerful utilities for scheduling and managing personal information and doing e-mail rather than a standard application program, such as Word or Excel. Among its useful utilities are the Contacts module (where you can store information about the people you deal with day in and day out), the Calendar module (where you can schedule your appointments), and the Tasks module (where you can keep track of all the thousands of things that you need to get done).

You can use Outlook's File➪Import and Export command to exchange data between an Excel spreadsheet and any Outlook folder, such as the Contacts, Calendar, or Tasks (heck, you can export your e-mail messages to an Excel workbook from the Inbox, Drafts, or Outbox folders).

When you select the File➪Import and Export command from the Outlook Menu bar, the program starts the Import and Export Wizard. Figure 3-11 shows the first dialog box in this wizard where you choose the type of action to perform. To bring data from an Excel worksheet file into one of the Outlook modules or folders, click the Import From Another Program or File item in the Choose an Action to Perform list box. To export Outlook data from one of its modules or folders into an Excel workbook, click the Export to a File item at the very top of this list box.

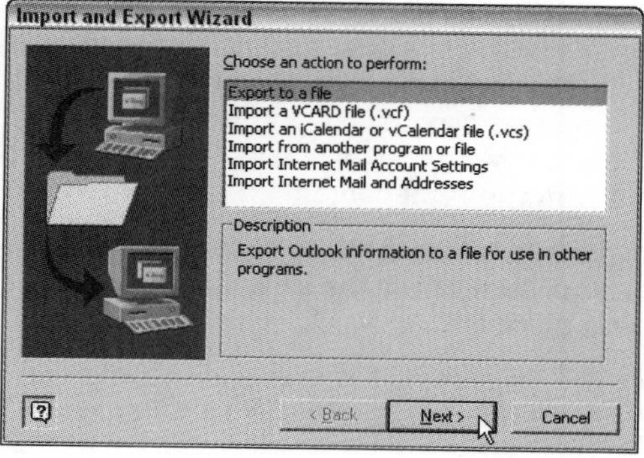

Figure 3-11: Using the Import and Export Wizard to transfer data between Excel and Outlook.

The following steps guide you through exporting the data in your Outlook Contacts folder into a new Excel workbook file. The steps for exporting other folders (such as the Inbox or Tasks folders) are almost the same. The steps for importing the data stored in an Excel worksheet into one of your Outlook folders are very similar, except that instead of specifying Excel as the type of file to create, you specify it as the type of file to import.

1. **Open Outlook and then choose File➪Import and Export from the Outlook Menu bar.**

   This action opens the first dialog box in the Import and Export Wizard (shown in Figure 3-11).

2. **Click Export to a File in the Choose an Action to Perform list box and then click the Next> button.**

   This action opens the second dialog box (now called Export to a File) in the Import and Export Wizard, where you indicate the type of file to create for the exported Outlook data.

3. **Click Microsoft Excel in the Create a File of Type list box and then click the Next> button.**

   This action opens the next dialog box in the Export to a File version of the Import and Export Wizard, where you select the Outlook folder whose information is to be copied into the Excel workbook.

4. **Click the Contacts folder icon in the Select Folder to Export From list box and then click the Next> button.**

   This action opens the next Export to a File dialog box in the Import and Export Wizard (shown in Figure 3-12), where you indicate the name and location of the new Excel workbook that is to contain the Outlook Contacts data.

5. **Click the Browse button to the right of the Save Exported File As text box.**

   This action opens the Browse dialog box (similar to the Save As dialog box), where you can select the folder and enter the filename for the workbook file where the Contacts data is to be stored. Enter a new filename in the File Name text box unless you specifically want to replace an existing workbook file with the exported Outlook data (at which time, you must confirm the replacement).

6. **Select the drive and folder in which to create the new file in the Save In drop-down list and then enter the new filename in the File Name text box before you click OK.**

   This action closes the Browse dialog box and returns you to the Export a File dialog box, where the complete path and filename of your new Excel workbook file appears.

7. **Click the Next button.**

   This action opens the next Export to a File dialog box in the Import and Export Wizard, which shows you what action the wizard will take as soon as you click the Finish button.

   Before you click Finish to start exporting the data to your new Excel workbook, you may want to specify exactly which fields in the Contact file to export. If you don't do this, the Import and Export Wizard copies all of the fields to the new Excel workbook (and there are a lot of them, to say the least). If you don't need all the data, follow Steps 8 through 11. If you do want all the data exported, skip to Step 12.

8. **(Optional) Click the Map Custom Fields button to specify exactly which fields to export.**

   This action opens the Map Custom Fields dialog box, where you specify exactly which fields to use (see Figure 3-13).

9. **Click the Clear Map button to completely clear the To list box.**

   After the To list box is clear, you're ready to drag the fields that you want exported out of the From list box to drop them in the To list box.

If you don't want all the fields within a particular category of the Contacts file, click the Expand button next to its name to display all of its subfields and then drag only the fields in that section that you want to export. For example, if you don't want the Title field and Suffix field in the Name category, click its Expand button and then drag the First Name, Middle Name, and Last Name fields over.

10. **Drag the fields that you want exported from the outline in the From list box over to the To list box.**

    Drag the fields over in the order in which you want them to appear in the resulting workbook file. If you drag a field and then discover that it's in the wrong order in the To list box, you reposition it by dragging it up or down in this list.

    After you have all the fields that you want exported in the To list box in the order in which you want them in the Excel workbook, proceed to Step 11.

11. **Click the OK button in the Map Custom Fields dialog box.**

    This action closes the Map Custom Fields dialog box and returns you to the final Export to a File dialog box, where you're ready to click the Finish button to begin the exporting of the Outlook Contacts data to your new workbook file.

12. **Click the Finish button in Export to a File dialog box.**

After the Import and Export Wizard finishes exporting the Contacts data in the fields that you specified, it saves it to the new Excel workbook file. You can then open this file in Excel and work with this data as though you had entered it directly into an Excel worksheet.

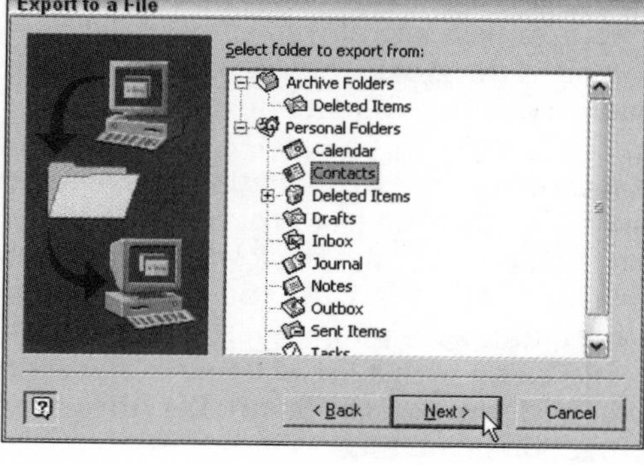

Figure 3-12: Selecting the Outlook folder to export in the Export a File dialog box.

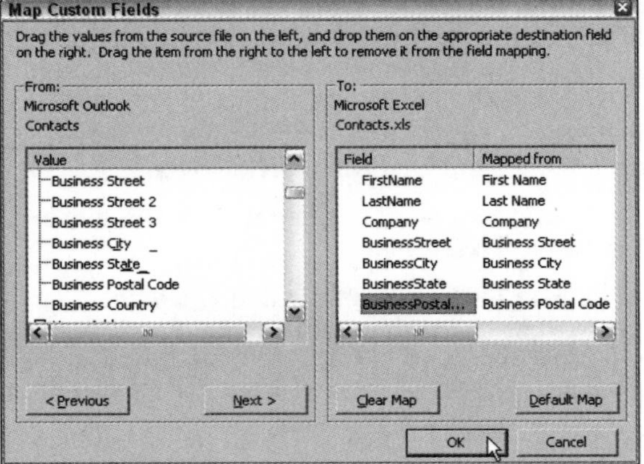

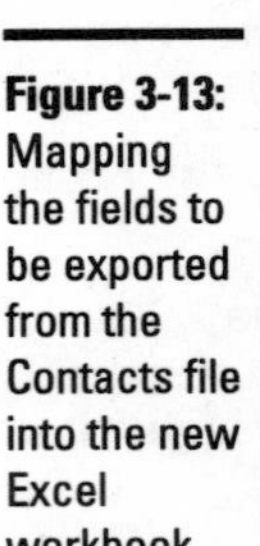

Figure 3-13: Mapping the fields to be exported from the Contacts file into the new Excel workbook.

Using Smart Tags

The Smart Tag feature provides the newest way to link certain types of information that you enter into your spreadsheet with other sources. A Smart Tag is automatically attached to a cell when Excel recognizes its contents as being of a certain type of data. For example, when you install Excel, it provides you with two basic types of Smart Tags:

- ✦ **Recent Outlook e-mail recipients** enable you to send e-mail, schedule a meeting, open the Contact information, add to the Contacts list, or insert the address for a person who is identified as someone from whom you've recently received an e-mail in Microsoft Outlook.
- ✦ **Smart tag lists (MSN MoneyCentral Financial Symbols)** enable you to insert stock quote information for a stock symbol that you enter — you can also visit the MSN MoneyCentral Web site and get information about the company who issued the stock, the stock performance, or any related news about the company and its business.

Excel indicates that it has recognized the data that you've entered into a cell as a type of Smart Tag data by inserting a purple triangle in the lower-right corner of the cell. When you position the thick white-cross pointer on the cell, this Smart Tag indicator appears. When you then position the mouse pointer on the Smart Tag indicator, a pop-up button appears, that, when clicked, displays a pop-up menu with a list of items representing the different actions that you can perform with the Smart Tag (these vary with the type of Smart Tag information involved).

Before you can use the Recent Outlook e-mail recipients and the Smart Tag lists (MSN MoneyCentral Financial Symbols Smart Tags that are installed with Excel) you must activate the Smart Tag feature in the program. To do this, follow these simple steps:

1. **Choose Tools⇨AutoCorrect Options from the Excel Menu bar.**

   This action opens the AutoCorrect dialog box with the AutoCorrect, AutoCorrect As You Type, and Smart Tags tabs.

2. **Click the Smart Tags tab to activate it.**

   This action displays the options on the Smart Tags tab (similar to the ones shown in Figure 3-14).

3. **Click the Label Data with Smart Tags check box and then click OK.**

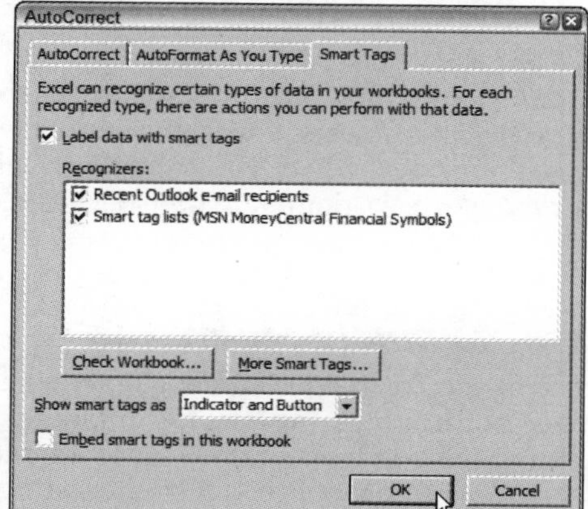

Figure 3-14: Activating the Smart Tags in the AutoCorrect dialog box.

After you activate Smart Tags in Excel, they start popping in the cells of the worksheet as you enter your data, indicated by both the purple triangle in the lower-right cell corner and the Smart Tag indicator.

If you think that both the triangle and Smart Tag indicator are a bit much, you can change how Smart Tags appear in the worksheet. Simply open the AutoCorrect dialog box (Tools⇨AutoCorrect Options), select the Smart Tags tab and then click the pop-up button attached to the Show Smart Tags As drop-down list box; you can then choose between the None and Button Only menu option. Of course, choosing None renders all your Smart Tags invisible (and thus, unusable). However, by choosing the Button Only option, you remove the purple triangles from the cells, while still retaining the ability to display the Smart Tag indicator by passing the mouse pointer over the cell — and to open its action menu by clicking the associated pop-up button.

Excel doesn't save the Smart Tags that it identifies in your worksheets unless you embed them in the sheet before saving the workbook. To do this, click the Embed Smart Tags in This Workbook check box at the bottom of the Smart Tags tab of the AutoCorrect dialog box (Tools⇨AutoCorrect Options), and then save the workbook.

Adding more Smart Tags

The eServices part of the Microsoft Office Web site has a bunch of different types of Smart Tags that you can download and add for use in Microsoft Office programs, such as Excel. These downloadable (and free) Smart Tags run the gamut from the Expedia Smart Tag — for getting travel-related information by entering destinations — all the way to the FedEx Smart Tag — for tracking your packages by its tracking number.

To get new Smart Tags for Excel, click the More Smart Tags button on the Smart Tags tab of the AutoCorrect dialog box (Tools⇨AutoCorrect). When you do this, Excel opens your Web browser, which then takes you to the Microsoft Office eServices home page, where you can follow links for getting Smart Tags in three major categories: Communication Services, Reference, and News & Travel.

Using the Financial Symbols Smart Tag

If your work involves tracking stocks in your spreadsheets, you'll appreciate the power and convenience of the Smart Tag lists (MSN MoneyCentral Financial Symbols) Smart Tag. All you have to do is enter a bona fide stock symbol in the cell of a worksheet to have it recognized as being a member of this type of data.

Figures 3-15 and 3-16 illustrate how this works. In cell A1, I input the text entry, MSFT, in all caps (which just happens to be the stock indicator for our beloved Microsoft Corporation). No sooner had I pressed the Enter key than Excel inserted a purple triangle in the lower-right corner of the cell, signifying that the program recognized this cell entry as constituting a Smart Tag.

In Figure 3-15 you see the particular Smart Tag pop-up menu associated with the Financial Symbol Smart Tag. You open this menu by clicking the pop-up button attached to its Smart Tag indicator. For this particular example, I clicked the Insert Refreshable Stock Price to insert a current quote on Microsoft's stock in the current worksheet.

Clicking this menu item opens the Insert Stock Price dialog box, where you indicate where to insert the MSN stock information on the MSFT stock. You can choose between inserting it on a new worksheet (the default setting) and inserting it in the current sheet starting at the cell of your choice. For this example, I choose the current worksheet cell B1 in the Insert Stock Price dialog box.

Figure 3-16 shows the result. As you can see, the Stock Quote information inserted into the worksheet includes links to Microsoft Corporation, Symbol Lookup (for looking up other stock symbols), a Chart link (to display a chart showing plotting the stock prices over the week), a News link to get business news involving Microsoft, and a MSN Money Home link for visiting the Home page of the MSN MoneyCentral Web site.

Better yet, Excel also displays the External Data toolbar (floating near the bottom of Figure 3-16). (You can display this toolbar by choosing View⇨Toolbars⇨External Data on the Excel menu bar, if it doesn't appear automatically.) The External Data toolbar contains a Refresh All button that you can click as often as you like to re-establish the link with MSN MoneyCentral and update the Microsoft stock quote data in your worksheet.

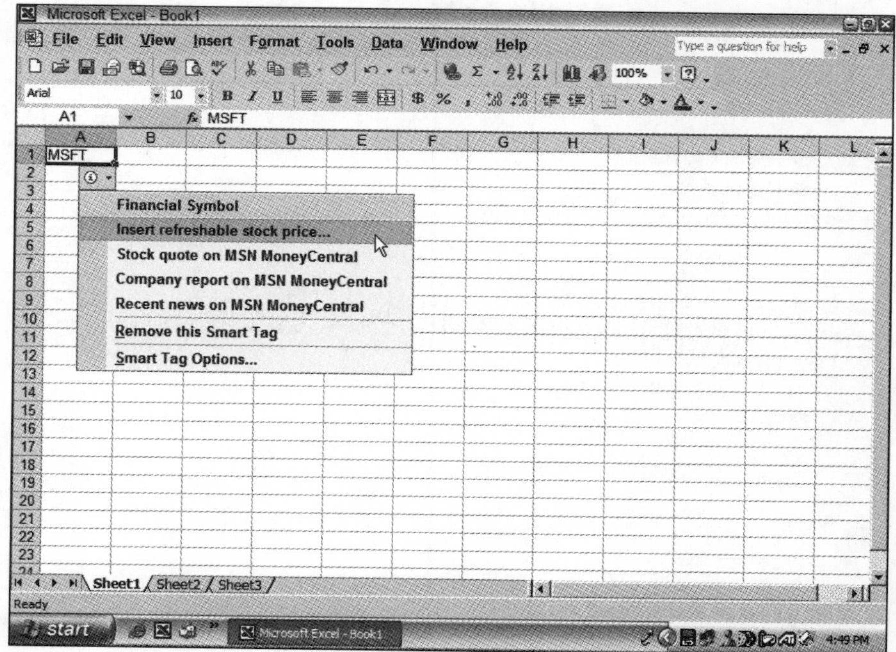

Figure 3-15: Selecting an action from the MSFT Smart Tag menu.

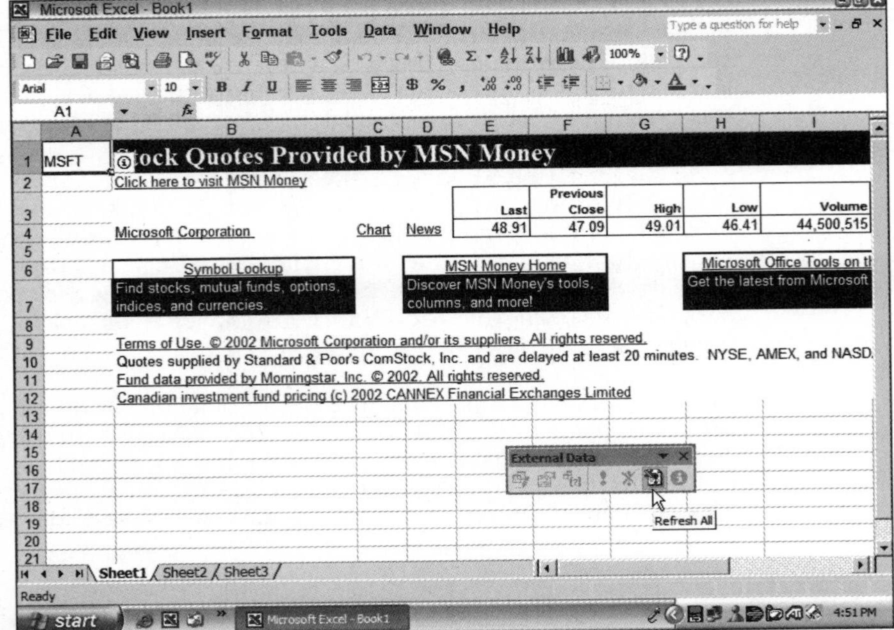

Figure 3-16: Worksheet after importing current stock information for the MSFT Smart Tag.

Book V

Charts and Graphics

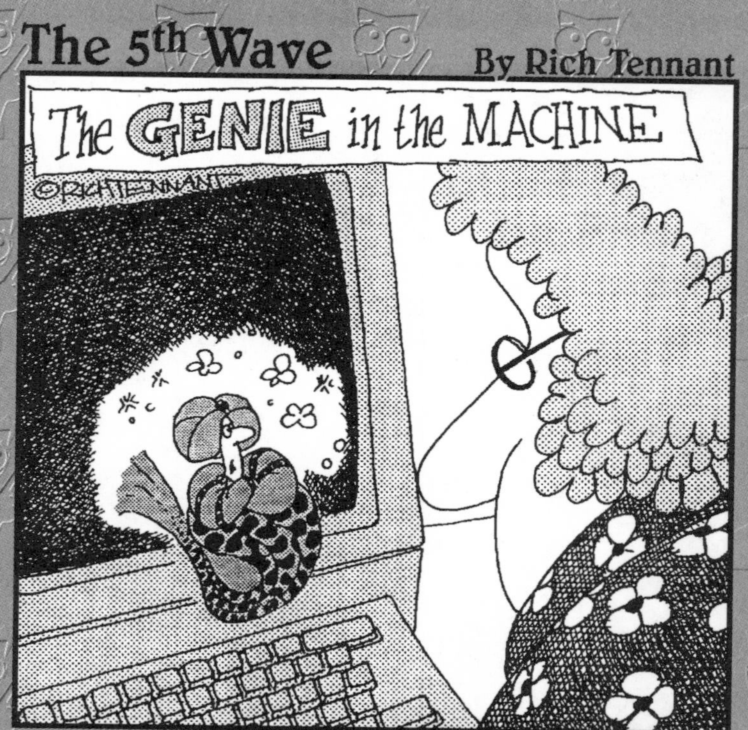

"Yes, I'm normally larger and more awe-inspiring, but I've got to squeeze into those tiny spreadsheet cells."

Contents at a Glance

Chapter 1: Charting Worksheet Data

In This Chapter

- **Understanding how to chart worksheet data**
- **Using the Chart Wizard to create an embedded chart or one on its own chart sheet**
- **Formatting the elements in a chart**
- **Editing an existing chart**
- **Selecting the right type of chart**
- **Adding a custom chart type**
- **Printing a chart alone or with its supporting data**

Charts present the data from your worksheet visually by representing the data in rows and columns as bars on a chart, for example, or as pieces of a pie in a pie chart. For a long time, charts and graphs have gone hand-in-hand with spreadsheets, because they allow you to see trends and patterns that you often can't readily visualize from the numbers alone. Which has more consistent sales, the Southeast region or the Northwest region? Monthly sales reports may contain the answer, but a bar chart based on the data shows it more clearly.

In this chapter, you first become familiar with the terminology that Excel uses as it refers to the parts of a chart — terms that may be new, such as "data marker" and "chart data series," as well as terms that are probably familiar already, such as "axis." After you get acquainted with the terms, you begin to put them to use with the ChartWizard, a tool that doesn't really require much specialized knowledge because it walks you through each of the steps required to create the kind of chart that you want.

The art of preparing a chart (and much of the fun) is matching a chart type to your purposes. To help you with this, you will take a tour through all the chart types available in Excel 2002, from old standbys such as bar and column charts to ones that may be new, such as radar charts and surface charts. Finally, you discover how to print charts, either alone or as part of the worksheet.

Workbook Charting 101

The typical Excel chart is comprised of several distinct parts. Figure 1-1 shows an Excel column chart in a separate document window with labels identifying the parts of this chart. Table 1-1 summarizes the parts of the typical chart.

Table 1-1 The Parts of a Typical Chart

Part	*Description*
Chart	Everything inside the chart window including all parts of the chart (labels axes, data markers, tick marks, and other elements in this table).
Chart toolbar	The toolbar that appears when you first create a chart that enables you to modify different parts of the current chart.
Data Marker	A symbol on the chart, such as a bar in a bar chart, a pie in a pie chart, or a line on a line chart that represents a single value in the spreadsheet. Data markers with the same shape or pattern represent a single data series in the chart.
Chart data series	A group of related values, such as all the values in a single row in the chart — all the production numbers for Part 100 in the sample chart, for example. A chart can have just one data series (shown in a single bar or line), but it usually has several.
Series Formula	A formula describing a given data series. The formula includes a reference to the cell that contains the data series name (such as the name Jan-92), references to worksheet cells containing the categories and values plotted in the chart, and the plot order of the series. The series formula can also have the actual data used to plot the chart. You can edit a series formula and control the plot order.
Axis	A line that serves as a major reference for plotting data in a chart. In two-dimensional charts there are two axes — the x (horizontal) axis and the y (vertical) axis. In most two-dimensional charts (except, notably, column charts), Excel plots categories (labels) along the x-axis and values (numbers) along the y-axis. Bar charts reverse the scheme, plotting values along the y-axis. Pie charts have no axes. Three dimensional charts have an x-axis, a y-axis, and a z-axis. The x- and y-axes delineate the horizontal surface of the chart. The z axis is the vertical axis, showing the depth of the third dimension in the chart.
Tick mark	A small line intersecting an axis. A tick mark indicates a category, scale, or chart data series. A tick mark can have a label attached.
Plot area	Area where Excel plots your data, including the axes and all markers that represent data points.

Part	Description
Gridlines	Optional lines extending from the tick marks across the plot area, thus making it easier to view the data values represented by the tick marks.
Chart text	Label or title that you add to the chart. *Attached text* is a title or label linked to an axis, data marker, or other chart object. If you move the object, you move the attached text as well. You can't move the attached text independently. *Unattached text* is text that you add with the Text Box button on the Drawing toolbar.
Legend	A key that identifies patterns, colors, or symbols associated with the markers of a chart data series. The legend shows the data series name corresponding to each data marker (such as the name of the red columns in a column chart).

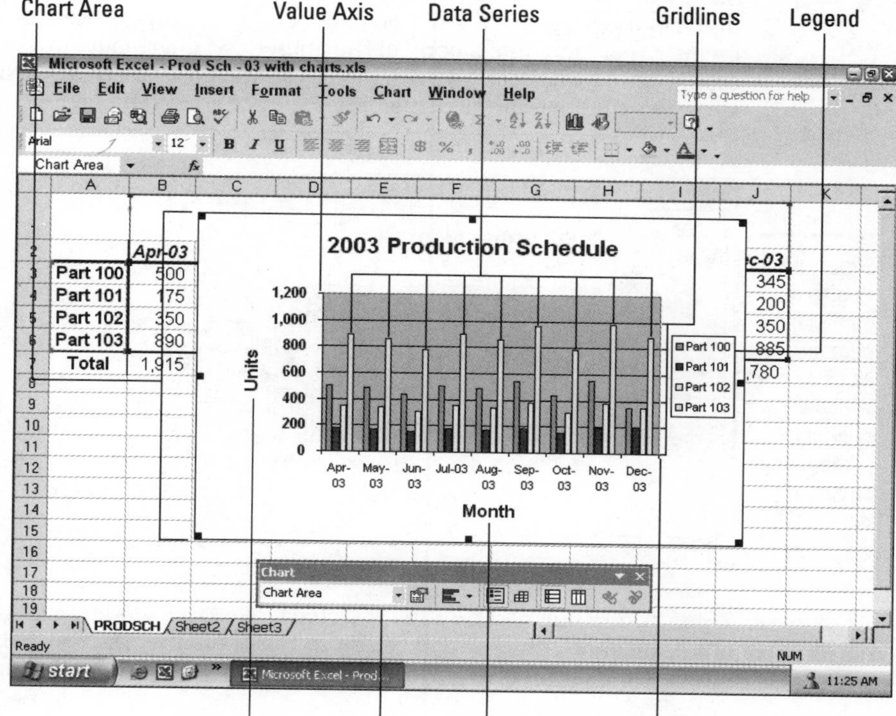

Figure 1-1: Typical column chart containing a variety of standard chart elements.

Embedded charts versus charts on separate chart sheets

An *embedded chart* is a chart that appears right within the worksheet so that when you save or print the worksheet, you save or print the chart along with it. Note that your charts don't have to be embedded. You can also choose to create a chart in its own chart sheet in the workbook at the time you create it. Embed a chart on the worksheet when you want to be able to print the chart along with its supporting worksheet data. Place a chart on its own sheet when you intend to print the charts of the worksheet data separately.

You can print any chart that you've embedded in a worksheet by itself without any worksheet data (as though it were created on its own chart sheet) by selecting it before you open the Print dialog box. You can also do this by putting the embedded chart in its own window. To do this, right-click the border of the embedded chart and then click the Chart Window item on its shortcut menu. Excel then puts a copy of the embedded chart in its own window, as shown in Figure 1-2. You can then print the chart by right-clicking the window's title bar and then clicking the Print command on its shortcut menu.

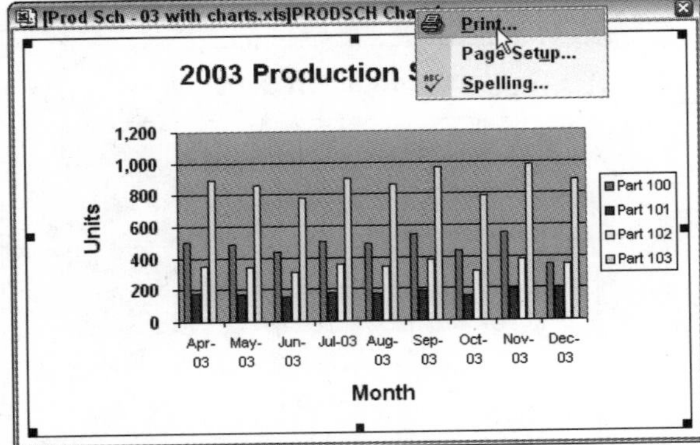

Figure 1-2: Putting an embedded chart in its own window to print it without any supporting data.

When you're finished printing the chart, click the window's Close button to close the chart window and return to the regular worksheet (where the chart is still embedded). Note that you can't save the chart window.

If it's really important that the chart remain a separate element in the workbook, you need to create the chart on its own chart sheet rather than embed it when you create the chart. If you embed a chart only to find that you would prefer that it be on a separate worksheet, you can switch by clicking the chart to select it and then choosing Chart⇨Location from the Excel Menu bar (note that Chart menu is only available on the Excel Menu bar in a regular worksheet when you've selected an embedded chart). This action opens the Chart Location dialog box. You then click the As New Sheet radio button and click OK to switch the embedded chart to a chart on a separate chart sheet.

Using the Chart Wizard to create a new chart

You use the Chart Wizard to create a new chart (at which time you decide whether or not to embed it or put it on a separate chart sheet). To use the Chart Wizard to create a new chart, follow these steps:

1. **Select the range of cells containing the data that you want to plot, including the column and row headings.**

   The labels in the top row of selected data become category labels in the chart. In other words, they appear along the x-axis in most charts to describe the data being charted. The labels in the first selected column on the left are used to name the data series in the chart. Excel assigns values to appear along the y-axis based on the data in those data series.

   To plot only the subtotals or totals in data table, outline the data table (see Book II, Chapter 4 for details), and then collapse the outline down to the level that just shows the subtotals or totals, which you can then select as a range by dragging through their cells.

   Note that you don't have to select the range of cells to plot before choosing the ChartWizard tool, although it is often easier to do so. If you don't select the range ahead of time, you can still type in the cell reference or even select the range after you open the Chart Wizard.

2. **Click the Chart Wizard button on the Standard toolbar (the button with the colorful column chart icon).**

   Excel then opens the Chart Wizard — Step 1 of 4 — Chart Type dialog box, shown in Figure 1-3, where you select the type of chart to create. This dialog box contains a wide variety of different types of charts and graphs on two tabs: Standard Types and Custom Types. Each of the types on the Standard Types tab offers two or more sub-types to choose from.

   To preview how the data that you've selected appears as the type of chart that you select, click and hold down the Press and Hold to View Sample button.

3. **Click the type of chart to create in Chart Type list box and then, if necessary, select its sub-type in the Chart Sub-Type list box before you click the Next > button.**

   Excel then opens the Chart Wizard — Step 2 of 4 — Chart Source Data dialog box, shown in Figure 1-4, where you verify the data to be plotted and whether the data series occur in the rows or columns of the selected worksheet on the Data Range tab. You can also use the options on the Series tab in this dialog box to make changes to the address of the range used as the category labels or the ranges that designate individual value ranges.

4. **Check the sample chart that appears at the top of Data Range tab and then make any modifications necessary to the source data used in the chart on both the Data Range and Series tabs before you click the Next button.**

   Excel then opens the Chart Wizard — Step 3 of 4 — Chart Options dialog box, shown in Figure 1-5, where you specify titles for the chart and category and value axes as well as change a wide variety of chart options (see the "Changing the Chart Options" section that follows for details).

   To enter titles for the chart, click the appropriate text box (Chart Title, Category (X) Axis, or Value (Y) Axis) and then enter the title that you want to appear (after a brief pause, the title you enter in the text box appears in the same chart shown in the preview area on the Titles tab).

5. **Enter the titles that you want to appear in the chart on the Titles tab and then click any of the other tabs and change their options as required before you click the Next > button.**

   Excel then opens the Chart Wizard — Step 4 of 4 — Chart Location dialog box, shown in Figure 1-6, where you indicate whether you want the chart to be embedded (the default selection) or you want it to appear on a new sheet (by selecting the As New Sheet radio button).

6. **(Optional) If you want the new chart to appear on its own chart sheet, click the As New Sheet radio button and then enter a descriptive name for the sheet in the associated text.**

   If you do select the As New Sheet radio button but you don't name the new chart sheet, Excel gives the sheet the default name Chart1 (assuming that it's the first chart sheet that you've added to the workbook).

7. **Click the Finish button to have Excel draw your new chart.**

   If you selected the As New Sheet in the Step 4 of 4 — Chart Location dialog box, Excel draws the chart on a new chart sheet, which is inserted in front of the current worksheet. If you left the default As Object In radio button selected, Excel draws the chart in the current worksheet and displays the Chart toolbar, shown in Figure 1-7. The new embedded chart remains selected (indicated by the appearance of the black square sizing handles around the perimeter) so that you can move and/or resize the chart.

   When you create the chart on a separate chart sheet, you can also reposition the chart sheet (if you want to) by dragging its tab to the proper place in the workbook. When you create an embedded chart, you can move and resize the chart in the worksheet. Move the chart by positioning the mouse pointer on its chart area and then dragging the double-cross pointer. Resize the chart by positioning the mouse pointer on one of the sizing handles (the black squares) and then dragging the double-headed arrow pointer in the appropriate direction. When you finish moving and resizing the embedded chart, click a cell outside of the chart to deselect its chart area (indicated by the disappearance of the sizing handles).

8. **Reposition the chart in the worksheet or the chart sheet in the workbook as desired and then save the workbook by choosing File⇨Save.**

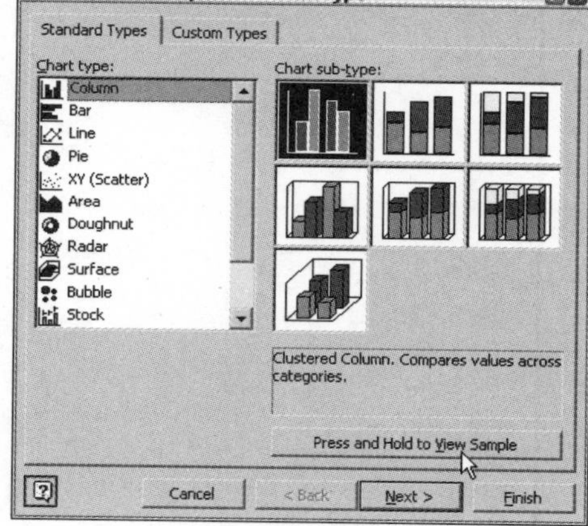

Figure 1-3: Selecting the chart type in the Chart Wizard — Step 1 of 4 — Chart Type dialog box.

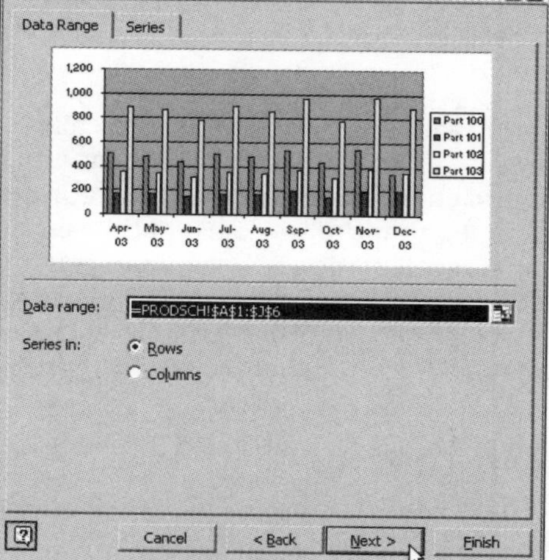

Figure 1-4: Verifying the chart data in the Chart Wizard — Step 2 of 4 — Chart Source Data dialog box.

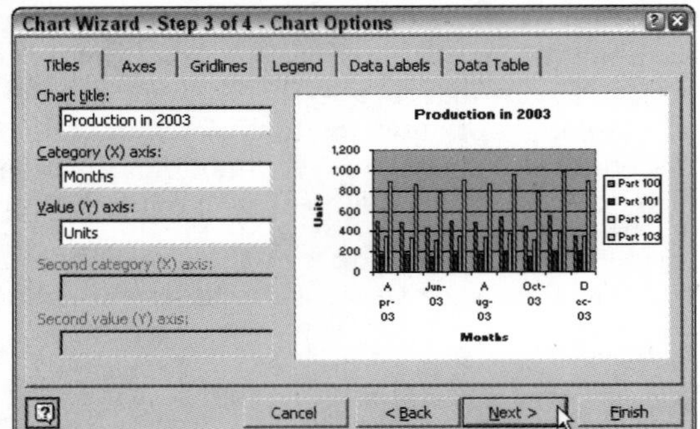

Figure 1-5: Adding titles and changing other options in the Chart Wizard — Step 3 of 4 — Chart Options dialog box.

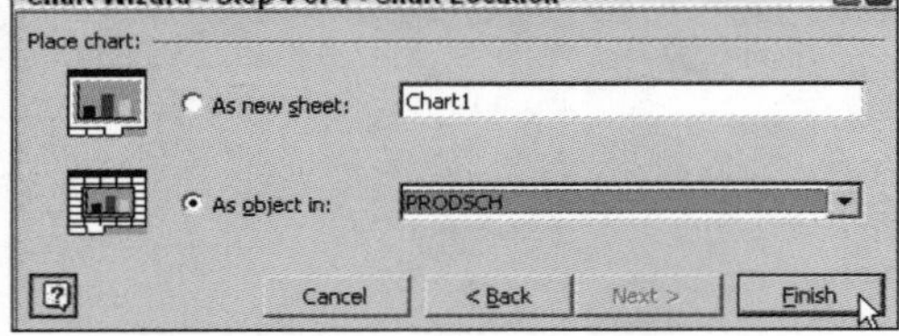

Figure 1-6: Indicating where to put the chart in the Chart Wizard — Step 4 of 4 — Chart Location dialog box.

You can immediately create a chart on its own chart sheet by using the default chart type and other default options (Clustered Column with the data series in rows) simply by selecting the worksheet data and then pressing the F11 key.

Keep in mind that all charts that you create are dynamically linked to the worksheet that they represent. This means that if you modify any of the values that are plotted in the chart, Excel immediately redraws the chart to reflect the change, assuming that the worksheet still uses automatic recalculation. When Manual recalculation is turned on, you must remember to press F9 or click the Calc Now (F9) button on the Calculation tab of the Options dialog box (Tools⇨Options) in order to get Excel to redraw the chart to reflect any changes to the worksheet values it represents.

Changing the Chart Options

The various tabs in the Chart Wizard — Step 3 of 4 — Chart Options dialog box gives you tons of options to choose from when creating a new chart. Of

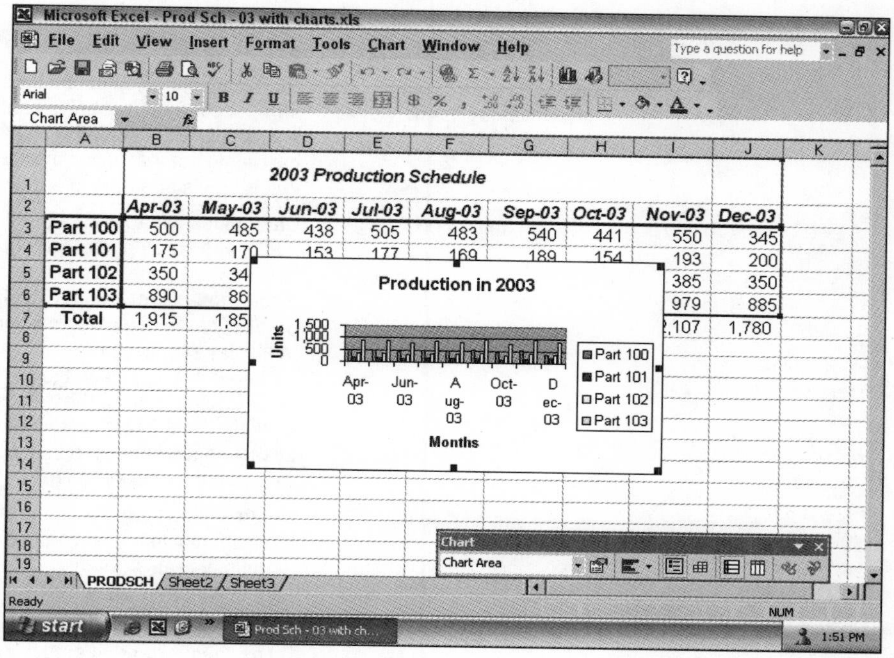

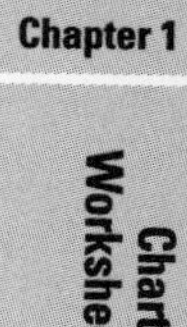

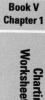

Figure 1-7: Embedded chart as it appears in the worksheet with Chart toolbar right after you create it.

course, many of these options don't apply to the type of chart that you're building. For example, if you're building a pie chart, you don't have the option of specifying Category (X) Axis and Value (Y) Axis title. So too, if you're building one of the 3-D charts, you're presented with options for adding a Series (Y) Axis Title and Value (Z) Axis Title in addition to the Chart Title and Category (X) Title options available for 2-D charts that use an x- and a y-axis.

Table 1-2 shows you the options on the various tabs in the Chart Options dialog box that are available to you when building the default Clustered Column chart.

Table 1-2 Chart Options for the Default Column Chart

Tab	*Option*	*Usage*
Titles	Chart Title	Centers the chart title you enter at the top of the chart area
	Category (X) Axis	Centers the title you enter for the x-axis at the bottom of the chart area beneath the category labels

(continued)

Table 1-2 (continued)

Tab	*Option*	*Usage*
	Value (Y) Axis	Vertical centers the title you enter for the y-axis at the left edge of the chart area running parallel to the y-axis and perpendicular to the y-axis labels attached to each tick mark
Axes	Category (X) Axis	Determines whether category labels and tick marks appear along the bottom of the plot area. Leave the Automatic radio button selected to display the row of column labels along the Category axis. Click the Category radio button to display evenly-spaced tick marks along the Category axis based on the values in the row of column labels even if the data is date formatted. Click the Time-Scale radio button to display evenly-spaced tick marks along the Category axis based on major and minor time units.
	Value (Y) Axis	Determines whether a series of value indicators with tick marks appear along the left edge of the plot area
Gridlines	Category (X) Axis	Determines whether horizontal gridlines are drawn out from the tick marks on the Value (Y) axis and extended across the chart: Click the Major Gridlines check box to draw gridlines from each category-axis tick mark. Click the Minor Gridlines check box to draw the major gridlines along with a series of other gridlines that evenly subdivide the area between each tick mark.
	Value (Y) Axis	Determines whether vertical gridlines are drawn up from the tick marks on the Category (X) axis and extended up the top of the plot area: Click the Major Gridlines check box to draw gridlines from each value-axis tick mark. Click the Minor Gridlines check box to draw the major gridlines along with a series of other gridlines that evenly subdivide the area between each tick mark.
Legend	Show Legend	Determines whether a legend appears in the chart, indicating what kind of data each type of data marker assigned a single data series represents
	Placement	Determines the placement of the legend in the chart area. By default, Excel places the legend to the right of the plot area. Choose the Bottom radio button to place it along the bottom of the plot area, Corner to place it in the upper-right corner of the chart area, Top to place it along

Tab	Option	Usage
		the top of the plot area, or Left to place it to the left of the plot area.
Data Labels	Label Contains	Enables you to add labels identifying each data series in the chart. Choose the Series Name check box to identify each data series with the series name taken from the row headings, the Category Name to identify each data series with corresponding category label taken from the column headings, or the Value to identify each data point with the value taken from the worksheet. Use the Separator drop-down list box to indicate how the contents of multiple data labels are separated (Space, Comma, Semicolon, Period, or New Line).
Data Table	Show Data Table	Enables you to display a data table beneath the chart area that contains all the charted values along with the column and row headings

Chart Formatting and Editing

Many times you find that you have to finesse the elements of the chart that the Chart Wizard produces for you. This is especially true in the case of embedded charts, where the overall size of the chart area may make the fonts used in the titles, legend, and data labels too big in relation to the data markers in the plot area.

You can change the formatting of particular parts of a chart either by clicking the chart elements to select them and then opening the associated Format dialog box or by selecting the element to format from the Chart toolbar and then opening its corresponding Format dialog box.

Formatting chart elements

The Chart toolbar, shown in Figure 1-8, enables you to select different parts of an embedded chart or the chart in the current chart sheet and then change its formatting:

1. **Click the Chart Objects pop-up button on the Chart toolbar and then click the name of the part of the chart you want to format.**

   The items listed on the Chart Objects pop-up menu vary, depending upon the type of chart that you're formatting and the options you used in originally building the chart.

2. **Click the Format button to the immediate right of the Chart Objects pop-up button to open the associated Format dialog box.**

   The Format button changes according to the chart object that you select. For example, when you select Chart Title in the Chart Objects combo box, the button becomes the Format Chart Title button and when you click this button, Excel opens the Format Chart Title dialog box with three tabs (Patterns, Font, and Alignment), each with its options for formatting the chart title.

3. **Use the options in the Format dialog box to format the chart element as desired and then click OK.**

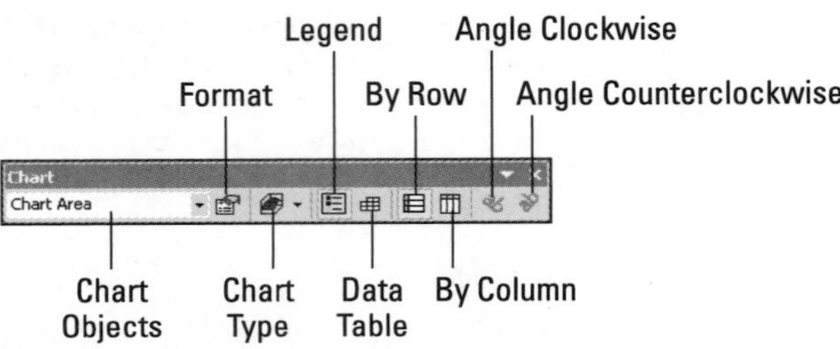

Figure 1-8: Using the buttons on the Chart toolbar to select and format specific elements.

You can also access the Format dialog boxes for formatting specific chart elements by right-clicking the part of the chart that you want to format. This action selects the chart element and displays its shortcut toolbar, where you click the Format *such-and-so* item to open its particular Format dialog box. For example, if you right-click one of the gridlines in the chart, the shortcut menu contains a Format Gridlines items that, once clicked, opens the Format Gridlines dialog box with options on its Patterns and Scale tabs for modifying the format of just the gridlines in the chart.

Note that you can also open the Format dialog box for the chart element that you select (either with the Chart Objects button on the Chart toolbar or by clicking the element within the chart) by pressing Ctrl+1. Note that you can also select different items in the chart by pressing the → or ← after selecting any part of the chart by clicking it. As you press an arrow, Excel selects the next part of the chart in the chart area and the name of the part selected appears in the Chart Objects combo box on the Chart toolbar.

Changing the orientation of category and value labels

The category labels run parallel to the Category x-axis and the value labels run perpendicular to the Values y-axis. When you're dealing with a chart that plots lots of data series, these labels may be too close together and, in some cases, actually overlap each other. For those situations, you can try using the Angle Clockwise and Angle Counterclockwise buttons on the Chart toolbar to display these labels diagonally, thus giving them more room to be displayed.

To put these labels on the diagonal, select the Category Axis or Values Axis in the chart (either by clicking them or selecting them by name in the Chart Objects pop-up menu on the Chart toolbar) and then click either the Angle Clockwise or Angle Counterclockwise button. Click the Angle Clockwise button to display the labels on the diagonal running down and the Angle Counterclockwise button to run the labels up.

Figure 1-9 illustrates how this works. In this figure, I selected the Value Axis on the Chart Objects pop-up menu and then clicked the Angle Counter-clockwise button on the Chart toolbar to run the labels up at 45 degrees. Then, I selected the Category Axis on the Chart Objects pop-up menu and then clicked the Angle Clockwise button to run these labels down at 45 degrees.

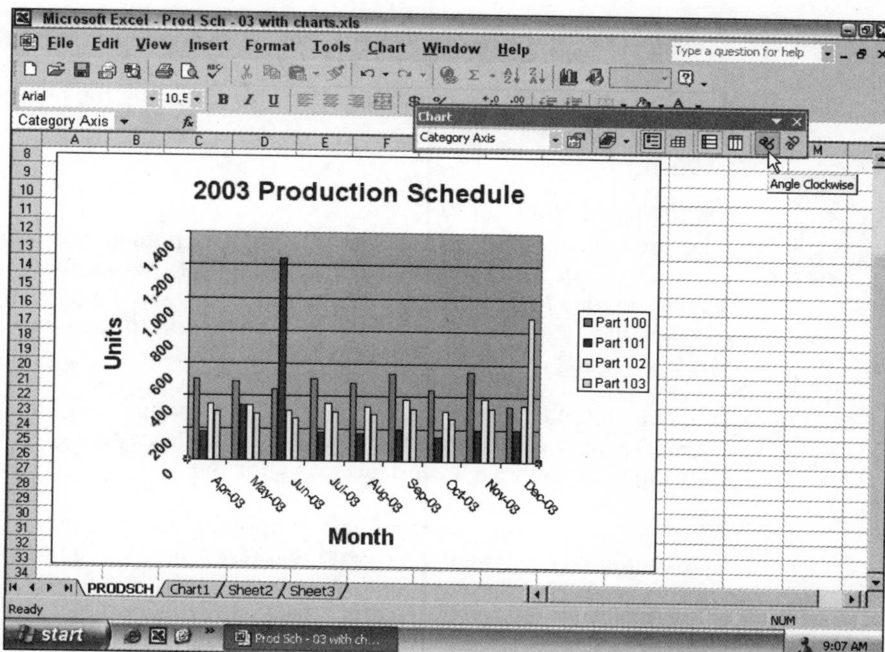

Figure 1-9: Using the Angle Clockwise button to display the category labels on a diagonal.

To return the Category- or Values-axis labels to their normal, 90-degree orientation, click the Angle Clockwise or Angle Counterclockwise button a second time (depending upon which one you use first).

Customizing the chart text

After you have all the titles and labels you need in the chart, you may still want to format them so that they appear exactly the way that you want them to. When formatting the text of chart, the chart object that you select determines which text is formatted. If you select the chart area, you can format all the titles and labels in the chart at once. You may do that if, for instance, you want to make all the text to use the same new font. To format the text of a particular object, you select just that object either by clicking it in the chart or selecting its name on the Chart Objects pop-up menu in the Chart toolbar.

To add bold or italics to the font of the selected chart object, click the Bold or Italic button from the Formatting toolbar, as usual. Likewise, to change the horizontal alignment of the text, click the appropriate alignment tool on the Formatting toolbar. To change the font, font style, font size, or some other attribute of the selected chart object, choose Format command on the object's shortcut menu (or press Ctrl+1), and then click the Font tab and make your choices using its standard options.

To change vertical alignment, orientation, or wrap the text, click the Alignment tab and its standard options. To change the text borders and the pattern of the area where the text appears, click the Patterns tab and then choose among its standard options for changing the border and background colors and patterns.

Customizing the chart legend

A legend lists each pattern or symbol used as a data marker in a chart and follows the pattern or symbol with the chart data series name. Generally, it's a good idea to use a legend in a chart where you're not using category labels. You can customize the legend that you add to the chart in various ways.

You can click the Legend button on the Chart toolbar to add or delete a legend for your chart. Click the legend tool to display a legend if none is showing or to delete a legend if one is showing.

When you select a legend in a chart, it appears with sizing handles around it that enable you to resize the legend markers and text. To move the legend, click the arrowhead pointer within its borders, and then drag its rectangle to the position you want. Be careful to drag the legend to a blank part of the chart area where it doesn't overlap and obscure other chart elements.

As with chart text, you can change the border around the legend and the pattern within the area of the legend box. The easiest way to make the changes is to double-click the legend to open the Format Legend dialog box and then use the options on the Patterns tab to format its border and background as you want.

Customizing the chart axes

The axis is the scale used to plot the data for your chart. Most chart types will have axes. All 2-D charts with the exception of pie charts and radar charts have an X and a Y-axis. Three-dimensional charts with a 3-D plot have an X, Y, and Z-axis.

When you initially create a chart, Excel sets up the axes for you automatically, based on the data you are plotting, which you can then adjust in various ways.

Perhaps the most common ways you will want to modify the axes of a chart is to assign a new number formatting to their units and to change the scale that they use.

To assign a number format to a scale, double-click the axis that you want to format (or click it and then press Ctr+1). This action opens the Format Axis dialog box where you click the Number tab, shown in Figure 1-10, and then select the number format that you want displayed.

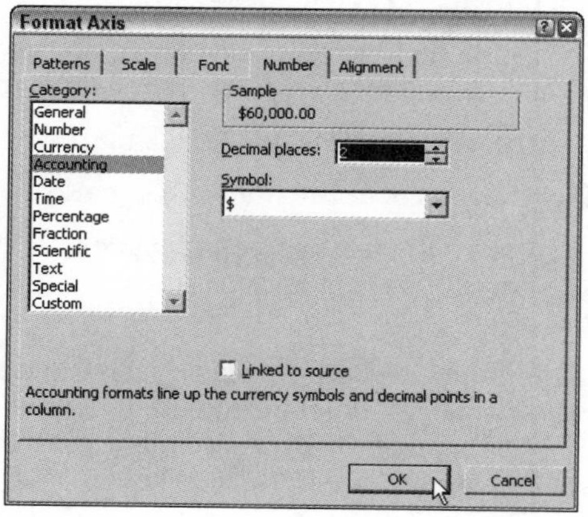

Figure 1-10: Assigning a number format to the Value (Y) axis in a Column chart.

Changing the scale can have a dramatic effect on the chart. Depending on which axis you are formatting, different options are available when you change the axis scale. To alter the scale used in a chart, double-click the axis (or click it and then press Ctrl+1). This action opens the Format Axis dialog box where you click the Scale tab. Figure 1-11 shows you the options on the Scale tab when the Value (Y) axis is selected in a typical 2-D Column chart.

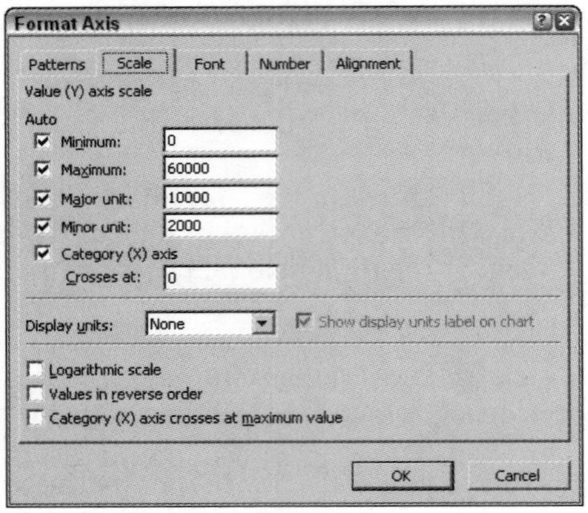

Figure 1-11: Altering the scale of the Value (Y) axis in a typical Column chart.

You can choose the following options for the Value (Y) axis (except on 3-D charts):

- **Minimum** to determine the point where the axis begins — perhaps $4,000 instead of the default of $0. If you choose a value higher than 0, data values smaller than 0 are not displayed at all (they do not, for instance, appear as a data marker that goes below the line).
- **Maximum** to determine the highest point displayed on the vertical axis. Data values greater than the value you specify here simply don't display.
- **Major Unit** to display the values at the major tick marks.
- **Minor Unit** to display the values at the minor tick marks.
- **Category (X) Axis Crosses At** to determine the value at which the X-axis crosses the Y-axis. If you choose this option, you can have data markers appear below the line.
- **Display Units** to divide the values on the axis by a basic unit that you select in its drop-down list box (Hundreds, Thousands, Millions, Billions, or Trillions). Click the Show Display Units Label Chart check box to also display a label designating the basic unit along the axis.
- **Logarithmic Scale** bases the scale upon powers of ten and recalculates the Minimum, Maximum, Major Unit, and Minor Unit accordingly.
- **Values in Reverse Order** places the lowest value on the chart at the top of the scale and the highest value at the bottom. You might use such a chart if you wanted to emphasize the negative effect of the larger values.
- **Category (X) Axis Crosses at Maximum Value** to place the Category (X) axis at the highest value.

If you select the Category axis (the X-axis in most cases) in standard two-dimensional chart, you can make these choices:

✦ **Value (Y) Axis Crosses at Category Number** text box to specify the number where you want the Value axis to cross the Category axis (similar to the Category (X) Axis Crosses at option for the Value axis)

✦ **Number of Categories between Tick Labels** text box to specify the number of labels that appear along the Category axis of the chart

✦ **Number of Categories between Tick Marks** text box to specify the number of tick marks that appear along the Category axis

✦ **Value (Y) Axis Crosses between Categories** check box to determine whether the Value axis displays at the edge of the category or in the middle of the category in a 2-D chart

✦ **Categories in Reverse Order** check box to reverse the order of the displayed categories.

✦ **Value (Y) Axis Crosses at Maximum Category** check box to display the Value axis after the last category in a 2-D chart. This option is useful if you have graphical material on the left side of the chart (such as a picture) and want to avoid a cluttered look. It is also helpful if you want the viewer to readily relate values to the last data marker.

In a 3-D chart, the X-axis is the category axis, the Y-axis is the Series axis, and the Z-axis is the Value axis. For the Series axis, you can make the following choices:

✦ **Number of Series between Tick Labels** text box to specify whether you want to have a label for every data series (an entry of 1), every other series (an entry of 2), and so on

✦ **Number of Series between Tick Marks** text box to specify the number of tick marks along the Series axis (rather than the number of labels as does the previous option)

✦ **Series in Reverse Order** check box to display the chart data series in reverse order (from March to January, for example, instead of from January to March)

Changing the scale, then, changes the appearance of the chart, sometimes in quite striking ways. You can also change other elements of the axes — the axis patterns, the tick marks, and the tick mark labels by choosing the appropriate tab in the Format Axis dialog box and then using its options.

Customizing the chart gridlines

Gridlines are the optional lines that extend from an axis across the plot area to help you relate the data marker to the scale represented on the axis. They can help you relate the values on the Value axis to the data markers representing those values.

If you don't put in the gridlines initially, you can add them by selecting the appropriate gridline options on the Gridlines tab of the Chart Options dialog box. To open Chart Options dialog box, right-click anywhere in the chart area and then click Chart Options on the chart area shortcut menu or choose Chart⇨Chart Options on the Excel Menu bar (note that Chart menu is available on the Excel menu bar in the regular worksheet only when you select an embedded chart).

Click the Major Gridlines check box in the Category (X) Axis section to add vertical gridlines between each data series in the chart. Click the Major Gridlines check box in the Value (Y) Axis section to add horizontal gridlines extending from the tick marks on the Y-axis. Click the Minor Gridlines check box in either or both sections to draw more gridlines that uniformly subdivide each major section.

To change the formatting of the gridlines in your chart, double-click one of them to open the Format Gridlines dialog box. You can then use the options on the Patterns tab to change what line style is used by those gridlines.

To delete a set of gridlines, click one of the gridlines to select all of them and then press the Delete key.

Customizing the chart's data series

The options available for formatting chart data series depend on the type of chart you are working with at the time. To open the Format Data Series dialog box, where you can make changes to the formatting of a particular data series, click one of its data markers to select them all and press Ctrl+1 (or you can double-click one of the markers to select them all and also open the Format Date Series dialog box).

To format a particular data marker in the data series, click the particular marker after selecting the data series before you press Ctrl+1. This action opens the Format Data Point where you can modify the formatting for just the selected data marker.

The Format Data Series dialog box contains many different kinds of tabs for changing the way your data series are formatted (and these tabs vary according to the type of chart). Figure 1-12 shows the tabs that are available in the Format Data Series dialog box for a data series in a standard 2-D chart.

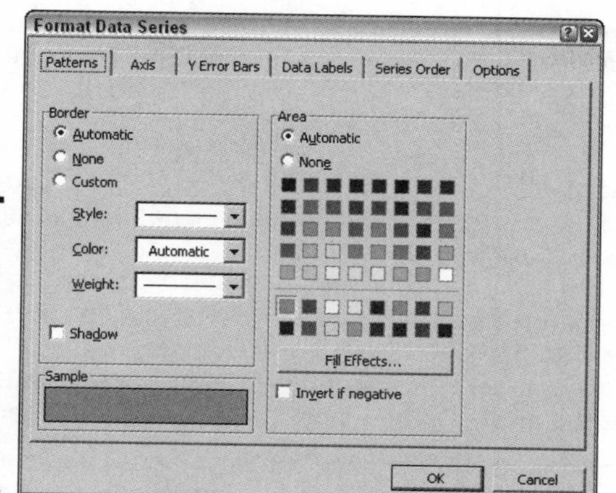

Figure 1-12: Formatting a data series with the options in the Format Data Series dialog box.

You can use the options on the Patterns tab to select a new color fill pattern for the selected data series. The Axis tab contains a single section called Plot Series On that enables you to have the values for the selected data series plotted on a secondary Y-axis by clicking the Secondary Axis radio button (the Primary Axis radio button is the default setting for all the various data series in a typical chart).

The Y Error Bars tab enables you to display y-error bars that show how much the data markers in the selected data series are above or below a particular value, percentage, or standard deviation. To display y-error bars for the selected data series, click the type of display: Both (to show y-error bars above every data marker that shows how much it is above or below the error amount), Plus (to show y-error bars only for data markers above the error amount), or Minus (to show y-error bars only for data marker below the error amount). Then, select the appropriate radio button in the Error Amount section (Fixed Value, Percentage, Standard Deviation(s), Standard Error, or Custom) and then fill in the amount of allowable error in the associated text boxes.

The Data Labels tab contains standard options for displaying the series name, category name, or value next to the selected data series (see the "Changing the Chart Options" section earlier in this chapter for more on using data labels).

The Series Order tab contains options that enable you to change the order in which the selected data series appears in the chart. To modify the order, you click the name of the data series you want to move up in the Series Order list box and then click the Move Up button until data series is where you want it (use the preview list box that shows the current chart to monitor the effect your moving the data series has on the appearance of the chart). By moving a data series, you can often make it data markers and therefore, the data they represent, more prominent in the chart.

The Options tab in the Format Data Series dialog box contains various options for controlling the appearance of the selected data series. For the typical 2-D chart, these options include:

- **Overlap** text box to enter a value between -100 and 100 that controls how much the data markers overlap or touch each other. When the value is zero, the markers are touching. Enter a negative value to create a gap between the markers and a positive value to have them overlap.
- **Gap Width** text box to enter a value between 0 (zero) and 500 that specifies the amount of space you want between each group of data markers for every data series in the chart. The larger the value you enter in this text box, the greater the amount of space between the groups.
- **Series Lines** check box to draw connecting lines between the data markers in the selected data series in a chart (this option is available for types of line charts)
- **Vary Colors by Point** check box to vary the color of each data marker in the data series (this option is available for charts that use a single data series)

Replacing a data series with a graphic image

You can replace the data markers that Excel assigns to a particular data series in a chart with artwork of your own choosing to make the chart even more graphic. For example, in Figure 1-13, you see that I replaced the normal, boring rectangular data markers with the Clip art image of an evergreen tree in a Column chart depicting the projected logging of redwood trees in 2003.

To replace the columns in the single data series (and there's only one in this particular chart), I first copied the evergreen tree Clip art image into the Clipboard (see Book V, Chapter 2 for details), and then selected the data series by clicking one of its data markers. Finally, I chose the Edit⇨Paste command on the Excel Menu bar to replace the selected column-shaped data markers with the tree Clip Art. As you can see, Excel automatically stretches or shrinks the tree graphic to fit the height of each data marker in the chart.

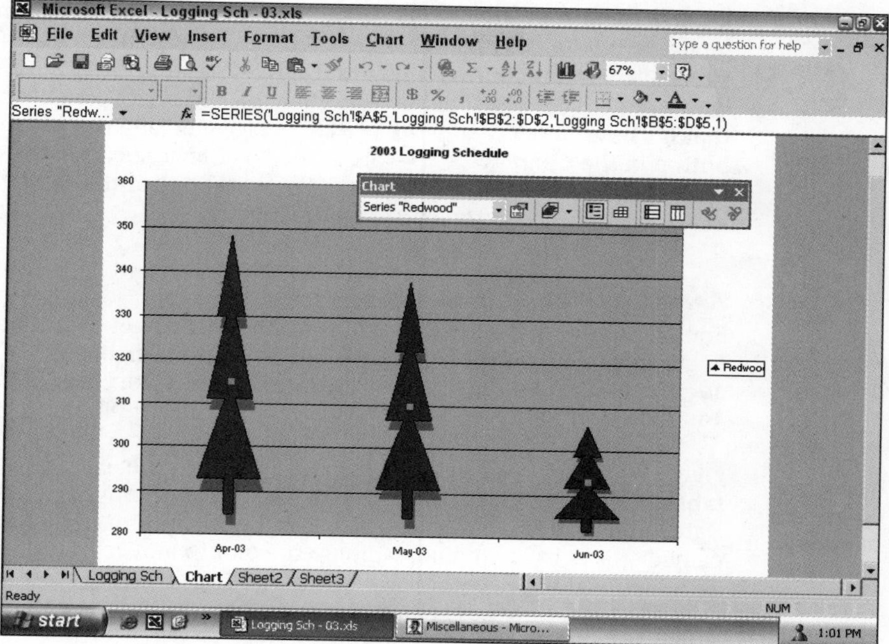

Figure 1-13: Replacing a data series in a chart with a Clip Art image.

Editing a chart

You can edit a chart by selecting the chart and then re-opening the Chart Wizard. If you need to edit an embedded chart, you take these two steps:

1. **Click the border of the embedded chart to select the chart area (indicated by the sizing handles around its border).**
2. **Click the Chart Wizard button on the Standard toolbar.**

After you have the Chart Wizard open, you can modify any parts of the chart using the options available on each of the four dialog boxes in the Chart Wizard. For example, to change the type of chart, you select the new Chart type in the Step 1 of 4 — Chart Type dialog box; to exchange the data series so that the each column of data is a new data series instead of each row, you click the Columns radio button in the Series In section of the Step 2 of 4 — Chart Source Data dialog box; to change any of the chart options (including adding titles that you didn't add when you first built the chart), you select the appropriate tab in the Step 3 of 4 — Chart Options dialog box, and, finally, to place the modified chart on its own chart sheet (assuming that it's currently embedded in the worksheet), you click the As New Sheet radio button in the Place Chart section of the Step 4 of 4 — Chart Location dialog box.

Keep in mind that when you change the location of a chart so that it's no longer embedded in the worksheet, Excel removes the chart from the worksheet at the same time as it places it on a separate chart sheet. Likewise, when you change the location of a chart placed on its own chart sheet so that it's now embedded in the worksheet (by clicking the As Object In radio button in the Chart Wizard — Step 4 of 4 — Chart Location dialog box), Excel removes the chart sheet from the workbook at the same time as it embeds the chart on the current worksheet.

Adding a data table to a chart

Sometimes you'll decide that you want the worksheet data that represented in graphic form in the chart displayed as table at the bottom of the chart. To add the worksheet data to your chart, you select the chart or its chart sheet and then click the Data Table button on the Chart toolbar.

Figure 1-14 illustrates how easy this is to do. For this figure, I added the table of worksheet data displayed at the bottom simply by clicking the Data Table button on the Chart toolbar. Because this data table automatically displays the column headings (the month and year in this example), I also removed the Category (X) Axis labels (by selecting the x-axis and then pressing the Delete key) since they were now redundant and just taking up valuable space in the chart area.

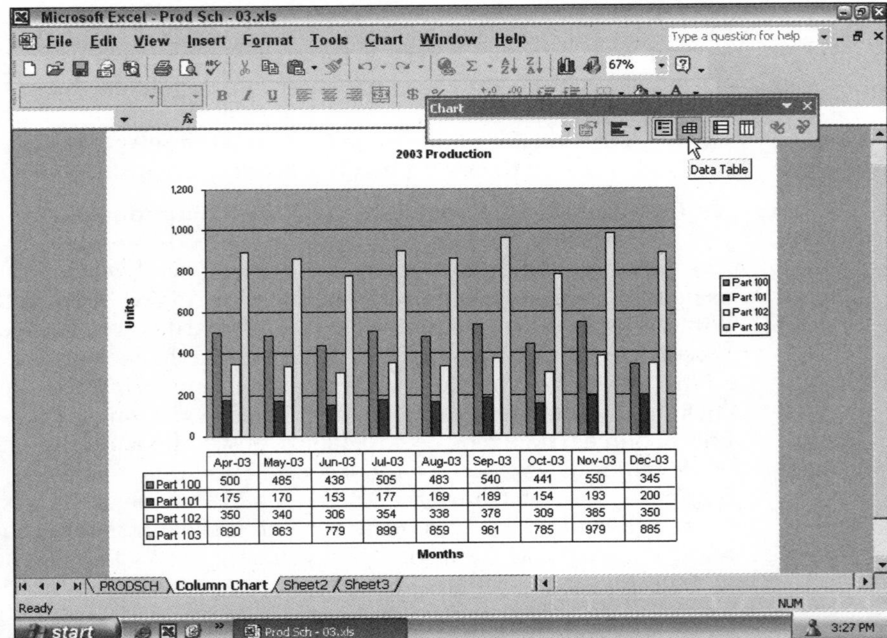

Figure 1-14: Adding a data table to a Clustered Column chart.

If you decide that having the worksheet data displayed in a table at the bottom of the chart is no longer necessary, simply click the Data Table button on the Chart toolbar to remove it when the chart is selected or its chart sheet is current to remove it.

Changing the way columns and rows of data are charted

When you first build a chart, Excel automatically uses the data in each row of the cell selection to form each data series in the chart. If you want to see how the chart looks when each column of data in the selection forms a data series, you switch the orientation of the chart, so to speak, by clicking the By Column button on the Chart toolbar. When you switch from rows to columns, Excel automatically modifies the chart legend at the same it switches the data series and redraws the data markers for each series.

Figure 1-15 illustrates how this works. For this figure, I removed the data table shown in Figure 1-14 and then switched the data series from rows to columns by clicking the By Column button on the Chart toolbar. As you can see, when each column of data represents a distinct data series, Excel must greatly expand the chart legend to accommodate all the months represented by the different groups of data markers.

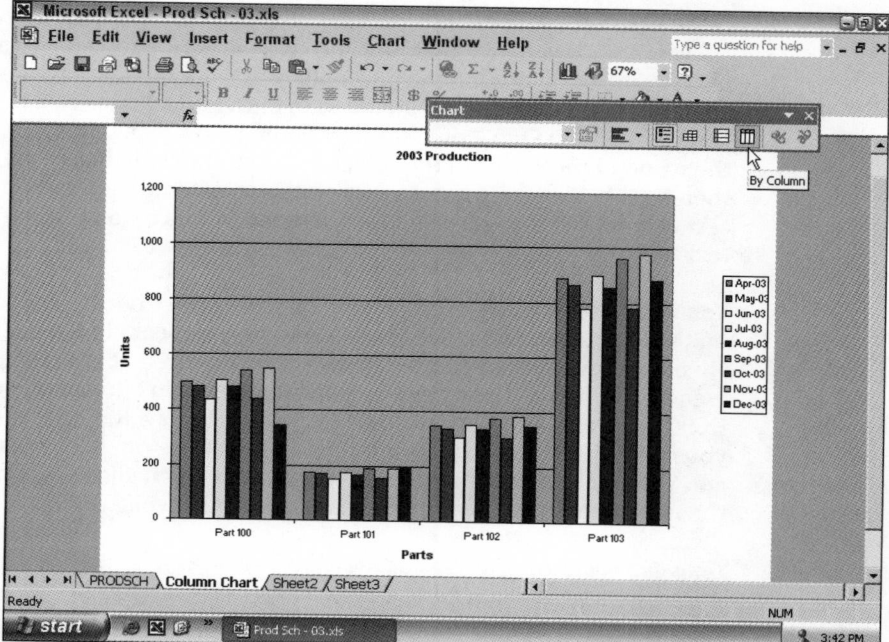

Figure 1-15: Switching the data series from rows to columns in a Clustered Column chart.

In this particular example, the Clustered Column chart reads much better when the rows form the four data series (for each part produced). To change the chart back to it original orientation, I have only to click the By Row button on the Chart Toolbar.

Editing the data series

The data that you initially select in the worksheet is the basis for the chart that you create with the Chart Wizard. Because the chart remains linked to the worksheet data, when you change the data used in a data series of a chart, Excel automatically redraws the chart. Excel creates the links between the worksheet data and the data series in your chart with linked formulas that use the SERIES function. You can add or delete data series from the chart using the Chart Wizard. You can also add data to a chart by dragging and dropping or cutting and pasting in new cell selections. You can edit the data included in a data series by modifying the arguments of the SERIES formula used to link the worksheet and chart data.

To use the Chart Wizard to edit its data series, click the embedded chart or activate its chart sheet and then click the Chart Wizard button on the Standard toolbar. Then click the Next button to select the Chart Wizard — Step 2 of 4 — Chart Source Data dialog box.

On the Data Range tab of this dialog box, you can add data to the chart by clicking the Data Range text box and then selecting the entire range of cells to be graphed, including the new ones you want included in the chart. You can also edit the cell range included in individual data series by clicking the Series tab in the Step 2 of 4 — Chart Source Data dialog box and then clicking the name of the series in the Series list box, shown in Figure 1-16. You can then modify the range name given to the selected data series in the Name text box and/or the cell selection included in this data series in the Values text box.

You can also add data to a chart by choosing the Chart⇨Add Data command on the Excel Menu bar (the Chart menu only appears in the regular worksheet window when an embedded chart is selected: it always appears on the menu bar when a chart sheet is active). When you choose this command, Excel opens an Add Data dialog box that contains a Range text box, where you can enter the cell range address or select the range of cells whose label and values are to be added to the chart. When you click OK, Excel redraws the current chart to include the data that you specified.

Dragging new data to an embedded chart

Excel enables you to drag selected cells in the worksheet to an embedded chart so that its data is included in the graph. As soon as you release the mouse button, the chart is redrawn, thus incorporating the added data. You can use this drag-and-drop technique to add columns or rows of data that were left out of the original chart (usually because they weren't yet part of the worksheet) as new data series.

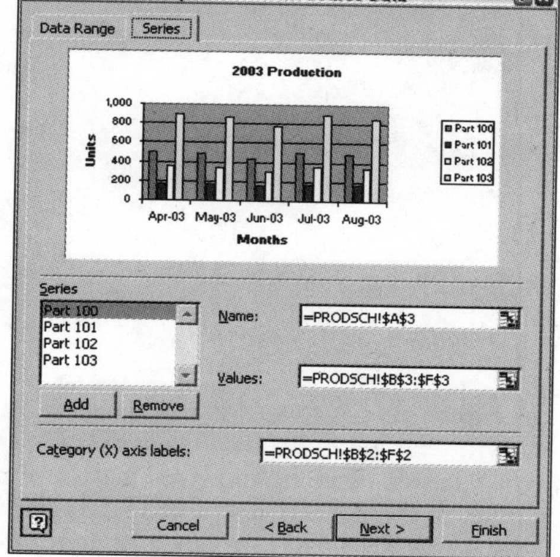

Figure 1-16: Modifying individual data series on the Series tab of the Chart Source Data dialog box.

When selecting the cells to drag onto the chart as a new data series, don't forget to select column or row heading as well as the values so that Excel can add the heading to its category labels and legend.

Pasting new data into a chart on its own chart sheet

To add new data to a chart that's on its own chart sheet, you use the cut-and-paste method rather than the drag-and-drop method. To have more control over the way the cell selection you copy to the Clipboard is pasted into the chart, you use the Edit⇨Paste Special command after you switch to the chart sheet.

When you choose Edit⇨Paste Special from the Menu bar in the chart sheet, the Paste Special dialog box, shown in Figure 1-17, appears. You can then use the radio buttons in this dialog box to indicate how the new data is to be added to the chart.

Editing a SERIES formula

For each chart that you create, Excel creates a linked formula using the SERIES function that you can change if you wish. To see the series formula, click the data series in the chart or click the name of the series in the Chart Objects drop-down list in the Chart toolbar.

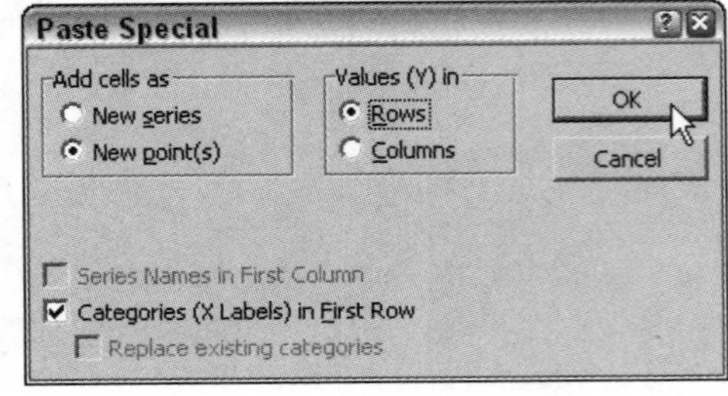

Figure 1-17: Using the Paste Special dialog box to paste a new data series into an existing chart.

The SERIES function uses the following syntax:

```
=SERIES(name_ref,categories,values,plot_order)
```

In the SERIES function, the *name_ref* argument is the name of the series (an external absolute reference to a single cell), the *categories* argument refers to the range containing the X labels (also an external absolute reference to the cells containing the names of the categories plotted), the *values* argument refers to the range containing the Y values (an external absolute reference to the cells containing the values), and the *plot_order* argument is a number, telling the order in which the data series is plotted in the chart (first, second, third, and so on).

Adding a trendline to a chart

You can add *trendlines* to your charts that display a trend implied by the charted data. Trendlines are often added to XY (Scattter) charts that correlate two different sets of numerical data to graphically point out the correlation between the two sets.

To add a trendline to your chart, you choose Chart⇨Add Trendline on the Excel Menu bar (note that the Chart menu appears on the regular Excel Menu bar only when you select an embedded chart). This action opens the Add Trendline dialog box shown in Figure 1-18. Here, you can choose the type of trend in the Trend/Regression Type section (Linear being the most common is the default) and the data series on which to base the trend in the Based on Series list box.

Changing the viewing angle on a 3-D chart

Oftentimes when you first create a 3-D chart, you find that the initial viewing angle selected by Excel obscures some of the data markers. You can easily rotate a 3-D chart to change the viewing angle and thus display more of the chart's elements. You do this by dragging any of corners of the 3-D chart frame. As soon as you start dragging, Excel reduces the chart to its wire frame that rotates in three dimensions as you drag the mouse around the chart area.

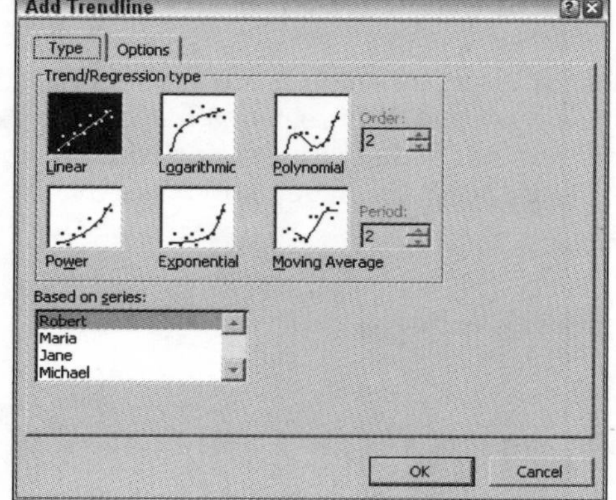

Figure 1-18: Adding a trendline to an XY (scatter) chart.

When you've got the wire frame positioned at what you think is a better angle, you simply release the mouse button to have Excel redraw the 3-D chart. With just a little experimentation, you should soon be able to settle upon the best angle for viewing all of the chart's information.

Deleting a chart

To delete an embedded chart, click the chart to select the entire chart area and then press the Delete key. To delete a chart on a separate chart sheet, right-click its tab, then click the Delete item on its shortcut menu and click the Delete button in the alert dialog box asking you to confirm the sheet's removal.

Selecting the Right Chart Type

Choosing the right chart is probably just as important in displaying your data visually as deciding to use a chart at all. A chart displays the data visually, but different charts display the data in very different ways. Certain general guidelines may be familiar to you already. Line charts are useful for showing changes over time. Pie charts are useful for showing the relationship of parts to the whole.

As you continue to work with Excel, you may find it beneficial to become more and more familiar with the chart types available and the formats available for those chart types. Using the best chart type and format will help you display your data visually in the most meaningful way. Following is a discussion of the major chart types available in Excel, with some simple guidelines on when to use each type.

Column charts

A column chart, unlike a bar chart to which it is often compared, emphasizes variation over a period of time. Whereas in a bar chart categories appear vertically, in a column chart they appear horizontally and values appear vertically. Figure 1-19 shows the seven sub-types available when creating a Column chart.

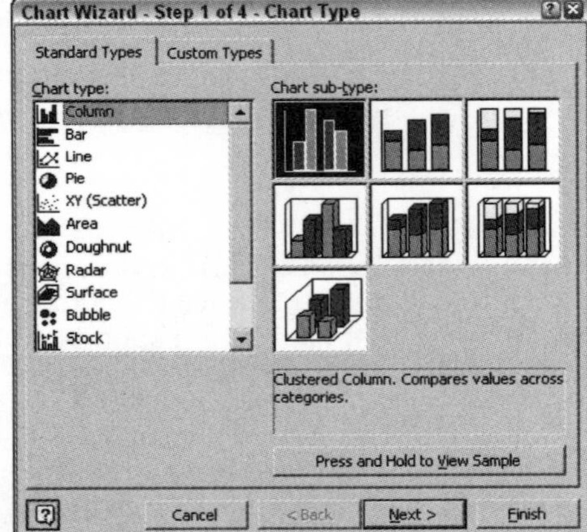

Figure 1-19: Column charts are available in seven different sub-types.

Excel includes Cylinder, Cone, and Pyramid chart types that are really just variations on the same seven column chart sub-types. Select one of these three chart types when you want to assign different shapes to the columns (cylindrical, conical, or pyramid-shaped) in your column chart.

Bar charts

Excel refers to charts with horizontal bars as "bar charts" and those with vertical bars as "column charts." A bar chart (horizontal) emphasizes the comparison between items at a fixed period of time. Figure 1-20 shows the six different sub-types available when building a bar chart.

Line charts

A line chart shows changes in data over a period of time. Although similar to an area chart, which shows the relative importance of values, the line

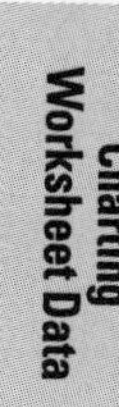

chart emphasizes trends rather than the amount of change. Figure 1-21 shows the seven different sub-types of Line chart from which you can choose.

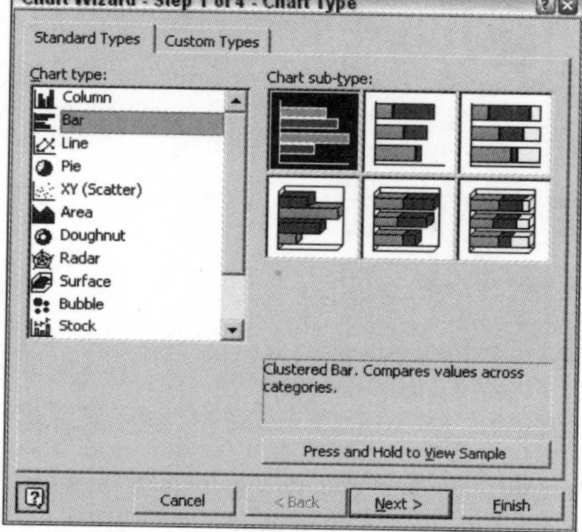

Figure 1-20: Bar charts are available in six different sub-types.

Pie charts

Unlike the other charts discussed so far, which can show multiple data series, pie charts contains just one chart data series. A pie chart shows the relationship of the parts to the whole. Figure 1-22 shows a sample 3-D pie chart that shows the relationship between the numbers of each type of part produced to the overall annual production.

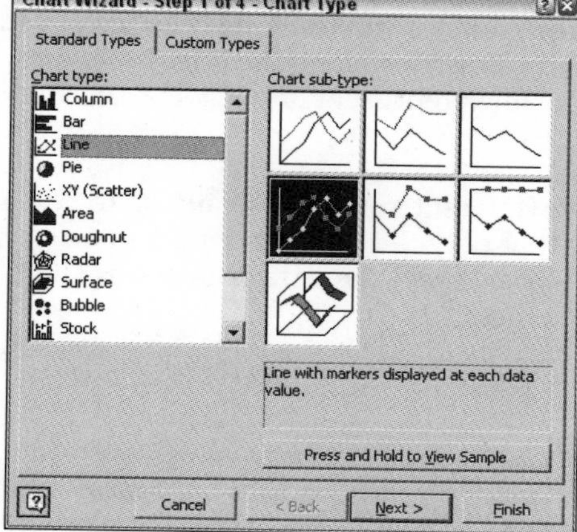

Figure 1-21: Line charts are available in seven different sub-types.

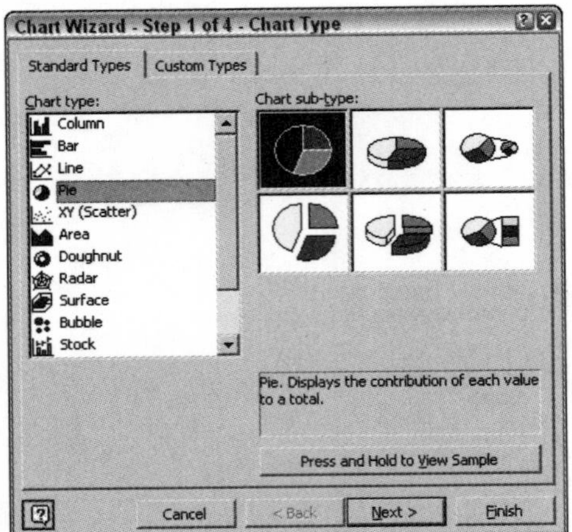

Figure 1-22: Line charts come in six different flavors.

To emphasize the importance of one part, emphasize one "slice" by making it a bright color or broad pattern or by labeling it clearly. This is best done by choosing one of the two exploded pie charts: Sub-type 4 (Exploded Pie) or Sub-type 5 (Exploded Pie with 3-D Visual Effect).

XY (Scatter) charts

Scatter charts are useful for showing a correlation among the data points that may not be easy to see from data alone. You may want to answer such questions as, "Does better nutrition mean that athletes have longer careers?" or "Do people with better insurance coverage have fewer accidents?" With an XY scatter chart, you can chart the two data series — for example, ad expenditures and overall sales — and look for a correlation.

An XY (scatter) chart uses numeric values along both axes instead of values along the vertical axis and categories along the horizontal axis. You then use a legend to show what the lines represent. If you wish, you can add axis labels of your own.

Figure 1-23 shows the five different sub-types available to you in creating an XY (Scatter) chart. Note that only the first sub-type for comparing pairs of values does not use lines to connect the data points. (creating, in effect, trendlines for each data series).

Area charts

An area chart shows the relative importance of values over time. For example, an area chart of the sales made by various account representatives over the first three months in the quarter might clearly reveal the relative importance of the sales from each person.

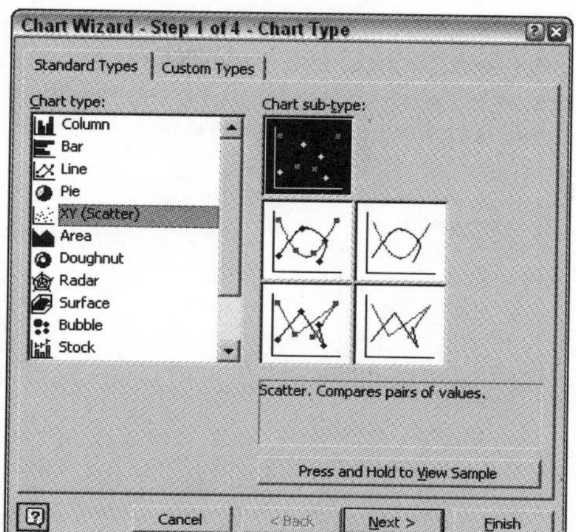

Figure 1-23: XY (Scatter) charts are available in five different sub-types.

An area chart is similar to a line chart, but because the area between lines is filled in, the area chart puts greater emphasis on the magnitude of values and somewhat less emphasis on the flow of change over time than the line chart (see Figure 1-24).

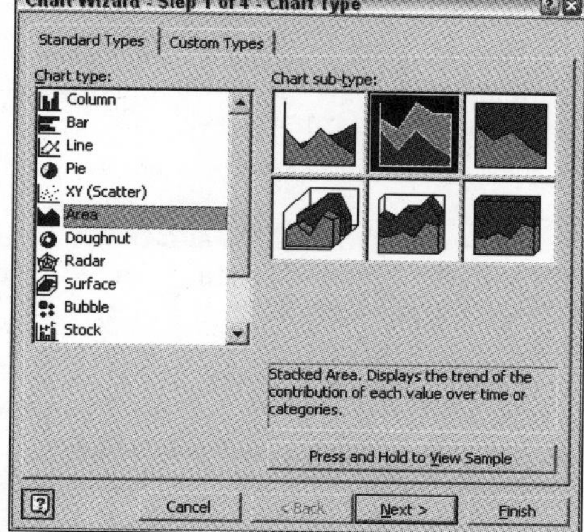

Figure 1-24: Area charts are available in six different sub-types.

Doughnut charts

A doughnut chart is similar to a pie chart except for its ability to display more than one data series (pie charts always graph just a single data series). Also, because the doughnut has a hole in the middle, you can use this space to display additional explanatory text.

Figure 1-25 shows the two types of doughnut chart sub-types. The only difference between the first and second sub-type is that the second type explodes the various segments, which can often be more effective when you want to emphasize one data group over another.

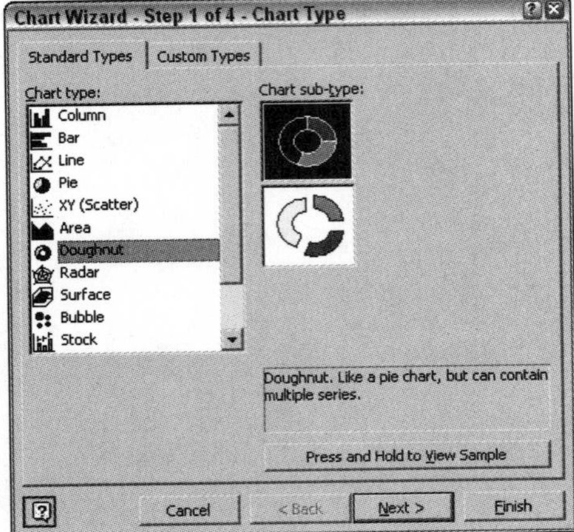

Figure 1-25: Doughnut charts are available in a standard and exploded sub-type.

Radar charts

A radar chart shows changes in data relative both to a center point and to each other. Each category in a radar chart has its own value axis radiating from the center point. Lines connect all the data markers in the same series. A radar chart is useful for making relative comparisons among items.

Figure 1-26 shows the three different radar chart sub-types available. The second sub-type places data markers at each data point, while the third sub-type fills the area covered by each data series in the chart.

Surface charts

Surface charts plot trends in values across two dimensions in a continuous curve. The trends in a surface chart imply the combined effects of two variables on a third. For that reason, all the different sub-types of surface charts (see Figure 1-27) are 3-D charts that have an X, Y, and Z axis (the last two sub-types are 3-D surface charts shown from above so that they appear to be two-dimensional). In order to use a surface, you need at least two data series, both of which are numeric as with an XY (Scatter) chart.

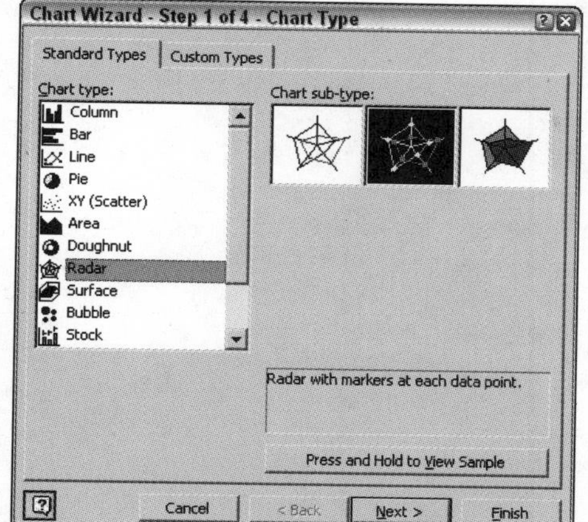

Figure 1-26: Radar charts are available in three varieties.

Bubble charts

Bubble charts compare sets of three values as kind of a combination of an XY (Scatter) chart with an Area chart. When you build a bubble chart, the size of each bubble represented on the x-y grid represents the third set of values being charted. The downside to using a Bubble chart to plot data is that each bubble takes up so much room that they often overlap each other unless you are plotting just a very few data samples. As Figure 1-28 shows, Bubble charts are available in only two varieties: The first sub-type draws the bubbles as 2-D circles, whereas the second sub-type draws them with a 3-D visual effect.

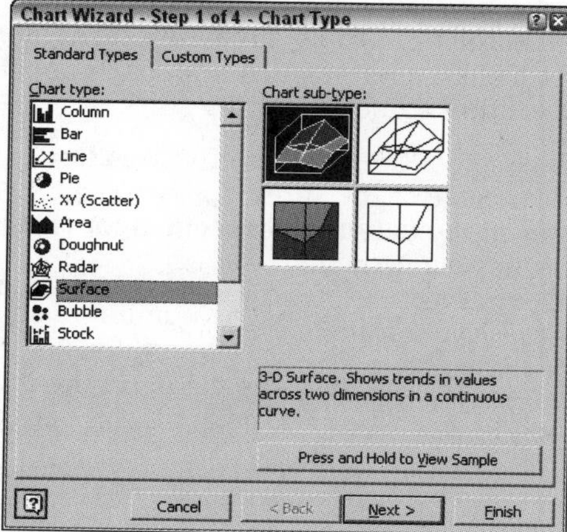

Figure 1-27: Surface charts come in four different sub-types.

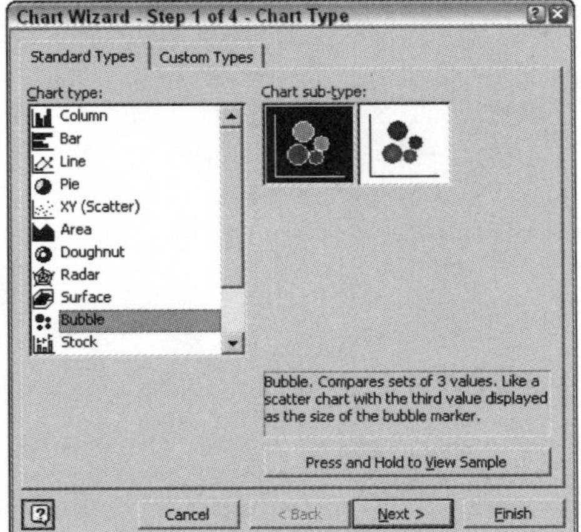

Figure 1-28: Bubble charts are available in a standard and 3-D version.

Stock charts

Stock charts, as their name implies, are used to plot stock quotes over a certain time period such as a single business day or week. As Figure 1-29 illustrates, Excel offers you a choice of four different sub-types of stock charts:

- **High-Low-Close** requires that you select three series of data in the high-low-close order. This means that the high values are in the leftmost column (or topmost row), the low values in the next column to the right (or next row down), and the close values in the rightmost column (or bottom-most row) of the data range used in the chart.
- **Open-High-Low-Close** requires the addition of the opening values to the high-close-low values in the order open-high-low-close (meaning that the open values must be in the leftmost column or topmost row of the data range with all the other values following suit).
- **Volume-High-Low-Close** plots the number of shares traded (the volume) along with the high-low-close of the stock. As with the other types of Stock chart, the values in the data range specified for this sub-type must be arranged in the order volume-high-low-close.
- **Volume-Open-High-Low-Close** combines the number of shares traded (the volume) with opening, high, low, and close values of the stock. As with the other types of Stock chart, the values in the data range specified for this sub-type must be arranged in the order volume-open-high-low-close.

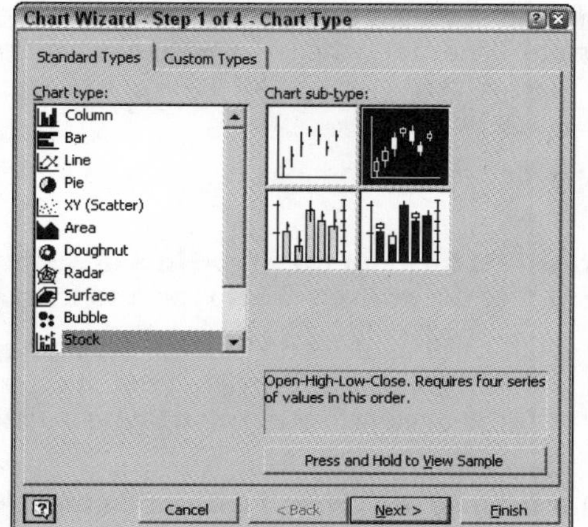

Figure 1-29: Stock charts are available in four different varieties.

Adding your own custom chart types

After going through extensive editing and formatting one of Excel's basic chart types, you may want to save your work of art as a custom chart type that you can then use again with different data without having to go through all the painstaking steps to get the chart looking just the way you want it. Excel makes it easy to save any modified chart that you want to use again as a custom chart type.

To convert a chart on which you've done extensive editing and formatting into a custom chart type, you take these steps:

1. **Click the chart to select it.**

   If the chart is on its own chart sheet, you click its chart sheet tab to do this.

2. **Choose Chart⇨Chart Type on the Excel Menu bar.**

   This action opens the Chart Type dialog box with two tabs: Standard Types and Custom Types.

3. **Click the Custom Types tab and then click the User-Defined button.**

   This action displays a Chart Type list box with all of the custom chart types you've defined and a Sample list box that shows a sample of the custom type currently selected.

4. **Click the Add button near the bottom of the Custom Types tab.**

   This action opens the Add Custom Chart Type dialog box where you enter a name for the custom chart type and a description for it. Note that the description you enter here appears at the bottom of the Sample list box on the Custom Types tab whenever you select this custom chart type in either the Chart Wizard — Step 1 of 4 — Chart Type dialog box or the Chart Type dialog box.

5. **Type the name by which the custom chart type is to be known in the Name text box.**
6. **Click the Description text box and then type in a description of the special characteristics of the custom chart type and then click OK.**

   As soon as you click OK to close the Add Custom Chart Type dialog box, Excel returns you to the Custom Types tab of the Chart Type dialog box, where the name for your new custom chart type is listed in the Chart Type list box.
7. **Click the OK button to close the Chart Type dialog box.**

After creating a custom chart type in this manner, you can then use it anytime you want in creating a new chart. Simply select the data to be charted, click the Chart Wizard button on the Standard toolbar. Then, in the Chart Wizard — Step 1 of 4 — Chart Type dialog box, click the Custom Types tab and the User-Defined button radio button. This action displays the names of all the custom chart types you've defined in the Chart Type list box. To use the custom type you just created, you click its name in this list box before clicking the Next button to advance to the Chart Wizard — Step 2 of 4 — Chart Source Data dialog box.

If you find that you're constantly using a particular chart type, be it one of the built-in types or a custom one that you've created, you can make that chart type the default chart type. Simply open the Chart Type dialog box (Chart⇨Chart Type) and then click the chart type in the Chart Type list box and, if necessary, the sub-type in the Chart Sub-Type list box on the Standard Types tab, or, in the case of a custom chart type, the Chart Type list box on the Custom Types tab (after clicking the User-Defined radio button) and then click the Set as Default Chart button before you click OK.

Printing Charts

To print an embedded chart as part of the data on the worksheet, you simply print the worksheet the File⇨Print command (Ctrl+P). To print an embedded chart by itself without the supporting worksheet data, click the chart to select it before you choose File⇨Print (you can also print the embedded chart by putting it in its own window and then selecting the Print command on the window's shortcut menu). To print a chart that's on a separate chart sheet, activate the chart sheet tab by clicking it and then File⇨Print.

When printing a chart alone, that is, without its supporting data or in its own chart sheet or chart window, the Page Setup dialog box includes a Chart tab that contains its own special chart printing options:

- **Use Full Page** radio button to print to scale the chart so that it takes up the entire page
- **Scale to Fit Page** radio button to have Excel scale the chart so that it prints on the page size you've selected
- **Custom** radio button to print the chart the size it assumes on the screen
- **Draft Quality** check box to print the chart using your printer's draft-quality setting
- **Print in Black and White** check box to have your color printer print the chart in black and white

Note that when you place an embedded chart in its own chart window, you can open the Page Setup dialog box to change these print settings on the Chart tab by right-clicking the title bar and then clicking Page Setup on the window's shortcut menu.

Chapter 2: Adding Graphic Objects

In This Chapter

- **Understanding what graphic objects are and how Excel treats them**
- **Creating graphics with the Drawing toolbar**
- **Adding text boxes**
- **Inserting WordArt in the spreadsheet**
- **Creating organization charts and other diagrams**
- **Adding Clip Art to the spreadsheet**
- **Importing graphics files in the worksheet**

Just as charts can really help to clarify trends and implications that aren't readily apparent in your worksheet data, graphics that you add to a worksheet can really spruce up your charts and make them read even better. Although you may often look to Excel graphic objects as chart enhancements, you can also use them to enhance regular spreadsheet data. Depending upon the type of spreadsheet, you may even end up using graphic elements not simply as a way to embellish the data but as a superior way to actually present it in the worksheet, especially when the data require diagrammatic presentation.

Excel supports two types of graphic objects: those that you create yourself by using the various tools on the Drawing toolbar within Excel and those created by other people and with other graphics programs that you import into the spreadsheet. This chapter covers how to use the Drawing toolbar to create graphics with text as well as basic graphic shapes. It also covers how to import two different types of graphics: Clip Art graphics that you keep and organize in a special Media Gallery, along with images stored in a variety of different graphics file formats that Excel can read.

Graphic Objects 101

It is important to understand that all graphic objects, whether you create them or import them, are discrete objects in the worksheet that you can select and manipulate. To select a graphic object, you simply click it. Excel lets you know that the object is selected by placing white circular sizing handles around the perimeter. The program also adds a green circular rotation handle that appears directly above and connected to the sizing handle on the top edge of the graphics' perimeter in the middle between the left and right edge. On some drawn objects (especially 3-dimensional ones), yellow diamond shaping handles also appear at the places at which and from which you can manipulate some part of the object's shape, as shown in Figure 2-1.

To select multiple graphic objects in the worksheet, hold down the Shift or the Ctrl key as you click each object. When you select more than one object, any manipulations that you perform on any of them affects all of them.

To deselect a graphic object, just click the thick, white cross pointer in any cell in the worksheet that it doesn't cover. To deselect an object when you have several graphics selected at one time, click an unobstructed cell or another graphic.

Manipulating graphics

When you position the mouse pointer on a graphic object's sizing handle, the pointer becomes a double-headed arrow that you can then drag to increase or decrease the overall size and shape of the object. To constrain a graphic while resizing it, click the sizing handle and then press and hold down the Shift key as you drag the mouse. Holding down the Shift key restricts your dragging so that the graphic retains its original proportions as you make it bigger or smaller. To constrain the proportions of an object in two dimensions, hold down the Shift key as you drag one of the corner sizing handles.

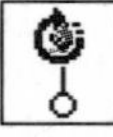

When you position the mouse pointer on a graphic objects' rotation handle, the pointer becomes a curved arrow pointing counterclockwise (shown in the left margin). When you click and hold down the mouse button to drag the rotation handle, the pointer becomes four curved arrows in a circle pointing in the clockwise direction. You can then rotate the graphic to any degree in a circle that pivots around the rotation handle.

When you position the mouse pointer on a shaping handle, the pointer becomes an arrowhead without any handle (shown in the left margin). You can then drag this pointer to reshape the side or section of the graphic. In the case of some 3-D graphic shapes, dragging the Shaping handle rotates a part of the graphic in such a way that it alters the object's perspective, thus changing the way it's viewed.

To move the selected graphic object, position the mouse pointer somewhere inside the object's perimeter. Then, when the pointer becomes an arrowhead with a double-cross at its point, drag the object to its new position within the worksheet. To copy the selected object, hold down the Ctrl key as you drag the graphic (when you press the Ctrl key, a plus sign, indicating that the object is being copied, appears above the arrowhead pointer).

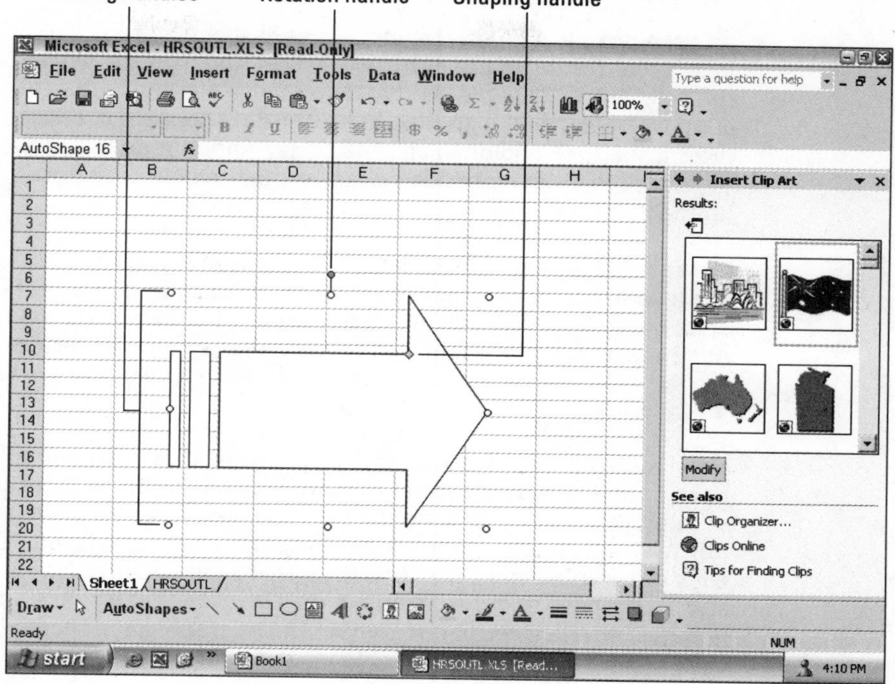

Figure 2-1: When you click a graphic to select it, the rotation and circular sizing handles appear.

When moving graphics in a worksheet, you can make use of an invisible grid to help you position them. This is especially helpful when you're trying to align one graphic with another (for example, when aligning two charts side by side in a worksheet). To turn on the grid, click the Draw button on the Drawing toolbar (View➪Toolbars➪Drawing) and then choose Snap➪To Grid on its pop-up menu. After the grid is turned, whenever you position an object very close to an invisible horizontal or vertical gridline, it snaps to this line as soon as you release the mouse button.

You can "nudge" a selected graphic object into its desired position by pressing the arrow keys (or if the Drawing toolbar is displayed, by clicking the Draw button and then choosing Nudge➪Up, Nudge➪Down, Nudge➪Left, or Nudge➪Right or pressing the ↑, ↓, ←, or → keys). When you press an arrow or choose one of the Nudge commands, Excel moves the object just a very little bit in that direction. Nudging is very useful when you have an object that's almost in place and requires very little handling to get it into just the right position.

If you no longer need a graphic object, you can get rid of it by clicking it to select the object and then pressing the Delete key to remove it.

Using layers

All graphic objects that you add to a worksheet lay on different invisible layers that reside on top of the worksheet and over the worksheet data in the cells below. This means that if you move a graphic object over a cell that contains an entry, the graphic hides the data beneath it. Likewise, if you draw a shape or add an image and then position it on top of another graphic object (such as an embedded chart or other shape or picture), it also covers up the graphic below.

Figure 2-2 illustrates this situation. In this figure, you see the Clip Art image of a map of Australia partially covering some worksheet data and an embedded Clustered Column chart on the layer below. On top of the map of Australia, I have placed the flag of Australia, which now resides on the very top layer, obscuring part of the map area and some of the worksheet data on the layers below it.

Excel makes it easy to move objects in layers above other graphics to the background or to move those that are below forward so that they're on top of other graphics or even on the very topmost layer. To move an object down a level so that it's below any graphics on the top layer, simply right-click the graphic and then choose Order⇨Send Backward on the object's shortcut menu. To move an object up a level so that it's now on top of graphics on the layer below, right-click the graphic and then choose Order⇨Send Forward on the object's shortcut menu.

If you're dealing with a number of levels and you want to send a graphic to the bottommost layer, right-click it and then choose Order⇨Send to Back on the object's shortcut menu. Likewise, if you want to send the graphic to the very topmost layer so that it lies on top of all other objects, right-click it and then choose Order⇨Send to Front on the object's shortcut menu. To move a graphic up just one level at a time, choose Order⇨Bring Forward. To move it back one level, choose Order⇨Send Backward instead.

Figure 2-3 illustrates how easy it is to move a graphic object to a different layer. In this figure, I right-clicked the map of Australia and then chose Order⇨Send Backward on its object's shortcut menu. As a result, Excel placed the map beneath the Column chart, leaving the flag on the topmost layer (so that it now appears to be sticking out of the chart rather than being planted in the land down under).

When you're dealing with two graphic objects, one on top of the other, and you want to align them with each other, you can use the Align or Distribute items on the Draw menu that appears when you click the Draw button on the Drawing toolbar (View⇨Toolbar⇨Drawing). Choosing the Align or Distribute item displays a sub-menu of items that includes the horizontal alignment options: Align Left, Align Center, Align Right, and the vertical alignment options: Align Top, Align Middle, and Align Bottom. When you choose one of the alignment options, Excel aligns the graphic on the top layer with the one underneath by using the horizontal or vertical direction chosen.

If you select three or more graphic objects at one time, you can also choose between two distribute commands on this sub-menu — Distribute Horizontally and Distribute Vertically. These commands attempt to equally distribute the objects horizontally or vertically within the relative space that they currently inhabit.

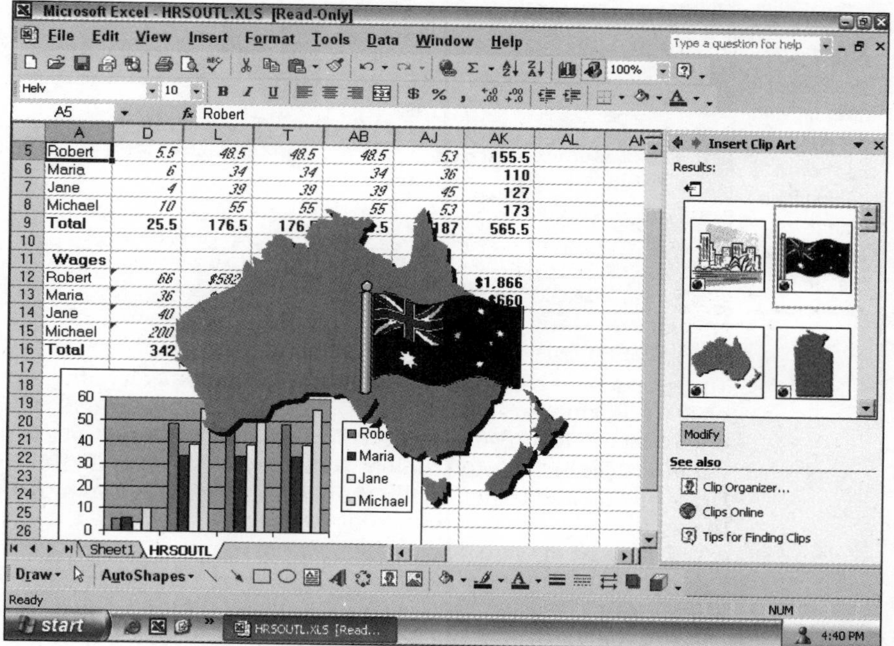

Figure 2-2: Graphic objects on top of obscure worksheet data and parts of other graphics below.

Grouping graphic objects

Sometimes you need to work with more than one graphic object (for example, my map of Australia and its flag). If you find that you're constantly selecting two or more objects at the same time in order to move them or rotate them together, you can make life a lot simpler by grouping the graphics. When you group selected graphic objects, Excel then makes them into a single graphic object, which you can then manipulate.

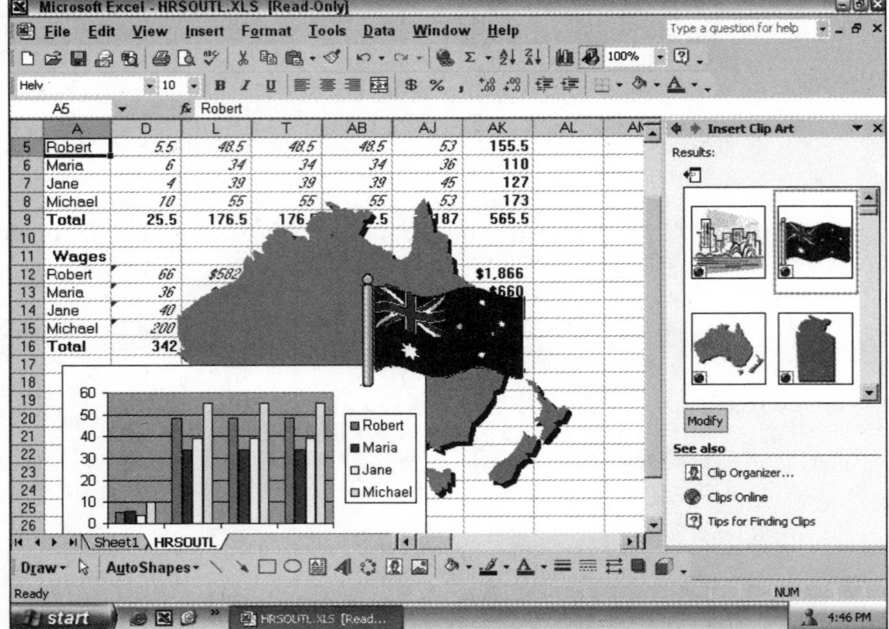

Figure 2-3: Worksheet after moving the map backward so that it no longer obscures the chart.

To group a bunch of graphics together, select them all (either by Shift+clicking or Ctrl+clicking each one of them). After they are selected, right-click the object on the top layer and then click Grouping⇨Group on the object's shortcut menu (if the Drawing toolbar is displayed, you can do this by clicking the Draw button and then clicking the Group item at the top of the Draw pop-up menu).

Excel indicates that the selected graphics are now grouped (and for all intents and purposes, a single graphic object) by placing a single set of sizing handles around the perimeter formed by all the former separate graphics. You can then manipulate the grouped graphic as a single entity by moving it, sizing it, rotating it, and so forth as you would any other object.

The great thing about grouping a bunch of different objects is that Excel never forgets that they were once separate objects that you could independently manipulate. This means that you can always turn them back into separate graphics by ungrouping them. To do this, right-click the composite graphic object and then choose Grouping⇨Ungroup on its shortcut menu (if the Drawing toolbar is displayed, you can do this by clicking the graphic to select it before you click the Draw button and then click the Ungroup item near the top of the Draw pop-up menu).

Excel shows that the composite object is once again separated into many different objects by displaying sizing handles around each object's perimeter. You can then deselect them all and manipulate each one once again independently by selecting it alone before moving, resizing, or rotating it. If you decide that you want the now independent objects to be joined as a group once again, you can do this by right-clicking any one of the graphics in the erstwhile group and then choosing Group➪Regroup on its shortcut menu (or, if the Drawing toolbar is displayed, click the graphic to select it before clicking the Draw button and then click the Regroup item near the top of the Draw pop-up menu).

Figure 2-4 illustrates grouping in action. For this figure, I selected both the flag of Australia and its map graphic below. In this figure, I'm in the process of choosing the Group command, which will turn them into a single composite graphic object. After choosing this command, not only will the flag move whenever I reposition the map but it will also resize when I modify the shape and would rotate together with it if I were to spin Australia on its head (putting a new spin on the term, *down under!*).

Object positioning relative to worksheet cells

By default, Excel automatically moves and resizes any graphic objects on the layer above whenever you move or resize the cells underneath on the layer below. Often, however, you won't want Excel to automatically resize the graphic when you change the width or the height of the column or row underneath because this ends up distorting the image. In those cases, you can have Excel automatically move the object with the cells underneath without also resizing it. In other cases, you may want to set it up so that the program neither moves nor resizes a graphic with the cells underneath (thus enabling you to move cell entries in a neighboring range without disturbing the object's original position).

To change the object positioning options for a graphic object, you select the Properties tab on the object's Format dialog box. To open the Format dialog box, double-click the object or click it and then press Ctrl+1. Figure 2-5 shows you the options on the Properties tab.

To prevent Excel from resizing an object but still enable the object to move with the cells underneath, click the Move but Don't Size with Cells radio button in the Object Positioning section. To prevent Excel from resizing and moving the object, click the Don't Move or Size with Cells radio button instead.

Note that if you don't want Excel to print the graphic object when you print the cells that it overlays, you click the Print Object check box to remove its checkmark.

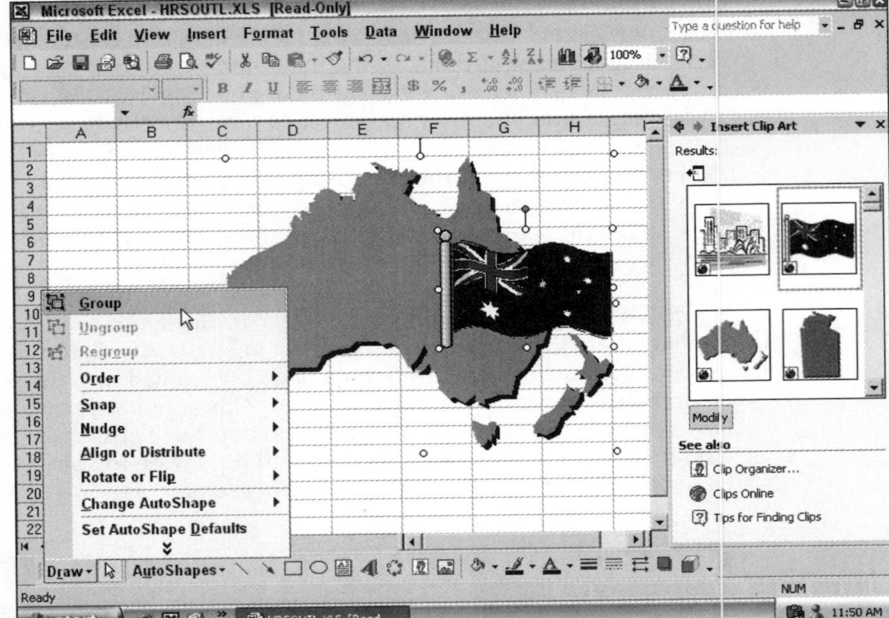

Figure 2-4: Grouping the flag and map of Australia to turn them into a single graphic object.

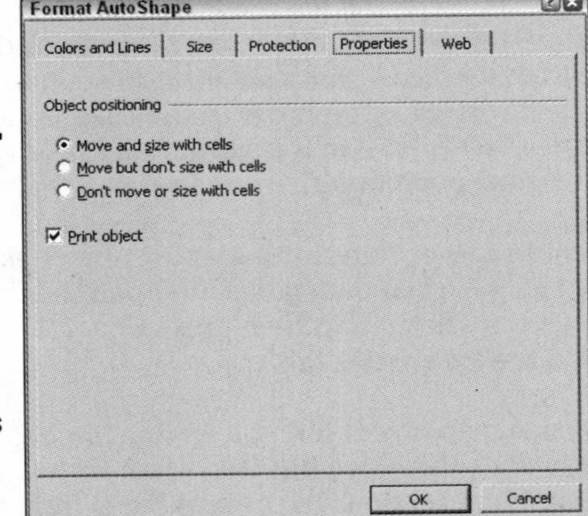

Figure 2-5: Use the Properties tab on an object's Format dialog box to control its relative positioning.

Sometimes you have to get pretty sneaky in order to select cells independently of a graphic object that partially obscures them or to select the object without selecting the cells. To select cells without a graphic that covers all or part of their borders, use the arrow keys to move the cell pointer to one of the first cells in the range that is partially covered and then hold the Shift key as you press an arrow key to select all the cells in a particular direction.

To select a graphic object without danger of selecting any cells underneath, click the Select Objects button on the Drawing toolbar (see Figure 2-6). This action temporarily hides the cell pointer so that you can only click and select graphic objects in the worksheet (it also enables you to draw a bounding box that selects all the graphic objects within the box's boundary). To return to the normal mode so that you can once again click cells to select them, click the Select Objects button on the Drawing toolbar a second time (this button acts like a toggle switch that switches you from one mode to the next).

Using the Drawing Toolbar

The Drawing toolbar is jam-packed with great tools for creating and adding all types of graphic objects. About the only graphic that you cannot bring in from this toolbar is one that you create on a scanner or import from a digital camera that's attached to your computer (to that, you have to choose Insert⇨Picture⇨From Scanner or Camera on the Excel Menu bar). For all the rest of your graphic needs, the Drawing toolbar is your ticket.

Figure 2-6 shows the Drawing toolbar and identifies the buttons that use only symbols. When you first open the Drawing toolbar (by choosing View⇨Toolbar⇨Drawing on the Excel menu bar), Excel automatically docks it at the bottom of the Excel window immediately above the Status bar. You can then move the Drawing toolbar to another side of the Excel window or even float it if you want (see Book I, Chapter 1 for details about docking and floating toolbars).

The Draw and AutoShapes buttons are attached to pop-up menus that open when you click their buttons. The Fill Color, Line Color, Font Color, Shadow Style, and 3-D Style buttons are all attached to pop-up palettes that open when you click their buttons and from which you can select new fill, line, and font colors; shading; and 3-D effects for selected graphic objects.

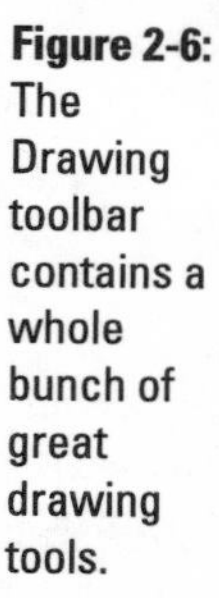

Figure 2-6: The Drawing toolbar contains a whole bunch of great drawing tools.

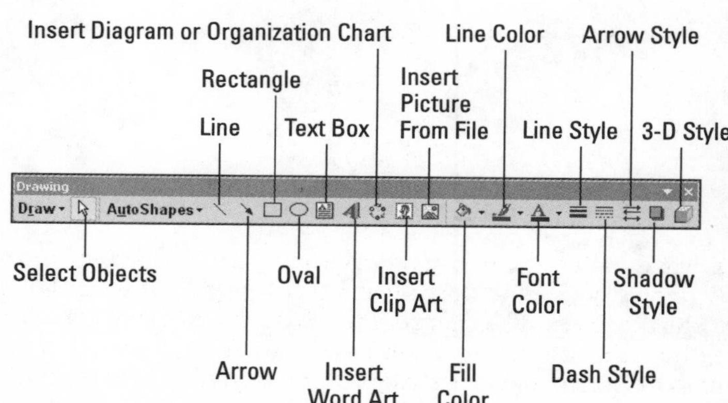

Drawing shapes

The Drawing toolbar enables you to manually draw straight lines, lines with arrowheads (simply referred to as *arrows*), rectangular and square shapes, and oval and circular shapes. To draw any of these shapes, click the appropriate button and then drag the thin, black cross pointer to draw its outline. When drawing a line or arrow, Excel draws the line from the place where you originally click the mouse button to the place where you release it.

When drawing a rectangle or an oval, you can constrain the tool to draw a square or circle by holding down the Shift key as you drag the mouse. Note that when drawing a two-dimensional shape, such as a rectangle, square, oval, or circle, Excel automatically draws the shape with a white fill that obscures any data or graphic objects that are beneath the shape on layers below.

After you've drawn the basic shape, you can then use the Fill Color, Line Color, Line Style, Dash Style, Shadow Style, and 3-D Style buttons on the Drawing toolbar to enhance the basic shape. Figure 2-7 shows a bunch of different shapes that I created with Line, Arrow, Rectangle, and Oval tools and then enhanced with these tools.

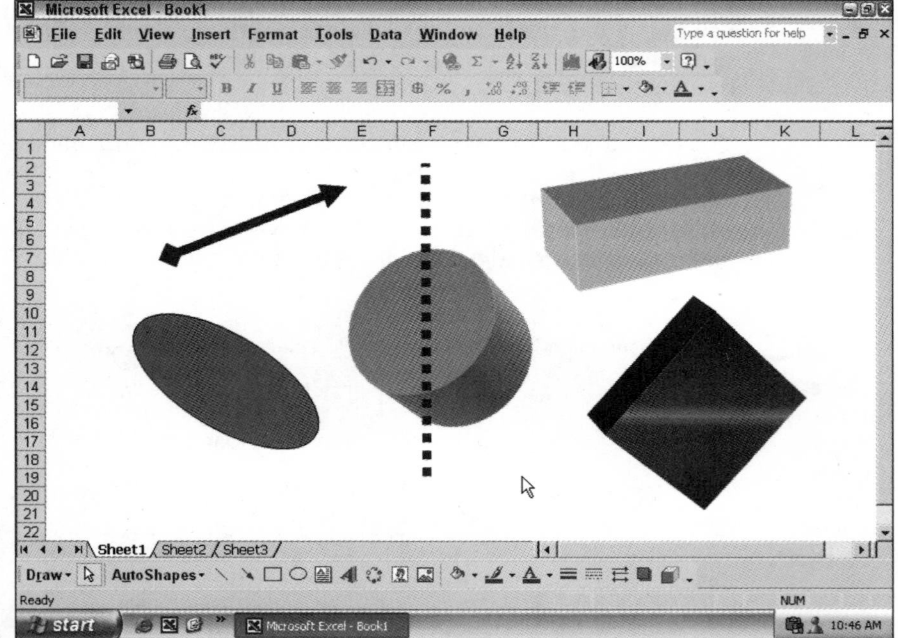

Figure 2-7: Worksheet with a bunch of different shapes created with various drawing tools.

I enhanced the basic arrow I drew on the left side of the worksheet by selecting a new arrow style from the Arrow Style pop-up menu as well as a new thickness from the Line Style pop-up menu. I enhanced the oval that I drew beneath it by selecting a dark green fill color from the Fill Color pop-up menu. For the vertical line that I drew with the Line tool, I made it as thick as possible by selecting the 6 pt. line on the Line Style pop-up menu and then made it into a dotted line by the smallest dotted style on the Dash Style pop-up menu. I then enhanced all three 2-D shapes that I drew (a circle, rectangle, and square) by selecting a fill color (or fill effect, in the case of the rotated square) from the Fill Color pop-up palette followed by a style of 3-D shading from the 3-D Style pop-up palette.

In addition to drawing your own shapes, you can insert any number of ready-made shapes (including lines, arrows, flow chart symbols, banners, and callouts) by selecting them from the AutoShapes pop-up menu and then sizing them in the worksheet. Figure 2-8 shows this pop-up menu with the cascading palette of shapes to choose from when you select Basic Shapes. This figure also contains a few shapes (the sun, crescent moon, and heart) that I drew and then filled by using a basic color on the Fill Color pop-up palette. In addition, you also see the Insert Clip Art Task Pane (opened by choosing Insert⇨Picture⇨Clip Art) that appears with more AutoShapes that you can paste into a worksheet when you click the More AutoShapes item, located at the bottom of the AutoShapes pop-up menu.

Figure 2-8: Worksheet with a bunch of different shapes created with the AutoShapes pop-up menu.

After selecting a shape from one of the AutoShapes menus, you position and size it in the worksheet by dragging the thin, black cross mouse pointer. To constrain the shape so that you can't possibly mess up its proportions when dragging the outline to size the AutoShape, hold down the Shift key as you drag.

Note that when you insert one of the callouts on the Callouts cascading palette, Excel positions the insertion point within the callout AutoShape, thus enabling you to then enter the text of the callout (callouts are the only AutoShapes that combine text and graphics). After you finish entering the text, click somewhere outside of the shape to deselect the callout (see the "Adding text boxes" section that follows for information on how to edit and format the callout text).

Adding text boxes

Text boxes are special graphic objects that combine text with a rectangular graphic object (the only other object that does this are the callouts that you insert from the AutoShapes Callout pop-up menu). They're great for calling attention to significant trends or special features in the charts that you create (see Book V, Chapter 1 for details).

To create a text box, click the Text Box button on the Drawing toolbar and then drag the mouse pointer to draw the outline of the box. As soon as you release the mouse button, Excel places the insertion point in the upper-left corner of the box.

You can then start typing the text that you want displayed in the text box. When the text that you type reaches the right edge of the text box, Excel automatically starts a new line. If you reach the end of the text box and keep typing, Excel then scrolls the text up and you then have to resize the text box to display all the text that you've entered. If you want to break a line before it reaches the right edge of the text box, press the Enter key. When you finish entering the text, click anywhere on the screen outside of the text box to deselect.

Keep in mind that although text boxes are similar to cell Comments in that they also display the text that you enter in a rectangular box, they do differ from Comments in that text boxes are *not* attached to particular cells and *are* always displayed in the worksheet (Comments only show when you position the mouse pointer over the cell or select the comment with the Reviewing toolbar — see Book IV, Chapter 1 for details).

Note that text boxes differ somewhat from other graphic objects that you add to the worksheet. Unlike other graphic objects in Excel, when you select text boxes, they only display sizing handles without any rotation handle (because Excel can't display text at just any angle you may select). Also, unlike other graphic objects, text boxes display two different border patterns when you select them: a single cross-hatched pattern is displayed when you click inside the text box, thus enabling you to format and edit the text, and a double cross-hatched pattern (that just looks like a bunch of fuzzy dots on my monitor) is displayed when you click the border of the text box or start dragging the box to reposition it, thus indicating that you can format and edit the box itself.

Formatting a text box

After you've added a text box, you can format its text by changing the font, font size, font style, alignment of the text (including its orientation); you can also format the text box by changing its background color and line style, object positioning properties, and — perhaps most important of all — its text margins.

To change the formatting of the text in a text box, you first select the text that needs changing by dragging through it in the box. You then have a choice of using the various buttons on the Formatting toolbar (just use the Bold button to bold text, the Center button to horizontally center the text) or opening the Format Text Box dialog box (Ctrl+1), which contains a single Font tab with all the standard options for formatting text.

To change the formatting of the text box itself, you need to double-click the border of the box or click the edge to select the box (indicated by the double cross-hatching around the border that looks just like fuzzy dots on my screen) and then press Ctrl+1. When you do this, Excel opens the version of the Format Text Box dialog box, as shown in Figure 2-9. As you can see, this version contains not only a Font tab but also seven other tabs with a whole bunch of options for formatting the box as well as modifying the relationship of the text in the box.

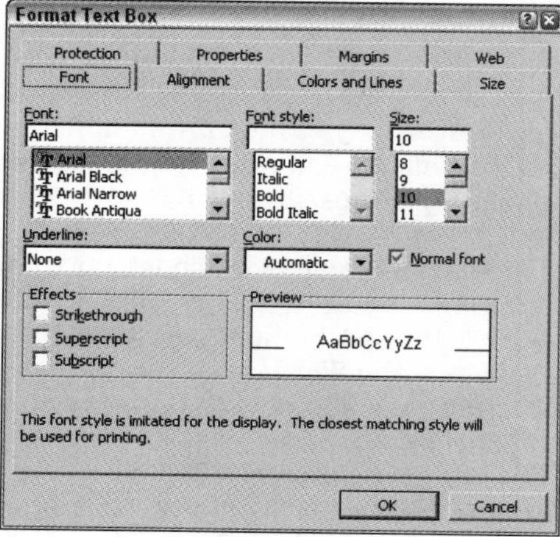

Figure 2-9: Using the options in the Format Text Box dialog box.

When you first enter the text in a text box, Excel doesn't use any margins so that there's hardly any white space between the text characters and the edge of the text box. If you're anything like me, one of the first things that you'll want to do is add decent margins to the text box by using the options on the Margins tab in the Format Text Box dialog box. On this tab, click the Automatic check box to remove its checkmark and then enter the values (in fractions of an inch) that you want for the top, bottom, left, and right margins in the text box.

Editing the text in a text box

You can edit the text in a text box as you would in any cell of the worksheet. To insert new text, click the insertion point at the appropriate place and start typing. To delete text, press the Backspace key to delete characters to the left of the insertion point or the Delete key to delete characters to its right. To delete an entire section of text, select it with the I-beam mouse pointer and then press the Delete key.

To spell check some or all of the text in the text box, select the text by dragging the I-beam mouse pointer through it and then choose Tools⇨Spelling on the Excel Menu bar (or just press F7).

To delete a text box from the worksheet, click its border to select the box (indicated by the fuzzy-looking, double cross-hatching) and then press the Delete key. Be sure that you don't click inside the box because this only selects the text (indicated by the single cross-hatching), in which case, pressing the Delete key doesn't get rid of anything.

Inserting WordArt

The WordArt button on the Drawing toolbar enables you to insert super fancy text in your worksheets (sometimes a little *too* fancy for my tastes). Keep in mind when using the WordArt feature that its text is really a graphic object that happens to have some text associated with it (meaning that you can't edit it directly as you can edit the text that you enter in a text box). Also, keep in mind that the WordArt styles are only intended with really large font sizes (36 points being the default) and many don't really work well with regular text font sizes (for example, those below about 24 points in size).

To insert a WordArt graphic object in your worksheet, you first click the WordArt button on the Drawing toolbar. This action opens the WordArt Gallery dialog box, shown in Figure 2-10, where you select the style that you want to use. As this figure shows, the WordArt Gallery contains a wide variety of different styles at different angles with some styles that even run the text down in a vertical line.

After selecting a WordArt style by clicking its picture in the WordArt Gallery dialog box and then clicking OK, Excel opens the Edit WordArt Text dialog box where you replace the dummy text, "Your Text Here" with the words or phrase that you want presented in the WordArt style that you just selected in the Gallery dialog box.

The Edit WordArt Text dialog box contains a Font drop-down list box and Size combo box that you can use to change the font and font size of the text that you enter. It also contains a Bold and Italic button that you can click to enhance the text that you enter by making it bold and/or italic.

After you finish entering and enhancing your text in the Edit WordArt Text dialog box and you click its OK button, Excel inserts your WordArt graphic object in the worksheet, while at the same time displaying the WordArt toolbar that you can use to further format or make changes to your WordArt masterpiece.

Figure 2-11 shows a sample piece of WordArt created by selecting the rainbow style in the WordArt Gallery. This figure also shows the WordArt toolbar that's automatically displayed whenever a piece of WordArt is selected in the worksheet. Note that the selected WordArt sample shown in Figure 2-11 contains sizing handles, along with a rotation handle and shaping handle. You can use the shaping handle to place the text characters on a forward slant (as though they were italicized) or a backward slant (as though they were written by a southpaw like myself).

Inserting diagrams and organizational charts

You can use the Insert Diagram or Organization Chart button on the Drawing toolbar to quickly add an organization chart or diagram to your worksheet (one place where a graphic object actually conveys the information rather than just embellishing the worksheet data or embedded chart already there). When you click the Insert Diagram or Organization Chart button, Excel opens the Diagram Gallery dialog box, shown in Figure 2-12, where you select the style of the chart or diagram that you want to insert.

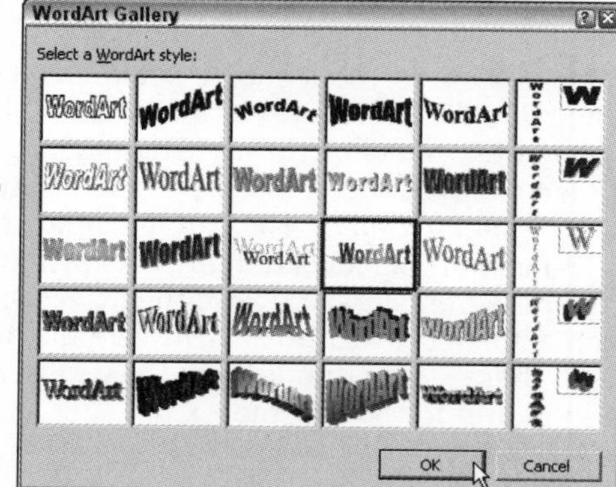

Figure 2-10: Selecting a WordArt style in the WordArt Gallery dialog box.

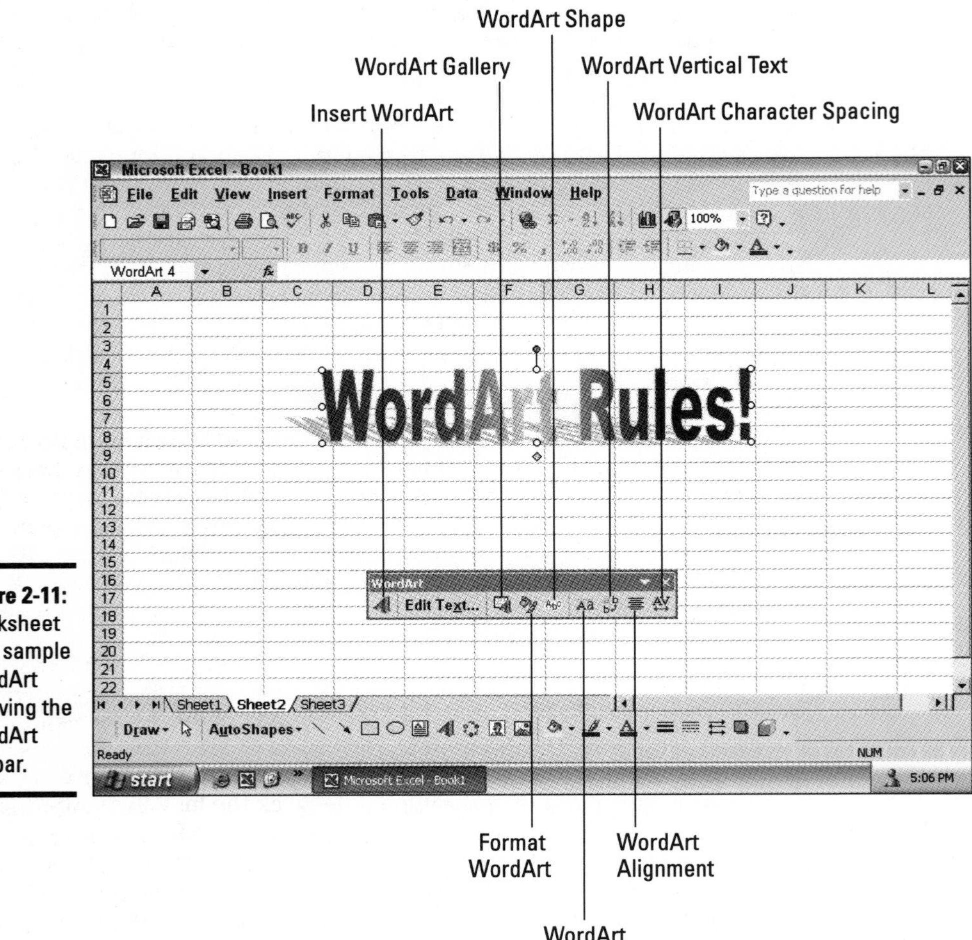

Figure 2-11: Worksheet with sample WordArt showing the WordArt toolbar.

The Diagram Gallery dialog box offers you a choice between an organization chart (the first picture) and five different types of diagrams (Cycle, Radial, Pyramid, Venn, and Target). After you click the style of diagram or the Organization Chart and then click OK, Excel inserts a blank chart or diagram into the worksheet as a new graphic object. You can then click the different parts of the chart or diagram and replace its dummy text with text of your own (organization charts or diagrams created with the Insert Diagram or Organization Chart button act like big text boxes with a bunch of graphics with little text boxes inside them — see the "Editing the text in a text box" section previously in this chapter for editing hints).

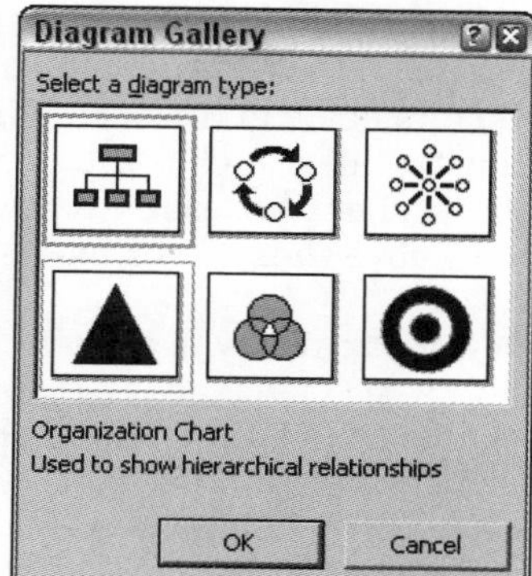

Figure 2-12: Selecting an organization chart type in the Diagram Gallery dialog box.

When you create a new organization chart, Excel opens an Organization Chart toolbar that contains buttons for editing the shape and layout, and for adding new levels and branches to the chart. When you create a new diagram (in any of the five available styles), the program opens a Diagram toolbar that contains its own tools for formatting and editing the diagram.

Adding Clip Art

Microsoft includes a wide variety of ready-to-use images called Clip Art that you can easily insert into your worksheets. To make this task easy, Excel has an Insert Clip Art Task Pane from which you can conduct word searches for the types of images that you want to use.

To choose a clip to paste into a worksheet, click the Insert Clip Art button on the Drawing toolbar. This action opens the Insert Clip Art taskbar where you can search for the type of clips that you want to use. The first time that you use Clip Art, Excel opens the Add Clips to Gallery dialog box that prompts you to collect and catalog all the media files on your computer system (including sound, pictures, digital movies, and Clip Art). Click the Now button to have Excel catalog your media files. When you do so, the program opens an Auto Import Settings dialog box where you can indicate which folders to search for the media files on your computer. After you finish indicating which folders to search, click the Catalog button to have the Microsoft Media Gallery catalog the media clips on your system.

After Excel finishes cataloging your system's clips, you can then use the Search For feature in the Insert Clip Art Task Pane to locate the Clip Art that you want to use (this works because the Microsoft Media Gallery includes the keywords assigned to the various clips when it creates the catalog). To display all the Clip Art images of a particular type, enter the keywords to search for in the Search Text box at the top of the Insert Clip Art Task Pane.

By default, Excel searches all collections on your computer system for all types of media files: Clip Art, Photographs, Movies, and Sounds. To limit the search to a particular collection, select its name in the Search In drop-down list. To limit the search to just the Clip Art images, click the Results Should Be drop-down list box and then click the check boxes in front of Photographs, Movies, and Sounds to remove their check marks.

If you want to limit the search to just a particular type of graphics file, click the Expand button (+) in front of the Clip Art check box to display the list of all the types of Clip Art graphics files. Next, click the Clip Art check box to remove its checkmark as well as the checkmarks from all the types of graphics files. Then, click the check box for each type of graphics file to search for to put a checkmark back into its check box.

When you finish specifying where and what type of Clip Art files to find, click the Search button to have Excel search your Clip Art collections for the Clip Art. When Excel finishes searching, thumbnails of the images that meet your search criteria appear in the Results list box inside the Insert Clip Art Task Pane (similar to the one shown in Figure 2-13). You can then scroll through the images, looking for ones that you want to use.

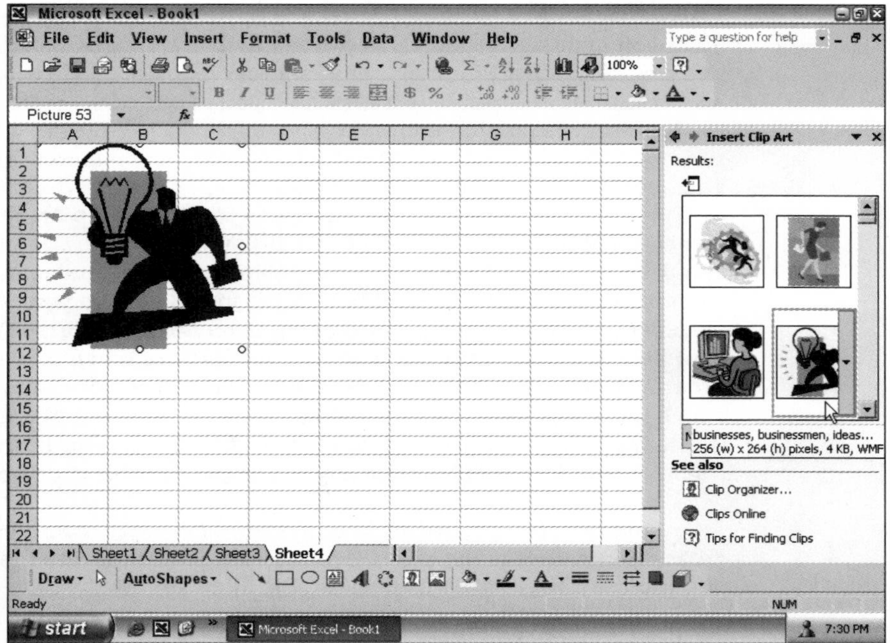

Figure 2-13: Inserting Clip art from the Results list box in the Insert Clip Art Task Pane.

When you locate an image that you want to use in the Results list box, click its thumbnail image to insert a full-size version of the Clip Art image into your worksheet. You can then move the image into its final position and use its sizing handles or rotation handle to size or rotate the image as needed.

Inserting pictures from files

In addition to the Clip Art images stored in collections on your computer system, you can also insert graphic files that you keep in your My Pictures folder on the hard disk (or another folder where you keep your artwork and digital photographs). To insert a picture into the worksheet, click the Insert Picture From File button on the Drawing toolbar (or choose Insert⇨Picture⇨From File on the Excel pull-down menus). This action opens the Insert Picture dialog box. This dialog box works just like the Open dialog box except that it's set to display only the graphics files that Excel can import, and it automatically looks in the My Pictures folder on your hard drive (which you can change by selecting another folder in the Look In drop-down list box).

After you locate the graphics file with the image that you want to insert in the worksheet, click its thumbnail in the Insert Picture dialog box and then click the Insert button to import it into the current worksheet. Excel then displays the image from the file you selected, along with the Picture toolbar, shown in Figure 2-14, in the current worksheet.

As with the other graphic objects that you work with, Excel places sizing handles around the perimeter with a rotation handle connected to the sizing handle in the middle at the top of the image. You can then reposition, resize, or rotate the image as needed.

You can also use the tools on the Picture toolbar (shown in Figure 2-14) to edit the photo. Among other things, these tools make it possible to heighten or lessen the brightness or contrast of the image, crop out unwanted areas around the edges, and compress the image so that it doesn't bulk up the size of your workbook (as only high resolution images can).

If you have a scanner or digital camera connected to your computer, you can use the Insert⇨Picture⇨From Scanner or Camera command on the Excel menu bar to bring a scanned image or digital photo that you've taken directly into your Excel worksheet.

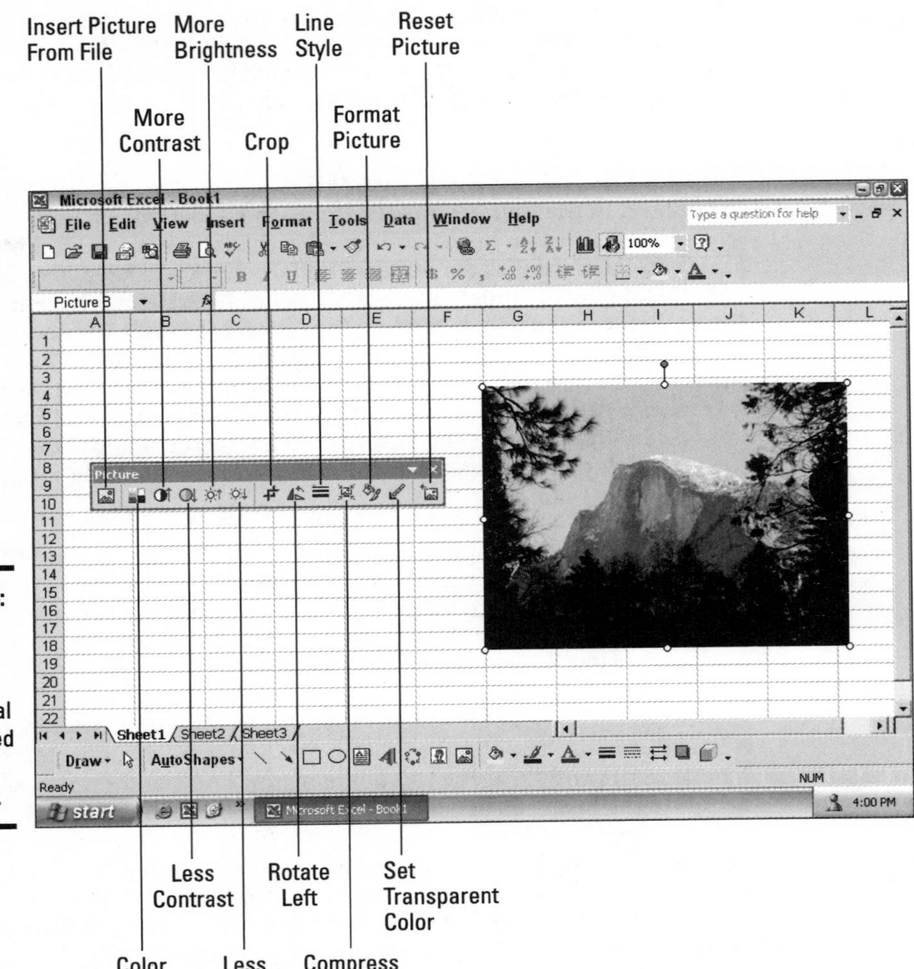

Figure 2-14: Using the Picture toolbar to edit a digital photo added to a worksheet.

Book VI

Data Management

Contents at a Glance

Chapter 1: Building and Maintaining Data Lists

In This Chapter

- **Understanding what goes into making a data list**
- **Adding data to a list using the data form**
- **Editing records in a data list**
- **Finding records in a data list**
- **Sorting data in a data list**
- **Subtotaling data in a data list**

In addition to its considerable computational abilities, Excel is also very accomplished at maintaining vast collections of related data in what are loosely referred to as *databases,* although the term *data list* is a little more accurate. This chapter covers all the basic procedures for creating and maintaining different types of data lists in the Excel worksheet.

This basic information includes how to design the basic data list and then create a data form that you can use to add new data to the list, as well as to edit existing data. This chapter also covers the procedures for sorting the data in a list, so that it's arranged the way you like to see the information and, for data lists that contain numerical data, how to subtotal and total the data. For information on how to find data in the data list and produce subsets of the list with just the data you need, refer to Book VI, Chapter 2.

Data List Basics

In Excel, a database or data list is a table of worksheet data that utilizes a special structure. Unlike the other types of data tables that you might create in Excel, a data list uses *only* column headings (technically known as *field names*) to identify the different kinds of items the data list tracks. Each column in the data list contains information for each item you track in the database, such as the client's company name or telephone number (technically known as a *field* of the data list). Each row in the data list contains complete information about each entity that you track in the data list, such as ABC Corporation or National Industries (technically known as a *record* of the data list).

After you've organized your data into a data list that follows this structure, you can then use a variety of commands on Excel's Data menu to maintain the data, as well as to reorder the information it contains. You can use the data form menu item to add new records, find and edit records, or to delete unwanted records from the data list. You can use the Data Sort menu item to rearrange the records in the data list by sorting one or more of its fields. In data lists with numerical fields, you can also use the Subtotals menu item to calculate subtotals and totals in the list when a certain field changes.

Designing the basic data list

All you have to do to start a new data list in a worksheet is to enter the names of the fields that you want to track in the top row of the worksheet and then enter the first record of data beneath. When entering the field names (as column headings), be sure each field name in the data list is unique and, whenever possible, keep the field name short. When naming fields, you can align the field name in the cell so that its text wraps to a new line by pressing Alt+Enter. Also, you should not use numbers or formulas that return values as field names. (You can, however, use formulas that return text, such as a formula which concatenates labels entered in different cells.)

When deciding on what fields you need to create, you need to think of how you'll be using the data that you store in your data list. For example, in a client data list, you split the client's name into separate first name, middle initial, and last name fields if you intend to use this information in generating form letters and mailing labels with your word processor. That way, you are able to address the person by his or her first name (as in *Dear Jane*) in the opening of the form letter you create, as well as by his or her full name and title (as in *Dr. Jane Jackson*) in the mailing label you generate.

Likewise, you split up the client's address into separate street address, city, state, and zip code fields when you intend to use the client data list in generating form letters, and you also want to be able to sort the records in descending order by zip code and/or send letters only to clients located in the states of New York, New Jersey, or Connecticut. By keeping discrete pieces of information in separate fields, you are assured that you will be able to use that field in finding particular records and retrieving information from the data list, such as finding all the records where the state is California or the zip code is between 94105 and 95101.

Figure 1-1 shows you a sample employee data list. This data list begins in row 1 of this worksheet, which contains the names for the ten fields in this data list (ID No through Profit Sharing). Note that employees' names are divided into separate First Name and Last Name fields in this list (columns B and C, respectively). Note too, that the first actual record of the data list is entered in row 2 of the worksheet, directly under the row with the field names. When entering your records for a new data list, you don't skip rows but keep entering each record one above the other going down successive rows of the worksheet.

When you're entering the row with the first data record, be sure to format all the cells the way you want the entries in that field to appear in all the subsequent data records in the data list. For example, if you have a salary field in the data list, and you want the salaries formatted with the Currency style number format without any decimal places, be sure to format the salary entry in the first record in this manner. That way all subsequent records will pick up that same formatting for the salary field when you enter them with Excel's data form.

Creating calculated fields

When creating a new data list, you can make full use of Excel's calculating capabilities by defining fields whose entries are returned by formula rather than entered manually. The sample employee list introduced in Figure 1-1 contains just such a calculated field (shown on the Formula bar) in cell I2 that contains the first entry in the Years of Service field.

The original formula for calculating years of service in cell I2 is as follows:

```
=YEAR(TODAY())-YEAR(H2)
```

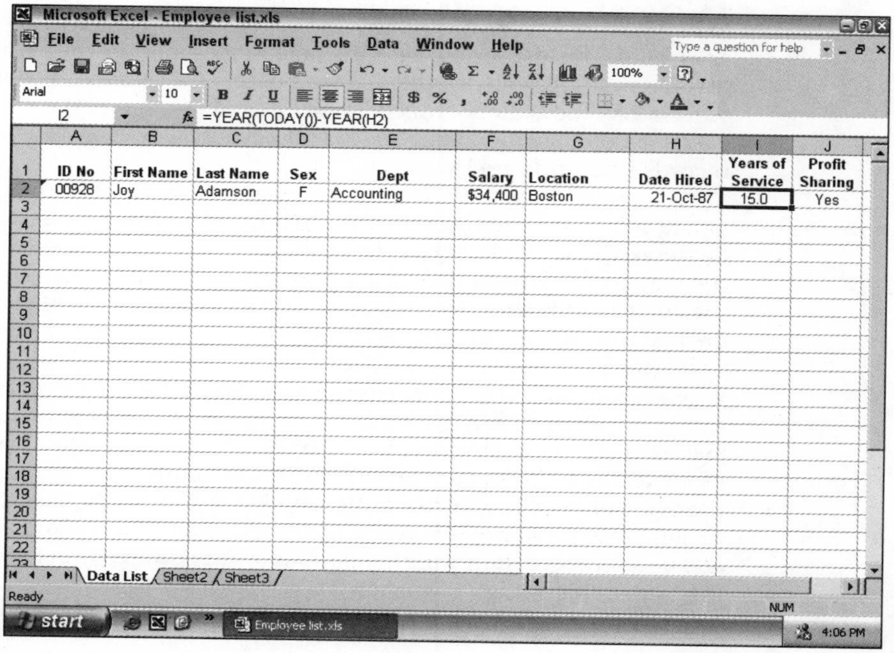

Figure 1-1: Creating an employee data list with the row of field names and first data record.

This formula uses the YEAR date function to subtract the serial number of the year in which the employee was hired (entered into the Date Hired field) in cell H2 from the serial number of the current year (returned by the TODAY function). After entering and formatting this original formula in cell H2, the data form picks up this formula and automatically copies it and applies it to any new record you add to the data list.

Modifying the structure of the data list

You may find after creating your data list that you need to modify its structure by adding or deleting some fields. To add a new field, you select the column (by clicking the column letter) where you want the field inserted, and then use the Insert⇨Column command on the Excel Menu bar to insert a new column. Enter the field name in the top row and then enter the entries for that field for each record in the data list. To delete an entire field from the data list (field name and entries), select its column, and then choose Edit⇨Delete from the Excel Menu bar.

To avoid losing data or disturbing the layout of data located outside of the data list caused by adding or deleting its fields, don't place any data tables or other entries in rows beneath the last row of data list. In other words, always keep the rows used by the columns of the data list free for new records by locating all related data in columns to the right of the last field.

Using the data form

After entering the top row with the field names and the next row with the first data record, you can then use the data form that Excel generates when you choose the Data⇨Form command to add the rest of the records. You can also then use the data form to edit entries in or even delete entire records from the data list.

Figure 1-2 shows you the data form that Excel creates for the sample Employee data list shown earlier in Figure 1-1. As you can see in this figure, the data form consists of a dialog box (whose title bar contains the name of the current worksheet file) that contains a vertical listing of each field defined for the data list.

When you choose the Data⇨Form command to display the data form, Excel automatically displays the field entries for the first record entered (which just happens to be the only record in the list at this point). On the right side of the dialog box, the data form indicates the current record number out of the total number of records in the data list (1 of 1 in this case). This part of the form also contains a number of command buttons that enable you to add a new record, find a particular record for editing, or delete a record from the data list.

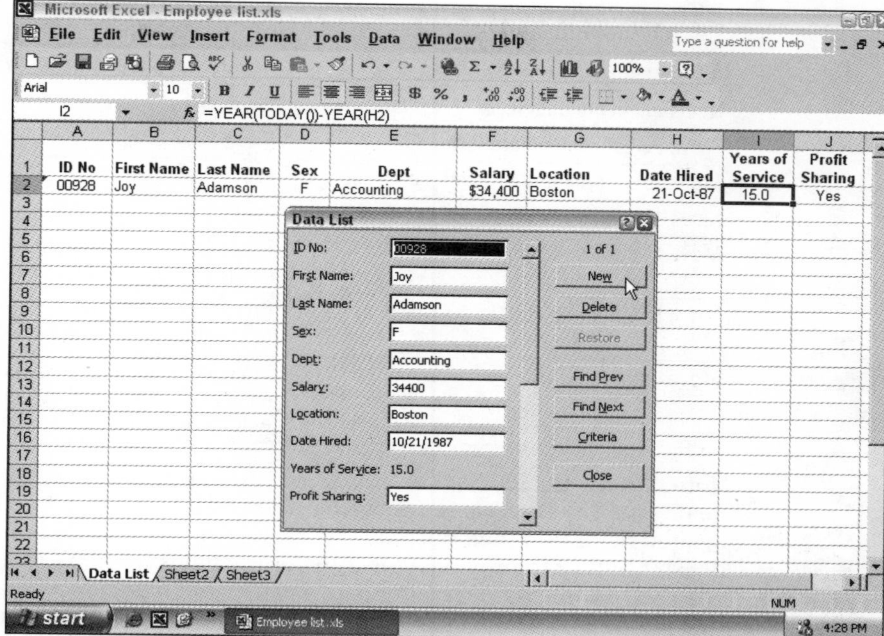

Figure 1-2: Opening the data form in the new data list to add a new record.

When the data form is displayed in the active document, you can use the scroll bar to the right of the fields to move through the records in the data list, or you can use various direction keys. Table 1-1 summarizes the use of the scroll bar and these keys. For example, to move to the next record in the data list, you can press the ↓ or Enter key or click the scroll arrow at the bottom of the scroll bar. To move to the previous record in the data list (assuming that there's more than one), you can press the ↑ key or Shift+Enter key or click the scroll arrow at the top of the scroll bar. To select a field in the current record for editing, you can click that field's text box or press the Tab (next field) or Shift+Tab key (previous field) until you select the field (and its current entry).

Table 1-1 Techniques for Navigating the Data Form

Movement	*Keystrokes or Scroll Bar Technique*
Next record, same field in the data list	Press ↓ or Enter key, click the downward-pointing scroll arrow, or click the Find Next command button.
Previous record, same field in the data list	Press ↑ or Shift+Enter key, click the upward-pointing scroll arrow, or click the Find Prev command button.

(continued)

Table 1-1 ***(continued)***

Movement	*Keystrokes or Scroll Bar Technique*
Next field in the data form	Press Tab.
Previous field in the data form	Press Shift+Tab.
Move 10 records forward in the data list	Press PgDn.
Move 10 records backward in the data list	Press PgUp.
Move to the first record in the data list	Press Ctrl+↑ or Ctrl+PgUp, or drag the scroll box to the top of the scroll bar.
Move to the last record in the data list	Press Ctrl+↓ or Ctrl+PgDn, or drag the scroll box to the bottom of the scroll bar.
Move within a field	Press ← or → to move one character at a time, press Home to move to the first character and End to move to the last character.

Note that the data form does not allow you to select and edit calculated fields (such as the Years of Service field shown in Figure 1-2). Although calculated fields and their current entries are listed in the data form, the form doesn't bother to provide a text box for the fields for making editing changes. To modify the contents of a calculated field, you would need to modify the original formula in the appropriate field in the first record and recopy the edited formula down to the other existing records in the list.

Of course, you don't have to use the data form to add records to your data list: You can just add the data to the cells of new rows at the end of the list, making entries as you would in any regular table of data. When you add data directly in the cells of the worksheet, just keep in mind that it's up to you to keep the new entries formatted in the same manner as the other existing records.

Adding new records with the data form

To add a new record to the data list, you can either move to the end of the data list (by dragging the scroll box to the very bottom of the scroll bar or by pressing Ctrl+↓ or Ctrl+PgDn) or simply click the New command button. Any way you do it, Excel displays a blank data form (marked New Record at the right side the dialog box), which you can then fill out. After entering the information for a field, press the Tab key to advance to the next field in the record (be careful not to press the Enter key because this inserts the new record into the data list).

When you're making an entry in a new field, you can copy the entry from the same field in the previous record into the current field by pressing Ctrl+" (double quotation mark). You can use this keystroke shortcut, for example, to carry forward entries in the text box for the State field when you are entering a series or records that all use the same state.

When you've entered all the information you have for the new record, press the ↓ or Enter key or click the New button again. Excel then inserts the new record as the last record in the data list and displays a blank data form where you can enter the next record. When you finish adding records to the data list, press the Esc key or click the Close button to close the data form dialog box.

Remember that some fields require you to enter their numbers as text rather than as values. For example, zip codes should be entered in a zip code field as labels rather than values, so that Excel will retain leading zeros, such as 00210, as should part numbers or other identification numbers that use leading zeros. To enter a value as text, you must preface the field entry with an apostrophe (') as in '00210 or '00105. Note that Excel does not copy this very important punctuation from the previous entry when you press Ctrl+" to copy into the current field — you must remember to enter it manually.

Editing records in the data form

The data form makes it easy to edit records in your data list. In a smaller data list, you can use the navigation keys or the scroll bar in the data form to locate the record that requires editing. In a larger data list, you can use the Criteria command button to quickly locate the record you need to change, as described in the next section.

When you've displayed the data form for the record that needs editing, you can then perform your editing changes by selecting the text boxes of the necessary fields and making your changes, just as you would edit the entry in its cell in the worksheet.

Finding records with the data form

You can use the Criteria button in the data form to find the records in your data list that you need to edit (or delete as described in the next section). When you click the Criteria button in the data form, Excel clears all the field text boxes so that you can enter the criteria to search for. For example, assume that you need to edit Sherry Caulfield's profit sharing status. You don't have her paperwork in front of you, so you can't look up her employee number. You do know, however, that she works in the Boston office and, although you don't remember exactly how she spells her last name, you do know that it begins with a C instead of a K.

To locate her record, you can at least narrow the search down to all the records where the Location field contains Boston and the employee's Last Name begins with the letter C (see Figure 1-3). To do this, you would open the data form for the Employee data list, click the Criteria command button, and then enter the following in the Last Name field:

```
C*
```

Then, in the Location field you enter

```
Boston
```

When entering the criteria for locating matching records in the data form, you can use question mark (?) and the asterisk (*) wildcard characters, just as you do when using Excel Find feature to locate cells with particular entries. (See Book II, Chapter 3 for a review of using these wildcard characters.)

When you click the Find Next button or press the Enter key, Excel locates the first record in the data list where the last name begins with the letter C and the location is Boston. This is William Cobb's record, as shown in Figure 1-4. Then, to locate the next record that matches your criteria, you click the Find Next button or press Enter, which brings you to Sherry Caulfield's record, as shown in Figure 1-5. Having located Sherry's record, you can then change her profit sharing status by selecting the Profit Sharing text box and replacing No with Yes. Excel inserts the editing change that you make in the record's data form into the data list itself as soon as you close the data form dialog box by clicking the Close button.

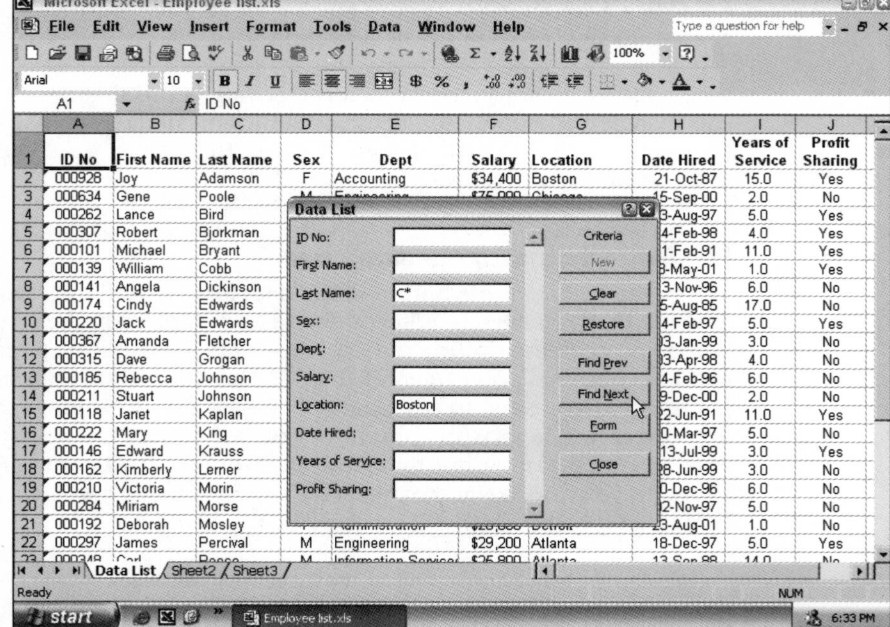

Figure 1-3: Entering the criteria to find records where Last Name starts with C and Location is Boston.

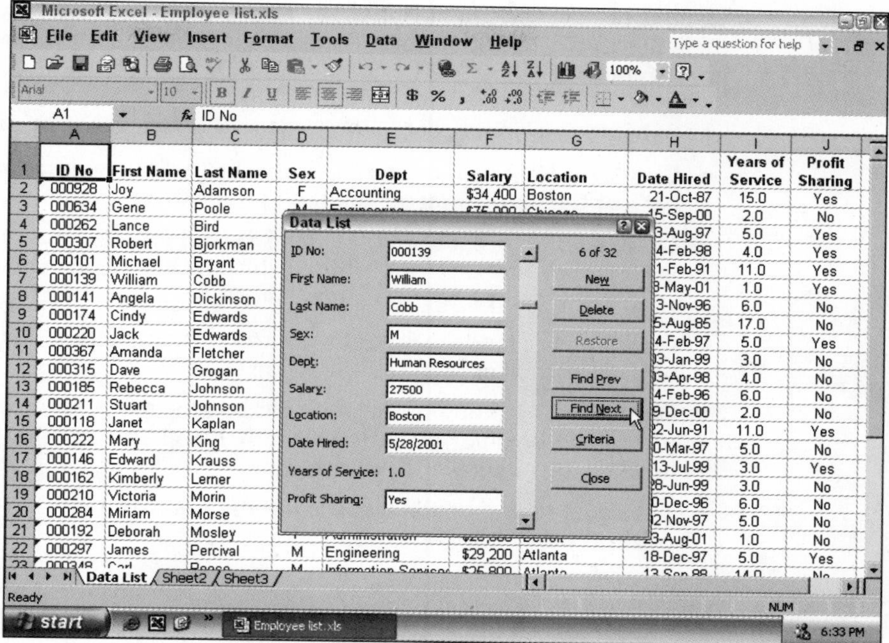

Figure 1-4: Locating the first matching record for William Cobb.

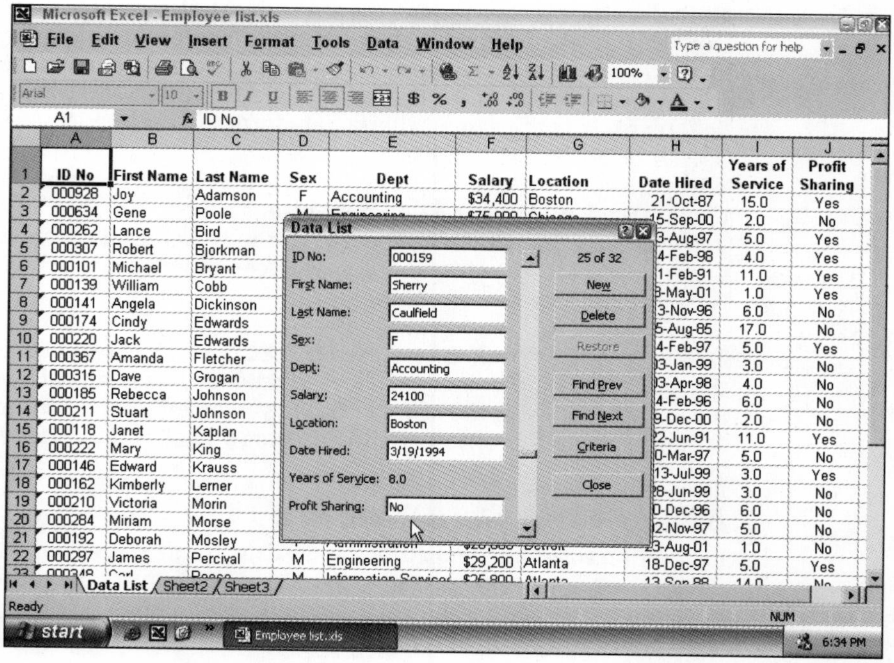

Figure 1-5: Locating the next matching record for Sherry Caulfield.

When using the Criteria button in the data form to find records, you can use the following logical operators when entering search criteria in fields that use numbers or dates:

- **Equal to (=):** Finds records the same as the text, value, or date you enter.
- **Greater than (>):** Finds records after the text characters (in the alphabet), or the date, or larger than the value you enter.
- **Greater than or equal to (>=):** Finds records the same as the text characters, date, or value you enter or after the characters (in the alphabet), after the date, or larger than the value.
- **Less than (<):** Finds records before the text characters (in the alphabet) or date or smaller than the value you enter.
- **Less than or equal to (<=):** Finds records the same as the text characters, date, or value you enter or before the characters (in the alphabet), or the date, or smaller than the value.
- **Not equal to (<>):** Finds records not the same as the text, value, or date you enter.

For example, to find all the records where the employee's annual salary is $50,000, you can enter =50000 or simply 50000 in the Salary field text box. However, to find all the records for employees whose annual salaries are less than or equal to $35,000, you enter <=35000 in the Salary field text box. To find all the records for employees with salaries greater than $45,000, you would enter >45000 in the Salary field text box instead. If you wanted to find all of the records where the employees are female *and* make more than $35,000, you would enter F in the Sex field text box and >35000 in the Salary field text box in the same Criteria data form.

When specifying search criteria that fit a number of records, you may have to click the Find Next or Find Prev buttons several times to locate the record you want to work with. If no record fits the search criteria you enter in the Criteria data form, your computer will beep at you when you click the Find Next or Find Prev button.

To change your search criteria, select the appropriate text box(es) and delete the old criteria and then enter the new criteria. To switch back to the current record without using the search criteria you enter, click the Form button (this button replaces the Criteria button as soon you click the Criteria button).

Deleting records with the data form

In addition to adding and editing records with the data from, you can also delete them. To delete a record, you simply display its data form and then click the Delete button. Be very careful when deleting records, however, as you cannot restore the records you delete with Excel's Undo feature. For this reason, Excel displays an alert dialog box whenever you click the Delete button, indicating that the record displayed in the data form is about to be permanently deleted. To continue and remove the record, you need to click OK or press Enter. To save the current record, press the Esc key or click the Cancel button instead.

Keep in mind that although you can use the Criteria data form to locate a group of records that you want to delete, you can only remove one record at a time with the Delete button.

Sorting Data

Excel's Data⇨Sort command makes it easy to rearrange the records or even the fields in your data list. You sort the records in your data list by sorting by rows, while you sort the fields in the data list by sorting by columns.

In sorting, you can specify either ascending or descending sort order for your data. When you specify ascending order (which is the default), Excel arranges text in A-to-Z order and values from smallest to largest. When you specify descending order, Excel reverses this order and arranges text in Z-to-A order and values range from largest to smallest. When sorting on a date field, keep in mind that ascending order puts the records in least-recent-to-most-recent date order, while descending order gives you the records in most-recent-to-least-recent date order.

When you choose the ascending sort order for a field that contains many different kinds of entries, Excel places numbers (from smallest to largest) before text (in alphabetical order) followed by Logical values (TRUE and FALSE), Error values, and, finally, blank cells. When you're using the descending sort order, the program uses the same general arrangement for the different types of entries, but numbers go from largest to smallest, text runs from Z to A, and the FALSE logical value precedes the TRUE logical value.

To sort your data, Excel uses *sorting keys* to determine how the records or fields should be reordered in the data list. When sorting records, you indicate by cell address which field (that is, column) contains the first or *primary* sorting key. When sorting fields, you indicate which record (row) contains the primary sorting key. Excel then applies the selected sort (ascending or descending) to the data in the key field or row to determine how the records or fields will be reordered during sorting.

When a key field contains duplicates entries, Excel simply lists these records in the order in which they were entered in the data list. To indicate how Excel should order records with duplicates in the primary key, you define a secondary key. For example, if, when organizing the data list in alphabetical order by the Last Name field, you have several records where the last name is Smith, you can have Excel order the Smiths' records in alphabetical order by first name by defining the First Name field as the secondary key. If the secondary key contains duplicates (let's say you have two John Smiths in your company), you can define a third key field (the Middle Name field, if your data list has one) that determines how the duplicate John Smith records are arranged when the data list is sorted.

Keep in mind that although sorting is most often applied to rearranging and maintaining data list records and fields, you can use the Data⇨Sort command to reorder data in any worksheet table, whether or not the table follows the strict data list structure.

Sorting the records in a data list

To sort the records in your data list with the Data⇨Sort command, you follow these steps:

1. **Position the cell pointer somewhere in one of the cells in the data list.**

   As long as the cell pointer is any cell in the data list, Excel automatically selects all the records in the list when you perform the next step. Note that you can manually adjust this range, should you ever want to sort less than all the records in the list.

2. **Choose Data⇨Sort on the Excel Menu bar.**

   Excel selects all the data in the list (excluding the row of field names at the top) and opens the Sort dialog box, similar to the one shown in Figure 1-6. If your data list doesn't have a row of field names at the top and you want to include it in the sort, you need to click the No Header Row radio button near the bottom of the Sort dialog box.

3. **Click the name of the field you want used as the primary key in sorting the records of the data list in the Sort By drop-down list.**

   By default, Excel selects the Ascending radio button for the all sorting keys. If you want to sort the records in descending order using the primary key, you must click the Descending radio button to the right of the Sort By combo box.

   If the primary key field contains duplicates, and you want to specify how these records are to be sorted, you need to define that field as the secondary sorting key by performing Step 4.

4. **(Optional) Click the first Then By combo box and then click the name of the field to sort by in the case of duplicates in the primary key.**

   To sort the records in descending order using the secondary key, you need to click the Descending radio button to the right of the first Then By drop-down list box.

   If the secondary key field contains duplicates, and you want to specify how these records are to be sorted, you need to define a tertiary sorting key in the second Then By combo box.

5. **(Optional) Click the second Then By combo box and then click the name of the field to sort by in the case of duplicates in the primary and secondary sorting keys.**

   To sort these records in descending order using the tertiary key, be sure to click the Descending radio button to the right of the second Then By combo box.

6. **When you finish defining all of the keys you need to use in sorting the records in your data list, click the OK button or press Enter to perform the sort.**

If, when Excel finishes rearranging the records, you find that you sorted the data list using the wrong key fields, click Edit➪Undo Sort command on Excel Menu bar or press Crl+Z to restore the data list records to their previous order.

By default, when you perform a sort operation, Excel assumes that you're sorting a data list that has a header row (with the field names) that is not to be reordered with the rest of the records in doing the sort. You can, however, use the Sort feature to sort a cell selection that doesn't have such a header row. In that case, you need to specify the sorting keys by column letter, and you need to be sure to select the No Header Row radio button in the Sort dialog box.

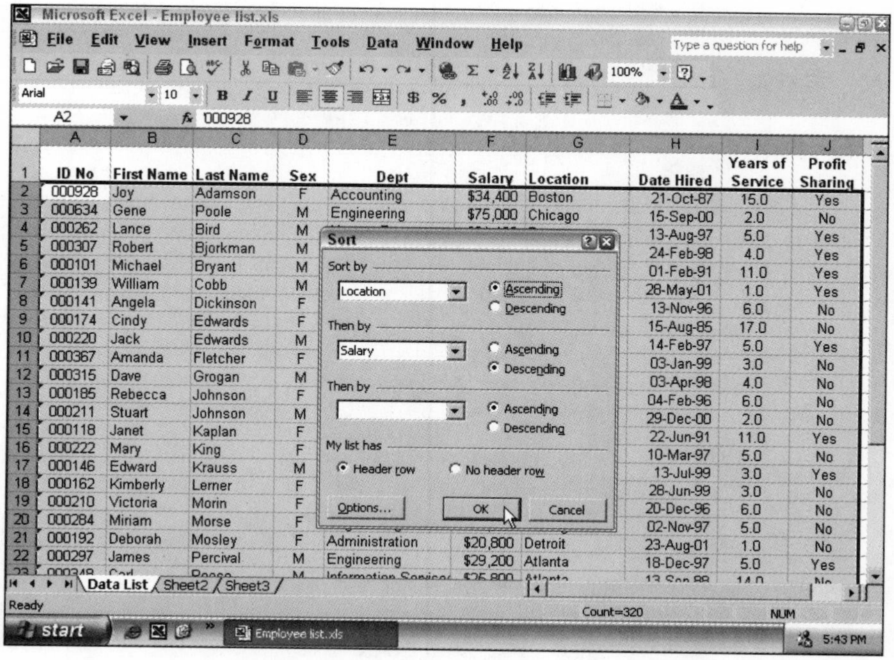

Figure 1-6: Defining the sorting keys in the Sort dialog box.

Also, the Sort dialog box contains an Options button that, when clicked, opens a Sort Options dialog box, which contains options for doing a case-sensitive sort on fields that contain text. This dialog box also contains options for changing the orientation of the sort from the normal top-to-bottom order to left-to-right order when you want to sort columns in a list.

Figure 1-7 illustrates sorting the employee data list first in ascending order by location and then in descending order by salary. For this sort, the Location field is designated as the primary key and the Salary field as the secondary key in the sort. Also, to have the records within each location sorted from highest to lowest salary, I chose the Descending radio button to the right of the first Then By combo box. Note in Figure 1-7 how the records are now organized first in ascending order by city listed in the Location field (Atlanta, Boston, Chicago, and so on) and within each city in descending order by Salary (38,900, 32,200, 29,200, and so on).

Keep in mind that you can use the Sort Ascending Tool (the one with A above Z) or the Sort Descending Tool (the one with Z above A) on the Standard toolbar to sort records in the data list, using any single field in the list as the sorting key. To sort the data list using these buttons, position the cell pointer somewhere in the field on which the records are to be sorted and then click the Sort Ascending Tool or Sort Descending Tool (depending upon which order you want to use).

	ID No	First Name	Last Name	Sex	Dept	Salary	Location	Date Hired	Years of Service	Profit Sharing
2	000247	Elaine	Savage	F	Engineering	$38,900	Atlanta	27-May-99	3.0	No
3	000220	Jack	Edwards	M	Engineering	$32,200	Atlanta	14-Feb-97	5.0	Yes
4	000297	James	Percival	M	Engineering	$29,200	Atlanta	18-Dec-97	5.0	Yes
5	000190	Elizabeth	Santos	F	Information Services	$27,200	Atlanta	17-Jul-96	6.0	Yes
6	000348	Carl	Reese	M	Information Services	$25,800	Atlanta	13-Sep-88	14.0	No
7	000185	Rebecca	Johnson	F	Human Resources	$50,200	Boston	04-Feb-96	6.0	No
8	000928	Joy	Adamson	F	Accounting	$34,400	Boston	21-Oct-87	15.0	Yes
9	000118	Janet	Kaplan	F	Engineering	$34,000	Boston	22-Jun-91	11.0	Yes
10	000139	William	Cobb	M	Human Resources	$27,500	Boston	28-May-01	1.0	Yes
11	000367	Amanda	Fletcher	F	Human Resources	$26,500	Boston	03-Jan-99	3.0	No
12	000159	Sherry	Caulfield	F	Accounting	$24,100	Boston	19-Mar-94	8.0	No
13	000262	Lance	Bird	M	Human Resources	$21,100	Boston	13-Aug-97	5.0	Yes
14	000146	Edward	Krauss	M	Administration	$86,200	Chicago	13-Jul-99	3.0	Yes
15	000634	Gene	Poole	M	Engineering	$75,000	Chicago	15-Sep-00	2.0	No
16	000162	Kimberly	Lerner	F	Human Resources	$34,900	Chicago	28-Jun-99	3.0	No
17	000324	George	Tallan	M	Human Resources	$29,700	Chicago	20-May-99	3.0	No
18	000284	Miriam	Morse	F	Engineering	$29,600	Chicago	02-Nov-97	5.0	No
19	000307	Robert	Bjorkman	M	Engineering	$25,000	Chicago	24-Feb-98	4.0	Yes
20	000222	Mary	King	F	Accounting	$38,000	Detroit	10-Mar-97	5.0	No
21	000361	Linda	Robinson	F	Engineering	$37,000	Detroit	11-Nov-98	4.0	No
22	000226	Adam	Rosenzweig	M	Accounting	$29,000	Detroit	01-Mar-01	1.0	No

Figure 1-7: Employee data list sorted by location and salary.

Sorting on more than three fields

Sometimes, you may need to sort on more than three fields (the maximum you can define in one sorting operation). For example, suppose you are working with a personnel data list like the one shown in Figure 1-8, and you want to organize the records in alphabetical order, first by department, then by supervisor, and finally by last name, first name, and middle name. To sort the records in this data list by these five fields, you have to perform two sorting operations.

In the first sorting operation, you define the Last Name field as the primary key, the First Name field as the secondary key, and the Middle Name field as the tertiary key. In the second sort, you define the Department field as the primary key and the Supervisor field as the secondary key. Figure 1-9 shows you the personnel data list after performing the second sorting operation. As you can see after performing the second sort operation, the records are now arranged in ascending order by department, then by supervisor within department, and finally by the last name, first name, and middle name under each supervisor.

SSN	Last Name	First Name	Middle Name	Department	Supervisor	Title	Salary
307-28-7613	Forbes	Janet	Ellen	Personnel	Williams	Director	53,500
600-44-8346	Grey	Eleanor	Marie	Marketing	Smith	Director	47,000
592-30-5112	Harris	Daniel	Michael	Administration	Johnson	VP Acct	62,500
359-45-8215	Jones	Allan	Jay	Sales	Jones	Acct Exec	31,000
677-94-0314	Jones	Ann	Marie	Sales	Johnson	Acct Exec	32,100
644-77-3598	Jones	Arthur	Clark	Sales	Johnson	Manager	47,500
450-34-8952	Jones	Sandy	Susan	Sales	Jones	Acct Exec	32,500
120-39-1157	Jones	Suzanne	Elizabeth	Sales	Jones	Acct Exec	30,000
561-54-2013	Manley	Philip	Robert	Accounting	Schnyder	Accountai	47,500
361-42-9002	Philips	Jon	Robert	Sales	Jones	Acct Exec	35,500
230-56-9512	Schnyder	Jay	Alan	Accounting	Johnson	Manager	48,500
430-47-9284	Smith	Andy	Edward	Administration	Gearing	Director	39,500
305-66-5214	Smith	Jeff	Michael	Personnel	Williams	VP Mktg	50,000
965-01-3422	Smith	Laura	Jean	Personnel	Williams	Manager	56,000
458-21-7791	Smith	William	Dennis	Administration	Johnson	VP Admn	62,500
360-22-0978	Smith	William	Mathew	Administration	Johnson	VP Sales	60,000
253-65-2234	Williams	Amy	Ann	Marketing	Smith	Manager	33,400
625-78-1364	Williams	Michael	Richard	Marketing	Johnson	Director	64,500

Figure 1-8: Personnel data list before sorting.

	A	B	C	D	E	F	G	H
1	SSN	Last Name	First Name	Middle Name	Department	Supervisor	Title	Salary
2	230-56-9512	Schnyder	Jay	Alan	Accounting	Johnson	Manager	48,500
3	561-54-2013	Manley	Philip	Robert	Accounting	Schnyder	Accountai	47,500
4	430-47-9284	Smith	Andy	Edward	Administration	Gearing	Director	39,500
5	592-30-5112	Harris	Daniel	Michael	Administration	Johnson	VP Acct	62,500
6	458-21-7791	Smith	William	Dennis	Administration	Johnson	VP Admn	62,500
7	360-22-0978	Smith	William	Mathew	Administration	Johnson	VP Sales	60,000
8	625-78-1364	Williams	Michael	Richard	Marketing	Johnson	Director	64,500
9	600-44-8346	Grey	Eleanor	Marie	Marketing	Smith	Director	47,000
10	253-65-2234	Williams	Amy	Ann	Marketing	Smith	Manager	33,400
11	307-28-7613	Forbes	Janet	Ellen	Personnel	Williams	Director	53,500
12	305-66-5214	Smith	Jeff	Michael	Personnel	Williams	VP Mktg	50,000
13	965-01-3422	Smith	Laura	Jean	Personnel	Williams	Manager	56,000
14	677-94-0314	Jones	Ann	Marie	Sales	Johnson	Acct Exec	32,100
15	644-77-3598	Jones	Arthur	Clark	Sales	Johnson	Manager	47,500
16	359-45-8215	Jones	Allan	Jay	Sales	Jones	Acct Exec	31,000
17	450-34-8952	Jones	Sandy	Susan	Sales	Jones	Acct Exec	32,500
18	120-39-1157	Jones	Suzanne	Elizabeth	Sales	Jones	Acct Exec	30,000
19	361-42-9002	Philips	Jon	Robert	Sales	Jones	Acct Exec	35,500

Figure 1-9: Personnel data list after sorting by department, supervisor, last, first, and middle name.

When sorting data list records on more than three key fields, you need to determine the order of the key fields from most general to most specific. In the preceding example, this arrangement would be as follows:

```
Department, Supervisor, Last Name, First Name, Middle Name
```

After arranging the fields in this manner, you then perform your first sort operation with the more specific key fields at the end of the list. In this example, these fields include the following fields as the primary, secondary, and tertiary keys:

```
Last Name, First Name, Middle Name
```

Next, you perform your second sorting operation with the more general key fields at the beginning of the list. In this example, the primary and secondary fields are

```
Department, Supervisor
```

Sorting the fields of a data list

You can use Excel's column sorting capability to change the order of the fields in a data list without having to resort to cutting and pasting various columns. When you sort the fields in a data list, you add a row at the top of the list that you define as the primary sorting key. The cells in this row contain numbers (from 1 to the number of the last field in the data list) that indicate the new order of the fields.

Figures 1-10 and 1-11 illustrate how you can use column sorting to modify the field order of a data list in the sample personnel data list. In Figure 1-10, I inserted a new row (row 1) above the row with the field names for this data list. As you can see, the cells in this row contain numbers that indicate the new field order. After the fields are sorted using the values in this row, the ID No field remains first (indicated by 1), the First Department field becomes the second (2), Supervisor field the third (3), followed by First Name (4), Middle Name (5), Last Name (6), Title (7), and Salary (8).

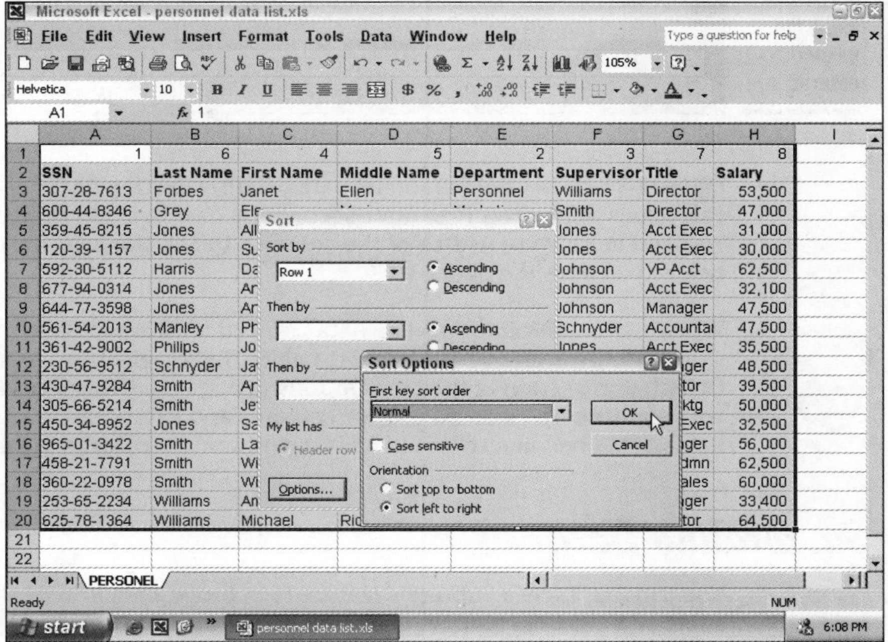

Figure 1-10: Personnel data list before sorting the columns.

	A	B	C	D	E	F	G	H
1	1	2	3	4	5	6	7	8
2	**SSN**	**Departmen**	**Supervisor**	**First Name**	**Middle Name**	**Last Name**	**Title**	**Salary**
3	307-28-7613	Personnel	Williams	Janet	Ellen	Forbes	Director	53,500
4	600-44-8346	Marketing	Smith	Eleanor	Marie	Grey	Director	47,000
5	359-45-8215	Sales	Jones	Allan	Jay	Jones	Acct Exec	31,000
6	120-39-1157	Sales	Jones	Suzanne	Elizabeth	Jones	Acct Exec	30,000
7	592-30-5112	Administrati	Johnson	Daniel	Michael	Harris	VP Acct	62,500
8	677-94-0314	Sales	Johnson	Ann	Marie	Jones	Acct Exec	32,100
9	644-77-3598	Sales	Johnson	Arthur	Clark	Jones	Manager	47,500
10	561-54-2013	Accounting	Schnyder	Philip	Robert	Manley	Accountai	47,500
11	361-42-9002	Sales	Jones	Jon	Robert	Philips	Acct Exec	35,500
12	230-56-9512	Accounting	Johnson	Jay	Alan	Schnyder	Manager	48,500
13	430-47-9284	Administrati	Gearing	Andy	Edward	Smith	Director	39,500
14	305-66-5214	Personnel	Williams	Jeff	Michael	Smith	VP Mktg	50,000
15	450-34-8952	Sales	Jones	Sandy	Susan	Jones	Acct Exec	32,500
16	965-01-3422	Personnel	Williams	Laura	Jean	Smith	Manager	56,000
17	458-21-7791	Administrati	Johnson	William	Dennis	Smith	VP Admn	62,500
18	360-22-0978	Administrati	Johnson	William	Mathew	Smith	VP Sales	60,000
19	253-65-2234	Marketing	Smith	Amy	Ann	Williams	Manager	33,400
20	625-78-1364	Marketing	Johnson	Michael	Richard	Williams	Director	64,500

Figure 1-11: Personnel data list after sorting the columns using the values entered in.

Figure 1-11 shows the personnel data list after sorting its fields according to the values in the first row. After sorting the data list, you then delete this row and modify the widths of the columns to suit the new arrangement before you save the data list.

When sorting the columns in a data list, you must remember to click the Options button and select the Sort Left to Right radio button in the Orientation section of the Sort Options dialog box. Otherwise, Excel will sort your records instead of your columns and in the process, the row of field names become sorted in with the other data records in your list!

Subtotaling Data

You can use Excel's Subtotals feature to subtotal data in a sorted list. To subtotal a data list, you first sort the list on the field for which you want the subtotals, and then you designate the field that contains the values you want summed — these don't have to be the same fields in the data list.

When you use the Subtotals feature, you aren't restricted to having the values in the designated field added together with the SUM function. You can instead have Excel return the number of entries with the COUNT function, the average of the entries with the AVERAGE function, the highest entry with the MAXIMUM function, the lowest entry with the MINIMUM function, or even the product of the entries with the PRODUCT function.

Figures 1-12 and 1-13 illustrate how easy it is to use the Subtotals feature to obtain totals in a data list. In Figure 1-12, I sorted the sample Employee data list first by the Department field in ascending order and then by the Salary field in descending order. I then chose the Data⇨Subtotals command on the Excel Menu bar to open the Subtotal dialog box shown in Figure 1-12.

Here, I selected the Dept field as the field for which the subtotals are to be calculated in the At Each Change In drop-down list box, Sum as the function to use in the Use Function drop-down list box, and the Salary check box as the field whose values are to be summed in the Add Subtotal To list box.

Figure 1-13 shows the results I obtained after clicking OK in the Subtotal dialog box. Here, you see the bottom of the data list showing the salary subtotals for the Engineering, Human Resources, and Information Services along with the grand total of the salaries for all the departments. The grand total is displayed at the bottom of the data list because I left the Summary Below Data check box selected in the Subtotal dialog box — if I hadn't wanted a grand total, I would have removed the check mark from this check box.

As you can see in Figure 1-13, when you use the Data⇨Subtotals command, Excel outlines the data at the same time that it adds the rows with the departmental salary totals and the grand total. This means that you can collapse the data list down to just its departmental subtotal rows or even just the grand total row simply by collapsing the outline down to the second or first level. (Remember that you can toggle between showing and hiding the outline symbols at the left edge of the data list by pressing Ctrl+8.)

In a large data list, you may want Excel to put in page breaks every time there is a change (often referred to as a *break*) in the data in the field on which the list is being subtotaled (that is, the field designated in the At Each Change In drop-down list box). To do this, you simply click the Page Break between Groups check box in the Subtotal dialog box to put a checkmark in it before you click OK to subtotal the list.

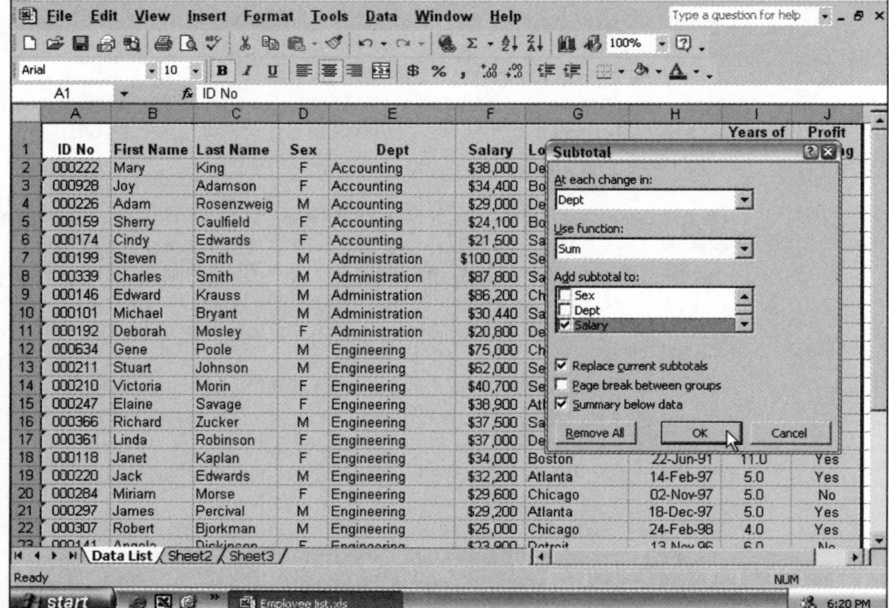

Figure 1-12: Using the Subtotal dialog box to subtotal the salaries for each department.

Microsoft Excel - Employee list.xls

	ID No	First Name	Last Name	Sex	Dept	Salary	Location	Date Hired
19	000361	Linda	Robinson	F	Engineering	$37,000	Detroit	11-Nov-98
20	000118	Janet	Kaplan	F	Engineering	$34,000	Boston	22-Jun-91
21	000220	Jack	Edwards	M	Engineering	$32,200	Atlanta	14-Feb-97
22	000284	Miriam	Morse	F	Engineering	$29,600	Chicago	02-Nov-97
23	000297	James	Percival	M	Engineering	$29,200	Atlanta	18-Dec-97
24	000307	Robert	Bjorkman	M	Engineering	$25,000	Chicago	24-Feb-98
25	000141	Angela	Dickinson	F	Engineering	$23,900	Detroit	13-Nov-96
26					**Engineering Total**	$465,000		
27	000185	Rebecca	Johnson	F	Human Resources	$50,200	Boston	04-Feb-96
28	000162	Kimberly	Lerner	F	Human Resources	$34,900	Chicago	28-Jun-99
29	000324	George	Tallan	M	Human Resources	$29,700	Chicago	20-May-99
30	000139	William	Cobb	M	Human Resources	$27,500	Boston	28-May-01
31	000367	Amanda	Fletcher	F	Human Resources	$26,500	Boston	03-Jan-99
32	000262	Lance	Bird	M	Human Resources	$21,100	Boston	13-Aug-97
33					**Human Resources Total**	$189,900		
34	000603	Sarah	Michaels	F	Information Services	$57,500	Santa Rosa	23-Mar-02
35	000315	Dave	Grogan	M	Information Services	$47,500	Seattle	03-Apr-98
36	000190	Elizabeth	Santos	F	Information Services	$27,200	Atlanta	17-Jul-96
37	000348	Carl	Reese	M	Information Services	$25,800	Atlanta	13-Sep-88
38					**Information Services Tota**	$158,000		
39					**Grand Total**	$1,285,140		

Figure 1-13: Bottom of the data list showing the subtotals and grand total for department salaries.

Chapter 2: Filtering and Querying a Data List

In This Chapter

- **Understanding how filtering and querying a data list works**
- **Using AutoFilter to filter out unwanted data**
- **Filtering a list with custom criteria**
- **Using Database functions to compute statistics from records that match your filter criteria**
- **Creating queries to import data from an external database**

It's one thing to set up a data list and load it with tons of data, and it's quite another to get just the information that you need out of the list. How you go about extracting the data that you consider to be important is the subject of this chapter. The procedure for specifying the data that you want displayed in an Excel data list is called *filtering* the data list or database. The procedure for extracting only the data that you want from the database or data list is called *querying* the database.

In addition to filtering and querying the data in your list, this chapter explains how you can use Excel's Database functions to perform calculations on particular numerical fields for only the records that meet the criteria that you specify. These calculations can include getting totals (DSUM), averages (DAVERAGE), the count of the records (DCOUNT and DCOUNTA), and the like.

Finally, this chapter introduces you to Excel's Microsoft Query feature that enables you to extract data from external databases and bring it into Excel, where you can work with the data in a more familiar setting. These external databases can be kept in other Windows database programs, such as Microsoft Access or dBASE, or in even more sophisticated, non-Windows database management systems, such as IBM's dB2 or Oracle Corporation's Oracle DBMS.

Database Filtering 101

If you ever have the good fortune to attend my class on database management, you'll hear my spiel on the difference between data and information in a database (or *data list*, in Excel-speak). In case you're the least little bit interested, it goes like this: A database consists of a vast quantity of raw data, which simply represent all the stuff that everybody in the company wants stored on a given subject (employees, sales, clients, you name it). For example, suppose that you're keeping a database on the sales transactions made by your customers. This database can very well track such stuff as the customers' identification numbers, names, addresses, telephone numbers, whether they have a charge account with the store, the maximum amount that they can charge, the purchases that they've made (including the dates and amounts), and whether their accounts are due (or overdue).

However, this vast quantity of *data* stored in the customer database is not to be confused with the *information* that particular people in the office want out of the database. For example, suppose that you're working in the marketing department and you're about to introduce a line of expensive household items that you want to advertise. You want to limit the advertising to those customers who have a charge account with the store and have purchased at least $5,000 of merchandise in the last six months. Use the *data* provided in the database to supply the *information* to weed out the customers that you need from the list.

On the other hand, suppose that you work in the accounting department and you need to send out nasty notices to all the customers who have charge accounts that are more than 90 days past due. In this case, you want only the data identifying those customers whose accounts are overdue. You couldn't care less about what was actually purchased. All you care about is reaching these folks and convincing them to pay up. You again use the *data* provided in the database to supply the *information* to weed out the customers that you need from the list.

From these simple examples, it should be clear that the data that supply information to one group in the company at a particular time are often not the same data that supply information to another group. In other words, for most people, the database dispenses information only when you are able to filter out the stuff that you currently don't want to see, and leaving behind just the stuff that you're interested in.

Filtering Data

Filtering the database to leave behind only the information that you want to work with is exactly the procedure that you follow in Excel. At the most basic level, you use the AutoFilter feature to temporarily hide the display of unwanted records and leave behind only the records that you wanted to see. Much of the time, the capabilities of the AutoFilter feature are all that you need, especially when your main concern is simply displaying just the information of interest in the data list.

You will encounter situations, however, in which the AutoFilter feature is not sufficient and you must do what Microsoft refers to as *advanced filtering* in your database. You need to use advanced filtering to filter the database when you use computed criteria (such as when you want to see all the records where the entry in the Sales column is twice the amount in the Owed column) and when you need to save a copy of the filtered data in a different part of the worksheet (Excel's version of querying the data in a data list).

Using AutoFilter

Excel's AutoFilter feature literally makes filtering out unwanted data in a data list as easy as clicking a button. When the cell pointer is located within any cell in your data list and you choose the Data⇨Filter⇨AutoFilter command from the Excel Menu bar, the program adds drop-down buttons to each of the field names in the top row of the list, as shown in Figure 2-1.

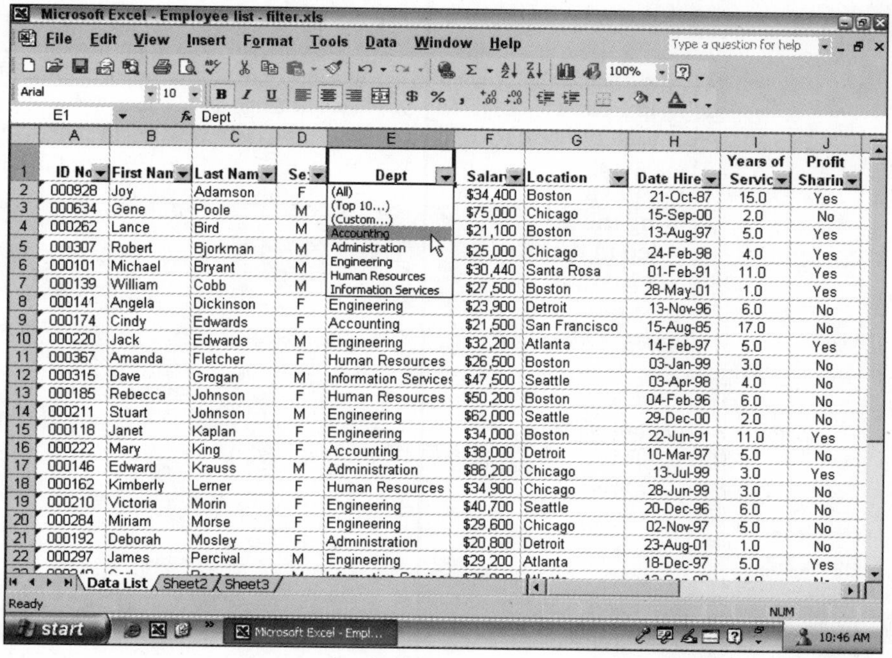

Figure 2-1: Employee data list with the AutoFilter feature turned on.

When you click a drop-down button next to a field, Excel displays a menu that contains the following three items at the top of the menu:

- **(All)** to display all records with an entry in that field
- **(Top 10...)** to display only the records with the top 10 values or in the top 10 percent
- **(Custom...)** to open the Custom AutoFilter dialog box, where you can specify multiple criteria for filtering the list by using either an AND or OR condition as well as criteria using logical operators, such as "is greater than," "is less than," "begins with," "ends with," and so on

Following the (Custom...) item, the field's drop-down list box displays all of the unique entries in that field in ascending order (lowest to highest in numeric and date fields and A to Z in text fields). To filter out all the records in the list except those that contain a particular entry or value, click that entry or value on the field's pop-up menu.

For example, Figure 2-2 shows the Employee data list after selecting the entry, Accounting, on the Dept field's pop-up menu. As this figure shows, Excel has now hidden all the rows in the data list containing records where the entry in the Dept field was anything but Accounting, thus essentially filtering the list down to just those records for the employees who work in Accounting.

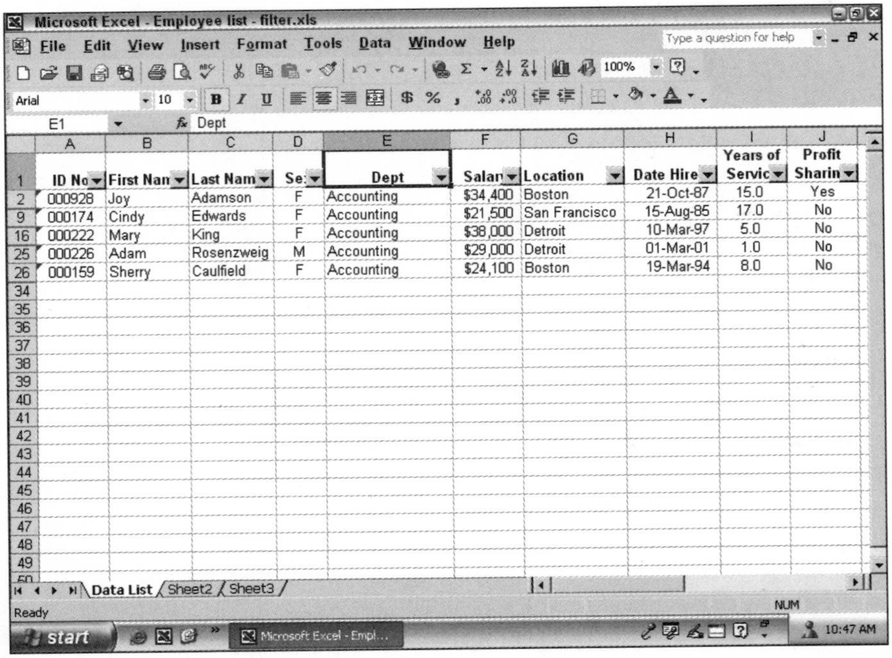

	ID No	First Nam	Last Nam	Se:	Dept	Salar	Location	Date Hire	Years of Servic	Profit Sharin
2	000928	Joy	Adamson	F	Accounting	$34,400	Boston	21-Oct-87	15.0	Yes
9	000174	Cindy	Edwards	F	Accounting	$21,500	San Francisco	15-Aug-85	17.0	No
16	000222	Mary	King	F	Accounting	$38,000	Detroit	10-Mar-97	5.0	No
25	000226	Adam	Rosenzweig	M	Accounting	$29,000	Detroit	01-Mar-01	1.0	No
26	000159	Sherry	Caulfield	F	Accounting	$24,100	Boston	19-Mar-94	8.0	No

Figure 2-2: Employee data list after filtering out all records except those where the Dept is Accounting.

To redisplay the entire data list, you can either click the (All) item at the very top of the Dept field's pop-up menu or you can choose the Data➪Filter➪ Show All command from the Excel Menu bar. When you're finished filtering the data list, you can then remove the drop-down buttons from the field names by choosing Data➪Filter➪AutoFilter on the pull-down menus (this command acts like a toggle switch so that selecting it a second time turns it off).

Making it to the Top Ten!

When the AutoFilter feature is turned on, you can select the (Top Ten...) item at the top of a field's pop-up menu to filter out all records except for those whose entries in that field are at the top or bottom of the list by a certain number (10 by default) or in a certain top or bottom percent (10 by default). Of course, you can only use the (Top Ten...) item in numerical fields and date fields; this kind of filtering doesn't make any sense when you're dealing with entries in a text field.

When you click the (Top Ten...) item on a numeric or date field's pop-up menu, Excel opens the Top 10 AutoFilter dialog box, shown in Figure 2-3, where you can specify your filtering criteria. By default, the Top 10 AutoFilter dialog box is set to filter out all records except those whose entries are among the top ten items in the field by selecting Top in the drop-down list box on the left, 10 in the middle combo box, and Items in the drop-down list box on the right. If you want to use these default criteria, you simply click OK in the Top 10 AutoFilter dialog box.

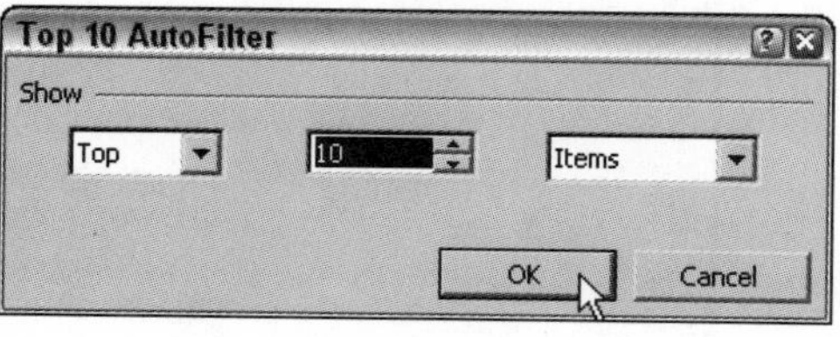

Figure 2-3: Using the Top 10 AutoFilter dialog box to filter out all records except for those with the top ten salaries.

You can also change the filtering criteria in the Top 10 AutoFilter dialog box before you filter the data. You can choose between Top and Bottom in the leftmost drop-down list box and between Items and Percent in the rightmost one. You can also change the number in the middle combo box by clicking it and entering a new value or using the Spin buttons to select one.

Custom AutoFilter at your service

You can use the (Custom...) item on a field's pop-up menu to open the Custom AutoFilter dialog box, where you can specify more complex filtering criteria by using AND and OR conditions. When you click the (Custom...) item on a field's pop-up menu, Excel opens the Custom AutoFilter dialog box, similar to the one shown in Figure 2-4.

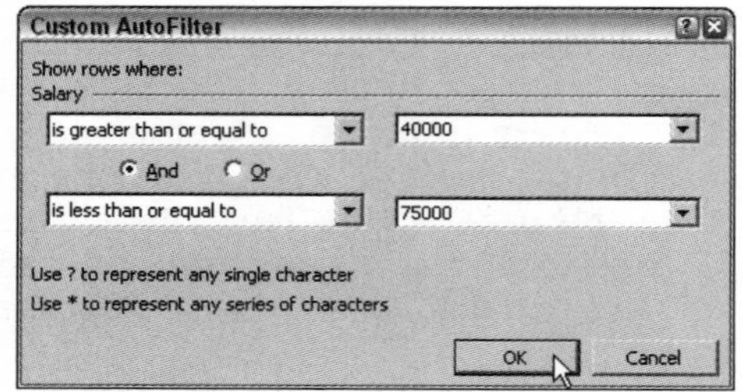

Figure 2-4: Using Custom AutoFilter to filter out records except for those within a range of salaries.

Here, you select the type of operator to use in evaluating the first and the second condition in the top and bottom drop-down list boxes and the values to be evaluated in the first and second condition in the associated combo boxes. You also specify the type of relationship between the two conditions with the And or Or radio buttons (the And radio button is selected by default).

When selecting the operator for the first and second condition in the left-most drop-down list boxes at the top and bottom of the Custom AutoFilter dialog box, you have the following choices:

- Equals
- Does not equal
- Is greater than
- Is greater than or equal to
- Is less than
- Is less than or equal to
- Begins with
- Does not begin with
- Ends with

✦ Does not end with

✦ Contains

✦ Does not contain

Note that you can use the Begins with, Ends with, and Contains operators and their negative counterparts when filtering a text field — you can also use the question mark (?) and asterisk (*) wildcard characters when entering the values for use with these operators (the question mark wildcard stands for individual characters and the asterisk stands for one or more characters). You use the other logical operators when dealing with numeric and date fields.

When specifying the values to evaluate in the associated combo boxes on the right side of the Custom AutoFilter dialog box, you can type in the text, number, or date, or you can select an existing field entry by clicking the box's drop-down list button and then clicking the entry on the pop-up menu.

Figure 2-4 illustrates setting up filtering criteria in the Custom AutoFilter dialog box that selects records whose Salary values fall within a particular range of values. In this example, I'm using an AND condition to filter out all records where the salaries are below $40,000 and above $75,000 by entering the following complex condition:

```
Salary is greater than or equal to 40000
   AND is less than or equal to 75000
```

You can also use the Custom AutoFilter feature to create an OR condition where records are displayed if they contain either value or entry that specify in any one of the two conditions. For example, suppose that you wanted to see only the records in the data list where the location is Boston or Chicago. To do this, you open the Custom AutoFilter dialog box from the Location field's pop-up menu. Then, select the Equals operator in both condition drop-down list boxes, select Boston and then Chicago in the respective combo boxes, and then click the OR radio button to create the following complex condition:

```
Location equals Boston OR equals Chicago
```

Using the Advanced Filter

When you use advanced filtering, you don't use the drop-down list boxes that appear next to the field names. Instead of selecting the filtering criteria from a field's pop-up menu or entering it in the Custom AutoFilter dialog box, you need to create a so-called Criteria Range somewhere on the worksheet containing the data list to be filtered.

If you're using the Advanced Filter feature to do a query — that is, to extract copies of the records that match your criteria by creating a subset of the data list — you can locate the Criteria Range in the top rows of columns to the right of the data list and then specify the Copy To range underneath the Criteria Range, similar to the arrangement shown in Figure 2-5.

To create a Criteria Range, you copy the names of the fields in the data list to a new part of the worksheet and then enter the values (text, numbers, or formulas) that are to be used as the criteria in filtering the list in rows underneath. When setting up the criteria for filtering the data list, you can create either comparison criteria or calculated criteria.

After you've set up your criteria range with all the field names and the criteria that you want used, you choose Data⇨Filter⇨Advanced Filter from the Excel Menu bar. This action opens the Advanced Filter dialog box, which is similar to the one shown in Figure 2-5. Here, you specify whether you just want to filter the records in the list (by hiding the rows of all those that don't meet your criteria) or you want to copy the records that meet your criteria to a new area in the worksheet (by creating a subset of the data list).

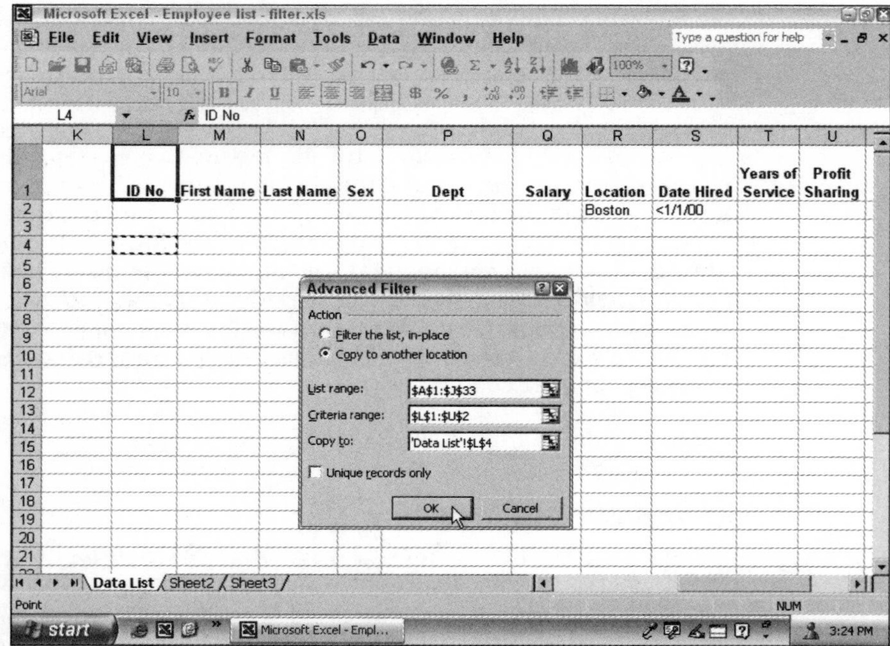

Figure 2-5: Using Advanced Filter to copy records that meet the criteria in the Criteria Range.

Only the unique need apply!

To filter out duplicate rows or records that match your criteria, select the Unique Records Only check box in the Advanced Filter dialog box before you start the filtering operation. You can remove the display of all duplicate records from a data list by selecting this check box and also removing all cell references from the Criteria Range text box before you click OK or press Enter.

To just filter the data in the list, leave the Filter the List, In Place radio button selected. To query the list and copy the data to a new place in the same worksheet (note that the Advanced Filter feature doesn't let you copy the data to another sheet or workbook), you click the Copy to Another Location radio button. When you click this radio button, the Copy To text box becomes available, along with the List Range and Criteria Range text boxes.

To specify the data list that contains the data that you want to filter or query, click the List Range text box and then enter the address of the cell range or select it directly in the worksheet by dragging through its cells. To specify the range that contains a copy of the field names along with the criteria entered under the appropriate fields, you click the Criteria Range text box and then enter the range address of this cell range or select it directly in the worksheet by dragging through its cells. When selecting this range, be sure that you include all the rows that contain the values that you want evaluated in the filtering or querying.

If you're querying the data list by copying the records that meet your criteria to a new part of the worksheet (indicated by clicking the Copy to Another Location radio button), you also click the Copy To text box and then enter the address of the cell that is to form the upper-left corner of the copied and filtered records or click this cell directly in the worksheet.

After specifying whether to filter or query the data and designating the ranges to be used in this operation, click OK to have Excel apply the criteria that you've specified in the Criteria Range in either filtering or copying the records.

After filtering a data list, you may feel that you haven't received the expected results — for example, no records are listed under the field names that you thought should have several. You can bring back all the records in the list by choosing Data⇨Filter⇨Show All. Now you can fiddle with the criteria in the Criteria Range text box and try the whole advanced filtering thing all over again.

Specifying comparison criteria

Entering selection criteria in the Criteria Range for advanced filtering is very similar to entering criteria in the data form after selecting the Criteria button. However, you need to be aware of some differences. For example, if you are searching for the last name *Paul* and enter the label Paul in the criteria range under the cell containing the field name Last Name, Excel will match any last name that begins with *P-a-u-l* such as Pauley, Paulson, and so on. To avoid having Excel match any other last name beside Paul, you would have to enter a formula in the cell below the one with Last Name field name, as in

```
="Paul"
```

When entering criteria for advanced filtering, you can also use the question mark (?) or the asterisk (*) wildcard character in your selection criteria just like you do when using the data form to find records. If, for example, you enter the J*n under the cell with the First Name field name, Excel will consider any characters between *J* and *n* in the first name field to be a match including Joan, Jon, or John as well as Jane, or Joanna. To restrict the matches to just those names with characters between *J* and *n* and to prevent matches with names that have trailing characters, you need to enter the following formula in the cell:

```
="J*n"
```

When you use a selection formula like this, Excel will match names like Joan, Jon, and John but not names such as Jane or Joanna that have a character after the *n*.

When setting up selection criteria, you can also use the other logical operators, including >, >=, <, <=, and <>, in the selection criteria. See Table 2-1 for descriptions and examples of usage in selection criteria for each of these logical operators.

Table 2-1 The Logical Operators in the Selection Criteria

Operator	*Meaning*	*Example*	*Locates*
=	Equal to	="CA"	Records where the state is *CA*.
>	Greater than	>m	Records where the name start with a letter after *M* (that is, N through Z).
>=	Greater than or equal to	>=3/4/02	Records where the date is on or after *March 4, 2002.*
<	Less than	<d	Records where the name begins with a letter before *D* (that is, A, B, or C).

Operator	*Meaning*	*Example*	*Locates*
<=	Less than or equal to	<=12/12/04	Records where the date is on or before *December 12, 2004*.
<>	Not equal to	<>"CA"	Records where the state is not equal to *CA*.

To find all the records where a particular field is blank in the database, enter = and press the spacebar to enter a space in the cell beneath the appropriate field name. To find all the records where a particular field is *not* blank in the database, enter <> and press the spacebar to enter a space in the cell beneath the appropriate field name.

Setting up logical AND and logical OR conditions

When you enter two or more criteria in the same row beneath different field names in the Criteria Range, Excel treats the criteria as a logical AND condition and selects only those records that meet both of the criteria. Figure 2-6 shows an example of a query that uses a logical AND condition. Here, Excel has copied only those records where the location is Boston *and* the date hired is before January 1, 2000 because both the criteria Boston and <1/1/00 are placed in the same row (row 2) under their respective field names, Location and Date Hired.

Microsoft Excel - Employee list - filter.xls

	L	M	N	O	P	Q	R	S	T	U
1	ID No	First Name	Last Name	Sex	Dept	Salary	Location	Date Hired	Years of Service	Profit Sharing
2							Boston	<1/1/00		
3										
4	ID No	First Name	Last Name	Sex	Dept	Salary	Location	Date Hired	Years of Service	Profit Sharing
5	000928	Joy	Adamson	F	Accounting	$34,400	Boston	21-Oct-87	15.0	Yes
6	000262	Lance	Bird	M	Human Resources	$21,100	Boston	13-Aug-97	5.0	Yes
7	000367	Amanda	Fletcher	F	Human Resources	$26,500	Boston	03-Jan-99	3.0	No
8	000185	Rebecca	Johnson	F	Human Resources	$50,200	Boston	04-Feb-96	6.0	No
9	000118	Janet	Kaplan	F	Engineering	$34,000	Boston	22-Jun-91	11.0	Yes
10	000159	Sherry	Caulfield	F	Accounting	$24,100	Boston	19-Mar-94	8.0	No

Figure 2-6: Copied records for the Boston location where the date hired is before January 1, 2000.

When you enter two or more criteria in different rows of the Criteria Range, Excel treats the criteria as a logical OR and selects records that meet any one of the criteria they contain. Figure 2-7 shows you an example of a query using a logical OR condition. In this example, Excel has copied records where the location is either Boston or San Francisco because Boston is entered under the Location field name in the second row (row 2) of the Criteria Range above San Francisco entered in the third row (row 3).

When creating logical OR conditions, you need to remember to redefine the Criteria Range to include all the rows that contain criteria, which in this case is the cell range L2:U2 (if you forget, Excel uses only the criteria in the rows included in the Criteria range).

When setting up your criteria, you can combine logical AND and logical OR conditions (again, assuming that you expand the Criteria Range sufficiently to include all of the rows containing criteria). For example, if you enter Boston in cell R2 (under Location) and <1/1/00 in cell S2 (under Date Hired) in row 2 and enter San Francisco in cell R3 and then repeat the query, Excel copies the records where the location is Boston and the date hired is before January 1, 2000, as well as the records where the location is San Francisco (regardless of the date hired).

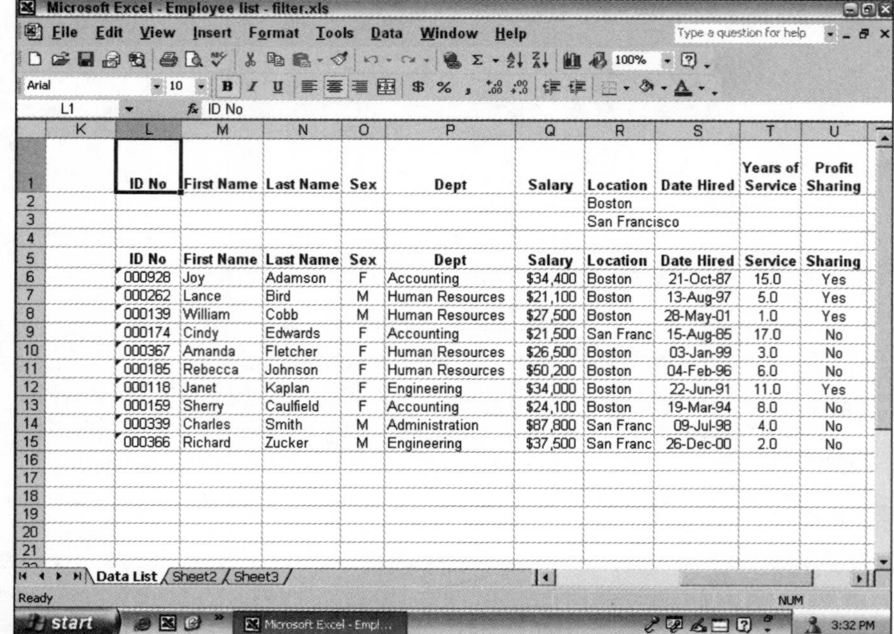

	K	L	M	N	O	P	Q	R	S	T	U
1		ID No	First Name	Last Name	Sex	Dept	Salary	Location	Date Hired	Years of Service	Profit Sharing
2								Boston			
3								San Francisco			
4											
5		ID No	First Name	Last Name	Sex	Dept	Salary	Location	Date Hired	Service	Sharing
6		000928	Joy	Adamson	F	Accounting	$34,400	Boston	21-Oct-87	15.0	Yes
7		000262	Lance	Bird	M	Human Resources	$21,100	Boston	13-Aug-97	5.0	Yes
8		000139	William	Cobb	M	Human Resources	$27,500	Boston	28-May-01	1.0	Yes
9		000174	Cindy	Edwards	F	Accounting	$21,500	San Franc	15-Aug-85	17.0	No
10		000367	Amanda	Fletcher	F	Human Resources	$26,500	Boston	03-Jan-99	3.0	No
11		000185	Rebecca	Johnson	F	Human Resources	$50,200	Boston	04-Feb-96	6.0	No
12		000118	Janet	Kaplan	F	Engineering	$34,000	Boston	22-Jun-91	11.0	Yes
13		000159	Sherry	Caulfield	F	Accounting	$24,100	Boston	19-Mar-94	8.0	No
14		000339	Charles	Smith	M	Administration	$87,800	San Franc	09-Jul-98	4.0	No
15		000366	Richard	Zucker	M	Engineering	$37,500	San Franc	26-Dec-00	2.0	No

Figure 2-7: Copied records for the Boston and San Francisco location using an OR condition.

Setting up Calculated criteria

You can use calculated criteria when filtering or querying your data list. All you need to do is enter a logical formula that Excel can evaluate as either TRUE or FALSE in the Criteria Range under a name that is *not* used as a field name in the data list (I repeat, is *not* a field name in the data list). Calculated criteria enable you to filter or query records based on a comparison of entries in a particular field with entries in other fields of the list or based on a comparison with entries in the worksheet that lie outside of the data list itself.

Figure 2-8 shows an example of using a calculated criterion that compares values in a field to a calculated value that isn't actually entered in the data list. Here, you want to perform a query that copies all of the records from the Employee data list where the employee's salary is above the average salary. In this figure, cell V2 contains the formula that uses the AVERAGE function to compute average employee salary and then compares the first salary entry in cell F2 of the data list to that average with the following formula:

```
=F2>AVERAGE($F$2:$F$33)
```

Note that this logical formula is placed under the label Calculated Criteria in cell V2 that has been added to the end of the Criteria Range. Cell F2 is the first cell in the data list that contains a salary entry. The cell range, $F$2:$F$33, used as the argument of the AVERAGE function, is the range in the Salary field that contains all the salary entries.

To use this calculated criterion, you must remember to place the logical formula under a name that isn't used as a field name in the data list itself and you must include this label and formula in the Criteria Range (for this query example, the Criteria Range is defined as the cell range L2:V2).

When you then perform the query by using the Advanced Filter feature, Excel applies this calculated criterion to every record in the database. Excel does this by adjusting the first Salary field cell reference F2 (entered as a relative reference) as the program examines the rest of the records below. Note, however, that the range reference specified as the argument of the AVERAGE function is entered as an absolute reference ($F$2:$F$33) in the criterion formula so that Excel won't adjust this reference but compare the Salary entry for each record to AVERAGE computed for this entire range (which just happens to be 40,161).

When entering formulas for calculated criteria that compare values outside the data list to values in a particular field, you should always reference the cell containing the very first entry for that field in order to ensure that Excel applies your criteria to every record in the data list.

Microsoft Excel - Employee list - filter.xls

V2 =F2>AVERAGE($F$2:$F$33)

	L	M	N	O	P	Q	R	S	T	U	V
1	ID No	First Name	Last Name	Sex	Dept	Salary	Location	Date Hired	Years of Service	Profit Sharing	Calculated Criteria
2											FALSE
3											
4	ID No	First Name	Last Name	Sex	Dept	Salary	Location	Date Hired	Years of Service	Profit Sharing	
5	000634	Gene	Poole	M	Engineering	$75,000	Chicago	15-Sep-00	2.0	No	
6	000315	Dave	Grogan	M	Information Services	$47,500	Seattle	03-Apr-98	4.0	No	
7	000185	Rebecca	Johnson	F	Human Resources	$50,200	Boston	04-Feb-96	6.0	No	
8	000211	Stuart	Johnson	M	Engineering	$62,000	Seattle	29-Dec-00	2.0	No	
9	000146	Edward	Krauss	M	Administration	$86,200	Chicago	13-Jul-99	3.0	Yes	
10	000210	Victoria	Morin	F	Engineering	$40,700	Seattle	20-Dec-96	6.0	No	
11	000199	Steven	Smith	M	Administration	$100,000	Seattle	11-Oct-00	2.0	Yes	
12	000339	Charles	Smith	M	Administration	$87,800	San Franc	09-Jul-98	4.0	No	
13	000603	Sarah	Michaels	F	Information Services	$57,500	Santa Ros	23-Mar-02	0.0	No	

Data List / Sheet2 / Sheet3

Figure 2-8: Extracted records for personnel whose salaries are above the salary average.

You can also set up calculated criteria that compare entries in one or more fields to other entries in the data list. For example, to extract the records where the Years of Service entry is at least two years greater than the record above it (assuming that you have sorted the data list in ascending order by years of service), you would enter the following logical formula under the cell labeled Calculated Criteria:

```
=I3>I2+2
```

Most often, when referencing to cells within the data list itself, you want to leave the cell references relative so that they can be adjusted because each record is examined and the references to the cells outside the database are absolute so that these won't be changed when making the comparison with the rest of the records.

When you enter the logical formula for a calculated criterion, Excel returns the logical value TRUE or FALSE. This logical value applies to the field entry for the first record in the data list that you refer to in the logical formula. By inspecting this field entry in the database and seeing if it does, indeed, meet your intended selection criteria, you can usually tell whether your logical formula is correct.

Using the AND and OR functions in calculated criteria

You can also use Excel's AND, OR, and NOT functions with the logical operators in calculated criteria to find records that fall within a range. For example, to find all of the records in the employee database where the salaries range between $55,000 and $75,000, you would enter the following logical formula with the AND function under the cell with the label Calculated Criteria:

```
=AND(F4>=55000,F4<=75000)
```

To find all of the records in the Employee data list where the salary is either below $29,000 or above $45,000, you would enter the following logical formula with the OR function under the cell with the label Calculated Criteria:

```
=OR(F4<29000,F4>45000)
```


Using the Database Functions

Excel includes a number of database functions that you can use to calculate statistics, such as the total, the average, the maximum, the minimum, and the count in a particular field of the data list only when the criteria that you specify are met. For example, you could use the DSUM function in the sample Employee data list to compute the sum of all the salaries for employees who were hired after January 1, 2000, or you could use the DCOUNT function to compute the number of records in the data list for the Human Resources department.

The database functions, regardless of the difference in names (and they all begin with the letter *D*) and the computations that they perform, all take the same three arguments as illustrated by the DAVERAGE function:

DAVERAGE(*database*,*field*,*criteria*)

The arguments for the database functions require the following information:

- ✦ *Database* is the argument that specifies the range containing the list and it must include the row of field names in the top row.
- ✦ *Field* is the argument that specifies the field whose values are to be calculated by the database function (averaged in the case of the DAVERAGE function). You can specify this argument by enclosing the name of the field in double quotes (as in "Salary" or "Date Hired") or you can do this by entering the number of the column in the data list (counting from left to right with the first field counted as 1).

* *Criteria* is the argument that specifies the address of the range that contains the criteria that you're using in determining which values are calculated. This range must include at least one field name that indicates the field whose values are to be evaluated and one cell with the values or expression to be used in the evaluation.

Note that in specifying the *field* argument, you must refer to a column in the data list that contains numeric or date data for all the database functions with the exception of DGET. All the rest of the database functions can't perform computations on text fields. If you mistakenly specify a column with text entries as the field argument for these database functions, Excel returns an error value or 0 as the result. Table 2-2 lists the various database functions available in Excel along with an explanation of what each one calculates (you already know what arguments each one takes).

Table 2-2 The Database Functions in Excel

Database Function	*What It Calculates*
DAVERAGE	Averages all the values in a field of the data list that match the criteria you specify.
DCOUNT	Counts the number of cells with numeric entries in a field of the data list that match the criteria you specify.
DCOUNTA	Counts the number of nonblank cells in a field of the data list that match the criteria you specify.
DGET	Extracts a single value from a record in the data list that matches the criteria you specify. If no record matches, the function returns the #VALUE! error value. If multiple records match, the function returns the #NUM! error value.
DMAX	Returns the highest value in a field of the data list that matches the criteria you specify.
DMIN	Returns the lowest value in a field of the data list that matches the criteria you specify.
DPRODUCT	Multiplies all the values in a field of the data list that match the criteria you specify.
DSTDEV	Estimates the standard deviation based on the sample of values in a field of the data list that match the criteria you specify.
DSTDEVP	Calculates the standard deviation based on the population of values in a field of the data list that match the criteria you specify.
DSUM	Sums all the values in a field of the data list that match the criteria you specify.
DVAR	Estimates the variance based on the sample of values in a field of the data list that match the criteria you specify.
DVARP	Calculates the variance based on the population of values in a field of the data list that match the criteria you specify.

Figure 2-9 illustrates the use of the database function, DSUM. Cell B2 in the worksheet shown in this figure contains the following formula:

```
=DSUM(A3:J35,"Salary",E1:E2)
```

This DSUM function computes the total of all the salaries in the data list that are above $55,000. This total is shown in cell B2 that contains the formula as $468,500.

To perform this calculation, I specified the range A3:J35 that contains the entire data list, including the top row of field names as the *database* argument. I then specified "Salary" as the field argument of the DSUM function because this is the name of the field that contains the values that I want totaled. Finally, I specified the range E1:E2 as the *criteria* argument of the DSUM function because these two cells contain the criteria range that designate that only the values in the Salary field that exceed 55000 are to be summed.

Microsoft Excel - Employee list - dbfunc.xls

B2 =DSUM(A3:J35,"Salary",E1:E2)

	A	B	C	D	E	F	G	H	I	J
1					Salary					
2		$ 468,500			>55000					
3	ID No	First Name	Last Name	Sex	Dept	Salary	Location	Date Hired	Years of Service	Profit Sharing
4	000928	Joy	Adamson	F	Accounting	$34,400	Boston	21-Oct-87	15.0	Yes
5	000634	Gene	Poole	M	Engineering	$75,000	Chicago	15-Sep-00	2.0	No
6	000262	Lance	Bird	M	Human Resources	$21,100	Boston	13-Aug-97	5.0	Yes
7	000307	Robert	Bjorkman	M	Engineering	$25,000	Chicago	24-Feb-98	4.0	Yes
8	000101	Michael	Bryant	M	Administration	$30,440	Santa Rosa	01-Feb-91	11.0	Yes
9	000139	William	Cobb	M	Human Resources	$27,500	Boston	28-May-01	1.0	Yes
10	000141	Angela	Dickinson	F	Engineering	$23,900	Detroit	13-Nov-96	6.0	No
11	000174	Cindy	Edwards	F	Accounting	$21,500	San Francisco	15-Aug-85	17.0	No
12	000220	Jack	Edwards	M	Engineering	$32,200	Atlanta	14-Feb-97	5.0	Yes
13	000367	Amanda	Fletcher	F	Human Resources	$26,500	Boston	03-Jan-99	3.0	No
14	000315	Dave	Grogan	M	Information Service	$47,500	Seattle	03-Apr-98	4.0	No
15	000185	Rebecca	Johnson	F	Human Resources	$50,200	Boston	04-Feb-96	6.0	No
16	000211	Stuart	Johnson	M	Engineering	$62,000	Seattle	29-Dec-00	2.0	No
17	000118	Janet	Kaplan	F	Engineering	$34,000	Boston	22-Jun-91	11.0	Yes
18	000222	Mary	King	F	Accounting	$38,000	Detroit	10-Mar-97	5.0	No
19	000146	Edward	Krauss	M	Administration	$86,200	Chicago	13-Jul-99	3.0	Yes
20	000162	Kimberly	Lerner	F	Human Resources	$34,900	Chicago	28-Jun-99	3.0	No
21	000210	Victoria	Morin	F	Engineering	$40,700	Seattle	20-Dec-96	6.0	No

Data List / Sheet2 / Sheet3

Figure 2-9: Using the DSUM to total the salaries over $55,000 in the Employee data list.

External Data Query

Excel makes it possible to query other external databases to which you have access and then extract the data in which you're interested into your worksheet for further manipulation and analysis. To create a query that acquires data from an external database, you must complete two procedures. In the first procedure, you define the data source; that is, the external database that contains the data that you want to query. In the second procedure, you specify the query itself, including all the columns of data that you want extracted along with the criteria for selecting them.

Creating a new data source definition

To perform the first procedure that creates the new data source, follow these steps:

1. **Choose Data⇨Import External Data⇨New Database Query from the Excel Menu bar.**

   The first time you choose Data⇨Import External Data⇨New Database Query, Excel displays an Alert dialog box stating that the Microsoft Query feature is not currently installed and asking if you want to install this feature now. Click Yes to have Excel install this feature (remember that you must have your Office XP CD handy or be able to specify the path on your company's network where the necessary files are stored in order to do this).

   After Microsoft Query is installed on your system, the Choose Data Source dialog box, shown in Figure 2-10, appears with the <New Data Source> item in the list box on the Databases tab automatically selected.

2. **Click OK to accept the default settings in the Choose Data Source dialog box.**

   This action opens the Create New Data Source dialog box where you need to name your new database query and specify the driver to be used in accessing the external database.

3. **Enter a descriptive name for the database query in the What Name Do You Want to Give Your New Data Source text box.**

   By naming the data source definition, you can reuse it without having to go through all these tedious steps for defining it. Next, you need to select a driver for your data source in the Select a Driver for the Type of Database You Want to Access drop-down list box. This list contains drivers for all the most popular PC databases, such as Access, dBASE, Paradox, and FoxPro, as well as an SQL driver for sophisticated database management systems, such as dB2 and an OBDC Oracle driver for querying an Oracle database (to name a few).

4. **Click the name of the driver to be used in the Select a Driver for the Type of Database You Want to Access drop-down list box.**

   Now you're ready to select the database to be accessed.

5. **Click the Connect button in the Create New Data Source dialog box.**

   This action opens a dialog box where you can select the database to be used. For example, if you select Microsoft Access Driver (*.mdb) as the driver in the Create New Data Source dialog box, Excel opens an ODBC Microsoft Access Setup dialog box.

6. **Click the Select button and then locate the folder that contains the database file that you want to query in the Select Database dialog box and then click OK.**

   After you've selected the database to work with, you have completed the first major step of specifying the data source to use in your external query.

7. **Click OK in the Setup dialog box for the type of database that you're accessing.**

   This action returns you to the Create New Data Source dialog box (shown in Figure 2-11), which now displays the name of the database that you selected. If you want, you can specify a default table to use in the database and, if you had to specify a username and password to gain access to the database, you can have this information saved as part of the data source definition.

8. **(Optional) Click the name of the default table in the Select a Default Table for Your Data Source (Optional) drop-down list box and click the Save My User ID and Password in the Data Source Definition check box to save this information.**

   Now you're ready to close the Create New Data dialog box and return to the Choose Data Source dialog box from which you can perform the second procedure of specifying your database query.

9. **Click the OK button in the Create a New Data Source dialog box.**

   This action closes the Create a New Data Source dialog box, returning you to the Choose Data Source dialog box where the name that you've given to the data source definition that you've just completed appears selected.

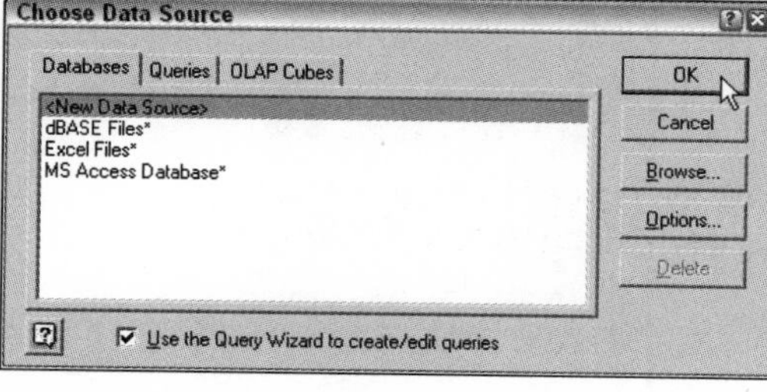

Figure 2-10: Using the Choose Data Source dialog box to create a new database query.

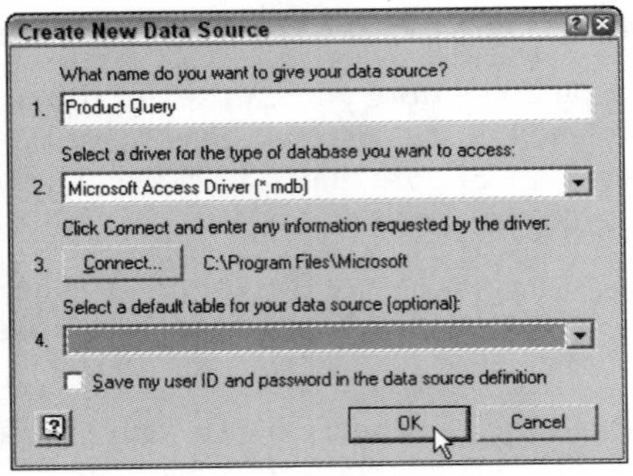

Figure 2-11: Creating a new data source for the external database query.

Specifying the database query

Now that you've finished the data source definition, you can use it with the Query Wizard to specify which fields in the database to acquire. At this point, the Choose Data Source dialog box is still open and the name of your new data source definition is selected along with the Use the Query Wizard to Create/Edit Queries check box.

To perform the second procedure in which you specify the conditions of the query by using your new data source definition, follow these steps:

1. **Make sure that the name of your data source is highlighted on the Databases tab and the Use the Query Wizard to Create/Edit Queries check box has a checkmark in it and then click OK in the Choose Data Source dialog box.**

   This action closes the Choose Data Source dialog box and opens the Query Wizard — Choose Columns dialog box, similar to the one shown in Figure 2-12. This dialog box contains two list boxes: the Available Tables and Columns list box on the left side and the Columns in Your Query list box on the right side.

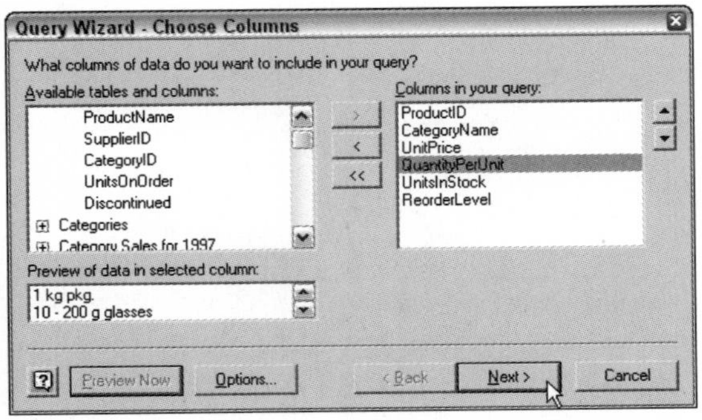

Figure 2-12: Specifying the fields to acquire in the new external database query.

To select the fields that you want to acquire, click the Expand button (+) in front of the name of each table in the external database that contains fields that you want. Then, click the name of the field followed by the > button to copy the field name to the Columns in Your Query list box. To preview the data in that field, click the Preview Now button when the field name is selected in the Columns in Your Query list box.

Note that the order in which you add the fields determines their column order in your Excel worksheet. To change the order after copying the fields to the Columns in Your Query list box, click the field and then click the button to the right with the triangle pointing upward to promote the field in the list or click the button with the triangle pointing down to demote it in the list.

2. **Select the fields that you want to use in the Available Tables and Columns list box on the left and then copy them to the Columns in Your Query list box on the right.**

   After you finish selecting the fields to use in the query, you're ready to move on to the next dialog box in the Query Wizard where you specify how the data is to be filtered.

3. **Click Next> to open the Query Wizard — Filter Data dialog box.**

   To set up the criteria by which records are selected in the Filter Data dialog box (similar to the one shown in Figure 2-13), click the field for which you want to set criteria and then click the criteria to use in the drop-down list box on the left and the value to be evaluated in the combo box on the right.

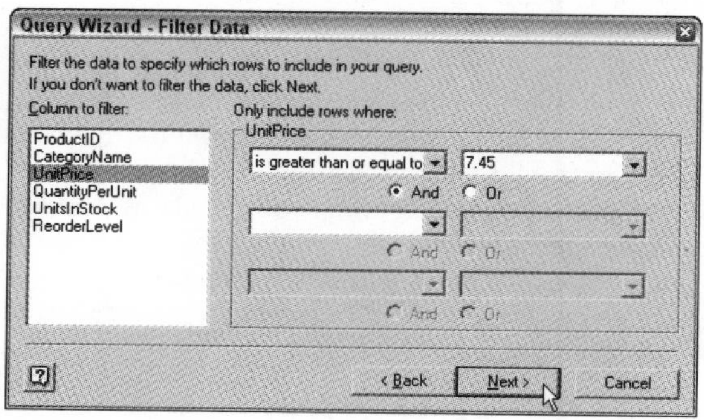

Figure 2-13: Specifying how the data are to be filtered in the new external database query.

The criteria available in the drop-down list boxes on the left are the same as those used with the Custom AutoFilter (see the "Custom AutoFilter at your service" section previously in this chapter for details) with the exception of the "like" and "not like" and "is Null" and "is Not Null" operators, which are not available when setting criteria for the Custom AutoFilter ("like" refers to entries that sound like one that you enter in the associated combo box on the right and "Null" refers to empty entries in the field).

When entering the values to be evaluated in the associated combo boxes on the right side of the Filter Data dialog box, you can use the question mark (?) and asterisk (*) wildcard characters (question marks for single characters and the asterisk for multiple characters) in the text that you enter in these boxes. You can also select data entries in a field from which to compare to by clicking them in the drop-down list.

To set up a logical AND condition, make sure that the AND radio button is selected when you specify the second, and even third set of filtering criteria (remember in an AND condition, records are selected only when all set of criteria are TRUE). To set up a logical OR condition, click the Or radio button before you specify the second, or even third set of criteria (remember in an OR condition, records are selected when any one of the sets of criteria are TRUE).

Note that if you want to acquire all data in a selected field, you don't specify any filtering criteria for that field in the Filter Data dialog box.

4. **Specify the filtering criteria, including any AND and OR condition, in the criteria drop-down list boxes on the left and evaluation combo boxes on the right for each field that should be filtered in the Column to Filter list box.**

   After you finish specifying the filtering to be used on the fields, you're ready to specify the order in which matching records are to be sorted.

5. **Click the Next> button to open the Query Wizard — Sort Order dialog box.**

   To sort the data that you acquire in the external database query, click the name of the field in the Sort By drop-down list box and then select either the Ascending (default) or Descending radio button (see Figure 2-14). To sort and duplicates in the field that you specify as the primary sorting key, you select the tie-breaking field for the secondary key in the Then By drop-down list box and then select between its Ascending (default) and Descending radio button.

   You repeat this procedure to sort the incoming data on up to three fields total (just as you can a standard Excel data list — for more on sorting data, see Book VI, Chapter 1). If you don't want the data sorted, click the Next> button without selecting any fields as sorting keys.

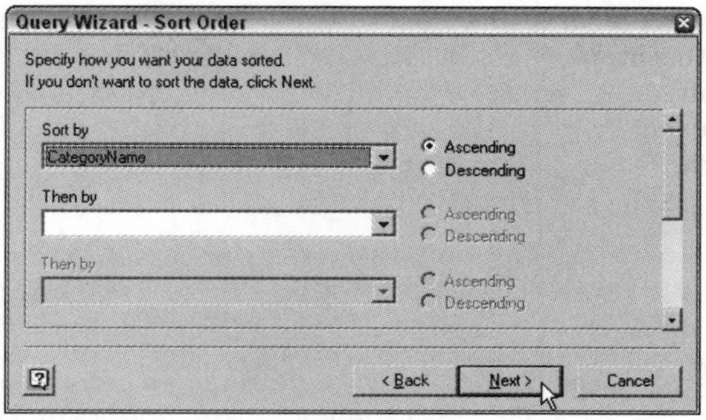

Figure 2-14: Specifying how the data are to be sorted in the new external database query.

6. **Specify the field or fields on which the external data is to be sorted and then click the Next> button.**

   Clicking Next> opens the Query Wizard — Finish dialog box shown in Figure 2-15. This dialog box contains several options that you can choose from in completing the query. You can return the data to the current or a new worksheet by leaving the Return Data to Microsoft Excel radio button selected. You can view the data and/or edit the query in the Microsoft Query dialog window by clicking the View Data or Edit Query in Microsoft Query radio button. You can create an OLAP (Online Analytic Processing) cube that summarizes the data being acquired by clicking the Create an OLAP Cube from this Query radio button. (This is useful when querying really huge databases that contain so many records that they need to be summarized before importing them into Excel.)

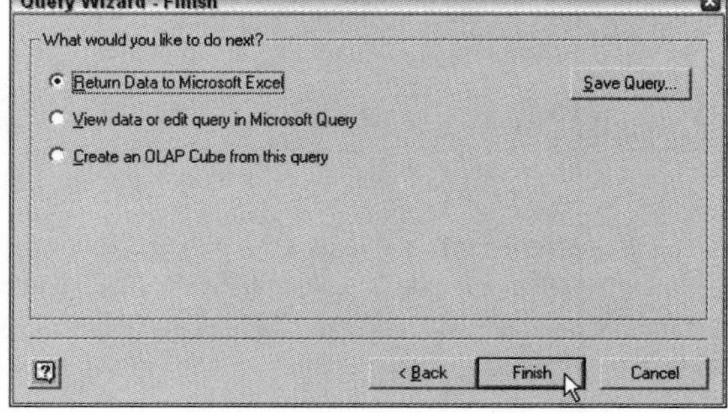

Figure 2-15: Selecting the options in the Query Wizard — Finish dialog box.

You can also save your new query by selecting the Save Query button in the Query Wizard — Finish dialog box. When you do this, Excel saves it as a separate query file (indicated by the `.dqy` file extension) so that you can reuse it from any workbook file. Note that Excel automatically saves the data source definition as file (indicated by the `.dsn`) when you next save the current workbook but not the query.

7. **Click the Save Query button and then enter the filename for the new query file in the Save As dialog box before you click the Save button.**

   If you want to see the data and review your query before you bring it into your Excel worksheet, you click the View Data or Edit Query in Microsoft Query radio button before you click OK in the Query Wizard — Finish dialog box. When you do this, Excel opens a Microsoft Query window similar to the one shown in Figure 2-16 where you can preview the way the acquired data will appear when you bring it into Excel. You can also edit the database query in this window.

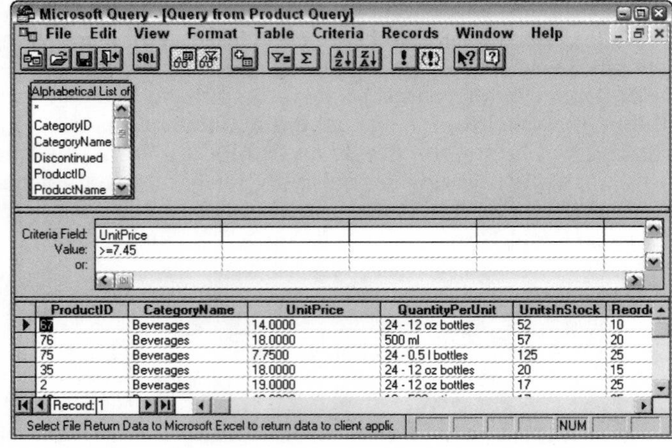

Figure 2-16: Viewing the data to be acquired by the query in the Microsoft Query window.

8. **(Optional) Click the View Data or Edit Query in Microsoft Query radio button and then click the Finish button to open the Microsoft Query window showing the fields and records to be acquired by the query along with the filtering criteria.**

   After you finish viewing the data in the Microsoft Query window, you can click its Close button. Doing this opens the Import Data dialog box described in Step 10.

The Import Data dialog box is also displayed when you click the Finish button when the Return Data to Microsoft Excel radio button is selected in the Query Wizard — Finish dialog box, which is described in Step 6.

9. **Click the Finish button in the Query Wizard — Finish dialog box.**

   This action closes this dialog box and opens the Import Data dialog box (shown in Figure 2-17) where you indicate where you want to put the data acquired from the external database. By default, the Existing Worksheet radio button is selected and cell A1 is designated as the start of the range. To change the starting cell, click it in the worksheet. To import the data into a brand new worksheet in the current workbook, click the New Worksheet radio button instead.

10. **Indicate where you want the data imported on the active sheet in the Existing Worksheet text box or select the New Worksheet option and then click OK to start importing the data.**

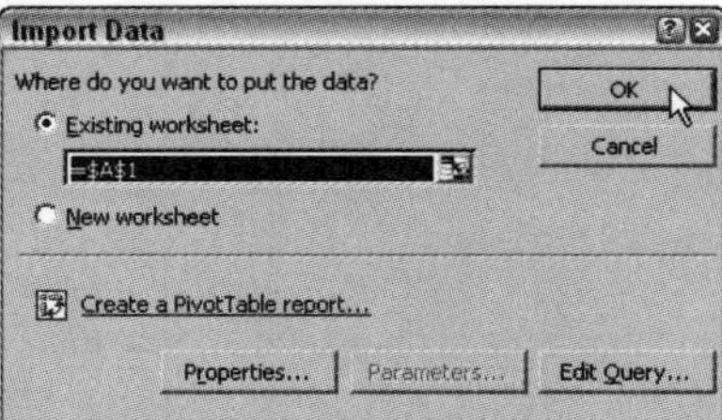

Figure 2-17: Indicating where to put the queried data in the Import Data dialog box.

As soon as you click OK, Excel executes the database query and acquires the data from the external database. After the program finishes importing all the records that match your filtering criteria, it also displays the External Data toolbar (shown in Figure 2-18 and opened by selecting View➪Toolbars➪ External Data on the Excel Menu bar, if it doesn't appear automatically). You can use the buttons on this toolbar to update the acquired data or edit the query.

After you've saved a data query, you can use it to connect to an external database and to acquire its data according to the query's parameters. To do this, choose Data➪Import External Data➪Import Data from the Excel Menu bar to open the Select Data Source dialog box. This dialog box displays the name of all the query files that you create and save (as outlined in the foregoing steps). Click the name of the query file (with the `.dqy` file extension) to use and then click the Open button. This action closes the Select Data Source dialog box and opens the Import Data dialog box where you indicate where to put the imported data in Excel.

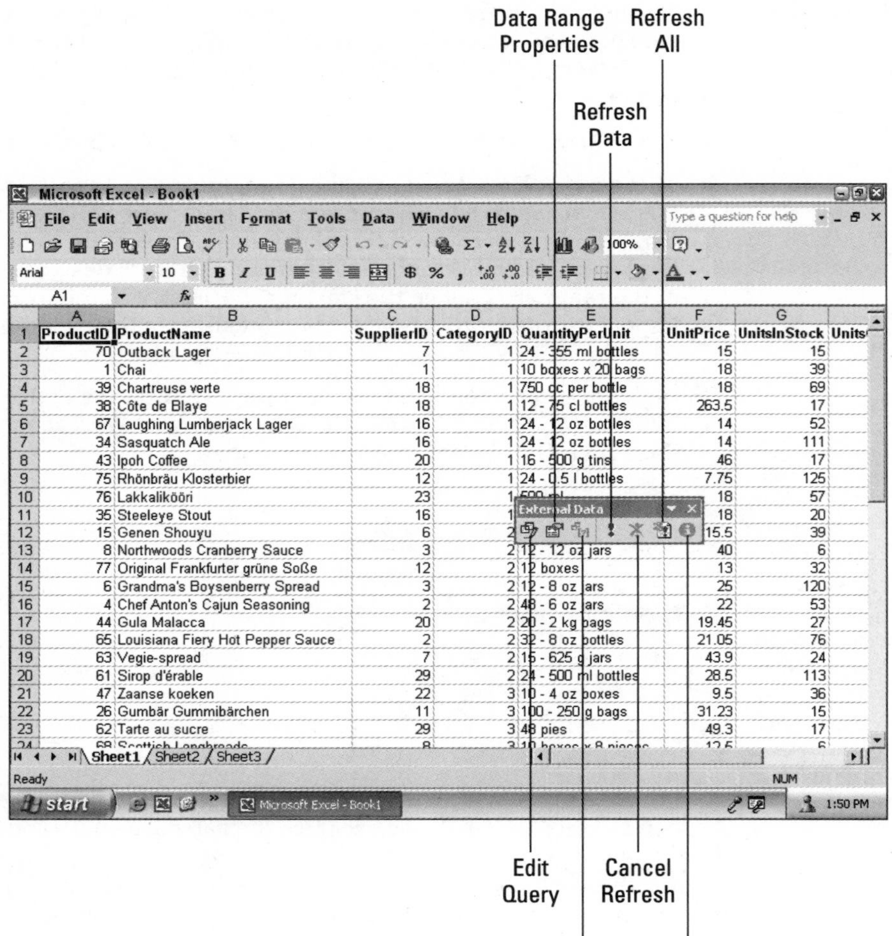

Figure 2-18: Worksheet after importing the data using the external database query.

Book VII

Data Analysis

The 5th Wave
By Rich Tennant
"WELL, SHOOT! THIS EGGPLANT CHART IS JUST AS CONFUSING AS THE BUTTERNUT SQUASH CHART AND THE GOURD CHART. CAN'T YOU JUST MAKE A PIE CHART LIKE EVERYONE ELSE?"

Contents at a Glance

Chapter 1: Performing What-If Scenarios

In This Chapter

- ✓ **Doing what-if analysis in one- and two-variable Data tables**
- ✓ **Performing goal seeking**
- ✓ **Creating and playing with different scenarios**
- ✓ **Using the Solver utility**

Because electronic spreadsheets are so good at updating their results by automatically recalculating their formulas based on new input, they have always been used (and sometimes, misused) to create financial projections based on all sorts of assumptions. Under the guise of what-if analysis, you will often find the number crunchers of the company using Excel as their crystal ball for projecting the results of all sorts of harebrained schemes designed to make the company a fast million bucks. As you start dabbling in this form of electronic fortune-telling, keep in mind that the projections you get back from this type of analysis are only as good as your assumptions. So when the results of what-if analysis tell you that you're going be richer than King Midas after undertaking this new business venture, you still need to ask yourself whether the original assumptions on which these glowing projections are based fit in with real-world marketing conditions. In other words, when the worksheet tells you that you can make a million bucks of pure profit by selling your lead-lined boxer shorts, you still have to question how many men really need that kind of protection and are willing to pay for it.

In Excel, what-if analysis comes in a fairly wide variety of flavors (some of which are more complicated than others). In this chapter, I introduce you to three simple and straightforward methods. *Data tables* enable you to see the effect on the bottom line of changing one or two variables, such as what happens to the net profit if you fall into a 45 percent tax bracket, a 60 percent tax bracket, and so on. *Goal seeking* enables you to find out what it takes to reach a predetermined objective, such as how much you have to sell to make a $20 million profit this year. *Scenarios* let you set up and test a wide variety of cases, all the way from the best-case scenario (profits grow by 20 percent) to the worst-case scenario (you don't make any profit).

At the end of the chapter, I introduce you to the Solver add-in utility that enables you to find solutions to more complex what-if problems involving multiple variables. You can use Solver to help you with classic resource problems, such as finding the correct product mix in order to maximize your profits, staffing to minimize your general costs, and routing to minimize transportation costs.

Using Data Tables

In an Excel spreadsheet you can see the effect of changing an input value on the result returned by a formula as soon as you enter a new input value in the cell that feeds into the formula. Each time you change this input value, Excel automatically recalculates the formula and shows you the new result based on the new value. This method is of limited use, however, when you are performing what-if analysis and need to be able to see the range of results produced by using a series of different input values in the same worksheet so that you can compare them to each other.

To perform this type of what-if analysis, you can use Excel's Data Table command. When creating a data table, you enter a series of input values in the worksheet, and Excel uses each of them in the formula that you specify. When Excel is finished computing the data table, you see the results produced by each change in the input values in a single range of the worksheet. You can then save the data table as part of the worksheet if you need to keep a record of the results of a series of input values.

When creating data tables, you can create a one-variable or a two-variable data table. In a one-variable data table, Excel substitutes a series of different values for a single input value in a formula. In a two-variable data table, Excel substitutes a series of different values for two input values in a formula.

Creating a one-variable data table

To create a one-variable data table, you need to set up the master formula in your worksheet and then, in a different range of the worksheet, enter the series of different values that you want substituted for a single input value in that formula. Figures 1-1 and 1-2 demonstrate how this is done.

In Figure 1-1, cell B5 contains a simple formula for computing the projected sales for 2004, assuming an annual growth rate of 3% over the annual sales in 2003. The 2004 projected sales in this cell are calculated with the following formula:

```
=Sales_03+(Sales_03*Growth_04)
```

This formula adds cell B2 (named Sales_03) to the contents of B2 multiplied by the growth rate of 3% in cell B3 (named Growth_04). Cell B5 shows you that, assuming an annual growth rate of 3% in the year 2004, you can project total sales of $901,250.

But what if the growth rate in 2004 is not as high as 3%, or what if the growth rate is even higher than anticipated? To create the one-variable table to answer these questions, you first bring forward the master formula in cell B5 to cell C7 with the formula = B5. Then, second, you enter the series of different growth rates as the input values in column B, starting in cell B8 (cell B7, at the intersection of the row with the master formula and the column with the input values, must be left blank in a one-variable data table). This series of input values for the data table can be created with the AutoFill feature (see Book II, Chapter 1 for details). In this example, a data series that increments each succeeding value by 1 percent is created in the cell range B8:B17, starting at 1 percent and ending at 10 percent.

After bringing the formula in cell B5 forward to cell C7 with the formula =B5 and generating the growth rate series in the cell range B8:B17, you then select the cell range B7:C17 and choose Data⇨Table from the Excel Menu bar. The blank cell range C8:C17 is the cell range where Excel put the projected sales figures based on the growth rate entered into the comparable cell in column B.

Excel opens the Table dialog box shown in Figure 1-1 where you must specify the row input cell in the Row Input Cell text box and/or the column input cell in the Column Input Cell. The cell that you designate as the row or column input cell in the Table dialog box must correspond to the cell in the worksheet that contains the original input value that is fed into the master formula.

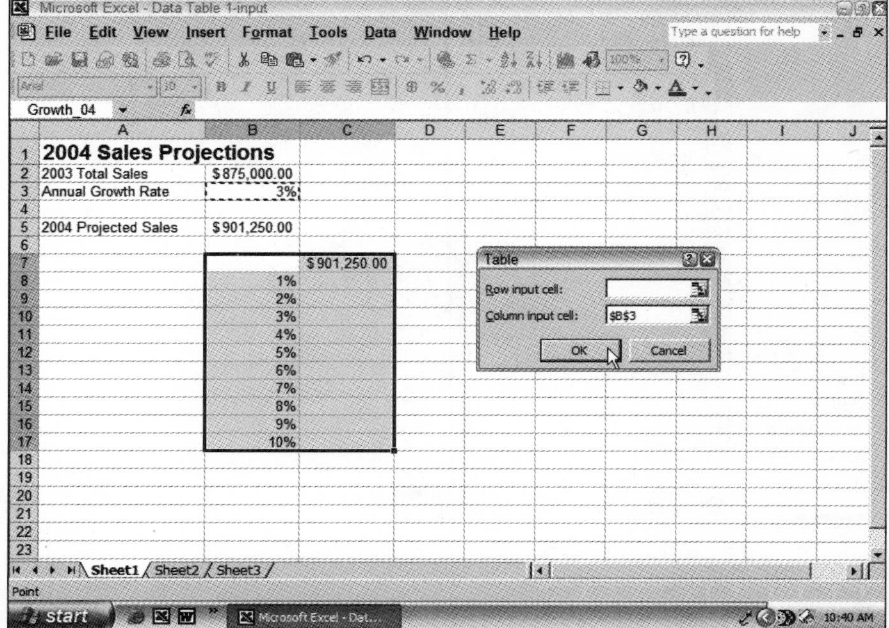

Figure 1-1: Creating a one-variable data table.

In the data table in this example, you only need to designate B3 as the column input cell. (In the case of Figure 1-1, when you click this cell or use an arrow key to select this cell, Excel enters the absolute cell reference, as in $B$3.) You choose cell B3 because this is the cell that contains the growth rate value used in the master formula.

After indicating the row or column input cells, Excel computes the data table when you click the OK button. In this example, the program creates the data table by substituting each input value in the data series in the range B8:B17 into the column input cell B3, whereupon it is used in the master formula to calculate a new result, which is entered in the correspon-ding cell in the cell range C8:C17. After the program has finished calculating the data table, Excel returns the original value to the row or column input cell (in this case, 3% in cell B3).

Figure 1-2 shows the completed data table. Here, you can see at a glance the effect on the projected sales for 2004 of changing a single percentage point for the growth rate. After creating the data table, you can then format the results and save the table as part of the worksheet.

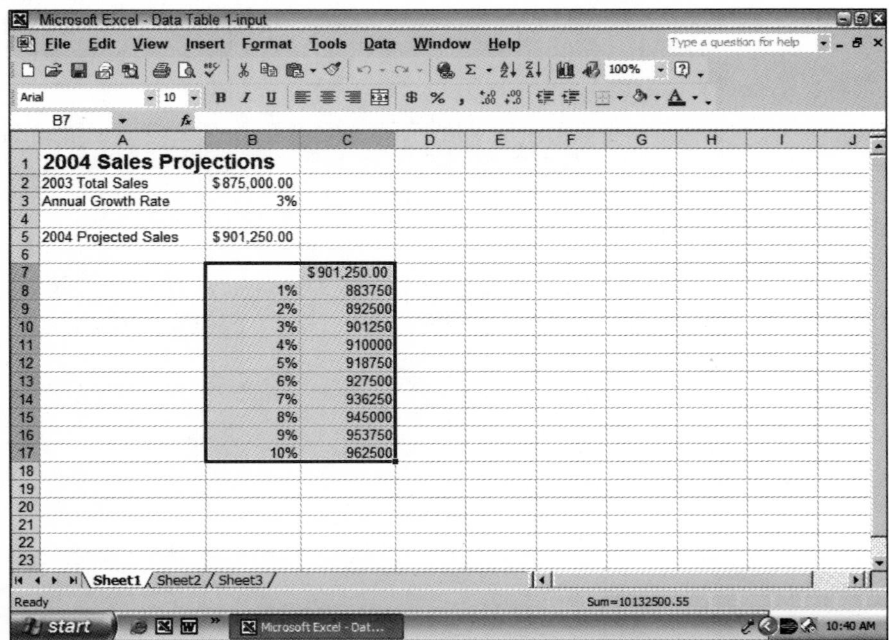

Figure 1-2: The completed one-variable data table.

If you want to see the effect on the results in the table of using a different range of variables, you only need to enter the new input values in the existing range. By default, Excel automatically recalculates the results in the output range of a data table whenever you change any of its input values. If you want to control when each data table is recalculated, while still allowing the formulas in the worksheet to be automatically recalculated, click the Automatic Except Tables radio button on the Calculation tab of the Options dialog box (Tools⇨Options).

Excel computes the results in a data table by creating an array formula that uses the TABLE function (see Book III, Chapter 1 for more information on array formulas). In this example, the array formula entered into the cell range C8:C17 is as follows:

```
{=TABLE(,B3)}
```

The TABLE function can take two arguments, *row_ref* and/or *column_ref*, which represent the row input cell and column input cell for the data table, respectively. In this example, the data table uses only a column input cell, so B3 is the second and only argument of the TABLE function. Because Excel enters the results in a data table by using an array formula, Excel won't allow you to clear individual result cells in its output range. If you try to delete a single result in the data table, Excel displays an Alert dialog box, stating that you can't change part of a table.

If you want to delete just the results in the output range of a data table, you must select all of the cells in the output range (cell range C8:C17, in the current example) before you press the Delete key or choose the Edit⇨Clear⇨All pull-down menu command.

Creating a two-variable data table

When you have a master formula in a worksheet in which you want to see the effect of changing two of its input values, you create a two-variable data table. When you create a two-variable data table, you enter two ranges of input values to be substituted in the master formula: a single-row range in the first row of the table and a single-column range in the first column of the data table. When you create a two-variable data table, you place a copy of the master formula in the cell at the intersection of this row and column of input values.

Figure 1-3 shows the typical setup for a two-variable data table. This figure uses the projected sales worksheet shown previously in the section on a one-variable data table. Here, however, a second variable has been added to projecting the total sales in 2004. This worksheet contains a value in cell B4 (named Expenses_04) that shows the projected percentage of expenses to sales, which is used, in turn, in the master formula in cell B5 as follows:

```
=Sales_03+(Sales_03*Growth_04)-(Sales_03*Expenses_04)
```

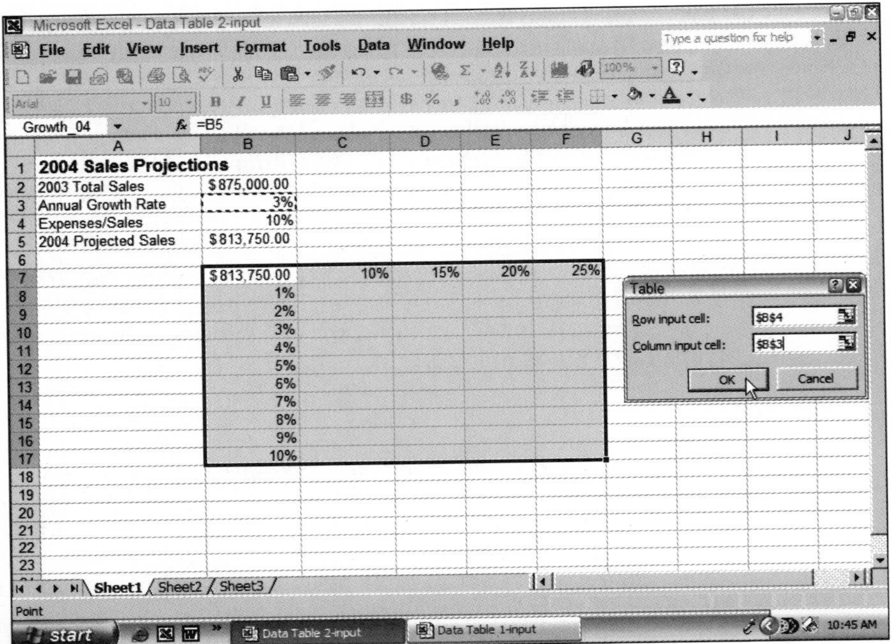

Figure 1-3: Creating a two-variable data table.

Note that when you factor in the expenses, the projected sales at an annual growth rate of 3% falls in cell B5 from $901,250 to $813,750.

To determine how changing both the growth rate and the percentage of expenses to sales will affect the projected sales for 2004, you create a two-variable data table. In setting up this table, you still enter the variable growth rates down column B in the cell range B8:B17. Then, you enter the variable expense rates across row 7 in the range C7:F7. This time, you bring forward the master formula by entering the formula =B5 in cell B7, the cell at the intersection of the row and column containing the two input variables.

After setting up the two series of variables in this manner, you are ready to create the table by selecting the cell range B7:F17 and opening the Table dialog box, as shown in Figure 1-3. For a two-variable data table, you must designate both a row input and column cell in the worksheet. In this example, the row input cell is B4, which contains the original expense-to-sales percentage, while the column input cell remains B3, which contains the original growth rate. After these two input cells are entered in the Table dialog box, you are ready to generate the data table by clicking the OK button.

Figure 1-4 shows the completed two-variable data table with the results of changing both the projected growth rate and the projected expenses. As with a one-variable data table, you can save this two-variable data table as part of your worksheet. You can also update the table by changing any of the (two types) input variables.

Microsoft Excel - Data Table 2-input

B7 =B5

	A	B	C	D	E	F
1	**2004 Sales Projections**					
2	2003 Total Sales	$875,000.00				
3	Annual Growth Rate	3%				
4	Expenses/Sales	10%				
5	2004 Projected Sales	$813,750.00				
6						
7		$813,750.00	10%	15%	20%	25%
8		1%	796250	752500	708750	665000
9		2%	805000	761250	717500	673750
10		3%	813750	770000	726250	682500
11		4%	822500	778750	735000	691250
12		5%	831250	787500	743750	700000
13		6%	840000	796250	752500	708750
14		7%	848750	805000	761250	717500
15		8%	857500	813750	770000	726250
16		9%	866250	822500	778750	735000
17		10%	875000	831250	787500	743750

Sheet1 / Sheet2 / Sheet3

Ready Sum= $31,613,751.25

Figure 1-4: The completed two-variable data table.

The array formula entered in the output range (C8:F17) to create this two-variable data table is very similar to the one created previously for the one-variable data table, only this time the TABLE function uses both a *row_ref* and *column_ref* argument as follows:

```
{=TABLE(B4,B3)}
```

Remember that because this data table used an array formula, you must select all the cells in the output range if you want to delete them.

Exploring Different Scenarios

Excel enables you to create and save sets of input values that produce different results as *scenarios* with the Tools⇨Scenario command. A scenario consists of a group of input values in a worksheet to which you assign a name, such as *Best Case*, *Worst Case*, *Most Likely Case*, and so on. Then, to reuse the input data and view the results that they produce in the worksheet, you simply select the name of the scenario that you want to use and Excel applies the input values stored in that scenario to the appropriate cells in the worksheet. After creating your different scenarios for a worksheet, you can also use Scenario Manager to create a summary report showing both the input values stored in each scenario as well as key results produced by each.

Creating new scenarios

When creating a scenario for your worksheet, you create a spreadsheet that uses certain cells that change in each scenario (appropriately enough, called *changing cells*). To make it easier to identify the changing cells in each scenario that you create (especially in any scenario summary reports that you generate), you should assign range names to the variables in the spreadsheet with the Insert⇨Name⇨Define or Create pull-down menu command before you create your scenarios.

To create your scenarios with Scenario Manager, follow these steps:

1. **Select the changing cells in the spreadsheet; that is, the cells whose values vary in each of your scenarios.**

   Remember that you can select non-adjacent cells in the worksheet by holding down the Ctrl key as you click them.

2. **Choose the Tools⇨Scenarios from the Excel Menu bar.**

   This action opens the Scenario Manager dialog box, similar to the one shown in Figure 1-5.

3. **Click the Add button in the Scenario Manager dialog box.**

   This action opens the Add Scenario dialog box, similar to the one shown in Figure 1-6. The Add Scenario dialog box contains a Scenario Name text box, where you give the new scenario a descriptive name such as *Best Case, Most Likely Case,* and so on. This dialog box also contains a Changing Cells text box that contains the addresses of the variable cells that you selected in the worksheet and a Comment box that contains a note with your name and the current date, so you'll always know when you created the particular scenario.

4. **Type a descriptive name for the new scenario in the Scenario Name text box.**

   Now, you should check over the cell references in the Changing Cells to make sure that they're correct — you can modify them if necessary by clicking the Change Cells text box and then by clicking the cells in the worksheet while holding down the Ctrl key. You can also edit the note in the Comment box if you want to add more information about your assumptions as part of the new scenario.

By default, Excel protects a scenario from changes when you turn on protection for the worksheet (see Book IV, Chapter 2 for details) so that you can't edit or delete the scenario in any way. If you want Excel to hide the scenario as well when worksheet protection is turned on, click the Hide check box. If you don't want to protect or hide the scenario when worksheet protection is turned on, click the Prevent Changes check box to remove its checkmark and leave the Hide check box as it is.

5. **Choose what kind, if any, of scenario protection that you need with the Prevent Changes and Hide check boxes in the Protection section of the Add Scenario dialog box.**

   Now you're ready to specify the changing values for the new scenario.

6. **Click OK in the Add Scenario dialog box.**

   This action closes the Add Scenario dialog box and then opens the Scenario Values dialog box, similar to the one shown in Figure 1-7. The Scenario Values dialog box numbers and shows the range name (assuming that you named each of the cells), followed by the current value for each of the changing values that you selected in the worksheet before starting to define different scenarios for your spreadsheet.

   You can accept the values shown in the text box for each changing cell if it suits the current scenario that you're defining, or you can increase or decrease any or all of them as needed to reflect the scenario's assumptions.

7. **Check the values in each of changing cells' text boxes and modify them as needed.**

   Now you're ready to close the Scenario Values dialog box, which completes the definition of the new scenario.

8. **Click the Add button in the Scenario Values dialog box.**

   This action closes the Scenario Values dialog box and returns you to the Add Scenario dialog box, where you can define a new scenario name for the changing cells.

9. **Repeat Steps 4 and 7 to add all the other scenarios that you want to create.**

   After you finish defining all the different scenarios you want to apply to the changing values in the spreadsheet, you can close the Scenario Values dialog box and then return to the Scenario Manager dialog box where you can use the Show button to display the effects that have been made to your spreadsheet by using different sets of changing values.

10. **Click OK in the Add Values dialog box and then the Close button in the Scenario Manager dialog box.**

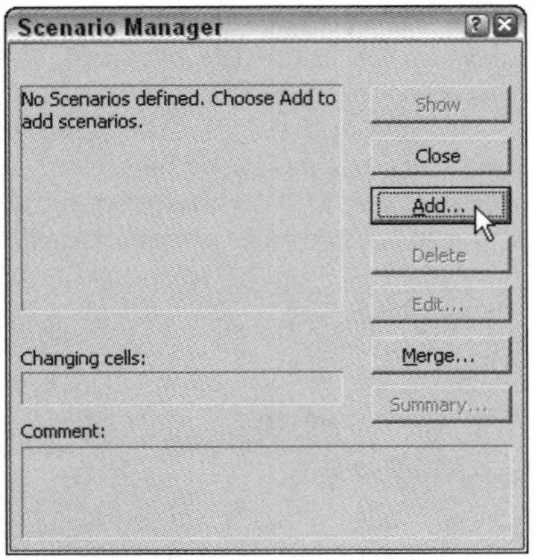

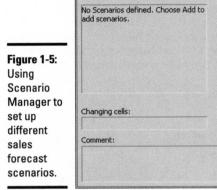

Figure 1-5: Using Scenario Manager to set up different sales forecast scenarios.

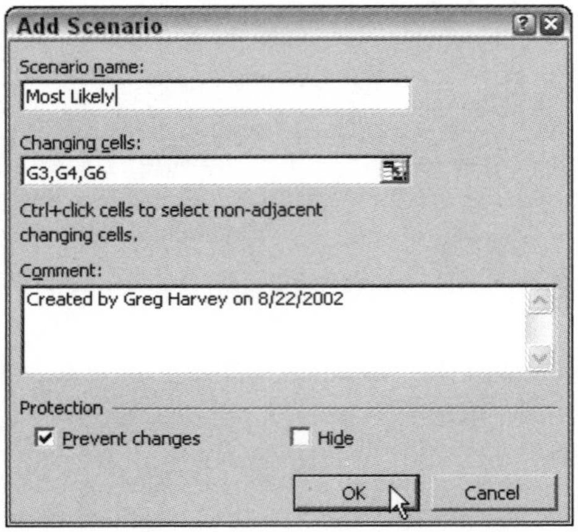

Figure 1-6: Adding a new Best Case scenario for the sales forecast.

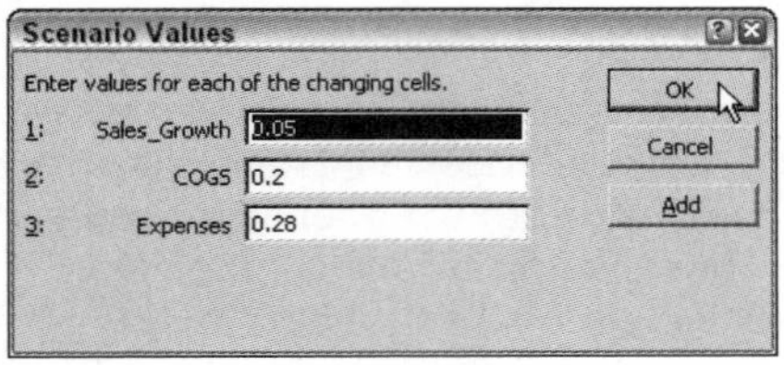

Figure 1-7: Specifying the changing values in the Scenario Values dialog box.

When you return to the Scenario Manager dialog box, the names of all the scenarios that you added appear in the Scenarios list box of the Scenario. For example, in Figure 1-8, you see that three scenarios — Most Likely, Best Case, and Worst Case — are now listed in the Scenarios list box.

To show a particular scenario in the worksheet that uses the values you entered for the changing cells, you simply double-click the scenario name in this list box or select the name and click the Show command button. Figure 1-8 shows the results in the sample forecast worksheet after selecting the Best Case scenario.

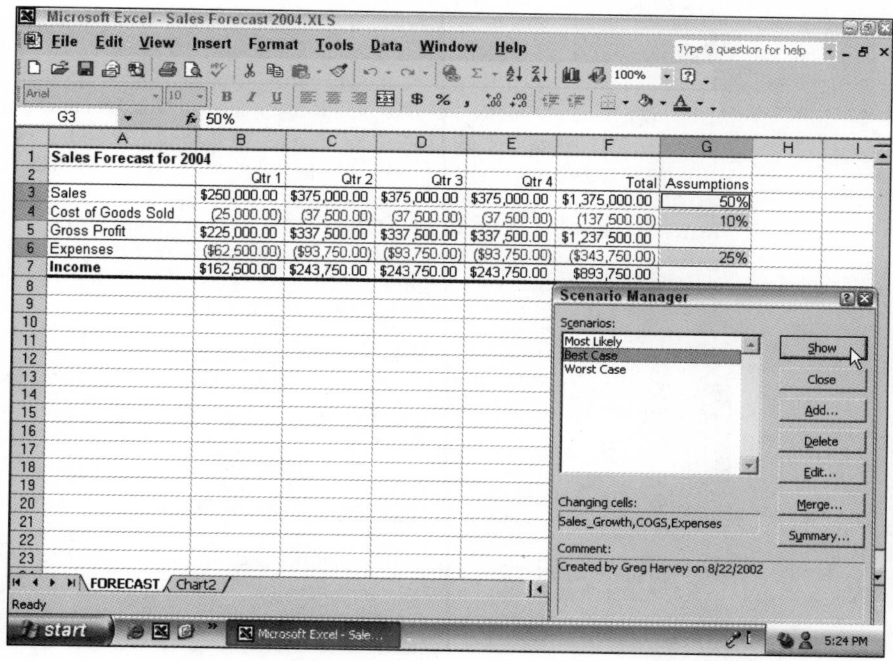

Figure 1-8: Spreadsheet after specifying the changing values from Best Case scenario.

If, after creating the scenarios for your worksheet, you find that you need to use different input values or you want to add or remove scenarios, you can edit the scenarios in the Scenario Manager dialog box. To modify the scenario's name and/or the input values assigned to the changing cells of that scenario, click the scenario name in the Scenarios list box and then click the Edit button so that you can make the appropriate changes in the Edit Scenario dialog box. To remove a scenario from a worksheet, select the scenario's name in the Scenarios list box and then click the Delete button. Note, however, that if you delete a scenario in error, you can't restore it with the

Edit⇨Undo Clear command. Instead, you must recreate the scenario by using the Add command button as outlined previously.

You can also merge scenarios from other Excel workbook files that are open (of course, the workbooks should share the same spreadsheet layout and changing cells). To merge a scenario into the current worksheet from another workbook, click the Merge button in the Scenario Manager dialog box, and then select the workbook in the Book drop-down list box and the worksheet in the Sheet drop-down list box before you click OK. Excel then copies all of the scenarios defined for that worksheet and merges with any scenarios that you've defined for the current worksheet.

Producing a summary report

After creating the different scenarios for your worksheet, you can use the Summary button in the Scenario Manager dialog box to create a summary report that shows the changing values used in each scenario and, if you want, key resulting values that each produces. When you click the Summary button, Excel opens a Scenario Summary dialog box, similar to the one shown in Figure 1-9, where you may designate a cell selection of result cells in the Result Cells text box to be included in the report. After selecting the result cells for the report, click OK to have Excel generate the summary report and display it in a new worksheet window.

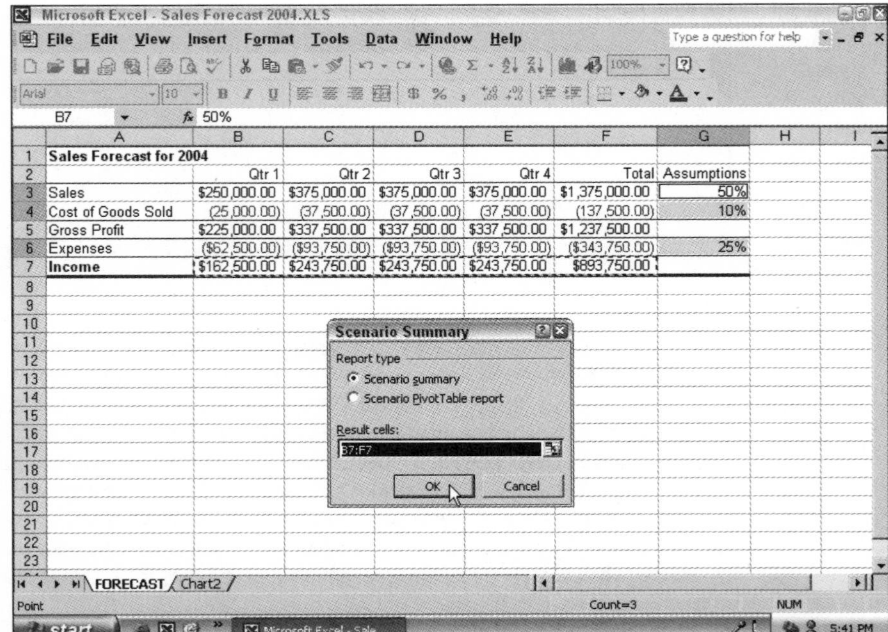

Figure 1-9: Designating the result cells in the Scenario Summary dialog box.

In the example shown in Figure 1-9, the cell range B7:F7, containing the projected income figures for the sales forecast, are designated as the result cells to be included in the summary report. Figure 1-10 shows the actual summary report generated for this sample worksheet in a new document window. Note that because all the changing and result cells in this worksheet are named, the summary report uses their range names in place of their cell references. Also, when Scenario Manager generates a summary report, it automatically outlines the summary data, thus creating two vertical levels — one for the changing cells and another for the result cells.

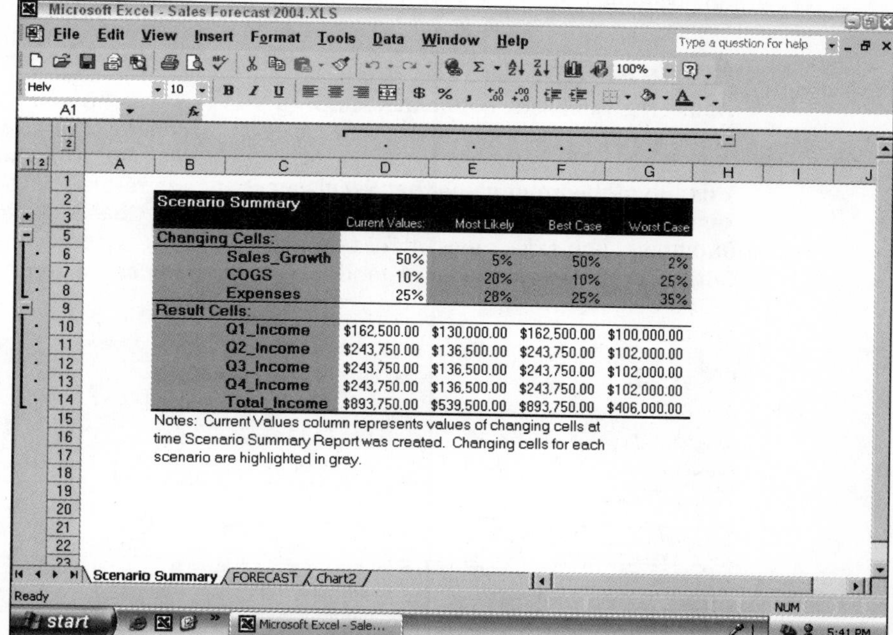

Scenario Summary	Current Values:	Most Likely	Best Case	Worst Case
Changing Cells:				
Sales_Growth	50%	5%	50%	2%
COGS	10%	20%	10%	25%
Expenses	25%	28%	25%	35%
Result Cells:				
Q1_Income	$162,500.00	$130,000.00	$162,500.00	$100,000.00
Q2_Income	$243,750.00	$136,500.00	$243,750.00	$102,000.00
Q3_Income	$243,750.00	$136,500.00	$243,750.00	$102,000.00
Q4_Income	$243,750.00	$136,500.00	$243,750.00	$102,000.00
Total_Income	$893,750.00	$539,500.00	$893,750.00	$406,000.00

Notes: Current Values column represents values of changing cells at time Scenario Summary Report was created. Changing cells for each scenario are highlighted in gray.

Figure 1-10: Scenario Summary report for the scenarios in the Sales Forecast table.

After generating a summary report, you can save it with the File⇨Save As command and/or print it with the File⇨Print command.

Note that the Scenario Summary dialog box contains an option, Scenario Pivot/Table Report, which enables you to view the scenario results as a pivot table. See Book VII, Chapter 2 for details on the uses of pivot tables.

Hide and Goal Seeking

Sometimes, you know the outcome that you want to realize in a worksheet and you need Excel to help you find the input values necessary to achieve those results. This procedure, which is just the opposite of the what-if analysis that I've been examining in this chapter, is referred to as *goal seeking*.

When you simply need to find the value for a single variable that will give the desired result in a particular formula, you can perform this simple type of goal seeking with the Goal Seek command. If you have charted the data and created a two-dimensional column, bar, or line chart, you can also perform the goal seeking by directly manipulating the appropriate marker on the chart. And when you need to perform more complex goal seeking, such as that which involves changing multiple input values to realize a result or constraining the values to a specific range, you can use the Solver command.

Performing goal seeking

To use the Goal Seek command, simply select the cell containing the formula that will return the result that you are seeking (referred to as the *set cell*), indicate what value you want this formula to return, and then indicate the location of the input value that Excel can change to return the desired result. Figures 1-11 and 1-12 illustrate how you can use the Goal Seek command to find how much sales must increase to realize first quarter income of $200,000 (given certain growth, cost of goods sold, and expense assumptions).

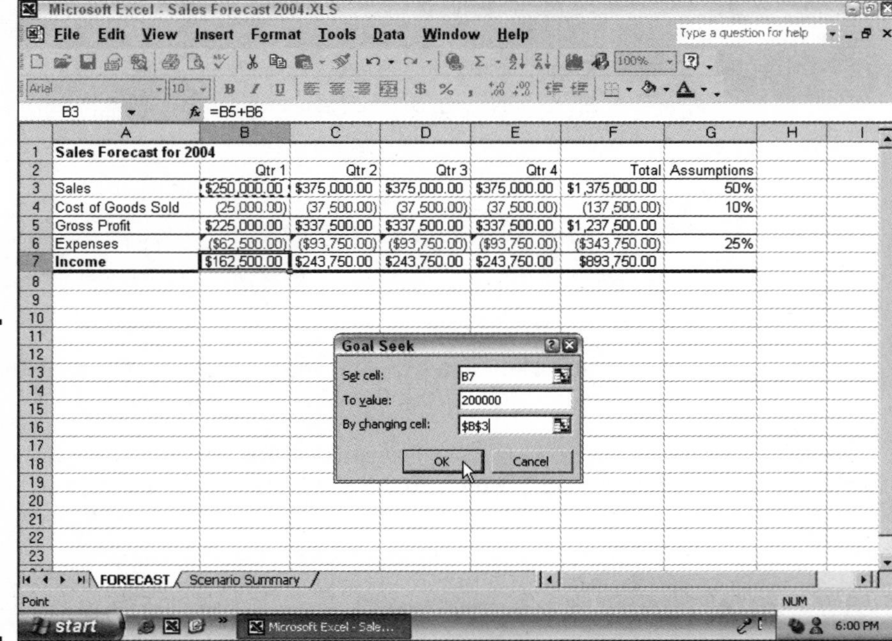

Figure 1-11: Using goal seeking to find out how much sales must increase to reach a target income.

To find out how much sales must increase to return a net income of $200,000 in the first quarter, you first select cell B7, which contains the formula that calculates the first quarter income before you choose Tools➪Goal Seek from the Excel Menu bar. This action opens the Goal Seek dialog box, similar to the one shown in Figure 1-11. Because cell B7 is the active cell when you open this dialog box, the Set Cell text box already contains the cell reference B7. You then select the To Value text box and enter **200000** as the goal. Then, you select the By Changing Cell text box and select cell B3 in the worksheet (the cell that contains the first quarter sales).

Figure 1-12 shows you the Goal Seek Status dialog box that appears when you click OK in the Goal Seek dialog box to have Excel go ahead and adjust the sales figure to reach your desired income figure. As this figure shows, Excel increases the sales in cell B3 from $250,000 to $307,692.31, which, in turn, returns $200,000 as the income in cell B7. The Goal Seek Status dialog box informs you that goal seeking has found a solution and that the current value and target value are now the same (if this were not the case, the Step and Pause buttons in the dialog box would become active, and you could have Excel perform further iterations to try to narrow and ultimately eliminate the gap between the target and current value).

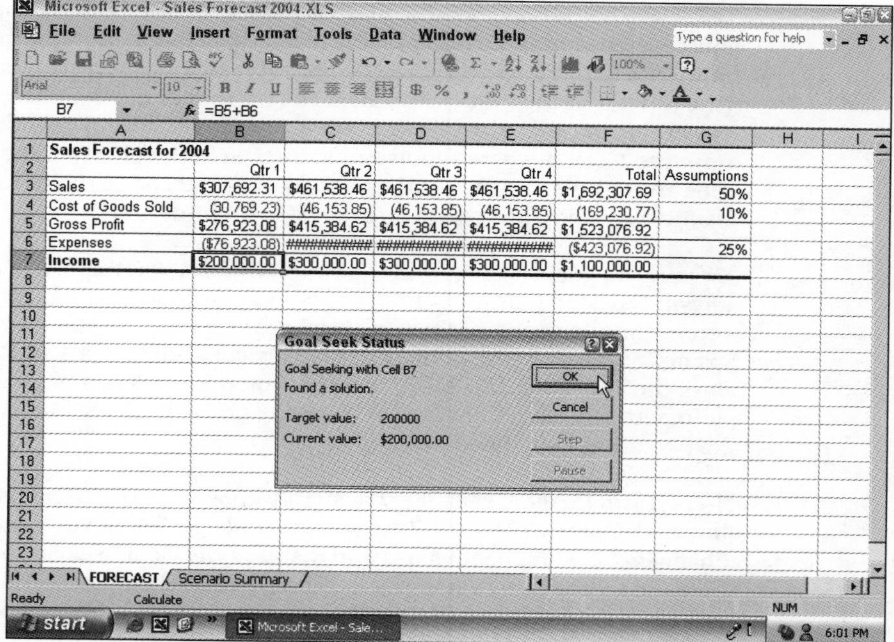

Figure 1-12: Spreadsheet showing goal seeking solution and Goal Seek Status dialog box.

If you want to keep the values entered in the worksheet as a result of goal seeking, click OK to close the Goal Seek Status dialog box. If you want to return to the original values, click the Cancel button instead. If you change the value by clicking OK, remember that you can still switch between the "before" and "after" input values and results by choosing the Edit⇨Undo Goal Seek command or by pressing Ctrl+Z.

To flip back and forth between the "after" and "before" values when you've closed the Goal Seek Status dialog box, press Ctrl+Z to display the original values before goal seeking and then Ctrl+Y to display the values engendered by the goal seeking solution.

Graphic goal seeking

If you create an embedded two-dimensional line, column, or bar chart for your data, you can perform goal seeking from the chart window by directly manipulating the line or bar (see Book V, Chapter 1 for details on how to create these types of charts). Figures 1-13 and 1-14 illustrate how this works.

In Figure 1-13, you see a two-dimensional bar chart embedded below the Sales Forecast table that graphs the projected sales and income for all four quarters. The top bar in each cluster represents the quarterly income, while the lower bar represents the quarterly sales. To find out how much sales must increase to realize an income of $200,000 in the first quarter, hold down the Ctrl key as you click the bar representing the first quarter income (the top bar in the first cluster near the bottom of the bar chart). When you select this bar with the Ctrl key depressed, Excel selects only this bar (as opposed to all the bars representing income in the chart) and draws handles around the bar. One of these handles at the end of the bar in the center handle is a solid black square (the rest are white).

To perform goal seeking from the chart window, you then release the Ctrl key and use the pointer to drag the black handle until you position the line representing the end of the bar at the desired value on the chart grid (in this example, you drag the pointer to the vertical gridline marked $200,000 and until the ToolTip reads 200000). When you release the mouse button, Excel automatically opens the Goal Seek dialog box with the Set Cell and To Value text boxes already filled in.

To perform the goal seeking, you simply choose the By Changing Cell text box and designate the worksheet cell to change. When you click OK, Excel changes the worksheet values and displays the Goal Seek Status dialog box (like the one shown previously in Figure 1-12). When you choose the OK button in the Goal Seek Status dialog box, Excel closes this dialog box and updates the chart as it changes the values in the spreadsheet, as shown in Figure 1-14.

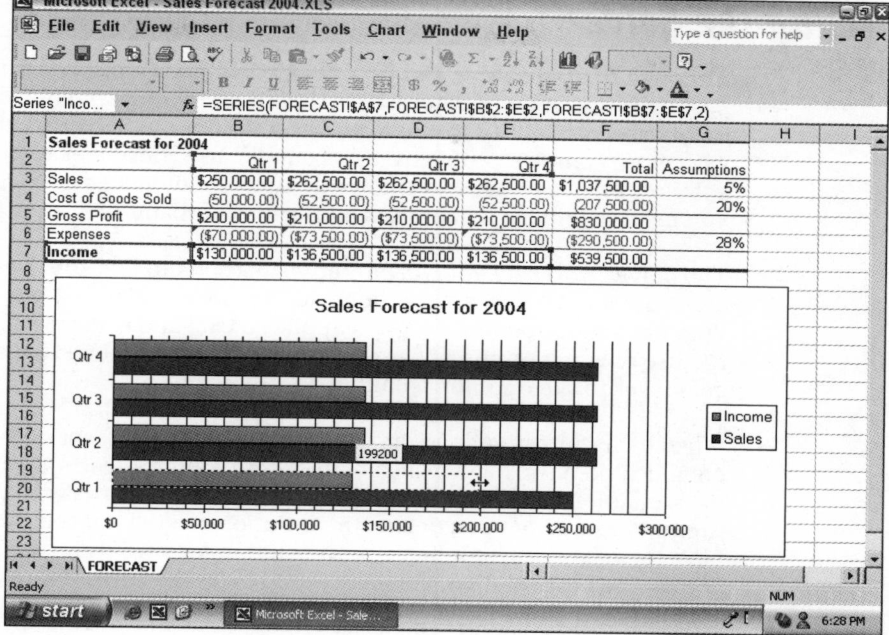

Figure 1-13: Doing goal seeking by manipulating the bar representing Qtr 1 Income in the chart.

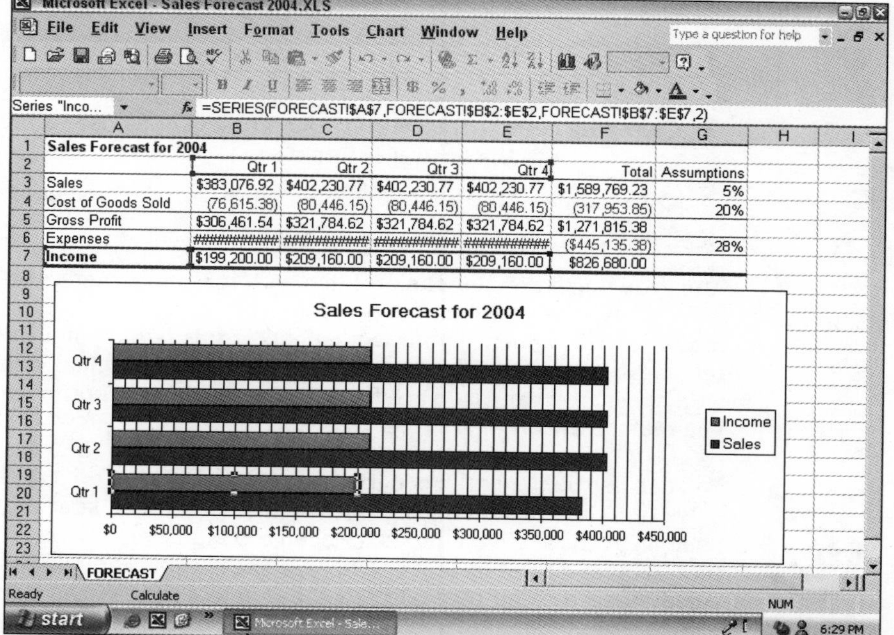

Figure 1-14: Spreadsheet showing goal seeking solution with updated bar chart.

Using the Solver

Although the Data Table and Goal Seek commands work just fine for simple problems that require determining the direct relationship between the inputs and results in a formula, you need to use the Solver when dealing with more complex problems. For example, use the Solver to find the best solution when you need to change multiple input values in your model and you need to impose constraints on these values and/or the output value.

The Solver works by applying iterative methods to find the "best" solution given the inputs, desired solution, and the constraints that you impose. With each iteration, the program applies a trial-and-error method (based on the use of linear or non-linear equations and inequalities) that attempts to get closer to the optimum solution.

When using Solver, keep in mind that many problems, especially the more complicated ones, have many solutions. Although Solver returns the optimum solution, given the starting values, the variables that can change, and the constraints that you define, this solution is often not the only one possible and, in fact, may not be the best solution for you. To be sure that you are finding the best solution, you may want to run the Solver more than once, adjusting the initial values each time you solve the problem.

When setting up the problem in your worksheet model to be solved by Solver, define the following items:

- **Target cell** — the cell in your worksheet whose value is to be maximized, minimized, or made to reach a particular value
- **Changing cells** — the cells in your worksheet whose values are to be adjusted until the answer is found
- **Constraints** — the limits that you impose on the changing values and/or the target cell

After you finish defining the problem with these parameters and you have Solver solve the problem, the program will return the optimum solution by modifying the values in your worksheet. At this point, you can choose to retain the changes in the worksheet or restore the original values to the worksheet. You can also save the solution as a scenario to view later before you restore the original values.

You can use Solver with Scenario Manager to help set up a problem to solve or to save a solution so that you can view it at a later date. The changing cells that you define for Scenario Manager are automatically picked up and used by Solver when you select this command, and vice versa. Also, you can save Solver's solution to a problem as a scenario (by clicking the Save Scenario button in the Solver dialog box) that you can then view with the Scenario Manager.

Setting up and defining the problem

The first step in setting up a problem for the Solver to work on is to create the worksheet model. Excel comes with a sample workbook called `solvsamp.xls` (for Solver samples) that comes with six classic resource problems that you can use as guides when setting up your worksheet models. This workbook contains a Quick Tour sheet that introduces how the Solver works along with the following models — each on its own worksheet:

- **Product Mix** finds the most advantageous profit mix for constructing TVs, stereos, and speakers from parts available in inventory
- **Shipping Routes** finds the least costly shipping routes for shipping goods from production plants to warehouses
- **Staff Scheduling** finds the most profitable scheduling of staff by using various shift changes
- **Maximizing Income** finds the maximum interest income from short-term versus long-term investments
- **Portfolio of Securities** finds the maximum rate of return for a specific level of risk in a portfolio of stocks
- **Engineering Design** contains an engineering problem that determines the appropriate value for a resistor to dissipate a charge to a particular percentage of its initial value within a particular length of time

The `solvsamp.xls` workbook is in the Samples folder located within the Office10 folder. This folder, in turn, is located inside the Microsoft Office folder that's put inside the Program Files folder on your hard drive. Note, however, that this workbook file is available only when you have installed the Excel sample files. Because these are not automatically copied when you do a standard installation of the Excel program, you may have to use the Windows Add or Remove Programs Control panel to install the Excel sample files on your computer.

Keep in mind that Solver is an add-in utility. This means that before you can use it, you need to activate the add-in. To do this, choose Tools⇨Add-Ins on the Excel pull-down menus and then click the Solver Add-in check box in the Add-Ins dialog box before you click OK to close the dialog box.

To define and solve a problem with Solver after you have created your worksheet model, take the following steps:

1. **Choose Tools⇨Solver from the Excel Menu bar.**

   This action opens the Solver Parameters dialog box, which is similar to the one shown in Figure 1-15.

2. **Click the target cell in the worksheet or enter its cell reference or range name in the Set Target Cell text box.**

   Next, you need to select the Equal To setting. Click the Max radio button when you want the target cell's value to be as large as possible. Click the Min radio button when you want the target cell's value to be as small as possible. Click the Value Of radio button and then enter a value in the associated text box when you want the target cell's value to reach a particular value.

3. **Click the appropriate radio button option in the Equal to section of the dialog box. If you select the Value To radio button, enter the value to match in the associated text box.**

   Next, designate the changing cells; that is, the ones that Solver can adjust to reach your Equal To goal.

4. **Click the By Changing Cells text box and then select the cells to change in the worksheet or enter their cell references or range name in the text box.**

   Remember that to select nonadjacent cells in the worksheet, you need to hold down the Ctrl key as you click each cell in the selection. To have Excel choose the changing cells for you based upon the target cell that you selected, click the Guess button to the right of this text box.

   Before having Solver adjust your model, you may add constraints for the target cell or any of the changing cells that determine its limits when adjusting the values.

5. **(Optional) Click the Add button to the right of the Subject to the Constraints list box in the Solver Parameters dialog box.**

   This action opens the Add Constraint dialog box, similar to the one shown in Figure 1-16. When defining a constraint, choose the cell whose value you want to constrain or select the cell in the worksheet or enter its cell reference in the Cell Reference text box, choose the relationship (=, <=, >=, or *int* for integer or *bin* for binary) in the drop-down list box to the right and (unless you chose int or bin), enter the appropriate value or cell reference in the Constraint text box.

   To continue to add constraints for other cells used by Solver, click the Add button to add the constraint and clear the text boxes in the Add Constraint dialog box. Then, repeat Step 5 to add a new constraint. After you finish defining constraints for the target cell and changing values in the model, click OK to close the Add Constraint dialog box and return to the Solver Parameters dialog box (which now lists your constraints in the Subject to the Constraints list box).

6. **Click the Solve button to have Solver solve the problem as you've defined it in the Solver Parameters dialog box.**

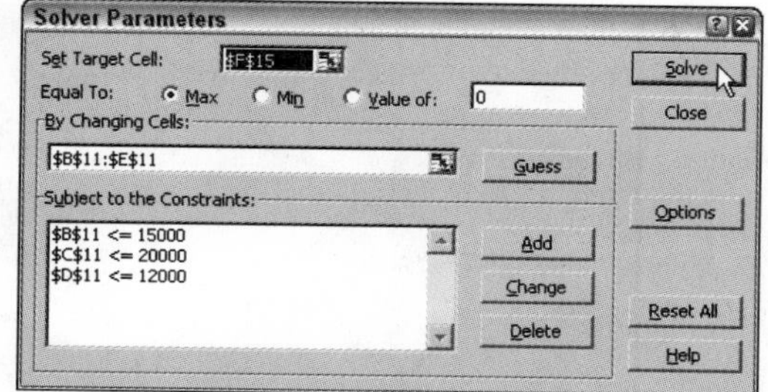

Figure 1-15: Specifying the parameters to apply to the model in the Solver Parameters dialog box.

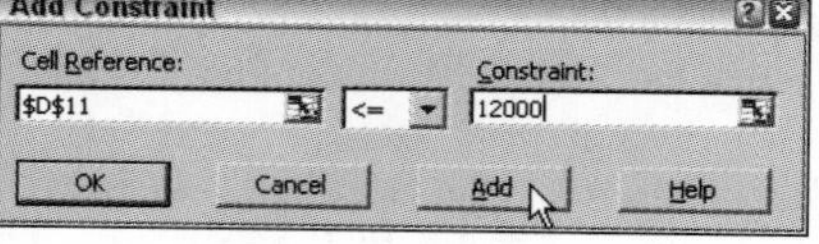

Figure 1-16: Adding a constraint to the target cell in the Add Constraint dialog box.

Solving the problem

When you click the Solve button, the Solver Parameters dialog box disappears and the status bar indicates that Solver is setting up the problem and then keeps you informed of the progress in solving the problem by showing the number of the intermediate (or trial) solutions as they are tried. To interrupt the solution process at any time before Excel calculates the last iteration, press the Esc key. Excel then displays the Show Trial Solution dialog box, informing you that the solution process has been paused. To continue the solution process, click the Continue button. To abort the solution process, click the Stop button.

When Excel finishes the solution process, the Solver Results dialog box appears, similar to the one shown in Figure 1-17. This dialog box informs you whether Solver was able to find a solution, given the target cell, changing cells, and constraints defined for the problem. To retain the changes made by Solver in your worksheet model, leave the Keep Solver Solution radio button selected and click OK to close the Solver Results dialog box. To return the original values to the worksheet, click the Restore Original

Values option button instead. To save the changes as a scenario before you restore the original values, click the Save Scenario button and assign a name to the current scenario before you click the Restore Original Values option and OK button.

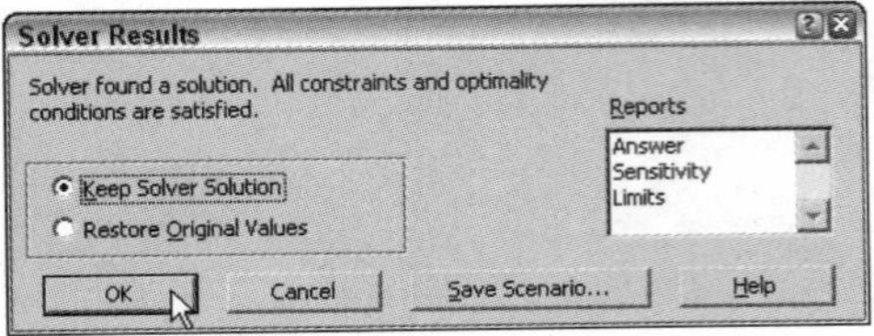

Figure 1-17: Solver Results dialog box showing that Solver has found a solution to the problem.

Unlike when using the Goal Seek command, after selecting the Keep Solver Solution radio button in the Solver Results dialog box, you can't use the Edit⇨Undo command to restore the original values to your worksheet. If you want to be able to switch between the "before" and "after" views of your worksheet, you must save the changes with the Save Scenario button and then select the Restore Original Values radio button option. That way, you can retain the "before" view in the original worksheet and use Scenario Manager to display the "after" view created by Solver.

Changing the Solver options

For most of the problems, the default options used by Solver are adequate. In some situations, however, you may want to change some of the Solver options before you begin the solution process. To change the solution options, click the Options button in the Solver Parameters dialog box. Excel then opens the Solver Options dialog box, shown in Figure 1-18, where you can make all necessary changes (refer to Table 1-1 for information on each option).

After changing the options, click OK to return to the Solver Parameters dialog box; from here, you can then click the Solve button to begin the solution process with the new solution settings that you just changed.

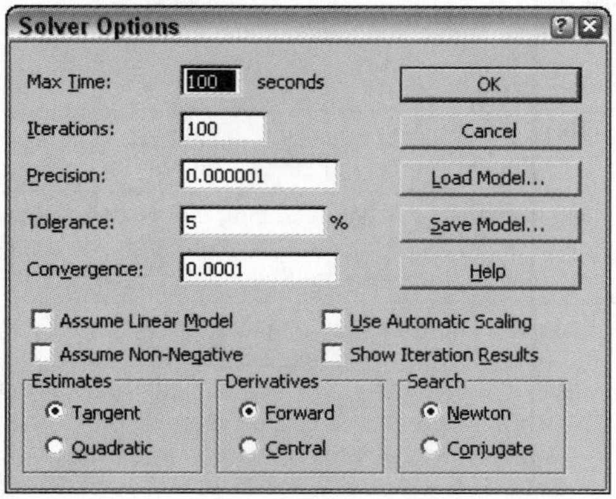

Figure 1-18: Modifying the solution options in the Solver Options dialog box.

Table 1-1 The Solver Option Settings

Option	*Function*
Max Time	Specify the maximum number of seconds that Solver will spend on finding the solution.
Iterations	Specifies the maximum number of times that Solver will recalculate the worksheet when finding the solution.
Precision	Specifies the precision of the constraints. The number that you enter in this text box determines whether the value in a constraint cell meets the specified value or the upper or lower limit you have set. Specify a lower number (between 0 and 1) to reduce the time it takes Solver to return a solution to your problem.
Tolerance	Specifies the integer tolerance. The number that you enter here is the maximum percentage of error allowed for integer solutions after you've constrained some of the changing cells to integers.
Convergence	Specifies the amount of relative change allowed in the last five iterations before Solver stops with a solution — the smaller the number you enter, the less relative the change allowed.
Assume Linear Model	Sets Solver to use linear programming method by using the Simplex method when solving your problem. Selecting this option can greatly reduce the amount of time it takes for Solver to return a solution to your problem when working on a linear problem.
Assume Non-Negative	Causes Solver to set 0 (zero) as the lower limit for all adjustable cells for which you have not already set a lower limit in the Add Constraint dialog box.
Use Automatic Scaling	Turns on automatic scaling for finding a solution to a problem where the magnitude of the changing cells differs greatly from the magnitude of the set cell and/or the constraint values.

(continued)

Table 1-1 *(continued)*

Option	*Function*
Show Iteration Results	Pauses the Solver at each trial solution so that you can see the intermediate results in the worksheet.
Load Model	Displays the Load Model dialog box where you can select the reference of saved Solver parameters that you want to load as the current problem into the Solver (see Save Model that follows).
Save Model	Displays the Save Model dialog box where you specify the reference for storing the current Solver parameters that you want to save in the worksheet so that you can reuse them later. You need to use this option to save a problem model only when you've already defined at least one problem for the worksheet and want to save all the problems in the worksheet.
Estimates	Specifies the approach used to obtain initial estimates for the basic variables in each one-dimensional search. Click the Tangent radio button to use linear extrapolation from a tangent vector. Click the Quadratic radio button to use quadratic extrapolation (which can improve the results on highly non-linear problems).
Derivatives	Specifies Forward differencing (the default) or Central differencing for estimates of partial derivatives. (Central requires more worksheet recalculations but can help when the Solver dialog box displays the message indicating that Solver could not improve the solution.)
Search	Specifies either a (quasi-) Newton (the default) or Conjugate gradient method searching (changing to Conjugate can be useful if, when stepping through iterations, you notice little progress between successive trial results).

Saving and loading a model problem

The target cell, changing cells, constraints, and Solver options that you most recently used are saved as part of the worksheet when you choose the File⇨Save command. When you define other problems for the same worksheet that you want to save, you must choose the Save Model button in the Solver Options dialog box and indicate the cell reference or name of the range in the active worksheet where you want the problem's parameters to be inserted.

When you select the Save Model button, Excel opens the Save Model dialog box, containing a Select Model Area text box. This text box will contain the cell references for a range large enough to hold all of the problem's parameters, starting with the active cell. To save the problem's parameters in this range, click OK. If this range includes cells with existing data, you need to modify the cell reference in this text box before you choose OK to prevent Excel from replacing the existing data.

After you click OK, Excel copies the problem's parameters in the specified range. These values are then saved as part of the worksheet the next time you save the workbook. To reuse these problem parameters when solving a problem, you simply need to open the Solver Options dialog box, click the Load Problem button and then select the range containing the saved problem parameters. When you click OK in the Load Model dialog box, Excel loads the parameters from this cell range into the appropriate text boxes in the Solver Parameters dialog box. You can then close the Solver Options dialog box by clicking OK and solve the problem by using these parameters by clicking the Solve command button.

Remember that you can use the Reset All button whenever you want to clear all of the parameters defined for the previous problem and return the Solver options to their defaults.

Creating Solver reports

You can create three different types of reports with Solver:

- **Answer report** lists the target cell and changing cells with their original and final values, along with the constraints used in solving the problem.
- **Sensitivity report** indicates how sensitive an optimal solution is to changes in the formulas that calculate the target cell and constraints. The report shows the changing cells with their final values and the *reduced gradient* for each cell (the reduced gradient measures the objective per unit increase in the changing cell). If you defined constraints, the Sensitivity report lists them with their final values and the *Lagrange multiplier* for each constraint (the Lagrange multiplier measures the objective per unit increase that appears in the right side of the constraint equation).
- **Limits report** shows the target cell and the changing cells with their values, lower and upper limits, and target results. The lower limit represents the lowest value that a changing cell can have while fixing the values of all other cells and still satisfy the constraints. The upper limit represents the highest value that will do this.

Excel places each report that you generate for a Solver problem in a separate worksheet in the workbook. To generate one (or all) of these reports, select the report type (Answer, Sensitivity, or Limits) in the Reports list box of the Solver Results dialog box (as shown previously in Figure 1-17). To select more than one report, just click the name of the report.

When you click OK to close the Solver Results dialog box (after choosing between the Keep Solver Solution and Restore Original Values option), Excel generates the report (or reports) that you selected in a new worksheet that it adds to the beginning of the workbook (report sheet tabs are named by report type, as in *Answer Report 1*, *Sensitivity Report 1*, and *Limits Report 1*).

Chapter 2: Generating Pivot Tables

In This Chapter

- **Understanding how pivot tables summarize data and how you can use them to analyze data lists**
- **Using PivotTable Wizard to create a pivot table**
- **Pivoting the elements in the data table**
- **Changing the summary function used in the pivot table**
- **Formatting a pivot table and changing the pivot table options**
- **Creating a pivot chart at the same time as your pivot table**

The subject of this chapter is the *pivot table*, which is the name given to a special type of data summary that you can use to analyze and reveal the relationships inherent in the data lists that you maintain in Excel. Pivot tables are great for summarizing particular values in a data list or database because they do their magic without making you create formulas to perform the calculations. Unlike the Subtotals feature, which is another summarizing feature (see Book VI, Chapter 1 for more information), pivot tables let you play around with the arrangement of the summarized data — even after you generate the table. (The Subtotals feature only lets you hide and display different levels of totals in the list.) This capability to change the arrangement of the summarized data by rotating row and column headings gives the pivot table its name.

Pivot tables are also versatile because they enable you to summarize data by using a variety of summary functions (although totals created with the SUM function will probably remain your old standby). When setting up the original pivot table — made really simple with the help of PivotTable and PivotChart Wizard — you make several decisions: what summary function to use, which columns (fields) the summary function is applied to, and which columns (fields) these computations are tabulated with. You can also use pivot tables to cross-tabulate one set of data in your data list with another. For example, you can use this feature to create a pivot table from an employee database that totals the salaries for each job category cross-tabulated (arranged) by department or job site.

Creating Pivot Tables

You open PivotTable and PivotChart Wizard by choosing Data⇨PivotTable and PivotChart Report from the Excel Menu bar; this enables you to create a new pivot table. This wizard consists of just three simple dialog boxes:

- **Step 1 of 3** (see Figure 2-1), where you indicate the source of the data that you want to summarize and choose between creating a simple pivot table or a pivot chart, which represents the summary data graphically with a supporting pivot table. The data source can be a Microsoft Excel List or Database, an External Data Source (as discussed in Book VI, Chapter 2), Multiple Consolidation Ranges, or Another PivotTable or PivotChart Report.
- **Step 2 of 3** (see Figure 2-2), where you indicate the data that you want to use in the Excel worksheet (when specifying a Microsoft Excel List or Database, Multiple Consolidation Ranges, or Another PivotTable or PivotChart Report as the data source), or execute an external data query that gets the data (when specifying an External Data Source).
- **Step 3 of 3** (see Figure 2-3), where you indicate whether the pivot table should be placed in a new worksheet or in a cell range somewhere in the current worksheet. When generating a pivot chart, Excel places the chart on its own chart sheet and places the support pivot table on the sheet that you specify in this dialog box.

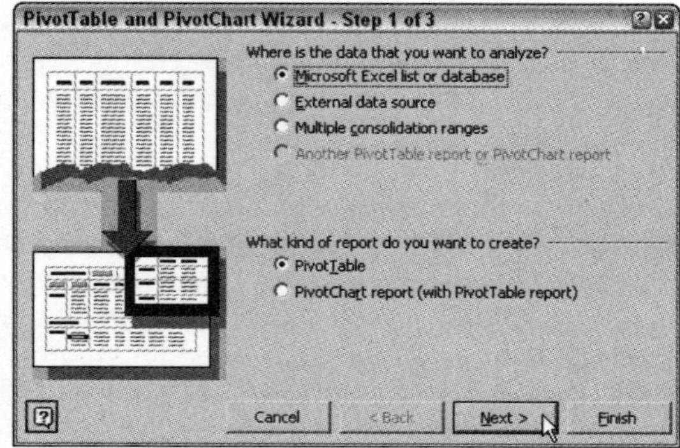

Figure 2-1: Indicating the source of the data in the PivotTable and PivotChart Wizard — Step 1 of 3 dialog box.

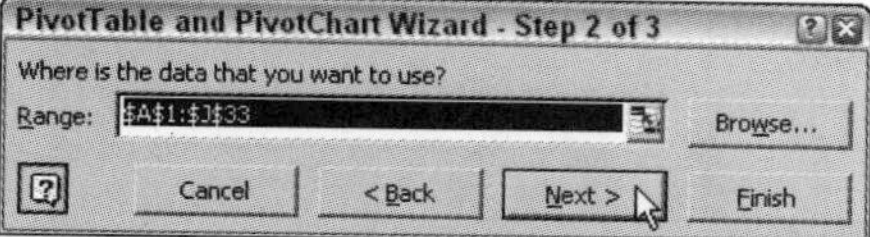

Figure 2-2: Indicating the data to use in PivotTable and PivotChart Wizard — Step 2 of 3 dialog box.

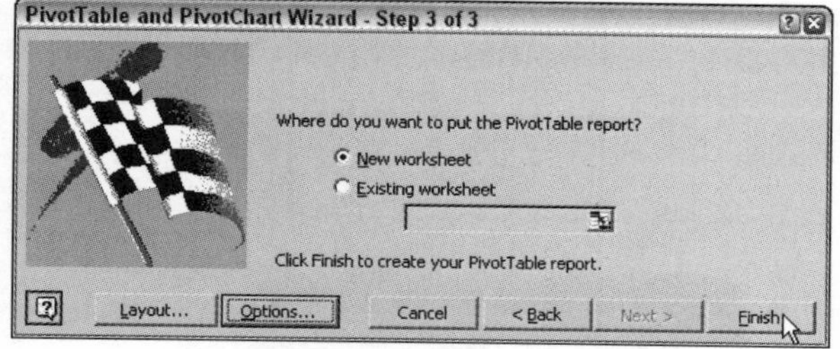

Figure 2-3: Indicating the location of the table in PivotTable and PivotChart Wizard — Step 3 of 3 dialog box.

After you finish going through the options offered in the three dialog boxes of PivotTable and PivotChart Wizard, you end up with a new (and somewhat blank) pivot table, similar to the one shown in Figure 2-4.

This new pivot table contains a blank framework with the various areas of the pivot table identified. Excel opens a floating PivotTable Field List task pane that contains a complete list of the names of the fields in your data source. You use these field names to bring the blank pivot table to life. In addition to the PivotTable Field List task pane, Excel also displays the PivotTable toolbar in the Excel window.

The key to completing the new pivot table is to assign the fields in the Field List task pane to the various parts of the table. You can do this in two ways: by dragging a field name from the task pane and then dropping it on a particular part of the pivot table; or by clicking the field name in the Field List task pane, selecting the part of the table to which to attach the field in its drop-down list box, and then clicking the Add To button at the bottom of the pane.

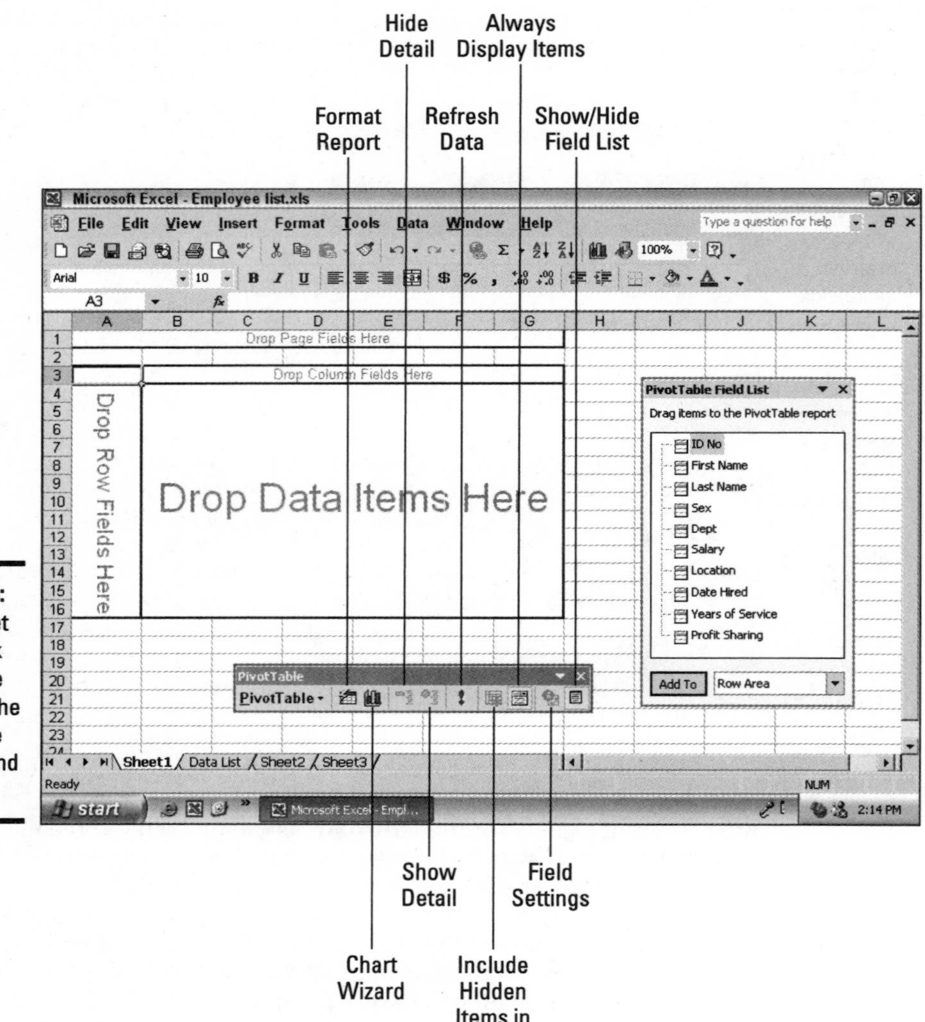

Figure 2-4: Worksheet with blank pivot table showing the PivotTable field list and toolbar.

Before you begin this procedure, however, you need to understand the use and significance of the various areas of a pivot table:

- **Drop Page Fields Here:** This area contains the fields that enable you to page through the data summaries shown in the actual pivot table by filtering out sets of data. For example, if you designate the Year Field from a data list as a Page Field, you can display data summaries in the pivot table for individual years or for all years represented in the data list.
- **Drop Column Fields Here:** This area contains the fields that determine the arrangement of data shown in the columns of the pivot table.
- **Drop Row Fields Here:** This area contains the fields that determine the arrangement of data shown in the rows of the pivot table.
- **Drop Data Items Here:** This area contains the fields that determine which data are presented in the cells of the pivot table and then summarized in its last column (totaled by default).

To better understand how you can use these various areas in a pivot table, consider the pivot table shown in Figure 2-5. For this pivot table, I assigned the Profit Sharing field from the data list (a logical field that contains Yes or No to indicate whether an employee is currently enrolled in the company's profit sharing plan) as the Page Field, the Dept Field (that contains the names of the various departments in the company) as the Column Field, the Location Field (that contains the names of the various cities with corporate offices) as the Row Field, and the Salary Field as the table's sole Data Item. As a result, the pivot table now displays the sum of the salaries for the employees in each department (across the columns) and then presents these sums by their corporate location (in each row).

Figure 2-6 demonstrates what happens when you change the Page Field from its default setting of (All), which displays the sums for all employees regardless of whether they're currently part of profit sharing, to Yes, which displays only the totals of the salaries for employees who are now part of the plan.

To change the Profit Sharing Page Field from (All) to Yes, click the pop-up button attached to the cell displaying this entry and then click Yes on the pop-up menu (to display the salary totals in the pivot table for those that aren't yet enrolled in the profit-sharing plan, click No in this pop-up menu instead) and then click the OK button at the bottom of the pop-up menu to close it.

In addition to changing the way the data in the pivot table is filtered by selecting a new item on a Page Field's pop-up menu, you can also collapse and expand the pivot table itself by selecting or unselecting particular items on the Column fields' and Row fields' pop-up menus.

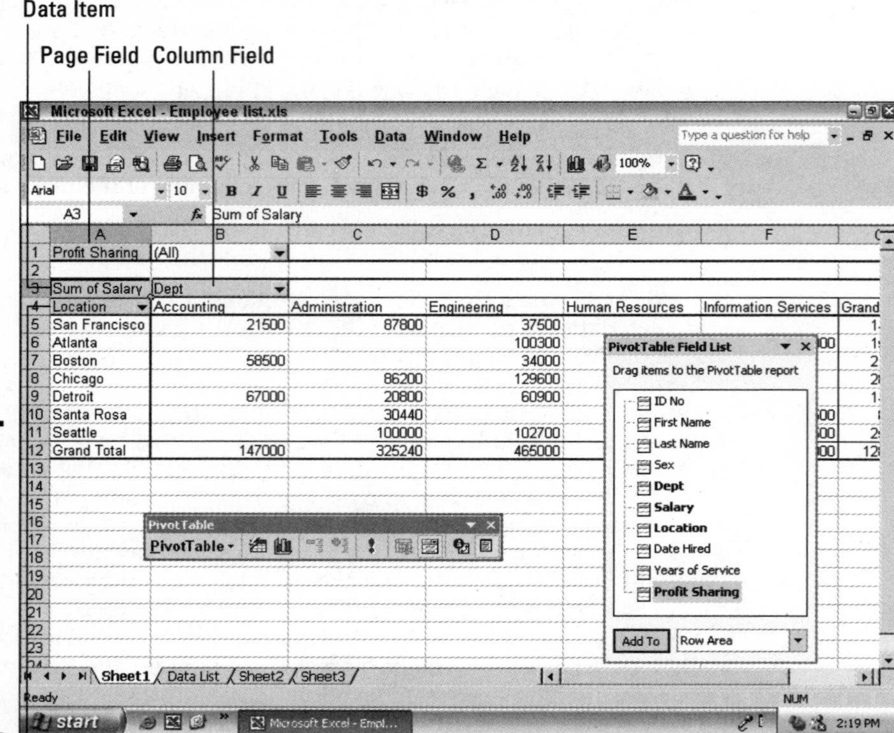

Row Field

Figure 2-5: Pivot table report after selecting the fields and data items from the PivotTable Field List.

When you click one of these pop-up buttons, Excel displays a pop-up menu showing each unique item in that field following a (Show All) option at the very top. Each of these pop-up menu items is preceded by a check box. To remove items that are currently shown in the pivot table, you click their check boxes to remove their checkmarks. To remove the checkmarks from all the items on the pop-up menu, click the (Show All) item to remove its checkmarks (and simultaneously all checkmarks for the other items). You can then click the items on the menu whose values are still to be displayed before you click the OK button at the bottom of the menu to close it.

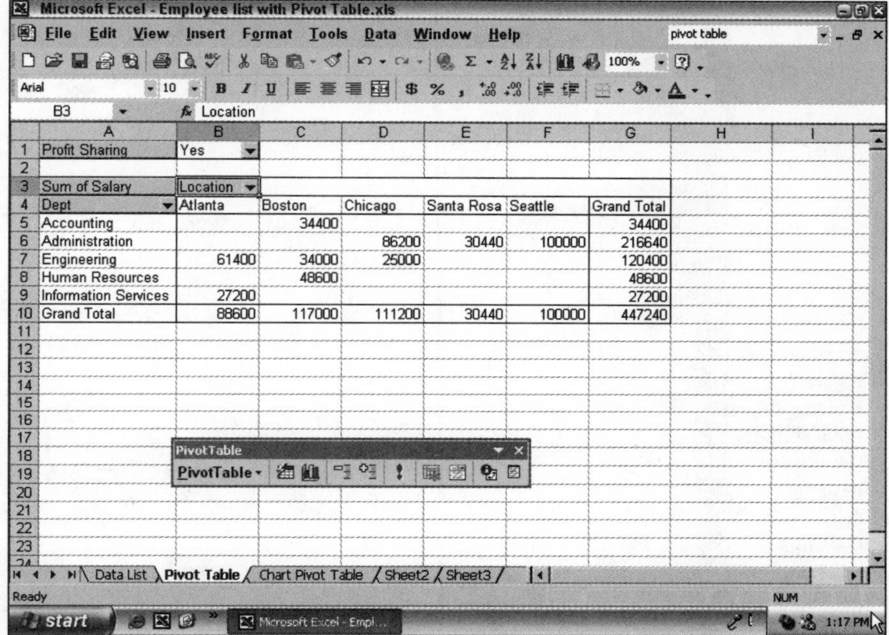

Figure 2-6: Pivot table report after changing Page Field from (All) to Yes.

Pivoting the Column and Row Fields

As the name "pivot" implies, the fun of pivot tables is being able to rotate the data fields by using the rows and columns of the table, as well as to change what fields are used on the fly. For example, suppose that after making the Dept Field the pivot table's Column Field, and the Location Field the Row Field, you now want to see what the table looks like with the Location Field as the Column Field and the Dept Field as the Row Field?

No problem: All you have to do is drag the Dept Field label from the top row of the table and drop it in the first column and then drag the Location Field label from the first column and drop it on the first row, and voila, Excel rearranges the totaled salaries so that the rows of the pivot table show the departmental grand totals and the columns now show the location grand totals. Figure 2-7 shows this new arrangement for the totals of the salaries for the employees enrolled in profit sharing (because the Profit Sharing Page Field is still set to Yes).

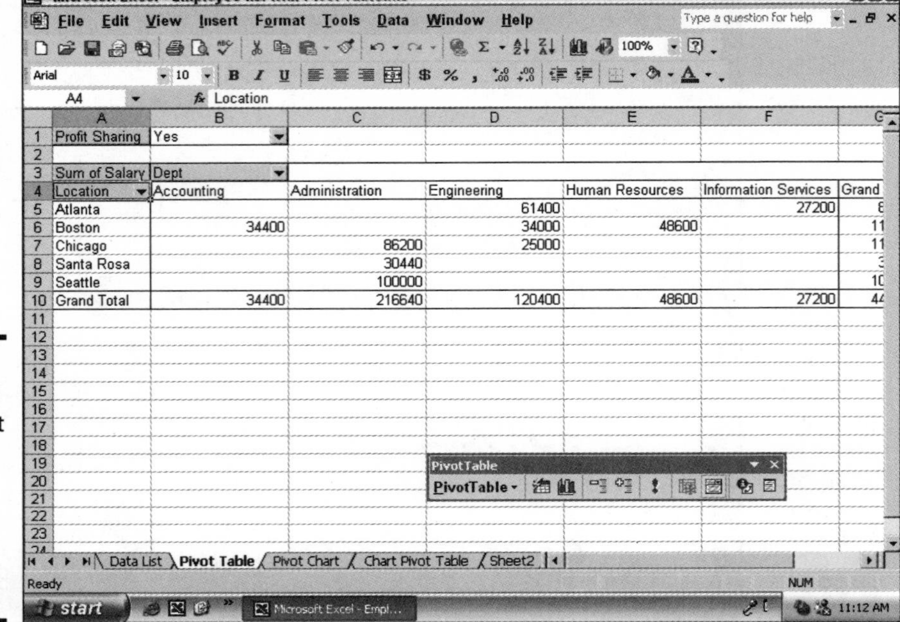

Figure 2-7: Pivoting the table so that Location is now the Column Field and Dept the Row Field.

In fact, when pivoting a pivot table, not only can you rotate existing fields, but you can also add new fields to the table or assign more fields to the table's Column Field and Row Field areas.

Figure 2-8 illustrates this situation. This figure shows the same pivot table after making a couple of key changes to the table structure. First, I added the Sex Field from the PivotTable Field List as a second Page Field by dragging it from the PivotTable Field List Task Pane (which I redisplayed by clicking the Show Field List button at the end of the PivotTable toolbar) and dropping this field on top of the Profit Sharing Page Field. Then, I added Location as a second Column Field by dragging it from the top row of the pivot table (as shown in Figure 2-7) and dropping it on top of the Dept Row Field. Finally, for this figure, I changed the setting in the Sex Page Field from the default of (All) to M and the Profit Sharing Page Field from Yes back to (All).

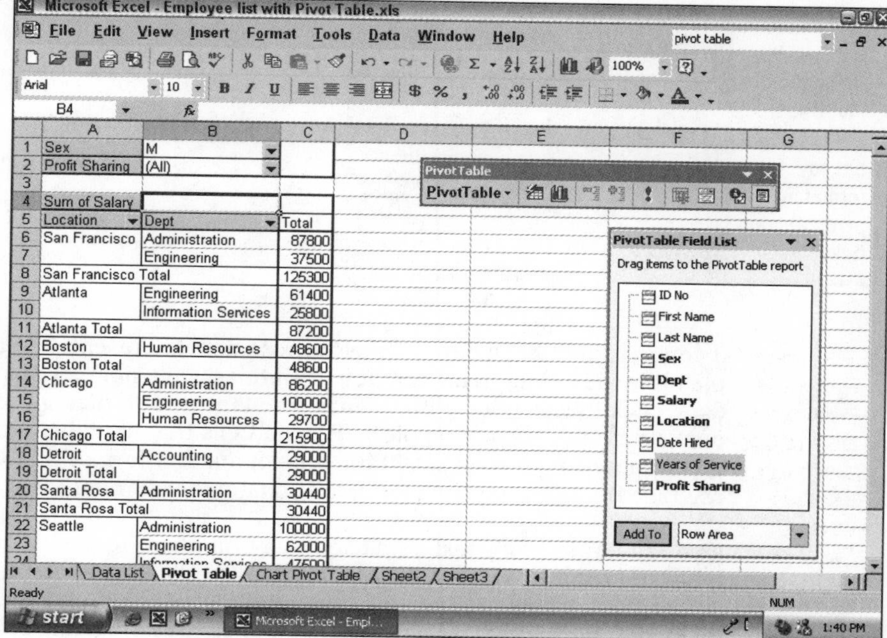

Figure 2-8: Pivot table after adding Sex as a Page Field and making Dept and Location Row Fields.

As a result, the modified pivot table shown in Figure 2-8 now shows the salary totals for all the men in the corporation arranged first by their location and then by their department. Because I added Sex as a second Page Field, I can see the totals for just the men or just the women who are or aren't currently enrolled in the profit sharing plan simply by selecting the appropriate Page Field settings.

Formatting the pivot table

The one thing that stands out like a sore thumb in pivot tables is the lack of formatting. When Excel creates a new pivot table, it doesn't pick any formatting from the original data source. This means that you have to manually apply whatever number formats and other kinds of table formatting that you want to apply. Fortunately, Excel makes it easy to format both the individual fields of the pivot table as well as the overall table itself.

To format a particular pivot table field, double-click the field label in the table or click the label and then click the Field Settings button on the PivotTable toolbar. Doing this opens a PivotTable Field dialog box for that field, similar to the one shown in the Figure 2-9.

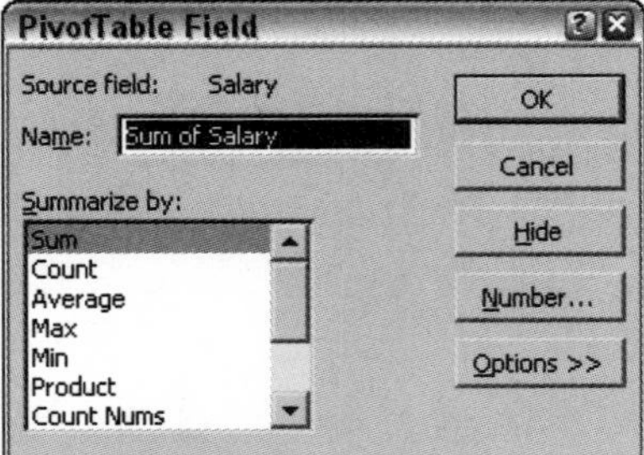

Figure 2-9: Using the PivotTable Field dialog box to format a pivot table field.

If you're formatting a numeric field whose data is presented in the body of the table (as a Data Item) and you want to assign a number format to this data, click the Number button in the PivotTable Field dialog box. This action opens a simplified version of the Format Cells that contains only a Number tab from which you can select the type of number format that you want to use (see Book II, Chapter 2 for details on number formats).

If you're formatting a text field used as a Column or Row Field in the pivot table and want to sort the field labels in ascending or descending order across the top row or down the first column, click the Advanced button in its PivotTable Field dialog box and then click the Ascending or Descending radio button in the AutoSort section of the PivotTable Field Advanced Options dialog box.

To select an AutoFormat for the pivot table, position the cell pointer in any one of the table's cells and then choose Format⇨AutoFormat from the Excel Menu bar or click the Format Report button on the PivotTable toolbar. This action selects all the cells in the pivot table and opens up an AutoFormat dialog box. This AutoFormat dialog box contains a list box with 10 different sample Report formats followed by 10 different sample Table formats, along with a sample PivotTable Classic format and a None format (that you select to remove another Report or Table formatting).

To assign a particular Report or Table format to your pivot table, click its sample in the AutoFormat dialog box and then click OK. Excel responds by closing the AutoFormat dialog box and assigning all the formatting in the selected Report or Table format to your pivot table. If you find that you're not happy with the one you selected, press Ctrl+Z to remove all the new formatting from the table and select another one from the AutoFormat dialog box.

Figure 2-10 shows the sample pivot table generated from the Employee data list after I formatted the Salary Field (assigned as the table's Data Item) with the Accounting number format with zero decimal places and applied the Table 8 AutoFormat to the entire table.

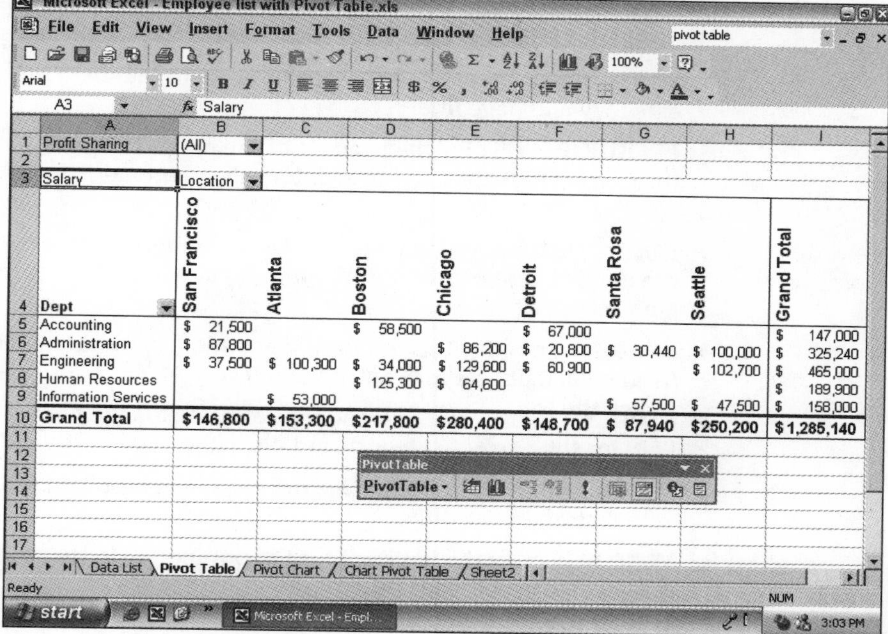

Figure 2-10: Pivot table with the Table 8 AutoFormat and formatting to the Salary Field.

Changing the summary functions

By default, Excel uses the good old SUM function to total the values in the numeric field(s) that you assign as the Data Items in the pivot table. Some data summaries require the use of another summary function, such as the AVERAGE or COUNT function. To change the summary function that Excel uses, open the Field dialog box for one of the fields that you use as the Data Items in the pivot table. You can do this by double-clicking the field's label or by clicking this label (this label is located at the cell intersection of the first Column and Row Field in a pivot table that has only one data field and uses the default or Classic Table format) and then clicking the Field Settings button on the PivotTable toolbar.

After you open the Field's dialog box, you can change its summary function from the default SUM to any of the following functions by selecting it in the Summarize By list box:

- **COUNT** to show the count of the records for a particular category (note that COUNT is the default setting for any text fields that you use as Data Items in a pivot table)
- **AVERAGE** to calculate the average (that is, the arithmetic mean) for the values in the field for the current category and page filter

- **MAX** to display the largest numeric value in that field for the current category and page filter
- **MIN** to display the smallest numeric value in that field for the current category and page filter
- **PRODUCT** to display the product of the numeric values in that field for the current category and page filter (all non-numeric entries are ignored)
- **COUNT NUMS** to display the number of numeric values in that field for the current category and page filter (all non-numeric entries are ignored)
- **STDDEV** to display the standard deviation for the sample in that field for the current category and page filter
- **STDDEVP** to display the standard deviation for the population in that field for the current category and page filter
- **VAR** to display the variance for the sample in that field for the current category and page filter
- **VARP** to display the variance for the population in that field for the current category and page filter

After you select the new summary function to use in the Summarize By list box of its PivotTable Field dialog box, click the OK button to have Excel apply the new function to the data presented in the body of the pivot table.

Adding Calculated Fields

In addition to using various summary functions on the data presented in your pivot table, you can create your own Calculated Fields for the pivot table. Calculated Fields are computed by a formula that you create by using existing numeric fields in the data source. To create a Calculated Field for your pivot table, follow these steps:

1. **Click any of the cells in the pivot table and then click the PivotTable button at the beginning of the PivotTable toolbar.**

   A pop-up menu attached to the PivotTable button opens.

2. **Highlight Formulas on the pop-up menu and then click Calculated Field on its submenu.**

   An Insert Calculated Field dialog box opens, similar to the one shown in Figure 2-11.

3. **Enter the name for the new field in the Name text box.**

   Next, you create the formula in the Formula text box by using one or more of the existing fields displayed in the Fields list box.

4. **Click the Formula text box and then delete the zero (0) after the equal sign and position the insertion point immediately following the equal sign (=).**

   Now you're ready to type in the formula that performs the calculation. To do this, insert numeric fields from the Fields list box and indicate the operation to perform on them with the appropriate arithmetic operators (+, -, *, or /).

5. **Enter the formula to perform the new field's calculation in the Formula text box, inserting whatever fields you need by clicking the name in the Fields list box and then clicking the Insert Field button.**

   For example, in Figure 2-11, I created a formula for the new calculated field called Bonuses that multiplies the values in the Salary Field by 2.5 percent (0.025) to compute the total amount of annual bonuses to be paid. To do this, I clicked the Salary field in the Fields list box and then clicked the Insert Field button to add Salary to the formula in the Formula text box (as in =Salary). Then, I typed *0.025 to complete the formula (=Salary*0.025).

   When you finish entering the formula for your calculated field, you can add the calculated field to the Pivot Table Field List by clicking the Add button. After you click the Add button, it changes to a grayed-out Modify button. If you start editing the formula in the Formula text box, the Modify button becomes active so that you can click it to update the definition.

6. **Click OK in the Insert Calculated Field dialog box.**

   This action closes the Insert Calculated Field dialog box and adds the summary of the data in the calculated field to your pivot table.

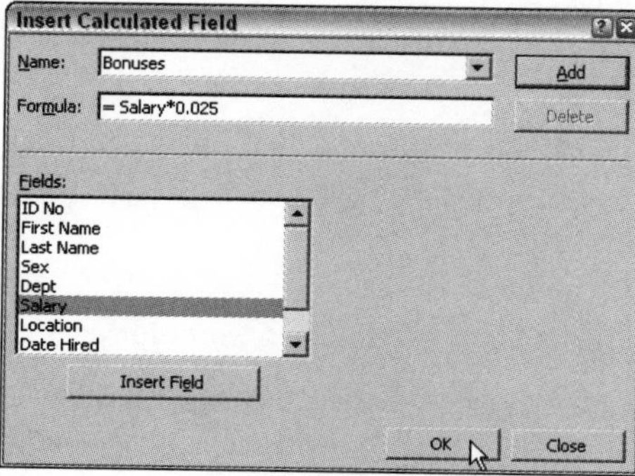

Figure 2-11: Creating a calculated field for a pivot table.

After you finish defining a calculated field to a pivot table, Excel automatically adds its name to the PivotTable Field List Task Pane and assigns it as a Data Item in the data area of the pivot table. The program also adds a new Data field and makes it the first Column Field in the pivot table.

If you want to hide a calculated field from the body of the pivot table, click the Data field's pop-up button to open the pop-up menu showing all the fields that you've added as Data fields (both calculated and not) and then click the name of the calculated field to remove the checkmark from its check box before you click the menu's OK button. To then add the calculated field back into the pivot table, click its field name in the PivotTable Field List Task Pane (opened by clicking the Show Field List button on the PivotTable toolbar), and then select Data Area in the drop-down list box at the bottom of the Task Pane before you click the Add To button.

Changing the PivotTable Options

You can use the PivotTable Options dialog box (shown in Figure 2-12) to change the settings applied to any and all pivot tables that you create in a workbook. You can open this dialog box when first creating a new pivot table by clicking the Options button in the PivotTable and PivotChart Wizard — Step 3 of 3 dialog box, or you can open it later by clicking the PivotTable button at the beginning of the PivotTable toolbar and then clicking Table Options on its pop-up menu.

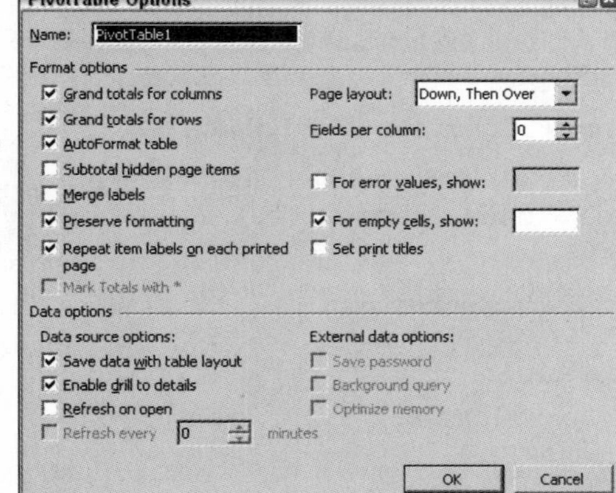

Figure 2-12: Modifying the pivot table options in the PivotTable Options dialog box.

The options in the PivotTable Options dialog box include:

- ✦ **Name:** Use this text box for giving the pivot table a little more imaginative name than PivotTable1, PivotTable2, and so on.
- ✦ **Grand Totals for Columns:** Selected by default, this check box automatically displays totals of the summarized data across the last row of the pivot table.

- **Grand Totals for Rows:** Selected by default, this check box automatically displays totals of the summarized data down the column of the pivot table.
- **AutoFormat Table:** Selected by default, this check box makes the Report and Table AutoFormats available for prettying up the pivot table.
- **Subtotal Hidden Page Items:** This check box includes hidden Page Field items in the pivot table's subtotals.
- **Merge Labels:** Select this check box to merge and center the labels in the top row and first column of the pivot table.
- **Preserve Formatting:** Selected by default, this check box retains the formatting that you assign to parts of the table even after refreshing the data or pivoting the fields.
- **Repeat Item Labels on Each Printed Page:** Selected by default, this check box repeats the outer field's item at the top of a page when a page break occurs before all of the items of an inner field have been printed (this option is useful when printing a pivot table that spans more than one page and has multiple Column and Row Fields that create the inner and outer items in the report).
- **Mark Totals with *:** Select this check box to display an asterisk (*) after each subtotal and grand total in pivot tables that are based on OLAP (Online Analytic Processing) source data to indicate that these totals include both hidden as well as displayed items in the table. This option is available only when the source of your pivot table is an OLAP data cube.
- **Page Layout:** Use this drop-down list box to change the order in which page fields appear. The default is to stack the fields vertically with the Down, Then Over option. You can change this to side by side by selecting the Over, Then Down on the Page Layout pop-up menu.
- **Fields Per Column:** Use this text box to indicate the number of fields that you want included in a row or column before beginning a new row or column for the Page Fields in the pivot table.
- **For Error Values, Show:** Select this check box to suppress error values from the pivot table by selecting other text or values to represent them. When you put a checkmark in this check box, its associated text box becomes available, and you can enter the character(s) to substitute for error values there.
- **For Empty Cells, Show:** Use this check box to display other text or values in blank cells in the pivot table. This check box is selected by default, although its associated text box is empty (so that blank cells appear empty in the table). To have text or a particular value (such as 0) represent blank cells, enter it in this text box.

- **Set Print Titles:** Select this check box to select the field and row labels in the pivot table as the column and row print titles for a printed pivot table report that spans more than one page (see Book II, Chapter 5 for more on using print titles in a report).
- **Save Data with Table Layout:** Selected by default, this check box saves a copy of the data used to generate the pivot table as part of the worksheet. If you clear this check box, you have to select the Refresh on Open check box in the PivotTable Options dialog box (see Refresh on Option description below) or click the Refresh Data button on the PivotTable toolbar to refresh the data in the pivot table each time you open its workbook. Not saving the data with the table layout can decrease the size of the workbook file considerably, especially in pivot table reports that are based on really large external databases.
- **Enable Drill to Details:** Selected by default, this check box enables you to double-click a cell in the data area of the pivot table and have Excel display the table's source data in the form of a data list on a new worksheet that's automatically added to the workbook.
- **Refresh on Open:** Select this check box to have Excel update the data in any pivot table in the workbook each time that you open its file. Select this check box when your source data is an external database and you have deselected the Save Data with Table Layout check box in the PivotTable Options dialog box (see previous description).
- **Refresh Every:** Select this check box to have Excel automatically update the data in your pivot tables at the time interval that you enter (in minutes) in the associated text box. This check box and associated text box options are available only when your pivot table uses an external data source.
- **Save Password:** Select this check box to save the password that you used to gain access to the external data source used in a pivot table. This check box option is available when your table uses an external data source.
- **Background Query:** Select this check box to be able to work while the query to the external data source used in your pivot table is being executed. When this check is cleared and you use external data in your pivot table, you can't do anything in the workbook until the database query is complete (which can take some time if you're querying a large database).
- **Optimize Memory:** Select this check box to have Excel take whatever steps it can to conserve computer memory while executing a database query on an external data source.

Creating Pivot Charts

Instead of generating just a plain old boring pivot table, you can spice up your data summaries quite a bit by generating a pivot chart along with a supporting pivot table. To do this, follow the same procedure for creating a sole pivot table (see the "Creating Pivot Tables" section earlier in this chapter for details) except that you click the PivotChart Report (with PivotTable Report) radio button in the PivotTable and PivotChart Wizard — Step 1 of 1 dialog box (refer to Figure 2-1).

When creating a new pivot chart with a pivot table, Excel always places the pivot chart on a new chart sheet regardless of whether you place the associated pivot table on a new worksheet or elect to place it somewhere on the worksheet that's current when you open PivotTable and PivotChart Wizard. Figure 2-13 shows how a typical pivot chart appears in its own chart sheet right after you click the Finish button in PivotTable and PivotChart Wizard — Step 1 of 3 dialog box (refer to Figure 2-3).

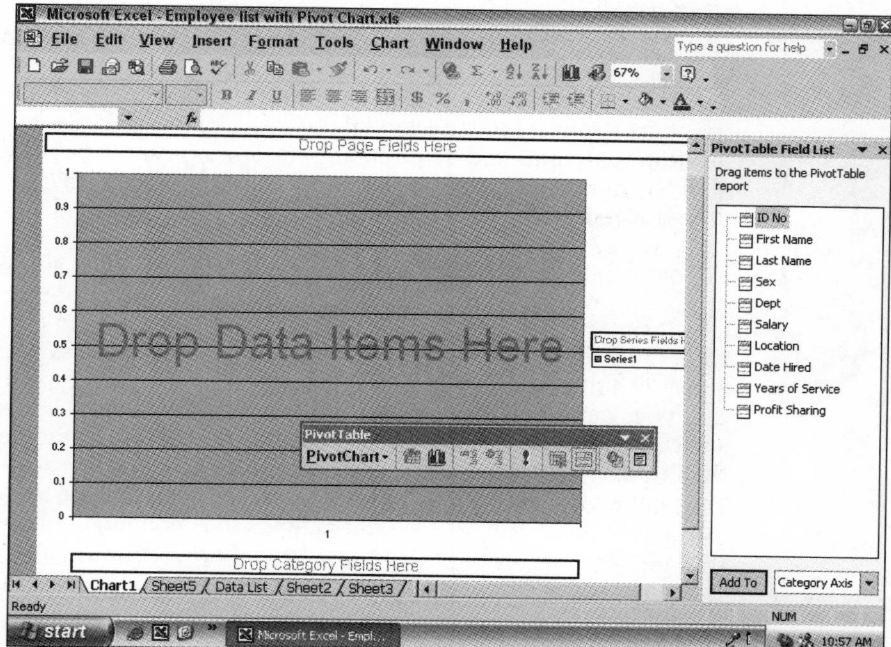

Figure 2-13: Generating a new pivot chart on a separate chart sheet from an Excel data list.

When you choose to generate a pivot chart with a pivot table, you actually generate the pivot table report by building the chart on its new chart sheet. As Figure 2-13 shows, building a pivot chart is similar to building a new pivot table: You do this by assigning fields from the data source (an Excel data list in this example) shown in the PivotTable Field List Task Pane (which I docked to the right of the chart area for this figure).

As with the pivot table, you can assign fields to the pivot chart either by dragging them to the designated areas in the chart (Drop Page Fields Here, Drop Data Items Here, Drop Series Fields Here, or Drop Category Fields Here) or by clicking the field name in the Task Pane Field List, and then selecting the name of the chart area to which to assign the field in the drop-down list box at the bottom of the Task Pane, and finally, clicking the Add To button to its immediate left.

Figure 2-14 shows the same chart sheet shown in Figure 2-13 after assigning the data fields to the various areas of the chart. In this example, I assigned the Sex Field as the chart's Page Field, the Salary Field as the Data Item, the Profit Sharing Field as the Series Field, and the Location Field as the Category Field. As a result, Excel generated a Stacked Column chart that shows the total salaries for each corporate location, differentiated in each column by those who are and those who are not enrolled in the profit sharing plan. Because I designated the Sex Field as the Page Field, I can restrict the chart to show only the sum of the men's or women's salaries at each location (differentiated by profit sharing status) simply by selecting the M or F option on the pop-up menu that appears when I click the Sex Field's drop-down button.

Although Excel always chooses the Column chart as the basic chart type for each new pivot chart that you generate, you can select another chart type for the pivot chart. To do so, simply click the Chart Wizard button on the PivotTable toolbar or on the Standard toolbar to open the Chart Wizard — Step 1 of 4 dialog box. There, you can select a new chart type from among the types displayed on the Standard Types or the Custom Types tab. When selecting a new chart type on the Standard Types tab, be sure that you click the Press and Hold to View Sample button so that you can see exactly how your pivot chart appears in the selected type (you may be surprised to see how Excel has to "pivot" the chart's fields to accommodate the new chart type — they don't call these babies *pivot* charts for nothing).

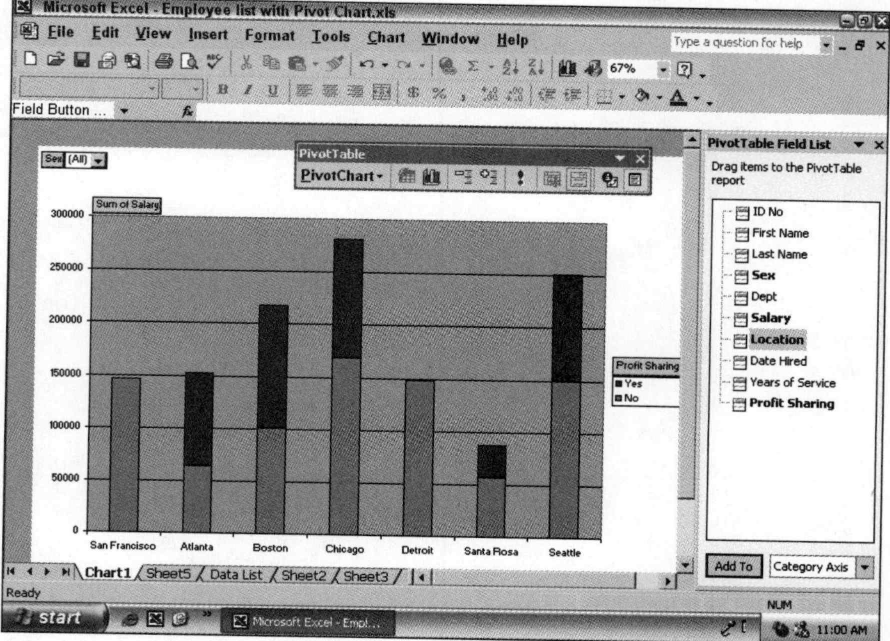

Figure 2-14: Chart sheet with completed pivot chart using the fields from the PivotTable Field List.

You can also use the Chart Wizard and Chart pull-down menu to enhance and further format your pivot chart. See Book V, Chapter 1 for details on how to use the chart options on the Chart Wizard — Step 3 of 4 dialog box and various items on the Chart pull-down menu to embellish your pivot chart.

Book VIII

Excel and the Web

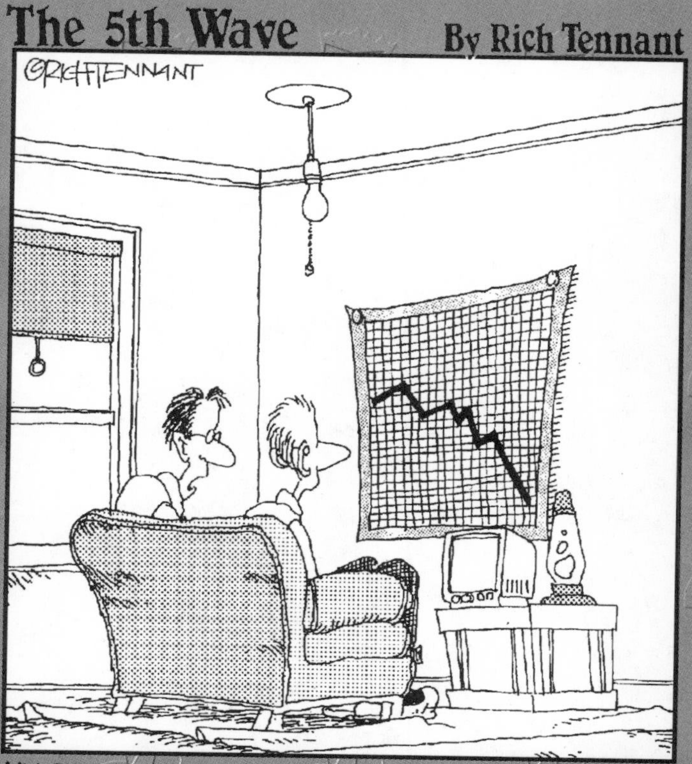

"MY GIRLFRIEND RAN A SPREADSHEET OF MY LIFE, AND GENERATED THIS CHART. MY BEST HOPE IS THAT SHE'LL CHANGE HER MAJOR FROM 'COMPUTER SCIENCES' TO 'REHABILITATIVE SERVICES.'"

Contents at a Glance

Chapter 1: Worksheets as Web Pages

In This Chapter

- **Previewing a spreadsheet as a Web page in your Web browser**
- **Saving Excel worksheet data and charts as HTML files**
- **Creating interactive Web pages**
- **Editing worksheet Web pages**
- **Exporting changes made to an interactive Web page back to Excel**
- **Performing Web queries in Excel**

With the continuing popularity of the World Wide Web, in recent years the HTML (Hypertext Markup Language) and XML (Extensible Markup Language) file formats — once pretty much exclusive to the arena of Web servers — have become more and more common file types understood and used by almost any program running on personal computers. In fact, any Office XP program, including Excel, can not only save its native documents as HTML files or XML files but also open these HTML or XML files for editing in their applications.

In this chapter, you find out how easy it is to convert your favorite Excel spreadsheets into HTML files, which you can then publish on a corporate intranet or on the Internet as part of the World Wide Web. When saving your worksheets in HTML, you have a choice between creating *static* and *interactive* Web pages. Static HTML files present all the worksheet data as HTML tables and your charts and other graphic objects as linked graphic files. Interactive HTML files enable users who view the pages with Microsoft's Internet Explorer, Version 4.0 or later (as of this writing, Version 6.0 is the latest), to manipulate the data and charts via a toolbar that provides the user with a set of limited controls for making basic changes to them.

Saving Spreadsheets as Web Pages

Converting your favorite spreadsheet into a Web page that's ready for publishing on the World Wide Web is no more difficult than opening the worksheet and then choosing File⇨Save As Web Page from the Excel Menu bar.

However, before you go off and choose the File➪Save as Web Page command to do the deed, you will normally want to see how the spreadsheet will appear in the HTML file format when viewed in your default Web browser. To do this, choose the File➪Web Page Preview command from the Excel pull-down menus. This action launches your computer's default Web browser (usually this is Internet Explorer unless you've specifically installed and selected a different browser) and displays the spreadsheet more or less as it will appear in that browser when saved as an HTML file. Figure 1-1 shows a preview of sample CG Media — 2003 Sales worksheet previewed in Internet Explorer 6.0.

After you finish previewing your spreadsheet in your computer's Web browser, you can click the browser window's Close button to close the preview with the browser program and return to Excel and your spreadsheet.

Keep in mind that you can't save your spreadsheet as an HTML file if it is password-protected. You can still convert a worksheet that is protected as long as you haven't used a password to prevent anyone from changing the removing protection from the sheet. If you've assigned a password to open the workbook or to remove a password, you need to remove the password before you try saving the worksheet as a Web page (see Book IV, Chapter 2 for details on how to do this).

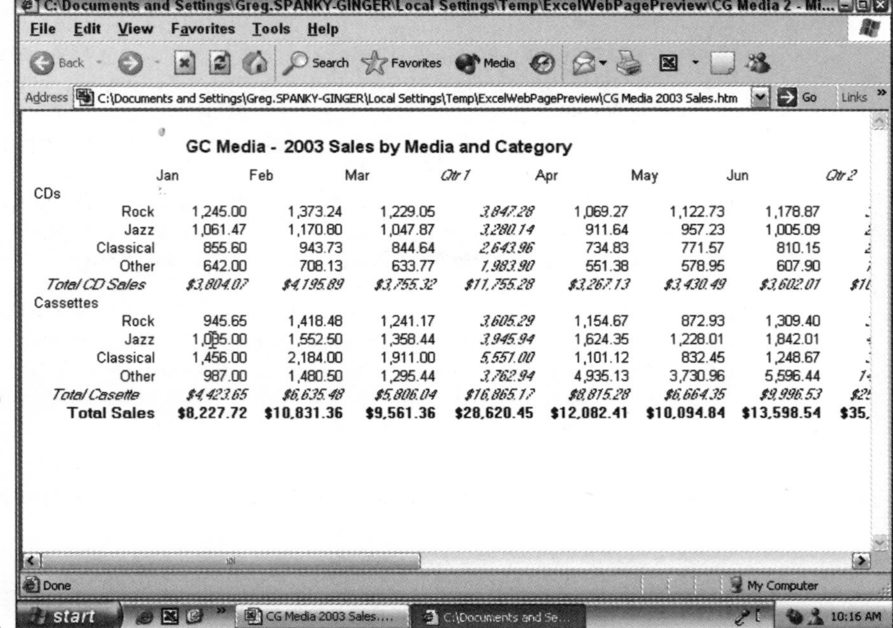

	Jan	Feb	Mar	*Qtr 1*	Apr	May	Jun	*Qtr 2*
CDs								
Rock	1,245.00	1,373.24	1,229.05	*3,847.28*	1,069.27	1,122.73	1,178.87	
Jazz	1,061.47	1,170.80	1,047.87	*3,280.14*	911.64	957.23	1,005.09	
Classical	855.60	943.73	844.64	*2,643.96*	734.83	771.57	810.15	
Other	642.00	708.13	633.77	*1,983.90*	551.38	578.95	607.90	
Total CD Sales	*$3,804.07*	*$4,195.89*	*$3,755.32*	*$11,755.28*	*$3,267.13*	*$3,430.49*	*$3,602.01*	
Cassettes								
Rock	945.65	1,418.48	1,241.17	*3,605.29*	1,154.67	872.93	1,309.40	
Jazz	1,0[illegible]5.00	1,552.50	1,358.44	*3,945.94*	1,624.35	1,228.01	1,842.01	
Classical	1,456.00	2,184.00	1,911.00	*5,557.00*	1,101.12	832.45	1,248.67	
Other	987.00	1,480.50	1,295.44	*3,762.94*	4,935.13	3,730.96	5,596.44	
Total Casette	*$4,423.65*	*$6,635.48*	*$5,806.04*	*$16,865.17*	*$8,815.28*	*$6,664.35*	*$9,996.53*	
Total Sales	**$8,227.72**	**$10,831.36**	**$9,561.36**	**$28,620.45**	**$12,082.41**	**$10,094.84**	**$13,598.54**	**$35,**

Figure 1-1: Previewing a worksheet as a Web Page in Internet Explorer 6.0.

If you still want to save the spreadsheet as a Web page after previewing it in your Web browser, go ahead and choose File⇨Save As Web Page from the Excel Menu bar. Choosing this command opens the Save As dialog box, which is similar to the one shown in Figure 1-2. After this dialog box is open, follow these steps to save the current worksheet or entire workbook as a Web page:

1. **Select the folder in which you want to save the HTML file in the Save In drop-down list box.**

   Next, you need to give a new filename to your Web page in the File Name text box. Note that Excel automatically appends the filename extension `.htm` (Hypertext Markup) to whatever filename you enter here. When selecting a filename, keep in mind that some file servers (especially those running some flavor of UNIX) are sensitive to upper- and lowercase letters in the name.

2. **Enter the filename for the new HTML file in the File Name text box.**

   By default, Excel selects the Entire Workbook radio button, meaning that all the worksheets in the workbook that contain data will be included in the new HTML file. To save only the data on the current worksheet in the HTML file, you need to take Step 3.

3. **(Optional) If you only want the current worksheet saved in the new HTML file, click the Selection: Sheet radio button.**

   If you want, you can have Excel add a Page title to your new HTML file that appears centered at the top of the page right above your worksheet data by taking Step 4. Don't confuse the Page title with the Web page header that appears on the Web browser's title bar — the only way to set the Web page header is to edit this HTML tag after the HTML file is created.

4. **(Optional) If you want to add a Page title to your HTML file, click the Change Title button, and then type the text in the Page Title text box in the Set Page Title dialog box before you click OK.**

   You're now ready to save your spreadsheet as an HTML file by clicking the Save button. If want to see how this file looks in your Web browser immediately upon saving it, click the Publish button to open the Publish as Web Page dialog box and save the file from there after selecting the Open Published Web Page in Browser check box.

5. **Click the Save button to save the file without opening it in your Web browser. Otherwise, click the Publish button so that you can see the Web page in your browser right after saving it.**

If you click the Save button, Excel closes the Save As dialog box, saves the file to the hard drive, and returns to the Excel window (that now contains the HTML version of your workbook or worksheet in place of the original `.xls` file).

If you click the Publish button to view the new HTML file in your browser, Excel opens the Publish as Web Page dialog box, where you click the Open Published Web Page in Browser check box to put a checkmark in it before clicking the Publish button.

6. **Click the Open Published Web Page in Browser check box and then click the Publish button.**

   When you click the Publish button, Excel closes the Publish as Web Page dialog box, saves the spreadsheet as an HTML file, and then immediately launches your default Web browsing program while at the same time opening the new HTML file in the browser. After you finish looking over the new HTML file in your Web browser, click its program window's Close button to close the browser and HTML file and to return to Excel and the original worksheet.

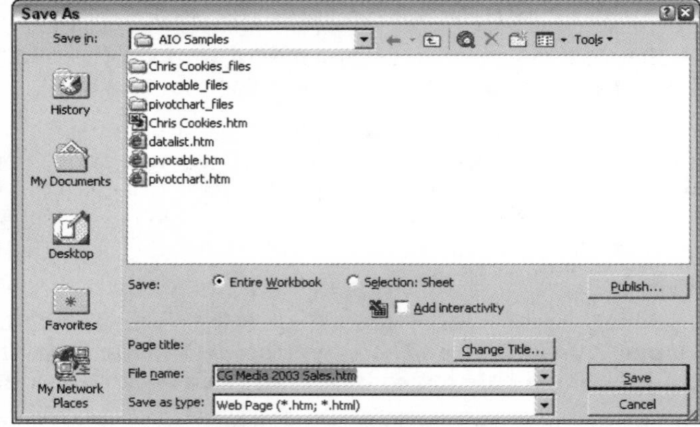

Figure 1-2: Saving a worksheet as a Web Page in the Save As dialog box.

Keep in mind that the big difference between saving the HTML version of your spreadsheet from the Save As dialog box as opposed to saving the file from the Publish as Web Page dialog box is not just that you get to see the new Web page immediately in your Web browser but also that Excel keeps the original `.xls` version of the spreadsheet open for you when you return to the program. When you save the HTML from the Save As dialog box, Excel replaces the original `.xls` file with the new `.htm` version (so in order to do anymore work with the original Excel file, you have to re-open it with the

File⇨Open command). When you save the new file from the Publish as Web Page, the browser closes the new `.htm` version of the spreadsheet when you close the browser, bringing you back to the good old original version of the spreadsheet when it returns you to Excel.

Saving just part of a worksheet

You don't have to save all the data and charts in a worksheet in a new HTML file. You can select just the particular data table, cell selection, or embedded chart that you want and save it in the Web page. The only thing you do differently when saving just part of a worksheet is to select the cell range or embedded chart to include before you choose the File⇨Save as Web Page command from the Excel menu bar. Then, after the Save As dialog box is open, you need to remember to click the Selection radio button instead of the Entire Workbook radio button before you click the Save or Publish button.

The name of the Selection option changes according to the type of selection that you make. When you select a named range to save in the new Web page, Excel displays the name of the range after Selection, as in Selection: sales_table. When you select a cell range to save in the new Web page, Excel displays the range address after Selection, as in Selection: $A$5:$H$35. When you select an embedded chart to save as a Web page, Excel makes Selection: Chart the radio button name.

Saving an entire workbook

When you save an entire workbook that contains several sheets of data, Excel saves all the data on each sheet. If you then open the new HTML file in Internet Explorer, the Web page retains even its original sheet structure and layout.

Figure 1-3 illustrates this situation. This figure shows a Web page created from an Excel workbook that contains two worksheets plus a single chart sheet. As this figure shows, when Excel converted this workbook to HTML, it retained the original three-sheet layout, which is then reproduced when the Web page is opened with the latest version of Internet Explorer.

To display the table of data on the Qtr1 sheet or the bar chart on the Bar Chart sheet, you simply click that tab. You can also page through the sheets in the HTML file by using the buttons shown to the immediate left of the first sheet tab: click the Next Sheet (>) button to display the next sheet or the Previous Sheet (<) button to display the previous sheet, or click the First Sheet (<<) button to display the very first sheet or the Last Sheet (>>) button to display the very last sheet of the file in the browser window.

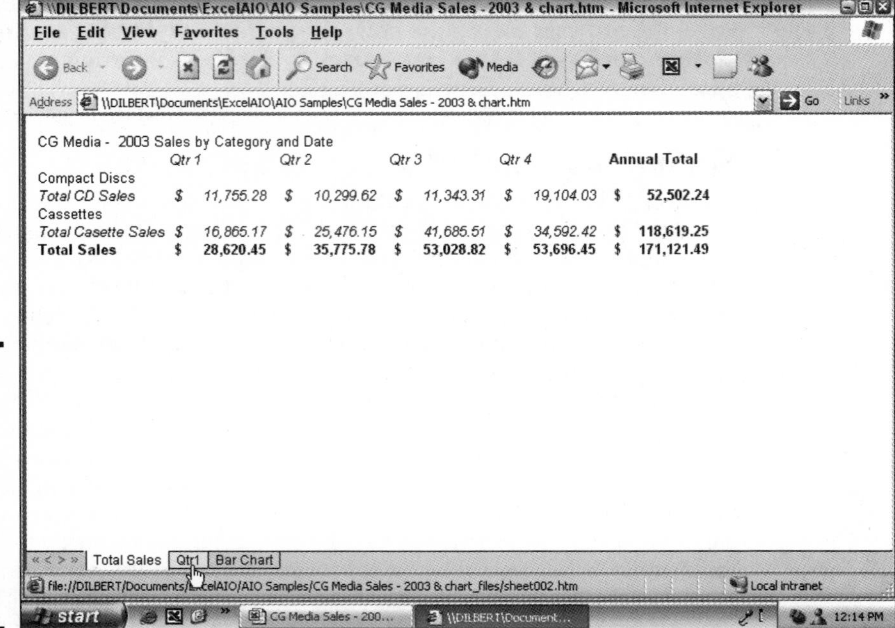

Figure 1-3: Worksheet saved as a Web Page opened in Internet Explorer right after saving.

Adding data to an existing Web page

Sometimes you'll want to save a worksheet as part of an existing HTML file rather than as a new HTML file. Just keep in mind that anytime you add a worksheet to an existing Web page, Excel appends the worksheet data to the very bottom of the existing Web page. If you want the data to appear at an earlier place on the existing Web page, you then have to edit the Web page and move the worksheet data up (see the "Editing worksheet Web pages" section later in this chapter for ideas on how to do this).

The steps for saving a worksheet as part of an existing HTML file are the same as for saving a worksheet in a new file with these two important differences:

- ✦ In the Save As dialog box, you enter or select the name of the existing file to which the new HTML version of the worksheet is to be appended in the File Name text box.
- ✦ In the Alert dialog box that appears when you click the Save button in the Save As dialog box, you click the Add to File button rather than the Replace File or Cancel button.

You can't save an entire workbook as part of an existing Web page. When you select the name of an existing HTML file when the Entire Workbook option button is selected, you only have a choice between replacing the file and canceling the action of saving it. If you click the Replace File button in the Alert dialog box that appears, you end up getting rid of the original file rather than adding new data onto it!

Make mine interactive!

If you know that the users of the spreadsheets you're going to save as Web pages are going to be using Internet Explorer (Version 4.0 or later) to view them, you can make it possible for them to modify the worksheet data on the Web pages by selecting the Add Interactivity button in the Save As dialog box at the time you first save them.

Note, however, that before users of one of these later versions of Internet Explorer can take advantage of the spreadsheet Web page interactivity in Internet Explorer, they must also have installed the Microsoft Office Web Components on their computer. These utilities aren't automatically installed when you do a standard installation of Office XP, so you may have to take time out and install them by using the Add or Remove Programs Control Panel (the Office XP Web Components are part of Office Shared Features group in the Features to Install list box in the Microsoft Office XP Setup dialog box).

The changes that users can make to the spreadsheet data in Internet Explorer to an interactive Web page depend upon the type of data involved:

✦ **Worksheet data tables:** Users can edit the cell entries and have the table's formulas updated either automatically or manually. They can also modify the formatting of the cells in the table (see Book II, Chapter 2 for details on formatting worksheets and Chapter 3 for details on editing worksheet data).

✦ **Data lists:** Users can sort and filter the data in the list as well as modify field entries and make formatting changes to the list (see Book VI, Chapter 1 for details on sorting data lists and Chapter 2 for details on filtering data lists).

✦ **Pivot tables:** Users can pivot the fields in a table as well as add new fields to the table. They can also refresh the table data from the external data source (assuming that this source is accessible from the Web page), show details for any of the summarized data in the table, add calculated fields to the table, and page through the summaries by using different items in the Page Fields (see Book VII, Chapter 2 for details on pivot tables).

- **Charts:** Users can edit supporting data (shown beneath the chart as an attached data table) and have the chart automatically updated on the page (see Book V, Chapter 1 for details on charts).

To turn your worksheet into an interactive Web page, follow the same steps as you do when saving a worksheet as a static Web page — outlined earlier in this chapter in the section, "Saving Spreadsheets as Web Pages" — except that you must be sure to click the Selection option button (which will read Selection: Sheet or Selection: Chart) and then click the Add Interactivity check box in the Save As dialog box. After that, follow these simple steps:

1. **Click the Publish button in the Save As dialog box.**

   This action opens the Publish as Web Page dialog box, which is similar to the one shown in Figure 1-4. This dialog box contains an Items to Publish section and a Viewing Options section, where you indicate which part of the worksheet to publish and the type of functionality to be used (Spreadsheet Functionality, PivotTable Functionality, or Chart Functionality).

2. **Check the items listed in the Choose combo box and make sure that they are the ones that you want to publish on the interactive Web page. If they aren't, click the name of the items to publish in the Choose drop-down list or click it in the Choose list box below.**

   Next, you need to check and make sure that the Add Interactivity Check Box in Viewing Options is still selected and that the type of functionality that you want to add is selected in the associated drop-down list box. Select Spreadsheet Functionality when creating an interactive page with a data table or data list; select PivotTable Functionality when creating an interactive page with a pivot table; and finally, select Chart Functionality when creating an interactive page with a chart.

3. **Make sure that the Add Interactivity check box has a checkmark and that the type of functionality listed in its drop-down list box is correct: otherwise, click the check box and then click the appropriate type of functionality in its drop-down list.**

   If you want to open the new interactive page in your Web browser, click the Open Published Web Page in Browser check box before you take Step 4.

4. **Click the Publish button in the Publish as Web Page dialog box.**

Figure 1-5 shows you how a typical interactive data table appears on a new Web page after opening it with Internet Explorer 6.0. Notice that the interactive table is self-contained with a toolbar at the top, a facsimile of the worksheet row and column header at the top, and vertical and horizontal scroll bars on the right and at the bottom. Notice also that this table uses gridlines to demarcate the cells and sports a sheet tab at the bottom, just like a regular Excel workbook window.

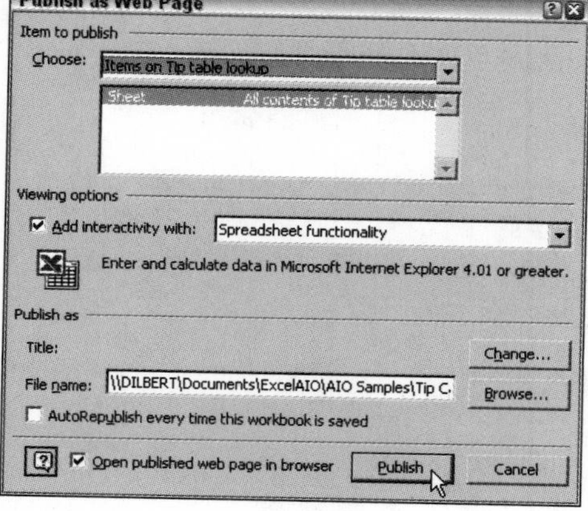

Figure 1-4: Selecting the items to publish and type of functionality for the interactive Web page.

The Office Web Components add a horizontal and vertical scroll bar to the interactive table because you have no way to resize the table. You must use the scroll buttons to bring new parts of the data table into view on the Web page. Likewise, they automatically display the row and column headers to give you a way to widen or narrow the columns and heighten or shorten its rows by dragging the appropriate border of a column letter or row number.

Despite the obvious similarities to the standard workbook window, you see some noticeable differences as well. Most significant is the fact that the interactive spreadsheet table has no Formula bar or Menu bar.

Without a Formula bar, you can't tell which values in the table are calculated by formula and which are input as constants. Also, the only way to edit any of the table cells is by double-clicking the cell and then editing the entry there (at which time, you can immediately tell whether it's a value or a formula that you're editing).

Without a Menu bar, you must pretty much rely upon the buttons on the toolbar to make changes that affect the entire table. The only other way to access commands that affect the table is by right-clicking one of the table cells to display its shortcut menu. The items on this shortcut menu duplicate the functions of the buttons at the top of the table with the exception of the Insert and Delete items. These menu items both lead to the Rows and Columns sub-menu options that enable you to either insert or delete the columns or rows that are currently selected in the table.

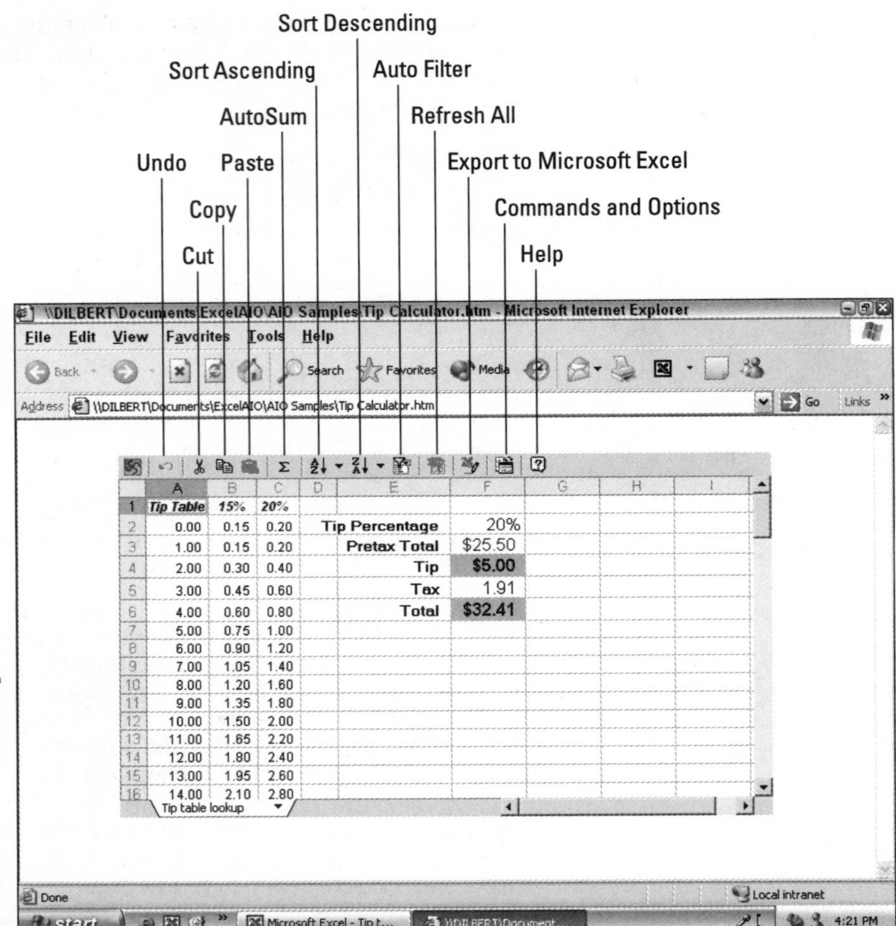

Figure 1-5: A Web page with interactive data table opened in Internet Explorer 6.0.

As Figure 1-5 shows, many of the buttons on the toolbar at the top of an interactive worksheet table are very familiar; they repeat buttons on Excel's Standard toolbar whose functions are already known to you. The most important buttons on this toolbar are:

- **Export to Microsoft Excel** button (the one with the XL icon above a pencil) that you use to open the table as an `.xml` file in Excel, where you can save your changes (see the "Exporting an interactive Web page to Excel" section later in this chapter for details).
- **Commands and Options** button (the one with the picture of a dialog box in front of a sheet) that opens the Commands and Options dialog box shown in Figure 1-6, which you can use to make global changes to the interactive data table.

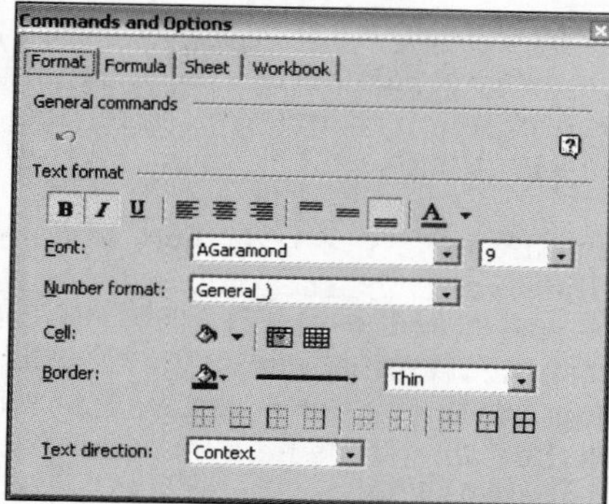

Figure 1-6: The Commands and Options dialog box enables you to make global changes to the table.

As you can see in Figure 1-6, the Commands and Options dialog box contains four tabs of options that you can use:

- **Format tab** with buttons and boxes for changing the font, size, alignment, border, and cell and text color of any cells that you've selected in the table.
- **Formula tab** with boxes that enable you to see the contents (very helpful when dealing with long formulas) and value of the active cell, along with all the range names defined in the table. You can even use its Define button to define a new range name for the current cell selection.
- **Sheet tab** containing Find What and Show/Hide sections. To find some text or values in the table, enter the search text in the Find What text box and then click the Find Next button (using the Match Case and Entire Cell Only check boxes if you need to refine the search). Select or deselect the Show/Hide check box options (Row Headers, Column Headers, Gridlines, and Display Right to Left) to control which interior table elements to display or hide.
- **Workbook tab** containing Calculation, Show/Hide, and Worksheets sections. Use the Manual and Automatic radio buttons to switch from automatic recalculation (the default) to manual recalculation (in which case, you click the Calculate button to update table formulas). Use the Show/Hide check box options (Horizontal Scrollbar, Vertical Scrollbar, Sheet Selector, or Toolbar) to control which overall table elements to display or hide (note that you can't remove the scroll bars when the table is too large to show all the data in the table). Use the Sheet Name text box to rename the table sheet that's selected in the list box below, the Insert button to insert a new sheet into the table, and the Delete button to remove the current sheet or the Hide button to hide the current sheet in the table. Use the Order buttons to move the current sheet ahead (with the button with the upward-pointing arrow) or behind (with the button with the downward-pointing arrow) the other sheets in the table.

Interacting with a Web page data list

In addition to the kinds of formatting and editing changes that you can make to a standard data table saved as an interactive Web page, you can also do basic sorting and filtering on a data list saved as an interactive Web page.

In sorting a data list, you can only sort its records on one column (that is, a single sorting key). To sort the records in ascending order, click the drop-down button attached to the Sort Ascending button and then click the name of the field for which you want the records ordered on its pop-up menu. To sort the records in descending order, you perform the same procedure; only this time, however, you click the name of the field on which to sort the data list from the Sort Descending button's pop-up menu.

To use the most basic of the AutoFilter functions, click the AutoFilter button on the table's toolbar. This action adds AutoFilter drop-down buttons, similar to the ones shown in Figure 1-7. To filter out unwanted records from the data list, click the drop-down button for the field (column) that you want to filter. Internet Explorer then displays a pop-up menu listing all the unique values in that field. To restrict the records to just those with certain values in the field, click the check box in front of the (Show All) item at the very top to remove its checkmark and then click the check box for each of the values for the records that you want displayed before you click OK.

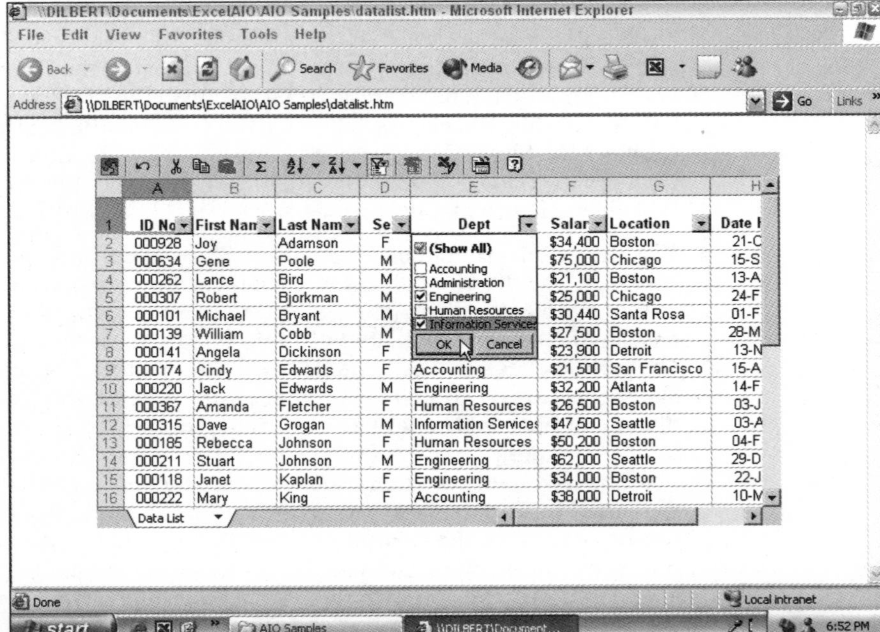

Figure 1-7: Using the AutoFilter buttons to filter an interactive data list.

When you click OK to close a field's pop-up menu, Internet Explorer redraws the table showing only the records for the items that you checked on that menu. To redisplay all the records, click the same field's pop-up button, click the check box in front of the (Show All) item and then click OK. To remove the AutoFilter pop-up buttons from the field names at the top of the data list, click the AutoFilter button on the table's toolbar.

Interacting with a Web page pivot table

When you work with an interactive pivot table, Internet Explorer displays the summary data in your data by using a simpler variation of a spreadsheet pivot table's classic layout. To page through the data summaries, click the Page Field's pop-up button and then clear and reselect the field's check boxes on the pop-up menu as appropriate before you click OK. To pivot the table by rotating the Column or Row Fields, drag their labels to the appropriate area of the pivot table.

To display the PivotTable Field List in a floating window, click the Field List button (the last one before the Help button on the table's toolbar). Figure 1-8 shows how this works. In this figure, I clicked the Field List button on the toolbar for an interactive pivot table that was created from the sample pivot table I used to illustrate their workings in Book VII, Chapter 2.

The floating PivotTable Field List window shown to the right of the table in this figure should be totally familiar to you, except for icons that precede the field names. The icon with 01 over the 10 in the square denotes a Calculated Field (the Totals Field summing all the salaries for the different corporate locations). The icon with the blue lines running across the square denotes a field that exists in the original data source (the Excel data list from which this table is generated, in this example).

You may have noticed another difference between the appearance of the interactive pivot table in Internet Explorer (as shown in Figure 1-8) and the way the table normally appears in Excel. Notice the small buttons in the data area beneath the Column Fields and to the immediate right of the Row Field. These are Show/Hide Details buttons that you can use to expand or collapse a detail of the pivot table. Click the Show/Hide Details button with a plus (+) sign to expand a part of the table to show the records used in creating its total or subtotal. Then click the Show/Hide Details button with the minus sign (-) to hide the records used in totaling that part of the table and to return to the original collapsed view.

TIP

If you want to expand the entire table and display all of the records used in the table at once, click the Show Details button on the table's toolbar. You can then return the whole table back to its original collapsed summary view by clicking the Hide Details button to the immediate left of the Show Details button.

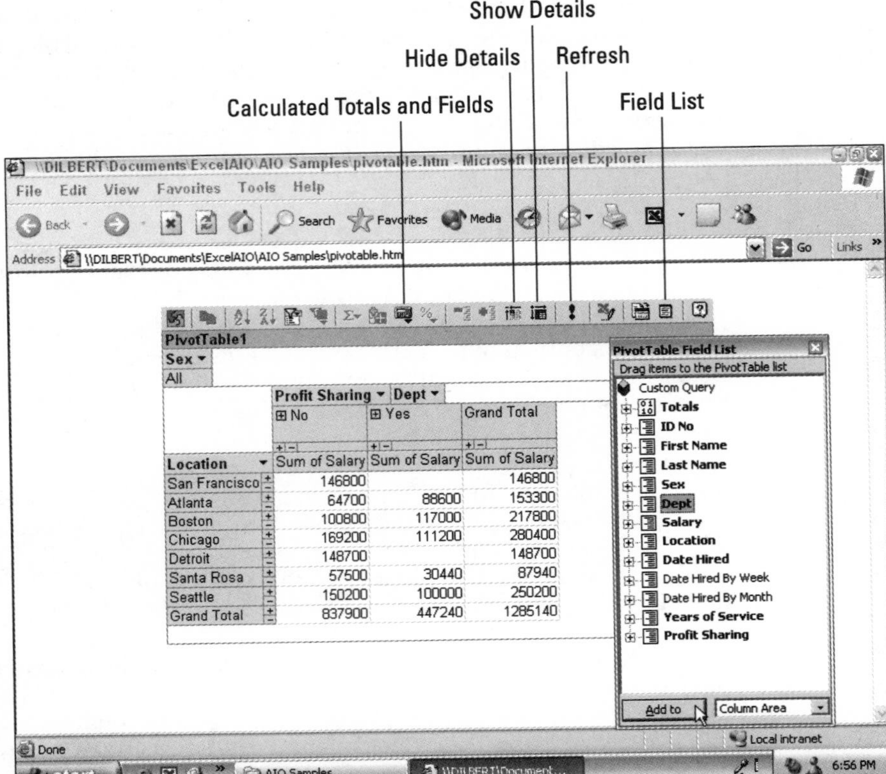

Location	No Sum of Salary	Yes Sum of Salary	Grand Total Sum of Salary
San Francisco	146800		146800
Atlanta	64700	88600	153300
Boston	100800	117000	217800
Chicago	169200	111200	280400
Detroit	148700		148700
Santa Rosa	57500	30440	87940
Seattle	150200	100000	250200
Grand Total	837900	447240	1285140

Figure 1-8: Using the Field List button to display the fields used in an interactive pivot table.

Note that the Commands and Options dialog box, which opens when you click the Commands and Options button on an interactive pivot table's toolbar, contains completely different tabs from those displayed in the Commands and Options dialog box for a regular interactive data table or interactive data list. This version of the Commands and Options dialog box contains only three tabs:

- **Captions tab:** This tab contains options that enable you to modify the captions that appear in different areas of the interactive pivot table, including the Report title bar that appears immediately below the table's toolbar. This tab also contains options for changing the basic formatting of the table data, including the font, size, alignment, style, and color.
- **Report tab:** This tab contains a series of radio button and check box options that enable you to control where the totals appear in the table,

whether to base the totals on visible items only or to include hidden items (important when using a really large external data source), and which items to always display in the table.

✦ **Behavior tab:** This tab contains a bunch of Hide/Show Elements options that enable you to hide particular components, such as the Expand Indicator (those Show/Hide Details buttons with the plus and minus signs), as well as the table's Title Bar, Drop Areas, and toolbar. It also contains General options for controlling whether items and details automatically expand and, if so, by how much.

Interacting with a Web page chart

When you generate an interactive chart, Excel automatically appends a supporting data table to the chart. This data table is then interactive when it appears immediately below the chart in Internet Explorer.

Figure 1-9 illustrates this situation. Here, you see an interactive pie chart that graphs the percentages of the planned part production for April, 2003. As this figure shows, the interactive data table with the production data that's represented graphically in the pie chart appears in a data table immediately below the chart.

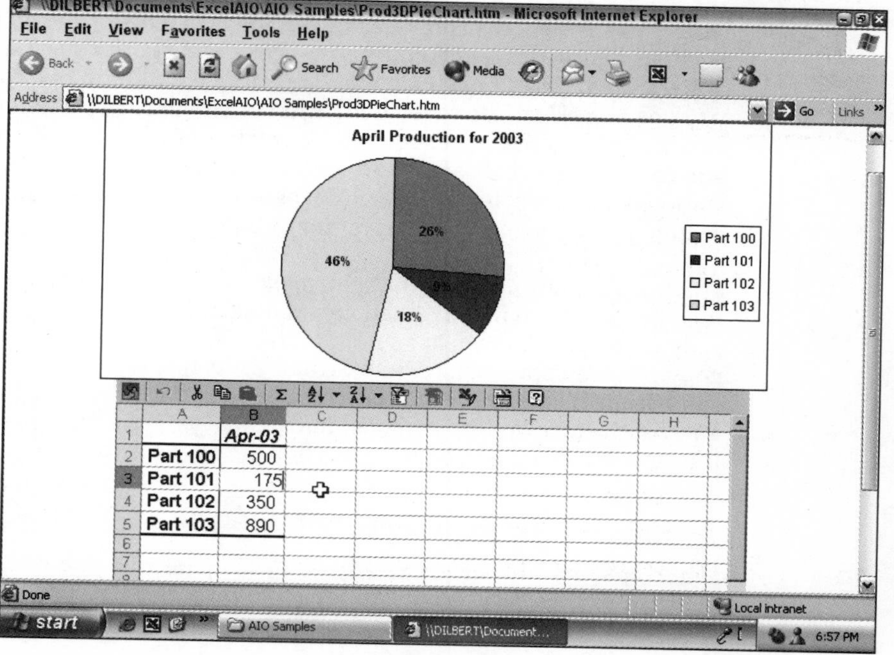

Figure 1-9: Changing a value in the data table attached to an interactive pie chart.

Because the chart's data table is interactive, you can format the table and modify its contents as you would any other interactive data table. However, because the data table is connected to the chart, all changes that you make to its data are automatically reflected in the chart that appears directly above the table, as the chart is immediately redrawn by the Internet Explorer Web browser.

Editing spreadsheet Web pages

Just as Excel can save workbooks as HTML files, it can also open them for editing. Opening an HTML file for editing is really no different from opening a regular Excel workbook. This is because the Files of Type drop-down list box contains an All Microsoft Excel Files option that not only looks for all types of Excel files but all types of HTML files, as well. In the Files of Type pop-up list, this particular item appears as follows:

```
All Microsoft Excel Files (*.xl*;*.xls;*.xlt;*.htm;*.html;
```

Because this option contains the `.htm` and `.html` file extensions along with the `.xls` (for Excel worksheets) and `.xlt` (for Excel templates), when you select this item on the Files of Type drop-down list, Excel displays all the Web pages in the folders that you select in the Open dialog box along with all the Excel workbook and template files.

After you've opened a spreadsheet Web page in Excel, you can make any necessary formatting and editing changes to its contents just as you would any standard Excel workbook file. The only exception to this rule is when you open an HTML file saved with interactivity in Excel. When you open an interactive Web page in Excel, the file retains its toolbar and scroll bars, and you can only use its toolbar and options on the tabs in its Command and Options dialog box to make your changes (see the "Make mine interactive!" section previously in this chapter for details).

You can save any changes that you make to spreadsheet Web pages by using the File⇨Save command. When you choose this command, Excel automatically saves the changes in its now, native HTML format. If you want to save a copy of a Web spreadsheet as a regular Excel file, you need to choose File⇨Save As command and then replace Web Page (*.htm;*.html) with Microsoft Excel Workbook (*.xls) in the Save as Type drop-down list box in the Save As dialog box before you click the Save button.

Exporting an interactive Web page to Excel

Unfortunately, you can't save any of the changes that you make to an interactive Web page in Internet Explorer. The only way that you can save any of the formatting or editing changes that you make to an interactive data table, data list, or pivot table is to export the page back to Excel as an `.xml` (Extensible Markup Language) file and then save the changes there.

To do this, click the Export to Microsoft Excel button on the toolbar at the top of the interactive table or list (shown in the left margin). Clicking this button launches Excel on your computer and opens the interactive table or list with your edits (in the case of interactive charts, only the data table attached to the chart opens in Excel, and not the chart itself).

The `.xml` file that opens in the Excel window is given a temporary filename, something like `OWCSheet1.xml` (OWC stands for Office Web Components), that appears on the window's title bar followed by the (Read Only) to indicate that the file is open in read-only mode. This means that you must choose the File⇨Save As command to make its changes on your disk. In the Save As dialog box, you can save the file by giving it a new filename in the File Name text box and selecting a new folder (all OWCSheet files are automatically saved in the Temp folder on your hard disk).

Note that Excel automatically saves the file as an `.xml` file, the type of HTML that enables you to interact with it in Internet Explorer. If you're not concerned about saving the interactivity and only want to be able to open the edited data table or list in Excel, remember to change the Save as Type setting from XML Spreadsheet (*.xml) to Microsoft Excel Workbook (*.xls).

Doing Web Queries

You can use Excel's Web Query feature to extract text or tables (or a combination of the two) from Web pages on the World Wide Web and bring their data into an Excel worksheet. Doing a Web query is a lot like performing an external database query (covered in Book VI, Chapter 2) except that instead of extracting data from an external database, you're taking it out of a Web page on the Internet.

The key to being able to do a Web query is having the URL address of the Web site whose data you want to query (you know, the `http://`-type address that appears on the Address bar of your Web browser when you visit a site). You must have this address handy at the time you start the new Web query because the New Web Query dialog box doesn't provide a way to search the Internet, nor does it give you access to your Web favorites as you have in your Web browser.

Often the best way to do capture the URL address for the page that you want to query is to visit the Web site in your Web browser (by using your Web favorites or its search capability), and then select the URL address that appears on the Web browser's Address bar and copy it into the Clipboard with the Edit⇨Copy command. Then, switch over to Excel, select the text currently displayed in the Address bar of the New Web Query dialog box (refer to the steps that follow), and paste the page's URL address in this text box by pressing Ctrl+V (you must use this shortcut because you don't have access to the Edit⇨Paste command on the Excel pull-down menus from within a dialog box).

To perform a new Web query in Excel, follow these steps:

1. **Open the worksheet where you want the Web data to reside and position the cell pointer in the first cell where you want the imported data to appear.**
2. **Choose Data⇨Import External Data⇨New Web Query from the Excel Menu bar.**

   This action opens the New Web Query dialog box, which is similar to the one shown in Figure 1-10.
3. **Click the Address and then enter the URL address of the Web site whose data you want to extract.**

   Next, you need to connect to the Internet and visit the site containing the data that you want to extract.
4. **Click the Go button to connect to the Internet and visit the page whose address is shown in the Address bar.**

   The first part of the page that you visit appears within the body of the New Web Query dialog box. Next, you need to select the page and indicate which tables and text to import into your Excel worksheet.

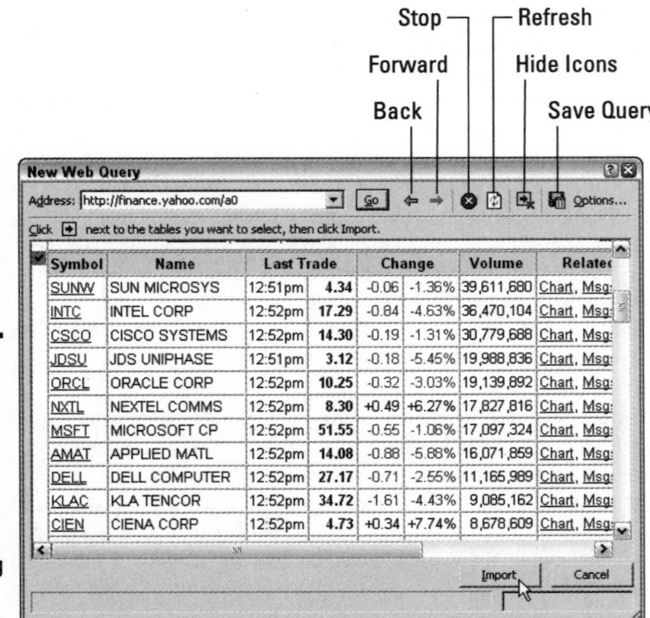

Figure 1-10: Selecting the data tables to bring into Excel in the New Web Query dialog box.

5. **Click somewhere on the Web page shown in the body of the New Web Query dialog box to make it active.**

   After the Web page is active, Excel shows which elements on the page you can import by displaying yellow buttons with black arrows pointing to the right in front of each table or text, and you can then move new parts of the Web page into view by pressing the arrow keys (→, ↓, ←, or ↑).

   To select a table or text on the page for importing, click its yellow button, whereupon it changes to a green button containing a black checkmark, indicating that it's selected.

6. **Use the arrow keys to move around the Web page as you click the yellow buttons for all the tables and text on the page that you want imported into your Excel worksheet.**

   After you've marked all the elements on the page, you can either click the Import button to go ahead and bring in the selected text and data or you can first save the Web query in a separate query file (by using the `.iqy` file extension for Internet query) by selecting the Save Query button.

   To save your query for reuse, follow Step 7. Otherwise, skip to Step 8.

7. **(Optional) Click the Save Query button to open the Save Query dialog box, where you enter the name for your Web query in the File Name text box before you click the Save button.**

   When importing data and text from Web pages into a worksheet, Excel doesn't bother to retain the Web page formatting. If you want the data in your worksheet to look exactly as it does on the Web page with all its fonts and colors, you need to take Step 8. If you're only concerned with the raw data, skip to Step 9.

8. **(Optional) Click the Options button and then click the Full HTML Formatting or the Rich Text Formatting Only radio button in the Web Query Options dialog box before you click OK.**

   When choosing between the HTML Formatting and Rich Text Formatting Only options, keep in mind that Excel is able to render RTF formatting more faithfully than the HTML formatting.

9. **Click the Import button in the New Web Query dialog box.**

   This action closes the New Web Query dialog box and opens the Import " Excel selects the Existing Worksheet radio button and selects the current cell as the place at which to start importing the Web data. If you want to import the Web data at the beginning of a new worksheet, click the New Worksheet radio button. If you want to import the data in the current worksheet but starting at a different cell, click the text box beneath the Existing Worksheet radio button and then enter its cell address or click it directly in the worksheet.

10. **Select the appropriate option in the Where Do You Want to Put the Data section and then click OK in the Import Data dialog box.**

As soon as you click the OK button in the Import Data dialog box, Excel begins importing the data. Because this can take some time — depending upon how much data you're importing and how fast your Internet connection is — Excel inserts a temporary message, "Getting data", in the current cell that is replaced as soon as your Web data comes into the current sheet.

After the data finishes coming into the worksheet, Excel displays the External Data toolbar on the screen, as shown in Figure 1-11. You can then click its Edit Query button to revisit the Web page in the Edit Web Query dialog box, where you can modify which tables and text are to be imported or click its Refresh button to update the data (a very important feature if you've imported a bunch of stock quotes like I did in Figure 1-11 and you want to keep them up-to-date).

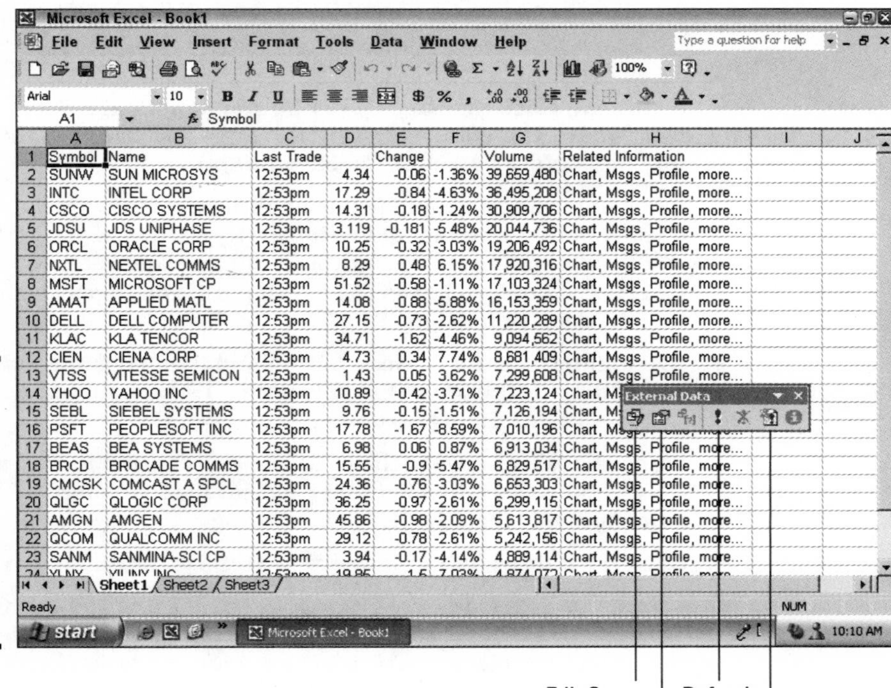

Figure 1-11: New worksheet with the stock quotes imported by the Web query.

You can save the data imported into a worksheet as the result of a Web query by saving the workbook file with the File➪Save command. You can then refresh its data when you open it at a later date by displaying the External Data toolbar (View➪Toolbars➪External Data) and then click its Refresh button.

If you saved the Web query, you can redo the Web query without having to redefine it at any time simply by choosing Data➪Important External Data➪Import Data from the Excel Menu bar and then selecting its `.iqy` file in the Select Data Source dialog box before you click the Open button. Then, all you have to do is specify where to place the imported data in the Import Data dialog box and click OK to once more get the data from the Web page.

Chapter 2: Adding Hyperlinks to Worksheets

In This Chapter

- **Adding hyperlinks to your worksheet**
- **Following hyperlinks that you create in a worksheet**
- **Editing hyperlinks in a worksheet**
- **Assigning hyperlinks to custom buttons on toolbars or custom menu items on pull-down menus**
- **Creating formulas that use the HYPERLINK function**

The subject of this chapter is linking your worksheet with other documents through the use of *hyperlinks*. Hyperlinks are the kinds of links used on the World Wide Web to take you immediately from one Web page to another or from one Web site to another. Such links can be attached to text (thus the term, *hypertext*) or to graphics such as buttons or pictures. The most important aspect of a hyperlink is that it immediately takes you to its destination whenever you click the text or button to which it is attached.

In an Excel worksheet, you can create hyperlinks that take you to a different part of the same worksheet, to another worksheet in the same workbook, to another workbook or other type of document on your hard drive, or to a Web page on your company's intranet or on the World Wide Web.

Hyperlinks 101

To add hyperlinks in an Excel worksheet, you must define two things:

- The object to which to anchor the link and then click to activate
- The destination to which the link takes you when activated

The objects to which you can attach hyperlinks include any text that you enter into a cell or any graphic object that you draw or import into the worksheet (see Book V, Chapter 2 for details on adding graphics to your worksheet). The destinations that you can specify for links can be a new cell or range, the same workbook file, or to another file outside of the workbook.

The destinations that you can specify for hyperlinks that take you to another place in the same workbook file include:

- **Cell reference** of a cell on any of the worksheets in the workbook that you want to go to when you click the hyperlink
- **Range name** of the group of cells that you want to select when you click the hyperlink — the range name must already exist at the time you create the link

The destinations that you can specify for hyperlinks that take you outside of the current workbook include:

- **Filename** for an existing file that you want to open when you click the hyperlink — this file can be another workbook file or any other type of document that your computer can open
- **URL Address** of a Web page that you want to visit when you click the hyperlink — this page can be on your company's intranet or on the World Wide Web and is opened in your Web browser
- **New Document** that you want to create in Excel or some other program on your computer when you click the hyperlink — you must specify the filename and file extension (which indicates what type of document to create and what program to launch)
- **E-mail Address** for a new message that you want to create in your e-mail program when you click the hyperlink — you must specify the recipient's e-mail address and the subject of the new message when creating the link

Adding hyperlinks

The steps for creating a new hyperlink in the worksheet are very straightforward. The only thing you need to do beforehand is to add the jump text in the cell where you want the link or to draw or import the graphic object to which the link is to be attached (as described in Book V, Chapter 2). Then, to add a hyperlink to the text in this cell or the graphic object, follow these steps:

1. **Position the cell pointer in the cell containing the text or click the graphic object to which you want to anchor the hyperlink.**

   After you have selected the cell with the text or the graphic object, you're ready to open the Insert Hyperlink dialog box.

2. **Choose Insert⇨Hyperlink from the Excel Menu bar, click the Insert Hyperlink button on the Standard toolbar, or press Ctrl+K.**

   The Insert Hyperlink dialog box opens, similar to the one shown in Figure 2-1. If you selected a graphic object or a cell that contains some entry besides text before opening this dialog box, you notice that the Text to Display text box contains <<Selection in Document>> and that this box is grayed out (because there isn't any text to edit when anchoring a link to a graphic). If you selected a cell with a text entry, that entry appears in the Text to Display text box. You can edit this text in this box; however, be aware that any change that you make to it here is reflected in the current cell when you close the Insert Hyperlink dialog box.

The ScreenTip button located to the immediate right of the Text to Display text box enables you to add text describing the function of the link when you position the mouse pointer over the cell or graphic object to which the link is attached. To add a ScreenTip for your link, follow Step 3. Note that if you don't add your own ScreenTip, Excel automatically creates its own ScreenTip that lists the destination of the new link when you position the mouse pointer on its anchor.

3. **(Optional) Click the ScreenTip button and then type the text that you want to appear next to mouse pointer in the Set Hyperlink ScreenTip dialog box before you click OK.**

   By default, Excel selects the Existing File or Web Page button in the Link To area on the left side of the Insert Hyperlink dialog box, thus enabling you to assign the link destination to a file on your hard drive or to a Web page. To link to a cell or cell range in the current workbook, click the Place in This Document button. To link to a new document, click the Create New Document button. To link to a new e-mail message, click the E-mail Address button.

4. **Select the type of destination for the new link by clicking its button in the Link to panel on the left side of the Insert Hyperlink dialog box.**

   Now all that you need to do is to specify the destination for your link. How you do this depends upon which type of link you're adding; see the following instructions for details.

   - **Linking to a cell or named range in the current workbook:** Enter the address of the cell to link to in the Type the Cell Reference text box and then click the name of the sheet that contains this cell listed under Cell Reference range in the Or Select a Place in This Document list box. To link to a named range, simply click its name under Defined Names in the Or Select a Place in This Document list box.
   - **Linking to an existing file:** Open its folder in the Look In drop-down list box and then click its file icon in the list box that appears immediately below this box. If you're linking to a Web page, click the Address text box and enter the URL address (as in `http://` and so on) there. If the file or Web page that you select contains bookmarks (or range names in the case of another Excel workbook) that name specific locations in the file to which you link, click the Bookmark

button and then click the name of the location (bookmark) in the Select Place in Document dialog box before you click OK.

- **Creating a new document:** Enter a filename for the new document in the Name of New Document text box. Include the three-letter filename extension if this new document is not an Excel workbook such as `.doc` to create a new Word document or `.txt` to create a new text file. To specify a different folder in which to create the new document, click the Change button to the right of the current path and then select the appropriate drive and folder in the Create New Document. If you want to edit the contents of the new document right away, leave the Edit the New Document Now radio button selected. If you prefer to edit the new document at a later time, click the Edit the New Document Later radio button.
- **Creating a new e-mail message:** Enter the e-mail address (as in `gharvey@mindovermedia.com`) in the E-mail Address text box and then click the Subject text box and enter the subject of the new e-mail message.

5. **Specify the destination for the new hyperlink by using the text boxes and list boxes that appear for the type of link destination that you selected.**

   Now you're ready to create the link.

6. **Click the OK button in the Insert Hyperlink dialog box.**

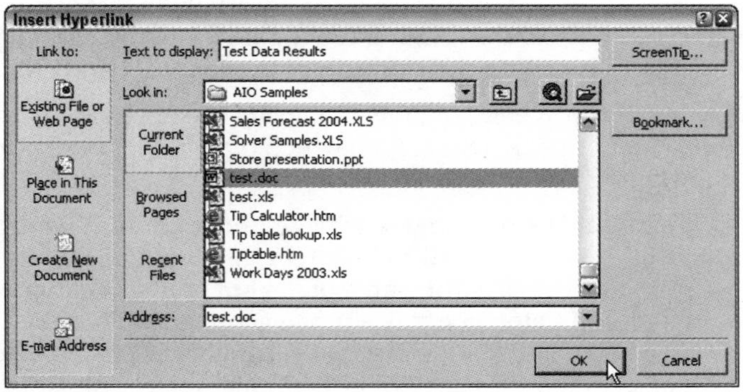

Figure 2-1: Creating a new hyperlink in the Insert Hyperlink dialog box.

As soon as you click OK, Excel closes the Insert Hyperlink dialog box and returns you to the worksheet with the new link (unless you specified that the new link is to create a new document *and* you left the Edit New Document Now radio button selected, in which case, you're in a new document — possibly in another application program such as Microsoft Word). If you anchored your new hyperlink to a graphic object, that object is still selected in the worksheet (to deselect the object, click a cell outside of its boundaries). If you anchored your hyperlink to text in the current cell, the text now appears in blue and is underlined (you may not be able to see the underlining until you move the cell pointer out of the cell).

When you position the mouse pointer over the cell with the hypertext or the graphic object with the hyperlink, the mouse pointer changes from the thick, white cross pointer to a hand with the index finger pointing up and the ScreenTip that you assigned appears below and to the right of the hand.

If you didn't assign your own ScreenTip to the hyperlink when creating it, Excel adds its own message that shows the destination of the link. If the link is a hypertext link (that is, if it's anchored to a cell containing a text entry), the message in the ScreenTip also says,

```
Click once to follow. Click and hold to select this cell.
```

Follow that link!

To follow a hyperlink, click the link text or graphic object with the hand mouse pointer. Excel then takes you to the destination. If the destination is a cell in the workbook, Excel makes that cell current. If the destination is a cell range, Excel selects the range and makes the first cell of the range current. If this destination is a document created with another application program, Excel launches the application program (assuming that it's available on the current computer). If this destination is a Web page on the World Wide Web, Excel launches your Web browser, connects you to the Internet, and then opens the page in the browser.

After you follow a hypertext link to its destination, the color of its text changes from the traditional blue to a dark shade of purple (without affecting its underlining). This color change indicates that the hyperlink has been followed (note, however, that graphic hyperlinks don't show any change in color after you follow them). Followed hypertext links regain their original blue color when you reopen their workbooks in Excel.

To help navigate your links, you can display the Web toolbar and use its buttons. To display the Web toolbar, choose View⇨Toolbars⇨Web on the Excel pull-down menus. Figure 2-2 shows the Web toolbar and identifies each of its unnamed buttons.

The Address combo box in the Web toolbar shows you not only the address of the current workbook but also stores all the addresses of the various documents that you've opened and Web pages that you've visited. You can then reopen a document or revisit a Web page simply by clicking its path or URL address on the Address drop-down list.

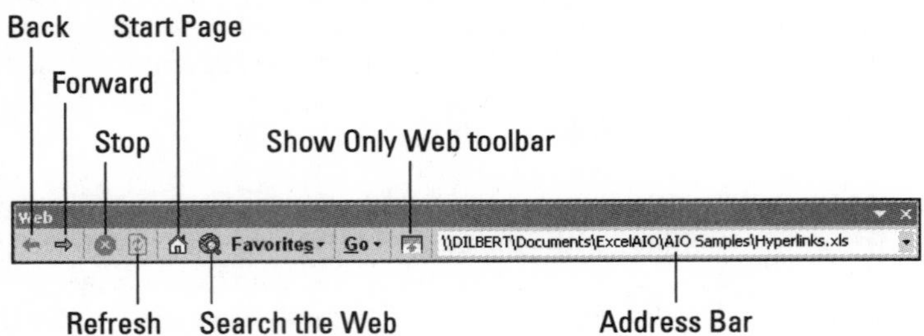

Figure 2-2: You can use the buttons on the Web toolbar to navigate hyperlinks in your spreadsheet.

When you follow a link to a Web page or to open another Office document, you can use the Back and Forward buttons to go back and forth between the Excel workbook with your hyperlinks and the destination document or Web page. For example, suppose that you create a hypertext link in a cell of your spreadsheet that opens your favorite financial page on the World Wide Web. When you click the hyperlink text, Excel launches Internet Explorer, connects you to the Internet, and takes you directly to that page.

After browsing the information on the financial Web page, suppose that you decide that you need to return to your Excel spreadsheet to check some data. Without closing the Internet Explorer window, click the Back button on the Internet Explorer toolbar to return to the worksheet. From there, you can go right back to your financial Web page by clicking the Forward button on the Web toolbar.

You can continue going back and forth between the Web page and the Excel spreadsheet as long as you like just by using the Back and Forward buttons on their respective toolbars. Note that this is a perfect way to get to and fro when you're copying and pasting information from the Web page into your worksheet.

Editing hyperlinks

Excel makes it easy to edit any hyperlink that you've added to your spreadsheet. The only trick to editing a link is that you have to be careful not to activate the link during the editing process. This means that you must always remember to right-click the link's hypertext or graphic to select the link that you want to edit, because clicking only results in activating the link.

When you right-click a link, Excel displays its shortcut menu. If you want to modify the link's destination or ScreenTip, click Edit Hyperlink on this shortcut menu. This action opens the Edit Hyperlink dialog box with the same options as the Insert Hyperlink dialog box (shown previously in Figure 2-1). You can then use the Link To buttons on the left side of the dialog box to modify the link's destination or the ScreenTip button to add or change the ScreenTip text.

Removing a hyperlink

If you want to remove the hyperlink from a cell entry or graphic object without getting rid of the text entry or the graphic, right-click the cell or graphic and then click the Remove Hyperlink item on the cell's or object's shortcut menu.

If you want to clear the cell of both its link and text entry, click the Delete item on the cell's shortcut menu. To get rid of a graphic object along with its hyperlink, right-click the object (this action opens its shortcut menu) and then immediately click the object to remove the shortcut menu without either deselecting the graphic or activating the hyperlink. At this point, you can press the Delete key to delete both the graphic and the associated link.

Copying and moving a hyperlink

When you need to copy or move a hyperlink to a new place in the worksheet, you can use either the drag-and-drop or the cut-and-paste method. Again, the main challenge to using either method is selecting the link without activating it because clicking the cell or graphic object containing the link only results in catapulting you over to the link's destination point.

To select a cell that contains hypertext, use the arrow keys to position the cell pointer in that cell or use the Go To feature (Edit➪Go To or Ctrl+G) and enter the cell's address in the Go To dialog box to move the cell pointer there. To select a graphic object that contains a hyperlink, right-click the graphic to select it as well as to display its shortcut menu, and then immediately click the graphic (with the left mouse button) to remove the shortcut menu while keeping the object selected.

After you have selected the cell or graphic with the hyperlink, you can move the link by choosing Edit➪Cut (Ctrl+X) or copy it by choosing Edit➪Copy (Ctrl+C) and then paste it into its new position with Edit➪Paste (Ctrl+V). When moving or copying hypertext from one cell to another, you can just click the cell where the link is to be moved or copied and then press the Enter key.

To move the selected link by using the drag-and-drop method, drag the cell or object with the mouse pointer (in the shape of a white arrowhead pointing to black double-cross) and then release the mouse button to drop the hypertext or graphic into its new position. To copy the link, be sure to hold down the Ctrl key (which changes the pointer to a white arrowhead with a plus sign to its right) as you drag the outline of the cell or object.

When attempting to move or copy a cell by using the drag-and-drop method, remember that you have to position the thick, white-cross mouse pointer on one of the borders of the cell with the cell pointer before it changes to a white arrowhead pointing to a black double-cross. If you position the pointer anywhere within the cell's borders, the mouse changes to the hand with the index finger pointing upward, indicating that the hyperlink is active.

Adding hyperlinks to toolbars and menus

You can assign links to custom buttons or custom menu items that you add to new or existing toolbars or pull-down menus in Excel (see Book I, Chapter 3 for complete information on how to create custom buttons for toolbars and pull-down menus in Excel).

To see how easy it is to add a hyperlink to a custom button on a toolbar, follow along with the steps that I used for assigning a hyperlink to a new button added to the Choice Tools custom toolbar (introduced in Book I, Chapter 3 on the discussion of creating a new toolbar):

1. **Add a new custom button to the end of the Choice Tools toolbar.**

   Figure 2-3 shows the Choice Tools toolbar after adding a custom button to the end of the toolbar (the one with the Smiley Face icon). To do this, I opened the Customize dialog box (View⇨Toolbars⇨Customize), clicked the Commands tab and then selected Macros in the Categories list box, before dragging the Custom Button item from the Commands list box to the end of the Choice Tools toolbar.

2. **Rename the custom button.**

   To do this, I right-clicked the Smiley Face button and then clicked Name on the button's shortcut menu and replaced the name "&Custom Button" with "Excel Support Center" and pressed the Enter key.

3. **Select a new graphic image for the Excel Support Center button.**

   To do this, I right-clicked the Smiley Face button again and this time clicked Change Button Image on the button's shortcut menu. This action opens a palette of images from which to select. I clicked the question mark icon at the bottom of this palette (see Figure 2-4).

4. **Assign the hyperlink to the custom button for visiting the Excel Support Center Web page.**

   To do this, I right-clicked the Question Mark button and clicked Assign Hyperlink⇨Open on the button's shortcut menu. This action opens the Assign Hyperlink: Open dialog box which looks just like and works just like the Insert Hyperlink dialog box discussed previously in this chapter. To assign the hyperlink, I clicked the Existing File or Web Page button in the Link To area and then filled in the URL address of the Excel Support Center page in the Address text box before clicking OK (see Figure 2-5).

5. **Close the Customize dialog box and test the Excel Support Center button on the Choice Tools toolbar.**

   To do this, I clicked the Close button in the Customize dialog box and then clicked the Excel Support Center button at the end of the Choice Tools toolbar. This action opens the Internet Explorer and takes you directly to the Excel 2002 Support Center page on the Microsoft Web site.

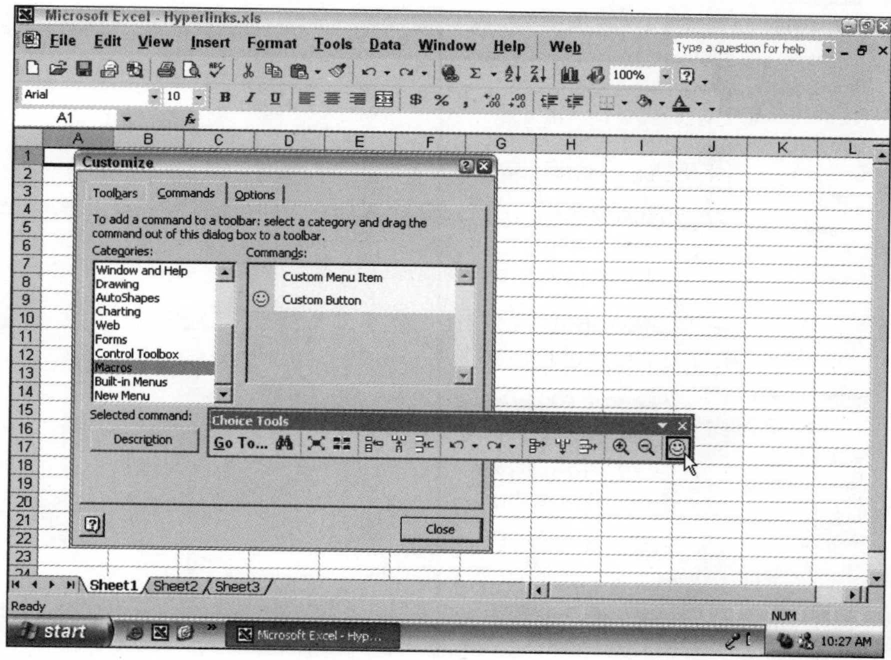

Figure 2-3: Adding custom button to the Choice Tools toolbar to which a hyperlink is to be attached.

The procedure for adding hyperlinks to custom menu items is very similar to the previous procedure. Follow along with the steps that I took to add a MS Office Home Page menu item to a custom Web menu at the end of the Excel Menu bar and then to assign a hyperlink to it that takes you to Microsoft Office Home Page on the Microsoft Web site.

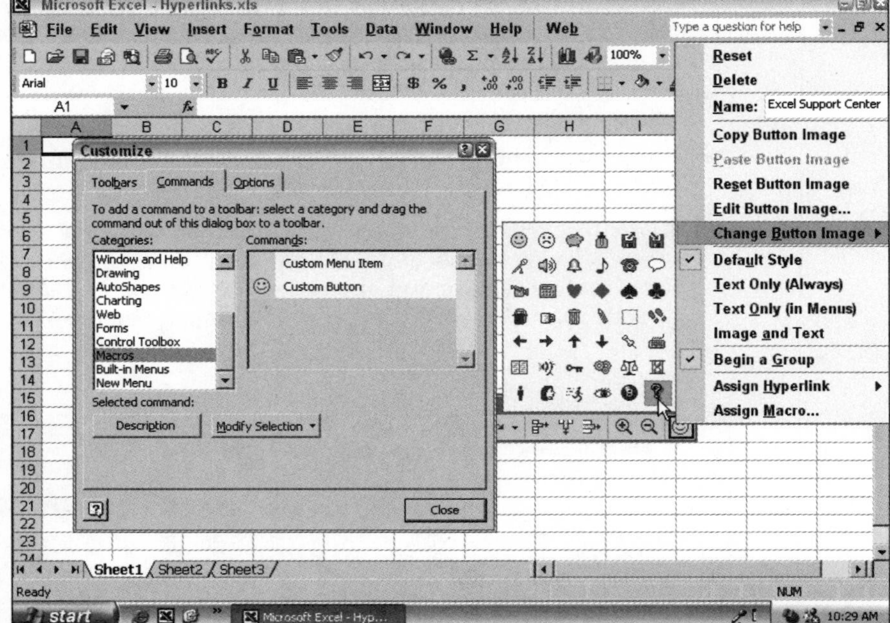

Figure 2-4: Selecting a new icon for the Excel Support Center button.

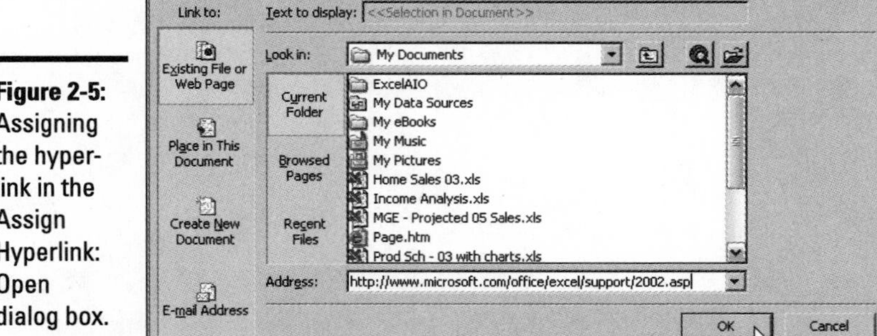

Figure 2-5: Assigning the hyperlink in the Assign Hyperlink: Open dialog box.

1. **Add the Web menu to the end of the Excel Menu bar.**

   To do this, I opened the Customize dialog box (View➪Toolbars➪ Customize), clicked the Commands tab and then selected New Menu in the Categories list box, before dragging the New Menu item from the Commands list box to the end of the Excel Menu bar.

2. **Replace the menu name, New Menu, with the new menu name, Web.**

   To do this, I right-clicked New Menu at the end of the Menu bar and then clicked Name on its shortcut menu where I replaced "New Menu" with "We&b" and pressed Enter. Remember that the ampersand (&) before the "b" in Web tells Excel to make that letter the hot key in the Menu name (I couldn't use "W" because that's already used by the Window menu or "e" because that's already used by the Edit menu).

3. **Add a Custom Menu Item to the Web menu.**

   To do this, I clicked Macros in the Categories list box in the Customize dialog box and then dragged Custom Menu Item from the Commands list box to the Web custom menu (see Figure 2-6).

4. **Rename the custom menu item.**

   To do this, I right-clicked Custom Menu Item on the Web menu at the end of the Menu bar and then clicked Name on its shortcut menu where I replaced "&Custom Menu Item" with "&MS Office Home Page" and pressed Enter.

5. **Assign the hyperlink to the MS Office Home Page menu item that takes you to this page on the Microsoft Web site.**

   To do this, I right-clicked the MS Office Home Page item on the Web menu and clicked Assign Hyperlink⇨Open on the button's shortcut menu. This action opens the Assign Hyperlink: Open dialog box, where I assigned the link by clicking the Existing File or Web Page button in the Link To area and then filling in the URL address of the Microsoft Office Home Page in the Address text box before clicking OK.

6. **Close the Customize dialog box and test the MS Office Home Page item on the custom Web menu.**

   To do this, I clicked the Close button in the Customize dialog box and then chose Web⇨MS Office Home Page from the Excel Menu bar. This action opens the Internet Explorer and takes you directly to the Microsoft Office Home Page on the Microsoft Web site.

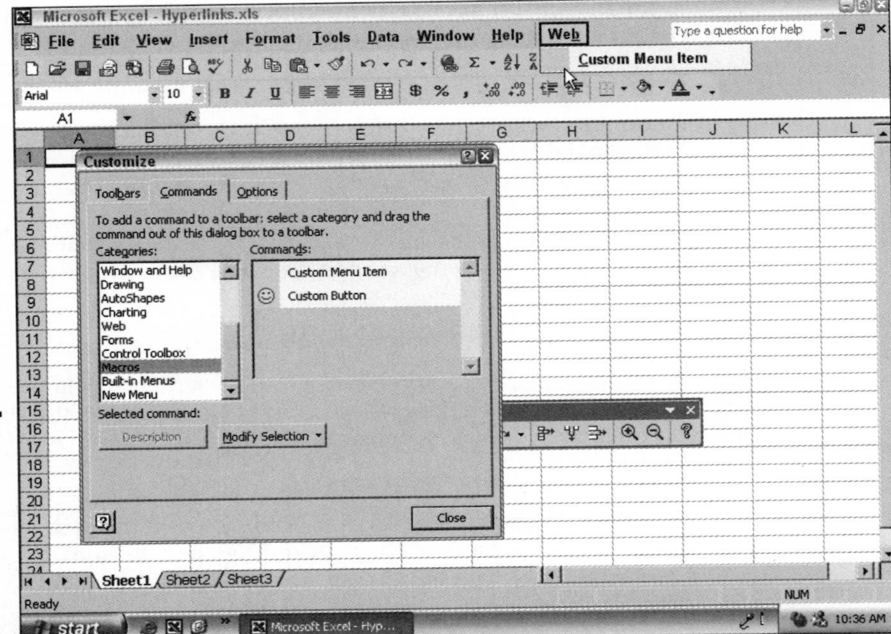

Figure 2-6: Adding a Custom Menu Item to the custom Web menu.

Using the HYPERLINK Function

Instead of using the Insert⇨Hyperlink command, you can use Excel's HYPERLINK function to create a hypertext link (you can't use this function to attach a hyperlink to a graphic object). The HYPERLINK function uses the following syntax:

```
HYPERLINK(link_location,[friendly_name])
```

The *link_location* argument specifies the name of the document to open on your local hard drive, on a network server (designated by a UNC address), or on the company's intranet or the World Wide Web (designated by the URL address — see the following sidebar for details). The optional *friendly_name* argument is the hyperlink text that appears in the cell where you enter the HYPERLINK function. If you omit this argument, Excel displays the text specified as the *link_location* argument in the cell.

When specifying the arguments for a HYPERLINK function that you type on the Formula bar (as opposed to one that you create by using the Insert Function feature by filling in the text boxes in the Function Arguments dialog box), you must remember to enclose both the *link_location* and *friendly_name* arguments in closed double quotes. For example, to enter a HYPERLINK function in a cell that takes you to the home page of the Dummies Web site and displays the text, "Dummies Home Page" in the cell, enter the following in the cell:

```
=HYPERLINK("http://www.dummies.com","Dummies Home Page")
```

How to tell a UNC from a URL address and when to care

The address that you use to specify a remote hyperlink destination comes in two basic flavors: UNC (Universal Naming Convention) and the more familiar URL (Universal Resource Locator). The type of address that you use depends on whether the destination file resides on a server on a network (in which case, you use a UNC address) or on a corporate intranet or the Internet (in which case, you use a URL address). Note that URLs also appear in many flavors, the most popular being those that use the Hypertext Transfer Protocol (HTTP) and begin with `http://` and those that use the File Transfer Protocol (FTP) and start with `ftp://`.

The UNC address for destination files on network servers start with two backslash characters (\\), following this format:

```
\\server\share\path\filename
```

In this format, the name of the file server containing the file replaces *server*, the name of the shared folder replaces *share*, the directory path specifying any subfolders of the shared folder replaces *path*, and the file's complete filename (including any filename extension, such as `.xls` for Excel worksheet) replaces *filename*.

The URL address for files published on Web sites follows this format:

```
internet service//internet
    address/path/filename
```

In this format, *internet service* is replaced with the Internet protocol to be used (either HTTP or FTP in most cases), *internet address* is replaced with the domain name (such as `www.dummies.com`) or the number assigned to the internet server, *path* is the directory path of the file, and *filename* is the complete name (including filename extensions such as `.htm` or `.html` for Web pages).

Book IX

Excel and Visual Basic for Applications

"Your database is beyond repair, but before I tell you our backup recommendation, let me ask you a question. How many index cards do you think will fit on the walls of your computer room?"

Contents at a Glance

Chapter 1: Building and Running Macros

In This Chapter

- Understanding how macros do what they do
- Recording macros
- Using the relative option when recording macros
- Playing back macros
- Assigning macros to custom buttons and menu items

Macros enable you to automate almost any task that you can undertake in Excel. By using Excel's macro recorder to record tasks that you perform routinely, you not only speed up the procedure considerably (because Excel can play back your keystrokes and mouse actions much faster than you can perform them manually), but you are also assured that each step in the task is carried out the same way each and every time you perform the task.

Excel's macro recorder records all the commands and keystrokes that you make in a language called Visual Basic for Applications (VBA), which is a special version of the BASIC programming language developed and refined by the good folks at Microsoft for use with all their Office application programs. You can then use Excel's Visual Basic Editor to display and make changes to the macro's VBA code.

In this chapter, you find out how to use Excel's macro recorder to record, test, and play back macros that you use to automate repetitive tasks required when building and using your Excel worksheets and charts. In the next chapter, you find out how to use Excel's Visual Basic Editor to debug and edit the macros that you record, as well as to create complex macros that run custom functions and set up and run custom Excel applications, complete with their own pull-down menus and dialog boxes.

Macro Basics

You can create macros in one of two ways:

- ✦ Use Excel's macro recorder to record your actions as you undertake them in a worksheet.
- ✦ Enter the instructions that you want followed in VBA code in the Visual Basic Editor.

Either way, Excel creates a special *module* sheet that holds the actions and instructions in your macro. The macro instructions in a macro module (whether recorded by Excel or written by you) are stored in the Visual Basic for Applications programming language.

You can then study the VBA code that the macro recorder creates and edit this code in Visual Basic Editor, which you open by choosing Tools➪Macro➪Visual Basic Editor or by pressing Alt+F11.

Recording Macros

With Excel's macro recorder, you can create many of the utility-type macros that help you to perform the repetitive tasks necessary for creating and editing your worksheets and charts. When you turn on the macro recorder, the macro recorder records all of your actions in the active worksheet or chart sheet as you make them. Note that the macro recorder doesn't record the keystrokes or mouse actions that you take to accomplish an action — only the VBA code required to perform the action itself. This means that mistakes that you make while taking an action that you rectify won't be recorded as part of the macro; for example, if you make a typing error and then edit it while the macro recorder is on, only the corrected entry will show up in the macro without the original mistakes and steps taken to remedy them.

The macros that you create with the macro recorder can be stored either as part of the current workbook, in a new workbook, or in a special, globally available Personal Macro Workbook named `personal.xls` that's stored in a folder called `xlstart` on your hard drive. When you record a macro as part of your Personal Macro Workbook, you can run that macro from any workbook that you have open (this is because the `personal.xls` workbook is secretly opened whenever you launch Excel and although it remains hidden, its macros are always available). When you record macros as part of the current workbook or a new workbook, you can run those macros only when the workbook in which they were recorded is open in Excel.

When you create a macro with the macro recorder, you decide not only the workbook in which to store the macro but also what name and shortcut keystrokes to assign to the macro that you are creating. When assigning a name for your macro, use the same guidelines as when you assign a standard range name to a cell range in your worksheet. When assigning a shortcut keystroke to run the macro, you can assign the Ctrl key plus a lowercase letter between a to z as in Ctrl+Q, or the Ctrl key plus an uppercase letter between A and Z (the equivalent of Ctrl+Shift), as in Ctrl+Shift+Q. You can't, however, assign the Ctrl key plus a punctuation or number key (such as Ctrl+1 or Ctrl+/) to your macro.

To see how easy it is to create a macro with the macro recorder, follow along with these steps for creating a macro that enters the Company Name in 12-point, bold type and centers the company name across rows A through E with the Merge and Center feature:

1. **Open the Excel workbook that contains the worksheet data or chart you want your macro to work with.**

   If you're building a macro that adds new data to a worksheet (as in this example), open a worksheet with plenty of blank cells in which to add the data. If you're building a macro that needs to be in a particular cell when its steps are played back, put the cell pointer in that cell.

2. **Choose Tools➪Macro➪Record New Macro from the Excel Menu bar.**

   The Record Macro dialog box opens, similar to the one shown in Figure 1-1, where you enter the macro name, define any keystroke shortcut, select the workbook in which to store the macro, and enter a description of the macro's function.

3. **Replace the Macro1 temporary macro name by entering your name for the macro in the Macro Name text box.**

   Remember that when naming a macro, you must not use spaces in the macro name and it must begin with a letter and not some number or punctuation symbol. For this example macro, you replace Macro1 in the Macro Name text box with the name Company_name.

   Next, you can enter a lowercase or uppercase letter between A and Z that acts like a shortcut key for running the macro when you press Ctrl followed by that letter key. Just remember that Excel has already assigned a number of Ctrl+letter keystroke shortcuts for doing common tasks, such as Ctrl+C for copying an item to the Clipboard and Ctrl+V for pasting an item from the Clipboard into the worksheet (see the Cheat Sheet at the beginning of this book for a complete list). If you assign the same keystrokes to the macro that you're building, your macro's shortcut keys override and, therefore, disable Excel's ready-made shortcut keystrokes.

4. **(Optional) Click the Shortcut key text box and then enter the letter of the alphabet that you want to assign to the macro.**

   For this example macro, enter **C** (uppercase) to assign Ctrl+Shift+C as the shortcut keystroke (so as not to disable the ready-made Ctrl+C shortcut).

Next, you need to decide where to save the new macro that you're building. Select Personal Macro Workbook on the Store Macro In drop-down list box to be able to run the macro anytime you like. Select This Workbook (the default) when you only need to run the macro when the current workbook is open. Select New Workbook if you want to open a new workbook in which to record and save the new macro.

5. **Click the Personal Macro Workbook, New Workbook, or This Workbook item on the Store Macro In drop-down list to indicate where to store the new macro.**

   For this example macro, select the Personal Macro Workbook so that you can use it to enter the company name in any Excel workbook that you create or edit.

   Now, you should document the purpose and functioning of your macro in the Description list box. Although this step is purely optional, it is a good idea to get in the habit of recording this information every time you build a new macro so that you and your co-workers can always know what to expect from the macro when they run it.

6. **(Optional) Click the Description list box and then insert a brief description of the macro's purpose in front of the information indicating the date and who recorded the macro.**

   Now you're ready to close the Record Macro dialog box and start recording your macro.

7. **Click OK to close the Record Macro dialog box.**

   When you do this, the Record Macro dialog box closes and a floating Stop Recording toolbar appears (although all you can see is "St" and half of the "o" in the title bar of this toolbar because it's too short — see Figure 1-2). You also notice that a message, "Recording" now appears on the Status bar to remind you that the results of all of the actions you take (including selecting cells, entering data, and choosing commands) will be now be recorded as part of your macro.

   The Stop Recording toolbar contains a Stop Recording button that you can click to turn off the macro recorder and a Relative Reference button that you click when you want the macro recorder to record the macro relative to the position of the current cell. For this example macro that enters the company name and formats it in the worksheet, you definitely need to click the Relative Reference button before you start recording commands. Otherwise, you can only use the macro to enter the company name starting in cell A1 of a worksheet.

8. **(Optional) Click the Relative Reference button if you want to be able to play back the macro anywhere in the worksheet.**

9. Select the cells, enter the data, and choose the Excel commands required to perform the tasks that you want recorded just as you normally would in creating or editing the current worksheet, using either the keyboard or the mouse or a combination of the two.

For the example macro, all you do is type the company name and click the Enter button on the Formula bar to complete the entry in the current cell. Next, click the Bold button and then click 12 on the Font Size drop-down list on the Formatting toolbar. Finally, drag through cells A1:E1 to select this range and then click the Merge and Center button, again on the Formatting toolbar.

After you finish taking all the actions in Excel that you want recorded, you're ready to shut off the macro recorder.

10. Choose Tools➪Macro➪Stop Recording or click Stop Recording button on the floating Stop Recording toolbar.

The Stop Recording toolbar and the Recording message on the Status bar immediately disappear, letting you know that the macro recorder is now turned off and no further actions will be recorded.

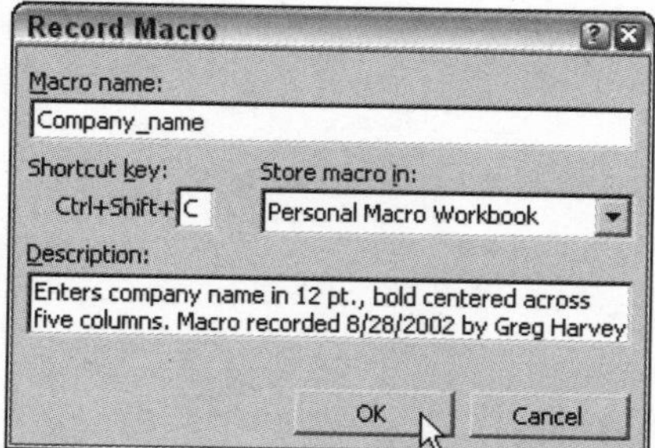

Figure 1-1: Getting ready to record the Company_name macro in the Record Macro dialog box.

Playing back a macro

After you record a macro, you can play it back by choosing Tools➪Macro➪Macros from the Excel Menu bar or by pressing Alt+F8. This action opens the Macro dialog box, which is similar to the one shown in Figure 1-3. As this figure shows, Excel lists the names of all the macros in the current workbook and in your Personal Macro Workbook (provided you've created one) in the Macro Name list box. Click the name of the macro that you want to play and click the Run button or press Enter.

If you assigned a shortcut keystroke to the macro, you don't have to bother opening the Macro dialog box to play the macro: simply press Ctrl plus the letter key or Ctrl+Shift plus the letter key that you assigned and Excel immediately plays back all of the commands that you recorded.

Before testing a new macro, you may need to select a new worksheet or, at least, a new cell range within the active worksheet. When recording cell references in a macro, the macro recorder always inserts absolute references in the macro sheet unless you click the Relative Reference button on the Stop Recording toolbar before you start choosing the commands and taking the actions in the spreadsheet that you want recorded as part of the macro. This means that your macro enters its data entries or performs its formatting in the same area of the active worksheet (unless the code in the macro itself causes the macro to first select a new area or select a new sheet in the workbook active).

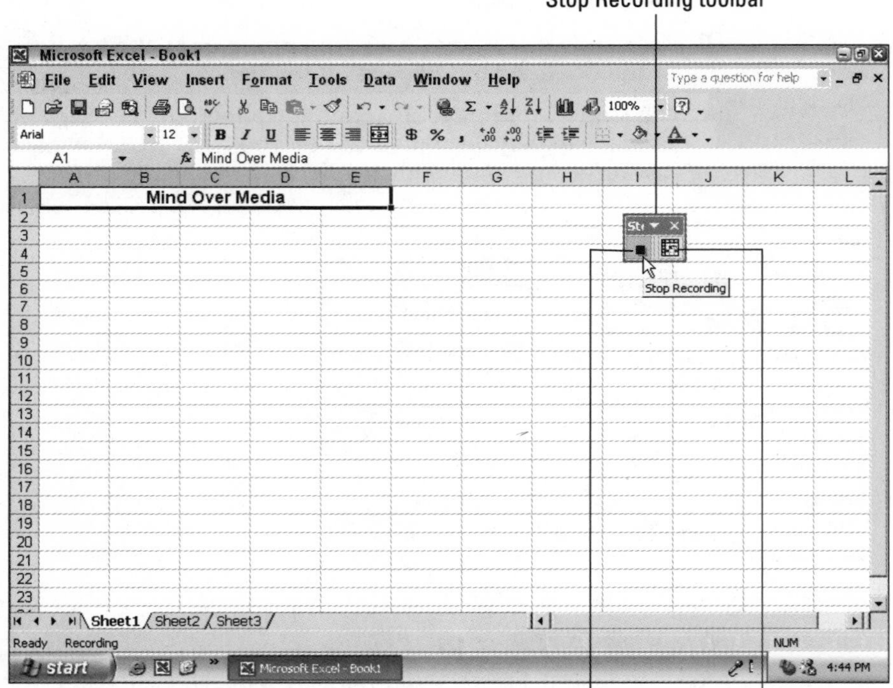

Figure 1-2: Recording the actions for the Company_name in the worksheet.

If you run your macro in a worksheet that already contains data in the cells that the macro uses, you run the risk of having existing data and/or formatting overwritten during the macro's execution. Keep in mind that although you can use the Undo feature to reverse the very last action performed by your macro, most macros perform a series of actions so that you may end up using multiple levels of Undo before you are able to successfully reconstruct your spreadsheet.

Macros and macro security

Excel 2002 uses a system called Microsoft Authenticode that enables developers to authenticate their macro projects or add-ins created with Visual Basic for Applications by a process referred to as *digital signing*. By default, Excel sets the level of macro security to the highest level so that only digitally signed macros can run. To enable Excel to run macros that aren't signed but that you know come from trustworthy sources (such as Fred in Accounting), you need to reset the macro security level to medium. To do this, choose Tools⇨Macro⇨Security to open the Security dialog box. To set the security level to medium so that you are always prompted whether to enable macros that are unsigned, click the Medium radio button in this dialog box before you click OK. Don't select the Low radio button option unless you are positive that your computer's virus scanning software is foolproof and that all the workbooks you come across that you haven't created are totally safe. Because this level of surety is almost impossible to come by, I strongly recommend that you never ever set the level in the Security dialog box any lower than the Medium setting!

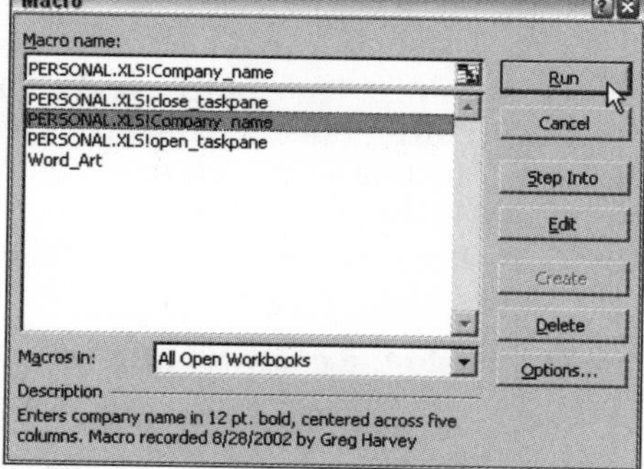

Figure 1-3: Selecting a macro to run in the Macro dialog box.

Assigning Macros to Toolbars and Menus

Excel makes it easy to assign macros to the custom buttons that you add to toolbars and to the custom menu items that you add to the Excel pull-down menus. You can also assign macros to any graphic object that you draw or import into Excel. When you assign a macro to a toolbar button, pull-down menu item, or a graphic object, you can then run the macro simply by clicking the button or graphic or by choosing the menu item from its pull-down menu.

To see how easy it is to assign a macro to a custom button, follow along with the steps for adding a couple of buttons to the Choice Tools toolbar (introduced in Book I, Chapter 3 in the discussion of creating a new toolbar) that run pre-recorded macros to open and to close the Task Pane in the Excel window:

1. **Add the two custom buttons to the new section near the end of the Choice Tools toolbar.**

   To do this, I open the Customize dialog box (View⇨Toolbars⇨Customize), select Macros in the Categories list box, and then drag the Custom Button item from the Commands list box to the custom Choice Tools toolbar two times (one time for each button) to create a new section near the end of it. Remember that you can add a separator bar to create a new section for these two buttons by slightly dragging the first custom button you add just slightly to the right.

2. **Rename the custom buttons.**

   To do this, I right-click the first Smiley Face button and then click Name on its shortcut menu and replace the name "&Custom Button" with "Open Task Pane" and press the Enter key. I then repeat this step for the second Smiley Face button, renaming it to "Close Task Pane."

3. **Select a new graphic image for Open Task Pane and the Close Task Pane buttons.**

   To do this, I right-click the Open Task Pane button and click Change Button Image on the button's shortcut menu. I then click the icon with the picture of the blue arrow pointing to the left to assign it this button. Next, I repeat this procedure with the Close Task Pane button, selecting this time, the icon with the blue arrow pointing to the right from the pop-up palette.

4. **Assign the appropriate macros to the custom buttons.**

   To do this, I right-click the Open Task Pane button and click Assign Macro on the button's shortcut menu. Doing this opens the Assign Macro dialog box which looks just like the Macro dialog box from which you can run macros. I assign the open_taskpane macro saved in the Personal Macro Workbook to Open Task Pane button by clicking PERSONAL.XLS!open_taskpane in the list box and then clicking OK (see Figure 1-4). I then repeat this process for the Close Task Pane button — this time assigning the PERSONAL.XLS!close_taskpane macro to this button.

5. **Close the Customize dialog box and then test out the Open Task Pane and Close Task Pane buttons on the Choice Tools toolbar.**

   To do this, I click the Close button in the Customize dialog box and then click the Open Task Pane button on the Choice Tools toolbar. This action runs the open_taskpane macro in the Personal Macro Workbook

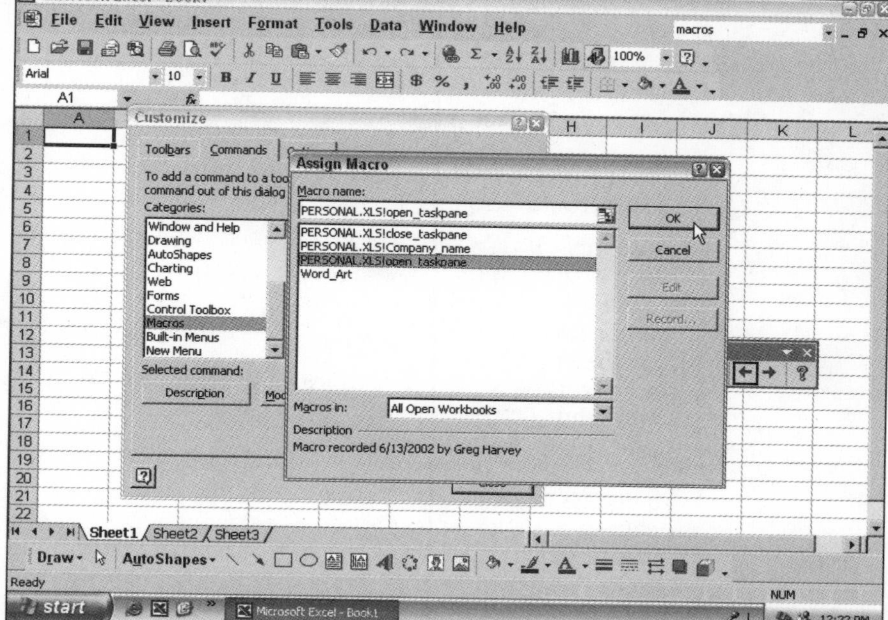

Figure 1-4: Assigning the PERSONAL.XLS!open_taskpane macro to the Open Task Pane button.

that opens the Task Pane window on the right of Excel window. I then click the Close Task Pane button on the Choice Tools toolbar to run the close_taskpane macro that immediately closes the Task Pane.

The steps for assigning a macro to a custom menu item or graphic object are very similar. After you add the custom menu item from the Macros category in the Customize dialog box (View⇨Toolbar⇨Customize), you right-click the menu item and then choose the Name and Assign Macro commands on the item's shortcut menu to rename the menu item and then to select the macro that runs when you choose the item from the Excel Menu bar.

To assign a macro to a graphic object that you draw or import into the worksheet (see Book V, Chapter 2 for details), right-click the object to display its shortcut menu and then click Assign Macro on its shortcut menu. Excel opens the Assign Macro dialog box from which you select the macro that you want assigned to the object by clicking the macro name followed by the OK button.

After assigning a macro to a graphic object, the mouse pointer assumes the shape of the hand with the index finger pointing up (the same pointer shape used to let you know when a graphic has a hyperlink attached to it). When you click the object with this pointer, Excel runs the macro as though you had selected it in the Macro dialog box and then clicked the Run button.

Chapter 2: VBA Programming

In This Chapter

- Getting familiar with Visual Basic for Applications and the Visual Basic Editor
- Installing and using VBA help
- Editing a macro in the Visual Basic Editor
- Creating a dialog box that prompts you for input for your macro
- Writing new macros in the Visual Basic Editor
- Using VBA to create user-defined functions
- Using your user-defined functions in your spreadsheets
- Saving user-defined functions as Excel add-ins

The subject of this chapter is Visual Basic for Applications (usually known simply as VBA), which is the official programming language of Excel, and how you can use it to both edit the macros that you record (as described in Book IX, Chapter 1) as well as to write new macros. The key to editing and writing macros in VBA is its editing program, the Visual Basic Editor (often abbreviated as VBE). The Visual Basic Editor offers a rich environment for coding and debugging VBA code with an interface that rivals Excel itself in terms of features and complexity.

VBA is a huge subject, well beyond the scope of this book. In this chapter, I simply introduce you to the Visual Basic Editor and I explain how to use it to do basic macro editing. I also show you how to use the Visual Basic Editor to create custom Excel functions that you can then use when building formulas in your Excel spreadsheets. Custom functions (also known as *user-defined functions* or UDFs) work just like built-in functions except that they perform only the calculations that you define, by using just the arguments that you specify.

If this basic introduction to Visual Basic for Applications and using the Visual Basic Editor inspires you to go on and try your hand at real VBA project development in Excel, I recommend *VBA For Dummies* by Steve Cummings as an excellent next step. His book gives you the lowdown on all the ins and outs of VBA programming in that old, familiar, down-home *For Dummies* style that you've come to know and love.

Using the Visual Basic Editor

The first question that you may have is where the heck did they stick this Visual Basic Editor that you've heard so much about? Actually, the Visual Basic Editor is always ready to step forward whenever you choose Tools⇨Macros⇨Visual Basic Editor or press Alt+F11. You can also start the Visual Basic Editor from the Visual Basic toolbar (View⇨Toolbars⇨Visual Basic) by clicking its Visual Basic Editor button, shown in Figure 2-1.

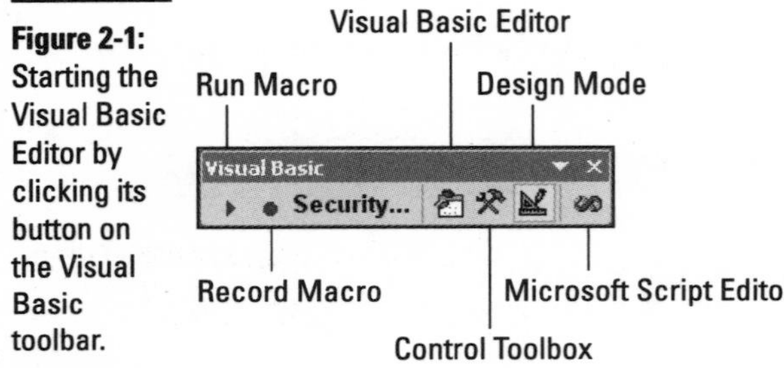

Figure 2-1: Starting the Visual Basic Editor by clicking its button on the Visual Basic toolbar.

Figure 2-2 shows the arrangement of the typical components shown in the Visual Basic Editor when you first open it. As you can see, this window contains its own Menu bar (with a few more menus than are used by the regular Excel window). Beneath the Menu bar, you find a Visual Basic Editor Standard toolbar. This toolbar, shown in Figure 2-3, contains a number of buttons familiar to you from the Standard toolbar in the regular Excel window.

Beneath the Standard toolbar in the Visual Basic Editor, you find a number of tiled windows of various sizes and shapes. Keep in mind that these are the default windows — they aren't the only windows that you can have open in the Visual Basic Editor (as though it weren't crowded and confusing enough) nor is this the only way that they can be arranged.

The two most important windows (at least, when you're first starting out using the Visual Basic Editor) are the Project Explorer window and the Code window. The Project Explorer window, which is located to the immediate left of the Code window (refer to Figure 2-2), shows you all the projects that you have open in the Visual Basic Editor and enables you to easily navigate their various parts. Note that in VBA, a *project* consists of all the code and user forms that belong to a particular workbook along with the sheets of the workbook itself.

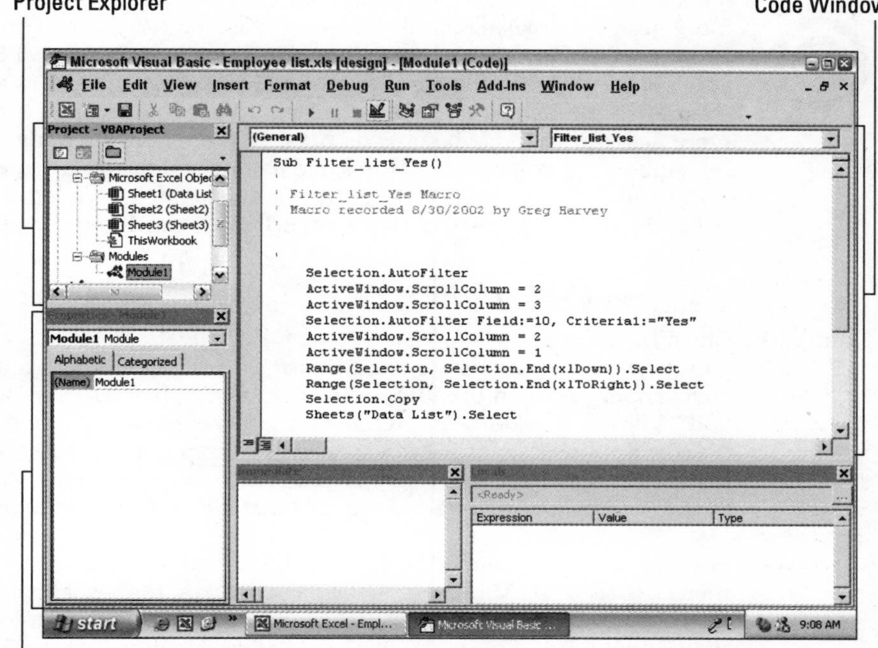

Figure 2-2: The Visual Basic Editor window as it normally appears when first opened.

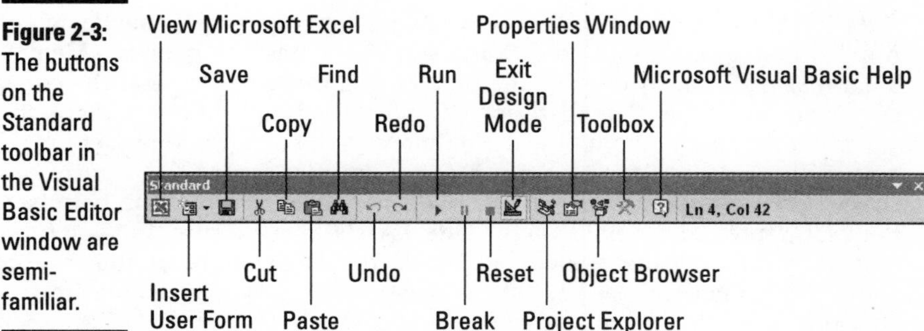

Figure 2-3: The buttons on the Standard toolbar in the Visual Basic Editor window are semi-familiar.

The macros that you record in the workbook, as well as any that you write for it in the Visual Basic Editor, are recorded on module sheets to which generic names are assigned, such as Module1, Module2, and so forth. The actual lines of VBA programming code for the macro that are stored on a particular module sheet appear in the Code window when you select its module in the Project Explorer window (the Code window appears to the immediate right of the Project Explorer window).

If you want to rename a module in your VBA project to something a little more descriptive than Module1, Module2, and so on, you can do this in the Properties window that appears immediately below the Project Explorer window. Simply click the name (such as Module1) that appears after the label (Name) on the Alphabetic tab in the Properties window and replace it with a more descriptive name before you press Enter. When renaming a module, remember that you must use the same naming guidelines as when naming a range name in a worksheet: Begin the module name with a letter of the alphabet and don't put any spaces (use underlines instead) between words.

Getting VBA Help

Given the richness of the Visual Basic for Applications language and the sophistication of the Visual Basic Editor, you will definitely want to become well acquainted with the VBA online help as you begin to use the language and its editor to modify and refine your recorded macros and develop custom applications of your own. The VBA Help system, although it works just like Excel's Help program (covered extensively in Book I, Chapter 2) is separate from it and not automatically installed as part of the program.

To install the VBA Help, open the Visual Basic Editor from Excel (Atl+F11) and then choose Help⇨Microsoft Visual Basic Help on the Visual Basic Editor's Menu bar or press F1. An Alert dialog box then appears, informing you that the VBA Help is not currently installed and asking you if you now wish to install it. Click the Yes button to install the VBA Help. (Remember that you must have your Office XP CD-ROM handy to install the Help files or be able to indicate where these files are located on your company's network.)

After the Help files are installed, you can get help on using Visual Basic for Applications by choosing Help⇨Microsoft Visual Basic Help on the Menu bar, pressing F1, or by clicking the Help button that appears near the end of the Standard toolbar. The first time you open the Help window, it displays general information about how the online VBA documentation is set up. Also, if you don't want to be stuck having Clippit or some other cutesy Office Assistant persona show up every time you access the VBA help (see Book I, Chapter 2 for details on the Office Assistant), be sure that you turn him off by right-clicking his icon and then choosing Options on the shortcut menu. Then, click the Use the Office Assistant check box to remove its checkmark on the Options tab before you click OK.

To get access to the topical information on Visual Basic, click the Show button on the Help window's toolbar to expand the Help window so that you have access to the Contents, Answer Wizard, and Index tabs (just like in the regular Excel Help window). To look up a particular help topic (and there are a slew of them), click the Contents tab and then expand the topical index as needed to reveal the help topic of interest. As with the regular Excel program Help, you can print the topic that you're viewing by clicking the Help button on its toolbar (see Book I, Chapter 2 for more on how to navigate the Help window and use the buttons on its toolbars).

You can also get help on a topic by typing keywords or simple questions into the Ask a Question text box, which appears near the end of the row with the Menu bar, and then pressing the Enter key. The Visual Basic Editor responds by displaying a pop-up menu of possible Help topics related to the keywords or question that you type into the Ask a Question text box (the one that says, "Type a question for help." You can then display one of the topics in the Help window by clicking it on the pop-up menu.

When you need help on a particular property that appears in a line of VBA code in your macro in the Code window, by far the best way to get help on it is to drag through the code and select the property in the Code window with the I-beam mouse pointer and then click the Help button on the Standard toolbar or press F1. When you do this, the Visual Basic Editor opens a Help window that gives you specific help information on the property that you selected.

For example, line 9 of my Filter_list_Yes macro contains the following line of VBA code:

```
ActiveWindow.ScrollColumn = 2
```

In order to understand the purpose of this statement in the macro, I selected "ActiveWindow.ScrollColumn" with the I-beam pointer in the Code window and then clicked the Help button on the Standard toolbar. This action opened the VBA Help window, shown in Figure 2-4, which explains the working of the ScrollColumn property in Visual Basic for Applications and gives an example of its usage that is almost identical to that in line 9 and 10 of the macro code.

By selecting unfamiliar statements in the code of the macros that you record and then edit in the Visual Basic Editor and then opening a context-sensitive Help window in this manner, you can quickly become familiar with the usage and syntax of the most commonly used statements and properties in the VBA language.

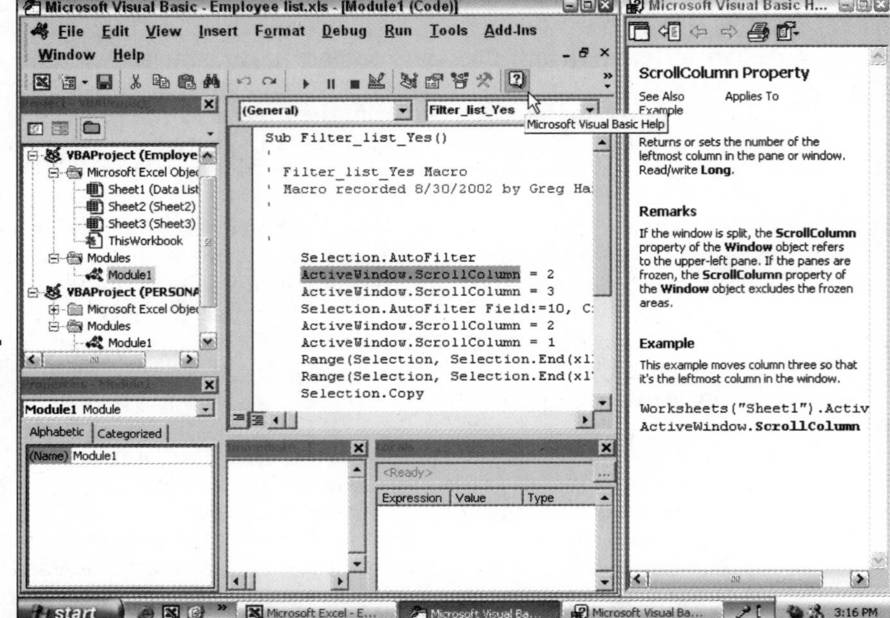

Figure 2-4: Getting help on the Scroll-Column property in the VBA Help window.

Editing recorded macros

After you've created a macro, you don't necessarily have to re-record it to change the way it behaves. In many cases, you will find it more expedient to change its behavior by simply editing its contents in the Visual Basic Editor. Note that if the macro you want to edit is stored in your Personal Macro Workbook (that `personal.xls` file in the XLSTART folder — see Book IX, Chapter 1 for details), you *must* unhide this workbook before you edit it in the Visual Basic Editor.

To unhide the Personal Macro Workbook, follow these steps:

1. **Choose Window➪Unhide on the Excel Menu bar.**

   This action opens the Unhide dialog box showing the workbook, `personal.xls` in its Unhide Workbook list box.

2. **Click** `personal.xls` **in the Unhide Workbook list box and then press Enter.**

   This action makes the Personal Macro Workbook visible and activates it so that you can now edit its macros in the Visual Basic Editor.

To open a macro for editing in the Visual Basic Editor, follow these steps:

1. **Choose Tools⇨Macros⇨Macro or press Alt+F8.**

   This action opens the Macro dialog box showing all the names of the macros that you've defined in the workbook and in your Personal Macro Workbook.

2. **Click the name of the macro that you want to edit in the Macro Name list box and then click the Edit button.**

   This action opens the Visual Basic Editor with the code for your macro displayed in the Code window unless you select the name of a macro saved in the Personal Macro Workbook and this workbook is still hidden. In that case, Excel displays an Alert dialog box telling you that you can't edit a hidden macro and informing you that you need to use the Window⇨Unhide command. You then need to click OK in the Alert dialog box, press Escape to close the Macro dialog box, and then follow the steps for unhiding the Personal Macro Workbook immediately preceding these steps before you repeat these first two macro editing steps.

   After you have the lines of code for the macro displayed in the Code window in the Visual Basic Editor, you can edit any of its statements as needed. If you want to obtain a printout of the lines of code in your macro before you begin making changes, choose File⇨Print on the Visual Basic Editor Menu bar or press Ctrl+P. This action opens a Print dialog box with the Current Module radio button selected in the Range section and the Code check box selected in the Print What section so that you can go ahead and click OK to have Excel print all the statements in the macro.

   When editing the macro's commands, remember that you can use the Edit⇨Undo (Ctrl+Z) command to undo any deletion that you make by mistake and you can find out what a particular statement or property does in the macro by selecting it with the I-beam mouse pointer and pressing F1, or by clicking the Help button on the Standard toolbar to get help on it in the Help window.

3. **Edit the statements in the Code window of the Visual Basic Editor as needed.**

   After you finish editing the macro, you're ready to return to your spreadsheet where you can test out the modified macro and make sure that you haven't added some wacky, unwanted command to the macro or, even worse, crippled it so that it no longer runs at all.

4. **Click the View Microsoft Excel button at the beginning of the Standard toolbar or click the workbook's minimized button on the Windows taskbar.**

Select an appropriate or safe place in which to test your modified macro and then run it, either by pressing its shortcut keys or by pressing Alt+F8, clicking it in the Macro list box, and then clicking the Run button.

If something doesn't work as intended or if the macro doesn't work at all, you need to return to the Visual Basic Editor and find and correct your error(s). Click the minimized Microsoft Visual Basic button on the Windows taskbar to return to the Visual Basic Editor and have a try at editing the code one more time.

If everything checks out and runs as planned, you need to save your changes as outlined in Step 5.

5. **Choose File⇨Save to save the changes to the modified macro if it's stored as part of the current workbook.**

   If you modified a global macro saved as part of the Personal Macro Workbook, you have to exit Excel in order to save your changes to the macro. When you choose File⇨Exit on the pull-down menus or press Alt+F4, Excel displays an Alert dialog box asking if you want to save the changes you made to the `personal.xls` file. Click the Yes button to save your macro modifications as you close down Excel.

Keep in mind that Excel automatically hides the Personal Macro Workbook when you exit Excel if you didn't choose the Window⇨Hide command when the `personal.xls` workbook is active some time before exiting the program. This means that you must remember to use the Windows⇨Unhide command to make this workbook visible before you can edit any of its macros during any subsequent editing session.

Maximizing the Code window for editing

After you have the macro open for editing in the Code window, you may want to maximize the Code window so that you can see as many of the lines and as many statements as possible on-screen. You can start by closing the Immediate and Locals windows that normally reside directly underneath the Code window. Although these windows can be helpful when debugging a macro (showing the results of executing certain lines of code and the values currently assigned to particular local variables), you usually don't have to have them open when you're just reviewing the macro's code and decide what modifications that you want to make.

When you click the close boxes on the Immediate and the Locals windows, the Code window expands to fill their space on the screen. If you want to devote the entire screen to the Code window (besides the Title, Menu, and toolbar at the top and Task bar at the bottom), close the Project Explorer window and Properties window as well by clicking their Close boxes. Figure 2-5 demonstrates how the Visual Basic Editor appears after closing the Project Explorer, Properties, Immediate, and Locals windows to maximize the screen space devoted to the Code window and the VBA code of the Company_name macro.

REMEMBER

Keep in mind that each time you open the Visual Basic Editor, its windows appear as they were when you last closed the editor, both in terms of the relative positioning and window size. To restore the Project Explorer or Properties windows to the Visual Basic Editor, you can click the Project Explorer or Properties button on the Standard toolbar or you can choose View➪Project Explorer (Ctrl+R) or View➪Properties Window (F4) on the Menu bar. To reopen the Immediate Window, choose View➪Immediate Window or press Ctrl+G. To reopen the Locals Window, choose View➪Locals Window.

To reposition a window after it's open in the Visual Basic Editor, drag the window by its title bar. To resize a window, position the mouse pointer on the appropriate edge of the window and then, when the pointer becomes a double-headed arrow, drag its border until it becomes the desired size.

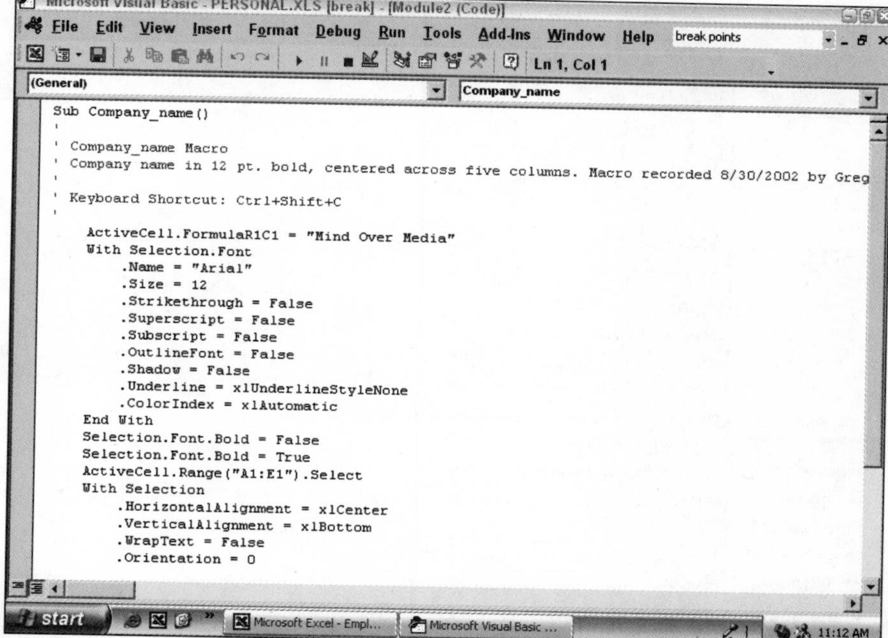
Microsoft Visual Basic - PERSONAL.XLS [break] - [Module2 (Code)]
File Edit View Insert Format Debug Run Tools Add-Ins Window Help
break points
Ln 1, Col 1
(General)
Company_name
Sub Company_name()
'
' Company_name Macro
' Company name in 12 pt. bold, centered across five columns. Macro recorded 8/30/2002 by Greg
'
' Keyboard Shortcut: Ctrl+Shift+C
'
ActiveCell.FormulaR1C1 = "Mind Over Media"
With Selection.Font
.Name = "Arial"
.Size = 12
.Strikethrough = False
.Superscript = False
.Subscript = False
.OutlineFont = False
.Shadow = False
.Underline = xlUnderlineStyleNone
.ColorIndex = xlAutomatic
End With
Selection.Font.Bold = False
Selection.Font.Bold = True
ActiveCell.Range("A1:E1").Select
With Selection
.HorizontalAlignment = xlCenter
.VerticalAlignment = xlBottom
.WrapText = False
.Orientation = 0
start
Microsoft Excel - Empl...
Microsoft Visual Basic ...
11:12 AM

Figure 2-5: Maximizing the Code window when editing a macro in the Visual Basic Editor.

Finding and replacing code in the macro

You can use the Find feature in the Visual Basic Editor to quickly locate the statements or properties that need editing in your macro. You open the Find dialog box, shown in Figure 2-6, by choosing Edit⇨Find on the Menu bar, clicking the Find button on the Standard toolbar, or by pressing Ctrl+F. This dialog box is very similar to the one you use when finding entries in your Excel spreadsheet. The main difference is that the Find dialog box gives you different choices for what to search for (in addition to the familiar options for finding whole words only and matching case):

- **Current Procedure** radio button to search only the current programming procedure in the Code window
- **Current Module** radio button (the default) to search only the macros in the current module
- **Current Project** radio button to search all the macros in all modules within the current project
- **Selected Text** radio button to search only the text that you've selected in the Code window (this option is not available unless you've selected a block of text in the current code)

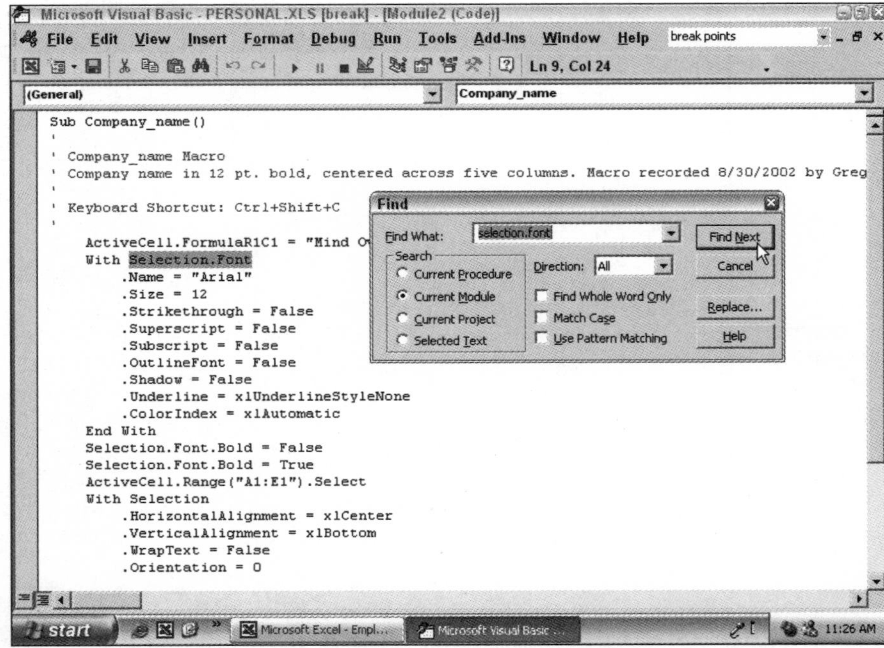
Microsoft Visual Basic - PERSONAL.XLS [break] - [Module2 (Code)]
File Edit View Insert Format Debug Run Tools Add-Ins Window Help
break points
Ln 9, Col 24
(General)
Company_name
Sub Company_name()
'
' Company_name Macro
' Company name in 12 pt. bold, centered across five columns. Macro recorded 8/30/2002 by Greg
'
' Keyboard Shortcut: Ctrl+Shift+C
'
ActiveCell.FormulaR1C1 = "Mind O
With Selection.Font
.Name = "Arial"
.Size = 12
.Strikethrough = False
.Superscript = False
.Subscript = False
.OutlineFont = False
.Shadow = False
.Underline = xlUnderlineStyleNone
.ColorIndex = xlAutomatic
End With
Selection.Font.Bold = False
Selection.Font.Bold = True
ActiveCell.Range("A1:E1").Select
With Selection
.HorizontalAlignment = xlCenter
.VerticalAlignment = xlBottom
.WrapText = False
.Orientation = 0
Find
Find What:
selection.font
Find Next
Cancel
Search
Current Procedure
Current Module
Current Project
Selected Text
Direction:
All
Find Whole Word Only
Match Case
Use Pattern Matching
Replace...
Help
start
Microsoft Excel - Empl...
Microsoft Visual Basic ...
11:26 AM

Figure 2-6: Using the Find feature to locate the code to edit in the Code window.

After you enter the Visual Basic property or statement as your search string in the Find What text box, select the search options, and click the Find Next button, Excel attempts to locate its first occurrence in the code. When it does, the program highlights that occurrence in the current procedure, module, VBA project, or selected text block (depending upon which Search option you use). To find the next occurrence, you can click the Find Next button in the Find dialog box again, or, if you close this dialog box, by pressing F3.

If you have a number of occurrences throughout the macro that require the same type of updating, you can use the Replace feature to both find and replace them in the macro code. This is particularly useful when you decide to change a particular value throughout a macro (such as selecting the cell range named "income_03" for processing instead of the range "income_02"), and you want to make sure that you don't miss any occurrences.

To open the Replace dialog box, choose Edit⇨Replace on the Visual Basic Editor Menu bar or press Ctrl+H. Note that you can open the Replace dialog box from within the Find dialog box by clicking its Replace button.

The Replace dialog box that then appears is just like the Find dialog box except that it contains a Replace With text box along with the Find What text box and has Replace and Replace All buttons in addition to the Find Next button. After entering the property or statement to find in the Find What text box and the one to replace it with in the Replace With text box, click the Find Next button to locate the first occurrence in the current procedure, module, VBA project, or selected text block (depending upon which Search option you use). After this occurrence is selected in the Code window, you have it replaced with the replacement text by clicking the Replace button. Excel then locates the next occurrence, which you can then replace by clicking the Replace button or pass over to find the next occurrence by clicking the Find Next button.

Don't use the Replace All button to replace all the occurrences in your macro unless you're 100 percent sure that you won't be globally replacing something that shouldn't be replaced and possibly screwing up your macro big time. I once typed "selection.font.bold = ture" into the Replace With text box when I intended to enter "selection.font.bold = true" as the replacement text when searching for the property "Selection.Font.Bold = False" in the macro. I then clicked the Replace All button only to discover to my dismay that I introduced this error throughout the code! Of course, I then had to turn around and use the Replace feature to find all the instances of "selection.font.bold = ture" and replace them with "Selection.Font.Bold = True."

Changing settings for VBA properties

Even when you don't know anything about programming in VBA (and even if you aim to keep it that way), you can still get the gist of some of the more obvious properties in a macro that change certain settings, such as number format or font attribute, by experimenting with assigning them new values.

In the Company_name macro shown previously in Figure 2-5, for example, you can tell that the section of VBA commands between the line

```
With Selection.Font
```

and the line

```
End With
```

contains the procedure for assigning various font attributes for the current cell selection.

Going a step further, you probably can figure out that most of these attributes are being reset by making the attribute equal to a new entry or value, such as

```
.Name = "Arial"
```

or

```
.Size = 12
```

Or an attribute is being reset by turning it on or off by setting it equal to True or False, such as

```
Selection.Font.Bold = True
```

to make the text in the current cell selection bold.

Now, it doesn't require a programming degree (at least, not the last time I checked) to get the bright idea that you can make your macro behave differently just by — *carefully* — editing these settings. For example, suppose that you want the final font size to be 24 points instead of 12. All you have to do is change

```
.Size = 12
```

to

```
.Size = 24
```

Likewise, you can have the macro apply single underlining to the cell selection by changing

```
.Underline = xlUnderlineStyleNone
```

to

```
.Underline = xlUnderlineStyleSingle
```

Many times, the alternate settings allowed in a particular Visual Basic code, such as the Underline property, are anything but obvious (how's that for an understatement?). When you encounter such a property in the macro code and you want to know what kinds of values it will accept, simply look it up in the online Visual Basic Reference. Click the property in the Code window without selecting its current setting (such as selecting .Underline rather than selecting .Underline = xlUnderlineStyleNone) and then Press F1 to open the VBA Help window with information on that property. Usually the Example section at the bottom of this Help window gives you an idea of the different types of values that the property can take. Remember, too, that you can obtain a printout of this Help information by clicking the Print button on the Help window's toolbar.

Getting macro input by adding a dialog box

One of the biggest problems with recording macros is that any text or values that you have the macro enter for you in a worksheet or chart sheet can never vary thereafter. If you create a macro that enters the heading "Bob's Barbecue Pit" in the current cell of your worksheet, this is the only heading you'll ever get out of that macro. However, you can get around this inflexibility by using the InputBox function. When you run the macro, this Visual Basic function causes Excel to display an Input dialog box where you can enter whatever title makes sense for the new worksheet. The macro then puts that text into the current cell and formats this text, if that's what you've trained your macro to do next.

To see how easy it is to use the InputBox function to add interactivity to an otherwise staid macro, follow along with the steps for converting the Company_name macro that currently inputs the text "Mind Over Media" to one that actually prompts you for the name that you want entered. The InputBox function uses the following syntax:

```
InputBox(prompt[,title][,default][,xpos][,ypos][,helpfile,con
   text])
```

In this function, only the *prompt* argument is required with the rest of the arguments being optional. The *prompt* argument specifies the message that appears inside the Input dialog box, prompting the user to enter a new value (or in this case, a new company name). The *prompt* argument can be up to a maximum of 1,024 characters. If you want the prompt message to appear on different lines inside the dialog box, you enter the functions, Chr(13) and Chr(10), in the text (to insert a carriage return and a linefeed in the message).

The optional *title* argument specifies what text to display in the title bar of the Input dialog box. If you don't specify a *title* argument, Excel displays the name of the application on the title bar. The optional *default* argument specifies the default response that automatically appears in the text box at the bottom of the Input dialog box. If you don't specify a default argument, the text box is empty in the Input dialog box.

The *xpos* and *ypos* optional arguments specify the horizontal distance from the left edge of the screen to the left edge of the dialog box and the vertical distance from the top edge of the screen to the top edge of the dialog box. If you don't specify these arguments, Excel centers the input dialog box horizontally and positions it approximately one-third of the way down the screen vertically.

The *helpfile* and *context* optional arguments specify the name of the custom Help file that you make available to the user to explain the workings of the Input dialog box as well as the type of data that it accepts. As part of the process of creating a custom help file for use in the Excel Help system, you assign the topic a context number appropriate to its content, which is then specified as the *context* argument for the InputBox function. When you specify a helpfile and *context* argument for this function, Excel adds a Help button to the custom Input dialog box that users can click to access the custom help file in the Help window.

Before you can add the line of code to the macro with the InputBox function, you need to find the place in the Visual Basic commands where the line should go. To enter the Mind Over Media text into the active cell, the Company_name macro uses the following Visual Basic command:

```
ActiveCell.FormulaR1C1 = "Mind Over Media"
```

To add interactivity to the macro, you need to insert the InputBox function on a line in the Code window right above this ActiveCell.FormulaR1C1 statement, as follows:

1. **Position the insertion point in the Code window at the beginning of the ActiveCell.FormulaR1C1 statement and press Enter to insert a new line.**

   Now that you've added a new line, you need to move the insertion point up to it.

2. **Press the ↑ key to position the insertion point at the beginning of the new line.**

   On this line, you want to create a variable that supplies the *prompt* argument to the InputBox function. To do this, you state the name of the variable (InputMsg in this case) followed by its current entry. Be sure to enclose the message text on the right side of the equal sign in a closed pair of double quotation marks.

3. **Type the following code to create the InputMsg variable on line 8 and then press the Enter key to start a new line 9:**

```
InputMsg = "Enter the title for this worksheet in the
text box below and then click OK:"
```

Next, you create a variable named InputTitle that supplies the optional *title* argument for the InputBox function. This variable makes the text, "Company Name" appear as the title of the Input dialog box. Again, be sure to enclose the name for the dialog box title bar in quotation marks.

4. **Type the following code to create the InputTitle variable on line 9 and then press Enter to insert a new line 10:**

```
InputTitle = "Company Name"
```

Next, you create a variable name DefaultText that supplied the optional *default* argument to the InputBox function. This variable makes the text, "Mind Over Media," appear as the default entry on the text box at the bottom of the custom Company Name Input dialog box.

5. **Type the following code to create the DefaultText variable on line 10 and then press Enter to insert a new line 11:**

```
DefaultText = "Mind Over Media"
```

Next, you create a final variable named CompanyName that specifies the InputBox function as its entry (using the InputMsg, InputTitle, and DefaultText variables that you just created) and stores the results of this function.

6. **Type the following code to create the CompanyName variable that uses the InputBox function on line 11:**

```
CompanyName = InputBox(InputMsg, InputTitle,
DefaultText)
```

Finally, you replace the value, "Mind Over Media," in the ActiveCell.FormulaR1C1 property with the CompanyName variable (whose value is determined by whatever is input into the Company Name Input dialog box), thus effectively replacing this constant in the macro with the means for making this input truly interactive.

7. **Select "Mind Over Media" on line 12 and replace it with CompanyName (with *no* quotation marks).**

Figure 2-7 shows the Code window with the edited Company_name macro after adding the statements that make it interactive. Figure 2-8 shows the Company Name Input dialog box in action in the worksheet. This Company Name dialog box now automatically appears and prompts you for input whenever you now run the edited and now fully interactive version of the Company_Name macro.

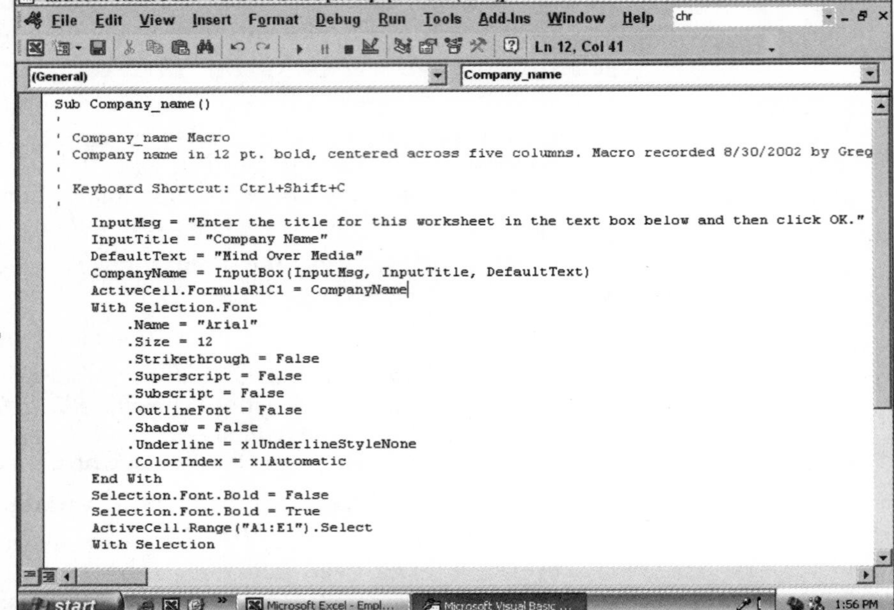
Microsoft Visual Basic - PERSONAL.XLS [break] - [Module2 (Code)]
(General)
Company_name
Sub Company_name()
'
' Company_name Macro
' Company name in 12 pt. bold, centered across five columns. Macro recorded 8/30/2002 by Greg
'
' Keyboard Shortcut: Ctrl+Shift+C
'
InputMsg = "Enter the title for this worksheet in the text box below and then click OK."
InputTitle = "Company Name"
DefaultText = "Mind Over Media"
CompanyName = InputBox(InputMsg, InputTitle, DefaultText)
ActiveCell.FormulaR1C1 = CompanyName
With Selection.Font
.Name = "Arial"
.Size = 12
.Strikethrough = False
.Superscript = False
.Subscript = False
.OutlineFont = False
.Shadow = False
.Underline = xlUnderlineStyleNone
.ColorIndex = xlAutomatic
End With
Selection.Font.Bold = False
Selection.Font.Bold = True
ActiveCell.Range("A1:E1").Select
With Selection

Figure 2-7: Company_ name Code window after adding variables and InputBox function.

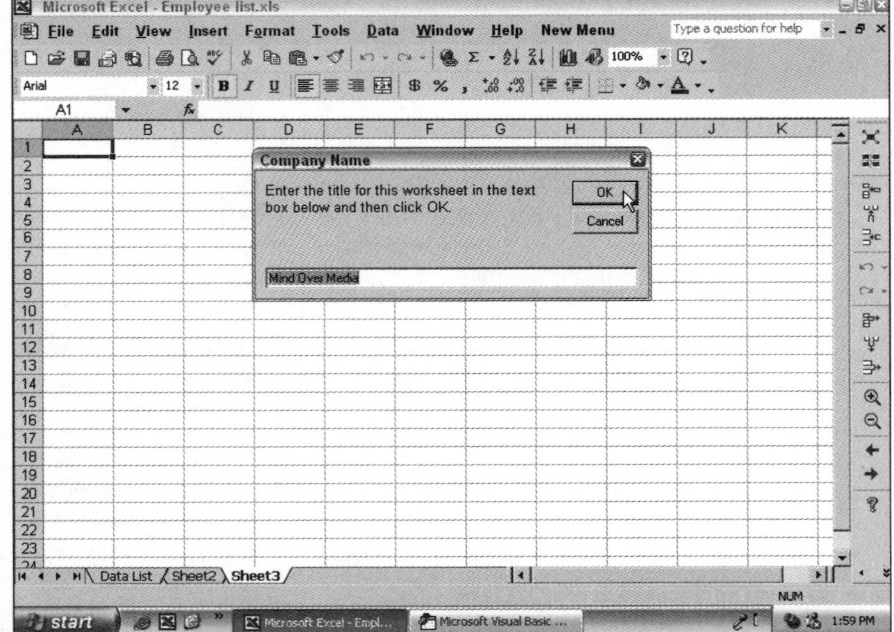
Microsoft Excel - Employee list.xls
Company Name
Enter the title for this worksheet in the text box below and then click OK.
OK
Cancel
Mind Over Media

Figure 2-8: The Company Name dialog box that appears when you run the Company_ name macro.

Why not simply type in the arguments of the InputBox function?

The biggest reason for using the variables InputMsg, InputTitle, and PromptText to supply the *prompt, title*, and *default* arguments of the InputBox function — rather than just typing them into the function — is their length. If you typed in all three pieces of text within the parentheses of the InputBox function, you would end up with one of the longest (and hardest to read) lines of code in history. When you use variables to do the job, as in the example shown previously, you end up with lines of code that fit on one screen, thus making the lines of code easier to read and also making it possible to print them on a normal piece of paper. If you use the variables on other procedures in the macro, declaring them all together at the beginning of the code also makes it easy to update their values.

To go ahead and enter Mind Over Media into the current cell and then format it by using the rest of the macro commands, you just click OK in this custom dialog box. To enter and format the name of another company, you simply type the name of the company (which automatically replaces Mind Over Media in the text box) before you click OK.

Writing new macros in the Visual Basic Editor

After you have the skill in the VBA language, you can write new macros from scratch in the Visual Basic Editor instead of just editing ones that you've previously recorded in your spreadsheet by using Excel's macro recorder. When creating a macro from scratch in the Visual Basic Editor, you need to follow these general steps:

1. **Click the name of the VBA project in the Project Explorer window where you want to add the new macro.**

   If you want to write a macro just for the current workbook, click the VBAProject function that contains its filename in parentheses, as in VBAProject (My Spreadsheet). If you want to write a global macro in the Personal Macro Workbook, click VBAProject() `personal.xls` in the Project Explorer window.

2. **Choose Insert⇨Module on the Visual Basic Editor Menu bar.**

   Excel responds by opening a new, blank Code window in the Visual Basic Editor window and by adding another Module icon (named with the next available number) in the outline in the Project Explorer window under the appropriate VBA Project.

Next, you begin your macro by creating a subroutine (all macros, even the ones you record in the spreadsheet, are really Visual Basic subroutines). To do this, you just type the word **sub** (for subroutine).

3. **Type** sub **and then press the spacebar.**

   Now, you need to name your new macro, which you do by naming your subroutine. Remember that in naming your new macro (or a subroutine) you follow the same rules as when naming a range name (begin with a letter and no spaces).

4. **Type the name of your macro and then press the Enter key.**

   As soon as you press the Enter key, the Visual Basic Editor inserts a closed pair of parentheses after the macro's name, a blank line, and an End Sub statement on its own line below that. It then positions the insertion point at the beginning of the blank line between the lines with the Sub and End Sub statements. It's here that you enter the lines of code for the macro that you're writing.

5. **Enter the lines of VBA code for the macro in between the Sub and End Sub statements.**

   Before you begin writing the VBA statements that your macro is to execute, you should first document the purpose and functioning of this macro. To do this, type an apostrophe (') at the beginning of each line of this text to enter it as a comment (Excel knows not to try to execute any line of code that's prefaced with an apostrophe). When you press the Enter key to start a new line that begins with an apostrophe, the line of text turns green, indicating that the Visual Basic Editor considers it to be a comment that's not to be executed when the macro runs.

   After you document the purpose of the macro with your comments, you begin entering the statements that you want the macro to execute (which must not be prefaced by apostrophes). To indent lines of code to make them easier to read, press Tab. If you need to outdent the line, press Shift+Tab For help on writing VBA code, refer to the VBA online help and Steven Cummings' excellent *VBA For Dummies*. When you finish writing the code for your macro, you need to save it before you test it.

6. **Choose File➪Save on the Visual Basic Editor Menu bar or press Ctrl+S.**

After you save your new macro, you can click the View Microsoft Excel button on the Standard toolbar to return to your worksheet where you can try it. To run the new macro that you've written, choose Tools➪Macro➪Macros or press Alt+F8 to open the Macro dialog box and then click the name of the macro that you just wrote before you click OK.

If Excel encounters an error when running the macro, it returns you to the Visual Basic Editor and an Alert Microsoft Visual Basic dialog box appears indicating (in very cryptic form) the nature of the error. Click the Debug button in this dialog box to have the Visual Basic Editor highlight the line of code that it can't execute. You can then attempt to find the mistake and edit it in the line of code. If you do eliminate the cause of the error, the Visual Basic Editor removes the highlighting from that line of code, and you can then click the Continue button (which automatically replaces the Run button when the Editor goes into debug mode) with the blue triangle pointing to the right on the Standard toolbar to continue running the macro.

Creating Custom Excel Functions

One of the best uses of VBA in Excel is to create custom spreadsheet functions also known as *user-defined functions* (*UDFs* for short). User-defined functions are great because you don't have to access the Macro dialog box to run them. In fact, you enter them into your spreadsheets just like you do any of the other built-in spreadsheet functions, either with the Insert Function button on the Formula bar or by typing them directly into a cell.

To create a user-defined function, you must do four little things:

- ✦ Create a new module sheet where the custom function is to be defined in the Visual Basic Editor by selecting its project in the Project Explorer window and then choosing Insert⇨Module on the Visual Basic Editor Menu bar.
- ✦ Enter the name of the custom function and specify the names of the arguments that this function takes on the first line in the Code window — note that you can't duplicate any built-in function names, such as SUM or AVERAGE functions, and so on, and you must list argument names in the order in which they are processed and enclosed in parentheses.
- ✦ Enter the formula, or set of formulas, that tells Excel how to calculate the custom function's result by using the argument names listed in the Function command with whatever arithmetic operators or built-in functions are required to get the calculation made on the line or lines below.
- ✦ Indicate that you've finished defining the user-defined function by entering the End Function command on the last line.

To see how this procedure works in action, consider this scenario: Suppose that you want to create a custom function that calculates the sales commissions for your salespeople based on the number of sales they make in a month as well as the total amount of their monthly sales (they sell big-ticket items, such as RVs). Your custom Commission function will then have two arguments — *TotalSales* and *ItemsSold* — so that the first line of code on the module sheet in the Code window is

```
Function Commission(TotalSales,ItemsSold)
```

In determining how the commissions are actually calculated, suppose that you base the commission percentage on the number of sales made during the month. For five sales or fewer in a month, you pay a commission rate of 4.5 percent of the salesperson's total monthly sales; for sales of six or more, you pay a commission rate of 5 percent.

To define the formula section of the Commission custom function, you need to set up an IF construction. This IF construction is similar to the IF function that you enter into a worksheet cell except that you use different lines in the macro code for the construction in the custom function. An ELSE command separates the command that is performed if the expression is True from the command that is performed if the expression is False. The macro code is terminated by an END IF command. To set the custom function so that your salespeople get 4.5 percent of total sales for five or fewer items sold and 5 percent of total sales for more than five items sold, you enter the following lines of code underneath the line with the Function command:

```
If ItemsSold <= 5 Then
      Commission = TotalSales * 0.045
Else
      Commission = TotalSales * 0.05
End If
```

Figure 2-9 shows you how the code for this user-defined function appears in the Code window for its module sheets. The indents that you see for the IF...END IF statements are made with the Tab key to keep it easy to differentiate the parts of the IF construction. The first formula, Commission = TotalSales * 0.045 is used when the IF expression ItemsSold <= 5 is found to be True. Otherwise, the second formula underneath the Else command, Commission = TotalSales * 0.05 is used.

After entering the definition for your user-defined function, you are ready to save it by choosing File⇨Save on the Visual Basic Editor Menu bar or by pressing Ctrl+S. Then, you can click the View Microsoft Excel button on the Standard toolbar to return to the worksheet where you can try out your new custom function.

If you want to be able to use your user-defined function in any spreadsheet you create, be sure that you select VBAProject(`personal.xls`) in the Project Explorer window before you open a new module and define the custom function there.

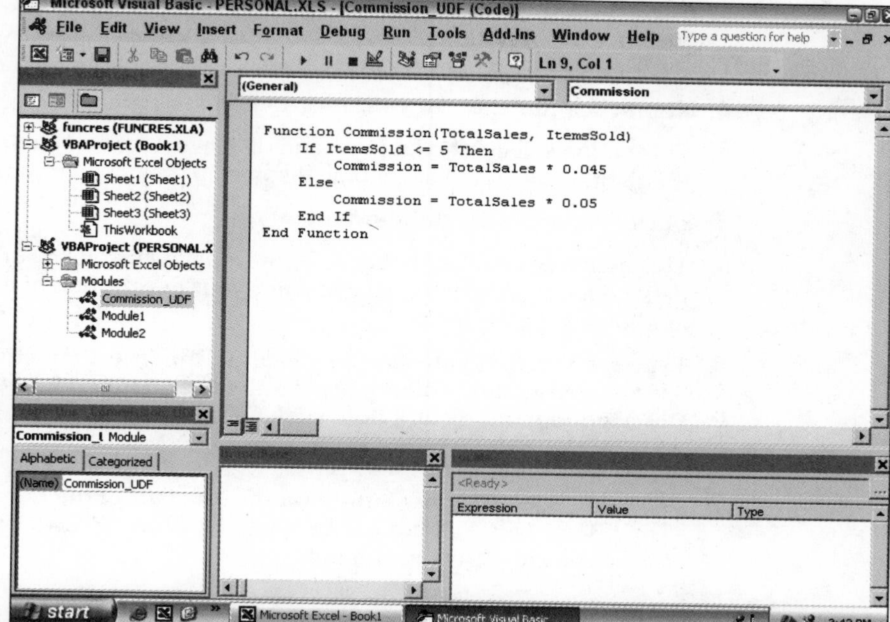

Figure 2-9: Entering the Commission user-defined function in the Personal Macro Workbook.

Adding a description to a user-defined function

To help your user understand the purpose of your custom functions, you can add descriptions that appear in Insert Function and Function Arguments dialog boxes that help explain what the function does. To add this kind of description to your user-defined function, you use the Object Browser, a special window in the Visual Basic Editor that enables you to get information about particular objects available to the project that you have open.

To add a description for your user-defined function, follow these steps:

1. **Open the Visual Basic Editor from Excel by choosing Tools⇨Macro⇨Visual Basic Editor on the Menu bar or press Alt+F11.**

   Now, you need to open the Object Browser.

2. **Choose View⇨Object Browser from the Visual Basic Editor Menu bar or press F2.**

   This action opens the Object Browser window, which obscures the Code window.

3. **Click the drop-down list box that currently contains the value <All Libraries> and then click VBAProject on the drop-down list.**

When you select VBAProject in this drop-down list, the Object Browser then displays your user-defined function as one of the objects in one of the Classes in the pane on the left.

4. **Right-click the name of your user-defined function.**

   This action selects the function and displays it in the Members pane on the right, while at the same time displaying the object's shortcut menu.

5. **Click Properties on the shortcut menu.**

   This action opens the Members Options dialog box for your user-defined function, where you can enter your description of this function, as shown in Figure 2-10.

6. **Type the text that you want to appear in the Insert Function and Function Arguments dialog box for the user-defined function in the Description text box and then click OK.**

   Now, you can close the Object Browser and save your changes.

7. **Click the Close Window button on the far right of the bar with the Visual Basic Editor Menu bar to close the Object Browser and then choose the File⇨Save command.**

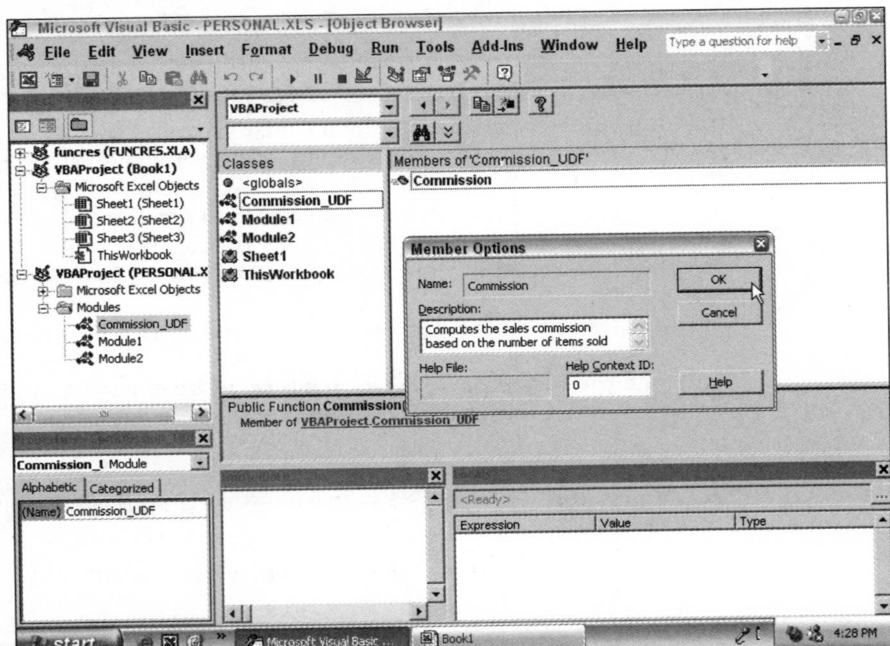

Figure 2-10: Adding a description for the Commission user-defined function.

Using a custom function in your spreadsheet

The great thing about custom functions is that they can be inserted into your worksheets with your old friend the Function Wizard on the Formula bar. Figures 2-11 through 2-13 illustrate how easy it is to enter the custom Commission function in a worksheet with the Function Wizard.

Figure 2-11 shows a worksheet that contains a table with the April 2004 RV sales for three salespeople: Fred, Holly, and Jack. As you can see, the Automatic Subtotals feature (covered in Book VI, Chapter 1) has been used to compute both the monthly total sales (with the SUM function) and the number of sales (with the COUNT function) for each of these three salespeople.

	A	B	C	D	E
1	Salesperson	RV Sold	Amount of Sales	Date of Sale	Commissions
2	Fred	Model RV456-78	$ 34,500	4/3/2004	
3	Fred	Model RV456-79	$ 24,500	4/25/2004	
4	**Fred Total**		$ 59,000		
5	**Fred Count**		2		
6	Holly	Model UV456-80	$ 45,000	4/2/2004	
7	Holly	Model UV456-81	$ 24,500	4/10/2004	
8	Holly	Model RV456-82	$ 26,900	4/30/2004	
9	**Holly Total**		$ 96,400		
10	**Holly Count**		3		
11	Jack	Model UV456-80	$ 45,500	4/1/2004	
12	Jack	Model UV456-84	$ 34,500	4/15/2004	
13	Jack	Model RV456-85	$ 28,500	4/15/2004	
14	Jack	Model RV456-79	$ 24,500	4/22/2004	
15	Jack	Model RV456-79	$ 24,500	4/25/2004	
16	Jack	Model RV456-79	$ 24,500	4/29/2004	
17	**Jack Total**		$ 182,000		
18	**Jack Count**		6		
19	**Grand Total**		$ 337,400		
20	**Grand Count**		11		

Figure 2-11: Selecting a cell in the RV Sales spreadsheet into which to enter the Commission function.

To calculate the April monthly commissions for each salesperson in this table, you select the cell where you want the first commission to be calculated (Fred's commission in cell E5). Click the Insert Function button on the Formula bar and then click User Defined at the very bottom of the Or Select a Category drop down list. Doing this displays the PERSONAL.XLS!Commission custom function in the Select a Function list box.

When you click the OK after selecting the `personal.xls`!Commission function in the Insert Function dialog box, the Function Arguments dialog box appears, shown in Figure 2-12. Here, you select cell C4 with Fred's total sales amount for April as the TotalSales argument and cell C5 with the number of sales made in that month as the ItemsSold argument.

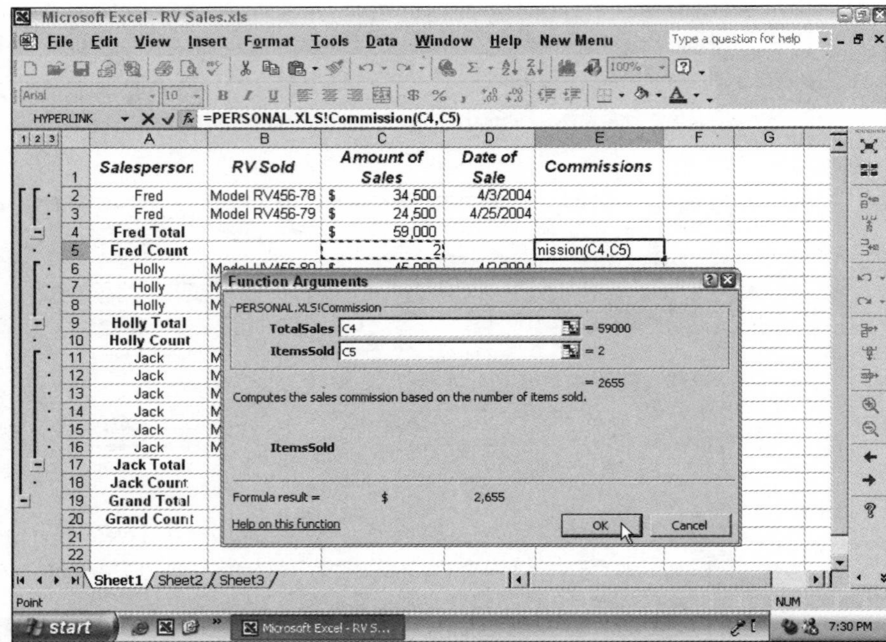

Figure 2-12: Specifying the TotalSales and ItemsSold arguments in the RV Sales spreadsheet.

When you click OK in the Function Arguments dialog box, Excel calculates Fred's commission by using the 4.5 percent commission rate because his two sales made in April are well below the five sales necessary to bump him up to the 5 percent commission rate used by the custom Commission function. Figure 2-13 shows the completed April sales table after calculating the monthly commissions for Fred, Holly, and Jack. In using the custom Commission function, both Fred and Holly fall into the 4.5 percent commission rate. Only Jack, the April RV sales king, gets paid the higher 5 percent commission rate for his six sales during this month.

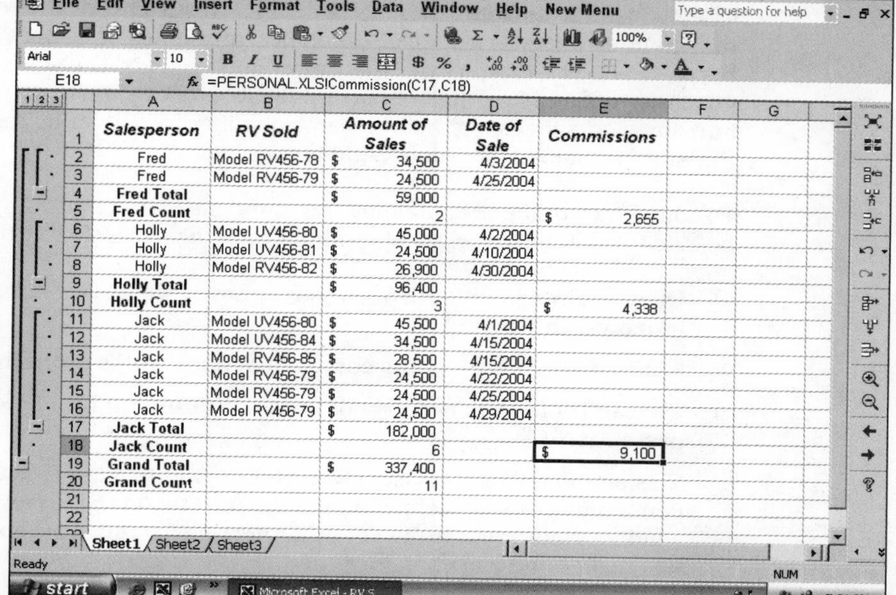

Figure 2-13: Completed spreadsheet for all sales people computed with the Commissions function.

Saving custom functions in add-in files

The only limitation to the user-defined functions that you save as part of a regular workbook files or the Personal Macro Workbook file is that when you enter them directly into a cell (without the use of the Insert Function dialog box), you must preface their function names with their filenames. For example, if you want to type in the custom Commission function that's saved in the Personal Macro Workbook and you enter the following formula:

```
=Commission(C9,C10)
```

(assuming that cell C9 contains the total sales and cell C10 contains the number of items sold), Excel returns the #NAME? error value to the cell. If you then edit the function to include the Personal Macro Workbook's filename as follows:

```
=Personal.xls!Commission(C9,C10)
```

Excel then calculates the sales commission based on the *TotalSales* in C9 and the *ItemsSold* in C10, returning this calculated value to the cell containing this user-defined function.

To be able to omit the filename from the custom functions that you create when you enter them directly into a cell, you need to save the workbook file that contains them as a special add-in file (for details on using add-ins in Excel, see Book I, Chapter 3). Then, after you've saved the workbook with your user-defined functions as an add-in file, you can start entering them into any worksheet sans their filename qualifier by activating the add-in in the Add-Ins dialog box (Tools➪Add-Ins).

To convert a workbook containing the user-defined functions that you want to be able to enter into worksheets without their filenames, follow these steps:

1. **Open the workbook in which you've saved your user-defined functions in Excel.**

   Make sure that each of the custom functions works properly.

2. **Choose Tools➪Macro➪Visual Basic Editor on the Excel Menu bar or press Alt+F11.**

   This action opens the Visual Basic Editor window with the workbook file containing the user-defined functions selected in the Project Explorer window. Now you want to set up protection for this workbook so that no one but you can change or modify its contents.

3. **Choose Tools➪VBAProject Properties from the Visual Basic Editor's Menu bar.**

   This action opens the VBAProject — Project Properties dialog box with a General and a Protection tab, shown in Figure 2-14.

4. **Click the Protection tab and then click the Lock Project for Viewing check box.**

   Putting a checkmark in this check box prevents other users from viewing the custom functions so that they can't make any changes to them. Next, you add a password that prevents them from removing the view protection status.

5. **Click the Password text box, enter the password there, and then click the Confirm Password text box and re-enter the password exactly as you entered it in the text box above before you click OK.**

   Now you're ready to return to the worksheet where you need to add a title and description for the new add-in file.

6. **Click the View Microsoft Excel button at the beginning of the Standard toolbar.**

   This action returns you to the worksheet in Excel. Before saving the workbook as an add-in, you should add a title and description of the user-defined functions that it contains (this information then appears in the Add-Ins dialog box whenever you select the add-in file).

7. **Choose File⇨Properties from the Excel Menu bar.**

   This action opens the Properties dialog box with the Summary tab already selected (similar to the one shown in Figure 2-15). Here you enter a brief name for the add-in in the Title field and a longer description of its custom functions.

8. **Click the Title text box and enter a descriptive title for the add-in, and then click the Comments text box and enter a description of its contents before you click OK.**

   Now you're ready to save the workbook file as a special add-in file.

9. **Choose File⇨Save As from the Excel Menu bar.**

   This action opens the Save As dialog box, where you need to change the file type from Microsoft Excel Workbook (*.xls) to Microsoft Excel Add-In (*.xla) and then specify the filename (to which Excel automatically appends the `.xla` filename extension) under which to save it.

10. **Click the Save as Type pop-up button and then scroll all the way down to the bottom of the list and click Microsoft Excel Add-In (*.xla).**

    This action selects the AddIns folder in the Save In drop-down list box showing the names of any add-in files that you've saved there.

11. **Click the File Name combo box and make any necessary changes to the filename (without changing the `.xla` filename extension) before you click the Save button.**

    After saving your workbook as an add-in file, you're ready to activate the add-in so that you can enter its user-defined functions in any worksheet.

12. **Choose Tools⇨Add-Ins from the Excel Menu bar.**

    This action opens the Add-Ins dialog box showing the names of all the available add-ins. You must now add the name of your new add-in to this list.

13. **Click the Browse button in the Add-Ins dialog box.**

    This action opens the Browse dialog box that shows the contents of your AddIns folder.

14. **Click the name of your new add-in file in the Browse list box and then click OK.**

    This action closes the Browse dialog box and returns you to the Add-Ins dialog box that now lists your new add-in file. Now all you have to do is click the check box in front of the name of the new add-in (which displays the title and description you gave the add-in at the bottom of the Add-Ins dialog box) and click OK (see Figure 2-16).

15. **Click the check box in front of the name of the new add-in and then click OK.**

As soon as you click OK, Excel closes the Add-Ins dialog box and you can then start entering the custom functions that this add-in file contains directly into the cells of any spreadsheet without having to open the Insert Function dialog box.

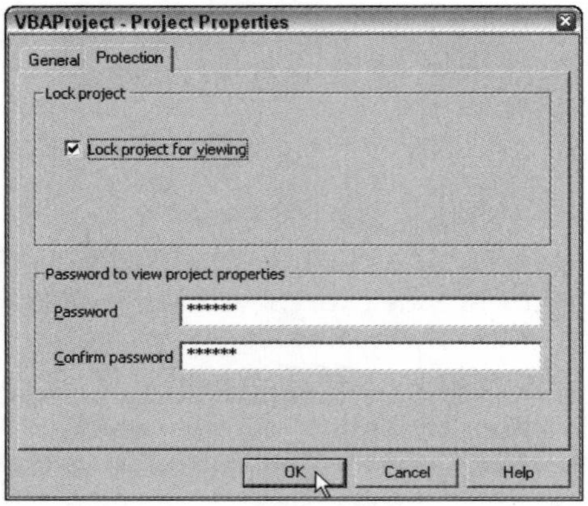

Figure 2-14: Protecting the VBA project so that its user-defined functions can't be changed.

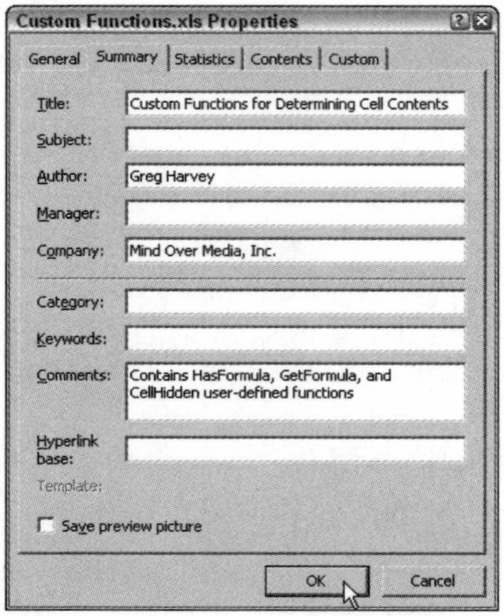

Figure 2-15: Adding a title and description for the new add-in file.

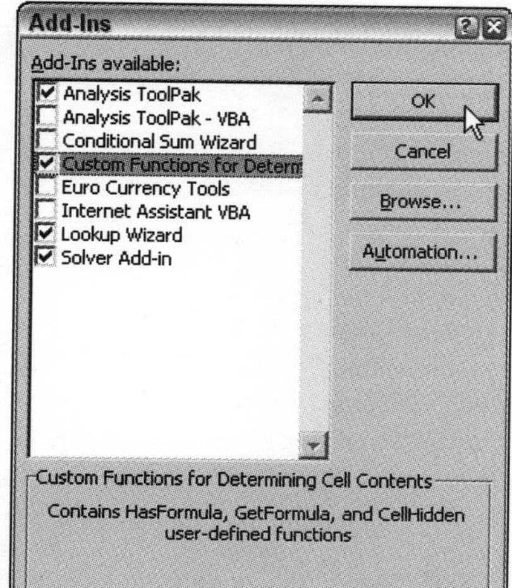

Figure 2-16: Activating the new add-in file in the Add-Ins dialog box.

Index

Numerics

A

B

C

D

E

F

G

H

I

J

K

L

N

O

P

Q

R

S

T

U

V

W

X

Y

Z

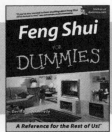

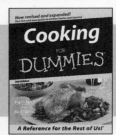

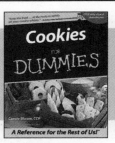

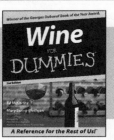

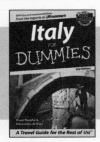

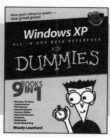

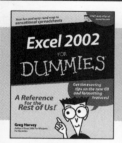

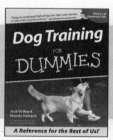

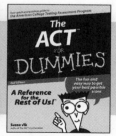

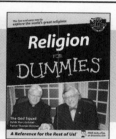